CHINA MADE

CONSUMER CULTURE AND THE
CREATION OF THE NATION

HARVARD EAST ASIAN MONOGRAPHS 224

CHINA MADE

CONSUMER CULTURE AND THE

CREATION OF THE NATION

Karl Gerth

Published by the Harvard University Asia Center and
Distributed by Harvard University Press
Cambridge (Massachusetts) and London, 2003

Printed in the United States of America

The Harvard University Asia Center publishes a monograph series and, in coordination with the Fairbank Center for East Asian Research, the Korea Institute, the Reischauer Institute of Japanese Studies, and other faculties and institutes, administers research projects designed to further scholarly understanding of China, Japan, Vietnam, Korea, and other Asian countries. The Center also sponsors projects addressing multidisciplinary and regional issues in Asia.

Library of Congress Cataloging-in-Publication Data

Gerth, Karl, 1966-
  China made : consumer culture and the creation of the nation / Karl Gerth.
    p. cm. -- (Harvard East Asian monographs ; 224)
  Includes bibliographical references and index.
  ISBN 0-674-01214-3 (alk. paper)
  1. Consumption (Economics)--China--History--20th century. 2. Nationalism--China--20th century. 3. Manufacturing industries--China--20th century. 4. Boycotts--China--History--20th century. I. Title. II. Series.
  HC430.C6G47 2003
  339.4'7'09510904--dc21

                                                                2003011610

Index by the author

⊗   Printed on acid-free paper

Last figure below indicates year of this printing
13 12 11 10 09 08 07 06 05 04 03

For Pamela

Acknowledgments

In the late 1980s, the U.S. mass media sounded an alarm. A steady stream of reports suggested that Japanese foreign direct investment was "invading" the United States. The acquisition of prominent symbols of American wealth and power, such as Rockefeller Center in Manhattan and Universal Pictures in Hollywood, was front-page news. *Newsweek* even published an issue with the Statue of Liberty draped in a kimono. The panic over "foreign" control of "our" economy made the consumption of Japanese imports controversial.

I experienced the angst of that era. One summer day as I drove with friends through Detroit, I felt acutely conscious of the make of our car, a Nissan. I wondered whether locals would assault us for brazenly driving a Japanese car through the heart of the nation's automobile industry. Since that time, I have continued to note the ties between consumerism and nationalism in the United States. Recently television advertisements accused owners of gas-guzzling sport utility vehicles (SUVs) of treason for indirectly funding those responsible for the September 11 tragedy. These feelings of fear and guilt were never enough to stop me (or most Americans) from buying Japanese products then or gasoline now. But I think there were other effects.

Anxiety over imports is neither new nor exclusively American. This book charts the development of a similar social anxiety in China during the early twentieth century, a time when China faced a genuine threat to its sovereignty and continued existence as an independent country. It was challenging to link nationalism and consumption in a vast country where the levels of both were usually low to nonexistent. Naturally, the responses varied. Apathy abounded. Many felt an obligation but, like me in the United States many decades later, stopped short of direct action. Given the state of mass communications in China, millions never even heard the call to action. Yet a broad history of this anxiety uncovers a wide range of effects and manifestations that collectively demonstrate how nationalism became a central part of consumer culture in China.

The path that turned a nervous motorist into a published author began at Harvard. Since my first semester of graduate school, Philip A. Kuhn has generously shared his time and knowledge. I see this book as a combination of the social history I studied with him and the political and economic history I explored through William C. Kirby's classes and scholarship. Their ongoing advice has been invaluable.

Many friends, colleagues, and students assisted me. Frank Bechter, John Carroll, Ken Chase, Hyung Gu Lynn, Rana Mitter, and Allison Rottmann critiqued all or large parts of the entire manuscript. Others who helped include Paul Frank, Chen Shiwei, Mary Buck, Caroline Reeves, Cheng Linsun, Anne Reinhardt, Eugenia Lean, Chang Li, Richard Belsky, Marc Busch, and Elaine Mossmann. Fellow scholars of China commented on various parts. Parks Coble, Sherman Cochran, Prasenjit Duara, Antonia Finanne, Akira Iriye, Peter Perdue, William Rowe, and Wen-hsin Yeh were particularly helpful. Several scholars of American consumerism also advised me: Susan Strasser, Lawrence Glickman, Katherine Grier, and Kathy Peiss. I am certain each will still find points of disagreement. At the University of South Carolina, I am especially grateful to Patrick Maney, W. Dean Kinzley, Anna Krylova, Lynn Shirley, Eric Cheezum, the staff at the Interlibrary Loan department, the students in my seminars on the history of consumer culture in modern East Asia, and the members of the Department of History. I am also indebted to three anonymous reviewers of the manuscript.

Numerous individuals and institutions supported my research in Japan, China, and Taiwan as well as my revisions. A Japanese Ministry of Education (Mombushō) scholarship allowed me to spend two years at Tokyo University studying under Hamashita Takeshi, who has been a source of countless suggestions. Linda Grove, Kawashima Shin, and Harald Fuess also assisted me in Japan. The financial support of Harvard University's Frederick Sheldon Fellowship, Graduate Society Fellowship, and the Weatherhead Center for International Affairs enabled me to make three research trips to China. In Shanghai, Li Yihai and the staff of the Foreign Scholars Section of the Shanghai Academy of Social Sciences arranged two of my trips. Many scholars at the Academy took time to suggest materials, including Huang Hanmin, Chen Zhengshu, and Luo Suwen. For sharing their own sources on the National Products Movement, I am indebted to Xu Dingxin and Pan Junxiang. I also thank the staffs of the Tianjin Municipal Archives, the Number Two Archives in Nanjing, the Shanghai Municipal Archives, especially Chen Zhengqing, and the Shanghai Municipal Library, particularly Jeff Qin. Fu Dehua of the History Department Library of Fudan University provided early encouragement. At the Suzhou Municipal Archives, Lin Zhilin and Shen Huiying ensured that I found everything that I needed. A Fulbright Foundation fellowship funded a year of research in Taiwan. I am grateful to the scholars and staff at my institutional home there, the Modern History Institute of the Academia Sinica, especially Lin Man-houng and Chang Rui-te. The Harold Gross Dissertation Award from the history department at Harvard along with grants from the University of South Carolina's College of Liberal Arts Scholarship Support and Taiwan's Chiang Ching-kuo Foundation funded my revisions.

Lastly, I thank my family, especially Pamela, to whom I dedicate this book.

K.G.

Contents

Map, Table, and Figures   xiii

Introduction   1

The Elaboration of the Movement 5/ "Chinese People Ought to Consume Chinese Products" 13/ Overview 24

PART I   CONTEXTS AND CASE STUDY

1 The Crisis over Commodities and the Origins of the Movement   29

Foreign Exposure 33/ Symbolizing Lost Sovereignty 40/ New Commodities as Conduits of Nationalism 49/ The Ideological and Institutional Foundations of the Movement 57

2 Nationalizing the Appearance of Men   68

Ascribing Meaning to Men's Appearance During the Qing 74/ The Visual and Economic Significance of Chinese Clothing 80/ Late Qing Interpretations of Appearance 83/ The Appearance of Revolution, 1898–1911 88/ Nationalizing Appearance 93/ Lobbying for National Clothing 105/ The Legacy of Nationalistic Appearance Under the Republic 111

PART II   CONSUMPTION AS RESISTANCE

3 The Movement and Anti-Imperialist Boycotts, 1905–1919   125

Institutionalization: The Anti-American Boycott of 1905 127/ Early Anti-Japanese Boycotts 131/ "National Humiliation" and Consumption in 1915 133/ The Movement and Continuity Between Boycotts 145/ The Boycott of 1919 146

4 The Movement and Anti-Imperialist Boycotts, 1923–1937   158

Part I: Boycotts, 1923–37 159/ _Boycott of 1925: The May 30th
Movement_ 168/ _Part II: Standardizing the Meaning of "National
Products"_ 185/ _The Practical Problem of Determining Product
"Purity"_ 187/ _The Formulation of National Products Standards_ 192/
The National Products Standards of 1928 194

PART III   THE EXHIBITIONARY COMPLEX

5 Nationalistic Commodity Spectacles   203

Remaking Commodity Spectacles for the Nation 205/ _Components
of the Exhibitionary Complex_ 208/ _Creating Nationalized
Exhibitions_ 222/ _Expansion Under the Nationalist Government_ 231

6 Creating a Nationalistic Visuality in the Exhibition of 1928   246

Making the Mythical 249/ _Profiting from a National Polity_ 252/
The Preparations 255/ _Creating a Nationalized Space_ 258/ _Mass
Mediated Spectacle_ 266/ _People and Products on Display_ 269/
Communities of Commodities Within the Nation 273/ _Conclusion:
A Commodity Nation_ 281

PART IV   NATION, GENDER, AND THE MARKET

7 Nationalizing Female Consumers   285

The Image of the Consuming Woman 289/ _A Year in the Life of a
Patriotic Female Consumer_ 309/ _Contesting Representations of Women
as Treasonous Consumers_ 328

8 Manufacturing Patriotic Producers   333

National Products Movement Biographies 334/ _A Capitalist with
Chinese Characteristics_ 337/ _The Limits of Patriotic Production_ 345

Conclusion   355

How Widely Elaborated Was the Movement? 358/ _A Meta-
Movement_ 360/ _Nationalistic Consumerism Viewed from North
America_ 363/ _Nationalistic Consumerism in Contemporary China_ 366

REFERENCE MATTER

Bibliography   371

Index   425

Map, Table, and Figures

Map

I.1   Treaty Ports as Showcases   36

Table

1.1   Chinese Foreign Trade   44

Figures

I.1   A Nation as Products   16

I.2   What Is Chinese?   22

1.1   Consumer and Consumed   31

1.2   Worshipping the Foreign   32

1.3   The Toothpaste Defense   59

2.1   Coercion and the Queue   69

2.2   Reinterpreting Qing Male Dress   72

2.3   The New Male Orthodoxy?   73

2.4   Antithetical Interpretations of the Queue   78

2.5   The Clothing Law of 1912   110

2.6   New Uniforms for Diplomats   113

2.7   The Sun Suit Compromise   116

2.8   Western-Style Chinese-Made Clothing   119

3.1	Marketing Humiliation in 1915	138
3.2	Marketing Humiliation in 1920	139
3.3	"National Humiliation Commemorative Poster"	153
4.1	"The Shamelessness of the Treasonous Merchant"	162
4.2	Publicizing the Latest National Humiliation	170
4.3	Boycott Banner, 1925	173
4.4	Fanning the Humiliation	174
4.5	The Myth of the Pure Product	188
4.6	National Product Certification, 1928	195
5.1	Nationalized Retail Space	210
5.2	The Chinese National Products Company	212
5.3	Nationalized Visual Spaces	214
5.4	Patriotic Smokers	215
5.5	Shanghai Commercial Products Display Hall	229
6.1	Chinese National Products Exhibition	250
6.2	Main Gate of the Exhibition	259
6.3	West Wing of the Exhibition	260
6.4	East Wing of the Exhibition	261
6.5	Textile and Beverage Displays	262
6.6	Nested Identities Within Pavilions	263
6.7	Microcosm of Nationalist Modernity	265
6.8	Mementos from the Exhibition	268
6.9	Students Visiting an Exhibition	271
6.10	Ceremonial Hall of the Exhibition	274
7.1	Women as National Saviors	288
7.2	"Practicing New Life"	295
7.3	Fashionable Traitors	303
7.4	Conduits of Imperialism	304
7.5	National Product Fashion Shows	310
7.6	Bashing Foreign Beer	320
7.7	Santa Selling Cigarettes	328

8.1   Commercial War   335

8.2   Patriotic Footwear   338

8.3   Domestic Status Earned Abroad   347

8.4   Heaven's Kitchen MSG Bomber   351

8.5   Packaging Nationalism   353

CHINA MADE

CONSUMER CULTURE AND THE

CREATION OF THE NATION

Introduction

What's a fashion-conscious teenager to do when all her favorite products are imported from a country that's attacking her own? In "The Lin Family Shop" ("林家鋪子," 1932), a short story by the famous Chinese writer Mao Dun 茅盾 (1896–1981), the spoiled teenaged daughter of a small merchant returns home from school distraught after her classmates and teachers harass her because her pretty new dress is made of Japanese rather than Chinese material. The girl understands their criticism. She knows that Japan has been expanding its control over China aggressively and that she is expected to boycott all things Japanese. Still, she loves her clothing, cosmetics, pencils, umbrella, and many other belongings, even though they are Japanese imports. She resents having to abandon them, but the social pressure has become unbearable. To avoid further torment, the girl informs her mother that she requires a new wardrobe made from Chinese fabrics immediately. This young woman's decision reveals the pervasive tensions between consumerism and nationalism that were, as this book argues, central to the creation of China as a modern nation.

Nationality-bearing commodities impinge on every character in Mao Dun's story. The schoolgirl's father comes under attack from local officials for selling Japanese products. Because every store sells such things, the father considers this harassment an arbitrary shakedown by local officials trolling for bribes rather than a genuine attempt to promote a nationalistic consumer culture. Yet he has no choice. He pays a bribe and begins trying to recoup his losses to earn enough to buy his daughter new clothing, but he does not remove the Japanese products from his shelves. On the contrary, desperate for sales, he displays them boldly with reduced prices. Customers jump at the chance to obtain a bargain; they do not avoid these imported products. Business picks up, but the merchant's success only renews his original problem. His store attracts the attention of another official who, under the pretext of prohibiting the sale of Japanese products, is looking for yet another payoff. By now, other area merchants have also paid bribes to secure permission to sell Japanese products. Showing their true colors, officials permit the sale of these goods once merchants remove the Japanese markings. Merchants and customers then participate in a charade of nationalistic consumerism by referring to the disguised goods as "Chinese products" or "national products" (國貨), as goods made in China, by Chinese workers, using Chinese materials, under the direction of Chinese managers, in Chinese-owned factories were known at the time of the story.[1] As a result, the local market becomes flooded, prices drop, and the merchant soon goes bankrupt.

In this classic Mao Dun satire, greedy merchants, unethical officials, and self-interested consumers participate in a nationalistic consumer culture, but not necessarily with genuine commitment.[2] Clearly, a new notion of "product-nationality" constrained consumers and enabled individuals to advance their interests by invoking that constraint. The constraint was real. None of the characters denies that goods possess nationality or that there are *nationalistic categories of consumption*. Indeed, even Mao Dun himself, although deeply cynical about the blatant manipulation of these categories by self-proclaimed patriots, did not directly challenge the notion of product-nationality. An exploration of the history of the categories that defined commodities as either Chinese or foreign must therefore transcend a simple identification of Chinese consumption patterns. The presence of these categories alone, for instance, enables the girl's classmates and teachers to humiliate her publicly and "legitimately," even if their actual motivation is envy rather than patriotism. Likewise, far from providing evidence against the emerging hegemony of a nationalized consumer culture, the decisions of Chinese merchants to misrepresent (and sell) "Japanese" goods as "Chinese" serve to confirm the reality of nationalistic categories of consumption. The question for us then becomes: How the disjunction between "did

---

1. In fact, the Chinese equivalent of the *Oxford English Dictionary* uses this story to define the term *guohuo* 國貨 (national product) (Luo Zhufeng 1990, vol. 3: 641).

2. I share Thomas Richards's concern over using the term "consumer culture," which "makes it sound like there is something uniquely modern about consumption" (1990: 268). By qualifying and contextualizing this culture (see esp. Chapter 1), I hope to avoid such confusion. The term "material culture" is broader and refers to "that sector of our physical environment that we modify through culturally determined behavior" (Deetz 1996: 35). I define consumer culture as a specific, mass-produced, and commodity-centered form of material culture. On the term "consumption," see D. Miller 1995c: 30 and D. Miller 1998.

do" and "ought to have done" creates room for political, social, and economic maneuverings.

Why do the consumers, merchants, and officials in "The Lin Family Shop" go to such extreme lengths to maintain the appearance of nationalistic consumerism? Indeed, this story accurately represents Chinese reality. In his classic study of the competition between the British-American Tobacco Company and Nanyang Brothers Tobacco Company (南洋兄弟煙草公司), for instance, business historian Sherman Cochran writes that both companies "recognized the need to disguise their foreign ties and appear as 'Chinese' as possible" (1980: 211, 218). But how and why did nationalism and consumerism intersect to create this deep and far-reaching constraint? What was the broader social context that made the appearance of nationalistic consumerism so important?

In early twentieth-century China, an emerging consumer culture defined and spread modern Chinese nationalism. China had begun to import and to manufacture thousands of new consumer goods. These commodities changed the everyday life of millions of Chinese who used, discussed, and dreamed about them. At the same time, the influx of imports and the desires they created threatened many in China. Politicians worried about trade deficits and the new consumer lifestyles exemplified by opium dens and addicts. Intellectuals, who had begun to read works on Western political economy, feared the loss of sovereignty implicit in the growing foreign dominance of the commercial economy. And manufacturers, faced with inexpensive and superior imports, wondered how they would preserve or increase their market share.

The growing conceptualization of China as a "nation" with its own "national products" influenced the shape of its consumer culture. This book demonstrates that consumerism played a fundamental role in defining nationalism, and nationalism in defining consumerism. Nationalism molded a burgeoning consumer culture by applying the categories "national" and "foreign" to all commodities, creating, in effect, the notion of "treasonous" and "patriotic" products. This nationalized consumer culture became the site where the notions of "nationality" and of China as a "modern" nation-state were articulated, institutionalized, and practiced. The consumption of commodities defined by the concept of nationality not only helped create the very idea of "modern China" but also became a primary means by which people in China began to conceptualize themselves as citizens of a modern nation.

Efforts to create a nationalistic consumer culture had innumerable social manifestations. A broad array of political, economic, and social forces placed cultural constraints on consumption through a massive but diffuse social movement. The National Products Movement (國貨運動; hereafter, "the movement"), as it was known at the time, popularized the meaning of material culture around the duality of "national products" (國貨) and "foreign products" (洋貨), and it made the consumption of national products a fundamental part of Chinese citizenship. This movement included new sumptuary laws mandating the use of Chinese-made fabrics in clothing (Chapter 2), frequent anti-imperialist boycotts (Chapters 3 and 4), massive exhibitions and myriad advertisements promoting the consumption of national products (Chapters 5 and 6), a Women's National Products Year (Chapter 7), and the mass circulation of biographies of patriotic manufacturers (Chapter 8). These aspects of the movement created a nationalistic consumer culture that drove modern Chinese nation-making.[3]

The role of consumerism in persuading people in China to see themselves as members of a modern nation-state in a world of similarly constituted nation-states, although critical to understanding modern China, is surprisingly absent from contemporary scholarship on Chinese nationalism. Early scholarship on the emergence of modern nationalism in China attempted to locate China along a "culturalism-to-nationalism" continuum stretching from the late nineteenth to the early twentieth century. In political scientist James Townsend's summary, "the core proposition is that a set of ideas labeled 'culturalism' dominated traditional China, was incompatible with modern nationalism and yielded only under the assault of imperialism and Western ideas to a new nationalist way of thinking" (Townsend 1996: 1; see also J. Harrison 1969). In recent years, historians have greatly expanded our knowledge of China's final dynasty and questioned the purported cultural unity of late imperial China by identifying regional and ethnic tensions (see, e.g., E. S. Rawski 1998; Crossley 1999; Rhoads 2000). Nevertheless, scholarship examining the emergence of modern nationalism continues to take two general forms: top-down and bottom-up. The first approach

---

3. Rather than the term "nation-building," which suggests the nation is a top-down construction, I use "nation-making" to emphasize the much broader social participation. On the difference between "nation-building" and "nation-making," as well as a discussion of the use of the term "nation" as employed here, see R. J. Foster 1995a.

explores the role of intellectual, military, and political leaders in creating a nation.[4] The second investigates the development of nationalism within specific contexts, such as the expansion of local customs and religious practices to broader arenas or sporadic anti-imperialist acts such as the killing of foreign missionaries or the picketing of foreign companies.[5]

A study of nation-making through consumerism allows us to connect all levels of Chinese society. This book extends the top-down approach to reveal the broader institutional and discursive environments in which notions of nationhood were conceived, diffused, and enforced. At the same time, examining nationalism through consumerism expands the bottom-up approach by integrating different levels of Chinese society and connecting diverse phenomena over time. This extension of the analysis of Chinese nation-making into consumerism should make it hard to imagine histories of Sino-foreign relations, business enterprises, the lives of leading figures, popular protest, the women's movement, urban culture, or even the Communist Revolution of 1949 that do not consider the rise of a nationalized consumer culture in early twentieth-century China.

The Elaboration of the Movement

Why did the Chinese government not nationalize consumer culture by banning or restricting imports through high tariffs? The answer is simple: because of imperialism, the Chinese state lacked the power to do so. As Chapter 1 demonstrates, successive defeats by imperialist powers after the Opium War (1840–42) compounded deep institutional problems within the Chinese state and culminated in the collapse of China's last dynasty in 1911–12. Imperialist countries imposed a series of "unequal treaties" that "opened" China to trade by, among other methods, denying China the ability to restrict imports by raising tariffs. When China recovered tariff autonomy in

---

4. Because the top-down approach is the predominant way of studying the rise of Chinese nationalism, there are too many citations to list here. The best-known example of this approach is Levenson 1965. For a dated but annotated introduction, see F. G. Chan 1981. For a recent critique of these approaches, see Mitter 2000: 7–15.

5. Two good examples are Watson 1985 and M. L. Cohen 1994. For a more recent study on the role of changing rituals in creating a new sense of Chinese ethnicity and nationalism, see H. Harrison 2000. On the homogenizing power of nationalist narratives that arose among diverse local social groups, see Duara 1995: 115–46.

the late 1920s, it used internationally accepted means of nationalizing consumer culture and immediately imposed tariffs to restrict market access. By one estimate, the tariff rate of 1934 was seven times the pre-1929 rate (Zheng Yougui 1939: 12). However, throughout the period discussed here, roughly 1900 to 1937, China saw itself as inundated with imports but powerless to use tariffs for a quick solution. Instead, interested parties tried to create other ways of restricting foreign access and enforcing nationalistic consumption. The National Products Movement was the expression of their manifold efforts.

There was never one centrally controlled national products movement (think the civil rights movement, not the National Association for the Advancement of Colored People). Silk manufacturers, student protestors, women's organizations, business enterprises, government officials, and ordinary citizens alike invoked the term "National Products Movement." Moreover, as the movement grew, its name, its slogans, and the categories of nationalistic consumption it created became ubiquitous in cities and even appeared in the countryside. Its manifestations included the Clothing Law of 1912, the *National Product Monthly* (國貨月報) and many other magazines, the government-sponsored "National Products" campaign of the late 1920s, official "National Products Years" in the 1930s (Women's in 1934, Children's in 1935, and Citizens' in 1936), weekly supplements published in a major national newspaper (*Shenbao*) in the mid-1930s, thousands of advertisements, regular national-product fashion shows, and specially organized venues— visited by millions—for displaying and selling national products, including museums, fixed and traveling exhibitions, and a chain of retail stores.

The movement, then, was not a bounded entity but an evolving, growing, and interactive set of institutions, discourses, and organizations, which sought new ways to incorporate reluctant producers, merchants, and, above all, citizen-consumers. The movement was initiated by a few groups, expanded by others into new domains, and appropriated by still others, for multiple purposes, many of them directly at odds with the interests of movement supporters. Participants ranged from men leading recognized movement organizations to women organizing movement events as a way to take part in public life to entrepreneurs jumping on the movement bandwagon to sell products to gangsters manipulating movement discourse as a means of extortion to consumers consciously or unconsciously acting on the nationalistic categories of consumption.

MOVEMENT TERMS AND LABELS

A key means for expanding the National Products Movement was the creation and popularization of a vocabulary that underwrote nationalistic categories of consumption. The most important terms were "national product" and "foreign product." *Guohuo* 國貨 is often translated "native goods" or "national goods." Although I occasionally use the term "Chinese goods" and others for variation, I prefer "national products" because this term invokes the attributes that movement participants aspired to associate with their products: nationalism and industrialism rather than localism and handicraft production.[6] For the same reason, I translate *Guohuo yundong* 國貨運動 as "national products movement" rather than "native goods" or "national goods" movement. Similarly, as I point out in Chapter 1, the influx of imported consumer goods that were given the prefix "foreign" (洋) helped to convey the notion of "foreign commodities" (洋貨) more generally, and, by implication, the idea of Chinese "national products."[7] Likewise, the circulation of goods labeled "domestic" and "foreign" served to teach "nationality" to consumers throughout China on a daily basis.

The creation and application of positive and negative nationalized social labels led to further elaborations of the movement's vocabulary. An "authentic Chinese woman," as Chapter 7 shows, did not consume imports, lest she "betray her nation." One participant in the Women's National Products Year of 1934 even suggested that such unpatriotic women be labeled prostitutes because they degraded their bodies by consuming imports. Moreover, decades before Chinese historians in the People's Republic contrasted the patriotic "national capitalist" (民族資本家), whose work aided the nation,

---

6. I also prefer to emphasize the exchange and sign values of merchandise by using the term "products" or "commodities." On the construction of the broader social meanings of such values, in particular, see Appadurai 1986a and Baudrillard 1998. For a lucid introduction to Baudrillard's notion of "sign value," see Kellner 1989. However, to avoid repetition, I also use the term "goods." Note that "commodities" refers to the more contemporary meaning of the term as all exchangeable goods rather than simply as primary materials such as grains. On these distinctions, see Rowling 1987: 7.

7. Another Chinese term for "foreign products" was *waiguohuo* 外國貨, often shortened to *waihuo* 外貨. The movement also used explicitly derisive terms to refer to imports. "Non-Chinese" products were commonly called "enemy products" (仇貨), although by the late 1920s this term usually referred specifically to Japanese products. The movement also used the term "inferior products" (劣貨) as a catchall for "imports."

and the treasonous "comprador capitalist" (買辦資本家), whose work benefited foreign companies, the movement sought to create a marketplace that automatically distinguished genuinely patriotic Chinese capitalists from the traitorous agents of foreign interests. Without relying on foreign assistance, the "authentic Chinese capitalist," as I show in Chapter 8, used *Chinese* capital, labor, raw materials, and management to produce goods that defended the domestic market by displacing imports.

Although I do argue that the process of nationalizing consumer culture was a primary mechanism for developing and extending nationalism in China, it was not the only one. Other aspects of Chinese life were being nationalized and given nationalized names with the addition of the prefix "nation" or "national" (國), including "national medicine" (國藥), "national language" (國語), "national father" (國父; i.e., Sun Yatsen or Sun Yixian 孫逸仙, 1866–1925), and "national opera" (國劇), as well as "national flag" (國旗) and "national anthem" (國歌).[8] These usages mutually reinforced and bolstered the idea of nation as a primary classification and further naturalized the notion of national products. Personal and national racial hygiene, a concept widely circulated through ideas of racial competition and eugenics in Republican China, mirrored the notions of a pure economy and of pure commodities.[9] The connection was not casual. National Products Movement literature often represented commodities as the "national blood" (國血) and invoked eugenics slogans.[10] Attempts to create representations of "pure"

---

8. On the recoding of the "Peking opera" (京劇) into "national drama" (國劇), see Goldstein 1999. For Chinese nationalists, perhaps the most important "national" term was "national essence" (國粹). On the history of this late Qing import from Japan, see Schneider 1976 and, more recently, L. H. Liu 1995: 239–56. For additional examples of similarly nationalized nouns, see Mathews et al. 1966: 550–52. The Mathews dictionary was originally compiled in 1931 at the height of the movement.

9. Scholar and reformer Liang Qichao 梁啓超 (1873–1929), for instance, conceptualized all of history in racial terms: "What is history? It is simply the story of racial development and racial strife" (quoted in Pusey 1983: 196). On the spread of racial discourses in China, see Dikötter 1992: 98–115. In East Asia more generally, see the essays in Dikötter 1997 and Kaiwing Chow 1997, 2001. For an overview of the popularity of racial competition in framing Chinese nationalism, see Mitter 2000: 158–65. The links between discourses of hygiene and cleanliness and consumer goods in China have not been studied. For a suggestive introduction to the connections in Europe and America, however, see Forty 1986: 156–81. On eugenics in China, see Dikötter 1998: 104–18.

10. For instance, the movement publication *Jilian huikan* 機聯會刊, the official magazine of one of the largest movement organizations, regularly printed the slogan "Emphasize eugen-

national products thus paralleled and may even have been derived from eugenics.[11]

The abundance of related strands of nationalized discourse clarifies my main point. My claim is not that early proponents of nationalism conceived their ideas wholly through the movement. By the early twentieth century, the idea of the nation, in specific individuals or specific discursive forums, took many different forms. Rather, the movement was a driving force behind the spread of nationalist sentiment throughout China as a whole. It put "nation" in front of everyone's eyes, on everyone's back, and on everyone's table and tongue. The elaboration, intensification, and institutionalization of this movement, in turn, provided new platforms and points of reference for further developments of nationalism.

INSTITUTIONAL ELABORATION

The movement involved much more than new coinages and name-calling. At its core, it also attempted to create, introduce, and reinforce new patterns of group behavior and new systems of social regulation and order and to integrate them into a nascent nationalistic consumer culture. The development of national product certification standards, examined in the second half of Chapter 4, can serve as a model for understanding this institutional elaboration of the movement as a whole. In the early stages, there was no clear-cut way of defining and identifying national products. Various systems of certification emerged in non-government organizations as makeshift centrifuges for separating foreign contaminants from the Chinese market. Then, growing links between organizations popularized the desire for a single standard of certification. Regular anti-imperialist boycotts intensified the need for explicit standards that identified precisely which products Chinese should and should not boycott. Finally, in 1928, a new national government

---

ics as the initial step in strengthening the country" (注重優生學為強國之初步). See, e.g., *Jilian huikan* 44 (1931.10.16): 50.

11. In another national context, Ohnuki-Tierney (1995) notes that Japanese "white rice" (*hakumai* 白米) was also known as "pure rice" (*junmai* 純米) and "became a powerful metaphor for the purity of the Japanese self" (ibid., p. 232). She further notes the ways Japanese identity was constructed first against the notion of Chinese rice and later against the meat-eating West. See also Ohnuki-Tierney 1993. Social scientists have long recognized the literal objectification of cultural identity; see Bourdieu 1977.

formalized national certification standards. It made these standards law and institutionalized incentives for their application.

Clearly, national product standards codified the pre-eminence of product-nationality, but consumers did not automatically come to view products in this way. The more elaborate the movement, the greater the efforts of recalcitrant individuals to circumvent it and hence the greater the need for further controls to persuade them to adhere to the movement's goals. Physical and visual spaces—what I call "nationalistic commodity spectacles"—functioned as forums to concentrate Chinese consumers' attention and condition them to recognize and valorize certified products. The movement, then, included a specific form of socialized or culturally constructed vision, a *nationalistic visuality* centered on training the eye to identify visual clues and to distinguish between the foreign and domestic across social life.[12] This attempt to construct a nationalistic visuality was part of all aspects of the movement; for this reason, examples of this visuality are reproduced and analyzed in every chapter. The National Products Exhibition of 1928, to take one example, essentially achieved the movement's goal in miniature by creating a completely nationalized visual and physical space intended for the nation as a whole. Everything—from the advertisements on the walls of the exhibition hall to the dress of attendees to every product on display to the towels in the men's room—was a certified national product. Within this miniature nation of national products, consumers learned that they themselves could lead a life that was materially pure Chinese. Indeed, within this nationalistic commodity spectacle, it was impossible to visualize or live any other life.

PARTICIPANTS

Prominent commercial and industrial leaders, individuals with clear economic interests at stake, formed the backbone of the movement throughout China. These entrepreneurs became living examples of two common expressions of the day: "Business enterprises rescue the nation" (實業救國) and "Establish factories for national self-preservation" (設廠自救). As Chapter 1 explains, they established the businesses that formed the foundation of this new consumer culture, manufacturing personal hygiene articles such as toothpaste and soap, textile products like towels and silk dresses, and

---

12. On the cultural conditioning of sight, see Walker and Chaplin 1997 and H. Foster 1988.

household goods such as light bulbs and electric fans, as well as the international icon of this culture, plastic (Gu Weicheng 1996). Zhang Jian 張謇 (1853–1926), the reformer of Nantong in Jiangsu province, for instance, tried to save China nearly single-handedly by industrializing one town, and founded dozens of companies, including the Dasheng Cotton Mill (大生紗廠) (Nakai Hideki 1996). Among the most active movement participants in north China was Song Zejiu 宋則久 (1867–1956), the Tianjin merchant-activist who established match and toothpaste companies as well as organized a local branch of a key movement organization. Among the many other leading industrialists who participated were the powerful Rong brothers of Shanghai, Rong Zongjing 榮宗敬 (1873–1938) and Rong Desheng 榮德生 (1875–1952), who became known as China's "flour and cotton kings" (Huang Hanmin 1996); China's "match king" Liu Hongsheng 劉鴻生 (1888–1956) (Yang Chengqi 1996); and the founders of China's modern chemical industry, Shanghai's Wu Yunchu 吳蘊初 (1891–1953) (see Chapter 8) and Tianjin's Fan Xudong 范旭東 (1883–1945) (Han Yin 1996).

The movement also included innumerable less widely known proto-industrialists, whose new consumer goods competed directly with imports. An example is Fang Yexian 方液仙 (1893–1940), the co-founder of the China Chemical Industries Company (中國化學工業社), which made mosquito coils, tooth powder, food-flavoring powder, and soap. He used movement ideology to promote his products and later helped establish a store on Shanghai's main commercial street, Nanjing Road, devoted exclusively to selling national products (Ma Bingrong 1996b). Likewise, the Jian 簡 brothers formed the Nanyang Brothers Tobacco Company and actively contrasted their "Chinese" cigarettes with the "foreign" British-American Tobacco products (see Cochran 1980). Chen Diexian 陳蝶仙 (1878–1940), the founder of the consumer goods company Household Enterprises (家庭工業社), was also a primary participant and wrote widely on movement and social issues under his pen name, Tianxu Wosheng 天虛我生. Other participants in the movement were Song Feiqing 宋斐卿 (1898–1956), a co-founder of the East Asia Wool Textile Company (東亞毛呢紡織股份有限公司), whose spun wool remains popular in China today (Zhao Zizhen 1996), and the founders of Three Friends Enterprises (三友實業社), whose company capitalized on anti-imperialist sentiment by manufacturing and marketing "freedom cloth" (自由布) and "patriotic blue cloth" (愛國藍布) in the 1920s (Li Daofa 1996). Xiang Songmao 項松茂 (1880–1932),

the founder of the Five Continents Dispensary Company (五洲大藥房股份有限公司), China's most important distributor and, later, manufacturer of pharmacological products such as soap and health tonics, also became an active participant (Xiang Zenan 1996). Indeed, every industrialist participated in the movement in one form or another.

Before the re-emergence of a relatively strong state in 1927–28, much of the organizational and financial strength of the movement came from economic interest groups formed by business leaders who owned consumer goods industries. Local chambers of commerce, native-place associations, and newer ad hoc organizations specifically devoted to the movement had a huge financial stake in linking consumerism and nationalism to protect what they had come to consider *their* home market. Throughout this period, as Chapter 1 shows, Chinese enterprises struggled to maintain market share and gain acceptance for manufactures that competed directly with imports. As Chapter 2 shows, economic interest groups such as silk and hat manufacturers spread the notion of nationalistic consumption.

However, we can also find participants in the movement in unexpected quarters. Many other people became involved in the movement, sometimes unwittingly and often unwillingly. During the frequent anti-imperialist boycotts discussed in Chapters 3 and 4, students of all ages joined in the movement. The more extreme among them vowed not to consume imports, forced merchants to adhere to boycotts, and even made and sold national products. Instead of settling on any one group that beat the drum of nationalism and drove the Chinese public to consume patriotically, this book identifies the multiple discourses and institutions that formed this context and thus reveals the consequences of a nationalized consumer culture, consequences unforeseen by the movement's original supporters and beneficiaries.

Nor did all the participants share the same motivation. As I show in Chapters 3 and 4, zealous students and opportunistic hooligans often appropriated these categories of national and foreign products to justify violence against anyone refusing to boycott foreign goods or to "donate" to "patriotic organizations." In fact, the U.S. consul in the southern coastal city of Fuzhou in the late 1920s concluded that movement organizations were "often a euphemism for black-mail gangs."[13] Indeed, according to two foreign

---

13. Fuzhou consul Samuel Sokobin, report to U.S. Secretary of State, 1929.8.21, File 893.504/62, Central Records of the Department of State, RG59 (National Archives) [hereafter, CRDS]: 3.

correspondents for the *New York Times*, "the confiscation and resale of Japanese goods and the illegal 'fining' of merchants" were typical parts of the frequent anti-imperialist boycotts (Abend and Billingham 1936: 45). In one notorious case, the leader of a large student organization used his position to enrich both himself and his cronies by extorting money from merchants. Angered by his betrayal, a group of more radical students—the Iron and Blood Society (鐵血團)—assassinated him "on behalf of our 400,000,000 country-men."[14] Throughout China, merchants who refused to stop selling Japanese products were murdered. Such activities discredited the movement but reinforced the hegemony of the notion that products had nationalities and that citizens within a nation owed their allegiance to its products.

We tend to associate social movements with conspicuous activities such as marches, incendiary handbills, and slogan-filled rallies or subtle actions such as donations to a movement's organizations or support for movement-backed politicians. The genius of this movement was that every consumer was a participant. Even those opting to buy foreign products were participants in a negative way. Because every consumer could choose to support the movement, its goal was to ensure that every consumer—every citizen—did.

"Chinese People Ought to Consume Chinese Products"

Consumerism has become a key concept in analyzing the modern history of North America and Western Europe. Many academic disciplines have begun to posit that individuals increasingly experience life as "consumers" living in "consumer cultures." Individuals are said to construct their identities increasingly through, as I have defined consumer culture, the consumption of branded, mass-produced commodities and the orientation of their social life and discourse around such commodities. In American history, the ideology of this culture, consumerism, has been called the "real winner" of the

---

14. Fuzhou consul to U.S. Secretary of State, 1920.12.10, CRDS File 893.43B62. The Iron and Blood Society circulated a handbill to explain its actions and serve notice to other "traitors." There are extensive reports of such organizations enforcing boycotts. See, e.g., the newspaper clippings on the attacks on the editor of the Shanghai mosquito press newspaper, *Dajingbao*, in Shanghai Municipal Police [hereafter, SMP] 5790, 1934.4–5: "Anti-Japanese Movement—Mosquito newspaper office attacked" and other articles. I examine this overtly coercive side of the movement in Part II.

twentieth century and "the 'ism' that won" (Cross 2000: 1).[15] Likewise, historians of Western Europe have identified a "consumer revolution" that accompanied or even predated the better-studied Industrial Revolution (McKendrick et al. 1982). Historians continue to push the origins of this revolution back by centuries and into historical subfields as diverse as gender and labor history.[16]

Although these concepts are less commonly applied to other areas of the world, it is a mistake to assume, as these studies often do, that consumerism is a uniquely "Western" phenomenon.[17] Consumerism, this book argues, was critical to the creation of modern China. More important, this book suggests that the development of consumerism was not uniform around the globe. Studies of the history and economics of consumerism routinely emphasize the role of the market in enabling the exercise of personal choice (for the classic statement of this position, see Milton Friedman and R. D. Friedman 1982: esp. 7–21); indeed, as sociologist Zygmund Bauman (1988: 7–8) observes, the very notion of individual freedom itself has been conceptualized in terms of consumer choice.[18] In contrast, consumerism in China was not only, or even

---

15. Cross continues: "Consumerism, the belief that goods give meaning to individuals and their roles in society, was victorious even though it had no formal philosophy, no parties, and no obvious leaders." Historians of the United States have begun to rethink every major aspect of the country's history through the lens of consumerism. For a collection of representative essays, see Glickman 1999.

16. Consumerism has already been interpreted as an important component of Western European society dating back through the Renaissance (see Jardine 1996) and into classical antiquity (see Davidson 1999). On consumption and gender alone, see, e.g., the broad range of essays and the literature review in de Grazia and Furlough 1996 and Scanlon 2000. On labor, see Glickman 1997.

17. Many of these studies begin by stating without evidence that their generalizations apply only to "the West." See, e.g., de Grazia 1996: 1. Paul Glennie (1995: 164) is more circumspect. Writing a review of the historiography of the study of consumption, he notes that his generalizations are limited by the dearth of scholarship on the history of consumption outside Europe and the United States. For an exception, see Burke 1996. For a critique, see Clunas 1991: 3.

18. Likewise, Don Slater identifies the common equation of consumerism and freedom: "Consumer culture denotes a social arrangement in which the relation between lived culture and social resources, between meaningful ways of life and the symbolic and material resources on which they depend, is mediated through markets. Consumer culture marks out a system in which consumption is dominated by the consumption of commodities, and in which cultural reproduction is largely understood to be carried out through the exercise of free personal choice in the private sphere of everyday life" (1997: 8). For a scathing critique of the conflation of American democracy and the discourse of the marketplace, see T. Frank 2000.

primarily, about individual freedom, self-expression, and pleasure, and it would be a mistake for students of consumerism to reach the same conclusions for China. Rather than solely providing agency- or freedom-generating mechanisms, the nationalization of consumerism in China also imposed serious constraints on individuals. The purpose of the movement was to stress the national implications of the behavior of the individual consumer. A consumer was either patriotic or treasonous. According to the movement's rhetoric (exemplified in the heading of this section, "Chinese people ought to consume Chinese products," a common slogan), Chinese, newly defined as "citizens" or "national people" (國民), were to envisage themselves as members of the new political collectivity known as the Chinese "nation" (國家) by consuming "national products" (國貨).[19] Through this simple equation of citizenship, nationality, and consumption, the movement denied the consumer a place outside the nation as economy and nation became coterminous. The movement did not recognize an abstract world of goods; rather, it divided the world into nations of products (see Fig. I.1).

Freedom in the marketplace may be more the exception than the rule in the histories of consumerism around the world. China is not the only country that attempted to nationalize its consumer culture and constrain personal choice. The *swadeshi* (belonging to one's own country) and non-cooperation movements in India (1904–8, 1920–22) are the best-known and best-studied equivalents of China's National Products Movement. Likewise, Americanists have been aware of links between consumerism and nationalism since late colonial times.[20] These are not isolated cases. Japan, Ireland, Korea, Britain, France, Germany, Nigeria, and Spain, among other countries, also experienced similar "national products movements" with varying intensity in nation-making projects from late colonial times to the present.[21]

---

19. Movement literature explicitly drew such equations. See, e.g., "'Guohuo' he 'guomin'" and "Zhongguo huo xianyao Zhongguoren ziji yong qilai." On the introduction of and connections between the concepts of citizenship and nationality by journalists, see Judge 1996: esp. 83–99.

20. The best studies of national products movements focus on late colonial American history. See, e.g., Schlesinger 1957 and Breen 1988. For a survey of "Buy American" campaigns since the Revolution, see D. Frank 1999.

21. The terms applied to the histories of other countries that overlap with the term "nationalizing consumer culture," as I use it here, include "indigenization," "indigenism," "domestication," "import-substitution," "decolonization," "autarky," and "de-foreignization." See, e.g.,

Fig. I.1 A Nation as Products

This advertisement, which appeared regularly in the national newspaper *Shenbao* in the early 1930s, illustrates the goals of the National Products Movement. Here an agglomeration of national products represents the Chinese nation. The advertisement cleverly plays on a widely shared fear of national destruction that predicted the imperialist powers would carve up China like a melon and gobble up the country bit by bit like silkworms eating a mulberry leaf. The Chinese characters superimposed on Manchuria (*upper right*), which in effect had been annexed by Japan in 1931, warn consumers that "buying foreign products" was the equivalent of arming China's enemies while consuming national products would place these enemies in a "hopeless situation." The implication was that the production, circulation, and consumption of national products acted as a figurative insecticide that ensured national salvation by preventing foreign products (silk worms) from gradually conquering the Chinese market (mulberry leaf).

Indeed, advocates of the movement in China regularly sought to inspire consumers with reports on the activities of similar movements in other countries.[22] The movement in China, then, should be seen as one among many rather than a unique phenomenon. That is not to suggest these movements unfolded in a uniform way. What makes the Chinese case particularly interesting for comparative purposes is that the country was not formally colonized yet lacked many aspects of sovereignty, including the ability to set tariffs. It was, to use the common Chinese term for its situation, "semi-colonial" (半殖民地的). And, for this reason, the movement was not, nor could it have been, solely state-directed.

Despite the emergence of such movements throughout the globe, historians have neither devoted much attention to them nor suggested that they are key aspects of nation-making. When mentioned at all, the nationalization of consumer culture is treated as a natural by-product of the creation of nation-states. In fact, the causes and consequences of nationalizing commodities played a crucial role in creating nations. I argue here that a Chinese nation did not precede the notion of "Chinese products." The two constructs evolved together. Nation-making included learning, or being coerced, to shape preferences around something called the Chinese nation and away from items deemed foreign—a problematic process reinforced by institutional elaborations.

Most discussions of consumerism have not placed it at the center of nationalism. None of the studies of India, the most promising parallel to China, provides comprehensive accounts of a national products movement; these studies generally subordinate aspects of the national products movement to either business strategy (e.g., attempts by Bengali textile producers to preserve their market share) or Mohandas Gandhi's (1869–1948) attempt to promote spiritual revival through self-reliance.[23] Indeed, the National

---

W. J. MacPherson 1987: 32; Constantine 1981; Robinson 1988: 92–100; Nelson 2000; and Balabkins 1982. For a survey of the various approaches to "indigenization" taken throughout Africa, see Adedeji 1981. On South America, see Orlove 1997. On Southeast Asia, see Golay et al. 1969. Similarly, consumption campaigns also create and solidify socially constructed categories other than nationality, such as ethnic awareness among African Americans (see, e.g., Skotnes 1994 and C. Greenberg 1999). Or, indeed, they may include both nationality and ethnicity, as in the anti-Jewish boycotts in pre–World War II Germany (see Barkai 1989).

22. See, e.g., "Aiyong guohuo fengqi zhi puji," 2.

23. See Sarkar 1973 and Chandra 1966: 122–41. On Gandhi's ties, see J. M. Brown 1989: 89–90, 163–64, and 203–5; and Bean 1989. A brief lecture by a prominent subaltern scholar, how-

Products Movement agenda provides a sharp contrast to Gandhi's emphasis on simple living and tradition.[24] Likewise, survey introductions to nationalism rarely discuss attempts to nationalize consumer culture (see, e.g., Smith 1998). Finally, studies of economic nationalism focus on the political discourse of economic and political leaders rather than on a widespread and multidimensional social movement.[25]

Studies that do integrate consumerism and nationalism emphasize voluntary participation in consumption (e.g., watching movies, reading newspapers, going bowling); because such consumption is "shared," it helps create the basis for a shared national identity (e.g., L. Cohen 1990). In contrast, consumption in China was often coerced. The movement contributed to nation-making not only by spreading a new consumer culture of mass-produced tastes and habits (that is, the basis of shared, nationwide consumption) but also by attempting to restrict consumption exclusively to national products, often through violence. "National products," moreover, were themselves closely scrutinized for national content in terms of the four categories of raw materials, labor, management, and capital. Thus, the emphasis in my study differs significantly from the histories of the late nineteenth- and early twentieth-century United States, which, when examining the role of consumption in creating a shared national identity, stress only that the consumption of a particular article or activity took place do-

---

ever, emphasizes the coercive component of the *swadeshi* movement; see Guha 1991: 1–18. For a subtle introduction to the origins of *swadeshi*, see Bayly 1986. As in the Chinese case, literature provides the most morally complex portrait of the participants. In 1919, the Nobel Prize-winning Indian writer Rabindranath Tagore captured the coercive side of the *swadeshi* movement in his novel *Ghare baire* (*The Home and the World*).

24. For an overview of the anti-materialistic emphasis in Gandhi's ideas, see Misra 1995. Despite Gandhi's emphasis on limiting material desires and creating self-sufficient villages, his ideas did overlap with the movement on one fundamental issue. Both rejected a simple embrace of capitalist relations that privileged price over provenance. Criticizing those who argued that the use of home-spun was costlier than mill-made cloth, Gandhi said that if expense were the most important issue, then, by the same logic, we should kill our aged parents and young children "whom we have to maintain without getting anything in return" (quoted in Misra 1995: 35).

25. Moreover, some studies recognize "nationality" as a significant category of consumption without explaining the historical origins. For instance, Joseph Tobin notes that "in Japan, before a food, an article of clothing, or a piece of furniture is evaluated as good or bad, expensive or cheap, it is identified as either foreign or Japanese" (1992a: 25–26).

mestically.[26] For the Chinese movement, it would not have been enough for citizens simply to read the same nationally circulated newspaper and imagine the same national events. Rather, regardless of the event being reported or editorialized, citizens were expected to read papers printed on the products of Chinese paper mills, produced by Chinese workers and managers, and owned by Chinese capitalists. Enforcing these principles led to the proliferation of specific institutions and laws. The modern Chinese nation was not simply "imagined"—it was made in China.

PROBLEMS OF PRE-EMINENCE

Participants in the movement clearly saw themselves as involved in an aggressive campaign, to use their own terms, of "cleansing China's national humiliations" (雪國恥 or simply 雪恥). Part of this campaign was the forcible removal of foreign elements from Chinese production and markets, thereby producing "authentic" (真正), "pure" (單純), and "complete" (完全) Chinese products. This was an impossible ideal, especially at this point of Chinese economic and political development, and it was certainly never fully realized before the re-emergence of a strong centralized state with the Communist Revolution in 1949.

Still, the central problem for the movement was how to make product-nationality the pre-eminent or most important meaning of a commodity— that is, to "nationalize consumer culture"—even in this problematic context. Price and quality certainly challenged the supremacy of product-nationality. It is safe to assume that consumers wanted to buy the least expensive and best-made goods, which were often mass-produced imports. Brand loyalty, including loyalty to foreign brands, also hindered the ability of the movement to assert the pre-eminence of product-nationality. Indeed, in 1937, Carl Crow, who established one of the first advertising agencies in China, claimed Chinese consumers scrutinized brands and packaging to avoid ever-present counterfeit goods: "[Once they] have become accustomed to a certain brand, no matter whether it be cigarettes, soap or tooth paste, they are the world's most loyal consumers, and will support a brand with a degree of unanimity

---

26. Early influential studies include Boorstin 1973: 89–164; Ewen and Ewen 1982; and Fox and Lears 1983. On this approach within studies of nationalism more generally, see, e.g., Anderson 1983: 39, on activities such as newspaper reading.

and faithfulness which should bring tears of joy to the eyes of the manufacturer" (Crow 1937: 17–18).

Considerations of style were also of clear importance to many urban consumers in China in the early twentieth century. In fact, foreign fashions, introduced by Japanese, British, American, French, and other imperialist powers, exerted a heavy influence. To a great degree, imports of any kind were by definition fashionable. Foreign residents of the treaty ports, Chinese students returning from abroad, missionaries in inland areas, and a plethora of new foreign and Chinese media exposed many in China to images that challenged the pre-eminence of nationality within the marketplace. As a result, the social requirement to appear cosmopolitan frequently overwhelmed the injunction to "Buy Chinese." Then, as now, the power of "Paris," and, more generally, "the West," was often unrivaled, certainly by any domestic equivalents.

The question for the movement was how to push product-nationality to the forefront, given all these competitors—how to make it the foremost consideration of consumers in China. As I have suggested, the campaign began with appeals to patriotism. But because the concepts of citizenship and patriotism were new and meaningless to many millions, such appeals were largely unsuccessful. The movement soon turned to more persuasive tactics ranging from legal institutions to brute force. Building national consciousness in China was a long and complicated process. The movement played a key role in this process, but it was neither a uniform movement at all times and in all places nor an uninterrupted success story. A triumph in Shanghai might not be matched in Nanjing, let alone further away in the communications grid; gains were often followed by setbacks.

Nationalizing consumer culture does *not* refer to the removal of products or product elements simply because of the non-Chinese origin of their *invention*. As one collection of essays on the history of imports in Latin America confirms, the notion of a national product is in fact an "almost infinitely plastic concept" (Orlove and Bauer 1997: 13). Both "Chinese" and "foreign" were flexible constructs. The definition of foreign could vary over time in order to stigmatize specific commodities, companies, and consumers (for instance, two extreme periods of hostility toward anything identified as "Western" occurred during the Boxer Uprising, 1899–1901, and the Cultural Revolution, 1966–76). For stylistic simplicity, I use the terms "imports" and "foreign products" synonymously. However, within the movement, the term "foreign products" came to include certain commodities made in China. Similarly, as I show in Chapter 2, in the controversy over "authentic styles" for Chinese men and women, movement advocates opposed certain clothing fashions not because the styles originated outside China but because they were made without (or with too few of) the four critical ingredients of a national product: raw material, labor, management, and capital. Indeed, traditional Chinese clothing was susceptible to the same scrutiny and action, whereas goods of Western invention might be worn without censure provided such commodities met the movement's production standards. The movement eventually enshrined these standards in a seven-tier classification scheme of product purity based on the percentage of domestic content in each of the four categories (see Chapter 4).

This attempt to draw sharp distinctions between foreign and domestic products is not unique to China and is common today. "National cultural content" regulations are routinely used throughout the world to preserve national identities (often, to resist "Americanization"). France, for instance, requires theaters to reserve twenty weeks of screen time per year for domestic feature films. Similarly, Australia demands that domestic programming occupy 55 percent of the television schedule. And in Canada, 35 percent of the daytime play list of radio stations must be devoted to Canadian content. In the Canadian case, music with "Canadian content" is defined not with respect to form, instrumentation, or lyrical content but according to its conditions of production, a direct parallel to definitions of national products in China considered here. "Canadian" songs are composed, written, and played by Canadians; presumably the subject matter or message of the song is unrestricted.[27] Similarly, within the National Products Movement, national product-brand tuxedos and electric fans qualified as perfectly "Chinese" (see Fig. I.2).

This recognition of the complexity of commodities is not new. As Karl Marx famously observed, analyzing them reveals that they are actually "a very queer thing, abounding in metaphysical subtleties and theological

---

27. On the problem of determining "nationality," see Anthony DePalma, "It Isn't So Simple to Be Canadian: Tough Rules Protecting the Culture Make for Confusion and Surprises," *New York Times* 1999.7.14: B1–2. For example, non-Canadian Lenny Kravitz's song "American Woman" is considered more Canadian than Canadian singer Celine Dion's "My Heart Will Go On." In contrast to Dion's song, Canadians wrote the lyrics and composed the music for "American Woman."

Fig. I.2 What Is Chinese?

What is "Chinese" and what is "foreign" in this calendar poster of women playing miniature golf in Shanghai from the early 1930s? The National Products Movement taught consumers to interpret the "nationality" of a product as its *pre-eminent* attribute. The conditions of production rather than the national origins of the style or type of good defined product-nationality. A pure "Chinese product" was made from Chinese raw materials, by Chinese laborers, under Chinese management, in a company owned by Chinese. Accordingly, the golf clubs could easily have been "more Chinese" than the silk *qipao* dresses, which quite likely were made from Japanese silk.

niceties" (1967, vol. 1: 71). Of course, Marx and, later, Chinese Marxists "de-fetishized" commodities and criticized capitalism and imperialism by argu-ing that commodities presented social relations between people as relations between things, thereby facilitating the alienation of workers and products (see Jhally 1990: 24–63). For Marxists, labor is the pre-eminent meaning of commodities. Chinese Marxists, in fact, had more in common with move-ment business people than might at first be imagined. Both focused on production. But movement supporters emphasized that the provenance of production, not the individual labor involved in production, was of para-mount importance as a unifying principle of a people ("Consumers of the Chinese nation unite!"). In essence, Chinese Marxists aided the movement in the 1920s and 1930s by promoting the elimination of what they consid-ered the concrete manifestation of imperialism in China: foreign commodi-ties. The business and government leaders involved in the movement did not return the favor; they asserted that "labor" and "capital" should "coop-erate" (勞資合作) in the interests of developing the national economy. Strikes were "unpatriotic."

There are clearly countless possible meanings that can be assigned to commodities. Today various social movements have sought to elevate other concerns to a position of pre-eminence in the marketplace (see Monroe Friedman 1999). For example, the environmental movement promotes the notion of ecological impact as the chief meaning of commodities. Environ-mentalists stigmatize manufacturers (and consumers) that undermine their agenda. Similarly, the civil rights movement in the United States adopted slogans such as "Don't buy where you can't work" to promote racial equality through consumer boycotts. When Americans became concerned that there was a "glass ceiling" for women at major companies, John Kenneth Galbraith (1990) created a fictional character who promoted the idea of disclosing the "female executive content" on all product labels.

In contrast to these and all other conceivable criteria, proponents of the National Products Movement claimed to uncover a different but truly pre-eminent meaning of commodities: nationality. Its advocates attempted to convince consumers that products—like Chinese consumers themselves (in-deed, like consumers of any country)—had essential or inalienable national identities. The movement insisted that wealthy and powerful nations in the industrial West as well as Japan had already established the supremacy of product-nationality. In classic hegemonic fashion, the movement, like the social movements just cited, advanced a universalistic claim. Ironically, the movement's claim functioned to particularize the world.

Overview

As the foregoing suggests, the movement was multidimensional. In this book, I do not provide an exhaustive treatment of the movement; rather, in four parts, I explore its primary dimensions. Part I (Chapters 1 and 2) answers the difficult questions of when, why, and how the movement began. Why did Chinese begin to define their material culture in terms of nationality by 1900? On what grounds did the movement attempt to nationalize consumption and impose a nationalistic visuality? Chapter 2 focuses on exactly how specific objects and practices became "national" or "Chinese" by showing how hairstyles and clothing were constructed as visual cues of patriotism and treason. Part II (Chapters 3 and 4) examines the movement as the foundation of regular anti-imperialist boycotts, which popularized links between nationalism and consumerism and made anti-imperial resistance available to, indeed increasingly mandatory for, all Chinese. Part III (Chapters 5 and 6) explores the ways nationalistic commodity spectacles such as product exhibitions, department stores, museums, and advertisements naturalized and coded the link between consumption and nationalism in subtler, less contentious ways than boycotts. The final part (Chapters 7 and 8) unravels the ways the movement helped define gender norms, particularly through its two central archetypes: the "treasonously wasteful female consumer" and the "patriotic male producer."

As the movement expanded, the notion that there were such things as national products to which citizen-consumers automatically owed their allegiance gained currency. Increasingly, the lines became drawn, and a nascent state apparatus backed by revolutionary elements in the society became willing and able to enforce nationalistic consumption. Thus, the movement was not important only, or even primarily, because of its influence on immediately expressed market preferences. When given the option, plenty of consumers still chose inexpensive imports over patriotic "national products." Rather, it was significant because it made such alternatives increasingly unavailable. The ultimate irony, discussed in the Conclusion, is that the largest economic interests supporting the movement, those Chinese capitalists who were involved in the production and circulation of domestically produced commodities, may have inadvertently provided the noose the Communists used to hang them after 1949. The logic of a movement which insisted that products were "national" was easily used to undermine the notion that profits derived from selling such goods ought to be "private." The legacies of the National Products Movement are visible across the twentieth century.

PART I

Contexts and Case Study

CHAPTER ONE

The Crisis over Commodities

and the Origins of the Movement

Everything which the people need for their well-being and sustenance, whether it be for food or clothing or even delicacies and superfluities, is abundantly produced within the borders of the kingdom and not imported from foreign climes.

—Oft-repeated seventeenth-century European assessment of the tremendous wealth and self-sufficiency of the Chinese economy (quoted in Lach and van Kley 1993: 1593)

$219,213,000

—China's deficit in 1905

The origins of efforts to nationalize consumer culture lie in a nineteenth-century crisis over commodities. The perception among people in China that they were members of a self-sufficient civilization that produced tea, porcelains, and silks desired by the rest of the world began to erode. They started to visualize themselves as members of a weak "nation" unable to control the flood of commodities displacing Chinese exports in foreign markets and streaming into China. Goods started to acquire nationalities; commodities produced in China became "Chinese products" or "national products" (國貨). This transition in the perception of China from the cultural center of the universe, the Middle Kingdom, to a single nation in a world of homologous nation-states was not simply a product of repeated military defeats. At least as important was this redefinition of commodities. As anxiety over the growth of imports and decline of market share for exports increased, there was a growing perception that China's material culture was being replaced subtly but pervasively by imports. Indeed, the names attached to many of these imports helped undermine this earlier self-image because embedded in the common terms for many categories of late nineteenth-century imports was the prefix "foreign" (洋).[1]

Two events bracket this long nineteenth-century economic crisis. In 1793, the Qianlong emperor (r. 1736–96) was sufficiently unimpressed with British wares to dismiss the diplomatic overtures of King George III with the now famous line: "There is nothing we lack, as your principal envoy and others have themselves observed. We have never set much store on strange or ingenious objects, nor do we need any more of your country's manufactures."[2] And many Europeans shared the emperor's sentiment; contemporary Europeans often expressed a variation on the remark "China produces everything necessary for human life and thus does not need foreign trade" (Lach and van Kley 1993: 1593).[3] However, as this chapter demonstrates, perceptions of the superiority of Chinese material culture declined markedly over the course of the nineteenth century. The fruits of industrialization in Europe, America, and eventually Japan—along with cheaper transportation costs—created among the Chinese many hungers in addition to opium, most notably the desire for Western military hardware. A little over a century later,

---

1. For example, "foreign fire" (洋火) for matches, "foreign oil" (洋油) for kerosene, "foreign needles" (洋針) for imported needles. Other examples include "foreign soap" (洋皂), "foreign yarn" (洋紗), "foreign thread" (洋線), "foreign umbrellas" (洋傘), and "foreign lamps" (洋燈). For additional examples, see Mathews et al. 1966: 1084. As I discuss below, not only did the varieties of imported goods grow, but also the quantities expanded. To cite one example, from the mid-1860s to the mid-1890s, the number of imported "foreign needles" grew from roughly 200 million to over 2.4 billion per year. Moreover, the market for such products, unlike some luxury goods, extended into the countryside (Shanghai baihuo gongsi et al. 1988: 4–6). Other popular consumer imports at this time were lace, towels, handkerchiefs, socks, cosmetics, perfume, and candies. The varieties and quantities of these imported mass-produced consumer goods were carefully recorded in the publications of the Chinese Maritime Customs Service, which during this time was run by foreigners, primarily British. The extensive statistical reports are summarized in many places; see, e.g., Hsiao Liang-lin 1974.

2. Qianlong's "Imperial edict to the King of England" of 1793, translated in Teng and Fairbank 1954: 19 and countless other places cited in Hevia 1995: 238n13. Hevia reinterprets the context and implications of this famous line and concludes that the Qianlong emperor was not rejecting trade with Great Britain but rather the excessive "claims about the gifts" sent by the English monarch (ibid.: 188, 238–39).

3. On the view among European visitors to late Ming and early Qing China that the country had an impressive and abundant material culture, Lach and van Kley note that the "usual reaction to the fertility of the land and the diversity of its products was one of amazement" (1993: 1593).

Fig. 1.1 Consumer and Consumed
(John Thomson 1874: vol. 1)

Between the late eighteenth and early twentieth centuries, in the minds of foreigners and Chinese alike, the image of China changed from an empire feared for its power and admired for its products to a country of poorly equipped soldiers and indolent consumers exemplified in the popular image of the prototypical wasteful Chinese consumer, the debauched addict of "foreign smoke" (洋煙 or "opium").

China's humiliation was complete. Not only had the Japanese, popularly known by the derisive term "dwarf pirates" (倭 寇), defeated China in war (1894–95), but by 1909 Japan also surpassed China as the largest exporter of silk, a product virtually synonymous with China for thousands of years (L. M. Li 1981: 83–84) (see Fig. 1.1).[4]

Despite the growing anxiety over the future of "Chinese products," nationalizing Chinese consumer culture proved to be difficult. In Chinese

---

4. Indeed, the term "silk" comes from the Greek name for an area thought to be China (Seres), where it was believed silk originated. The export market for another commodity synonymous with China, tea (the English term for which is derived from a Chinese dialect), also collapsed in the early twentieth century, becoming the subject of the same sort of anxiety (Gardella 1994: 8, 142–60). In modern times, the Japanese, too, reconstructed "China" through a negative image; see, e.g., Fogel 1996: 75–78.

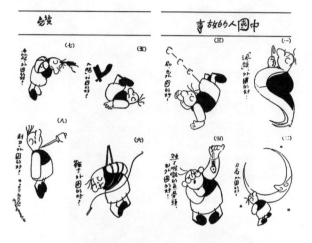

Fig. 1.2 Worshipping the Foreign
(*Jilian huikan* 169 [June 15, 1937])

Attempts to nationalize consumer culture usually insisted that the provenance of a style was not the issue. Any style (Chinese or Western) was acceptable as long as the products themselves were Chinese made. At the same time, the movement sought to counter the perception that spread during the nineteenth century that everything foreign was superior to anything Chinese, an equation that heightened demand for imports. Moving from top to bottom and from right to left, the eight captions, in what is billed as "The Story of the Chinese," read: "(1) Foreign mannerisms are superior! (2) The moon overseas is brighter! (3) Foreign farts are superior! (4) Foreign fish bones and fish heads are also superior! (5) What about being kicked around by foreign boots, is that a good thing? (6) Are foreign whips better? (7) Are foreign handguns superior? (8) And are foreign knives better?"

cities, efforts to nationalize consumption evolved in a milieu in which "foreign" implied "better" seemingly everywhere—from concepts of male and female beauty to forms of sport and entertainment to styles of architecture and personal appearance to new institutions of government, commerce, and leisure. Even (perhaps, especially) in places known as "antiforeign" such as Guangzhou (Canton), imports simultaneously created admiration and animosity (see Fig. 1.2).[5]

5. On the popular ambivalence toward "the West" in Guangzhou, see Ho 1991. This fascination with imports was not entirely new. On interest in exotic imports and their influence on China during the Tang dynasty (618–907), see Schafer 1963.

Foreign Exposure

National consciousness in China did grow from direct exposure to Western peoples and ideas. More significantly, however, it also grew indirectly from exposure to Western material culture. During the nineteenth century, Europeans and Americans demanded access to China and eventually achieved it through force. As the number of foreigners living in China grew, so did the opportunities for Chinese to encounter a different material culture. By the mid-1870s, thirty years after first gaining the right to reside in five Chinese cities, some 4,000 Westerners (Americans and Europeans) were living in China. By the Revolution of 1911, the foreign population exceeded 150,000, and by 1927, it was over 300,000.[6] During this period, a growing number of Chinese diplomats, merchants, and students traveled abroad and returned to China; along with a zeal for reform, they shared an acquaintance with new products and new technologies. By 1911, for instance, tens of thousands of students had returned from studies abroad.[7] In the late nineteenth century, the number and variety of contact opportunities rose geometrically.[8] And for most Chinese, contact with imperialism came not through encounters with foreign soldiers, officials, and merchants but through exposure to a new material culture.

The basic history of the Western, and later Japanese, entrance into China is well known. From 1757, the "Canton system" of trade severely restricted Western economic relations.[9] Under this system, the Chinese government

---

6. These numbers are rough estimates and do not accurately reflect the influx of White Russians after 1917, Koreans on the Chinese side of the Yalu, or the growing Japanese population in Manchuria following the Russo-Japanese War (1904–5) (Feuerwerker 1976: 16–17).

7. The influence of "returned students" (留學生) cannot be overemphasized. Beginning with Yung Wing (Rong Hong 容閎, 1828–1912), who returned to China in 1855 and later joined the staff of the famous reformer Zeng Guofan 曾國藩 (1811–72), such students played a critical role in introducing new ideas and institutions. Like so many of the reforms discussed in this chapter, the loss to Japan in 1895 greatly accelerated government reforms, including support for sending students abroad. On the early period, see La Fargue 1942. On the impact of these students in the Republican period, see Y. C. Wang 1966. The number of Chinese students studying in Japan, for example, went from a few dozen before 1898 to thousands by the 1900s (Sanetō 1939: 544).

8. For a comprehensive treatment of the rapid proliferation of American companies and private investment in China, see Luo Zhiping 1996.

9. For an argument that the trade was somewhat freer than is generally assumed, see the revisionist account in Hao 1986: 14–33.

quarantined Western traders to an area outside the walls of the southeastern city of Guangzhou. Chinese officials forbade these traders to settle with their families and forced them to work through a limited number of government-approved Chinese merchants (cohong). Beginning in the late eighteenth century, Great Britain repeatedly tried to negotiate better access to Chinese markets. But efforts such as the Macartney Mission in 1793 (which elicited the Qianlong emperor's response noted above) and the Amherst Mission of 1816 met with Chinese refusal to change trade practices, open more ports, or allow foreign diplomats to live in Beijing (see Mui and Mui: 1984).

Nevertheless, trade relations had already begun to change by the late eighteenth century. In a pattern repeated many times in the early twentieth century, Westerners first discovered a product that could stimulate demand and then battled for market access. For the British, the opium trade quickly became the critical final link in a lucrative triangle of trade (India-China-Britain) on which its entire empire rested.[10] By the 1830s, the Chinese were importing more than 35,000 chests (approximately 130–60 pounds per chest) of opium from British traders each year (Morse 1910, vol. 1: 173–74, 209; Hsin-pao Chang 1964: 223). By the middle of the nineteenth century, opium accounted for nearly half of China's imports and remained the country's primary import until 1890. In the seventeenth century, the silver China obtained in exchange for exports fueled economic growth. The growing importation of a single consumer good, however, contributed to a net outflow of silver, a trend that had disastrous consequences in the bimetallic world of Chinese taxpayers, who had to exchange the copper coins they used for everyday transactions into silver at increasingly unfavorable rates (Morse et al. 1908: 323–51). This outflow of silver, combined with the corruption by officials colluding in the illegal opium trade, alarmed Chinese observers, who recognized the profound political, economic, and social impact of the growing consumption of opium at all levels of society.[11]

In the mid-eighteenth century, the central government thought it had sufficient power to regulate consumption by prohibiting imports and ban-

---

10. "The entire imperial system on which Britain's trade was delicately balanced depended on the funds it could extract from other commodity trades through opium, either in tax or profit" (Brook and Wakabayashi 2000a: 7). On the place of opium in the British trading system, see J. Y. Wong 1998 and Blue 2000.

11. Opium is a good example of the mass consumption of imports that crossed social classes. Members of every social group seem to have consumed opium, from eunuchs and members of the imperial clan to coolies and farmers.

ning the use of opium, the prototypical wasteful consumer product. The court issued several edicts prohibiting its cultivation, trade, and use (M. Greenberg 1951: 110). But the problem persisted: by the 1820s, there were more than a million addicts.[12] The Qing policy became more severe in 1839, when the Daoguang emperor (r. 1820–50) sent Lin Zexu 林則徐 (1785–1850) to Guangzhou to suppress the opium trade.[13] Lin's approach quickly escalated from moral appeals to the British government to the suspension of Western trade and the imposition of an embargo. After Lin confiscated the opium stocks of British traders, the British government applied force to gain access to the Chinese market. In a series of military confrontations lasting from 1840 to 1842, the British convincingly demonstrated the superiority of one aspect of their material culture, their military, and forced the Chinese to seek a settlement. Soon the British would introduce other aspects of their material culture.

The Treaty of Nanjing (1842) that ended the Opium War became the first of many nonreciprocal "unequal treaties" that broadened foreign access to China. These treaties required China to open an increasing number of "treaty ports" and cede or lease territory that became bases for foreign operations in China; to pay huge indemnities that hindered the Qing dynasty's ability to finance reforms; to permit foreign control of institutions such as the Maritime Customs; to relinquish the power to set tariffs ("tariff autonomy"); and to surrender judicial sovereignty over foreign nationals living in China ("extraterritoriality"). The Treaty of Nanjing marked the end of even the *possibility* of an aggressive state-led "Lin Zexu approach" to managing consumption by limiting imports. For the next hundred years, treaty restrictions prevented Chinese elites from using the state to raise tariffs or deny market access to imports by any direct or simple means. Thus, Chinese nationalists could not use conventional approaches to ensure that their fellow Chinese consumed only domestic goods—they could not rely on the state to enforce a nationalistic interpretation of consumer culture. Moreover, foreign aggression and encroachment on China as embodied in the Treaty of Nanjing initiated a century-long string of treaties that contained many overt and subtle challenges to Chinese sovereignty.

---

12. For a discussion of the number and location of opium addicts, see Lodwick 1996: 17–26.

13. On the politics behind this approach to solving the opium problem, see Polachek 1992.

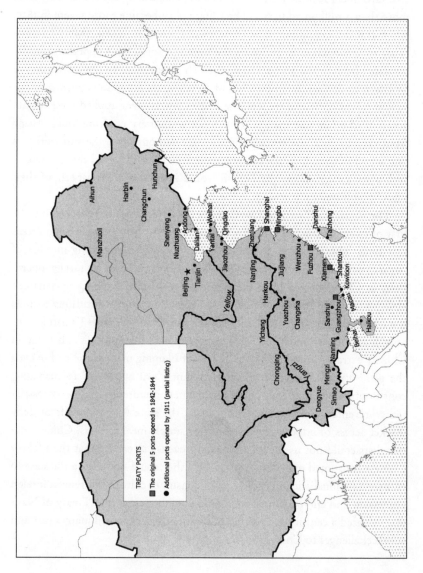

Map 1.1 Treaty Ports in China as Showcases of Western Consumer Culture

CREATING LIVING SHOWCASES OF
WESTERN CONSUMER CULTURE

Histories of the "opening of China" rarely emphasize the countless ways treaty ports eased the entry into China not only of foreigners but also of their material culture. The five ports stipulated in the Treaty of Nanjing— Shanghai, Ningbo, Fuzhou, Xiamen, and Guangzhou—immediately became the most important channels for introducing Western goods, customs, and ideas. The opening of the treaty ports and other annexed or leased territories also attracted increasing numbers of foreigners, not only traders but also missionaries, teachers, adventurers, and opportunists, as well as their families, not to mention the troops necessary to protect the newly acquired legal rights of foreign nationals. These foreigners became walking advertisements and displays of foreign goods.[14] The number of treaty ports grew to nearly fifty by the time of the Revolution of 1911; a few years later there were almost one hundred, spanning the entire coast of China and lining its major rivers (see Map 1.1) (Feuerwerker 1976: 2).[15]

As expanding and interactive showcases for a new, Western-inspired, industrialized consumer culture, the treaty ports provided a vision of what was in store for the rest of China. These living showcases gave Chinese firsthand knowledge not only of foreign technology and ideas but also of the West's consumer and visual culture through department stores, advertisements, drugstores, museums, zoos, parks, restaurants, dance halls, and many other businesses and forms of entertainment originally designed to serve foreigners. Many of these institutions had Chinese managers, who soon established equivalents for elite Chinese patrons. But Chinese of any social class merely

---

14. As Chinese animosity toward the treaty system grew in the late nineteenth and early twentieth century, some foreigners increasingly came to understand that the treaty rights that permitted them to enter China also tainted their products, both commercial and religious. Christian missionaries, who often worked unprotected in the Chinese hinterland, were perhaps the most outspoken opponents of extraterritoriality and the treaty system. See, for example, the case of the American Presbyterian Gilbert Reid (1857–1927), discussed in Tsou 1996: 87–88. Indeed, the movement of missionaries into the Chinese interior, where they became "the only concrete manifestation of the foreign intrusion," led to the growth of antiforeignism after 1860 (P. A. Cohen 1963: 269).

15. The latter total includes ports open to foreigners by treaty and by the Chinese voluntarily on a restricted basis. The Chinese Maritime Customs maintained stations at nearly fifty of these sites.

had to enter the city to experience aspects of this new culture.[16] And enter they did, as urbanization accelerated in the late nineteenth and early twentieth centuries.[17] With or without new consumer goods and habits, a growing number of sojourners in these cities returned to their rural hometowns with stories of this urban-based culture.[18]

New Chinese media also extended awareness of this culture throughout China. In late nineteenth-century Shanghai, for instance, an intellectual class emerged that made its living "peddling words" and promoting an image of the city as a "big playground" (大樂園) (W.-H. Yeh 1997: 421–27).[19] These words and pictures reached Chinese through a quickly expanding mass media of newspapers and periodicals as well as novels and books.[20] By 1910, there were some twenty-five times as many letters, newspapers, and magazines in circulation in China as there had been in 1901 (M. C. Wright 1968: 30).[21] Even those who could not read could still gaze at representations of this new culture in advertisements and illustrations. Soon new visual and aural forms of mass communication emerged, including movies, radio, gramophones, and Western-style plays.[22]

---

16. Indeed, even within the treaty port cities, the foreign aspects of these living showcases, as I call them, were particularly concentrated. In Guangzhou, for instance, the foreign presence was concentrated on Shameen (Shamian) Island. Locals considered the island a symbol of foreign imperialism but also admired its beauty and order as an "artifact of Western creativity and transforming power" (Ho 1991: 89–90).

17. For instance, the population of Shanghai grew from nearly 1.3 million in 1910 to over 3.8 million in 1937 (Zou 1980: 1–14, 90–91).

18. Indeed, in Shanghai, throughout the twentieth century, the majority of the population came from other places (ibid.: 114–17). On the institutional basis for the continuing links between Chinese living in Shanghai and their places of origin, see Goodman 1995.

19. Yeh notes, as I do, that Shanghai "simultaneously represented China's humiliation and its cosmopolitan modernity" (W.-H. Yeh 1997: 421). Likewise, I argue that *imports* simultaneously represented humiliation and modernity.

20. The widespread use of advertising was critical to the creation of the thousands of new newspapers and periodicals established around the time of the Revolution of 1911. Some publications devoted more space to advertisements than to articles. By the early twentieth century, even government gazetteers carried advertisements (Zhen 1997: 40–44).

21. On the rapid proliferation of print media at the end of the Qing dynasty, see L. Lee and Nathan 1985.

22. This culture is the subject of intensifying scholarly attention. For an overview, see L. Lee 1999: 3–42. On the rapid expansion of the Chinese press in Shanghai, see Ma Guangren 1996. On the introduction of the gramophone and the creation of a market for popular music, see Jones 1999. At first, most films were imported. However, by the mid-1920s, Shanghai had over 300 film companies, which by 1937 had produced over 1,000 films (Rimmington 1998: 24).

MISSIONARIES OF CONSUMER
CULTURE IN THE INTERIOR

The presence of missionaries throughout China extended the reach of Western consumer culture beyond the treaty ports. Even before the establishment of the treaty system, Christian missionaries had proselytized in China—first Jesuits, Franciscans, and Dominicans during the sixteenth through eighteenth centuries, and then Protestants from the early nineteenth century. But their numbers and field of operations were extremely limited. The Treaty of Nanjing, however, allowed missionaries to proselytize in the treaty ports, and the Beijing Convention (1860) extended the permitted area of operations to the rest of the country. At the end of the nineteenth century, several thousand foreign missionaries were spread out across China. By 1919 nearly 10,000 Catholic and Protestant missionaries lived in all except 106 of the 1,704 Chinese counties. These Christian missionaries may have had as many as several million communicants. In addition, hundreds of thousands of children came into contact with Westerners and Western material culture through missionary schools (the students of which were not restricted to Chinese converts) and through charitable organizations such as hospitals, the YMCA, and the Salvation Army (Feuerwerker 1976: 39, 42–43).[23]

These missionaries may have had mixed success in making permanent converts to Christ, but their role in exposing Chinese outside the treaty ports to Western consumer and visual culture was pivotal. Literally carrying Western consumer culture on their backs through their dress and deportment, missionaries acted as walking billboards for an alternative form of life centered on new kinds of commodities, and not only on new forms of worship. Their missionary compounds provided even more local exposure to a new material culture and lifestyle.[24] In many instances, missionaries even

---

23. The most comprehensive study is still Latourette 1929. See also P. Cohen 1963. On the YMCA, see S. S. Garrett 1970.

24. The innumerable memoirs of Christian missionaries to China relate the introduction of these new commodities and commodity-centered forms of life to Chinese. The long-time Presbyterian missionary to Hainan island, Margaret Moninger, for instance, introduced new conceptions of time through her strict work schedule and even more informally, but no less significantly, through birthday parties. The lifestyles of such missionaries became the subject of intensive local interest, so much so that she and other missionaries opened their compounds to groups of curious Chinese women (Lodwick 1995: 85, 59). This does not, of course,

introduced production techniques for foreign commodities (e.g., straw hats, lace, and hairnets) to alleviate rural poverty.

Westerners brought this material culture to China, but the Chinese embraced it. Even before the establishment of treaty ports, foreign firms employed Chinese. Naturally, these numbers grew after 1842, and by the turn of the century some 20,000 Chinese were working for foreign businesses (Hao 1970: 102). These individuals became the basis of a "new urban elite" that already counted well over one million "affluent entrepreneurs" by the mid-nineteenth century (Bergère 1986: 20). They, in turn, employed millions of Chinese assistants and servants, who had direct experience with this new culture through their employers. The exact number is less significant than the fact that wealthy groups and their emulators increasingly turned to consumption to express and reinforce social standing, especially after the abolition in 1905 of the primary road to social standing for over a thousand years, the imperial examination system.

By the early twentieth century, the Chinese had experienced nearly six decades of direct and indirect exposure to Europeans and Americans and their material culture. These Sino-foreign interactions provided the intellectual and social foundations for applying a new notion of nationality not only to peoples but also to an emerging consumer culture and its representations.

Symbolizing Lost Sovereignty

By the last third of the nineteenth century, increasing numbers of Chinese had concluded that a foreign commercial assault on China was accompanying the more conspicuous military confrontations. Decades before the National Products Movement popularized the issue, a discourse of trade statistics within elite political and intellectual circles was already a primary means of comprehending China's lack of sovereignty. In this discourse, China's weakness was symbolized by a single number: the trade deficit. Within this discourse, which became the foundation stone of the movement, tariff autonomy and the unfair access to Chinese markets enjoyed by foreigners were singled out as undermining China's sovereignty. Participants in this discourse pointed to China's tariff history. For nearly one hundred years, China's tariff rate remained at 5.0–7.5 percent of the estimated value of

---

mean that missionaries themselves did not adopt aspects of Chinese material culture. See Chapter 2 and Stapleton 2000: 43–45.

goods. On top of this, despite inflation, the assessment of the value of imports using price tables that were decades old resulted in even lower actual tariff rates.[25] Once the tariff had been paid, imports were exempted from all further levies, including internal transit tolls (or *lijin* 厘金), a privilege that gave imports a distinct advantage over their Chinese competitors.[26] In the initial years following the Treaty of Nanjing, tariff control did not seem to be an important issue, and it did not even seem clear that the Chinese had ceded such control (M. C. Wright 1957: 178–79). As nation-states came to see tariff control as central to sovereignty, regaining control became a focal point of Chinese nationalism and anti-imperialism.[27]

Within the discourse of trade statistics, China was engaged in a zero-sum game with the imperialist powers over the China market. All imports came at the expense of domestic economic development. The dominant popular conception of political economy was that the recovery of economic sovereignty was more important than expanding economic activity and raising per capita incomes. Chinese control over a Chinese economy was seen as more important than economic development controlled by foreigners. Not surprisingly,

---

25. On China's attempts to regain autonomy or, at least, to renegotiate higher rates, see S. F. Wright 1938. By contrast, Japan, whose economic policies China closely watched, successfully began raising its tariffs at the turn of the century and regained tariff sovereignty formally in 1911. By 1908, Japan's average import duty had increased from 3.6 to 16 percent, and by 1911 it was 20 percent (Hirschmeier and Yui 1975: 146–47). Nor could Chinese policymakers tax goods at different rates; so imported luxury goods and raw material were taxed at the same rate. Chinese leaders were aware that whereas Japan could protect its domestic cigarette market with a 355 percent tax on tobacco, China could not. This difference allowed consumer goods such as British-American Tobacco Company products unhindered access to Chinese markets, in sharp contrast with that company's inability to gain market share in Japan (Cochran 1980: 41–42).

26. Similarly, beginning in the late Qing, the same Chinese calling for tariff autonomy also promoted the abolition of the transit tolls, which was not accomplished until 1931 (Mann 1987: 145–51).

27. As one of the early scholars to note the relationship between tariff autonomy and nationalism concluded, the disadvantage to China of its lack of tariff autonomy was "keenly felt by Chinese intellectuals" and the issue was used by leaders such as Sun Yatsen to "arouse patriotic sentiment" (Loh 1955: 71–72). Similarly, by the 1930s, politicians around the industrializing world recognized the utility of protective tariffs—what one contemporary observer called a country's "main weapon"—to enforce economic nationalism at home. The treaty system not only denied China tariff control but also prohibited other "weapons," including quotas, embargoes, and international exchange controls. For an overview of contemporary writings on this issue in the United States, see Hodgson 1933 (the quote comes from p. 8).

successive Chinese governments and popular pressure repeatedly brought foreign governments to the bargaining table to discuss domestic control over tariffs. However, until 1925 the treaty powers refused to negotiate the restoration of tariff autonomy and even then delayed a final agreement. As a result, China did not achieve tariff autonomy until the start of the 1930s.[28]

As the trade deficit grew along with anger over the lack of tariff autonomy, trade statistics became a well-publicized index of the nation's health. In 1864, the foreign-administered Chinese Maritime Customs office began publishing annual trade statistics. These numbers—ironically, the foreign tabulation of them strengthened their aura of scientific objectivity—announced a yearly Chinese deficit, even though in actuality a deficit did not exist until after 1887 (Hazama et al. 1996: 21; Hou 1965: 93–94).[29] Official concern over the outflow of silver had begun much earlier and contributed to the tensions leading up to the Opium War (Hsin-pao Chang 1964: 95–96). In the 1880s, prominent Chinese scholar-officials such as Xue Fucheng 薛福成 (1838–94) and Ma Jianzhong 馬建忠 (1845–1900) (both trained under the great Qing statesman Li Hongzhang 李鴻章, 1823–1901) used trade statistics to argue that foreign trade exacerbated poverty in China. By the publication at the turn of the century of the translation of Adam Smith's *Wealth of Nations* by the famous scholar Yan Fu 嚴 復 (1854–1921), Chinese elites considered the trade deficit a critical issue, a symbol of economic decline that was continually noted.[30] This

---

28. In 1928, the newly established Nationalist government made achieving economic sovereignty and recovering tariff autonomy a top priority. The Chinese foreign minister, Wang Zhengting 王正廷 (1882–1961), ultimately forced the issue by announcing the new government's intention to terminate all treaties unilaterally in 1928. In response, the Americans concluded a new agreement, and shortly thereafter nearly all the other treaty powers followed suit. The new treaty, set to take effect at the start of 1929, promised to end the era of unequal treaties on tariff matters. Even at this point, a deal could not be concluded. Because the United States stipulated that the "most-favored-nation" clause remained in effect, the new treaty did not take effect until China renegotiated tariff autonomy with the other powers. The Japanese, however, had much more vested in lower rates. And although, as promised, the Chinese government promulgated new rates in early 1929, it could not fully implement them until the Japanese consented in May 1930. After recovering tariff autonomy, the Nanjing government raised tariffs. See Kubo 1980.

29. Feuerwerker (1969: 50) notes that until 1887 imports from Hong Kong into China were included, thereby exaggerating Chinese imports and underestimating its exports.

30. Yan Fu completed translating the *Wealth of Nations* in 1900. On his reinterpretation of Smith's concepts of "general interest" and "society" into state interest, see Schwartz 1964: 113–29. The outpouring of elite writings on trade and commerce included Ma Jianzhong's *Fumin shou* (Discussion on the wealth of the people), Chen Chi's 陳熾 (1855–1900) *Fuguo ze* (Poli-

mundane issue became a central concern to all, including eventually well-known intellectuals such as Liang Qichao 梁啓超 (1873–1929), who grudgingly recognized the importance of the crass world of trade and merchants. Recovering tariff autonomy so that China could reverse its trade deficit became a widely shared goal, especially after the defeat by Japan in 1895. It was also a key objective of the National Products Movement (see Table 1.1).[31]

THE SIGNIFICANCE OF THE
"CHINA MARKET MYTH"

By the early twentieth century, the highly publicized trade statistics and foreign-controlled industries became prime evidence in the argument that the economy was falling under foreign control. Between 1900 and 1905, for instance, China's trade deficit quadrupled. The influence of foreigners can further be seen in the rapid expansion of foreign investment in China. Between 1902 and the eve of the World War I in 1914, foreign investment nearly doubled.[32] Likewise, the number of British, American, French, Russian, and Japanese firms operating in China in the first decade of the twentieth century rose from just over 1,000 in 1902 to nearly 10,000 by 1921.[33]

These numbers provide ammunition for two connected and long-running debates. First, was there a market for foreign products in China, and, if so, did foreigners profit from it? And second, in accessing that market, did

---

cies for enriching the state), and Wang Kangnian's 王康年 (1860–1911) *Lun Zhongguo qiu fu-qiang yizhou yixing zhi fa* (Feasible paths on China's search for wealth and power) (see W. Chan 1977: 251n41).

31. Countless articles relate the movement to trade; see, e.g., Lu Shouqian, "Tichang guo-huo zhi yuanyin." I am grateful to Shanghai historian Xu Dingxin for allowing me to copy his personal collection of materials on the movement, including this article. See also W. Chan 1977: 26–33, 250–51n32.

32. Rising from U.S.$787.9 million in 1902 to U.S.$1.61 billion in 1914. By 1931, total foreign investment had roughly doubled again, reaching U.S.$3.3 billion (Remer 1933a: 58). Adjusted for the wholesale price index, however, the rate of increase in the second period (i.e., during the movement) was considerably lower than the numbers suggest: "Only about 20 percent during the seventeen years from 1914 to 1931" (Hou 1965: 211). Using a broader definition of "foreign investment," however, the prominent Chinese historian Wu Chengming (1958: 45) found even greater foreign investment.

33. These statistics, compiled from Maritime Customs data, are very rough estimates. "Firm" included everything from a small shop to a large company with many branches (Feuerwerker 1976: 17–18).

Table 1.1

Chinese Foreign Trade: Import and Export Statistics, 1900–1937

(1900–1932 in 000s of Haiguan taels and 1933–37 in 000s of Chinese National Dollars)

Year	Net imports	Exports	Total foreign trade	Trade balance
1900	211,070	158,097	370,067	−52,074
1901	268,303	169,657	437,960	−98,646
1902	315,364	214,182	529,545	−01,182
1903	326,739	214,352	541,092	−112,387
1904	344,061	239,487	583,547	−104,574
1905	447,101	227,888	674,989	−219,213
1906	410,270	236,457	646,727	−173,813
1907	416,401	264,381	680,782	−152,021
1908	394,505	276,660	671,166	−117,845
1909	418,158	338,993	757,151	− 79,165
1910	462,965	380,833	843,798	− 82,132
1911	471,504	377,388	848,842	− 94,166
1912	473,097	370,520	843,617	−102,577
1913	570,163	403,306	973,468	−166,857
1914	569,241	356,227	925,468	−213,015
1915	454,476	418,861	873,337	− 35,615
1916	516,407	481,797	988,204	− 34,610
1917	549,519	462,932	1,012,450	− 86,587
1918	554,893	485,883	1,040,776	− 69,010
1919	646,998	630,809	1,277,807	− 16,188
1920	762,250	541,631	1,303,882	−220,619
1921	906,122	601,256	1,507,378	−304,867
1922	945,050	654,892	1,599,942	−290,158
1923	923,403	752,917	1,676,320	−170,485
1924	1,018,211	771,784	1,789,995	−246,426
1925	947,865	776,353	1,724,218	−171,512
1926	1,124,221	864,295	1,998,516	−256,926
1927	1,012,932	918,620	1,931,551	− 94,312
1928	1,195,969	991,335	2,187,324	−204,614
1929	1,265,779	1,015,687	2,281,466	−250,092
1930	1,309,756	894,844	2,204,599	−414,912
1931	1,433,489	909,476	2,342,965	−524,014
1932	1,049,247	492,989	1,542,236	−556,258
1933	1,345,567	612,293	1,957,860	−733,274
1934	1,029,655	535,733	1,565,399	−493,932
1935	919,211	576,298	1,495,510	−342,913
1936	941,545	706,791	1,648,336	−234,754
1937	953,386	838,770	1,792,156	−114,616

SOURCE: Hsiao Liang-lin 1974: 23–24.

foreigners "exploit" China? Historians of Sino-American relations have generally come to regard the period between 1890 and 1915 as one of excessive optimism regarding the potential for trade in China; in other words, the lucrative Chinese market was a myth.[34] Whatever the actual conditions for foreign business, historians agree that Westerners rushed to China expecting to find, as the title of a popular book in the 1930s promised, a country of *400 Million Customers* (Crow 1937).[35]

The actual economic effect of foreign involvement in the Chinese economy is an issue not explored in this book. The information presented here cannot settle the issue of whether foreign capital undermined the Chinese economy by ruining the handicraft industry, forcing a reorganization of the agricultural sector, or "draining" (漏卮) the Chinese economy through the repatriation of profits earned in China.[36] For the same reason, the main issue here is not whether the superior access of foreign enterprises to capital, technology, and trained management gave these enterprises an "unfair" advantage over domestic enterprises.[37]

34. Sherman Cochran (1980: 10) has qualified attempts to portray the China market as largely a myth that required enormous effort for little returns and notes in his study of Sino-foreign competition that the cigarette industry was enormously profitable for the British-American Tobacco Company. Prominent studies on the "myth of the China market" include Varg 1968: esp. chap. 3 and M. B. Young 1968.

35. The related issue of the nature of foreign involvement in the Chinese economy has been even more contentious. As the economic historian Thomas Rawski argues, "The direct and specific influence of foreign activity on the size and composition of farm output, the money supply, the level of capital formation, the rate and pattern of modern-sector growth, interest rates, the size of government budgets, and other significant economic indicators was generally small" (1989: 4). According to Rhoads Murphey (1970), foreigners did very little business outside treaty ports.

36. For a recent survey of this debate, see Xiao 1999: 3–16.

37. For an overview, see Cochran 1980: 1–9. See also Feuerwerker 1968 on Communist historiography. Feuerwerker and Cheng 1970 introduces works on foreign exploitation by Chinese historians writing in the first decades after 1949.

Rather, the Chinese *perception* of exploitation is the critical issue. After all, the Chinese market myth had a Chinese side, too. In contrast to an earlier generation of scholarship that sought mainly to debunk this myth, I hold that the actual economic impact of foreign companies is less important than the domestic reverberation of this myth. The growing perception that China had lost economic sovereignty was critical to the conceptualization of the modern Chinese nation. Foreign involvement in a largely agricultural country may have been minuscule as a percentage of the gross domestic product.[38] However, it was huge symbolically. Chinese believed foreign capital had inundated China. Both the expectations of foreign companies of endless profits to be made in China and the perception on the Chinese side that foreigners had engineered a "hostile takeover" of the Chinese economy shaped notions of international commerce at this time. The discourse of trade statistics reinforced this perception of growing control, and these statistics were constantly cited as indisputable evidence of expanding foreign control and, within the movement, were used to attack the unpatriotic consumers of imports.[39]

FOREIGN CONTROL OVER
MODERN INDUSTRY

Foreign control over new, high-profile industries came to signify "foreign domination" of the Chinese economy as a whole. In the opening decade of the twentieth century, for example, foreign shipping companies controlled more than four-fifths of the commercial shipping market (K. C. Liu 1962). This control Chinese readily interpreted as a product of imperialism because the unequal treaties enabled foreign firms to send ships into domestic ports and inland waterways. Despite joint government-private efforts to establish domestic competitors such as the China Merchants' Steam Navigation

---

38. Or, in the words of economic historian Albert Feuerwerker, "Foreign trade and investment played a relatively small role in the Chinese economy—even in the twentieth century" (1977: 92).

39. For a typical example, see Yu Zuoting 1935. Movement literature often divided import statistics into its component parts to legitimize attacks on specific consumers. As Chapter 7 shows, for example, statistics for cosmetics and perfume were used as evidence of female betrayal. The statistics were also cited to demonstrate the growing threat of Japan, especially after 1931. See, e.g., Shiyebu 1933, which supplies 46 charts, diagrams, and tables to document Japan's expanding role in the Chinese economy. I provide other examples throughout the book.

Company (est. 1872), foreign companies continued to control the majority of the market right up to the eve of the Second Sino-Japanese War (1937–45). In the 1930s, some thirty foreign shipping companies with over 700 vessels operated in Chinese ports (Hou 1965: 60).

The introduction of one foreign industry often required the creation or expansion of another; shipping, for example, spurred the growth of coal mining (Tim Wright 1984: 50–76). Foreign shippers wanted cheap local sources of the high-quality coal required by steamships in order to avoid importing large amounts of coal. Mining thus became another highly symbolic industry dominated by foreign interests. Once again, the turn of the twentieth century marked a turning point in foreign involvement in the Chinese economy. Between 1895 and 1913, foreigners opened scores of mines. Mining also led to the extension of foreign economic operations beyond the treaty ports, something not sanctioned by the unequal treaties, deep into the Chinese interior.[40]

Similarly, in commercial banking, foreign banks completely controlled the financing of international trade and exchange transactions until the first modern Chinese bank opened in 1898. Even after the Chinese government banks began issuing banknotes, Chinese continued to favor the more stable foreign banknotes. Because of ongoing political and economic uncertainty, foreign banknotes remained popular during the Republic until the 1930s (Hou 1965: 52–58). These notes were a potent and omnipresent symbol in everyday life of the foreign "control" of the Chinese economy.

Attempts by foreign companies to build railways in China fueled fears that foreign-controlled technology would facilitate the "draining" of the Chinese economy by introducing technology that would displace the laborers who transported goods, allow greater foreign troop movement, disrupt local geomancy, and create yet more demand for imported materials to construct the railways (C.-A. Chang 1943). After a few false starts, a highly visible scramble by foreign powers to secure railway concessions began at the end of the First Sino-Japanese War in 1895 (L. Cheng 1935; Yang Yonggang 1997). The imperialist powers deemed railroads critical for carving out a

---

40. The French obtained the first concession in 1895 in the southwestern province of Yunnan. Shortly thereafter, the Russians concluded agreements for mines in Manchuria. Then, the Japanese, Germans, and British arranged to open mines within their spheres of interest. Affected provinces included Xinjiang, Mongolia, Hebei, Henan, Shandong, and Sichuan. See Hou 1965: 68–79 for a survey of these initial foreign mining efforts.

sphere of interest, and by the time of the Revolution of 1911, Russian, Japanese, French, German, and British interests owned over 2,000 miles of track, or some 40 percent of China's relatively meager total railroad mileage (Huenemann 1984: 37–80; Hou 1965: 65).[41]

MADE IN CHINA, BUT
NOT "CHINESE"

The earliest foreign-dominated industries—shipping, mining, banking, and railroads—became the first targets of Chinese efforts to "recover" control over the domestic economy. At the turn of the century, however, foreign involvement in manufacturing in China emerged as a much more widespread symbol of imperialism. What emerged was anxiety not only over imports but also over commodities manufactured by foreign companies within China. Within the nascent National Products Movement, products made by foreign companies in China were not "Chinese." The presence of *any* foreign capital became symbolically significant, and this symbol grew as foreign investment intensified.

The increasing volume of imports and the growing trade deficit were not the only indicators of the expanding presence of foreign commodities and capital. As foreigners began seeking better access to the domestic market and cheaper labor costs in the late nineteenth century, the number and variety of foreign manufacturing companies in China grew quickly. Before 1895, there were already over one hundred foreign-owned "factories."[42] After the First Sino-Japanese War and the Treaty of Shimonoseki (1895), which granted Japanese extensive financial and territorial gains in China, this number expanded dramatically. Further, a treaty concluded the following year gave all treaty powers the legal right to build factories in China and led to the quick

---

41. Moreover, foreign loans financed many of the "Chinese-owned" lines; see Morse 1910, vol. 3: 449. Russia aimed to control Manchuria and northern China; Germany wanted to secure its interests in Shandong; Britain concentrated on the Yangzi valley and a line to Burma; Japan eyed Fujian; and France had plans for Yunnan. Zhang Zhidong 張之洞 (1837–1909), governor-general of Hunan and Hubei, expressed a fear that railways would act as scissors with which the powers could cut up China. For a comprehensive table of foreign investment in Chinese railroads, see Yang Yonggang 1997: 169–77.

42. For a list of such companies, see Sun Yutang 1957, vol. 1: 234–41. On the various types of foreign business operations outside the treaty ports before 1895, see Allen and Donnithorne 1954: 31–51.

expansion of modern industries in China. For this reason, historians usually assign 1895 as the start of the modern industrialization of China.[43]

These companies did not export all their products. In the mid-nineteenth century, foreign firms had begun to manufacture items for domestic consumption, first for foreigners living in treaty ports and then gradually for an emerging Chinese market. For instance, in the 1850s several foreign companies manufactured pharmaceuticals, cosmetics, and soaps. In the 1860s, other companies made Western foods, candies, spirits, and flour. In the following decades, foreign-owned companies in Shanghai began producing ice, glass, bricks, concrete, and furniture. Oftentimes, foreigners established local companies to supply a Chinese demand created by imports. Matches, paper, soap, cigarettes, and cotton textiles all fall into this category. Because there was a huge Chinese demand for imported cotton goods, many foreign textile operations were set up shortly after foreigners gained the legal right to establish factories in 1895. And foreigners continued to launch consumer goods companies aimed at local markets after the Revolution of 1911.[44]

New Commodities as Conduits of Nationalism

As the numbers, varieties, and uses of new commodities expanded dramatically in the early twentieth century,[45] the burgeoning consumer culture in urban China became inseparable from social and political changes. The two most important of these were the abolition of the imperial examination system in 1905 and the Republican Revolution of 1911, which overthrew much more than the Qing dynastic polity. Eliminating the examination system ended the traditional and primary road to wealth, power, and status. For

---

43. James Reardon-Anderson summarizes the impact of 1895: "In industry, as in other fields, 1895 marked a turning point, after which central authority declined and new forces took charge. This meant the bubbling up, here and there, of new products, methods, forms of management, and expertise that in the long run would shake China to the core" (1991: 169–70). For the exact dimensions of this economic expansion, see Wang Jingyu 1957: 2–13, and the tabulations in Feuerwerker 1969: 38–39.

44. For example, in the decades preceding World War II, the Japanese and the British established over 100 machine works companies throughout China, making everything from bicycles and electrical goods to motors and other machines (Hou 1965: 83, 85).

45. Unfortunately, there are only a few full-length studies of the cultural history and impact of the new Chinese commodities discussed here. Contrast this dearth with U.S. historiography, where even a popular line of plastic containers (Tupperware) has its own scholarly treatise (Clarke 1999).

several decades, alternative routes had been developing, most conspicuously through modern schools and study abroad. Ending the examination system, however, eliminated in one fell swoop the basis of sumptuary legislation that reinforced the status of officials through regulations governing all aspects of their public lives, from the clothing they and their wives wore to the architectural style of their houses. Abolishing the primary means of certifying status, in effect, facilitated the semiotic reconfigurations discussed in the following chapters.[46]

In the decade immediately following the Revolution of 1911, Chinese began to use a wide variety of commodities to alter their personal appearance and to define their social standing visually. A whole range of new Chinese industries emerged both to create and to serve these new needs. A growing number of Chinese altered their appearance from head (hats) to toe (shoes and socks). This transformation affected such accessories as watches, eyeglasses, and canes. These changes even extended to notions of how Chinese ought to maintain their bodies, as new ideas of hygiene accompanied the adoption of particular commodities. Toothbrushes and tooth powders, perfumes and soaps, and new kinds of cosmetics simultaneously created and filled new needs. In that first decade, industries emerged to supply these consumer products. In short, the decade surrounding the Revolution of 1911 saw a transformation in personal appearance in China rivaled only by, first, the decades following the Communist victory in 1949 and, second, Deng Xiaoping's 鄧小平 (1907–1997) decision in 1978 to introduce market reforms and re-establish extensive ties with capitalist countries.

Chinese government sources introduce the new or improved commodities of this emerging consumer culture. A 1935 Ministry of Industry guide to the Jiangsu provincial economy lists factories producing fabrics (e.g., cotton ginning, spinning, and weaving; silk reeling and weaving; knitting; and leather tanning), food (flour, rice, and oil milling), chemicals, building materials (cement, bricks, and tiles), and power plants, to name several basic categories. These and other industries produced a growing percentage of

---

46. In China as elsewhere, an increasingly fluid social structure in the late Qing dynasty undoubtedly contributed to the need for and rise of sumptuary laws. The percentages of men with imperial degrees participating in elected assemblies reflected the dramatic transformation of the Chinese social structure by the time of the 1911 revolution. On the eve of the revolution, nearly 70 percent of the members of the Zhejiang provincial assembly had imperial degrees. However, by 1921, under 3 percent had degrees (Bergère 1986: 125).

commodities in circulation, such as clothing, processed foods and season-ings, pharmaceuticals, educational supplies, and hardware. In addition, these industries supplied many consumer items that began as luxuries but often became necessities: cigarettes; hats; buttons; umbrellas; eyeglasses; toilet articles such as soaps, perfumes, toothbrushes, and combs; and household supplies such as ice, matches, thermoses, light bulbs, and towels.[47]

The best description of the total transformation in the material culture in actual lives comes from literary sources, particularly the writings of Mao Dun. In his massive and widely read novel *Midnight* (子夜, 1933), Mao Dun captures this profound transformation as a temporal, spatial, and vis-ual gap. In the opening of the novel, the Chinese civil war forces the father of one of the main characters to flee his comfortable but rustic country residence for Shanghai. Through the response of a member of an older, ru-ral generation to a son's extravagant urban lifestyle, Mao Dun describes the new material life. The father, overwhelmed by a radically different material culture of abundance (that, in the son's home alone, includes everything from Western furniture to electric fans), drops dead after a few hours' ex-posure to China's most modern and cosmopolitan city. Of course, it was not just the wealthy families at the center of *Midnight* who participated in this transformation. Many ordinary Chinese observed and participated, al-though often only in inexpensive new forms of leisure or simply in their discussions and daydreams.[48] Poorer urban denizens, for instance, might have looked at magazines that advertised the new culture but could not have bought the products themselves. Likewise, they participated in this new culture through less expensive items—made possible, for example, by the emergence of cigarettes as a substitute for pipe smoking, a transforma-tion wrought by tobacco companies.[49]

---

47. "Factories" included both relatively advanced cotton-spinning plants and simpler handicraft shops, which were considered factories because several people worked in a com-mon location (NII 1935: xxii–xxiv, table of contents of "manufacturing industries"). For an in-troduction to many of these industries in China, see Dingle and Pratt 1921.

48. On the popularization of new forms of commodified leisure, especially opium smok-ing, see Des Forges 2000. By the late nineteenth century, thousands of opium dens served every social stratum in Shanghai alone.

49. Cf., e.g., the critical role London maids and servants played in the development of fashion trends; see McKendrick et al. 1982: 9–33.

THE PATTERN OF PROLIFERATION

The entry and spread of Western consumer goods in China followed a pattern: first, a new item filled foreign demand within China; then, the market expanded to create and meet domestic demand; and, eventually, particularly during World War I, Chinese companies entered the market. Most of these industries and their products did not exist before the turn of the twentieth century. The National Products Movement, then, began at the start of China's late, rapid, and uneven industrialization.

Ironically, foreign representatives of companies and creeds introduced many of the products that Chinese soon recast as "national products." In the late nineteenth century, French missionaries, for instance, introduced the lace industry to Shanghai by teaching Chinese girls and women how to make lace at home (NII 1935: 446). Indeed, many of the schools set up by missionaries taught the skill, which quickly became an important component of the local economy in places such as Shandong province's Zhifou (Chefoo), which until 1919 was the largest exporter of Chinese lace (Dingle and Pratt 1921: report no. 116).

This pattern occurred with many items. For instance, at the turn of the century, German manufacturers began selling underwear and hosiery in China. The German success attracted a host of competitors from Japan, America, and England. As with so many of China's consumer industries, shortly after the outbreak of World War I, when imports from Europe virtually ceased, Chinese companies quickly emerged to supply substitutes for those imports. For instance, within two decades of the start of the war, there were 136 factories in Shanghai alone. Import/export statistics demonstrate this massive transformation in the Shanghai-based market for underwear and hosiery. On the eve of World War I, Shanghai alone imported 1,786,296 pairs of underwear. However, by the end of the war in 1918, imports had dropped by over a third. Meanwhile, domestic manufacturers not only won customers at home but also became net exporters of underwear during this period, sending overseas more than a million pairs a year by the mid-1920s.[50] The Japanese also introduced many new consumer products and initiated this pattern. Toward the end of the Qing, for example, Japanese began

---

50. These statistics do not differentiate between Chinese and foreign control in these domestic manufacturers. See NII 1935: 429, 443.

selling woven towels that were favored over the cloth towels that up to then had dominated the market. Once again, the world war created opportunities for the first major Chinese competitor, which did not begin operations until 1917.[51]

The stiffest competition in China, indeed throughout East Asia, occurred over another recently introduced product: straw hats (that is, flat-topped boaters and not the conical hats worn by farmers for centuries). Straw hats originated in Europe in the late seventeenth century and quickly spread around the globe, arriving in America just before the Revolution. They appeared in China in the 1860s. Foreigners living in Fujian province introduced the technique for making these hats, which missionaries working in that province used. But they became popular elsewhere as a way to keep cool in the summer. The treaty port of Ningbo became an early headquarters for hat production. Export of these hats began in the late 1860s, and within ten years, the industry employed thousands of women and children and exported some fifteen million hats a year (Allen and Donnithorne 1954: 87; Dingle and Pratt 1921: report no. 93).

Before the Revolution of 1911, it was uncommon for Chinese to wear such hats. Upper-class men, for example, favored the black skullcap, which helped keep the queue hairstyle in place. However, after the Revolution, when men were forced to cut their queues, straw hats, particularly boaters, became extremely fashionable and spread throughout the country and across all classes.[52] In contrast to Western-style suits, these hats became symbols of new Western/modern dress and were affordable and widely available, especially because of inexpensive Japanese imports. In many ways, this new commodity was the ideal national product: it was easy to make and required very little technology.[53] Moreover, the raw materials were available domestically, because most straw braids came from the northern provinces of Shandong and Hebei. Originally, women working at home made these hats. Because the quality was considered inferior to European and Japanese hats, gradually production was centralized. Thus, by the early 1930s, there were

---

51. This company was the Three Friends Enterprises, which became a primary backer of the movement and was known for its Triangle Brand products (NII 1935: 451–59).

52. According to one foreign observer, such straw hats were something that "even coolies" could afford (van Dorn 1932: 259–62).

53. The two simple steps involved were sorting and sewing the plaited straw (McDowell 1992: 52, 60, 83).

nearly 90 factories in Shanghai alone producing nearly 100,000 straw hats. During the frequent anti-imperialist boycotts, Japanese hats became a common target of protestors.[54]

Like straw hats, umbrellas were widely embraced as accessories of modern/Western dress and new lifestyles. The history of this object in China also underscores another broader change within Chinese consumer culture: the democratization of fashion. During the Qing dynasty, parasols were used primarily by the wealthy, and the poor usually wore large straw hats. (China did not distinguish parasols and umbrellas; traditionally both were made from bamboo ribs on which paper was pasted and oiled.) The spread of the new type of umbrellas followed the usual pattern. First, foreigners introduced them. German and Japanese traders imported foreign-style umbrellas made of silk or cloth with metal ribs to China, but, as with so many other Western fashions, they did not become popular until a few years after the Revolution of 1911.[55] In the 1910s, there were several attempts by Chinese to set up companies to compete with these imports. As with so many companies founded during the movement, company names reflected the nationalist economic agenda. For example, the first Chinese factory (est. 1912) in Shanghai to make foreign-style umbrellas and parasols was called the People's Livelihood Foreign-Style Umbrella Factory (民生洋傘廠). And a locally produced product that was a combination of a parasol and an umbrella was known as a "patriotic umbrella" (愛國傘). During this initial period of the movement, Chinese manufacturers openly used some foreign components. Even "patriotic umbrellas" used Japanese frames, and traditional paper umbrella manufacturers used German dyes and Japanese cotton cords. However, the movement continually created new pressures for such companies to produce purely Chinese products. For example, in the mid-1920s, three prominent Chinese companies substituted hand-made rods, ribs, and struts for Japanese imports (NII 1935: 486–89).

The market for soap, modern cosmetics, toothbrushes, toothpaste (or powder), perfumes, and other items in the toiletries category expanded

---

54. Some factories also produced more expensive felt hats, which were made out of Australian or Chinese wool. See Yang Dajun 1933: 572ff and NII 1935: 471–74.

55. According to Mao Zedong 毛澤東 (1893–1976), in the rural county of Xunwu in south China, foreign-style umbrellas controlled only 30 percent of the market before the Revolution of 1911 but had gained 70 percent of the market by 1930 (Mao 1990: 96–97). His report also includes a list of 131 types of foreign-style goods (ibid.: 69–70) sold in this county.

greatly at the start of the twentieth century. These items quickly replaced their early analogues, particularly in treaty port cities and among the upper and middle classes. Until 1921, nearly all the toothbrushes used in Shanghai and the rest of Jiangsu came from Japan. In that year, Zhao Tieqiao 趙鐵橋 (1886–1930) set up the Shuanglun Toothbrush Company (雙輪牙刷公司); other Chinese entrepreneurs soon followed. Although most toothbrushes were produced to satisfy local demand, quite a few were exported to overseas Chinese communities, particularly in Southeast Asia. By the end of the 1920s, Shanghai was exporting nearly 750,000 toothbrushes a year (NII 1935: 515–17).[56] Similarly, the modern cosmetics market also boomed in the early twentieth century, leading to the establishment of Chinese companies in Shanghai by 1911. Before the establishment of these companies, cosmetics were luxury items. In cities, however, they soon became a daily necessity for a growing number of women.[57]

In the early twentieth century, Chinese not only changed what they put on themselves but also what they put into themselves, creating one more area where new commodities became part of everyday lives. The milling of rice and wheat and the extraction of vegetable oils were considerably less arduous with machine power than with traditional methods. Milling rice kernels into an edible grain, for instance, meant removing the husks and the thin brown skins and then grinding the kernels with stone powder to whiten them (NII 1935: 521–26).[58] Modern flour milling in China began with the establishment of a German-owned mill in Shanghai in 1886; the first Chinese competitor set up shop in 1898 (Lieu 1936: 41). Up to World War I, China had fewer than a dozen modern flourmills, most of which were owned by foreigners. Major cities such as Shanghai imported their flour. As with so many other domestic industries, however, the war stimulated the development of Chinese-owned mills. Between 1917 and 1922, 26 flourmills were established. The manufacturing of cooking oil changed in a similar way. During the war, Chinese acquired large foreign factories such as the Hengyu Company, which Germans had established in 1910 (Bergère 1986: 72–73).

---

56. On soap and perfume, see NII 1935: 498–508.

57. The two most important Shanghai-based manufacturers (Fang Yexian's China Chemical Industries Company and Chen Diexian's Household Enterprises) were heavily involved in the movement and sold their products throughout China and in Southeast Asia.

58. Even in the 1930s, companies continued to use older techniques, some as simple as crushing grains manually between millstones; see NII 1935: 527–28.

In this rapidly changing consumer culture, cigarettes lay somewhere between fashion accessories and food and medicine. The development of the
foreign-owned cigarette industry in China followed the pattern of other
products. First, imports developed the domestic market.[59] Foreign companies soon realized that it would be cheaper to supply Chinese demand with
domestic factories. Cigarettes were first imported from Britain in 1890 by
the American Tobacco Company's agent, Mustard & Company, which
began manufacturing cigarettes in China the following year. The scale of
cigarette production grew dramatically when, in 1902, the newly merged
British-American Tobacco Company commenced production in China
(Hou 1965: 87–88). By 1934, some 300,000 Chinese families were growing
American tobacco (Hou 1965: 88). The cigarette companies engaged in extensive marketing efforts; the growth of the domestic market—from 300
million cigarettes sold in 1902 to over 88 billion by 1933—confirmed their
success (Cochran 1980: appendix table 9, 234). British-American Tobacco,
for instance, established a main factory near Shanghai as well as facilities in
Hankou, Qingdao, Tianjin, Harbin, and other cities, and employed 25,000
workers (Allen and Donnithorne 1954: 169–72). During the movement, the
simple act of smoking cigarettes, itself a new practice, placed millions of
Chinese directly in the midst of battles to nationalize the country's emerging consumer culture.[60]

---

59. Although cigarettes were a new element in this emerging consumer culture, tobacco
was not. Chinese had been growing tobacco, along with other New World crops, for several hundred years, and had smoked tobacco with pipes. The existence of this practice, in
fact, helped create a market for the quintessential import of the nineteenth century, opium,
because "the habit of opium smoking in China was an offshoot and development of tobacco
smoking" (Spence 1992: 231). The history of cigarettes in China is the best studied of all the
commodities discussed here; see Cochran 1980.

60. NII 1935: 622 reports that after the May Thirtieth Incident of 1925, the subsequent
anti-imperialist boycott intensified "the feeling among the masses that it was unpatriotic to
smoke foreign cigarettes." In response, many Chinese tobacco companies sprung up to serve
these patriotic smokers. The total number of cigarette factories in the Shanghai area increased from just 14 on the eve of the incident to 182 three years later. After 1928, sharp
price reductions by foreign companies helped drive many of these Chinese factories out of
the market, proof that patriotism had its financial limits. Chinese were willing to spend
only so much more for national products and often only under pressure (see Chapters 3
and 4).

The Ideological and Institutional Foundations of the Movement

The growth of Chinese industrial competition heightened trade tensions.[61] Neither the level of foreign investment nor the actual level of growth—the number and net contribution of new Chinese companies in new industries—is the key to understanding the origins of the movement. The critical issue is that Chinese industrialists, along with their political and public supporters, grew convinced that the number of Chinese companies would be vastly higher without imperialism. Not surprisingly, Chinese industrialists became the most vocal agents behind the popularization of the movement agenda, as well as its strongest financial supporters.

Sino-foreign competition in modern light industry began around the time of the start of the movement. Before the Revolution of 1911, fewer than 600 Chinese-owned enterprises used mechanical power. Less than ten years later, however, there were approximately 2,000 such factories employing over 270,000 workers (Feuerwerker 1977: 16–17; Chen Zhen 1957–61, vol. 1: 55–56).[62] This rapid growth led movement participants (as well as later PRC historians) to enshrine the era surrounding World War I,

---

61. This actual level of growth remains contested, but, as noted, is largely irrelevant here. Scholarship extending back into the period itself has emphasized economic stagnation in the warlord period (1912–27) (see Yang Quan 1923 and Eckstein 1977). According to this line of interpretation, political chaos undermined the possibility for economic growth; see, e.g., Ch'i 1976 and Sheridan 1975. Scholars inside and outside China have demonstrated that there was much more growth than previous interpretations acknowledged. For example, Chi-ming Hou finds "unquestionably that there was a significant trend toward 'economic modernization' before 1937" (Hou 1965: 125). In his revisionist index of industrial production in fifteen industries spanning the entire Republican era (1911–49), John K. Chang (1969: 71) found a high rate of growth. And Xiao Yanming (1999: 10–11) does Chang one better, concluding that the growth rate averaged 15 percent between 1912 and 1927 and was even higher from 1912 to 1915. Likewise, in a study of this period, economic historian Thomas Rawski concludes, "The sustained expansion of output per head became a regular feature of Chinese economic life in the early [twentieth century]" (1989: 344). For positive assessments of the role of foreign investment in this period, see Dernberger 1975: 46 and Perkins 1969: 133.

62. The vast majority of these companies were located in Shanghai: 1,186, according to D. K. Lieu's influential estimate (Liu Dajun 1937). This count made use of the 1929 Factory Law, which defined "factory" as a company using mechanical power and employing at least 30 workers. For a detailed table that shows the creation of the larger enterprises by year, see Du 1991: 107. By 1933, there were over 3,000 Chinese factories employing over a half million people. For a breakdown by industry, see "1933 nian Huashang gongchang tongji" (Statistics on Chinese merchants' factories for 1933) in Chen Zhen 1957–61, vol. 1: 57.

which greatly reduced competition from Western firms not to mention the Western imperialist presence as a whole, as a nearly mythical Golden Age (黃金時期) of modern yet autarkic economic development.[63] Although this modern industrial economy grew quickly, it was still a tiny part of the entire economy, accounting for only 3 percent of the gross domestic product in 1933 (T.-C. Liu and K.-C. Yeh 1965: 66). Its importance, however, lay in its power as a symbol of China's future. Regardless of the actual size of foreign involvement, Chinese reformers and, later, the leaders of these new Chinese-owned industries became vocal proponents during the subsequent decades of the movement of the notion that "foreign presence" equaled "foreign domination." Even the arguments of historians that the years preceding the Golden Age were actually more golden (see Xiao 1999) do not undermine my point: popular opinion in China (expressed through the movement) held that Chinese economic growth (i.e., the national attainment of wealth) was closely tied to limiting foreign participation in the Chinese economy. Indeed, the prominent Chinese economist H. D. Fong remembered this period as "the most propitious moment in the history of China's industrialization," a period "when imports had to be suspended and local products soared in prices" (Fong 1975: 9).

In the late nineteenth century, a newly industrializing United States (and later Germany) adopted a "home-market ideology" or protectionism as a means to protect the domestic market from cheap, mass-produced imports (see Crapol 1973; Wolman 1992: 1–16). Similarly, Chinese elites came to believe that uncontrolled foreign access to Chinese markets undermined the country's ability to assert its sovereignty and build an industrial economy. This belief became the basis of a discourse of "commercial warfare" (商戰), an ideology that spread rapidly and became the basis for institutional reform.[64] The language of commercial warfare provided the vocabulary and concepts through which these elites articulated China's relationship with the outside world. It formed the ideological frame through which the growing

---

63. The most comprehensive account remains Zhou Xiuluan 1958. See also Bergère 1986: 63–98.

64. On the shared economic ideology of "commercial warfare" in late nineteenth-century China, see P. Cohen 1987: 185–208. Cohen finds that Wang Tao 王韜 (1828–97) was "almost totally preoccupied with nonagricultural matters: transportation, mining, manufacture, and, above all, commerce" (ibid.: 185).

Fig. 1.3 The Toothpaste Defense
(*SB* 1935.6.3)

This advertisement illustrates the popular notion of commercial warfare. Here a Chinese national product, Sincere toothpaste, is a cannon poised to repel ships delivering imports. The banner reads: National Product Sincere Toothpaste. The slogan on the lower left explicitly invokes the terminology of commercial warfare: "Let's collectively strive to promote national products to recover economic rights." The advertisement illustrates several key tensions within the National Products Movement. First, it was increasingly difficult to separate Chinese and foreign things. Sincere was a large department store that featured imports. Under the growing pressure of the movement, the company began manufacturing and selling national products. The advertisement, then, also reminds consumers and movement activists that it did so. Second, as the prominent foreign translation of the product name on the label suggests, the advertisement also illustrates the persistent appeal of appearing foreign.

trade deficit became the leading indicator of national economic decline.[65] Moreover, it became the ideological basis for nationalizing consumer culture during the movement in the early twentieth century (see Fig. 1.3).

The famous reform-minded official Zeng Guofan first advanced the concept of "commercial war" in 1862. Zeng based his ideas on the ancient Legalist concept of "agricultural warfare" (耕戰 or 農戰), whose origins lay in the fourth-century B.C. philosophy of Shang Yang. Shang Yang advocated supporting war efforts by taxing commerce but concurrently giving merchants more leeway to generate taxable income. Zeng adapted these ideas to the times and saw international trade as a weapon weakening China's economy and enabling its military conquest. The imperial censor Li Fan 李璠 extended these ideas, arguing in 1878 that a policy of commercial warfare would focus China's energies on developing domestic industry and commerce and gradually eliminating the potential for foreign economic domination (Pong 1985). As Ding Richang 丁日昌 (1823–82), then the

---

65. Between 1886 and 1905, China's trade imbalance grew from around 10 million Haiguan taels to nearly 220 million. See also Guo Xianglin et al. 1995: 65–83.

Shanghai intendant, put it, if China adopted the strategy of commercial warfare, foreigners would not make money in China and would soon depart
(Hao 1986: 166–67).

The comprador-scholar Zheng Guanying 鄭觀應 (1842–1921) popularized the concept of "commercial war" in essays written in the late 1870s and
1880s and later compiled in his *Warnings to a Prosperous Age* (盛世危言, ca.
1893).[66] This bestseller, which profoundly influenced Mao Zedong as a
youngster and remains in print today, pushed the conceptualization of "defense industries" to industry itself as defense and explicitly articulated the
threat posed by imports (Zheng Guanying 1998: 292–98).[67] According to
Zheng, trade represented a more insidious form of warfare because it was
slow and peaceful: "Being swallowed up by troops is a disaster men perceive
easily, [but] conquest by commerce envelops the nation invisibly" (quoted in
Fewsmith 1985: 26). Therefore, Chinese nation-builders had to go beyond the
narrow "self-strengthening" focus on defense-related industries and develop
the domestic economy as a whole, particularly the modern industrial sector. It
was not enough to build battleships, erect gun towers, establish arsenals, and
create modern military forces. In Zheng's oft-repeated phrase, "Practicing
armed warfare is not as good as practicing commercial warfare." To survive
this war, Zheng argued, China needed to "stimulate commerce" (振興實業)
and practice "mercantilist policies" (重商政策) by promoting exports and
reducing imports. This would prevent the "draining" of Chinese capital (Hou
1965: 93–94, 131). Above all, the Chinese state needed to recognize the important role merchants played in national survival.

RECOGNIZING THE IMPORTANCE
OF COMMERCE

During the late nineteenth century, Chinese provincial leaders gradually
expanded their support for industrial development, initially focusing on
producer goods, particularly conspicuous heavy industries such as railroads,
mining, and armaments. The efforts of reform-minded provincial leaders

---

66. On Zheng and the spread of this concept among Chinese elites, see Wang Ermin 1995:
233–381, C.-C. Wu 1974: 96–152, and Xia Dongyuan 1985. For a survey of recent studies on
compradors, including Zheng, see Xie Wenhua 1994.

67. Mao told Edgar Snow that Zheng's book "stimulated in me the desire to resume my
studies" (Snow 1968: 133–34; see also Spence 1999: 5–6). The fact that Mao, then living in rural Hunan, had access to the book suggests how widely the text and its ideas spread.

such as Zeng Guofan, Li Hongzhang, and Zuo Zongtang 左宗棠 (1812–85) to develop Western military technology inaugurated a period of "self-strengthening" (自強運動) and "Westernization" (洋務運動) beginning in the early 1860s and extending to the end of the century. Among such leaders, there was a growing acceptance of the need to update China's military and improve China's understanding of modern science and technology to preserve domestic order and resist imperialism.[68] During the 1870s, self-strengthening and Westernization broadened from a focus on producing armaments to competing with foreign companies. Qing reformers, for instance, established the China Merchants' Steam Navigation Company to challenge Western domination of coastal shipping and the Kaiping Coal Mines to compete with foreigners in mining (Hao 1986: 167; Carlson 1957).[69]

As China began importing goods such as cigarettes and textiles, the notion of a commercial war came to encompass consumer goods. By the end of the 1870s, government-sponsored industries included profit-oriented light industries designed to supply the country's chief imports, particularly machine-made yarn and cotton goods. Li Hongzhang was especially active in these efforts, and the Shanghai Cotton Cloth Mill (1878) became one of his many new "government-supervised, merchant-run" (官督商辦) enterprises.[70] The establishment of these enterprises marked an important transition toward a "conscious tapping of expertise and a voluntary cooperation in the pursuit of policy" (Fewsmith 1985: 28). In contrast with earlier cooperation between government and merchants in the salt monopoly, the government's role in these new enterprises was to encourage the development of industry and commerce. In theory, these enterprises operated under government protection and were granted

---

68. These changes included the establishment of several government-backed heavy industrial complexes, including several dozen modern provincial arsenals such as the Jiangnan Arsenal and Shipyard (est. 1865) and the Fuzhou Naval Dockyard (est. 1866). Between 1861 and 1894, over 25 arsenals of varying sizes were established throughout China. For an overview, see Liao Heyong 1987: 58–78.

69. Interestingly, some 30 years before the start of the National Products Movement made this standard practice, the founder of the Merchants' Steam Navigation Company tried to ensure foreigners did not own any of the company stock by requiring the disclosure of shareholders' names and hometowns on share certificates.

70. On the importance of Li's sponsorship to such enterprises, see Lai 1994.

monopoly rights to ensure profitability. In practice, these experiments were not successful economically.[71]

Despite their failures as economic enterprises, these businesses became powerful symbols that embodied an early version of the nationalistic economic vision manifest in the National Products Movement. These enterprises propagated the notion that Chinese companies should avoid foreign capital and serve the nation by preventing the foreign domination of domestic markets. Likewise, despite the difficulties of working under "official supervision," merchants understood that, in the face of fierce foreign competition and without strong legal institutions, they needed state protection to survive and prosper. As a result, reformer-officials such as Zhang Zhidong gave more control to private investors (Bays 1978; Ayers 1971). He embraced a reformulated "government-supervised, merchant-run" model: "government-merchant joint management" (官商合辦). Two such undertakings were the Hubei Cotton Cloth Mill (est. 1889) and the Hubei Cotton Spinning Mill (est. 1894). Despite promising starts, however, these efforts faced familiar problems: low levels of reinvestment and a struggle between officials and merchants over control. These failures continued to undermine merchants' faith in government-led projects, and new efforts such as Zhang's attempts to raise capital for a carpet factory met with tepid responses (W. Chan 1978: 433). Finally, by the early twentieth century, official-entrepreneurs such as Sheng Xuanhuai 盛宣懷 (1844–1916), Nie Qigui 聶緝槻 (1855–1911), Zhang Jian, and Zhou Xuexi 周學熙 (1866–1947) had begun to organize their own "merchant-run" (商辦) companies. Their official ties enabled them to operate with little government control, an important development, but such efforts, too, were hampered by limited capital (W. Chan 1977: 9).[72]

At the same time, a new business class in major cities such as Shanghai and Guangzhou pushed for more control. Gradually, the idea took hold that privately financed and privately operated modern industries could help China achieve wealth and power.

---

71. The existence of government-backed monopolies hindered the state's industrial goals by stifling domestic competition. In turn, the lack of competition left little incentive for private investors to reinvest any profits in the fledgling enterprises. Industries were also at the mercy of government officials, who often viewed the projects as private cash cows. Management positions were often assigned through nepotism and cronyism. By the end of the 1880s, fewer and fewer Chinese merchants were willing to invest in these projects, and, ironically, many of these enterprises eventually turned to foreign expertise and capital to survive.The most complete account remains Feuerwerker 1958.

INSTITUTIONAL SUPPORT FOR COMMERCE
ON THE EVE OF THE MOVEMENT

State support for a "commercial war" fought by private enterprises expanded in the aftermath of China's humiliating defeat by Japan in 1895. In the summer of 1898, reformers called for the enactment of copyright and patent laws, rewards for inventors, and the general encouragement of commerce. The most famous reformer, Kang Youwei 康有為 (1858–1927), who had been deeply influenced by the notion of "commercial war," proposed that China follow Meiji Japan's example by creating business schools, organizing trade fairs, and publishing business journals. He also endorsed the creation of a bureaucratic infrastructure to promote commercial and industrial development, such as a ministry of commerce, provincial trade offices, and local chambers of commerce (K.-C. Hsiao 1975: 311–12, 319–31). Although entrenched bureaucratic interests soon overturned or undermined many of the reforms, the setback was only temporary (Kwong 1984; K.-C. Hsiao 1975).

During the Xinzheng 新政, or New Systems Reforms, of the late Qing government (1901–10), institutional support for commerce expanded dramatically at the national, provincial, and local levels. At the national level, the Qing established a new bureaucratic apparatus to develop the Chinese economy, including new ministries for finance, industry and commerce, and education (Reynolds 1993: 1).[73] Provincial leaders followed Zhang Zhidong's example and established commercial bureaus. These dramatic changes in the dynasty's policy toward commerce extended to the local level, particularly in the establishment of a legal framework for chambers of commerce and the creation of a system of awards and titles for those investing in modern enterprises (W. Chan 1977: 25–26). The state further codified support for industry in the second half of the first decade of the twentieth century with a series of business laws dealing with, among other matters, patents, bankruptcy, and incorporation.[74] Within a decade, there were over a thousand chambers of commerce, with a quarter-million members, spread across

---

73. For a brief history of the establishment of the Ministry of Commerce, see W. Chan 1977: 161–69. The famous diplomat and statesman Wu Tingfang 吳廷芳 (1843–1922), who became a prominent participant in the movement, led the efforts to create this ministry (Pomerantz-Zhang 1992).

74. For an overview of these reforms, see Zhang Yufa 1992: 13–21. On the company law and its legacy, see Kirby 1995.

China and in overseas Chinese communities.[75] For the first time in Chinese history, "the state had recognized the legitimacy of a private sphere distinct from and outside the scope of the state" (Fewsmith 1985: 35).

PRECURSORS TO THE MOVEMENT
IN EARLIER SOCIAL MOVEMENTS

A growing number of overlapping social movements centered on economic nationalism in the 1900s directly contributed to the start of the National Products Movement. At the beginning of the twentieth century, increasing foreign visibility engendered local Chinese opposition. Protests politicized foreign economic involvement in China and insisted that the Chinese themselves should control *their* economy. By the early 1900s, the vocabulary for describing China's predicament continued to expand, and terms such as "national sovereignty" and "recovery of sovereign rights" seemed to be "on nearly every page" (M. C. Wright 1968: 4). Vocabulary and action came together in several social movements, often led by local gentry-business leaders, including the Resist Russia Movement (1901–5), the Mining and Railroad Rights Recovery Movement (1905–11), and the anti-American boycott of 1905.

Foreign involvement in China was an extremely volatile political issue, frequently used against the Qing government in its final decade and against subsequent Chinese governments. In the early twentieth century, the Qing government's inability to defend Chinese economic interests and territorial integrity became the focus of increasing popular criticism. At the end of the Boxer Uprising, for example, Russian forces refused to withdraw from China. Russia clearly intended to consolidate its control over Manchuria, Mongolia, and Xinjiang by forcing China to sign a treaty. In protest, Chinese elites and merchants in Shanghai organized meetings and passed out handbills protesting Russian aggression and calling on the government to rebuff Russian demands. Chinese students and elites in many cities, such as Shanghai, Beijing, Tianjin, Hangzhou, Suzhou, Tokyo, San Francisco, and Singapore, formed Resist Russia associations (拒俄會) (K.-S. Liao 1984: 57–58; see also Zhongguo shehui kexueyuan, Jindai shi yanjiusuo 1979). In

---

75. For a yearly breakdown of the establishment of new chambers of commerce during this first decade, see Ma Min 1995: 256. The formation of new professions and the establishment of countless professional associations in the early Republic accompanied the creation of chambers of commerce (see Xu Xiaoqun 2001).

Japan, Chinese students led protests against ongoing Russian activities in Manchuria and even formed an "Anti-Russia Volunteer Army" (拒俄義勇軍) in the spring of 1903 (Harrell 1992).[76]

Although the origins of the National Products Movement predate 1905, the anti-American boycott of 1905 is a very clear reason for emphasizing this year as its starting point.[77] To protest discriminatory U.S. immigration policies, Chinese merchants throughout China and overseas led a boycott of American products in the summer of 1905. As Chapters 3 and 4 of this book elaborate, this and subsequent boycotts were the backbone of the movement. This first nationwide boycott inaugurated decades of escalating anti-imperialism expressed through consumption, or rather nonconsumption, and ushered in the widespread use of nationality as the primary mark by which to evaluate commodities and consumers.

Local efforts to recover mining and railway concessions from foreign control, collectively known as the "Rights Recovery Movement" (收回利權運動), politicized *ownership* by fomenting popular anger against imperialism and government reliance on foreign capital (E.-H. Lee 1977; Tim Wright 1984). Foreigners had begun building railroads several decades earlier, but they became a top priority for the imperialists after the Sino-Japanese war. Competition to finance Chinese railway construction became a part of the Western and Japanese "scramble for concessions." Beginning in Sichuan and quickly spreading to Hubei, Hunan, and Guangdong provinces, popular resentment, fueled by local elites, led to provincial and local attempts to build lines without government-backed foreign assistance (Esherick 1976: 82–91; Mi 1980). These protests yielded early successes, for example, in recovering the right to construct the Guangzhou-Hankou railroad from an American

---

76. By mid-1901, the movement began to dissipate. However, in April 1903 anti-Russian agitation flared up again as Russia delayed its withdrawal from Manchuria. Students formed "patriotic associations" (愛國會) in many cities. Criticism also emerged in China. In one notorious case during the anti-Russian campaign of 1903, the *Subao* (*Jiangsu Journal*) published openly anti-Manchu articles. Although Qing authorities wanted to arrest the authors for sedition, they could not do so. Ironically, the individuals accused of treason lived in Shanghai's International Settlement, outside the reach of Qing law. In another ironic twist, the Qing's inability to extradite the accused from their imperialist-controlled sanctuary further undermined Qing authority and emboldened its critics (Lust 1964). For many additional examples of similar sentiments voiced in the first decade of the 1900s, see Rankin 1971.

77. Because of this boycott, Chinese reference books usually name 1905 as the inaugural year of the movement. See, e.g., Yang Tianliang 1991a. As this chapter makes clear, this date might easily be pushed back into the nineteenth century.

firm. The Guangdong provincial section of the railway was supported by the issuance of low-priced shares of stocks that encouraged students, merchants, overseas Chinese, and others active in protests to take a direct role in recapturing the national economy (Rhoads 1975).

Although economic development based on patriotism quickly encountered financial, technical, and managerial problems, these efforts contributed to an environment in which growing numbers of Chinese thought they needed to "recover" the Chinese economy from foreign control (M. C. Wright 1984: 117–38). At the highest level of government, these sentiments led Sheng Xuanhuai, who became minister of communications in 1910, to work out a compromise. He used foreign loans and technical assistance to build and run all the trunk lines, which he nationalized in 1911, but left the branch lines to provincial interests. This set a pattern seen throughout the movement and highlights an important change in local elite protest: gone were the days, as in Guangdong province in earlier decades, of direct attacks on foreigners and their economic interests.[78] Now, local elites used more sophisticated tactics—for instance, replacing Confucian canon with international law—to outmaneuver foreigners at the local level without resorting to violence. Opposition to perceived foreign control spread throughout China with the support of native-place associations and the new chambers of commerce (Yu Heping 1995: 329–40). These expressions of economic nationalism further discredited the dynasty, fueling anti-dynastic sentiment and contributing to the revolutionary environment.

The history of many new commodities introduced in the early twentieth century reveals the full circle made by the National Products Movement. Initially, as the next chapter demonstrates, groups of traditional Chinese industries such as silk and satin guilds opposing changes in clothing led the movement. Later, however, the movement came to include domestic manufacturers of Western-style items such as buttons and hats. The button industry, for instance, began in Shanghai only during World War I. In 1917, two new Chinese companies began producing buttons from domestic materials, especially oyster shells and animal bones. Business boomed, although misinformed participants in the movement periodically attacked these Chinese products. By the early 1930s, however, domestic manufacturers were competitive enough to begin cutting into button imports (NII 1935: 477–80).

---

78. See, e.g., the description of the Sanyuanli Incident (1841) in Wakeman 1966.

All these new Chinese companies, producing seemingly "foreign" products, became active participants in promoting the consumption of their own and other "national" products.

What does this commodity-centered revision of the old story of "China's struggle to modernize" reveal about the country at the start of the movement around 1900? Above all, the foreign presence in China influenced that country in profound but often overlooked ways. Indeed, foreign direct investment in China is significant for reasons different from those usually cited. By introducing and endorsing a consumer culture, foreigners—whatever their stated purpose for being in China—undermined confidence in the traditional economy and created new needs and desires. The Chinese, however, actively found ways to appropriate this new culture for their own purposes. The everyday presence of foreigners and foreign products became conspicuous reminders to the Chinese of their lack of sovereignty. On the eve of the movement, this lack of sovereignty was acutely on display in the Russo-Japanese War (1904–5), in which two foreign countries fought a war on Chinese soil. From political leaders to local elites to Chinese students, economic sovereignty—defined as Chinese control of a Chinese economy—became a primary way of interpreting China's path to self-preservation and to wealth and power. By 1900, as reformers began demanding broader political participation, they also expected popular participation in the "commercial war" through the consumption or nonconsumption of a growing variety of everyday consumer products.[79] The growing production of national products—the very measure of a successful movement—symbolized and facilitated not only the elimination of imperialism and the creation of national identity and pride but also the restoration of China to its former glory as a land of desirable commodities rather than a destination for them. Many Chinese were, however, unwilling to relinquish their newly acquired desire for imports. In the following decades, under the unifying principle of modern national identity, the movement made participation in the "war" increasingly mandatory.

---

79. Allowing merchants to formally participate in areas formerly reserved for the state was, of course, part of a much broader effort to expand elite participation in governance, most notably the "local self-government movement" (地方自治運動); see Kuhn 1975, Thompson 1995, Zhu Ying 1991a, and 1991b: 225–39. As Mary Rankin notes, "A culture of elite civic participation was developing, with an agenda that was not always the same as that of government officials" (1990: 273).

CHAPTER TWO

Nationalizing the Appearance of Men

Cut your queue, change your style of dress, and revolt.
—Common slogan during the Revolution of 1911

Respectable citizens who were not disposed to change the habits of a lifetime, or who saw no need to evidence a political change by an inconvenient change of clothes and hairdress, were frequently forced to conform to the prejudices of the new school.
—Percy Kent, a British lawyer in Beijing (1912: 289–90)

If it's not a national product, don't wear it.
—Popular slogan of the National Products Movement

The National Products Movement began by nationalizing specific aspects of Chinese material culture. It began by creating, disseminating, and enforcing a new orthodoxy in male appearance, a new *nationalistic visuality*. The previous chapter examined the general origins of the movement; by focusing on men's appearance, this chapter provides a case study of the complexities encountered in nationalizing Chinese material culture, especially its visual representations. This example highlights several critical aspects of the movement. First, it demonstrates the general instability of material culture and the highly malleable, multiple, and linked interpretations of things. This phenomenon allowed the movement to create and impute new meanings such as nationality onto material culture, particularly commodities. Maintaining those constructions proved difficult, however. Direct appeals did not always work. Second, the chapter underscores the willingness of the movement to impose its interpretations, and even to legitimate violence in the name of "national survival." Third, because the Chinese state was weak both internally and internationally, the movement could not simply compel nationalistic consumption by relying on such tools as laws and tariffs. It had to find new ways to ensure popular participation. Yet, without a powerful state apparatus (that emerged only after 1949), its success was limited and tentative.

Fig. 2.1 Coercion and the Queue
(Harlingue-Viollet)

Coercion and violence lay behind efforts to create a new visual and material culture. During the Revolution of 1911, Chinese men voluntarily removed or were forced to cut their queues by Republican soldiers (*above*) and their sympathizers. The queue had numerous associations. For many, a well-groomed, thick queue had become a symbol of virility and civility. However, the new Republican government standardized and enforced an interpretation of the queue as a symbol of backwardness and issued a law requiring all men to remove them immediately.

By early 1912, revolutionary forces had overthrown China's last dynasty throughout southern China and established a Provisional Government in Nanjing. Like revolutionaries in France, the United States, and other countries (see Ribeiro 1988; Lauer and Lauer 1981: 171–201), the leaders of the Revolution of 1911 promoted and enforced their political agendas through a nationalistic visuality manifest in clothing and personal appearance. Ordering Chinese men to remove their queues of hair was one of the first acts of this government (see Fig. 2.1).[1] To the new leaders, the hairstyle was the most visible and repellent custom enforced by the Manchu-led Qing dynasty (1644–1912). It literally embodied China's backwardness. Yet, this was only the most conspicuous symbol of Manchu rule targeted for elimination. Defining queues as un-Chinese or even anti-Chinese was part of a larger rein-

---

1. Throughout this book, "queue" refers to both the single long braid of hair *and* the shaved forehead and front part of the scalp.

terpretation of *all* aspects of male personal appearance that accompanied the rise of the anti-Qing revolutionaries.[2] To these revolutionaries, imposing a new nationalistic visuality by redefining the orthodox male appearance was inextricably a part of creating a modern nation-state.

Not everyone agreed with the new orthodoxy. As a result, a uniform revision of male appearance did not emerge immediately. Unlike the queue, other aspects of male appearance were tied to powerful economic interests whose beneficiaries opposed any change.[3] Above all, the rise of Western-inspired clothing styles for men—such as replacing Chinese silk "long-gowns" (長袍) with suit pants and jackets made of imported wool—threatened the powerful silk industry. Members of the silk industry appropriated the nationalism and anti-imperialism of the revolutionaries and redefined silk. Chinese silk—not silk as such or particular garments made with silk—became the actual indicator of a product's nationality. In this way, manufacturers of Chinese silk claimed status as the truly revolutionary force modernizing China, a claim premised on the division of the world into "nations." Yet the uncertainty caused by the inability to enforce Qing sumptuary laws had accelerated status competition through the consumption of Western styles and materials and made it difficult to elevate "Chinese" silk

---

2. Although I focus on hair and clothing, the controversy surrounding changes in "appearance" extended to hats (shapes and fabrics), shoes (traditional cotton versus new leather styles), and adornments (belts, watches, cigarettes, and many more "Western" items). Moreover, I see "appearance" as a subcategory of "self-presentation," which includes actions such as handshaking, blowing one's nose, table manners, and everyday activities discussed in Elias 1994. For an introduction to the symbolic transformation of China wrought under the early Republic—including the meanings associated with hair, dress, calendars, flags, postures, etiquette, and much more—see Harrison 2000: esp. 14–85.

3. The economic interests that supported the queue were considerably weaker. This style required almost constant attention from barbers, who not only had to braid and rebraid the queue but also had to shave the forehead. According to one European traveler to Qing China, barbers owed their very existence to the Qing conquest and the imposition of the queue (cited in Lach and van Kley 1993: 1695–96). However, until the Yongzheng emperor (r. 1723–36) abolished formal class distinctions, barbers were members of the most reviled and powerless legal class in China, the "mean people" (賤民), a category that also included prostitutes, actors, peddlers, and government runners (Ch'ü 1961: 128–35). More recently, Harry Hansson (1988: 50) has classified barbers along with sedan chair carriers, cooks, and a few other kinds of workers as "semi-mean" and finds that, although treated as inferior, barbers were not subjected to formal legal restrictions prohibiting them from participating in examinations. Hansson also enumerates the reasons for the low status of barbers, such as their work with hair, considered "polluted," and their association with homosexual brothels.

to a position as the pre-eminent quality of products.[4] Dissuading elites from switching to Western material culture would require organization and considerable work.

One group of Shanghai guilds or "native-place associations" (公所, 會館, 同鄉會) immediately responded to the challenge by forming a new organization that became an archetypical movement group. Shortly after the outbreak of revolution in October 1911, representatives from eight powerful Shanghai native-place associations established the National Products Preservation Association (中華國貨維持會; hereafter NPPA), one of many movement organizations designed to disseminate the perception that protecting the economic interests of domestic manufacturers was closely tied to the survival of China as an independent country.[5] In a brief speech at the inaugural meeting of the NPPA on December 12, 1911, one of the participants, Mei Zuolü 梅作侶, illuminated this emerging connection between products and patriotism when he urged the assembled to consider him the very embodiment of the new group's agenda. As he told the group, "People should hold me up as an exemplar of patriotic and appropriate appearance

---

4. This use of consumption to achieve and maintain status was not new in China. Like their European counterparts, scholars of late imperial China have begun to identify the origins of modern consumer culture in the consumption patterns of earlier centuries. For a summary of this research that argues that popular consumption of goods once deemed luxuries—agricultural goods such tea, tobacco, sugar, and textiles as well as more specialized objects such as books—was at or above European levels until the early nineteenth century, see Pomeranz 2000: 116–27, 138–42. As he also notes, the importance and popularity of this sort of competition varied by region, just as it did in Europe (ibid.: 149). For instance, in the Jiangnan region, this style of consumption was an essential part of elite status by the late sixteenth century (Brook 1998: 218–22).

5. Translating the Chinese name for the NPPA (中華國貨維持會) poses problems. I chose a middle course between two issues—describing the purpose of the organization versus finding a more literal translation. Rather than more common interpretations such as "promote," I elected to translate *weichi* 維持 as "preservation" to contrast it with its implied antonym, which often appeared in the phrase "national annihilation" (亡國). "Preservation" implies preserving not only the industries involved in the NPPA but also the Chinese nation through the "preservation" of all industries, a core tenet of the movement. A NPPA document from 1925 translates the organization's name as "China Products Improvement Association" (SZMA File 397). Although improving Chinese products was an explicit and central part of the agendas of movement groups such as the NPPA, "product improvement" does not adequately invoke the foreign threat that promoting Chinese products implied. Other translations for Zhongguo guohuo weichi hui are "Chinese Product Protection Society" and "Society to Encourage Use of National Goods" (Pomerantz-Zhang 1992: 235).

Fig. 2.2 Reinterpreting Qing Male Dress
(Kent 1912)

Statesman and future NPPA president Wu Tingfang wearing the brimless cap, silk long-gown, padded silk vest, and cotton shoes that were typical upper-class male dress during the Qing dynasty. The Revolution of 1911 not only required men to cut their queues and adopt Western-style haircuts, but also threatened to transform this style of clothing into a symbol of Chinese backwardness. However, members of China's powerful silk industry led the fight to reinterpret such dress as a symbol of modern Chinese nationalism.

because my brimless cap, long-gown, and cloth shoes are all made of domestic materials" (see Fig. 2.2) (ZGWH 1912: 9a).

The significance of these orthodox articles of clothing as new signs of patriotic fervor and elements of nation-making is not at first obvious. Although Mei Zuolü's physical appearance was orthodox under the pre-revolutionary government, this was not the case in the early days of the new Republic, which had swiftly and forcefully moved to impose a new orthodoxy in male appearance: the queueless hairstyle, with an unshaven forehead, and the Western-style suit (see Fig. 2.3).

This organization contributed to the broader nationalization of Chinese material culture by successfully fighting the symbolic shifts surrounding the Revolution of 1911. In the process, the NPPA helped uncouple two funda-

Fig. 2.3 The New Male Orthodoxy?
(Tang Weikang and Huang Yixuan 1991: 8)

Republican revolutionary Sun Yatsen (*seated*) and his son, Sun Ke (Sun Fo, 1891–1973), on the
eve of the Revolution of 1911. Following the overthrow of the Qing dynasty in 1911–12, participants in the National Products Movement feared that the style of clothing photographed
here would fast become the new orthodoxy and the foundation of an emerging visuality that
blindly emulated the industrial West, an appearance that for men included a queueless hairstyle, unshaven forehead, Western-style wool suit, and leather shoes.

mental and long-linked aspects of male appearance—queues and clothing
styles. Advancing its members' interests, the NPPA sought to make wearing
Chinese-style clothing a clear sign of patriotism and fought the reactionary,
pro-dynastic, and pro-Manchu linkages that traditional clothing was rapidly
acquiring. The group also aimed to make it unpatriotic to wear Western
styles and even traitorous when those suits were made of imported fabrics.
Ultimately, this second qualification would supplant all other concerns. The
organization opposed Western styles not because the styles themselves were
"foreign" but because the imported fabrics threatened to destroy a major
Chinese industry. For the NPPA and every other movement organization,
nationalizing consumer culture meant supporting or opposing the assimila-
tion of novel Western products based on China's ability to manufacture the
given products itself.

The NPPA promoted an *ethic of nationalistic consumption* as part of its strategy to compete against foreign companies in Chinese markets. To understand the process of constructing this ethic, we must examine the highly charged conflict over the competing interpretations of material culture to see how everyday artifacts could be imbued with nationalistic significance. Movement organizations such as the NPPA made the act of consumption a powerful locus for creating of a new Chinese nation, a nation that was materially bound to the individual through the consumption of Chinese goods.

This case study explores the development of these links between consumption and nationalism. The first half examines the battles over the meaning of the Qing hairstyle and clothing for men. The history of the Qing interpretation of male appearance and the challenges to its authority in terms of male appearance illuminates the shifting role that objects and materials play in nation-making at the social, economic, and political levels. The intense competition among contradictory visions of appearance surrounding the revolution confirms the difficulties of recoding Qing styles as fashionably nationalistic in the new Republic. The second half returns to the NPPA and explains how its interpretation of appearance successfully challenged an ascendant Republican orthodoxy. Revealing how one movement organization began labeling objects "Chinese" and "foreign"—that is, how it began nationalizing consumer culture—will provide a foundation for understanding the nascent National Products Movement.

Ascribing Meaning to Men's Appearance During the Qing

Personal appearance is never personal. Bound into the word "appearance" is the notion of an audience who sees. One appears to others. Nor is the meaning of appearance ever singular or straightforward. Rather than being unproblematically controlled by the "sender," appearance always has the capacity to mean many things to different "receivers." NPPA efforts, then, to get Chinese male appearance to pre-eminently signify product-nationality was difficult, if not impossible. The ascribed meanings of clothing, hairstyles, the body, adornment, and other aspects of appearance have always, regardless of area or epoch, been fundamental to the social construction of gender, age, caste, class, and ethnicity, indeed to every category of sociocultural subjectivity.[6]

---

6. The body of social science literature on the meaning of fashion is vast and growing. For general introductions, see Barnard 1996 and F. Davis 1992: 24–26. As the citations that follow

Orthodox male appearance in China was long a primary marker of these differences. For millennia, cultural differences between China and its Inner Asian neighbors, in terms of personal appearance, customs, and manners, defined Chinese culture. Indeed, an oft-quoted line from the *Analects* highlights this use of appearance to establish cultural difference: "Without [court retainer] Guan Zhong, we would have been reduced to barbarians with our hair down and robes folded to the left" (*Analects* 14.18). Queues and clothing buttoned on the left were in fact styles borrowed from "barbarian" peoples and were regarded by the time of the revolution as "the diplomatic expression for non-Chinese ways and speaking of all Tartars."[7] The initial framing of these styles by Republican revolutionaries as impositions of ethnically alien imperial rulers made the NPPA's advocacy of them a formidable task. With the crumbling of the Qing dynastic order, the use of clothing and other objects remained key to the reintegration of individual Chinese into a larger community but with a fundamental difference. Rather than simply emphasizing the type of fabric or style of clothing, Chinese manufacturers and merchants hoped to persuade others to assign primary importance to the national origin of the fabric. The attempt to do this would eventually require their participation in much broader political and cultural battles.

The Qing, like its predecessors, reinforced its military hegemony and reproduced its authority to govern by defining and enforcing an orthodox interpretation of personal appearance. Studies of personal appearance usually focus either on Qing hairstyle or on Qing clothing, without integrating the two.[8] This is a mistake because these two aspects shared a common history and formed a mutually reinforcing semiotic system. The history of this system includes the initial imposition of meaning in the early years of the Qing dynasty, followed by the repeated challenges of revolutionaries, such as the Taipings in the mid-nineteenth century, and finally the system's demise with the dynasty itself in the second decade of the twentieth century.

The intensely politicized nature of physical appearance, particularly hair, is apparent throughout the entire history of the dynasty. As the Manchus swept south and west, conquered men were forced to adopt the queue hair-

---

indicate, much less that addresses the meaning of fashion in China specifically has been written.

7. "The Renascence of Queue Cutting," in *NCH* 1914.7.25. See also Shiratori 1929.

8. On clothing, see any of the recent books by Valery Garrett, esp. Garrett 1987. See also C. Roberts 1997b. On queues, see Qiu 1936, 1938; W. Cheng 1998; and Godley 1994.

style as an unambiguous sign of surrender and submission, rather than allowing all their hair to grow and coiling it into a topknot, as had been the case in the Ming dynasty (1368–1644) (Kuhn 1990: 12, 52, 58–59).[9] The Manchu ruler, the regent Dorgon (1612–50), was initially reluctant to impose the Manchu hairstyle on the conquered ethnic Han men, who constituted the vast majority of the male population. But by the middle of 1645, he made the Manchu hairstyle obligatory for all laymen (Wakeman 1985, esp. vol. 1: 646–50).[10] The battles over the meaning of the queue would continue even after the abdication of the Manchu rulers in 1912.

The battles were so intense because many levels of Chinese society contested these issues. Anti-Manchu Chinese assigned meaning to the changes in appearance even before the establishment of the new dynasty, and refusal to adopt the hairstyle quickly became a rallying point for opposition. Resistance came in many forms. Some Chinese fought to the death out of loyalty to the recently toppled Ming dynasty; others justified opposition as a refusal to commit the unfilial act of altering the body received from one's parents.[11] Chinese men also sought less martial ways of dodging the edict by taking advantage of a loophole. Because the order exempted Buddhists and Daoists, there were widespread accounts of Han men becoming monks and priests to avoid persecution (J. C. Lynn 1928: 157).

In response, imperial authorities reinforced the official interpretation of the queue with the full power of the state. Because of the seditious implications of refusing to shave the forehead and maintain a queue, imperial authorities strictly enforced the law. A popular expression put it this way: "If

---

9. Historian Philip Kuhn suggests that the "Manchus probably adopted the style to avoid obstructing the eyes while riding" (1990: 243n6). Although braided hair was popular among Han men by the end of the Mongol Yuan dynasty, the Ming dynasty quickly reversed the trend. Chinese men who wished to be considered "Han" were ordered to discontinue the hairstyle and revert to a more "Chinese" style, namely, wearing the hair long and tied up in a topknot (Godley 1994: 55). For illustrations and descriptions of hairstyles and clothing under the Ming and Qing dynasties, see Zhou Xibao 1996: 378–532 and Huang Nongfu and Chen Juanjuan 1995: 312–83.

10. Among those exempted were Daoist and Buddhist clergy. The Qing code eventually mandated severe punishment for anyone who became a priest without first obtaining a license (W. C. Jones 1994: 106).

11. Yishan, Qingdai tongshi, shangce [first part: 294]. Resistance was particularly fierce in Jiangnan, a center of Chinese fashion. See, e.g., Dennerline 1981 and Struve 1984. This sentiment was expressed in the phrase: "One's hair and skin is a gift from one's parents and should not be damaged" (身體髮膚受之父母不可毀傷). See also Hua 1989: 76.

you want to keep your head, don't let your hair grow; if you let your hair grow, you won't keep your head" (留頭不留髮留髮不留頭). Imperial power eventually crushed overt resistance, and Chinese men adopted the hairstyle. However, abandoning the style potentially signified anti-dynastic sentiment throughout the Qing—as rebels such as those in Taiwan and the Taipings demonstrated. The Qing leadership was ever watchful for cases of queue-cutting as a harbinger of political unrest.[12]

RECEDING HAIR LINES

Initially a source of bitter antipathy between conquerors and conquered, the overwhelmingly political significance of the Manchu-imposed hairstyle gradually receded. Instead, the style became a visual means of representing and reinforcing social status. As a foreign observer noted at the end of the nineteenth century, "Chinese people are now more proud of their [queues] than of any other characteristic of their dress, and the rancorous hostility to the edict of the Manchus survives only in the turbans of the natives of the provinces of Canton and Fukien, coverings once adopted to hide the national disgrace" (A. H. Smith 1894: 118–19).

Indeed, the significance of the queue as a status symbol grew over the course of the dynasty, as customs, traditions, regulations, and even superstitions surrounding the queue bolstered its position in Chinese society. Social practices suggested that the longer the queue, the higher a man's social rank. Those who could afford it added additional hair; others often lengthened their queues by adding a piece of black cord, changing the color of the cord to white, the traditional color of mourning, at the appropriate times. As a result, queues often reached the knees or even the ankles (Godley 1994: 62n52; Ball 1911: 13). Other regulations on body hair reinforced the status symbol of a long, full queue. For instance, beards were prohibited to all males under the age of 45, and even then men could only grow a goatee.[13] And just as difficult-to-maintain white collars have been used to indicate status in indus-

---

12. For an exploration of Qing sensitivity to the potentially seditious significance of cutting even parts of the queue, see Kuhn 1990.

13. Prestige was often enhanced by wearing a tiny comb attached to a coat button and by stroking the growth of the beard. Only much older men, 65 and older, were allowed to grow a full beard. There was one exception to these hirsute rules: mole hairs were allowed free reign (Ball 1911: 15; Conger 1909: 51–52).

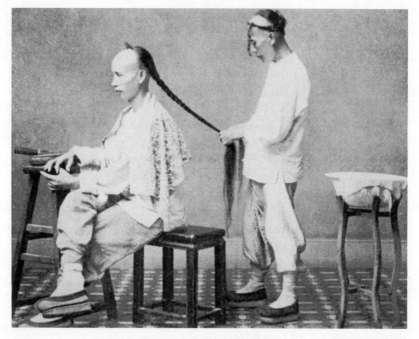

Fig. 2.4 Antithetical Interpretations of the Queue
(Ball 1911: 12)

When the Manchus conquered China in the mid-seventeenth century, they forced Han Chinese men to adopt the queue as a symbol of submission. During the Qing dynasty, the hairstyle acquired multiple and antithetical associations. Anti-Qing rebels usually cut their queues and allowed the hair on their foreheads to grow as a symbol of rebellion. However, for other men, the customs, traditions, regulations, and even superstitions surrounding the queue transformed the hairstyle into a status symbol.

trial societies, the maintenance of the hairstyle helped identify social status and reinforce social divisions; the length of the hair in those areas of the forehead that were properly kept shaven revealed one's financial capacity to keep the forehead cleanly shaven. A clean forehead required frequent trips to the barber (Ball 1911: 18).[14] When working, a man usually either rolled his queue into a knot at the back of the neck or head or coiled it loosely around the head (see Fig. 2.4). However, this was considered informal, as one Western observer put it, "the equivalent of our Western condition of being in

---

14. For a description of a typical visit to a Chinese barber and of the pain involved, see Ball 1911: 16–17.

one's shirt-sleeves." In the presence of superiors, one was expected to unfurl the entire queue (Ball 1911: 14).

The regulations governing queues reinforced this hierarchy of hair. Indeed, the social stigma attached to not having a queue was intense, and the queueless were the object of mockery by "even the lowliest beggar" (Crow 1944: 23). Although universally prescribed for laymen, there was one significant exception: criminals. No male in jail or guilty of a crime was permitted to maintain a queue; he was often derided as "tailless" (無辮). Those released from jail had to resort to wearing, as one observer put it, a "falsey" to avoid social stigma (Gutzlaff 1838, vol. 1: 479–80).[15] Because of the low status associated with those without queues, Jesuit missionaries, who usually remained in China for life, usually opted to grow queues. Protestants stationed inland often elected to wear fake queues, which they detached when they needed to move between social worlds. Roman Catholic and Protestant missionaries considered this practice so essential that, as one Western observer recounts, nobody doubted that Paul, the most famous Christian missionary, would have also adopted the custom; the only point of contention being whether he would have grown or bought his queue (Crow 1944: 23; see also Peterson 1994).

The accrued cultural significance of the queue demonstrates that the military power of the Qing was not the only force upholding the queue. As studies of the major rebellions during the Qing have shown, challenges to the orthodox Qing interpretation of appearance were frequent and violent.[16] Nevertheless, it seems clear that the hairstyle wove itself into popular culture. Clothing styles and fabric hierarchies were even more deeply ingrained in Chinese society.

---

15. For such examples, see Hardy 1905: 130–37. Conversely, Qing code also prescribed harsh punishments for removing someone else's hair. Completely shaving off the hair of another was punished with "60 strokes of heavy bamboo and penal servitude of one year" (W. C. Jones 1994: 285–86).

16. The best-known challenge to Qing orthodox appearance came during the Taiping Rebellion (1851–64). The radical social policies of these "hair bandits" (髮賊), as they were called, included cutting queues and changing clothing styles. For a comprehensive survey of these changes, see Li Wenhai and Liu Qingdong 1991: 31–52.

The Visual and Economic Significance of Chinese Clothing

Although the queue was the most conspicuous symbol of orthodox appearance, the Qing also regulated clothing by law and custom.[17] Shortly after decreeing the universal adoption of the Manchu hairstyle for laymen, the court ordered Chinese officials to adopt Qing clothing styles. Adherence was initially lax, and again in early 1653 the court ordered Chinese to conform to Qing styles. As the order put it: "Each dynasty has its own regulations regarding hats and clothing, and Ours was issued long ago. Yet the colors and dimensions of Han official clothing are not in accordance with this code. Because the Han must imitate Manchu styles, they cannot wear different clothes. From now on, Han must wear Manchu styles and no others" (quoted in Yan Changhong 1992: 238).[18]

As with the regulations on queues, these laws on clothing were strictly enforced. Officials had to observe explicit, detailed regulations on all items of clothing, hats, and adornments, including styles and materials (E. T. Williams 1923: 479–80).[19] Officials assumed summer and winter outfits on the day specified in the Beijing Gazette, and special buttons and feathers on their caps indicated rank (Hardy 1905: chap 12, esp. 130–37).[20] On the other hand, women, babies, Buddhists, Daoists, actors, and temple statues were permitted to wear the styles of the previous dynasty (J. C. Lynn 1928: 157; Vollmer 1977: 21).

Throughout Chinese society, fabrics also had a hierarchy of prestige, with silk at the top (Vollmer 1977: 16). Silk from China was recognized internationally and domestically as a precious commodity and was used by Chinese and foreigners as a form of currency (Rossabi 1997: 7). For thousands of years, silk had played a critical role in Sino-foreign trade: silk was a

---

17. By the late eighteenth century, there were 48 official categories of clothing determined by sex, status, rank, office, event, and season. Most of these categories addressed the clothing of the emperor and imperial family (Guoli lishi bowuguan 1988: 5). This book contains an illustrated overview of these styles.

18. The Qianlong emperor reviewed and reinforced sumptuary legislation for all officials in the mid-eighteenth century and in 1759 issued the *Huangchao liqi tushi* (Illustrated precedents for the ritual paraphernalia of the imperial court). See also Medley 1982 and G. Dickinson and L. Wrigglesworth 2000. On the widespread observance of clothing etiquette across social classes, see Walshe 1906: 12–13.

19. For a survey of clothing rules for officials over several thousand years, see Yang Shufan 1982.

20. The best-illustrated study of these regulations is V. M. Garrett 1990.

major component of Chinese gifts to foreign envoys and was bartered for Mongol horses and traded for Japanese specie. Most important, from the mid-sixteenth to the eighteenth century, silk exports to the Spanish American market (via Manila) attracted vast quantities of Mexican and Peruvian silver bullion, profoundly altering the Chinese economy (L. M. Li 1981: 62–65; Yü Ying-shih 1967: 158–59; Atwell 1977).

Although most Chinese wore cotton or hemp clothing, officials and wealthy men and women wore many articles of silk, including hats, long-gowns, petticoats, and detachable collars (L. C. Johnson 1995: 43–44; V. M. Garrett 1994: 12). This proliferation of silk products led to the massive consumption of silk, socially reinforced by centuries of prestige surrounding its use. The significance of silk as a luxury item and critical ingredient of upper-class life seemed immune to a revolution that could make or break the queue—that is, until the wool suits and khaki uniforms of anti-dynastic forces in the late nineteenth and early twentieth century began to threaten the privileged position of silk.

Because those directly and indirectly involved in the silk industry were so important to the initial development of the National Products Movement, it is worth noting the growing fears concerning silk in Chinese life. China's declining share of the world market and the possible destruction of the domestic market by cheaper, better-made imported silk (and later rayon) generated alarms, as did the switch from silk gowns to wool suits.[21]

Silk was not only a symbol deeply embedded in Chinese material culture but also a critical part of the Chinese economy, particularly in the major silk-producing areas of Jiangnan (south of the Yangzi River) and Guangdong. It is easy to imagine, then, why the possible destruction of the silk industry caused such anxiety. Many people stood to lose their livelihoods. Silk production was an extremely labor-intensive industry at every stage of its production.[22] From the planting and cultivating of mulberry trees to the raising of silkworms to reeling and finally to weaving, each step required massive labor inputs, even after the introduction of machines.

For instance, silk production was extremely important in the Lower Yangzi–Lake Tai area. During the Ming and Qing dynasties, silk became

---

21. On the gradual decline of the Chinese silk export market, see Allen and Donnithorne 1954: 60–68.

22. For an excellent description of silkworms and their cultivation, see C. A. S. Williams 1933: 127–28.

the foundation of the local economy. Not surprisingly, the Qing government understood sericulture's critical role in relieving the growing pressure on land due to the rapid population growth and worked hard to promote it. The state encouraged the planting of mulberry trees, bought cocoons from isolated farmers, and recruited experts to train locals (Shih Min-hsiung 1976: 5–7). The silk industry also provided critical supplemental and primary income opportunities for off-season and female laborers. With the introduction of silver from the Americas into China and the development of a market economy, silk and silk textiles became an increasingly important part of many local economies.

The silk industry was intimately connected with everyday life in these regions. It was much more than a luxury commodity whose fate would affect only a small fraction of the population. Local social customs and taboos reflected the supreme importance of the silkworms. Because the cocoons were sensitive to weather conditions and so valuable, families usually kept the cocoons indoors, expending precious resources and risking disaster by using oil lamps and charcoal ovens to keep the rooms warm. In some places, women incubated silkworm eggs with the warmth of their bodies. In other places, families kept the eggs under their blankets (Ball 1925: 574). During the most critical weeks leading up to the boiling of the cocoons and the reeling of the raw silk, normal social intercourse completely stopped, and local custom proscribed "the making of social calls, prying into one's neighbor's methods of raising the silkworms, loud or profane talk in the silkworm room, tax collection, and wedding celebrations or funerals" (Shih Min-hsiung 1976: 10).

The late nineteenth, early twentieth century was a tumultuous time for the silk industry in China, which had already begun to undergo massive change.[23] In the 1870s, just as the industry was recovering from the devastation wrought by the Taiping Rebellion, the introduction of steam-powered filatures (which reeled the silk cocoons) began to facilitate the shift from household to factory production. This shift rapidly displaced hand-reeled silk and those working by hand, particularly in the export market where machine-reeled silk fetched significantly higher prices. By 1900, some thirty years after the introduction of the first steam-powered filatures, 97 percent of the silk exported at Guang-

---

23. These changes are summarized in Shih Min-hsiung 1976: 29–32. In contrast to reeling, weaving remained largely a handicraft industry until the eve of the Revolution of 1911 (L. M. Li 1981: 30–33).

zhou came from these modern plants.[24] The resulting unemployment caused widespread social unrest but did not stop the spread of the new steam technology into the principal silk-producing centers.

In a pattern that would repeat itself frequently during the National Products Movement, industry after industry came to blame "foreign" (particularly Japanese) competition both for causing China's relative decline and for preventing Chinese companies from effectively competing with foreign commodities. As noted in Chapter 1, in the aftermath of the First Sino-Japanese War, foreign companies gained the right to set up factories in China. Foreigners with better access to capital began to provide stiff competition for Chinese-owned filatures and, later, textile companies.

Japanese ascendancy in silk production and export relative to the Chinese threatened the long-term viability of this Chinese industry. This caused considerable panic among Jiangnan silk producers, even as absolute output increased. Before Japanese companies could legally open factories in Chinese cities, Japan was already well along the road to replacing China as the primary supplier of the world's silk. China went from producing 41.5 percent of the world's silk in the decade preceding the Revolution of 1911, to 26 percent by 1914; in contrast, Japan accounted for 20.7 percent in 1900 and 44.5 percent in 1914, a near reversal of the two countries' fortunes. Similarly, Japanese silk production expanded nearly sixfold between 1883 and 1912 (Shih Min-hsiung 1976: 66, 70). Even so, Chinese raw silk and silk fabric production and exports expanded throughout this period and surpassed declining tea exports by 1887 to become China's primary export item (L. M. Li 1981: 72–81). Ironically, this expansion gave more and more Chinese a stake in the survival and prosperity of this key industry.

Late Qing Interpretations of Appearance

Toward the end of the Qing dynasty, pressure to officially reinterpret changes in male appearance came from many directions, not least from within the Manchu leadership itself.[25] Both Manchu and non-Manchu officials were anxious to link Qing rule with newer symbols. Some members of the Chinese

---

24. Data from Chinese Imperial Maritime Customs *Decennial Reports*, compiled in Shih Min-hsiung 1976: table II.1: 17.

25. Other East Asian countries faced similarly complex decisions over men's hair. On the controversy over cutting the topknot in Korea, see Jang 1998. For a survey on these changes throughout East Asia, especially China, see Ryū 1990.

elite began to argue that the dynasty should allow the removal of queues. Officials advocating reform of appearance usually downplayed the political symbolism of abandoning a hairstyle associated with the ethnic Manchu court. Instead, they argued that the queue was incompatible with modern appearance, with its emphasis on hygiene (among the many consequences, the queue left deep, dark stains along the backs of clothing) and convenience. For these advocates of change, such reform of appearance fell within the purview of a dynasty trying to protect the welfare of its subjects and was not necessarily a sign of anti-Manchu sentiment (Li Shaobing 1994: 51).[26]

The Qing military supplied a powerful internal source of pressure to reinterpret appearance. During the New Systems Reforms of the late Qing government, the uniforms of the New Army followed the Western example, by way of the Prussian-style uniforms used in Japan.[27] By 1905, for example, the troops of the two most important military commanders of the late Qing, Yuan Shikai 袁世凱 (1859–1916) and Duan Qirui 段祺瑞 (1865–1936), began using Western-style military uniforms. Abolition of the queue followed, because it was difficult to wear under Western military caps and because the troops objected to the trouble of maintaining it (E. T. Williams 1923: 478–79). To be sure, for some, the queue continued to be a "badge of loyalty." In the most famous case, General Zhang Xun's 張勳 (1854–1923) army gained the label the Queue Army (辮子軍) because the soldiers kept the traditional hairstyle.

Many diplomats, students, and officials became aware of negative images of the queue during their time abroad. Some of these people attempted to appropriate the meaning of changes in appearance and strengthen the image of the imperial state as reformer. After returning from a tour abroad, for instance, the powerful Manchu court member Zaize 載澤 (1868–1930), a grandson of a Qing emperor, "also urged the abandonment of the queue

---

26. The first of many such arguments for clothing reform came in 1890. Such opinions are quoted extensively in Wang Ermin 1981: 61–65. For instance, during the Hundred Days Reforms of 1898, a low-ranking official in the Board of Rites submitted a memorial advocating a lengthy list of suggestions for reviving the ailing dynasty, including the abolition of the queue and the replacement of Chinese-style dress with Western-style clothing (A. H. Smith 1901, vol. 1: 145–46). He was not the only reformer to make such a suggestion. In fact, the inspirational leader of the reforms, Kang Youwei, suggested that China follow Japan's lead in reforming dress and hairstyle (K.-C. Hsiao 1975: 341n146).

27. I follow Douglas Reynolds's (1993) use of the term "revolution" to underscore the profound changes begun during this period.

and the national costume, as usage unsuited to the energetic life necessary in the modern world" (*NCH* 1906.8.31). By the start of 1910, many princes and high officials supported limited changes in clothing styles. Opponents and proponents met to discuss the matter and concluded in a report that the court should allow diplomats, military officers, and policemen to cut their queues and adopt Western dress. However, they explicitly prohibited students from making these changes ("Change of Costume," *NCH* 1910.1.7). Shortly thereafter, the Prince Regent decided to order Chinese men to change their clothing style the following year ("The Change of Costume," *NCH* 1910.1.14).

Throughout the country and in Chinese communities overseas, pressure was mounting to modify appearance. An observer said that the entire country was talking about the queue, and the discussions were nearly paralyzing the government. Although a newspaper article on the subject said that most people in the country were in favor of abandoning the queue, there were dissenting opinions. One rumor held that cutting queues would profit foreigners because clothing would inevitably change with the removal of queues. The assumed link between hair and clothing led Hangzhou hat manufacturers to oppose the removal for fear of subjecting China to the "fickle goddess of fashion" (*NCH* 1910.9.30).

QUEUELESS BUT LOYAL: ONE
REFORMER'S INTERPRETATION

The famous Chinese diplomat and statesman Wu Tingfang, who served as the president of the NPPA from 1913 to 1916, provides a good example of these early, vocal efforts to redefine one dimension of China's visual culture.[28] His ideas offered the Qing a way to appropriate the potentially revolutionary meaning of queue cutting by suggesting the court itself sanction it. For the purposes of the movement, however, he was especially important for his early efforts to separate and assign distinct meanings to the queue and Chinese dress. Before returning to Shanghai from the United States in the spring of 1910, Wu began to lobby for the abolition of the queue but the re-

---

28. For a biographical sketch of Wu Tingfang, see Boorman and Howard 1967–71, vol. 3: 453–56. Although Wu's relationship to the NPPA and dress and queue reform is covered only briefly, Linda Pomerantz-Zhang's biography (1992) introduces his life and reform efforts.

tention of Chinese clothing styles.[29] He submitted a memorial to the court advancing an interpretation of appearance that remained unchanged even after the Revolution of 1911: one could be queueless and loyal to the Qing, but one could not wear Western clothes and still be patriotic.

To support his contention that removing the queue had no political significance, Wu Tingfang referred to practices among ethnic Chinese living in other countries. Based on visits to Chinese communities throughout North and South America, Wu concluded that 80–90 percent of Chinese men overseas had already cut their queues, and the rest hid them coiled under their hats. For these men, he argued, the queue was an "empty form" devoid of political significance. Getting rid of one's queue was a practical choice. The queue was unhygienic and dangerously hindered the mobility necessary for the new demands of factory life. Moreover, Wu argued, China should follow the example of Japan and the powerful nations of Europe by abandoning long hair. Finally, ordering the removal of the queue would also "show the world a sign of renovation" and send an encouraging sign to the Chinese populace that the government was willing to make practical changes.

While trying to reinterpret the meaning of Chinese hair by denying its political significance, Wu opposed sartorial changes by emphasizing the profound meaning of clothing. As Wu informed the court, clothing was an integral part of the body politic. In this area, the state, he wrote, should not allow "divergent practices." Clothing "should by no means be changed." Chinese clothing was sensible for all seasons, unlike the "starched collars, stiff sleeves, leather boots and silk hats of foreigners." In short, Chinese clothing had its own tradition and was more comfortable and more elegant, not to mention less expensive. Like other reformers, Wu pointed to Japan as the example to follow. According to Wu, the majority of the Japanese continued to follow traditional clothing styles but had cut their hair ("Removal of the Queue," NCH 1910.8.5). The court rejected the reinterpretation of appearance in these arguments and did not act on Wu's first memorial on clothing (Pomerantz-Zhang 1992: 188). He responded by writing an even longer one in July 1910, elaborating on the importance of maintaining Chinese clothing styles.

---

29. Wu's most complete statement on the subject of hair and clothing is "Zouqing jianfa bu yifu zhe" (A petition to the emperor requesting the cutting of the queue but not the changing of clothing), Dongfang zazhi 1910.8.25; reprinted in Ding and Yu 1993, vol. 1: 358–60. See also Pomerantz-Zhang 1992: 186–87.

Other reformers wanted to eliminate both the queue and traditional clothing styles. After returning from abroad, Prince Zaizhen 載振 became a vocal advocate of abolishing the queue and reforming Chinese clothing. The prince observed that Chinese were often treated badly because of their appearance, citing the queue and court dress, which looked "ridiculous." On his return to Beijing, the prince asked his father to support removal of the queue and reform of dress "as if it were the most vital question." Although unable to get his father's support, Prince Zaizhen convinced the regent of the importance of clothing and hair reform and persuaded the regent to pass his suggestions on to the Cabinet. Eventually, the National Assembly received a draft ("Prince Tsai Chen's [Zaizhen's] Proposal," *NCH* 1911.8.26).

With growing pressure to sanction changes in appearance, economic interests stepped forward and began to push their own interpretation. These forces scored an early victory in 1910, when the newly convened National Assembly took up the issue. In December 1910, the Assembly passed a resolution calling for the abolition of the queue and recommending changes in dress style. This caused a panic among Chinese in the clothing industry (Pomerantz-Zhang 1992: 188). Under pressure from commercial groups in Beijing, the court issued a decree on December 21, 1910, forbidding the cutting of queues and rejecting appeals to sanction clothing changes; it cited the deleterious effect such changes would have on domestic industries. In response, the National Assembly again passed a resolution requesting both changes. However, on the eve of its final collapse, the court again refused to approve additional changes in appearance and insisted that cutting queues and changing clothing styles remain unambiguous signs of sedition. By continuing to tie the dynasty to symbols increasingly associated with backwardness and other undesirable attributes, Manchu rulers conceded a powerful symbolic weapon to anti-Manchu revolutionaries.

A CONFLUENCE OF QUEUE-CUTTING AGENDAS

Pressure for change continued to mount outside the government. Frustrated in his efforts to get the dynasty to promote reform from within, Wu Tingfang began to support unilateral action in defiance of court decrees. Over 40,000 Chinese and hundreds of foreign observers converged on one of Shanghai's most famous parks, the Zhang Gardens, on January 15, 1911, for a rally. In a letter, Wu informed the assembled that he had already cut his queue, and he encouraged the assembled to follow suit. Some one thousand men did so. This was only one of many such public acts of defiance against the waning Qing authority held throughout the winter and spring of 1911 (NCH 1911.1.20; Rhoads 1975: 205–6).

Once the revolution was well under way, the court made a last-ditch effort to undermine the revolutionary import of changing one's appearance by sanctioning the change. After the court rejected the National Assembly's October bill to abolish the queue, the second session again raised the issue of queues (see *Japan Weekly Mail* 1911.11.25, 12.9, and 12.16; E. T. Williams 1923: 478–79).[30] This time, however, the throne agreed. In an imperial decree of December 1911, it authorized the immediate removal of queues: "All Our servants and subjects are hereby permitted to cut (remove) their hair (queue) at their own free will" ("Queues and Calendars," NCH 1911.12.16).[31] But it was too late for the court to associate itself with these highly charged changes.

The Appearance of Revolution, 1898–1911

The imposition of a new, revolutionary orthodoxy in male appearance followed an old pattern of attempting to create a standard interpretation of material culture, a pattern repeated throughout the National Products Movement. By the late 1800s, aspects of orthodox Qing appearance had acquired, lost, and re-acquired often contradictory layers of meaning. A single physical attribute could have many imputed meanings: the Manchu hairstyle could mean backwardness and subservience to a revolutionary, loyalty and obedience to Qing officials, outlandishness to a foreigner, or the heart of Chinese identity to a farmer. These interpretations increasingly came into conflict as their advocates struggled to impose—or maintain—identities for China. As a new generation of anti-Manchu nationalists gained the power to impose its interpretation, however, the growth in the number of cases of queue-cutting became a sign of the revolutionary times. Increasingly, widespread anti-queue and anti-Manchu slogans blended into the revolutionary lexicon, as opponents of the Qing urged their countrymen to embrace their politics through their interpretation of material culture: "Revolt, cut your queue, and overthrow the dynasty" (Yue 1994: 62–64). Moreover, revolutionaries com-

---

30. An earlier decree did allow diplomats to cut queues; see Wang, "The Abolition of the Queue," *Atlantic Monthly*, June 1911.

31. The same set of decrees also called for the adoption of the solar calendar. See also CRDS File 893.763 (1911.12.8).

pelled their "compatriots" (同胞), as fellow Chinese began to call one another, to adopt their interpretation of queuelessness as an expression of nationalism. This growing conflict culminated with the toppling of imperial power and the creation of a new state-sanctioned appearance. Like the Qing some 270 years earlier, the new rulers imposed a new orthodoxy that included hairstyles and dress. Queuelessness and the unshaven forehead quickly became badges of surrender and submission to the Republic. However, a new orthodoxy for clothing took longer to define.

Sun Yatsen, the leader of the 1911 Republican Revolution, had gradually become aware of the important symbolism of the queue and clothing by the late nineteenth century. Following China's loss to Japan in 1895 and the collapse of imperial support for the reforms of 1898, he fled China and went on a world tour. Because the Qing had put a price on his head, once in Japan Sun sought to hide his identity by adopting the hairstyle and European dress favored by his Japanese associates. As one historian observed, his repudiation of the queue was a final rejection of constitutional monarchy. Henceforth, the queueless and Western-dressed Sun was a confirmed republican revolutionary (T'ang 1930: 23).

Revolutionaries actively promoted their interpretation of Qing appearance through innumerable representations that forcefully cast the queue and its wearers as backward and delegitimated those who defended Qing styles.[32] One pamphlet circulated in Hong Kong provides typical examples of the interpretation of queues that revolutionaries disseminated. The pamphlet tells a sarcastic story of a visit by the "God of the Queue" to a Chinese man in a dream. The god details the practical uses of the queue and argues that the Chinese race will be finished if it continues to remove the queue. The pamphlet satirizes these supposedly beneficial uses of the queue: a wife may tie a thread to it to keep track of an errant husband; with a queue a Chinese man may imitate a dog to avoid being attacked by one; and the queue may protect its owner from vultures and eagles, which, upon seeing it blowing in the wind, mistake it for a snake and will not attack the man. In the pamphlet, the god also reminds Chinese men that queues can cushion blows to the head and protect the brain, and act as a safety rope when climbing trees or walls. In an explicit reference suggesting that Chinese men with queues are

---

32. For a comprehensive list of justifications for removing the hairstyle that, among other things, "befouls your shoulder with oily stains," see the circular of the Chinese Sociological Party of Nanjing, CRDS File 893.1044.

animals, the god suggests they sell their hair to foreigners when it falls out. Taking this last application one step further, the god also gives one legitimate reason for cutting the queue: to sell it, grow it again, and continue to harvest the hair, like a shepherd and his sheep ("The Uses of the Queue," *NCH* 1911.6.3).[33]

MANDATING AND ENFORCING
THE NEW ORTHODOXY

As the revolt against Qing rule spread, the revolutionaries quickly sought to consolidate their gains by forcing the Chinese to separate themselves from the Qing through their appearance, most notably by forcing men to cut their queues, the figurative umbilical cords connecting them to an earlier political and cultural order. Newly independent provinces issued orders regarding the queue and clothing even before the establishment of the provisional government in late 1911. The Hubei provincial military governor, for instance, issued a civil dress code that forbade the use of Qing dress. In Beijing, people were ordered not to wear the clothing styles of officials.

The newly established national government moved first to regulate hair. President Yuan Shikai, who himself had removed his queue only after the formal abdication of the Qing house in February, began imposing the new orthodoxy in March 1912, by having the Cabinet explicitly order Chinese men to remove their queues. The order addresses three themes raised throughout this chapter. First, advocates of the reform underscored the political significance. The order informed the populace that the government was not simply asking that it shed an old custom; rather, it reminded the Chinese that the Manchus had forced the hairstyle on the Han. It also reminded them that many Chinese had died heroically resisting the initial imposition of the queue. In other words, Qing appearance did have a negative political meaning. Second, the order to remove queues was part of a larger effort to reform customs associated with the old order. Clothing and hats were explicitly made a part of this larger bundle of targeted relics, which the new government said had to be "washed away" before China could establish

---

33. For other examples, see Thomson 1913: 69–70, 81. He notes: "The Chinese of Bangkok, Siam, were humorous in their methods [of promoting queue cutting]. The republican tricolor was hoisted to the peak, and two hundred sheered queues were hoisted under it, up the flag pole!" (ibid., 81–82).

a modern polity. Third, as in the Qing, the order demonstrates the authoritarian way the new government expected to address the issue: it came from the top, required immediate compliance, and threatened to punish those who disobeyed.[34] While acknowledging widespread resistance to initial attempts to remove queues, the order urged that those who had not already cut their queues should "follow the lead of urbanites" and do so. It ordered the Ministry of Domestic Affairs (内務部) to have all provincial military governors command their subordinates to carry out the order everywhere ("The Queue-Cutting Campaign," *NCH* 1912.5.4). Citizens had twenty days to submit to the shears; holdouts were threatened with punishment.[35]

Republican-era definitions of orthodox appearance were highly contested. Those who sought to express anti-Manchu, pro-republican sentiments cut their queues long before the proclamation of these national and local orders. However, not everyone was eager to conform to the new orthodoxy. For most Chinese, the forcible removal of the queue was, as one observer put it, a "humiliating disfigurement." In their eyes, the queue was less a "badge of conquest" and more a badge of nationality and identity (Crow 1944: 22). These Chinese had forgotten the original terms under which the hairstyle had been imposed and had no idea that it could signify allegiance to the Qing. As one observer noted, these men were not interested in "esoteric meanings of fashion" and worried more about the present government enforcing "a matter of personal taste" ("The Queue-Cutting Campaign," *NCH* 1912.5.4).[36] Indeed, some sixty years later, the famous Chinese economist H. D. Fong recalled that as an eight-year-old boy living in the coastal city of Ningbo he hid under the counter of the family's jewelry shop to avoid the compulsory shearing of his "long and beautiful pigtail." It was only after he had learned to interpret the queue as a "symbol of servitude" that he had it removed (Fong 1975: 2).

The new orthodox interpretation of objects and customs justified violence through forced compliance against those implicitly labeled as deviants. In the months immediately after the establishment of the Republic, the revolution-

---

34. *Lanshi zhengfu gongbao*, no. 29 (1912.3.5); republished in Luo Jialun 1968: 628.

35. Ibid.

36. Reports from Shandong indicate that residents in cities such as Zhifou feared that if they cut their queue, they would be mistaken for Japanese during any conflict among foreign powers over control of the province. See, e.g., "Queue Cutting at Chefoo," *NCH* 1912.7.20, and "The Queue-Cutting Crusade," *NCH* 1912.7.20.

aries, like their Qing predecessors, vigorously enforced the new orthodox hairstyle. Although many men willingly cut their own queue, in some cities troops set up roadblocks and forcibly removed the queues of unwilling Chinese men; "better class men" were escorted to a barbershop ("Queue Cutting Campaign" [Nanjing] 1912.1.1, CRDS File 893.1044). Perpetrators of the unsolicited haircuts, often pro-republican volunteers known as the "Dare-to-Die Corps" (敢死队), justified their acts as patriotic (Crow 1944: 25). Contemporary newspapers are rife with accounts of queue-cutting teams throughout China (e.g., SB 1911.12.4, 12.12, 1912.1.6). Men in Guangdong province shed their queues quickly. In one particularly active day alone, more than 200,000 men had their queues cut. In Changsha, the provincial capital of Hunan, as in many Chinese cities and towns, retention of the queue was viewed as an explicit sign of traitorous allegiance to the Manchus, and students and others removed the queues of fellow students and pedestrians (Yue 1994: 62–63).

Similar to the military revolution raging throughout China, battles were fought over the queue. One group near Shanghai established a society to encourage the reintroduction of the queue. Its members were not necessarily expressing pro-Manchu sympathies; more likely they were expressing general resistance to government involvement in local life (NCH 1912.9.7). Reports from Zhifou in Shandong province reveal the depth of local resistance; after an evening during which 1,000 queues were forcibly removed, merchants refused to open their shops because overzealous queue-cutters had injured the ear of the leader of the local chamber of commerce (NCH 1912.7.20). Things got so bad that residents sent telegrams to Beijing warning that friction between soldiers and civilians could escalate (NCH 1912.7.20). Another observer confirmed that the new government encountered resistance at all social levels and had a "great deal of trouble" imposing the new hairstyle on workers (Pott 1913: 130–31).

One man's decision to cut his queue personalizes the dilemma caused by the multiple meanings associated with this modification of personal appearance. The length and texture of his queue had been a source of pride for this man. But his queue came to signify an awkward backwardness that he longer wanted to convey. He decided to cut it. However, the head of his household, his mother, held a different opinion. For her, queue-cutting was a dangerous foreign fad that could get him killed. She also recognized the revolutionary significance of removing the queue and warned him that, just as they had vanquished the Taiping rebels a half-century earlier, Qing forces would eventually suppress the rebellion and kill its adherents, who would be easily identified by their queueless appearance. For a while, the authority of his mother served to prevent this forty-year-old from cutting his queue. Under relentless pressure from friends and strangers who continually threatened to cut his queue, he finally decided to abandon the hairstyle (Crow 1944: 25–26).

THE NEED TO REDEFINE CLOTHING

Like the Qing and earlier dynasties, the revolutionaries sought not only to regulate hair but also to effect a dramatic alteration in appearance in general. As imperial power and queues fell throughout China, confusion and competing interpretations came to surround the question of what Chinese ought to wear. Some Chinese suggested returning to pre-Qing (i.e., pre-Manchu) styles, including those detailed in one of the most famous Ming novels, the *Water Margin* (水滸傳) (Yan Changhong 1992: 239–40). Others promoted Western-style clothing, arguing that it was an integral part of building modern, Western institutions. The resulting confusion was visible in Chinese cities. One newspaper reported "men were dressing like females, females like males, and prostitutes like female students and vice-versa." Most alarming in a country with a millennia-long tradition of highly regulated official clothing, "commoners were dressed like officials and officials like commoners" (*SB* 1912.3.20, cited in Yue 1994: 49), a situation that persisted until the Sun Yat-sen jacket (中山裝) became popular a decade later.

The destabilizing challenge to clothing norms came especially from revolutionaries popularizing non-Qing styles. During and after the revolution, Western-style dress, particularly the khaki uniforms of the Republican troops, became a symbol of the new order. The slogan of the day was "Cut your queue and change your style of dress" (剪辮易服). The emerging orthodoxy seemed to be Western-style clothing, and major Chinese cities experienced a "Western clothing craze" (洋服熱). The government quickly sought to impose order by example, law, and force.

Nationalizing Appearance

The National Products Preservation Association stepped into this morass of unstable meaning surrounding personal appearance and promoted its own interpretation of how Chinese men should dress. Inaugurated at the end of 1911, the NPPA tried to shape the economic impact of political and social changes on its members' industries by severing the link between hair and clothes and attaching distinct meanings to each. This effort helped ensure the survival of Chinese clothing, but in linking consumption and nationalism it also had a long-term, subtler significance.

The remainder of this chapter examines the development of an ethic of nationalistic consumption through the early history of this key organization in the movement. The creation of this powerful interest group, its agenda, and its channels of dissemination reveal the growing coherence of the movement to nationalize consumer culture. As we shall see, the nationalistic interpretation of clothing advanced by the NPPA (and the movement in general) continued to be debated in the 1920s and 1930s and transformed the traditional styles worn by Chinese men such as Mr. Mei, whose patriotic dress is noted above, into a symbolic and literal male uniform of the movement.

THE NPPA'S ROLE

The nationalizing of consumer culture was an integral part of many changes occurring in China. The Revolution of 1911 that led to the downfall of China's last dynasty, for example, overturned state-sponsored symbols, institutions, and ideologies. There was, however, more than one group contending to provide replacements. These contenders were anxious to consolidate power, and at the local level their struggles were often expressed in battles over symbols such as anti-footbinding campaigns, the cutting of queues, the modification of clothing, the reorganization of time through holidays, and the introduction of the solar calendar (Li Shaobing 1994).[37] These conflicts over rival state-building agendas usually appear to be battles among political, military, and intellectual elites at one end of the social hierarchy and students, secret societies, and other mass movements of resistance at the other. However, powerful economic interests also mobilized resources to redefine the new symbols of state. These reinforced and extended competing narratives of the nation, its people, and its route to "national salvation" (救國).[38]

---

37. The new government initiated many of these changes, including converting to the solar calendar, changing terms of address, and prohibiting footbinding. For a summary, see Yue 1994. On the controversy surrounding the replacement of the reign-year system with a new calendrical method, see Wang Ermin 1981: 66–70.

38. Indeed, I would argue that this ethic of nationalistic consumption was very competitive and contributed largely to the emerging dominant narrative of history rather than to "al-

The NPPA had pressing reasons for linking consumption and Chinese nationalism at a time when the new Republican government was vigorously attempting to eradicate queues and introduce Western-style dress for men. Because of the close association between queues and Chinese-style clothing, the NPPA had a legitimate concern that the domestic silk industry was in grave danger. The immediate goal of the NPPA was to prevent political leaders throughout China from sanctioning the changes in dress that were accompanying queue-cutting, and they were successful in lobbying to mandate that Chinese clothing be made of domestically produced materials, especially silk and satin. What may have been an immediate economic objective had symbolic consequences. In the recoding process, the organization managed to prevent traditional-style clothes from acquiring the negative connotations associated with the queue. Above all, the NPPA helped redefine the Chinese-style long-gown as a patriotic style. Such reinterpretations not only ensured the survival of Chinese clothing but also built an ethic of nationalistic consumption that would define other products as national interests.

To defend against the threatening change in clothing styles, the powerful interests in the NPPA quickly built a sophisticated organization. This organization immediately sought to take advantage of many opportunities created by the fall of the Qing, which allowed economic interests to form new, even more focused interest groups than the recently introduced chambers of commerce. Indeed, the organizations of Chinese sojourning in Shanghai (or native-place associations) that eventually formed the NPPA began organizational activities shortly after the outbreak of the revolution. After two months of preparations, the association held its inaugural meeting in Shanghai on December 12, 1911, at the main hall of the Qianjiang (Hangzhou) native-place association (*SB* 1911.12.9).[39]

---

ternative" ones. For a discussion of the concepts of nationalism and narrative as they relate to modern Chinese history, see Duara 1995: 3–82.

39. The goal of the organizers was to create a permanent group, and they specified every aspect of the new organization including the name, membership rules, financing, recruitment, and election procedures. For more information on the preparatory meetings, see ZGWH 1932: "Huiyi jilu" section. Many scholars label the NPPA the first national products organization; see, e.g., Pan Junxiang 1989: 55; and Yang Tianliang 1991a: 348. However, a reporter attending the inaugural meeting of the NPPA informed those present that there were already three smaller organizations in Shanghai. See Li Zhuoyun's short speech in ZGWH 1912: 9a. Because most of the native-place associations I discuss were in Shanghai and Jiangnan, "native-place association" denotes both *huiguan* 會館 (meeting hall) and *gongsuo* 公所 (public office), the institutions established by sojourning merchants. On these terms, see Goodman 1995: 39.

Although the NPPA eventually became a large organization with hundreds of members representing native-place associations, industries, students, and many other groups, it began as a small, ad hoc, 32-member group of four representatives from each of eight native-place associations (ZGWH 1912: 4b–5b).[40] These associations represented the three industries most threatened by changes in clothing—silk/satin, hats, and pawnshops—and all were based in the prosperous coastal provinces of Jiangsu and Zhejiang.[41] Of these three, the silk industry was the most influential.[42] Despite these narrow origins, membership grew quickly, from slightly over 100 in its first year to nearly 500 members in its second, with more joining every year during its first few years. The group also actively encouraged women to join (SZMA File 454: 0, 12, and 20–21). The initial bylaws of the organization imposed strict criteria for membership (ZGWH 1912: 3b). However, in response to the outpouring of anti-imperialism following Japan's presentation of the Twenty-One Demands in early 1915, the categories of membership were expanded to native-place associations, commercial and industrial operations, and individuals. In addition, as the next chapter explains in detail, after 1915 domestic industries flocked to join the NPPA

---

40. This document (ZGWH 1912) clears up some of the confusion in the secondary and, indeed, primary literature concerning the establishment of the NPPA. The exact number of native-place organizations and representatives in the founding group is not clear. In its twentieth-year anniversary volume, the NPPA official history lists ten groups and forty members, see ZGWH 1932: "Huiyi jilu" section. This is the number given by, among others, Pan Junxiang (1989: 55) and Xin Ping et al. (1991: 348–49). Several scholars list the founding date for the organization as 1914 or 1915. Chen Zhengqing (1987), for example, gives 1915, and Linda Pomerantz-Zhang (1992: 235) suggests that Wu Tingfang organized the group in 1914.

41. The threat to pawnshops may be less obvious. The vast majority of items pawned were clothes. By one estimate, clothing occupied "perhaps ninety per cent in value and ninety-nine per cent in space and labour required for storage." These shops often acted as community attics for both poor and rich, who might not otherwise have the space or time to care for their clothing. See NCH 1914.7.4 and Gamble 1921: 281.

42. The results of the group's first elections show the importance of the silk industry. In accordance with the bylaws, the association held an election at its inaugural meeting. Yao Diyuan 姚滌源, a representative from the pawnshop industry, received the most votes, and Zhang Ziyin 張紫薇 and He Jiafu 何架甫 were elected vice-presidents. However, Yao Diyuan said that because the most pressing issue confronting NPPA related to the silk industry, someone from that industry should lead the organization, and so he deferred to Zhang Ziyin (ZGWH 1932: "Kaihui" section, 13; ZGWH 1912: 6b, 8a).

and similar organizations as a way of reinforcing their status as "Chinese" companies.[43]

HIERARCHIES OF DISSEMINATION

From the start, the NPPA faced three major obstacles. First, it needed the backing of Chinese military and political leaders, many of whom were already endorsing changes in clothing. It initially focused on cultivating leaders in and around Shanghai, where its influence was strongest. Second, it needed support from national leaders. Finally, it had to gain support beyond the narrow group of political and economic elites. With the collapse of imperial power and the growth of regional power centers, the members understood that they would not be able to rely exclusively on state and elite patronage. In cultivating relations with individuals and organizations throughout China, the NPPA directly contributed to the establishment of a nationwide National Products Movement.

The NPPA prized the support of powerful patrons and worked hard to gain early endorsements from influential politicians. The NPPA invited Shanghai leaders, county and provincial officials, and representatives from military, political, commercial, and academic circles to its inaugural meeting and gave them prominent roles. In the months following the inaugural meeting, the NPPA lobbied these political and military elites by writing letters, sending telegrams, and encouraging their attendance at organization functions. These efforts yielded public letters of support from such prominent Chinese as Sun Yatsen and Shanghai military governor Chen Qimei 陳其美 (1876–1916). Shortly after its establishment, the NPPA received a letter of endorsement from Wu Tingfang inquiring about membership. The NPPA immediately asked him to join and, as noted, in less than a year elected him president.[44] This early support helped establish the legitimacy and prominence of the NPPA.

---

43. The number of companies participating in the NPPA, for instance, grew from 49 in 1915 to 109 by the end of the decade (ZGWH 1932: "Huishi" section, 12).

44. Sun Yatsen's letter to the NPPA was published in Nanjing's *Lanshi zhengfu gongbao* 7 (1912.2.4); for Chen Qimei's assurances to the NPPA that clothing would be regulated, see his letter to the NPPA reprinted in the newspaper *SB* 1911.12.20 and republished in Shanghai shehui kexueyuan 1981: 423–24. On Wu Tingfang, see ZGWH 1932: "Huiwu" jilu section, 3. The NPPA also received early letters of support from lower-ranking officials, including one

From its inception, the NPPA hoped to provide a model for similar groups throughout China. It immediately began cultivating ties to chambers of commerce and local governments in other provinces. The aim of the correspondence was not only to secure support for the NPPA agenda but also to urge other cities and towns to set up similar groups, propagate common economic goals locally, and lobby local, regional, and national authorities. To assist in the formation of these organizations, the NPPA circulated materials on all aspects of its organization. The earliest and most comprehensive of these was a 1912 booklet that provided detailed information on the new group, including its initial membership roster, bylaws, and copies of speeches from the inaugural meeting.[45] It also provided form letters to use in lobbying local, regional, and national authorities. Other movement organizations used these NPPA templates as the basis for establishing their own organizations and writing their own petitions.[46]

The NPPA's appeal found immediate success in provinces and cities across China, including Tianjin, Fuzhou, Changsha, Tonghai, Anqing, Beijing, Nanjing, Jiaxing, Zhenjiang, Hankou, and Ji'nan, to mention only a few. By the mid-1920s, there were hundreds of such organizations.[47] The Shanghai-based NPPA had varying degrees of contact with these organizations. It was directly involved in setting up some organizations; with others it only exchanged correspondence and official literature. Its relationship with

---

from the chairman of the Commerce Bureau of the Shanghai Municipal Government; see ZGWH 1912: 2.

45. Nearly every speech in this booklet addresses the importance of helping to establish similar organizations in cities throughout China. See, e.g., the speech by Li Zhuoyun in ZGWH 1912: 9a. There was a large pool of potential contacts. As noted in Chapter 1, by the end of the 1911, there were over a thousand local-, county-, and provincial-level chambers of commerce in China.

46. Indeed, it became a common practice for movement organizations to send one another copies of their bylaws and organizational literature. Similarly, newspapers and movement publications reprinted such materials.

47. For a partial list of cities with such groups, see Huang Yiping and Yu Baotang 1995: 182. The NPPA log in ZGWH 1932 lists the establishment of these groups by year. See Pan Junxiang 1996c: 19–20 for a list compiled from this log. The log also shows the breadth of the NPPA correspondence with movement groups throughout China and among overseas Chinese. The number of movement organizations constantly changed. For a more general breakdown of the kinds of movement organizations active in the spring of 1925, see Jiang Weiguo 1995: 75–83, which classifies the NPPA as a "producer/marketer" movement organization (76–77). On the NPPA in Tianjin, see Rinbara 1983: 21.

the group in Suzhou was particularly close. In July 1912, Suzhou became one of the earliest cities to follow the NPPA lead in establishing an organization to promote the movement agenda. With a third of its population working in the silk industry, Suzhou had much to lose if the silk industry continued its downward slide.[48] An influential Suzhou native-place association in the silk trade, the Brocade Guild (雲錦公所), had been involved in the establishment of the NPPA in Shanghai. This association, working through the Suzhou General Chamber of Commerce, oversaw the establishment of a local branch.

In writing to the office of the Jiangsu provincial governor and city authorities, eight members of the new Suzhou group explained their purpose and requested official recognition in a petition drawn directly from the 1912 NPPA template. Their petition, for example, blamed imports, especially wool, for the country's economic problems and dependence on foreign countries, which the Suzhou branch also held responsible for destroying Chinese industries. Furthermore, it tied the interests of the silk industry to China as a whole by reminding Jiangsu officials that "enriching the country starts with commerce" and that the government had a responsibility to "prevent the leakage" (塞漏溢) of Chinese wealth abroad. In addition to acknowledging the need to improve silk products, the petition stressed the need to alter the Chinese "desire for imports" by reforming Chinese laws on clothing (SZMA File 840: 8–12, 27).

POPULARIZING THE MOVEMENT AGENDA

From its beginnings, the NPPA used diverse channels to popularize its agenda, both formal (letters and petitions) and informal (word-of-mouth within native-place associations) and both new (telegrams, newspapers, periodicals) and traditional (meetings at teahouses, restaurants, and native-place association halls).[49] At the most elemental level, the NPPA worked through personal contacts by honoring members who brought in new recruits. For example, participants in the inaugural meeting agreed to solicit

---

48. On the establishment of the Suzhou NPPA branch and its relationship to the local silk industry, see Wang Xiang 1992.

49. The NPPA also continually developed new communication channels, such as the parades, expositions, and periodicals discussed in subsequent chapters. For a brief introduction to such channels, see Pan Junxiang 1989: 55–59.

applications from fellow native-place association members by the end of the month. The status afforded members who brought in new recruits is evident in the many lists of new members in the organization's log, which carefully recorded the name of the recruiter (e.g., ZGWH 1932: "Huwu jilu" section, 5–8).

From its inception, the NPPA was concerned with conveying its message to as many Chinese as possible. For instance, one of the documents in the booklet of informational templates mentioned above was a synopsis of what might be termed the NPPA's "mission statement" in colloquial Chinese (ZGWH 1912: 24a–25b). Additionally, the NPPA frequently printed and distributed handbills, leaflets, and newspaper advertisements nationally and overseas to boost membership, advertise NPPA activities, increase awareness of the movement, and promote specific national products. Print runs varied by subject and year, from several thousand to several tens of thousands of copies. The total for all categories of propaganda literature ranged from the tens of thousands to the hundreds of thousands of pieces each year (ZGWH 1932: "Huishi" section, 16–18).[50] By the early 1930s, the NPPA would claim that these efforts to publicize the notion of "national products" had been so successful that even "all women and children know" about the importance of buying Chinese products (ZGWH 1932: "Huishi" section, 2).

In Shanghai, the NPPA also organized lectures and a variety of forums to disseminate its message. At the inaugural meeting in December 1911, members decided to hold a Promote National Products Rally, which drew over 3,800 persons. Buoyed by the success of this event, NPPA members initiated a program of Saturday evening lectures to teach Chinese that it was their responsibility to buy national products. The meetings started out slowly: only four persons attended the first lecture. Gradually, the organizers learned how to attract crowds by varying the time and inviting famous figures to make speeches. Soon attendance grew into the thousands (ZGWH 1932: "Kaihui" section, 13).[51] These efforts culminated in the inauguration of

---

50. See ZGWH 1932, "Huiwu jilu" section, for hundreds of instances of printing up handbills, circulars, special "product catalogs" (樣本) on silk and other products, and so on. For instance, in its first year (Dec. 1911 to Dec. 1912), the NPPA circulated over 5,000 copies of a handbill encouraging Chinese to use domestic silk.

51. Meetings were held at both the Qianjiang (Hangzhou) and Ningbo native-place associations. From 1912 to 1924, the NPPA held 59 such meetings. The first such rally was held in July 1912, and three more were held in September. From then until January 1914, meetings were held nearly every week. The NPPA log of these talks gives the names of speakers and brief summaries of their talks.

the annual National Products Salvation Rally, along with many other spectacles designed to nationalize consumer culture (see Chapters 5 and 6).

The NPPA publicized its agenda through the rapidly expanding mass media, which it considered an effective tool for shaping public opinion. This use of the media began with the NPPA's inaugural meeting, during which several reporters gave speeches expressing support for the organization. The NPPA invited reporters to attend subsequent meetings and urged its members to write newspaper articles and place advertisements in periodicals (ZGWH 1912: 15a–16b). In addition, summaries published in the local press gave NPPA rallies, and consequently its agenda, a wider reach.[52]

As we shall see in subsequent chapters, the NPPA developed many more tactics to nationalize consumer culture. For example, it created a process to certify national products, established stores that sold only these products, assisted area manufacturers in marketing their products outside the region, and participated in organizing national expositions for Chinese products. This network of movement organizations quickly spread the NPPA interpretation of Chinese clothing and facilitated the initiation and spread of anti-imperialist boycotts and other activities in support of Chinese manufacturers. In short, the organization and the network it helped form were instrumental in creating the institutions behind the efforts to cleanse the Chinese economy of imports and imported product elements.

ELEMENTS OF AN ETHIC OF
NATIONALISTIC CONSUMPTION

The messages transmitted through these numerous channels evince the ethic of nationalistic consumption at the heart of the NPPA and the movement agenda. The ethic reinforced the notion of commercial war that had been developing since the late nineteenth century (see Chapter 1). In practical terms, the early documents of the NPPA and the group's early activities demonstrate how the NPPA sought to separate the issue of abolishing the queue from the question of reforming Chinese dress by supporting the elimination of the queue while arguing for the preservation of Chinese-style

---

52. For a good overview of one such rally, see SB 1912.11.4. The NPPA convened its fifteenth rally on November 4, 1912, from 8 to 10 P.M. at the powerful Hangzhou native-place association, the Qianjiang huiguan. Over 200 men and women attended the meeting, which featured nine speakers.

dress. The NPPA aimed to save the silk industry by establishing a link between its interests and those of the entire country. Clothing, the NPPA argued, was more than a matter of the health of a few industries—it was an issue of national survival. To strengthen this link, the NPPA advanced arguments that blended economic, political, symbolic, and nationalistic reasoning in an effort to appeal to a broad spectrum of Chinese.

Linking the health of the economy and the well-being of the nation was fundamental to the discourse animating this new ethic of nationalistic consumption. The NPPA framed the economic consequences of switching to wool suits, for example, as more important to China than the desire to appear "modern" to foreigners by wearing Western-style clothing. As movement publications and speakers frequently warned, the scrapping of cotton and silk gowns would have a devastating effect on the Chinese economy because of silk's central role in the Chinese economy. The switch to wool would destroy a key Chinese industry without creating one in its place because China produced almost no wool products.[53] The raw materials would have to be imported, at least until China could develop a wool industry. In the meantime, NPPA literature warned, the destruction of the silk industry would throw millions out of work and affect the entire economy.

At the personal level, the NPPA's economic argument also featured an appeal to the pocketbook of its audience. It would cost an individual a fortune to convert to Western-style clothing. The notion that hundreds of millions of Chinese men stood ready to alter their mode of dress may seem ludicrous now, but as the rise of a Republican interpretation of appearance suggests, and indeed as Sun Yatsen's initial preference for suits indicates, the possibility of a shift, at least among the upper classes, was seen as imminent.

NPPA literature also frequently argued that international trade was even more detrimental to the nation than a zero-sum scenario would imply: buying foreign products not only hurt the domestic market for Chinese goods but also helped the nation's enemies. To reinforce this claim, the organization regularly invoked the concept of commercial war. As noted in Chapter 1, the main popularizer of this concept in the late nineteenth century was the

---

53. Among the fabrics used in clothing, wool was "noticeably absent" (Vollmer 1977: 16). In Jiangsu, for example, the first wool factory was founded in 1906 but went out of business the year before the Revolution. It was several decades before the region had factories that were competitive with imported wool fabrics (NII 1935: 429). On the growing market, see Bard 1905: 198.

compradore-scholar Zheng Guanying, who, in *Warnings to a Prosperous Age*,
contended that international commercial relations represented even more of
a threat to China than the territorial ambitions of imperialist powers. To
survive this war, China needed to "stimulate business." The NPPA invoked
this phrase to enhance the social position of economic elites and pressure
governments to adopt mercantilist policies.

However, the NPPA and the movement added newer, universal implications to the concept of commercial war. Whereas Zheng had aimed his recommendations at Chinese elites, modern mass communication extended the
reach of the message by encouraging Chinese consumers to enlist in the
"war" by not buying what, after 1915, would increasingly come to be known
as "enemy products" (仇貨).[54] The spread of the notion of commercial war
accompanied a growing obsession with China's trade deficit. The balance of
payments continued to serve as the single most important measure of how
the "war" was going. As noted above, a discourse of trade statistics emerged
in the constantly published and republished tables, charts, graphs, and essays on China's foreign trade.[55] At the NPPA's inaugural meeting, a speech
of a key figure throughout the organization's history, Wang Jie'an 王介安,
typifies this preoccupation with the "loss of economic control to foreigners"
and the "drainage of profits" (利權外溢 and 漏卮), to name two central
terms of the ideology of commercial warfare. Wang was a member of a
Suzhou native-place association with a long history of representing the interests of the silk industry, and he remained a leader of the NPPA and the
movement for decades:

Today we convene this organization to preserve national products. China is an ex-
pansive land, rich in natural resources, with more than enough to meet its own
needs. Why, then, are commerce and the economy in such dire straits? It is all because China does not understand the Way of Commercial Warfare [商戰之道].
Foreigners say that "Military warfare makes a state powerful, and commercial warfare makes a state wealthy" [兵戰強商戰富]. But, China does not understand
commercial warfare. It continually exports raw materials and imports finished products and thus allows the profits to flow into foreign hands. . . . When profits are
drained in this way, China is losing in commercial warfare. Consequently, the
economy faces hard times. Compatriots should research how to improve semi-

---

54. On the extensive use of military metaphors in the movement, see Chapter 7.

55. For a typical example of trade statistics as a scorecard for the movement, see Guangdong jianshe ting 1930.

finished products and sell finished ones. Everyone should make preserving national products a main objective and not simply blithely follow fashionable trends. In this way, the preservation of national products will be great. . . . Although the scope of this group is small now, it is my hope that it will reach all provinces and get them to preserve national products. (ZGWH 1912: 8b)

But NPPA leaders such as Wang Jie'an also understood that it would take more than a "buy China" campaign to strengthen the Chinese economy. The ultimate key to success lay in making Chinese industry more competitive, and NPPA members made frequent mention of the need to make improvements. For example, the first NPPA president Zhang Ziyin went so far as to say that finding new uses for Chinese silk was akin to cherishing the "essence of the Chinese nation" (黃族國粹) (ZGWH 1912: 7b). In the interim, however, members, in a proto–import substitution argument, sought to prevent imports from destroying their industries. These leaders understood that without tariff autonomy China could not use protective tariffs to shield the domestic market. In the absence of a strong, stable government with the financial means to support economic development, Chinese commercial and industrial leaders sought to erect non-tariff barriers to trade by encouraging clothing styles made of nationally produced fabrics.

The NPPA also tied its interests to those of political elites by warning that the widespread economic disruption that would accompany any switch in clothing styles would have immediate political reverberations. A chain reaction, begun by massive dislocations in the silk industry, would destabilize China as millions went hungry and began to wander the country in search of food. Moreover, allowing foreigners to benefit at the expense of the Chinese economy would delegitimize the government. While re-establishing political order, the revolutionaries ought not allow the masses to navigate cultural changes on their own.[56]

In its initial months, the NPPA tried to convey a sense of urgency surrounding the clothing issue. As one speaker described it, "The masses are using the opportunity created by the revolution to get rid of old customs and habits of clothing and adornment." The result was chaos, since nobody knew what the new orthodoxy was (ZGWH 1912: 5b). Because the revolutionaries were preoccupied with re-establishing a political order and too busy to impose a new orthodoxy, they were leaving the masses to sort through conflict-

---

56. See, e.g., Zhang Ziyin's speech in ZGWH 1912: 5b.

ing signals regarding cultural changes (ZGWH 1912: 1). As a result, many Chinese were adopting Western-style clothes made of imported wool.

In addition to bringing the consequences of this decision to the attention of the government, NPPA leaders tried to convince their "compatriots" to use Chinese fabrics. Through the ethic of nationalistic consumption, organizations such as the NPPA sought to create a bounded Chinese ethnic market based on the consumption of Chinese products that elided all divisions between Han and non-Han. From the first NPPA president on, leaders of movement organizations continually stressed that "all 400 million Chinese have this responsibility" to promote the NPPA agenda (ZGWH 1912: 5b). In addition to the economic well-being of the nation, Chinese independence was at stake because switching to wool clothing would not only benefit foreign economies but also encourage foreign imperialist powers to become more deeply entrenched in China. As the next chapter explores, this anxiety grew quickly after the Japanese presented the Twenty-One Demands in early 1915.

Lobbying for National Clothing

A combination of the new government's relentless efforts to eradicate queues and the long-standing links between queues and clothing gave the NPPA a legitimate concern that the two would disappear together, destroying the Chinese silk industry along the way. The immediate goal of the NPPA was to prevent political leaders throughout China from sanctioning the clothing changes accompanying queue-cutting throughout China.[57] Another aim was a law mandating that Chinese clothing be made of domestically produced materials, especially silk. As noted above, in an attempt to build political support, NPPA members immediately began sending petitions and letters to, among others, officials, commercial organizations, and overseas Chinese.

Shortly after the inaugural meeting, the NPPA sent petitions to the military governors of Shanghai, Jiangsu, and Zhejiang. In a long document, later circulated throughout China, the NPPA repeatedly stressed the importance of the silk industry to China and reminded the governors that the clothing, hat, and pawn industries depended heavily on the silk industry. It blamed the

---

57. At the preparatory, inaugural, and subsequent meetings, speakers stressed the need to seek government intervention. See, e.g., *SB* 1911.12.9; SZMA File 404; ZGWH 1912: 9b; and *SB* 1912.1.12.

precarious position of industry on the rush to abolish the queue and to change
clothing styles. It also encouraged the new leaders of China to consider the
Japanese example: although the Meiji Restoration had occurred some 40
years earlier, commoners still adhered to pre-Meiji clothing styles (ZGWH
1912: 10b–11b). The draft of a telegram sent to the Guangzhou and other
chambers of commerce put the NPPA message in its most distilled form:

Our organization has been established to promote the cutting of queues and to oppose changes in dress clothing [常服]. Moreover, dress and formal clothing [禮服]
should be made exclusively of pure domestic materials. We have already petitioned
the heads of various places to implement this agenda. We hope that your honorable
organization will pass this along to all other groups so that we can collectively preserve national products and prevent the massive outflow of profits. This would be of
great benefit to the whole nation. (ZGWH 1912: 12a)

An early sign of political patronage came on December 20, 1911, when the
influential, Shanghai-based newspaper *Shenbao* published a response to the
NPPA appeals from the military governor of Shanghai, Chen Qimei, who
had attended the organization's inaugural meeting a week earlier. In his letter, he assured the NPPA, as well as the reading public, that formal and
dress clothing as well as the uniforms of the military, police, and other
groups would be regulated; he promised that after the establishment of the
provisional government, regulations stipulating the use of national products
would be issued. In addition to publicly endorsing the NPPA agenda, Chen
also adopted the phrases and terminology, along with the logic, of the
NPPA letter. In doing so, he further sanctioned and popularized the terms
the NPPA hoped would inform the debate over clothing. Most fundamentally, he repeated the NPPA contention that switching from Chinese silk to
Western wool would be ruinous to "national products" and thereby would
allow "economic rights to go to foreigners" (SB 1911.12.20).[58]

An even more important endorsement came a few months later when
Sun Yatsen himself responded to an NPPA letter. To enhance the status of
the organization and disseminate its goals, the NPPA reprinted the letter
and distributed it to commercial and governmental organizations throughout China and to Chinese communities abroad. In the NPPA's letter, which
Sun summarized in his response, the group had urged Sun to be careful not

---

58. At the same time, Chen also urged the NPPA to respond to the growing popularity of
Western-style clothing by devising ways to use silk and satin to make such articles.

to give the Chinese people too much freedom in selecting clothing. Although the writers of the NPPA letter took pains not to appear authoritarian by agreeing that the people themselves must ultimately decide what to wear, they quickly added that there must be a clear procedure for moving from traditional clothing to any new style. The people, the NPPA letter warned, were unaccustomed to the absence of political authority and were blindly abandoning old customs and practices regardless of merit. The NPPA suggested the new government step in and restore order by issuing guidelines so that the people did not foolishly begin wearing Western-style clothing made of imported wool (*Lanshi zhengfu gongbao* [Nanjing] 1912.2.4).

Although Sun's response underscored many NPPA positions, it was far short of a full endorsement. After all, Sun himself had already begun wearing a suit and tie. First, Sun acknowledged the current chaos in clothing styles and conceded that formal and dress clothing was an important matter of state. He also conceded that Western-style clothing left "much to be improved" and that it might not be appropriate for China. Lastly, he accepted the NPPA link between the use of national products and the state of the domestic economy. He concluded that both dress and informal clothing should be manufactured from Chinese materials. But he left open the most important question—what Chinese ought to wear in the interim. Rather than endorsing Qing dress and ceremonial clothing, he recommended that the NPPA conduct more research to find clothing that was clean and hygienic, allowed for greater mobility, and was inexpensive. He even supplied the names of several Western-style tailors (*Lanshi zhengfu gongbao* [Nanjing] 1912.2.4).

By the summer of 1912, the power to make a national decision on clothing shifted from Nanjing to Beijing and from Sun's hands and into Yuan Shikai's. In mid-1912, the new government seemed poised to issue regulations on clothing (*Zhengfu gongbao* 1912.8.1). The initial draft, however, encouraged the use of both silk and wool. To avert the disaster of state-endorsed use of wool, the NPPA immediately sent its vice-president, Lü Baoyuan 呂葆元, to Beijing to lobby the newly established government to pass explicit regulations stipulating the use of nationally produced fabrics, especially silk, in the manufacture of Chinese clothing. As with earlier NPPA propaganda, Lü's petition stressed the close relationship between clothing and the state:

Now that we are starting to build our nation, it is not easy to make laws regarding clothing styles for everyone or to get everyone to use materials exclusively made of national products. . . . We humbly request that the Provisional Council of Provincial Representatives suggest that dress clothing continue to adhere to the traditional styles, in accordance with the wishes of the people, and that these articles be made purely of silk and cotton and make use of national products.

Lü Baoyuan also specifically addressed the threat of wool. Since the establishment of the Republic, he wrote, Chinese have anxiously awaited clarification on the clothing question; the uncertainty alone has hurt the silk and related industries in Zhejiang and Jiangsu provinces. Regulations permitting the use of both silk and wool would be more harmful than one might think. Although the proposed regulation did not call for the use of foreign wool, this would be its unintended consequence, because China's wool industry was still in its infancy. For Lü Baoyuan, there was a clear link between patriotism and what one wore—no Chinese could wear wool and be a patriot. Each use of wool was one less use of silk. This replacement would do double damage to the country by increasing imports and decreasing work and money within China. Lü pointed out that at least several hundred thousand people derived a livelihood from the silk industries and argued that China should adopt the practice of other countries and use domestic products to make clothing for the domestic market. In short, he urged the elimination of the character "wool" from the law.[59]

The NPPA's efforts to enlist the help of other organizations began to pay off, as different groups began to use NPPA literature to lobby the government. The most important support for the NPPA cause came from allies in Beijing. The Silk and Satin Guild (綢緞行), which controlled these trades in Beijing, sent a petition to the Beijing General Chamber of Commerce (京師商務總會), which forwarded it to the Cabinet (國務院).[60] In forwarding the original petition, the Beijing Chamber added an endorsement requesting that the government take steps to ensure the "preservation" (維持) of the silk industry by quickly adopting the petition's suggestions (*Zhengfu gongbao* 1912.8.1).[61]

---

59. "Weichi hui daibiao Lü liji cheng Canyiyuan wen" (NPPA representative Lü petitions Council of Provincial Representatives), *SB* 1912.7.19.

60. The Yuan-Ning dong guan, a large lodge for sojourners from Nanjing, housed the Silk and Satin Guild (Richard Belsky, pers. comm., Jan. 20, 1996).

61. The NPPA also received support from other allies. In summer 1912, for example, the Suzhou silk industry repeatedly sent telegrams to the Ministry of Industry and Commerce (工商部) on the importance of using domestic silk. The head of the Ministry of Industry and Commerce, Wang Zhengting, responded on July 2 with a reassurance that a favorable decision by the government was imminent: "The clothing case is presently being considered

In language reflecting the concerns of the NPPA, the Silk and Satin Guild repeated the arguments to de-emphasize the use of wool in the production of clothing by removing the characters "joint use of silk and wool." The guild's petition noted that China was presently unable to supply wool and that emphasizing its use would only lead to continued massive imports of wool, the decline of domestic industry, and further disorder. Although encroachment by foreign goods and the substitution of wool for domestic silk had begun before the Revolution, the petition implicitly blamed the revolutionaries for worsening the situation because of their failure to promulgate new clothing regulations. The guild urged the government to address both issues by quickly issuing regulations that emphasized the use of "pure" (純) domestic materials. Furthermore, it argued that opponents of foreign fabrics were acting in the interests of the nation by attempting to preserve "economic rights" (利權). Finally, the petition appealed to the self-interest of the new government by reminding it that taxes on silk helped pay the salaries of both soldiers and bureaucrats (*Zhengfu gongbao* 1912.8.1).

Unlike earlier petitions on clothing such as the one sent by the NPPA to Sun Yatsen, the one forwarded by the Beijing Chamber of Commerce explicitly rejected the need to change Chinese clothing styles. It challenged the contention of the proponents of wool that silk and satin were inappropriate for fall and winter and encouraged Chinese to continue the traditional practice of wearing furs. For winter wear it suggested a fur lining under an outer layer made of silk or satin and confidently concluded that improving and expanding rather than discarding the use of these Chinese materials would obviate the need for imported wool. Any clothing law ought to reinforce these goals (*Zhengfu gongbao* 1912.8.1).

The lobbying paid off. In October 1912, President Yuan announced the Clothing Law (服制案) (see Fig. 2.5).[62] The law confirms the success of the NPPA and the silk industry in influencing state policy. In effect, it halted and reversed the initial official policy that had emphasized Western styles and fabrics. Instead, it allowed, even encouraged, the use of Chinese-style

---

by the Cabinet. It has decided to promote the use of national silk as its basis. After the Provisional Council of Provincial Representatives passes the bill, it will be announced."

62. *Shenbao*, which actively promoted the NPPA and the movement, beat the *Zhengfu gongbu* by publishing a copy of the law, including the illustrations, on its front page on 1912.8.20.

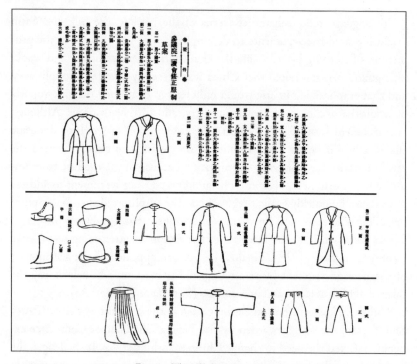

Fig. 2.5 The Clothing Law of 1912
(*SB* 1912.8.20: front page)

Participants in the National Products Movement successfully lobbied the new Republican government to pass a sumptuary law in 1912, a reprint of the draft of which appears above. The law ensured the survival of traditional clothing styles by approving their continued use alongside Western styles. For the movement, however, the more important victory lay in the wording of the law, which mandated that *all* clothing, regardless of style, was to be made of Chinese materials.

clothing, particularly articles using Chinese-manufactured fabrics. The NPPA immediately published an eighteen-page illustrated pamphlet on the new law; this widely circulated text explained the importance of supporting the silk industry by continuing to favor Chinese-style clothing (Zhonghua guohuo weichi hui 1912). The law and NPPA efforts prevented the state from symbolically sealing the fate of Qing-style clothing by forbidding its continued existence within the new nation. And for many decades, these traditional styles continued to be worn (although not with the same set of associations).

To be sure, the law was not a complete victory for the NPPA. The law divided men's formal and dress clothing into formal wear for official occasions (大禮服) and for ordinary activities (常禮服). The law stipulated that the former should be a frock coat and pants but mandated that the outfit be made of Chinese black silk. For ordinary dress clothing, men could opt either for the black morning coat and pants or the long-gown and coat (長袍 and 馬褂). These two styles had to use three nationally produced fabrics: silk, cotton, or flax (linen). Depending on the category, a man could wear either a silk top hat or a silk or cotton bowler. Almost as an afterthought, the law reaffirmed the long-gown and pleated skirt as the style for women's clothing. The law granted significant exceptions to students, soldiers, police officers, judges, bureaucrats, and others with specific dress codes. It also stated that public officials could not ordinarily wear the long-gown and vest (褂袍). The NPPA targeted these exceptions in ensuing years.

The Legacy of Nationalistic Appearance Under the Republic

Successfully persuading political elites to sanction the use of domestically produced fabrics and to reverse their support for Western styles was an impressive victory. It was, however, only a partial one. The law had no provisions for enforcement. Even if the law had included fines and punishments, it is doubtful the fragile coalition of interests within the various Republican governments could have afforded the time and energy necessary to enforce it.

Thus, the immediate impact of the new law is not clear. However, the Republic's new National Assembly (國會) quickly embraced the changes. A longtime Western observer of politics in Beijing summarized the law's impact:

Manchu law prescribed in minutest detail the official dress of every man and woman according to their class. Now that China was being modernised it was perhaps not unnatural that the introduction of Western political institutions should be accompanied by Western costume. So a bill was submitted and carried prescribing the sort of dress to be worn by officials of the government—the business suit, the morning frock coat, the informal dinner jacket and the swallow-tail; starched shirts, collars, neckties, silk hats, bowler hats and shoes. Patterns for all these were supplied. The change in the appearance of the Assembly was startling. The new members of the National Assembly in 1911 and 1912 were clothed in silk and satin robes of brilliant colors (Williams 1923: 479–80).[63]

---

63. See also Farjenel 1915: 183.

By 1913, all members dressed in the prescribed Western outfits. But this same Western observer misinterpreted these outfits: "The change was the more distressing because the patterns were not understood by some of the tailors in the interior cities. Trousers of black satin and frock coats that touched the ankles . . . ." This observation misses the purpose of the change. The intent was not to appear more "Western" but to support the Chinese economy. These men wore Western-style suits made of silk in compliance with the law, itself a compromise between Western form and Chinese content.

As with initial changes made by Republican officials, it was not the massive adoption of such changes in clothing that the NPPA and other participants in the movement feared. Rather, they worried that changes in styles at the top of government—legislators in Beijing falling "under the spell of clothes"—would accelerate and legitimize similar changes throughout China. There was also considerable concern that people would disregard the regulations on using Chinese fabrics and that the growing popularity of Western styles would continue to undermine the Chinese silk industry. These anxieties provoked widespread worry and anger, especially among the silk, hat, and other industries that had lobbied against the preliminary version of the Clothing Law. In public meetings in cities throughout China, the new dress was roundly condemned as unsuitable (Wu Tingfang 1914: 158–60).

The prominent early NPPA leader Wu Tingfang, who had a long-standing interest in the issue, led the opposition to this trend. After helping to lobby the new Republican state to alter its law on clothing, getting them to permit two distinct forms of dress clothing—one Western and the other more traditional—Wu set out to change the regulations of the Clothing Law regarding formal wear. The new law stipulated that men were to wear morning coats on formal occasions. It did not, however, define "formal occasion." The ambiguity in the law worried Wu, who feared that in the absence of clear regulations, such as those for military uniforms, everyone would wear Western clothing at formal events such as weddings and funerals, to the detriment of national products. As a compromise measure, and perhaps in a nod to Western fashion, Wu urged the government to find a Sino-foreign blend. In a long petition submitted to President Yuan Shikai, he went so far as to include exact forms, colors, and fabrics of such a Sino-Western hybrid, while consistently stressing the importance of using

Fig. 2.6 New Uniforms for Diplomats
(Wu Tingfang 1914: 160)

In the 1910s, Wu Tingfang passionately argued for the continued use of Chinese clothing styles. Wu was an early leader of the NPPA and understood that making clothing from silk was essential to the health of the Chinese economy and, therefore, the strength of the nation. At the same time, he acknowledged that Chinese needed to make compromises in their dealings with the imperialist powers. Wu, himself a former diplomat, designed the outfit above, which combines Western (pants and shoes) and Chinese elements (long-gown and jacket), as a uniform for Chinese diplomats.

Chinese materials (Ding Lanjun and Yu Zuofeng 1993, vol. 2: 615–18; Wu Tingfang 1915: 62–65; Pomerantz-Zhang 1992: 186–88; Crow 1944: 125–26). He also tried to undermine Western formal wear by designing an alternative that appeared somewhat Western but made use of Chinese styles and, more important, Chinese silk (see Fig. 2.6) (Wu Tingfang 1914: 160).

Although preserving important Chinese industries was always a central part of arguments against the adoption of Western styles, supporters of Chinese-style clothing bolstered their case with other points. Wu, for instance, attacked the purported superiority of Western dress, which was often cited as healthier, more hygienic, and more suitable to the mobility demanded by modern industrial life. He identified four reasons for wearing

clothing—protection from the elements, comfort, modesty, and ornament—and argued that Chinese clothing was equal or superior to Western
dress in each category. Wu alleged that Westerners suffered many more ill-
nesses due to improper protection from the elements. Chinese, he claimed,
got fewer colds and never suffered from heatstroke. Wu reserved his sharp-
est criticisms for corsets, which he called inconvenient and dangerous, and
proclaimed that the "death-rate among American women would be less if
the corset and other tight lacing were abolished." On the subject of modesty,
he argued that this was a relative concept and that Chinese would be just as
shocked to discover how Westerners dress as vice versa. Chinese, he felt, selected clothing based on practicality rather than fashion, a phenomenon he
labeled "the work of the devil" (Wu Tingfang 1914: 131–32, 140–41, 157).

Like those who argued that Chinese clothing made the country seem
backward, Wu endorsed clothing as a yardstick of civilization and reason,
but he turned the pro-Westerners' argument on its head by suggesting that
Chinese clothing was advanced and Western clothing was inferior and defi-
cient. The high collar and tight clothing of Western men represented the
height of impracticality. In contrast, Chinese habits of dress were superior
because "fashions are set by the weather." Wu joked that "death by unsuitable clothing" should be cited on many death certificates in the West.
Therefore, the Americans should adopt Chinese styles. Wu, of course, knew
he was fighting a losing battle. As he put it, "might is right" in clothing fashions (Wu Tingfang 1914: 141, 154–57). Moreover, because of imperialist
penetration of his country, Chinese were aping the inferior styles associated
with Western power, a process that accelerated following the collapse of the
Qing government. Still, he hoped to convince his compatriots that military
strength did not determine sartorial quality.

What Wu offered was a solution to a question debated in China since
the second half of the nineteenth century: To what degree did Chinese need
to adopt the material trappings of lifestyles associated with the contemporary West? Wu thought it understandable and practical for Chinese living
abroad, particularly diplomats, to dress in Western clothing (Wu Tingfang
1914: 160). Western prejudices against Chinese dress were simply insur-
mountable. However, he adamantly opposed the adoption of Western dress
in China. His solution can be found in his summary of the opinions of a
friend. After studying in the United States and adopting Western dress
there, she reverted to Chinese clothing upon her return. Wu quotes her ex-

planation: "If we keep our own mode of life it is not for the sake of blind conservatism. We are more logical in our ways than the average European imagines. I wear for instance this *'ao'* dress as you see, cut in one piece and allowing the limbs free play—because it is manifestly a more rational and comfortable attire than your fashionable skirt from Paris." Wu could not have put it better himself. He admitted that he had adopted Western-style dress himself while studying law in London under pressure from his British classmates. Doing so made him cold in the winter and hot in the summer. Moreover, his leather shoes gave him corns. All these ailments disappeared when he returned to China and resumed Chinese dress (see Fig. 2.7) (Wu Tingfang 1914: 139–40).

ONGOING EFFORTS TO NATIONALIZE APPEARANCE

The Clothing Law and Wu Tingfang's efforts were not the only attempts to nationalize consumer culture through new clothing regulations. In the early years of the Republic, successive Chinese administrations approved or reissued orders and regulations pertaining to national-product clothing. Many of these regulations were aimed at government employees, the Chinese whom the state could most easily control. Among the earliest regulations were those dealing with uniforms for judges, prosecutors, and lawyers, which were announced in January 1912. The following autumn the government issued new rules for army uniforms, and in spring 1913, it announced dress regulations for local civil servants, diplomats, and counselor officials. By 1915, similar regulations were in place for mining officials and prison officers, and in 1918, the Chinese navy got new uniforms (Huang Shilong 1994: 235).

The government and organizations in the National Products Movement continually reaffirmed the regulation requiring the use of national products for civilian dress, especially during the frequent anti-imperialist boycotts.[64] After the establishment of the Nationalist government in 1928, the NPPA successfully lobbied the new government to regulate dress to preserve the interests of domestic manufacturers and thereby enforce nationalistic

---

64. On the NPPA's promotion of Chinese-made clothing during the boycott of 1925, see SZMA File 367: 6a–b. For additional NPPA petitions to the government to expand and enforce clothing regulations, see SZMA Files 752: 47 and 1020: 16–18.

Fig. 2.7 The Sun Suit Compromise
(Tang Weikang and Huang Yixuan 1991: 54)

After the fall of the Qing dynasty, revolutionaries such as Sun Yatsen began to back away from complete support for Western-style clothing. The Sun Yatsen suit (known later in English as the Chairman Mao suit) represented a sartorial compromise for politicians such as Sun (photographed here in November 1924, four months before his death). In the early years of the Republic, politicians and other Chinese men found choosing a clothing style difficult. On the one hand, there was growing hostility to imperialism and its sartorial representations in the Western suit, hostility generated in the early years of the National Products Movement. On the other hand, Qing-style clothing appeared old-fashioned and was associated with the corruption of dynastic officialdom. The lack of a clear national identification associated with the Sun style, which may have arrived in China from Germany by way of Japan, made it an attractive compromise, especially after it became closely identified with Sun and after national product manufacturers began to market the style. These three styles (Western, Chinese, and compromise) did not represent fixed stages; Sun used all three styles. Nor was Sun the only world leader expressing anti-imperialism through clothing style. Chinese were aware that Gandhi's clothing choices also evolved away from Western styles and emphasized domestic products (see Tarlo 1996). Movement literature invoked Gandhi as a role model of opposing imperialism through patriotic dress.

consumption.[65] Such non-governmental efforts also grew as China's anti-imperialist struggle continued. Since the time of the Twenty-One Demands in 1915, industrialists such as Song Zejiu of Tianjin had marketed "patriotic cloth" (愛國布) to compete with Japanese textile imports (Rinbara 1983: 29–42). And in the aftermath of the Japanese invasion of Manchuria in 1931, savvy merchants marketed "cloth for erasing humiliation" (雪恥布) (Fang Xiantang 1996: 436). Likewise, the movement reminded Chinese that they needed to resist Japanese imperialism by selecting Chinese fabrics.[66] And the NPPA repeatedly petitioned the central government to enforce clothing regulations by ordering all provinces to investigate "unorthodox clothing" (奇裝異服).[67] Women became primary targets of the movement efforts (see Chapter 7). Students, often self-appointed leaders of the nationalist/anti-imperialist struggle, were frequently ordered to match their patriotic rhetoric and their personal practice. In spring 1930, for instance, the Ministry of Education in Nanjing ordered the educational bureaucracy throughout China to instruct students that they must wear uniforms made of Chinese-made cloth.[68] Similarly, the Shanghai municipal government required all civil servants to buy only clothing made of national products.[69] Regulations varied from place to place. In Shandong province, civil servants were

---

65. On the implementation of these regulations in Suzhou, see SZMA File 1332: 78–81; NJ 613.463, which also describes Nationalist attempts to create an umbrella organization for the movement; NJ 613.462: 28, which describes the new government's efforts; SB 1928.7.10: 8; "Guohuo lifu yundong zhi tuijin"; and Shandong sheng guohuo chenlieguan 1936: 57–58. See also H. Harrison 2000: 191.

66. These reminders to dress in Chinese-made clothing were especially common and pronounced on anniversaries such as the September 18th anniversary of the Manchurian Incident of 1931, which led to Japan's formal annexation of the area. See, e.g., "9-18 yu fuzhang" (September 18th and clothing), SB 1933.9.18: 19, and the numerous advertisements promoting nationalistic consumption.

67. "Guohuo weichi hui dianqing zhongyang lixing guohuo fuzhi tiaoli" (The NPPA telegraphs the central government to petition to enforce the Clothing Law regulations strictly), SB 1936.5.22.

68. "Chinese Students Must Wear Native-Made Cloth," CWR 1930.5.24: 500. On May 16, the Ministry of Education in Nanjing ordered public schools at all levels throughout the country to instruct students that their uniforms had to be made of Chinese cloth and that they should also try to avoid imports. For a discussion of the laws attempting to resolve the "problem of what to wear" (穿衣問題), see the title essay in Wang Keyou 1931: 1–4.

69. These same regulations also prohibited the consumption of imports, especially alcohol and tobacco, at official parties and mandated that all office supplies be national products (see "Shanghai shi zhengfu tichang guohuo shiyong shixing banfa").

required not only to wear national products but also to register any non-national product clothing that they might own.[70] Movement organizations and publications reminded Chinese both of the laws and of their duties in this time of national crisis with slogans such as "If it's not a national product, don't wear it" and "Clothing to the rescue of the nation" (see Fig. 2.8).[71]

From the establishment of the Qing dynasty in 1644 to the Republican Revolution in 1911, Chinese hair and clothing styles absorbed, lost, and acquired multiple meanings. By examining the politics of defining visuality in China, we can clarify the negotiated relationship between the physical and the imputed characteristics of objects. This chapter suggests that despite the always tenuous relationship between symbols and their referents, these relationships can become particularly unstable during a period of rapid political, economic, and social change. Republican leaders and their supporters considered establishing and enforcing their own orthodox definition of appearance as undertakings of utmost significance to the new nation. However, politicians and intellectuals did not define this new nationalistic visuality on their own. The early history of a key movement organization, the NPPA, demonstrates that powerful economic interests participated in this process by re-establishing the relationships among the economy, society, and politics in ways that linked the consumption of their products to nationalism and associated abstention from consuming products labeled "foreign" to anti-imperialism.

More broadly, this case underscores the importance of material culture in defining and sustaining nationalism. For the NPPA, material culture such as fabrics and clothing styles played a direct role in connecting individuals to the nation: individual bodies were key sites of a national symbology and hence for the construction of modern Chinese nationalism as such. The proliferation of "national products" not only transformed ways of living but also raised consciousness of membership in the Chinese *economic* community.

---

70. See the "Yizhou jian guohuo xinxun" (Weekly news of the National Products Movement) sections in SB 1934.11.12 and many other issues, which report on all kinds of government orders for various groups to wear only national products.

71. Virtually every movement publication reproduces these slogans. On the connection between the Japanese invasion and such slogans, see, e.g., Lu Baiyu 1931. See also "Guohuo zhidao" 1931 and "Fuzhuang jiuguo" 1933.

Fig. 2.8 Western-Style Chinese-Made Clothing
(*Shangye zazhi* 5, no. 7 [1930]; SSGC 1930)

As Chinese companies began to produce wool suits and Western-style clothing, it became easier for the movement to maintain its original interpretation of male clothing advanced during the Revolution of 1911 (product-nationality was the issue, not style). It became more tolerable to movement participants to embrace Western styles, even wedding tuxedoes and gowns, as confirmed by this photograph (*top*) of a group of women modeling a wedding party at the Shanghai National Products Fashion Show in 1930. Long-gowns remained the de facto male uniform of the movement. Nevertheless, the movement also utilized advertising, fashion shows (*bottom*), and other spectacles to promote nationally produced Western-style suits.

These goods made many more Chinese aware of a new and increasingly global economy. Being Chinese came to be associated with wearing "Chinese" clothing. Crucially, the nationality of articles of clothing was increasingly determined by content rather than by style; Chinese labor, management, raw material, and capital and not the shape of the garment made it Chinese.

With the disappearance of the Qing, Chinese elites and organizations sought new ways of defining personal appearance both to integrate Chinese "national people," as they now became known, into a new collectivity and to oppose "foreign" symbolic interpretations and economic penetration. People such as Mei Zuolü in his patriotic outfit initiated the lengthy effort to naturalize a connection between "nationalistic" consumption and nascent Chinese national consciousness. Institutionalizing a nationalistic consumer culture and a form of visuality to support it was not easy; nor did it go unchallenged. In the face of conflicting demands, urban elites might, for example, opt for cosmopolitanism over patriotism. Nevertheless, the process of nationalizing material culture was well under way. A broad movement greatly expanded this process in subsequent decades.

Despite frequent alarms, the Republican period never witnessed a revolution in men's dress. Although many Chinese men switched to (or simply occasionally wore) Western-style suits and formal wear, NPPA leaders had good reasons to claim victory in the mid-1930s. However, to judge from the movement's relentless attacks on imported fabrics, the use of distinctively Chinese styles did not necessarily ensure the use of domestically produced materials such as silk. Nonetheless, by the 1930s, although China's silk and satin industries faced new threats such as rayon, members of the NPPA considered their efforts to preserve Chinese industries and hundreds of thousands of jobs by promoting traditional silk-based styles to have been successful.[72]

By salvaging traditional styles and recasting them as "patriotic," stodgy Chinese economic elites had successfully reinvented themselves as cultural intermediaries, interpreters of a new post-dynastic, nationalistic aesthetic. They possessed both an interest in the production of new symbols of state

---

72. ZGWH 1932: "Huishi," section 2, claims that NPPA efforts saved these two industries and preserved the livelihoods of several hundred thousand people. For an example of NPPA efforts to discourage the use of rayon and imported clothing made of it, see "Guohuo hui qing nüjie wuyong waihuo" 1934.

and better means of imposing them than many of their competitors. Not only did they place "national products" at the top of a new nationalistic hierarchy, but they (and their peers) were also their own best customers. These styles became the de facto uniform of the movement and continued to reinforce the connection between national-product fabrics and nationalism until the Communist victory in 1949, when new uniforms—along with a different visuality—were imposed.

PART II

Consumption as Resistance

The Movement and Anti-Imperialist

Boycotts, 1905-1919

Always remember and never forget May Ninth.

—A 1915 poster written in its author's blood
(for photographs, see Zhichi hui 1915)

Japan indeed oppresses us,
and selfish are its claims.
Yes, boycott all things Japanese—
a duty evermore.

—A 1915 protest poem (*XWB* 1915.4.1)

The main problem facing advocates of the National Products Movement was to convince their compatriots to "buy Chinese." How did one convince people to think in terms of product-nationality? How did one reach those who wanted to buy foreign goods? One solution was the anti-imperialist boycott. Boycotts played a pivotal role in instilling the notions that every product had a nationality and that product-nationality should determine purchasing decisions. The frequent boycotts affected not only consumers but also merchants and manufacturers. Merchants contributed to the production of a nationalistic visuality by removing or disguising imports, and manufacturers purged "foreign" elements from their goods to make them appear as Chinese as possible.

Boycotts figured prominently in Sino-foreign relations in the first third of the twentieth century. During this period, boycotts precipitated or accompanied major turning points in China's relations with the imperialist powers—there were significant boycotts in 1905, 1908, 1909, 1915, 1919, 1923, 1925, 1928, 1931, and then nearly continuously into the Second Sino-Japanese War. Moreover, the policies behind the boycotts may have even provoked the war with Japan (Jordan 1991). In other words, a century after the Opium War "opened" Chinese markets, Japan initiated a new war to ensure market access at least partially out of the fear that a successful National Products Movement would severely restrict access to the Chinese market.

This and the following chapters study boycotts as a series of linked events and as part of the broader, continuous effort to nationalize consumer culture.[1] Individual boycotts were more than isolated events. They were not simply self-contained cycles in which a foreign "humiliation" prompted a popular protest that included a boycott that ended when government suppression from above, inertia from below, and the profit motive among merchants undermined the commitment of participants, to be followed in time by a recurrence of the same cycle.[2] Boycott supporters remained active between "cycles." Nor, contrary to the claims of contemporary foreign observers, were efforts to promote a nationalistic consumer culture mere "camouflage" for boycotts. These efforts did not emerge at the conclusion of a boycott to legitimize continued "anti-foreign" behavior (although movement rhetoric was certainly used this way).[3] Rather, I argue, boycotts were merely the most visible—and violent—aspects of the attempt to nationalize consumer culture.[4]

---

1. As will be apparent from the citations in these chapters, my study has benefited both from histories of individual boycotts and from studies of boycotts in general. Two important studies that cover boycotts as a phenomenon are Remer 1933b and Kikuchi 1974. Although occasionally mentioning some of the long-term effects of boycotts, such as the replacement of Japanese products with Chinese ones, Remer focuses on "economic effectiveness" from the perspective of trade statistics, not institutions, activities, or symbols. Kikuchi does a superior job of connecting boycotts by analyzing them alongside the growth of domestic Chinese industry. He examines the appearance of movement organizations within the narrow context of individual boycotts. Additional works subsume boycotts under other subjects. For example, see Wasserstrom 1991 on the connection between boycotts and student demonstrations.

2. Contemporary coverage, especially in Japanese sources, reinforced this interpretation by numbering boycotts. See, e.g., Ōsaka shōgyō kaigisho 1928: 1–6; and Ōsaka shōkō kaigisho 1931: 5.

3. For a representative view of the movement as "camouflage," see Matsumoto 1933. Western observers such as the *New York Times* correspondents Hallett Abend and Anthony Billingham also mistook the movement as a boycott by another name (Abend and Billingham 1936: 44–45).

4. The Shanghai economic historian Pan Junxiang (1996a: 577–78) has studied boycotts as a manifestation of the movement but does not explore the links between the two. On the difficulty of assessing the success of boycotts in general, see the discussion of the "criterion problem" in Monroe Friedman 1999: 17–20.

Boycotts were part of a sustained expression of anti-imperialism within the National Products Movement. They did not emerge from nowhere as an emotional response to an act of foreign aggression in China. The Chinese had always actively combated foreign incursions. Given the deep roots of the movement in the late nineteenth-century ideology of commercial warfare and the subtler work of movement organizations in tying nationalism and consumerism, boycotts were simply a particularly overt manifestation of a much deeper ideological commitment to constructing a nationalistic consumer culture. The National Products Movement provided a common social, economic, and ideological basis for the various boycotts. By examining events such as boycotts from the perspective of a movement that promoted a refusal to buy foreign products in general, and increasingly Japanese products in particular, we can more accurately understand popular resistance to Japanese and other foreign activity in China.[5] Indeed, viewing individual boycotts in isolation tends to devalue important dimensions of Chinese nationalism and forms of anti-imperialism produced throughout China.[6] The social arena of consumption was a primary arena for constructing resistance. By placing the frequent anti-imperialist boycotts in the context of the larger movement, I hope to show how they acted as a coercive force that publicized, imposed, and enforced a nationalistic interpretation of China's emerging consumer culture. Chinese constructed foreign activity as aggression and inculcated the nonconsumption of "foreign products" as an appropriate response.

Institutionalization: The Anti-American Boycott of 1905

The outbreak of an anti-American boycott in 1905 is, as noted in Chapter 1, a primary reason for dating the start of the movement to that year. Like subsequent boycotts, this one had an identifiable spark. The boycott was a direct outgrowth of friction over U.S. immigration policies. In the late nine-

---

5. In contrast with studies that concentrate on the economic dimension of Sino-foreign rivalries, I focus on the broader context of organizations, activities, and symbols that shaped these rivalries. For surveys of the growth of Chinese domestic industry and its implications for Sino-Japanese economic rivalry, see Du 1991: 158–59, Bergère 1986: 63–98, and Kikuchi 1974. On specific rivalries between Chinese and foreign enterprises, see, e.g., Cochran 1980 and Takamura 1982: esp. 140–56.

6. Although beyond the scope of this study, the Japanese also encountered these forms of nationalism among overseas Chinese communities, especially in Southeast Asia. See, e.g., Namikata 1997 and Yoji 1963.

teenth century, the U.S. Congress enacted increasingly restrictive immigration measures against all Chinese, culminating in 1904 with a measure that
excluded all Chinese workers for ten years. Although the treaties recognized
the difference between workers and Chinese elites, both groups were often
treated poorly.[7] Outraged Chinese of all classes, particularly in south China,
immediately protested, prompting negotiations between the Chinese government and Washington. To express their outrage and help pressure the
United States, Chinese merchants in cities throughout China began to boycott American products in the summer of 1905 (Field 1957).[8] Although U.S.
pressure on the Qing government led to an imperial decree at the end of August that largely quelled the boycott in cities outside the south, boycotts
continued into 1906.[9]

This boycott was critical to the development of the movement for four
reasons. First, it initiated a long series of anti-imperialist boycotts. Second, it
was national in scope. Earlier boycotts against foreigners had been considerably more circumscribed.[10] In 1905, at least ten provinces and many major
cities throughout China (and within Chinese communities abroad such as
San Francisco) participated. Third, the boycott cut across class lines. Because U.S. immigration officials had mistreated all Chinese—from manual
laborers to aristocrats—all social classes supported the boycott, and the
United States became a common enemy for more than just a single native-
place association or a single industry.[11] Fourth, as with the other social

---

7. One high-profile case occurred during the preparations for the Louisiana Purchase Exposition of 1904 in St. Louis. When Chinese exhibitors en route to St. Louis arrived in San
Francisco, customs officials treated them shabbily. The Chinese press covered this mistreatment extensively. For an overview, see J. W. Foster 1906.

8. See also Wong Sin-kiong 1995, Guanhua Wang 1995, and, most recently, Guanhua
Wang 2001. Wu Tingfang, who, as noted above, became a vocal supporter of the movement
and president of the NPPA, played an active role in supporting the boycott (Pomerantz-
Zhang 1992: 165). Wu described this coordinated movement as "enlightened antiforeignism"
(文明排外).

9. Participation in the boycott varied by city and product (Remer 1933b: 37). The boycott
of cigarettes produced by the British-American Tobacco Company, for instance, did not
cease until the end of 1906 (Cochran 1980: 50).

10. Earlier events presaged the sort of economic protests seen in boycotts. In 1874 and 1898,
for instance, the Ningbo native-place association of Shanghai led anti-imperialist protests
against French attempts to appropriate their mortuary and cemetery. See Belsky 1992 and
Goodman 1995: 158–69.

11. Wong Sin-kiong (1995: 44) sees the 1905 boycott as the "first cross-social-group popular protest." See also McKee 1986.

movements in this decade, the boycott fostered popular participation in the anti-imperialist and national salvation project.[12]

After compiling the names of blacklisted products, boycott leaders used many methods both to disseminate their message and to compel participation, such as writing posters, modifying popular songs, destroying stocks of American products, soliciting pledges to participate in the boycott, tearing down advertisement posters for American goods, spreading rumors (for example, that American cigarettes contained poison), and using advertisements to identify products as Chinese and encourage their consumption (Cochran 1980: 46–51). Protestors used different media to reach as many people as possible. Newspapers targeted the cultural elite; songs, lectures, slogans, drama performances, and cartoons of mistreated Chinese reached a wider audience; and handbills, leaflets, and placards written in the colloquial language informed intermediate groups (Wong Sin-kiong 1995: 12).

Aspects of this boycott anticipated future developments. The boycotts politicized merchants through native-place associations and the fledgling chambers of commerce, which were largely responsible for initiating the boycotts (Xu Dingxin and Qian Xiaoming 1991: 67–92). As political scientist Joseph Fewsmith notes in his study of merchant activism, this was the "first time that merchants used their collective strength to try to influence national political issues" (Fewsmith 1985: 42).[13] Moreover, although the boycott developed differently in cities across China, its scope demonstrated the possibility for national cooperation and coordination.[14] Among the participants were students, who become a common ingredient in subsequent decades. The boycott demonstrated to would-be Chinese entrepreneurs and policy-

---

12. In Shanghai, for instance, more than twenty ad hoc organizations were established to promote the boycott, and at least 76 professional organizations participated (Pan Junxiang 1996c: 3).

13. Kuang-sheng Liao (1984: 59) makes a similar point: "The Anti-American boycott of 1905 was a demonstration of the power of this newly-developed class of merchants and industrialists."

14. Tianjin joined the boycott a month after it began in Shanghai. Its major paper, the *Dagongbao*, reprinted Shanghai boycott articles and actively promoted local participation. However, General Yuan Shikai quickly intervened to end the Tianjin General Chamber of Commerce's support of the boycott. On differences between Shanghai and Tianjin, see Zhang Xiaobo 1995: 53. Zhang cites the Tianjin commercial elites' ties to the government, their need for American materials such as cotton, and their lack of commitment to the issue of emigration as reasons for their lack of interest. On the differences between the organization of the boycott in Shanghai and Guangzhou, see Wong Sin-kiong 1995: 3.

makers the utility of shutting out foreign capital: in the absence of foreign competitors, Chinese-owned companies sprang up and owed their survival to the forced absence of foreign competition.[15]

As with all boycotts, it is nearly impossible to gauge the economic impact of the events of 1905. We cannot say what long-term import statistics would have been in the absence of a boycott. In this particular case, Sino-American trade actually peaked. Although monthly statistics do not exist for the period 1904–5, imports from America grew during 1905 by over 250 percent. This suggests the boycott was a tremendous failure. Yet, three items imported into regions largely unaffected by the boycott—copper, plain gray cotton sheeting, and cotton drills—accounted for much of the increase. In contrast, U.S. export statistics show a reduction of over 50 percent between April and October. Again, research suggests that this was probably a result of more than simply the boycott (Remer 1933b: 36–39).[16] In other places, particularly Guangzhou and Shanghai, the boycott was very effective,[17] and it did achieve part of its goal. Although the United States continued to exclude Chinese laborers, it started to treat non–working class Chinese visitors with more respect (Remer 1933b: 34–35).

More important, the boycott began to popularize product-nationality consciousness among Chinese consumers, and a growing sense of empowerment through consumption and nonconsumption laid the groundwork for the expansion of the movement. As a foreign observer noted, "The Chinese boycott of American goods is striking evidence of an awakening spirit of resentment in the great Empire against the injustice and aggression of foreign countries" (J. W. Foster 1906: 118). However, the long-term implications of this "awakening spirit" were not always apparent to contemporaries. For instance, the classic study by Charles Remer focused on the economic costs of the boycott to China: "If it is effective, it is costly to the nation doing the boycotting." To support this contention, Remer's study cited Chinese offi-

---

15. For example, before the start of the boycott, there were only four Chinese cigarette companies, but by the end there were twenty (Cochran 1980: 50–51). These companies did not long survive the boycott, but their bankruptcy only served to strengthen the movement position that foreign companies inhibited the development of Chinese-owned industry. On the importance of the boycott in the early industrial history of China, see Kikuchi 1974: 2–56.

16. However, Remer (1933b) confirms that, particularly in Guangzhou, the boycott adversely affected imports of kerosene oil, wheat flour, and cotton piece goods.

17. The well-known observer of China Julean Arnold, then working in the U.S. consulate in Shanghai, concluded the boycott was 90 percent effective (cited in Cochran 1980: 48).

cials bragging about the large amount of money they had spent on telegrams urging others to support the boycott, Chinese merchants in America sending donations, and other resources wasted on the boycott (Remer 1933b: 35). However, these same anecdotes here and in future boycotts underscore the growing commitment to this form of economic nationalism and the desire to create a sustained and universally supported boycott.

Early Anti-Japanese Boycotts

The anti-American boycott of 1905 was an anomaly in one respect. The immediate causes of subsequent boycotts were infringements of Chinese sovereignty within China rather than affronts to Chinese overseas. The next major anti-imperialist boycott occurred a few years later. In early 1908, Chinese officials in Guangzhou seized a Japanese ship, the *Tatsu Maru II*, which they believed to be smuggling weapons to anti-Qing revolutionaries.[18] To legitimize the seizure, these officials had replaced the Japanese flag with a Chinese one. The Japanese government protested the act as an affront to the Japanese flag and demanded the immediate release of the ship, an indemnity, and a formal and elaborate apology. After protracted negotiations, the Chinese agreed.

The agreement angered Chinese in southern China, who wanted their government to stand up to the Japanese. The event quickly became an "incident" (事件), another opportunity to express nationalism and anti-imperialism through commodities. The chamber of commerce and native-place associations in Guangzhou, for instance, proposed a boycott of Japanese products until the aggregate value of the boycotted goods matched the indemnity. Longshoremen refused to unload Japanese ships, local shipping companies vowed not to use these ships, and merchants burned Japanese products. As with other boycotts, ad hoc organizations formed to support this one. The boycott spread to other cities, particularly those with populations of merchants from Guangzhou such as Shanghai and in overseas communities such as Honolulu, Manila, and even the Japanese city of Nagasaki (NCH 1908.4.24). Participation was not voluntary, as riots in Hong Kong over cheating confirm (NCH 1908.11.7).

---

18. There were several other minor boycotts around this time. For instance, there was a small boycott of German products due to violence in Qingdao in 1908.

Once again, an emphasis on the economic efficacy of the boycott would be misleading. Remer's study of boycotts shows the limitations of such an interpretive framework: "References to boycotting in customs reports and newspapers are so numerous that it is difficult to believe that trade was not affected" (Remer 1933b: 45). But Remer's assertion misses the point that regardless of its impact on trade, the boycott provided another symbolic victory: in an attempt to pacify Chinese critics, Japan recalled its official in charge of negotiations. Moreover, this boycott provides more evidence of the growing institutionalization of "the boycott" by demonstrating how quickly locals formed boycott organizations consisting of broad social coalitions.[19] Of particular note for the movement, these groups simultaneously promoted both the boycott and the development of Chinese industries. Seventy-two leading merchants in Guangzhou, for example, were asked to finance the establishment of a large commercial firm, where merchandise of every description would be collected from all over the country and sold at a designated price to encourage and to help improve Chinese industry (Matsumoto 1933: 19). The boycott also broke, if only temporarily, established trade relationships and thus opened up the possibility that domestic manufactures would replace Japanese imports. The boycott allowed Hangzhou umbrella manufacturers, for instance, to gain a toehold in a market dominated until then by popular Japanese-manufactured umbrellas (Lieu 1927: 669).[20] Above all, the boycott provided a lasting reminder that Chinese outside the government could take foreign policy into their own hands and express nationalism and anti-imperialism through commodities (NCH 1910.12.30). The dream of a "China market" among foreign merchants attempting to sell goods in China must have begun to seem much more nightmarish.

Nor was this the only boycott of Japan. As discussed in Chapter 1, the first decade of the twentieth century witnessed several overlapping social movements, including the anti-dynastic revolutionary movement and the

---

19. This broad social coalition included, on March 17, a gathering of tens of thousands in Guangzhou for a rally. These protests included women and girls who formed their own organizations, such as the National Humiliation Society (國恥會), which vowed not to use Japanese goods. Many schoolgirls signaled their participation in the protests and organizations by wearing white, the color of mourning (Collins 1976: 333).

20. The boycott also temporarily removed Japanese tobacco products from the south China market. Ironically, the boycott hurt Nanyang Brothers, at that time a fledgling "Chinese" tobacco company, which had anticipated a longer boycott and had invested accordingly (Cochran 1980: 58–59).

Rights-Recovery Movement. Protests against foreign ownership in the Rights-Recovery Movement featured a major boycott against Japan in Manchuria. The boycott began in 1909 as a response to dramatic growth of Japanese power and influence in that region following the Russo-Japanese War (see Kikuchi 1974: 107–52). In August, Japan announced that it would assume full control over the construction of a railway from Shenyang (Mukden) to Andong (Fengtian) on the Korean border on the grounds of procrastination from China. Begun by Chinese students living in Japan, the boycott spread to other overseas communities of Chinese and finally expanded to Manchuria and North China itself. It was most intense in Manchurian cities—Shenyang, Andong, Fushun, and Changchun—but smaller boycotts also occurred in Shanghai and Guangzhou.

Boycotters creatively altered their consumption habits to signify their protest. Chinese students in boycott areas, for instance, substituted flint and tinder for widely used Japanese matches (Orchard 1930: 254). Under pressure from Japan, the Chinese governor-general of Manchuria finally issued an ordinance prohibiting the boycott. The formal boycott, which began in August and ended in October, did not last long. Nevertheless, this form of protest had been introduced to new areas of China and would soon be repeated.

"National Humiliation" and Consumption in 1915

Japan's treatment of China during World War I, particularly the Twenty-One Demands of 1915, led to the first nationwide, prolonged boycott of Japanese goods. The movement appropriated the political opportunism, ultimatums, demands, threats, and abundance of Sino-Japanese friction of 1915 as raw materials for the creation of powerful anti-Japanese symbols. In view of the activities of movement organizations and the ethic of nationalistic consumption discussed in the previous chapter, 1915 takes on deeper significance. The boycotts of that year were not simply ephemeral events, "five minutes of enthusiasm," as foreigners and many Chinese often derided them, but overt manifestations of, and fuel for, a growing movement. Long after the boycotts dissipated, student organizations disbanded, and more relaxed Sino-Japanese economic intercourse resumed, the National Products Preservation Association and a growing number of similar organizations continued to disseminate interpretations of 1915 that linked consumption of Chinese products with anti-imperialism.

The politics behind the imposition and acceptance of the Twenty-One Demands are complex, but the basic elements are simple (see Li Yushu 1966, Dickinson 1999, and Yamane et al. 1996: 109–15). On January 18, 1915, Japan secretly presented Chinese president Yuan Shikai a list of demands divided into five groups. The first four groups stipulated the formal recognition of the transfer of German rights in Shandong province to Japan, the extension of leases and rights that Japan had won from Russia in 1905, joint control over the Hanyeping Iron Works, and a Chinese commitment not to cede territory to a third country. The final group of demands triggered the most intense Chinese opposition, however, because they would have virtually eliminated Chinese sovereignty by placing Japanese advisors in all branches of government and specifying joint policing of troublesome areas, contracting with the Japanese to build railways, and establishing special economic rights for Japan in Fujian province.[21] Negotiations dragged out for the next five months. Under pressure, Japan withdrew the fifth set of demands but presented the remaining groups as an ultimatum on May 7, which the Chinese were forced to accept on May 9.

The movement swiftly redefined these two dates as two more days in a calendar of "national humiliations" (國恥) and institutionalized the yearly commemoration of May Seventh and May Ninth.[22] Organizations and individuals across China quickly spread this interpretation, denouncing Japan's "latest, most serious humiliation." Local newspapers printed daily reminders "not to forget the national humiliation."[23] In a manifesto sent to chambers of

---

21. For a complete translation of the Demands, see La Fargue 1937: 241–43.

22. Symptomatic of the fragmented political state of China, Chinese commemorated this humiliation on two different days. May 7 was the focus of commemoration in north China, and May 9 in the south (Sun Fanjun and He Husheng 1991: 57). This difference betrays the sources and focus of a given text. One textbook on Sino-Japanese relations, for example, mentions only the commemoration of May Seventh (Jansen 1975: 209–23). Humiliations at the hands of foreigners are so common in Chinese modern history that enumerating them could fill, and indeed has filled, thick encyclopedias. They include every imaginable variety, from the unequal treaties to foreign wars fought on Chinese lands to countless acts of violence against individual Chinese. However, this chapter suggests that, as with other historical events, "national humiliations" neither are immediately self-evident nor have fixed interpretations for all time. They, too, are sites of contention, often defined by those with the power to get a definition to stick. A few of the many recent volumes include Zhu Hanguo 1993, He Yu and Hua Li 1995, and Renmin chubanshe ditu shi 1997.

23. In Guangzhou, they did so every day until Japanese pressured the local authorities to prohibit the practice. "China's National Disgrace Day" (1915.8.13), CRDS File 893.2309, and "China's National Disgrace Day" (1915.12.1), File 893.2332.

commerce and newspapers across China, the Beijing Chamber of Commerce expressed a popular Chinese response to the events that the NPPA helped to disseminate in the Shanghai area:

Japan is taking advantage of war in Europe to have its way in East Asia. The ultimatum of May Seventh is the best manifestation of this opportunism. If Chinese wish to live as human beings, we must never forget the humiliation of May Seventh. . . . The memory should be passed on to our children and grandchildren, from one generation to the next, for all eternity. From this May Seventh onward, we 400,000,000 Chinese must struggle wholeheartedly to help our country. Although our bodies may perish, our will cannot die, and we must forever remember this humiliation.[24]

In addition to constructing these days within an expanding trope of "national humiliations," public statements such as this one implicitly or explicitly signified how to "cleanse the humiliation" (雪恥).

FROM HUMILIATION TO RESISTANCE

The movement aimed to sustain and channel popular outrage. The lengthy negotiations over the Demands gave Chinese plenty of time to grow impatient. It also gave them time to organize opposition by creating new (and appropriating old) ways of expressing dissent through activities ranging from violent boycotts to a rejection of popular Japanese hairstyles.[25] Such forms of protest expressed varying levels of commitment to an ethic of nationalistic consumption, but all these actions contributed to the movement. Once defined, these events became signals not to consume Japanese products.

Local governments shaped the forms of dissent, which fed into the movement. The massively unpopular Twenty-One Demands put these governments in a difficult position. On the one hand, local and provincial lead-

---

24. "Beijing shanghui guochi tongxin tongdian" (The Beijing Chamber of Commerce's public statement regarding distress over the national humiliation), reprinted in Zhichi hui 1915. For similar sentiments, see the widely distributed Beijing Education Ministry telegram reprinted in SB 1915.6.14. On the NPPA's role in spreading this document, see SB 1915.5.20; the same issue says that the Jiangsu Provincial Education Association vowed to host yearly commemorations to remind students and staff at all schools of the meaning of this "humiliation."

25. According to one observer, patriotic Chinese women promptly abandoned the Japanese style of dressing the hair high over the forehead (pompadour style) in the wake of the presentation of the Twenty-One Demands (Tyau 1922: 86).

ers received a constant stream of orders from the top to suppress demonstrations and agitation that might further provoke Japan or further delegitimize the central government in Beijing. On the other hand, local governments were often sympathetic to the outpouring of anti-Japanese sentiment and were reluctant to try to suppress all manifestations of dissent; others wanted to further erode the dwindling credibility of Yuan Shikai because of his unwillingness to confront Japan. The national government was well aware of growing resentment, and officials continually tried to reassure an anxious populace with optimistic pronouncements about the negotiations.[26]

Meanwhile, local governments tried to balance the tension between maintaining order and yielding to popular pressure by cracking down on overt manifestations of dissent. They prohibited and disbanded public gatherings, confiscated inflammatory circulars, prevented the removal of advertisements of Japanese products, and heightened police visibility near Japanese businesses (XWB 1915.3.27, 29, 31, and 1915.4.1). But more subtle forms of dissent flourished. Japanese targets certainly got the message. In March 1915, a Japanese shopkeeper in Shanghai frustrated by the Chinese boycott allegedly posted the following six-character verse outside his shop:

> We are among the strongest of nations.
> Why should we fear you bastards?
> The current boycott of Japanese goods
> Is just empty talk.
> If you continue to protest in this way
> We will order your president to suppress it.
> Qingdao, Taiwan, and Korea.
> No, we are not jesting.
> Soon you will be an extinct nation.
> And assuredly you will become slaves. (Shibao 1915.3.29)

The verse expressed much more than the anger and bravado of a Japanese shopkeeper. Its reprinting in a Chinese newspaper was a clever use of a purportedly Japanese text to articulate the frustration and suspicions of a growing number of Chinese about Japan and its intentions. Here was proof positive that Japan, flush with its startling success over Russia a decade earlier,

---

26. For a summary of the role of domestic politics in negotiations over the Twenty-One Demands, see E. P. Young 1977: 186–92. On the eve of the settlement, these reassurances become more frequent and insistent; see, e.g., XWB 1915.5.7. These same papers printed editorials denouncing leaked versions of what they derided as a sham "peace" settlement.

now considered itself a world power able to push its own agenda in Asia; it was merely looking for an excuse to humiliate China further. The references to three recent additions to an expanding Japanese empire were an unambiguous statement of China's fate, the long-feared "national extinction."[27] Moreover, the verse emphasized the powerlessness of the Chinese, whose boycotts and politicians were mere short-term obstacles to the inevitable.

By reprinting the inflammatory verse, the Chinese paper also implied an appropriate response, a challenge to redouble resistance to Japanese imperialism and prove the Japanese wrong. It was a call to action. The events of May confirmed that the Chinese could not depend on their politicians to preserve China's immediate interests, much less the integrity of the nation. Despite growing government pressure, movement organizations such as the NPPA found ways to signal this threat as well as relate it to a desired Chinese response in the form of an ethic of nationalistic consumption.

SIGNIFYING NATIONALISTIC
CONSUMPTION BY INVOKING JAPAN

Under increasing pressure from the government, organizations and individuals created subtle ways to signify "Japan" without specifying it. Even after the formal boycotts and government pressure subsided, these signs continued to exist. The movement's invocation of Japan reminded China of Japanese "humiliations" and the need to reject Japanese products and services.[28] The dates of these and later humiliations were vivid and common symbols. For instance, the numbers "5-9" unambiguously represented the ninth day of the fifth month, May Ninth. On one level, simply writing "5-9"

---

27. Chinese intellectuals immediately added the acceptance of the Twenty-One Demands to a rapidly expanding narrative of "national humiliations" that they feared would climax with "national extinction." By June, one group that included Liang Qichao had compiled a set of essays on "extinct nations" (亡國) such as Poland and India and detailed how China was headed for the same fate (Yan Ruli 1919). On the popularity of this discourse, see Karl 2002.

28. Thousands of Chinese students in Japan protested by returning to China. In her memoirs, Buwei Yang Chao describes the tremendous pressure on students to participate in anti-Japanese protests in Japan. Women who chose to stay were accused of wanting to "marry the Japs" (B. Y. Chao and Y. R. Chao 1947: 145). Three years later, in 1918, Zhou Enlai 周恩來 (1898–1976), the future Communist Party leader and Prime Minister of China, and seven hundred other Chinese students participated in similar demonstrations against Japan in Tokyo on the eve of the May 7 National Humiliation Day (C.-J. Lee 1994: 94–95).

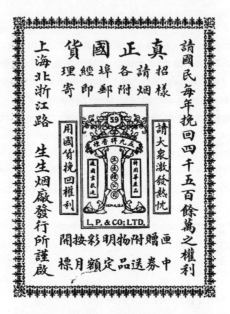

Fig. 3.1 Marketing Humiliation in 1915
(Wang Hanqiang 1915: 64)

This advertisement from 1915 for a Chinese cigarette company illustrates how Chinese companies immediately incorporated reminders of "national humiliations" into their logos and advertisements. Here the cigarette brand itself is "5-9," in reference to May 9, 1915, when Japan required China to agree to the Twenty-One Demands. The advertisement also utilizes movement ideology to connect resistance to the consumption of "authentic national products" (真正國貨). The inner vertical lines read "Everyone please arouse your enthusiasm and use national products to recover sovereign rights."

signified "humiliation at the hands of the Japanese." These numbers were widely used as symbols in posters, illustrations, and handbills throughout China. Naturally, they often signified more than one message. Within the movement, for example, "5-9" also came to signify a response to humiliation: Do not buy Japanese products. Often, such signs were explicitly linked, especially in advertisements and product names. Within months, companies had co-opted the "5-9" symbol into product names, including cigarettes and silk products (see Figs. 3.1–2).

With Japanese pressure on the Chinese government to crack down on boycotts, movement participants used many less explicit, but equally comprehensible, ways of disseminating boycott messages by referring to Japan itself in not-so-subtle ways. A common locution was "a certain empire"

Fig. 3.2 Marketing Humiliation in 1920

This advertisement, published in *Shenbao* on May 9, 1920, illustrates the way Chinese companies continued to associate resistance to Japanese imperialism with nationalistic consumption. It reminded readers of the significance of the anniversary of the Twenty-One Demands and the proper way to commemorate it through nationalistic consumption: "Compatriots! Pay attention! May Ninth is our National Humiliation Day. Fellow citizens, please be certain not to forget. In boycotting foreign products, one must begin by promoting national products. Our company's brands—Great Happiness, Peace, Mandarin Duck, Patriotic, and other brands— are one sort of national product. Wouldn't it be great if everyone quickly supported them."

(某帝國). For example, in Guangzhou, Chinese newspapers regularly received letters from readers offering money to support armed resistance against the "unwarranted aggression of a certain empire" (*NCH* 1915.3.27: 895–96). Likewise, Chinese were enjoined not to buy "inferior products" (劣貨), which along with "enemy products" became code words for Japanese goods (Reinsch 1922: 373).

Initially, references to this "certain empire" were reminders of the humiliations perpetrated by Japan. Increasingly, however, these references signified an appropriate response, instructions on forms of resistance. One carefully crafted pamphlet written in simple prose was open to several interpretations. In the most straightforward reading, the pamphlet discussed problems caused by the Japanese in China. Under scrutiny, it conveyed a more emotional statement: "Our country is becoming a second Korea!" The most inflammatory and central message had to be read from right to left, rather than from top to bottom, as was ordinary: "Citizens, don't buy Japanese goods" (*NCH* 1915.4.10: 84).

As rumors spread and tensions mounted, Shanghai police became more aggressive, often searching the houses of returned students, especially those who had been in Japan, and other known activists (*XWB* 1915.4.2 and 3).[29] In response, advocates of more aggressive anti-Japanese activities began expressing dissent by adopting the organizational forms, slogans, and techniques of the movement. This led contemporary observers and historians to misinterpret the movement as a whole as simply an extension of the boycott led by students and opportunistic business leaders. Matsumoto Shigeharu's interpretation of movement activities during 1915 is typical:

The movement for the 'Encouragement of the Use of Native Products' [i.e., the National Products Movement] which was still no more than a camouflaged boycott movement, came into existence first in Shanghai, where by March 16th an Association for the Encouragement of the Use of Native Products was formed under the auspices of the Chinese students who returned from Japan. Later in Hanyang, Hankow, Changsha, and in many other cities similar organizations were established. These associations carried on the boycott, carefully evading the law and authority. (Matsumoto 1933: 40)

Clearly, the founding of the NPPA in 1911 and the subsequent development of the movement into all the areas described in this book demonstrate that the movement was much more than a superficial "camouflage" for boycotts. Still, Matsumoto and others were certainly correct about two things. First, the patriotic rhetoric and nonconfrontational techniques of the movement insulated many of its activities from official censure. Indeed, local and national agencies sponsored many movement activities such as exhibitions and fashion shows (see Chapters 5–8). Second, the movement grew rapidly because of popular outrage over the Twenty-One Demands. Boycotts contributed directly to the popularity and development of non-boycott movement activities.

ORGANIZING FOR NATIONAL SURVIVAL

The threat of government retaliation encouraged protestors to adopt the tactics and vocabulary and organizational strategies of the movement.[30] At the same time, Chinese business leaders, students, intellectuals, and many others worked from below to form organizations to develop this sentiment.

---

29. One case of the police confiscating handbills from students returned from Japan received much attention at the time; see *XWB* 1915.4.10, 19, and 29.

30. President Yuan Shikai repeatedly ordered provincial authorities to end local boycotts, prohibit discussions of the negotiations, disband organizations, and censor telegrams (M. Chi 1970: 60).

For instance, contributing to a National Salvation Fund (救國儲金) became a popular and less risky way of participating in the movement. In April 1915, the Awareness of the Humiliation Association (知恥會) set up a fund in Shanghai to solicit $50 million (here and below, these are Chinese *yuan*) to "ensure national survival" by constructing arsenals, raising an army, and building a navy as well as financing domestic industries. As the immediate threat of war with Japan receded, the economic elites in charge of the fund gradually shifted the emphasis to the objective of economic development.[31]

The National Salvation Fund quickly became a socially and legally acceptable way to express what one observer called "practical nationalism." In just three weeks in April, the campaign raised and deposited $250,000 in the Bank of China. As money poured in from all over China and overseas, the management of the fund became more sophisticated and formed special committees to explain the purposes of the fund to depositors. In allowing only Chinese to contribute and setting no limits on subscriptions, the fund's regulations reflected the larger goals of the movement. The appeal found broad support, even among poor Chinese. It provided such a seemingly innocuous way to express anti-imperialism that many government officials, civil servants, members of the armed forces, and policemen agreed to contribute one month's salary, which was expected to raise over $10 million (*XWB* 1915.5.10; *NCH* 1915.6.19: 825–26). Naturally, the Japanese understood the deeper meaning of these deposits and claimed that donations to such funds by Chinese officials revealed these officials' support for boycotts and their cover, the National Products Movement (*NCH* 1915.6.26: 944). Although initiated in Shanghai, by May there were 70 branch committees for the fund throughout China.[32] Within a few months, Shanghai had collected $640,000, along with pledges of another $700,000; $1,940,000 was amassed in Beijing; and $2,100,000 in other provincial cities. By June, $20 million of the $50 million target had been raised (*XWB* 1915.4.15 and 28).

Many of the most powerful economic and political magnates openly supported the fund.[33] Under the direction of such elites in Shanghai, deposits

---

31. See "Jiuguo chujin" (National Salvation Fund) and "Shexu" (The society's manifesto) in *Zhichi hui* 1915, vol. 1. This volume also contains the bylaws of the group set up to administer the fund. See also *NCH* 1915.4.24: 255.

32. For a partial list of these locations, see Kikuchi 1974: 164–65.

33. In cities such as Fuzhou, prominent local men created their own fund to establish Chinese industries; see "Association for Promoting Chinese Industrial Interests Formed at

quickly expanded, as did new ways of finding participants. The success of the fund spawned more ambitious plans and organizations. A group of Shanghai business leaders that included NPPA leader Wu Tingfang established a group modeled after the National Salvation Fund. The new group had a sharper focus. Knowing that even with $50 million China could not build an army, navy, and industry, the new group, the League of China, placed development of domestic industry at the top of its agenda (*NCH* 1915.6.19: 825–26).[34]

Movement organizations also took more overtly pro-boycott positions. In March 1915, for example, some one hundred representatives from twenty major native-place associations met in the International Settlement of Shanghai to form the Association to Encourage the Use of National Products (專用國貨會). The members of this group resolved not to accept consignments of Japanese goods or use Japanese ships to transport goods. They also resolved to sever relations with Japanese merchants. Despite the Beijing government's ban on explicitly pro-boycott organizations, within a few months, the association had members in seventy cities and towns and counted politicians among its ranks, including a future minister of foreign affairs, Wang Zhengting (Kikuchi 1974: 164; Cochran 1980: 68).[35] Even a Japanese paper that favored compelling China to end the boycott acknowledged that because these organizations often did not explicitly support the boycott, there was little Japan could force the Chinese government to do (*Ōsaka Mainichi shinbun*, quoted in *NCH* 1915.7.10: 87–88).

THE NPPA THROUGH 1915

The events of 1915 fueled tremendous growth within movement organizations such as the NPPA, which expanded the frequency and scope of its activities. The Chinese resistance increasingly resorted to forms of expression typical of the National Products Movement because Japan could not be confronted directly by state-sponsored military confrontations or tariffs.

Foochow" (1919.7.29), CRDS File 893.60/12. This local consul's report observes that "the aim of the association is an anti-Japanese one."

34. The frequent newspaper reports on these funds also underscore their popularity and innocuous appearance. See, e.g., the run of articles in *XWB* 1915.4.7, 8, and 10.

35. The NPPA also sent one of its leading members, Wang Wendian, to help establish the group and write its bylaws (Shanghai Nippon shōgyō kaigisho 1915: 65; SB 1915.5.17 and 31).

Boycotts acted as a sort of membership drive. From slightly over a hundred members during its first year, the NPPA grew steadily for the first few years. During 1915, however, membership soared to 688, a 26 percent increase over the previous year, the highest single-year increase (ZGWH 1932: "Hu-ishi" section, 12). Moreover, the structure of the membership changed, as the group encouraged women to join.[36] Generally, however, new types of members largely account for this growth in membership. The initial bylaws of the association made joining difficult; native-place associations "with common interests" had to receive approval from the representatives of all other associations (ZGWH 1912: 3b). During 1915, however, membership expanded to include three new types. In addition to native-place associations and individual members, enterprises also began sending representatives—49 in 1915, with more joining every year.

In its first three years of activities, the NPPA published and distributed over 100,000 pieces of literature per year, including membership information, circulars on and promotions of national products, verification of the status of products, group advertisements, and so on. During 1915, however, the total expanded to over 300,000. The numbers alone do not tell the full story—the NPPA explicitly instructed recipients to circulate copies.

Because local, regional, and national Chinese government officials advocated policies promoting national products, investigations and certifications of the status of goods became an increasingly important function of movement organizations. These "certifications" became especially important during boycotts, when teams of students would scour local stores looking for imports to impound, confiscate, or destroy.[37] Because "treasonous

---

36. By 1919, the only year for which there is a complete membership list, 41 of the 749 members were women; see "Zhonghua guohuo weichi hui tongzhi quanlu" (A complete record of the NPPA membership), SZMA File 454: 20–21. On the role of women and representations of women in the movement, see Chapter 7.

37. The Chinese press across China carried accounts of student investigation teams. On these teams in Jiangsu province, for instance, see "Liuhe xian xuesheng fenhui Rihuo" (Liuhe county students burn Japanese products), *Nanjing xuesheng lianhehui rikan* 1919.7.21, reprinted in ZDLDG 1992: 229–30. Merchants also participated in such investigations. In one town on the Yangzi, an ad hoc product investigation office was established right at the dock; see "Qingjiang pu shangjie you fenhui Rihuo" (At the Qingjiang port, commercial circles again burn Japanese products), *XWB* 1919.7.16, and "Qingjiang shangxuejie fenhui Rihuo" (Qingjiang commercial and student circles burn Japanese products), *XWB* 1919.7.7, republished in ZDLDG 1992: 236 and 241. See also W.-H. Yeh 1996: 147–48.

merchants" (奸商) often relabeled products during boycotts and companies intentionally mislabeled products, every product came under suspicion.[38] In this environment, such classifications could make or break a company. Before the NPPA allowed a commercial or industrial enterprise to join, it sent a team to investigate the applicant's products for, among other things, the national origins of the raw materials used in its products, its source of capital, and the nationalities of its employees. In its first year, 1912, the NPPA conducted only eleven such investigations. As with other activities of the NPPA, however, things took off in 1915, when it conducted 383 such investigations, a total only equaled or exceeded in two other years with widespread boycotts, 383 in 1925 and a high of 464 in 1928 (ZGWH 1932: "Huishi" section, 14–16).

The NPPA published the results of these investigations along with other propaganda in an increasing array of publications. Two of the more innovative were the *Records of National Products Investigations* (國貨調查錄) and *The National Products Monthly* (國貨月報). The purpose of the *Records* was to disseminate an approved list of domestically manufactured products; this gave both domestic manufacturers a place to promote their wares and merchants a means of finding replacements for imported products. Along with lists of boycotted products, publishing lists of products that were sufficiently Chinese became a standard part of the movement.[39] Each addition to the list strengthened the concept of a national product defined implicitly against presumably "non-Chinese, unpatriotic products." This distinction made the benefits of attaching a national products label to one's products more compelling to domestic producers. Advertisements also made the distinction between national and foreign products more apparent.

---

38. Companies went to great lengths to conceal the foreign origins of their products. One investigation team, for instance, uncovered Japanese matches that had "Long live the Chinese Republic" printed on their covers; see "Qingjiang xuesheng jixu cha Rihuo" (Qingjiang students continue to investigate Japanese products), *XWB* 1919.10.11, republished in ZDLDG 1992: 232–33.

39. Wu Tingfang's Foreword to Wang Hanqiang 1915. These *Records* were widely circulated. For instance, see the reprint in Shanhai Nippon shōgyō kaigisho 1915: 77–127. For an example from the anti-Japanese boycott of 1928, see "Rihuo yilan biao" (Japanese goods at a glance), a chart published in Zhongguo Guomindang, Hebei sheng dangwu zhidao weiyuanhui 1928: 19–65.

The Movement and Continuity Between Boycotts

It is understandable that many observers and historians have concluded that the movement was an aftereffect of boycotts or a sideshow to them. By late 1915, the political confrontation between Japan and China had slipped from the front pages of Chinese and foreign newspapers, Chinese authorities had successfully suppressed open anti-Japanese boycotts, and some of the more strident activism within the movement had disappeared. According to trade statistics, Sino-Japanese economic relations returned to their pre-1915 levels.[40] From this perspective, the nationalistic sentiments and activities underlying the boycott were, perhaps, merely "five minutes of excitement" or a "cycle."

But this conclusion is mistaken. The broader movement had been building for decades. Even after boycotts began to flag in cities such as Changsha, the provincial capital of Hunan, the sentiments behind them remained, sustaining the movement. As one foreign reporter noted: "No one seems to have a good word to say about Japan. . . . [There] seems to be a general idea that Japan has asked for and has gained certain things that will eventually land China into the plight that Korea is in" (NCH 1915.6.19: 826).[41] These attitudes became part of everyday Chinese life. A year after the spring of 1915, the "humiliation" surrounding the Twenty-One Demands continued to be inculcated in new ways (Reinsch 1922: chap. 12). For instance, a book on Chinese chess named strategies after diplomatic humiliations in Chinese modern history. Each lesson illustrated chess positions and contained a brief history of the humiliation at the center of the lesson.[42] The boycott had also provided an opportunity for Chinese goods to replace Japanese ones. Hundreds of new Chinese factories sprung up, producing Chinese substitutes for popular Japanese products such as soap, matches, towels, cotton products, shoes and boots, umbrellas, and candles.[43]

---

40. In Remer's words (1933a: 53), "Trade statistics show that the effect of the boycott was temporary disturbance of the trade rather than any falling off."

41. Another reporter for the same paper noted that not only did the boycott severely affect trade, but it also left a lasting impression and distrust of Japan; see "China's Boycott of Japan: Decrease in Japanese Trade," NCH 1915.7.24: 220.

42. Guochi jiannian xiangqi xinju 1916. The foreword confirms that the purpose of the book was to connect China's most recent humiliation (1915) to the nation's much longer history of such humiliations.

43. Chinese Maritime Customs, Returns of Trade 1915: 1; quoted in Remer 1933a: 48.

The events of 1915 provided fuel to the movement, but it was neither the first nor the last source. The number of "national humiliation days" (國恥日) continued to grow, as did the intensity surrounding their commemoration. More specifically, movement organizations such as the NPPA continued to expand their hierarchies of dissemination, for example, by helping to establish leading organizations during the turmoils of 1919 and 1923 and other years.[44] The movement also sought to amplify its ethic of nationalistic consumption, especially by stressing the importance of having women and children keep the nation in mind when making purchases (see Chapter 7). Although some forms of movement activism may have declined temporarily between boycotts, the history of the NPPA suggests that resistance through forms of consumption persisted and spread, ever ready to generate, define, and absorb new expressions of nationalism and antiimperialism.

The Boycott of 1919

The protests surrounding the Versailles Peace Conference (1919) provide another example of the significance of boycotts. As we shall see, the activities, organizations, and rhetoric surrounding one of the most famous episodes in modern Chinese history were part of the National Products Movement. The history of the movement suggests that conventional interpretations of this era overemphasize the role of students in forging political and elite cultural change and overlook the significance of the boycott at the heart of the May Fourth Movement in nationalizing consumption.[45] It is

---

44. These organizations include the Industrial and Commercial Study Society of China for the Preservation of International Peace (中華工商保存國際和平研究會), formed in early 1919, and the Shanghai Citizens Association on Sino-Japanese Relations (上海對日外交市民大會), established in 1923.

45. Chow Tse-tsung 1960 is the premier example of studies that emphasize student agency. Many textbooks take a similar approach. See, e.g., the cursory coverage of this boycott in Hsü 1983: 504. This overemphasis on students and the intellectual aspects of the May Fourth Movement may be a result of the inordinate attention paid to Beijing. In Shanghai, the movement was a "total, popular, patriotic protest movement of the Chinese *people* for direct political action, as distinct from the 'thought' oriented, iconoclastic, new culture movement of the Chinese intelligentsia" (J. T. Chen 1971: xi). It may also result from the fact that many of the subsequent Chinese historians of the May Fourth movement had participated in it as students.

easy to dismiss the activities of non-student actors in the May Fourth Movement, since they appeared to be following the lead of students, forming less contentious versions of student organizations, and participating in less strident activism under the politically safer rubric of "promoting domestic products." However, the vigorous student support of the boycott itself strongly suggests the importance of regarding the movement as a primary force in modern Chinese history rather than a mere epiphenomenon or minor subset of "student protest."

As with earlier boycotts, a specific "national humiliation" was at the center of protests in 1919. This time the issue was a shift in the foreign control of Shandong province. In 1898, Germany began to carve out a "sphere of interest" in the province, with a naval base and colony at Jiaozhou Bay (at Qingdao) and extensive mining and railroad interests (see Schrecker 1971). During World War I, however, Japan took over and expanded the German possessions in Shandong and required China to recognize its interests there as part of the Twenty-One Demands. China had expected to recover control of the Shandong concessions as a reward for entering the war against Germany. Woodrow Wilson's rhetoric of self-determination heightened this expectation. However, Japan had carefully laid the groundwork for assuming control. Early on, Japan solidified its hold over Shandong through additional arrangements and treaties with the Beijing government. In September 1918, for instance, Japan signed a secret agreement with Beijing that acknowledged Japanese control in exchange for a loan of 20 million yen. The publicizing of these agreements during the Versailles Peace Conference sparked Chinese demonstrations. Despite the outcry in China, the conference formally recognized Japanese interests in Shandong in April. The "Shandong Question," as it came to be known, became emblematic of the two fundamental threats to Chinese sovereignty: internal division created by warlordism and external menaces from imperialism.

This latest humiliation was soon integrated into larger narratives directly connected to 1915. On May 4, several thousand students gathered at Tiananmen Square at the entrance to the Forbidden City to advocate the return of Qingdao and denounce the Versailles settlement. The students had originally planned to hold the demonstration on May Seventh, the symbolically charged anniversary of the Twenty-One Demands. When it became clear, however, that other groups were planning demonstrations for this date, student leaders opted to advance the date of their protest to May 4 (Jansen

1975: 250–51).[46] In the following weeks and months, the inhabitants of some 200 Chinese cities spread over twenty provinces participated in strikes and boycotts that lasted, depending on the place, until 1920 or 1921 (Chow Tse-tsung 1960: 144).[47]

THE BOYCOTT

The demonstrations in Shanghai reveal the salience of the "5-9" anniversary.[48] On May 7, at least 10,000 persons, including 3,000 students, attended the first major rally to support the students in Beijing at the Public Recreation Ground, outside the West Gate in the Chinese city (SB 1919.5.7 and 8; NCH 1919.5.10: 370).[49] Many students brought pennants that read "National Humiliation" and "5-9" (SB 1919.5.7; see the photograph in SB 1919.5.8). Furthermore, on the anniversary itself, announcements covered the front page of the Shenbao regarding theaters, schools, businesses, social organizations, and public offices closed for the day (SB 1919.5.7–9). These protests were widely observed. Some prostitutes even participated in commemorating the May Ninth anniversary by closing their workplaces for the day and leaving explanations on their doors (SB 1919.5.10).

The protest aimed to translate humiliation into retaliation. Protestors urged Chinese to respond to the latest humiliation by boycotting Japanese products, ships, and currency.[50] Posters announcing the boycott appeared in store windows throughout the Chinese-controlled part of the city (SB 1919.5.10). Movement organizations such as the NPPA sent detailed direc-

---

46. In other cities, including Ji'nan, the commemoration of 1915 and new protests did converge; see "A Conference for the Commemoration of National Humiliation," Dadong ribao 1919.5.7 (extra), translated in the consular report, CRDS File 893.3165.

47. For a mammoth collection of Japanese newspaper articles on this boycott, see Fujimoto and Kyōto daigaku, Jinbun kagaku kenkyūjo 1983.

48. Many comprehensive histories of national humiliations published during 1919 incorporated the latest humiliations. The cover of one, published shortly after the May Fourth Incident of 1919, emphasized May Ninth. It shows a hatchet inscribed with the numbers 5-9 splitting a Chinese man's head. Unlike previous histories, however, this one focuses exclusively on Japanese humiliations of China (Gongmin jiuguo tuan 1919).

49. The newly formed Citizens Association (國民大會) organized the event. The association grew out of 30 or so commercial and educational groups. For the entire list of members, see SB 1919.5.6.

50. Japanese newspapers carried extensive reports on the Chinese use of the term "humiliation." See, e.g., Ōsaka Asahi shinbun 1919.5.6, 8, 9, and 14, reprinted in Fujimoto and Kyōto daigaku, Jinbun kagaku kenkyūjo 1983: 43, 46–47, 51, and 61.

tions to other cities on how to conduct a boycott, noting, among other things, how to publicly humiliate merchants caught selling contraband goods (SZMA File 690: 12a–b). Like many other merchant organizations, the Book Guild called on members to close on May Ninth and post signs outside their shops using the characters "National Humiliation," clearly linking the shop closing to the economic protest (SB 1919.5.8; see also Shanghai shehui kexueyuan, Lishi yanjiusuo 1960: 186–91). Other stores made a more explicit connection by posting signs that read: "As of today, this store will never sell Japanese products" (Shanghai shehui kexueyuan, Lishi yanjiusuo 1960: 189).[51]

THE ROMANCE OF STUDENT RESISTANCE

What was the role of students in boycotts? Did they "lead" the boycotts, or was their participation in boycotts motivated by the ideology of the National Products Movement? Student organizations undoubtedly played the most visible role in every aspect of the May Fourth boycotts. As a result, observers and scholars have implied or concluded that students were the driving force behind this and later boycotts.[52] The best study of the boycotts acknowledges as much: "It was a movement which was initiated by students and which depended chiefly upon students for its perpetuation" (Remer 1933b: 55). Ironically, Japanese opponents of the boycott were as anxious as contemporary Western observers and latter-day Communist historians to give full credit to student leadership. Doing so made it possible to dismiss the boycotters as irrational, unrealistic, and unruly hotheads. In contrast, such accounts downplay the role of merchants: "A close study [of the 1919 boycott] will reveal that many of the merchant class were very passive and not much interested in the movement."[53]

---

51. For three photographs of shuttered stores covered with such placards, see "The Chinese Boycott at Shanghai," *FER* 1919.7: 503–4.

52. This "student" category was, of course, a heterogeneous one, and each element had its own relationship to the boycotts and the movement. Two important studies, Israel 1966 and Wasserstrom 1991, highlight the conflicting interests of student organizations. On the gender disputes between such organizations, see Graham 1994. As with other studies of student activism, in this article, the links between organizations, activities, and discourses and the movement are a central but implicit part of the analysis.

53. See Matsumoto 1933: 63. He continues: "There is no denying that the local students' federations were the real focal point of the whole movement. It was these student organiza-

Yet student activities evinced, and depended centrally on, movement ideology. Indeed, student textbooks were full of its rhetoric (see Peake 1932: 164–65, 171, 172, 179).[54] In addition to supplying the ideology behind the boycott, the movement also contributed directly to its organization.[55] For instance, the NPPA and other commercial organizations began positioning themselves to assert their agenda vis-à-vis the Peace settlement. The growing activism underscored distrust of the Beijing government and popular fears that it would not act in the interests of domestic producers. As early as December 1918, the NPPA organized a conference to discuss the Paris Peace Conference. Hundreds of representatives from many groups showed up for the inaugural meeting and agreed to form an umbrella organization to push for the equal treatment of all countries at Versailles. Naturally, recovering economic and political sovereignty was at the top of their agenda, which demanded the abolition of the unequal treaties. Shortly after the opening of the Paris Conference in Versailles on January 13, 1919, the NPPA helped form one of the first groups to promote Chinese concerns at the talks, the Industrial and Commercial Study Society for the Preservation of International Peace (SZMA File 690).[56] This group's open letter to chambers of commerce soliciting support for a more favorable peace plan "probably represented the first spontaneous response of the Shanghai Chinese to the Versailles developments" (J. T. Chen 1971: 67).

The problem with this interpretation is that the NPPA not only cowrote the letter but also used its contacts with other organizations to form the new group. Therefore, it makes more sense to think of this new organization as an ad hoc group formed to represent pre-existing groups that had pre-existing agendas and ways of disseminating them. In any case, in quick

---

tions which prevailed upon the Chambers of Commerce and other mercantile bodies to resort to the boycott."

54. These textbooks were critical to the circulation of modern ideas of the nation. Various Japanese ministries and organizations kept close track of their contents. The editors of one collection of textbook materials charged such books instilled "a violent anti-foreign sentiment in the hearts of China's young millions" (Sokusha 1929: ii).

55. In other cities, however, the subordinate role of students was more discernable. One observer of the boycott in Shandong, for instance, concluded that chambers of commerce were the real power behind the boycott and the students merely propagandists; see Upton Close, "A Distressing Five Minutes," CWR 1919.8.2: 357–62.

56. The formation of the group was announced in an open letter dated Jan. 1, 1919, to the National Chamber of Commerce and chambers all over China. It was republished the next day in Minguo ribao (Shanghai shehui kexueyuan, Lishi yanjiusuo 1960: 141).

succession, other organizations, many already involved in the movement, sent telegrams to foreign and Chinese leaders in Paris, the Beijing authorities, other organizations, and to the Chinese press, all affirming opposition to the proposed treaty.[57] As it had during the 1915 boycotts, the NPPA stepped up its activities.

ENFORCING NATIONALISTIC CONSUMPTION

Within the movement, boycotts were most important for the ways they forcefully linked the idea of nationality to commodities. Because historians of modern Chinese history have long viewed the May Fourth era as a turning point, there are many studies and collections of documents covering the events of that year. These collections include material on boycotts, the formation of new organizations in the movement, and the promotion of national products through exhibitions, children's songs, expeditions to larger cities to find national products to introduce to smaller cities—a countless variety of activities.[58] Together, these materials provide extensive firsthand accounts of the fostering of an ethic of nationalistic consumption at the local level.

Choices in personal appearance continued to be highly politicized, and activists throughout the country abandoned imported clothing in favor of domestically made substitutes. The universally popular straw hats (which were often made in Japan) became a particular target of student enforcers of nationalistic consumption. Many students chose to wear white cloth caps instead (Chow Tse-tsung 1960: 153). There were many reports of students confiscating Japanese-made hats, kicking out the tops, and destroying them. One observer noted that public notice boards were "decorated with straw

---

57. These were the first of the numerous telegrams circulated by movement groups. See, e.g., *SB* 1919.5.7 or Shanghai shehui kexueyuan, Lishi yanjiusuo 1960: 178–81. For a translation of one such telegram, see *NCH* 1919.5.17: 413.

58. For examples of such collections, see Zhongguo shehui kexueyuan, Jindai shi yanjiusuo 1959; Shanghai shehui kexueyuan, Lishi yanjiusuo 1960; Hu Wenben and Tian Geshen 1980; Tianjin lishi bowuguan and Nankai daxue, Lishixi 1980; Zhang Yinghui and Gong Xiangzheng 1981; Henan sheng difangzhi bianji weiyuanhui 1983; Zhonggong, Sichuan sheng wei, Dangshi gongzuo weiyuanhui 1989; and ZDLDG 1992. Many smaller cities compiled similar, though unpublished, collections not intended for public circulation (e.g., *Suzhou Wusi, Wusa yungdong ziliao xuanji* 1984). Other cities published colloquial histories (e.g., Xiong Zongren 1986).

hats, umbrellas, thermos flasks, and other Japanese goods taken from pedestrians and destroyed by students" (Orchard 1930: 254).[59] Alternative hats were also used to signify support for the protests. In Shanghai, for instance, students at fourteen girls' schools pitched in to make 20,000 white mourning caps to express their protest (J. T. Chen 1971: 101).[60] Likewise, the carpenters' and masons' guilds resolved not to buy Japanese materials and supplied lists of approved materials to their members (NCH 1919.5.24: 508). At one point, Chinese even boycotted all foreign goods arriving on Japanese ships (Reinsch 1922: 369).[61] Naturally, the boycott extended to Japanese-controlled railways.[62]

Boycotts were particularly remarkable for speedily producing import-free spaces *outside* the specially designated "national product" spectacles (the boycott also generated a dramatic expansion in the size and number of the nationalistic commodity spectacles; see Part III). Overnight, physical and visual spaces throughout China became completely devoid of the targeted commodities. Not only did students and other participants stop wearing foreign goods, but smaller shops also destroyed, hid, or repackaged their stocks of Japanese goods (Ch'en Li-fu 1994: 15).[63] Even Wing On (Yong'an 永安) and Sincere (Xianshi 先施), two large Shanghai department stores that featured imports, removed Japanese products from their shelves and replaced them with products made in China and non-Japanese imports (SB advertisements 1919.5.20, 30, cited in J. T. Chen 1971: 94). Imports also disappeared from visual media. For instance, Chinese newspapers printed

---

59. For another instance of attacks on straw hats, see J. T. Chen 1971: 98n1. Similarly, the British consuls in Wuhan and Ningbo reported attacks on individuals suspected of wearing Japanese-made hats; see "Report on anti-Japanese Agitation in the Wu-Han cities" in British FO 371/3695 and Acting Consul Platt, 1919.5.29 in FO 371/3695.

60. The use of protest clothing became so widespread that the Shanghai Municipal Council forbade the use of clothing to indicate dissent (NCH 1919.6.14: 718).

61. In another instance of guilt by association, the missionary Margaret Moninger reported that her maid refused to buy Horlick's Malted Milk because Japanese merchants owned the shop selling the product. The enthusiasm for the boycott reported on Hainan Island also confirms how widely the boycott spread (Lodwick 1995: 53–54).

62. For instance, even students attending Ji'nan Women's Normal College in Shandong with families living near Japanese-controlled railways refused to take the train home for summer vacation (Lü and Zheng 1990: 302–3).

63. Japanese shopkeepers in Shanghai tried to get around the boycott by erasing the "Made in Japan" labels (NCH 1919.5.31–30: 551).

Fig. 3.3 "National Humiliation Commemorative Poster" (1920)
(courtesy of the Japanese Ministry of Foreign Affairs Archives, Tokyo)

This large poster shows two middle-school students (as indicated by their school flag) passing out leaflets in anticipation of the May Ninth anniversary. It reads: "Compatriots Who Love Our Nation, Please Use National Products and Please Don't Forget This May 9." The flag fluttering above their heads similarly urges people not to forget the anniversary. Students of all ages were an important and highly visible part of the movement, particularly during anti-imperialist boycotts and on commemoration days.

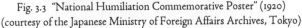

notices that they would not accept advertisements for Japanese products (Jordon to Curson, F.O. 405/226/72, 1919.7.7). Eight major Shanghai newspapers vowed not to accept Japanese advertisements or publish Japanese commercial news (*NCH* 1919.5.17: 415–16; Zhen 1997: 47–48).[64]

The irony, of course, was that students were now demanding that Chinese manufacturers aid the boycott and anti-imperialist efforts by doing precisely what generations of "commercial war" proponents, many of whom were manufacturers, had been advocating (see Fig. 3.3). Students had clearly

64. In Tianjin, Zhou Enlai's short-lived publication, the *Tianjin Federation of Students News* (*Tianjin xuesheng lianhehui bao*), not only provided extensive coverage of the boycotts and protests but also aided the movement in a direct way by refusing to publish any advertisements for Japanese goods and by offering a 50 percent discount to companies advertising Chinese products (C.-J. Lee 1994: 126).

embraced the movement agenda as their own (see *NCH* 1919.5.17: 416). The Shanghai Federation of Students (上海學生聯合會) and the Industrial College of Shanghai, for instance, issued a manifesto calling on Chinese manufacturers to produce cheap, stylish, and high-quality substitutes for Japanese products. The students themselves even pitched in to produce items such as cloth umbrellas, handkerchiefs, book bags, and children's toys, on which they printed slogans such as "Don't Forget the Humiliation" and "Boycott Japanese Goods" (Lü and Zheng 1990: 303).[65] In Zhenjiang, students established "national product peddler squads" (國貨負販團) to hawk such items in the city and surrounding countryside.[66]

PLEDGING TO CONSUME PATRIOTICALLY

The most radical advocates of the boycott were members of small groups that vigorously enforced nationalistic consumption. The May protests saw the re-emergence and dramatic expansion of the Groups of Ten for National Salvation (救國十人團).[67] At their most basic level, each group had ten members. Ten of these basic groups formed the next higher level of organization, and a hundred of these formed the highest level (i.e., 1,000 groups, or 10,000 participants) (J. T. Chen 1971: 96–97).[68] Participants pledged to consume only Chinese products, ensure that their group-mates did the same, and attempt to persuade others to form new groups.[69] In Shanghai, such groups had been established in 1915. And in 1919, these groups sprung up among male and female students and spread to workers,

---

65. There is evidence that students set up such national product companies in many cities. On one such company in Suzhou, see "Suzhou Taowu zhongxue xuesheng hui kaiban guohuo gongsi" (Students at Taowu Middle School in Suzhou open a national products store), *Shibao* 1919.8.8, reprinted in ZDLDG 1992: 231.

66. On one such team, see "Zhenjiang xuesheng zuzhi guohuo fufan tuan" (Students in Zhenjiang organize a national product peddler team), *SB* 1919.8.5, reprinted in ZDLDG 1992: 231.

67. For the most comprehensive study of these organizations, see Ono 1994.

68. This mutual-responsibility system was modeled on forms of community responsibly practiced in imperial China, particularly the household responsibility (*baojia* 保甲) system, which was used as late as the Qing; see K.-C. Hsiao 1967.

69. Of course, members of other organizations made similar pledges, though usually in milder language. See, e.g., the membership card for the Shandong Promote National Products Research Association (山東提倡國貨研究會). See Academia Sinica, Modern History Institute Archives, Foreign Ministry Archives File 114: "Shandong pai-Ri fengchao an (2)."

merchants, and other social classes in Beijing, Tianjin, Ji'nan, Changsha, and other urban centers (Chow Tse-tsung 1960: 140).[70] By the end of the summer, in Tianjin there was a citywide alliance of hundreds of such groups.

Members vowed to cleanse their own consumption of imports, swearing "by death not to buy any of our enemy's goods and not to allow the enemy to paste his advertisements on our house" (*NCH* 1919.5.17: 415–16). They also swore not to use Japanese banks or banknotes. To encourage others to follow their lead, groups organized lectures and participated in fundraisers to support the establishment of Chinese companies.[71] As pressure to end the boycott mounted, these groups shifted their overt activities toward the movement agenda, and, indeed, throughout the movement there were milder and more informal groups.[72] In Beijing, for example, they "acted as volunteer sales agents for Chinese industrialists and for the merchants who sold native goods." As with other movement activities, promoting "native goods" required having a list of "Chinese" companies and products. One of the first orders of business was to survey locally marketed products and compile a list of acceptably "Chinese" products. The groups distributed a list of 80 such enterprises to help retailers identify domestic substitutes for Japanese products (Chow Tse-tsung 1960: 147–48). They also monitored the activities of merchants suspected of betraying the boycott. The investigations of such groups, for example, forced at least one major department store to take out daily advertisements vowing that it would discontinue selling Japanese products (Shanghai Hualian shangxia dang wei 1991: 15; SB 1919.5.20). At the very least, such groups "played an important function as watchdog structures that made their own members and outsiders stick to the 'laws' of the anti-Japanese boycott" (Wasserstrom 1991: 66–67).

---

70. On the movement and these groups in 1919 in Changsha, see McDonald 1978: 95–107. On these groups in smaller towns, see, e.g., "Xuzhou xuesheng zuzhi shirentuan" (Xuzhou students organize Groups of Ten), *XWB* 1919.12.4, in ZDLDG 1992: 355–56. In Suzhou, women participating in all-women groups passed out fliers door-to-door; see "Suzhou nüzi aiguo shirentuan tichang guohuo" (Suzhou women's patriotic Groups of Ten promote national products), *Shibao* 1919.7.19, republished in ZDLDG 1992: 246–47.

71. These groups may have influenced the formation of Communist Party cells in Shanghai two years later (J. T. Chen 1971: 97–98*n*3).

72. For a suggestion that friends form such informal groups, see "Funü fuyong guohuo she de changyi" (Proposals by the Women's Use National Products Society), *SB* 1934.9.27. On the use of pledges in the movement, see "Xuanshi fuyong guohuo" (Pledging to use national products), *SB* 1935.4.18.

BENEFITING FROM THE MOVEMENT

The boycott motivated Chinese, for reasons of both patriotism and profit, to form new companies. Even scholars who downplay merchant participation in the events of 1919 reluctantly concede that the movement agenda promoted domestic industry and proactive industrial policies. The governor of Hubei, for instance, lowered taxes on 77 Chinese-produced fabrics to promote their local manufacture (Matsumoto 1933: 64). There is much anecdotal evidence that Chinese products were supplanting Japanese ones throughout China (Remer 1933b: 58). The Maritime Customs commissioner for the port of Changsha observed that the boycott and efforts to promote national products had made it easy to buy "most articles of daily use 'made in China,' whereas before this movement, similar articles were mostly Japanese in origin."[73]

A few perceptive foreign observers also discerned the movement underlying the boycott and demonstrations.[74] As a French diplomat told the American minister to China Paul S. Reinsch (1869–1923): "We are in the presence of the most astounding and important thing that has ever happened—the organization of a national public opinion in China for positive action." Reinsch understood that the movement was more than student camouflage for boycotts. He also viewed the events of 1919 in a similar way: "It gave great impetus to the development of Chinese industry, and gave both the manufacturers and the Government a clue as to what a definite campaign for the stimulation of the home industries might accomplish" (Reinsch 1922: 373).

Most important, although impossible to measure, was the growth of a nationalistic consumer consciousness by the conspicuous broadening of the movement through the boycott, which made a much greater attempt to enlist and demand the participation of all Chinese. As one reporter noted, in contrast to earlier boycotts that appealed directly to merchants and storeowners, "It is the consumer that is being appealed to, and it is the consumer that is answering the call" (CWR 1919.6.21: 119).

---

73. Maritime Customs, *Trade Report* 1919, vol. 1: 469, quoted in McDonald 1978: 101.

74. However, other foreign observers mocked the Chinese inability to successfully boycott Japanese goods; see, e.g., "The Failure of the Boycott," *FER* 1920.8: 389–90. Earlier, this same periodical had termed the boycott "immoral," "illegal," and "foolish" and its leaders "overgrown children" ("End the Anti-Japanese Boycott," *FER* 1920.7).

LOCAL BOYCOTTS AS LOCAL
FUEL FOR THE MOVEMENT

New humiliations continually stoked anti-imperialist sentiments and kept the boycotts alive. Indeed, it is not clear that boycotts ever "ended." In most places, they gradually declined, only to be rekindled by new humiliations. Local variation makes it difficult to generalize about the specific timing and role of boycotts within the movement across all of China. Because the boycotts (and the movement) were entwined with other issues, some cities had their own particular outrages to commemorate. These local incidents were sometimes protested nationally and other times not. For instance, the Fuzhou Incident of November 1919 gave new life to several boycotts. The trouble began with fighting between Chinese students and Taiwanese working to protect Japanese commercial property. Shots were fired, and students were killed. Word of this latest humiliation reignited the boycott in Fuzhou, Shanghai, and other cities. Similarly, in early 1920, when the peace treaty with Germany went into effect, Japanese officials contacted Chinese leaders to discuss various aspects of the transfer of control over German interests in Shandong. Although the Beijing government kept a low profile to avoid inciting further popular condemnation, word of the talks eventually slipped out and prompted rallies across China.

Recasting the boycotts of 1919 in the context of the movement confirms the conclusion of a comprehensive study of the May Fourth Movement in Shanghai. According to Joseph Chen (1971: 198):

In the economic realm, one of the most notable effects was that mounting economic nationalism stimulated the further growth of national industries and commerce in China. The effectiveness of boycotts and commercial strikes in the city taught the Chinese that to curtail and combat effectively Japanese economic interests in China, they must first have better organization, abundant capital, government protection, better management and improved products. Most important, they must first secure the abolition of extraterritoriality and the unequal treaties. Until all the vested economic interests in China were removed, the nascent Chinese industries and commerce would continue to suffer from overpowering foreign economic competition.

As we have seen, none of this was new in 1919. Consideration of the broader history of the National Products Movement reveals many aspects of May Fourth to be less a great turning point in modern Chinese history than a dramatic acceleration and expansion of the movement agenda of nationalizing consumer culture.

CHAPTER FOUR

The Movement and Anti-Imperialist Boycotts, 1923-1937

Commercial Warfare can defeat Military Warfare. By remembering May Ninth and May Thirtieth, Triangle towels will destroy Anchor Brand towels.

—Advertisement in a Shanghai newspaper for Chinese Triangle towels, which competed against Japanese Anchor towels, June 1925

"I'm sorry. We don't have foreign products. We only have national products."

—The suggested response for patriotic merchants to use when customers ask for a foreign-brand product

Frequent anti-imperialist boycotts continued to nationalize Chinese consumer culture in the 1920s and 1930s. These new boycotts strengthened the link between objects and nationalities through increasingly violent and vigorous means. Individual boycotts are part of the larger narrative of the National Products Movement: the movement shaped each boycott, and, in turn, boycotts expanded the movement. Boycotts were significant not for their short-term economic impact on trade but for their role in producing a specific type of nationalistic consciousness centered on the consumption of "Chinese" commodities and the nonconsumption of "foreign" products. At the same time, the absence of imports during boycotts created economic opportunities for domestic manufacturers. Part I of the chapter continues the exploration of boycotts and ends by briefly considering the impact of the formation of the Nationalist government in 1927–28. As with other aspects of the movement such as commodity spectacles (see the next two chapters),

---

EPIGRAPH 2: "Riben de tichang guohuo fangfa." The article claimed that Japanese merchants discouraged consumption of imports in Japan with a similar response to requests for foreign-brand products.

the new government contributed additional resources to boycott institutions and, more generally, to the movement.

Part II of this chapter shifts away from the boycotts themselves and addresses the fundamental problem underlying boycotts and the movement: What exactly is a "national product"? How were boundaries established between Chinese and foreign products? Since the inception of the movement, activists had been struggling to create and disseminate explicit product categories. Such categories—however arbitrary and unstable—were essential to all movement activities. Although the Nationalist government cannot be credited with inventing these categories, the re-establishment of a relatively centralized political authority in 1927–28 helped greatly in codifying and popularizing national product definitions.

PART I

BOYCOTTS, 1923–37

In spring 1923, Japan remained a focus of Chinese anti-imperialism and a target for the activities of a re-energized movement.[1] A series of reports prepared in 1923 by American consulates across China observed the links between foreign, particularly Japanese, "humiliations" of China and a growing sense of anti-imperialism. A report from Ji'nan, the provincial capital of Shandong, for instance, concludes: "Aggression on the part of Japan . . . arouses feelings of intense antagonism and opposition and a sense of injustice, humiliation and degradation suffered at foreign hands." But this animosity was directed against others as well. The report also observes a changing attitude among children, who now brazenly call foreigners "foreign devil[s]" and are "not rebuked or checked by their elders."[2] On the eve of a rejuvenated boycott, these reports also note that this environment was undermining the ability of foreigners to live in China: "There exists in the breast of every Chinese an inherent emotion of intense aversion for the Japanese." As a result, foreigners were having "great difficulty" buying or leasing land from Chinese.[3]

---

1. For detailed reports on the anti-Japanese boycotts in major cities throughout China, see "Chōsho, taisaku ikken, chinjō-sho, oyobi kō-shi dantai hōkoku, kyūmin kyūsai, zatsu."

2. "Changing attitude of the Chinese towards foreigners in China" (Ji'nan, 1923.3.28), CRDS File 893.4974: 4.

3. "Changing attitude of the Chinese towards foreigners in China" (Zhifou, 1923.4.7), CRDS File 893.4972. See also CRDS File 893.4973 (Hankou, 1923.4.2): 2–3.

Shortly thereafter, the situation worsened. At the center of a new controversy was the old issue of Japanese territorial expansion. After defeating Russia in 1904–5, Japan took control of Russian possessions in Manchuria, including the Liaodong Peninsula on the Manchurian coast west of Korea. The Sino-Russian treaty of 1898, which allowed Russia to lease the ice-free shipping center of Lüshun (Port Arthur) and Dalian (Dairen) on the peninsula for 25 years, was scheduled to end on March 26, 1923. However, in the settlement to the Twenty-One Demands of 1915, the Chinese under Yuan Shikai had agreed to extend the lease to 99 years (as, for example, the British had obtained for Kowloon, the peninsula opposite Hong Kong Island) (see Lensen 1966). Chinese nationalists argued that because the treaty had been signed under duress and because the Chinese National Assembly had never ratified this new lease, it was invalid even according to international conventions. Chinese politicians repeatedly refused to acknowledge the treaty, and there were popular demonstrations over the issue, including the boycotts of 1915 and 1919. In spring 1923, as the original 25-year lease was set to expire, Chinese nationalists wanted the territories returned.

In late March, when it became clear that Japan would not return the leased territories, another anti-Japanese boycott began. The boycott spread throughout north and central China in April, especially the Lower Yangzi area. It was particularly active in Changsha, the provincial capital of Hunan, where there was a large Japanese community. It lasted around five months, dropping from the headlines by early September. Although it was shorter than earlier boycotts, many accounts suggest that it was much more intense (Kikuchi 1974: 201–3). A new term, "severance of economic relations" (經濟絕交) (see Zhou Shouyi 1923), which became popular during the boycott, indicates the increasingly radical role of boycotts within the movement. Previous boycotts had promoted the nonconsumption of boycotted products and services. In 1923, boycotters began to use much more aggressive techniques to disrupt sales by intimidating Japanese merchants and their families, urging landlords not to rent to Japanese, and advocating the complete cessation of all relations with Japan, including the refusal to sell to or work for Japanese (NCH 1923.3.31: 867; CWR 1923.3.31: 180).

This boycott also witnessed stricter enforcement of nationalistic consumption on Chinese. One segment of society, in the name of patriotism, sought to deny those Chinese consumers deemed insufficiently patriotic the power of consumer choice. For instance, Chinese caught riding Japanese ships had "traitor" stamped on their clothes upon disembarking. In other cases, Japanese boats were prevented from docking (see, e.g., CRDS File 893.4995 [1923.5.17]). Chinese who had worked for Japanese were forced to march at the head of demonstrations and apologize for their unpatriotic behavior for the "heinous crime of forgetting their own country" (Matsumoto 1933: 73–74).

THE MERCHANT MENACE

The harshest attacks were reserved for Chinese merchants. Like the situation depicted in the short story "The Lin Family Shop" (see the Introduction), this and later boycotts used movement rhetoric to legitimize violence and coercion directed at merchants. Throughout Chinese history, merchants were frequently stereotyped and demonized for contributing little or nothing to society, for practicing a secondary or nonessential occupation (末業), and for being "cunning and crooked and interested only in profit" (L.-S. Yang 1970: 187). Although the "merchant" category encompassed various social statuses, Chinese norms assigned "merchants" as a whole to the lowest status within a social order consisting of the "four peoples" (四民): scholars, peasants, artisans, and merchants (see Mann 1987: 18–21, 96–99).

The movement redefined *jianshang* 奸商 from the traditional meanings of "treacherous," "villainous," or "crafty merchant" to "treasonous merchant." In the context of national crisis, the merchant archetype—formerly under suspicion merely as "crafty" or "unethical" (奸)—was now censured for putting profits ahead of patriotism. Such merchants sold "the national products of foreign devils" (洋鬼子的國貨).[4] In contrast, movement supporters defined a new "merchant morality" (商人道德) that, above all, required storekeepers to refuse to sell imports, not tamper with labels, and "not charge exorbitant prices for popular national products." In return, the status of merchants dealing in national products would be elevated (see Fig. 4.1).[5]

"Treasonous" merchants posed not simply a personal or local ethical threat but a national danger. This created an environment in which

---

4. There are innumerable examples of such descriptions in movement literature. See, e.g., "Zhufu tichang guohuo de ge fangmian" (Each aspect of a wife's promotion of national products), *SB* 1933.12.7; and "Lao taitai de guohuo shizhuang" (An elderly lady's national product fashions), *SB* 1933.5.11.

5. This morality is thoroughly explicated in "Tichang guohuo juti banfa."

Fig. 4.1 "The Shamelessness of the Treasonous Merchant"
(SB 1934.7.26)

Chinese civilization had long reviled merchants as unscrupulous and crafty characters. The National Products Movement, however, added a new and popular layer to this image by depicting merchants as *treasonous*. By selling foreign products, "treasonous merchants" (奸商) undermined the health of Chinese industries and, by extension, the Chinese nation. This illustration conveys the deep anxiety of the movement that merchants regularly added the label "Chinese national products" (中華國產) to imports (the ships are named after the major Japanese exporting cities). The unreliability of merchants made them a primary target of the movement.

merchants linked to the sale of foreign products were attacked. During the 1925 boycott in Zhengzhou in Henan province, for example, a Chinese manager for the British-American Tobacco Company was forced "to march in a huge parade through the streets with a large cigarette carton on his head."[6] Indeed, Japanese and Western observers claimed the boycotts were illegal by regularly and loudly citing the arbitrarily brutal and "lawless" acts directed against *Chinese* merchants.[7] As one longtime foreign resident observed of a

---

6. "The Shanghai Incident and the Anti-Foreign Reaction in the Interior" (Hankou, 1925.7.8), CRDS File 893.6512: 1–2.

7. See, e.g., Kawakami 1932: 124, which labels boycotts a "a racketeering system." Kawakami also reprinted numerous stories from China-based English-language newspapers that recount cases of intimidation of Chinese merchants, including reference to a government

later boycott, it "was enforced by barefaced terrorism and theft," which included the arrest of merchants alleged to be dealing in imported products and their imprisonment until a fine had been paid. Even when one such "gang of ruffians" was "caught red-handed" confiscating Chinese products, a Chinese judge let gang members off with a suspended sentence. In another case, someone caught throwing a bomb into a store alleged to be selling Japanese clothing also received a suspended sentence (Woodhead 1935: 165, 226).[8]

MOVEMENT ORGANIZATIONS AND THE BOYCOTT

Movement organizations played both direct and indirect roles in the boycotts of 1923. Contrary to the contentions of a contemporary observer, they did not "sit this one out" by merely adopting a resolution in support of the anti-Japanese boycott (Matsumoto 1933: 73). The level of direct participation (aside from ongoing movement programs) in boycott activities is not clear because movement organizations invariably contributed to the formation and activities of ephemeral, ad hoc groups that are more difficult to trace. Nevertheless, movement groups such as the NPPA helped establish the key organizations behind anti-imperialist activities in 1923.[9]

On March 24, two days before the date set for the retrocession of the Liaodong territories, movement activists from three native-place associations and representatives of the Shanghai General Chamber of Commerce rallied some 20,000–40,000 supporters. This event, chaired by the educator and Shaoxing (Zhejiang province) native-place-association member Cao Muguan 曹慕管, saw the establishment of the Shanghai Citizens Association on Sino-Japanese Relations (上海對日外交市民大會; hereafter the "Citizens Association"). A key contribution of this group was its founding of what became one of the most active movement organizations, the Shanghai

---

regulation from 1931 mandating that anyone caught "smuggling" Japanese goods have the word "traitor" marked on his or her face.

8. Not surprisingly, Woodhead and many other foreigners used such incidents to oppose the ending of extraterritoriality. Japanese generated innumerable lists of such actions directed against Chinese and Japanese merchants in China who sold Japanese merchandise. See, e.g., the translation of an official list, "Illegal Actions Committed against Japan in China," in Zumoto 1932: 231–90.

9. The NPPA branch in Changsha, formed during the boycott of 1919, was a primary organization behind the activities of 1923. The Changsha NPPA was an umbrella organization for many other occupational and professional organizations (McDonald 1978: 100–101, 200–205). McDonald translates NPPA as the "Society for the Promotion of National Goods."

Citizens Association for the Promotion of National Products (上海市民提倡國貨會; hereafter "Association for National Products").[10] By 1925, the Association for National Products had become a highly organized body with representatives from many social groups. The initial Executive Committee, for instance, incorporated 24 groups, including native-place associations, merchant federations, student groups, and other movement organizations such as the NPPA and the Groups of Ten for National Salvation.[11] These representatives themselves were selected from a pool of nearly 200 companies, schools, and special interest groups (Cao 1925: 12).

Members of these groups expressed their antipathy toward Japan through the now-familiar tropes. They were alarmed by the continuing spread of foreign commodities in Chinese markets, which came at the expense of Chinese products. Participants in the Citizens Association came to the conclusion reached by earlier generations of Chinese nationalists: the Chinese lacked patriotism. The absence of universal education, which would inculcate nationalistic values, and the ignorance of Chinese merchants, who were unaware of the advances made in the domestic production of consumer goods, compounded the problem. Above all, these new movement/boycott organizations saw their main task as raising the consciousness of fellow Chinese.

The Citizens Association immediately began to promote itself and its agenda by sending telegrams to groups throughout China and to foreign governments. These telegrams reveal the continued popularity of resistance to the Twenty-One Demands and to Japanese interpretations of Chinese anti-imperialist activism. In a telegram to "friendly nations," for instance, the organization stressed that the revived boycott of Japan was a response to Japan's "illegal enforcement of an illegal treaty." In all its documents, the Citizens Association placed Japanese claims to Liaodong within the broader history of encroachment. The Citizens Association also appealed directly to the

---

10. The relationship between these two organizations, as with many other movement organizations, is unclear. It seems that the group first formed during 1919, but to limit problems caused by having an overtly anti-Japanese name, in 1921 it changed its name to Shanghai shimin tichang guohuo hui (Jiang Weiguo 1995: 77). In contrast, Pan Junxiang (1996c: 542) says that the group was established in November 1921. It seems that both are incorrect. The Suzhou Municipal Archival (see SZMA File 696) has copies of the introductory materials circulated by the Citizens Association in April 1923. Based on this material, I use the official date of March 24, 1923.

11. See Cao 1925: 71 for the bylaws of the Executive Committee. For the general bylaws, see "Shanghai shimin tichang guohuo hui huizhang."

Japanese people through the Tokyo *Asahi shinbun* and other Japanese news services. One message begins: "Using the pretext of the Twenty-One Demands, your government refuses to return [Lüshun and Dalian]. This is destroying the goodwill between our countries and will forever be an obstacle to world peace." The letter attempted to build mass awareness and support through direct appeals in the same manner as other movement groups. It also demonstrates the broad dissemination of the movement agenda through telegrams and letters to all levels of government.[12]

Once again, the boycott and the official and foreign responses to it fed each other. Among the more contentious events in this escalation was the Changsha Incident of June 1, 1923. In Changsha, as in many other cities, boycott supporters attempted to block the unloading of Japanese steamships. On this date, Japanese marines supervising the disembarkation of Japanese passengers from a Japanese-owned steamer killed three Chinese attempting to block their arrival (*NCH* 1923.6.9: 663). This fueled local animosity and commitment to the boycott, and the following day there was a huge demonstration.[13] Through movement organizations such as the Citizens Association, news of the incident immediately circulated throughout China—and, as with previous incidents, this one was integrated into the growing list of national humiliations enumerated by organizations across China.[14] The events in Changsha, the Citizens Association concluded, provided further evidence that China could be saved only through a successful movement and the severance of all economic relations with Japan.

MAKING MEMORIES

National humiliation commemoration days continued to play an important symbolic and functional role in fueling boycotts. To place Japan's latest "humiliation" of China, its refusal to return the Liaodong territories, in a broader context, the Citizens Association worked hard to reinforce the movement interpretation of the May Ninth anniversary of the Twenty-One Demands. It not only provided a narrative of the date but also reinforced its

---

12. For a report on one of their rallies, see "Faqi guochi jinian yanjiang" (A lecture on launching a national humiliation commemoration), *SB* 1925.5.6.

13. Hostility toward Japan became so virulent in Changsha that all Japanese-owned shops were forced to close, and most Japanese residents fled (*CWR* 1923.6.16: 84).

14. For a copy of July 5, 1923, notice, see Cao 1925. For copies of the telegraphs sent by similar organizations with identical interpretations, see Xie Guoxiang 1996: 360–79.

significance through ritual. Because anniversaries and holidays of all sorts already cluttered the Chinese calendar, movement organizations drew attention to these particular dates and reproduced their meaning through yearly events and publications. Organizers of commemorations of May Ninth annually produced hundreds of documents on the event.[15] In 1923, the Citizens Association sent telegrams to every conceivable civil and government organization. The telegrams reminded recipients of the impending anniversary; recounted the Citizens Association's narrative of the events, which ended with the formation of their group as a form of righteous resistance to imperialist encroachment; shared its plans for commemorating the date and encouraged others to make similar plans; and invited patriotic Chinese of all walks of life to attend a National Humiliation Commemoration Rally. Above all, the telegrams reminded readers that they did have the means to respond to Japanese humiliations by boycotting "enemy products." On the eve of the "5-9" anniversary in 1924, the group again sent a similar telegram. This time their frustration was even more palpable. China, the telegram announced, had been subjugated by a "puny island nation" that had formerly depended on it (Cao 1925: 43).[16]

The Citizens Association continued to organize commemorations of May Ninth. For the 1925 anniversary, the group compiled a list of Chinese killed by Japanese since 1923, headed by the names of two merchants. The examples came from across China (e.g., Changsha, Xiamen, Fuzhou, Hankou, Tianjin, and Fengtian). These cases had similar features. In each, Chinese (usually "students") protesting Japanese policies in China were killed without genuine provocation. The Citizens Association tabulation claimed that since 1923 the Japanese had murdered several hundred Chinese, including the 289 killed in Japan by angry mobs in the aftermath of a major earthquake. By documenting these cases, the group attempted to add legitimacy and urgency to its agenda. Moreover, they made the explicit connection between these "humiliations" and their agenda by concluding with an appeal to all Chinese to participate through active nonconsumption.

---

15. See the documents collected by the Japanese consulate in Nanjing regarding activities in that city in 1921; e.g., "Guochi jinian ge" (National humiliation commemoration song) in "Shina ni oite teikoku shōhin dōmei haiseki ikken," p. 74.

16. On one commemoration in 1924, see "Chinese Humiliation Day at Harbin," CRDS File 893.5451.

The Citizens Association also developed specific tactics for disseminating its message, such as sending representatives to theaters throughout Shanghai on May Ninth to give speeches, establishing a committee that trained representatives from all area schools to spread the message of the movement, and formulating a twenty-one-item propaganda handbill (the number was presumably chosen to evoke the Twenty-One Demands). The Citizens Association even asked Chinese movie companies to insert a simple but graphic illustration in their previews that drew attention to the theme of May Ninth, a glass slide that read: "Since [Lüshun and Dalian] have not yet been recovered, everyone please persist in not buying enemy products." The Citizens Association also urged newspapers not to print Japanese ads, requested all local traditional theaters perform special "5-9" plays, asked the China Steam and Navigation Company to refuse passage to anyone wearing Japanese clothing, required that merchants discontinue stocking Japanese products, enlisted the support of other groups in Shanghai to join the Citizens Association, and lobbied other ports to set up similar organizations.[17] At the same time, association members such as Wang Jie'an, the NPPA leader who had lobbied the Beijing government for clothing laws in 1912, sent direct appeals to the Japanese government urging it to treat the Chinese as equals in the interests of "world peace."[18]

The Great Kanto earthquake in Japan helped subdue the boycott. On September 1, 1923, one of the worst earthquakes in modern times struck the area in and around Tokyo and Yokohama. Over 100,000 people were killed, 550,000 buildings were destroyed, and two million persons were left homeless by the earthquake and the fires that followed. Even as there were sympathetic calls to stop the boycott, reports of Japanese attacking Chinese and Koreans living in Japan revived calls for boycotts. As one Citizens Association document from October explained, Chinese should sympathize with the plight of the Japanese people, but they should not relent on the boycott. After all, the document argued, the Japanese still occupied Chinese territory,

---

17. The volume of correspondence and publications confirms the wide-ranging activism of the Citizens Association. In only two years, the group composed 42 different handbills, wrote 22 telegrams for mass circulation, and responded to nearly 200 letters from organizations from across China. For a summary of these activities, see Cao 1925: 52.

18. "Zhonghua guohuo weichi hui daibiao gongshang yijian shang Riben zhengfu shu" (The NPPA represents the opinions of industry and commerce in a petition to the Japanese government), SZMA File 605: 33–36.

and the atrocities committed against Koreans and Chinese in Japan after the earthquake demonstrated its contempt for its neighbors (Cao 1925).

The origins of the outbreak of the boycott of 1923 are presented as a mystery in Charles Remer's oft-cited study of Chinese boycotts. He noted that in contrast with earlier boycotts, this one was not a response to a specific event or humiliation. Rather, it was part of a larger attempt to change Japanese policy (Remer 1933: 83). What Remer neglects to explain is the continuing organizational and discursive foundations of such attempts. Placing the boycott of 1923 not only alongside other boycotts, as Remer does, but also within the context of a burgeoning National Products Movement reveals the continuity. To fully appreciate the boycott's influence on Chinese history, one must go beyond its short-term impact on trade.[19] Its long-term significance lay in raising awareness of the meaning and purpose of nationalizing China's consumer culture. In this specific boycott, we also see a longer-term intensification of the scope of movement efforts to impose controls on Sino-foreign interaction from below the level of the state.

Boycott of 1925: The May 30th Movement

One of China's most famous boycotts, that of 1925, may appear unique because it was the first time two countries were boycotted at once. In contrast to earlier actions, Chinese demonstrators explicitly targeted both the British and the Japanese. But this fact becomes less remarkable when we view the boycott in the context of the movement, which had from its start stigmatized the consumption of *all* imports. Many have seen the boycott of 1925 as an event run by the fledgling Communist party, whose labor activism undoubtedly played an important role.[20] I do not try in this section to demonstrate conclusively that one or another group launched the boycott of 1925. Indeed, others have published excellent case studies of the immediate causes (e.g., Rigby 1980). Rather, the point here is to place 1925 within the context

---

19. As Remer summarized the events of 1923, "It may be best described as an important temporary disturbance of trade" (1933: 90).

20. Matsumoto concluded "the Communist Party of China was the real headquarters of the boycott movement in 1925, but it remained always behind the curtain" (1933: 105). "Communist agitators" seemed to be blamed (or credited) for all anti-imperialist activism in this period, and "the Communists" were a favorite Japanese scapegoat. One scholar of colonial Korea argues the Japanese habit of blaming all agitation and social unrest on the Communists gave them enormous (and undeserved) prestige (Park 1999: 126).

of the movement and thereby underscore the fact that social groups ranging from Communists to manufacturers drew on a popular discourse of nationalistic consumption.[21] Of course, the NPPA also helped define the new boycott by immediately circulating handbills and sending petitions to the government that promoted its agenda of tariff autonomy and a renewed commitment to using only national product fabrics in clothing.[22] The organization also distributed model pledges similar to ones used by the Groups of Ten to other groups throughout China.[23] However, many other segments of society joined the boycott. And, in doing so, each group, even when seemingly diametrically opposed in political ideology, shared and reinforced the common agenda and language—even a common culture or hegemony—of nationalizing consumer culture.

THE IMMEDIATE CAUSE

The 1925 boycott resumed the pattern broken in 1923 when a specific incident rekindled support for an anti-imperialist boycott. The demonstrations and strikes grew out of months of escalating conflict, following the death of a Chinese factory worker at the hands of his Japanese boss. On May 30, 1925, Chinese responded to the broader mistreatment of workers at a local Japanese-owned textile mill by holding a demonstration on Shanghai's Nanjing Road. British-led police officers from the International Settlement, of which Nanjing Road was a part, fired on the crowd, killing eleven and wounding a few dozen more Chinese. Within days, strikes broke out across Shanghai and spread throughout the country.

In an attempt to contain the strikes, the Shanghai Municipal Council, the body that governed the International Settlement, pressured Chinese newspapers into toning down coverage. In response, students spread word of the deaths of the protestors and the factory worker by organizing public speeches in the streets, setting up the confrontation later that month. At the

---

21. Indeed, even ethnic Chinese living in Thailand promoted knowledge of the May Thirtieth Incident and the replacement of all British products with Chinese ones. Legation report (Bangkok, 1925.8.7), CRDS File 893.6600.

22. For copies of such NPPA petitions and handbills from summer 1925, see SZMA File 367.

23. "Xuanshi fuyong guohuo banfa ruxia" (Ways to swear to use national products include the following), SZMA File 340: 28–34.

Fig. 4.2 Publicizing the Latest
National Humiliation, 1925
(Weale 1926: 122)

This poster, which was attached to a busy gate at the Beijing city wall, graphically depicted the killing on May 30 of Chinese (seen lying in pools of blood) by British soldiers, who stand nonchalantly beside the corpses. Here an economically diverse group learned of the clash between the imperialists and Chinese in Shanghai. The movement used such posters, which according to one observer were "everywhere," to cultivate and channel national outrage.

same time, Chinese political parties circulated propaganda that reinterpreted the strikes through the lens of anti-imperialism (see Fig. 4.2). As one Nationalist (Guomindang or Kuomintang 國民黨) cable published in newspapers outside the Settlement put it, "Our party expresses strong opposition to such wanton violence and killing of Chinese within the borders of their own country by the Japanese" (quoted in Rigby 1980: 30).[24]

---

24. Wing On employees, for instance, organized "lecture teams" (宣講團) that passed out fliers promoting the boycott (Shanghai Hualian shangxia dang wei 1991: 17).

GROWING CONTACT WITH FOREIGN
PEOPLES AND PRODUCTS

Sino-foreign tensions were a consequence of the growing contact between Chinese and foreign peoples and products (examined in Chapter 1), which accelerated throughout the first quarter of the twentieth century. For instance, the Shanghai Tariff Conference of 1918 established a differential tariff schedule that forced Japanese textile manufacturers to shift yarn production increasingly to China. Between 1918 and 1921, the number of Japanese-owned spindles in China increased from 29,000 to 867,000 (King and Lieu 1929: 3). By the mid-1920s, Japanese investors owned over a third of the cotton mills in China (*China Yearbook, 1926–27*: 914–15). Over this period, the number of Japanese nationals in Shanghai, where most of these new factories opened, rose from under 400 in 1905 to 20,000 in 1931, or 70 percent of the foreign population (Goto-Shibata 1995: 5–6). In Shanghai, nearly 60,000 Chinese made a living from Japanese mills alone (King and Lieu 1929: 18).

These new factories created more contact points between Japanese and Chinese. In addition to a long-standing grudge against Japan for its presence in China, Chinese came to associate the excesses of industrialization with Japan through its factories, and these factories became places where Chinese expressed anti-imperialist sentiments. Although foreign observers considered working conditions and pay at Japanese-owned mills the best in China, there were more strikes at these mills than elsewhere. The nationality of the ownership was a primary cause. As the Social Bureau (社會局) of the Shanghai Municipal Government concluded in a 1933 report, "In disputes in foreign establishments, racial and national animosities were frequently involved" (Shanghai shi zhengfu, Shehuiju 1933: 16; trans. in Rigby 1980: 13).

In the mid-1920s, labor mobilization and activism led to an increasing number of strikes (see Perry 1993: 66). The nationality of the owners of the factories became a central issue. The heightened sense of national consciousness within the movement can be seen in the tendency to recast disputes between labor and management as disputes between Chinese and foreigners. Several months before the events of May 1925, for instance, Chinese demonstrators protesting the dismissal and arrest of fellow workers in a Japanese mill carried banners that read, "Oppose the Japanese beating people." In the following days, Chinese protestors attacked Japanese employees of the mill (Rigby 1980: 23–24). As with so many other events, each new instance of labor conflict, which in another context may have highlighted tension between workers and managers, was cast as additional evidence of China's national humiliation at the hands of the imperialists. Each new national humiliation fueled labor unrest, and vice versa. By emphasizing the foreign nationality of the factories where they worked, Chinese workers and labor activists helped construct nationalistic categories of consumption. Indeed, the labor movement and counter-movement was one more venue for National Product Movement rhetoric at this time. When the Nationalist army swept into Shanghai and brutally crushed the Chinese Communist Party and labor organizations in April 1927, Nationalist leaders immediately used the notion of "national products" to attack the strikers as *treasonous*: "When a strike is in effect the factories are closed. Consequently the Nationalist government and the Nationalist armies are forced to buy foreign made goods merely because there are no native productions. This is death not only to the country's commerce, but to patriotism as well."[25]

REMEMBRANCE OF
HUMILIATIONS PAST

The private memories and public commemorations of the Twenty-One Demands continued to fuel anti-imperialist sentiment surrounding the May Thirtieth Movement (see Fig. 4.3). According to one Chinese group in 1925, "Within the period of ten years we not only have not wiped out our shame, but we are ten times more oppressed by the Japanese imperialistic ideas. Our shame is tenfold."[26] With or without the approval of local authorities,

---

25. "A Proclamation, Headquarters of the Twenty-Sixth Nationalist Army," Chow Vung Chee, Commander, 1927.4.22; trans. in P.-K. Cheng et al., 1998: 266. These words anticipated the Nationalists' use of the movement over the next decade.

26. "Announcement of the Tenth Anniversary of May Seventh," reprinted and trans. in CRDS File 893.6273. This handout also measured the humiliation in terms of the trade deficit. The commemorations, of course, were used to serve more than immediate movement interests. In Changsha, for instance, the local branch of the Nationalist party printed a circular that linked revenge for the Twenty-One Demands, all other foreign humiliations (which were "just as ruthless as [the demands]"), and warlord rule with their own state-building project; see "Announcement of the [Nationalist] Branch Office in Hunan on May Seventh—The Humiliation Anniversary," reprinted and trans. in CRDS File 893.6273. For two additional

Fig. 4.3 Boycott Banner, 1925
(Shanghai shehui kexueyuan, Lishi yanjiusuo 1986)

Here is one of the countless banners that flew in Chinese commercial spaces in the aftermath of the May 30th Incident of 1925. The slogan, which reads "Be Resolute and Do Not Use British and Japanese Enemy Products," explicitly advocates boycotting British and Japanese "enemy products" (仇貨). The movement used such banners to continually remind consumers that nationalistic consumption was a powerful form of retribution for this latest national humiliation.

activists throughout China organized observances of the Humiliation Day.[27] Other groups produced fans that enumerated the Twenty-One Demands (see Fig. 4.4). Writing on the tenth anniversary of the Twenty-One Demands, Li Jianhong 李劍虹, a member of the Citizens Association, reflected on the formative influence of the demands on his experience as a fifteen-year-old protestor. His article reflects the way the date May Ninth had iconically come to represent China's precarious position:

handbills circulated in Guangzhou, see "Our Shame" and "May 7, Humiliation Day's Declaration to Laborers, Peasants and Commoners," trans. in CRDS File 893.6271.

27. "Humiliation Day," *North China Standard*, 1925.5.10; "Angry Mob of Students Parade Streets of Peking. Anti-Foreign Demonstration," *Peking Leader*, 1925.5.10; "The Government's Humiliation Day," *Peking & Tientsin Times*, 1925.5.13; and other newspaper clippings from CRDS File 893.6320.

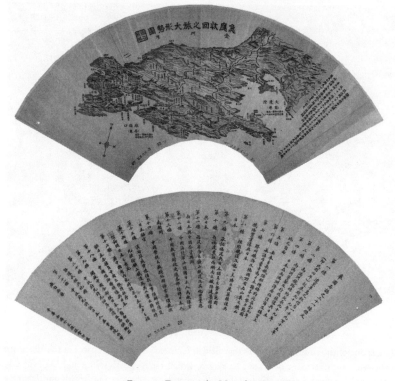

Fig. 4.4 Fanning the Humiliation

Movement organizations played a key role in defining and publicizing "humiliations" of China by the imperialist powers. This fan comes from a 156-page report on "propaganda fans" produced by the Japanese Ministry of Foreign Affairs ("Senden yō sensu," 1924–25). On one side of the fan (*top*) are pictured the territories of Lüshun (Port Arthur) and Dalian (Dairen) on the Liaodong Peninsula opposite Korea, which came under Japan's rule after it defeated Russia in 1905. The other side (*bottom*) supplies a complete list of Japan's Twenty-One Demands.

Chinese history is replete with humiliations at the hands of foreigners. But of these, none is more humiliating than the May Ninth imposition of the inhumane Twenty-One Demands, which have all but destroyed our nation and enslaved our people. They represent the cruelty of the Japanese. The treaty, which was made privately with Mr. Yuan [Shikai], sickens the hearts of 400,000,000 compatriots. We will never accept it. It serves as a warning to our nation. Time is of the essence. It is already the tenth anniversary of the completion of the lease on Lüshun and Dalian, but they continue to be forcibly occupied. Others want to treat us with equally cruel methods. Indeed, in commercial affairs, not a day passes without the continuation of evil hegemonic policies perpetuated against China. Foreigners are not satisfied each day unless they have extracted new concessions from China. O! My dear compatriots, take a moment to consider the situation! We already have a long history of relations with Japan. We were born on the same continent and of the same seed. Racially, we should help one another. Chinese are magnanimous, and it was originally our responsibility to assist Japan. Yet now they oppress us—moreover, they have been doing so for over ten years. However, as always, in our magnanimity, we are unwilling to blame them and continue to consider them enlightened, mistakenly thinking that the Japanese want to do right by us. O! Compatriots, please take a careful and sober look at whether they are enlightened and desirous of cordial relations. I fear this is just a dream. At present, we need to reconsider our magnanimity, which is no longer an appropriate way to deal with them. We must quickly adopt extremely severe methods. Otherwise, we will continue to observe this national humiliation without ever having the means of erasing it. And I fear that national humiliations such as this one will endlessly multiply. To put it another way, unless we are able to cleanse the national humiliation associated with this day, our nation will soon be no more. (Li Jianhong 1925a)

Li Jianhong saw national salvation in the movement. It was clear, he argued, that the Chinese government was hopelessly corrupt, immoral, and unable to save China. As a result, Li called for circumventing the government through massive popular participation in the movement. China must have "the entire nation promote national products. And, as for their [Japanese] products, we must get rid of them completely and not buy any more. This would prevent them from profiting economically and stave off an economic crisis" (Li Jianhong 1925b). Just weeks before the rejuvenation of boycott efforts, participants in the movement continued to circulate the notion that national salvation lay in popular awareness and participation in nationalistic consumption.

NATIONAL SCOPE AND
ANTI-IMPERIALIST TROPES

Richard Rigby, in his study of the May 30th Movement, concluded that "during the month of June there can have been few towns of any size which did not respond in some way." Specific incidents were recorded in nearly forty cities and towns across much of China (Rigby 1980: 63; for a complete list of these cities, see 217n4).[28] Many of these incidents began as seemingly insignificant tiffs between Chinese and foreigners but quickly worsened in this highly volatile context. The most notorious of these was the Shamian

---

28. For a collection of newspaper articles on the boycott and movement in Tianjin in 1925, see Zhonggong, Tianjin shi wei, 1987: 150–65.

(Shameen) Incident of June 23 in Guangzhou. Demonstrations in Guangzhou and Hong Kong against the British and Japanese began in early June
and escalated throughout the month. By the third week in June, strikes had
spread from longshoremen in Hong Kong to Chinese servants working in
the foreign settlement on tiny Shamian Island in Guangzhou. On June 23, a
massive anti-imperialist parade marched on the riverbank opposite the island. Foreign troops were stationed on Shamian to protect its residents, and
at some point, one side began firing at the other. In the ensuing bloodbath,
several dozen Chinese and a few Europeans were killed (CWR 1925.7.25: 127;
Orchard 1930: 256–57). The violence intensified the boycott and strikes,
which lasted longer in this city than in any other part of China.

As with every local anti-imperialist incident throughout China, local influences clearly shaped the choice of targeted countries and the scale of activities.[29] In Changsha, for example, because reaction to the May 30th Incident in Shanghai coincided with the commemorations of the June 1 Incident
of 1923, the boycott included Japan (CWR 1925.6.27: 78).[30] In Hong Kong
and Guangzhou, the rising power and activism of the Nationalists did much
to intensify the strikes and boycotts (Wilbur 1983: 24–26). For this reason,
the anti-imperialist activity there is often viewed as unique: more a part of
Nationalist history than the history of boycotts. As Nationalist power grew
in China, so did its level of involvement with boycotts and the movement.
Nevertheless, it is wrong to see boycotts (or the movement) as primarily the
product of the Nationalists or a simple response to a local provocation.

THE BOYCOTTS OF 1928,
1931, AND BEYOND

By 1925, the Nationalists had begun to strengthen their relationship with the
movement and all its activities, including the organization of boycotts and
the commemoration of national humiliation days.[31] Boycotts in 1928 and 1931,

---

29. In Chengdu, for instance, anti-imperialist boycotts also explicitly targeted France
(CWR 1925.7.18: 122).

30. For an overview of the boycott and movement efforts in Changsha, see McDonald
1978: 206–17.

31. On the Nationalists' participation in national humiliation days, see, e.g., Guoshiguan
(Academia Historica) Presidential archives, 141: 969–82. For an overview of the Nationalist
government's comprehensive commitment to the movement, see its detailed regulations and

the most effective to date, demonstrate the spread of the nationalistic categories of consumption through boycotts.[32] The Nationalists greatly extended the scope of these boycotts, but they never completely controlled (and certainly did not invent) these events. Indeed, the movement used the Nationalist government as much as the government used it. Movement organizations remained active.[33] In the boycott of 1931, for example, the NPPA continued to publicize "treasonous merchants" who sold "enemy products" (SMA Q230-1-93: 31–48). Indeed, the label "unpatriotic" was attached to anyone who got in the way of the boycotts. The movement also appropriated other government efforts; for instance, it used an official government campaign against cigarette smoking in the mid-1930s as a pretext for confiscating *foreign* cigarettes (for additional examples, see Chapter 7).[34] Movement organizations continued to publish guides on how to distinguish between Chinese and foreign products (e.g., Diyi Jiaotong daxue fan Ri yundong weiyuanhui 1928; *Guohuo Rihuo duizhao lu* 1932). Ultimately, heavy pressure from

---

files on promoting national products in Guoshiguan (Academia Historica) Presidential archives, 267: 613–906.

32. The best introductions to these boycotts are still Remer 1933: 137–96 and Kikuchi 1974: 361–438. Many Chinese and Japanese sources provide overviews. See, e.g., the report of the Tianjin-based newspaper *Dagong bao: Ershiwu nianlai dizhi Rihuo yundong zhi jingguo ji qi yingxiang* (The process and influences of twenty-five years of the movement to boycott Japanese products) (1933) collected in Guoshiguan (Academia Historica), *Kangzhan shiliao* (War of Resistance materials): esp. 17–26. On the intensity of the boycott that "began" in 1931, see also Israel 1966: 57–58. Because of their connection with the Nationalists, the League of Nations, and the Lytton Commission, these boycotts attracted more international attention and coverage. The British embassy reported that the Japanese Ministry of Foreign Affairs described the boycott of 1931 as the "most severe Japan has experienced"; see F520/1/10 (1931.12.24), reprinted in Bourne et al. 1996, Part 2, Series E, vol. 40 (China, January 1932–July 1932): 31. See also Koo 1932.

33. The SMA contains records of the activities of movement organizations' activities throughout the 1930s. See, e.g., SMA Q201-1-602. See also Gaimushō 1937.

34. On the connection between the New Life Movement and an anti-imperialist boycott in Wenzhou, see SMP File 5729, 1935.5.31: "Boycott over New Life Movement" and 1935.6.3: "[Wenzhou] Boycott said Anti-Foreign Under a Disguise," which reports that 1.7 million foreign cigarettes were confiscated and burned as part of the New Life Movement's efforts to eliminate smoking.

The common assertion by foreign observers, especially Japanese, that the boycotts were run by the Nationalists was similar to the concurrent attempts to suggest that the anti-Christian movement was both "xenophobic" and "manipulated by Communists." Such claims, it seems to me, systematically ignore the social bases of these popular movements. On contemporary foreign attitudes toward the anti-Christian movement, see Yip 1980: 1–14.

Japan and the policy of "first internal pacification, then external resistance" convinced Nationalist leader Chiang Kai-shek (Jiang Jieshi 將介石, 1887–1975) to withdraw support for boycotts (Coble 1991: 74–76). Nevertheless, even after the Nationalist government withdrew overt support and began suppressing the boycott in May 1932—attempting to ban, for instance, the popular term "enemy products"—many Chinese continued to pressure merchants by picketing stores, confiscating goods, sending intimidating anonymous letters and postcards, disrupting distribution channels, pasting posters on storefronts, and forcing shopkeepers to place advertisements in local newspapers in which they vowed not to sell imports.[35] Some industries formed ad hoc committees to prevent the sale of imports. In Shanghai, fishmongers formed the Enemy Fish Inspection Committee to enforce a ban on the sale of fish caught by Japanese.[36]

The harassment of merchants caught selling foreign products not only continued to discourage others from openly selling imports but also warned the public not to engage in unpatriotic consumption. Movement publications extended this message by publishing fictionalized accounts that reveal the wider social effects of merchant intimidation. One short story explains how a youngster learns to refuse to eat any imported candy, which he derisively refers to as "stinking candy" (臭糖), by witnessing merchant intimidation. While walking down a street with his uncle one day, the boy comes upon a number of "bird cages" (鳥籠) into which merchants caught selling Japanese products had been placed. Their names are printed on a plate on top of the cage, along with the words "treasonous merchant," and the merchants were paraded down the street as a warning to others. As a final act of dehumanization, the merchants were forced to wear such hideous makeup that the boy at first fails to recognize them as human. The boy turns to his uncle for an explanation. The uncle explains that these are "bad people" who do not love China because they specialize in selling products from "foreign

---

35. For examples, however, of the ongoing enforcement of the boycott during the 1930s, see SMP 3358, 1933.7.1: "List of Branches," which details the activities of Japanese goods inspection groups throughout the International Settlement. In addition to sealing and confiscating goods, these groups denounced stores that broke the boycott. See SMP 3358, 1933.4.21: "Anti-Japanese Boycott—Intimidation of Shops by Citizens' Federation" and "Citizens' Federation inspects Nanking Road shops for Japanese goods." For a list of the techniques used to intimidate merchants, see SMP 3753: "Index."

36. For translations of the newspaper clippings on the Enemy Fish Inspection Committee, see SMP 4847, 1933.5: "The Boycott of Japanese Fish."

countries." The boy, however, fails to grasp the meaning of "foreign countries," thinking instead that the world consists only of "China." His uncle explains to the boy, and indeed to the readers, that in fact the world consists of many nations, of which China is only one. Because many of these countries, especially Japan, are China's enemies, nobody should sell or buy Japanese goods. Thereafter, the boy refuses to consume what he recognizes as foreign goods, even candy, and whenever he sees a foreigner, he yells out: "Foreign devil! What the heck are you doing in China?" (Ye Kezhen 1935).

This story illustrates the profound ways the movement and boycotts continued to grow outside the control of the Nationalists. Moreover, it also suggests the growing intensity of the movement, especially in its hostility toward Japan following the Manchurian Incident in 1931 and the Japanese bombardment of Shanghai in 1932. Eyewitnesses such as the American reporter Edna Lee Booker concluded that the boycott of 1931 was "such as China, the past master of the art of boycott, had never before known." For Booker, the level of violence in this boycott was unprecedented. In a scene reminiscent of the story above, she observed a wealthy merchant who was thrown in a wooden cage and "left there to be gazed at by all—a strange 'beast' who betrayed his country by selling enemy goods!" In another incident, she saw a crowd threaten to brand the words "foreign slave" (洋奴) on the forehead of a merchant caught handling Japanese cotton cloth. When she asked a bystander whether the threat was genuine, the response was "'What do you think . . . it is an economic war! . . . Branding is too easy for these bloody traitors—they should have their eyes burned out!" (Booker 1940: 247–49). Clearly, the violence generated by boycotts continued to create opportunities for Chinese to participate in "recovering economic sovereignty" by obstructing local markets for imports while simultaneously creating opportunities for Chinese entrepreneurs to establish new industries to compete against imports.[37]

BOYCOTTS AND THE PREDICAMENT
OF NATIONAL PRODUCT COMPANIES

The nationalistic consumer culture created by the movement was never all-embracing and universally enduring. Rather, this culture, even during boycotts, placed Chinese companies in a predicament. On the one hand, such

---

37. For a year-by-year breakdown of the opportunities created by boycotts for domestic cigarette manufacturers in the 1920s and 1930s, see Fang Xiantang 1989: 41–71.

companies wanted to use the movement to promote the consumption of their products. To do so, they had to present their products as purely Chinese. Indeed, boycotts forced companies to present their products and themselves in this way. On the other, the companies wanted to tap into the allure of the foreign, with its associations of power and superior quality at a lower price. In any case, it is clear that boycotts created the demand for national products that led to the establishment of entire industries in China. The memoirs of owners and managers of dozens of national product companies credit the boycotts for their success (see Pan Junxiang 1996c).

One of the many national products that appeared during boycotts as substitutes for imports was Hundred Happiness Condensed Milk (百好煉乳), which competed against the imported Flying Eagle (飛鷹) brand. According to Wu Baiheng 吳百亨 (1894–1974), the manager of the Wenzhou-based company that produced Happiness, the boycott of 1925 and movement ideology inspired investors who envisioned the company as a means of making China wealthy (1996: 160–61). Another Chinese enterprise that owed its success to boycotts was the China Chemical Industries Company, which became China's earliest and biggest manufacturer of everyday chemical products (Xu Youchun 1991: 132–32). In 1912, nineteen-year-old co-founder Fang Yexian noted that foreign products completely dominated the cosmetics and tooth powder industries. China Chemical began producing domestic alternatives shortly thereafter. However, it was only the boycott of 1919, during which orders poured into Shanghai for any and all national products, that finally allowed his products to compete with imports. With his windfall, he reinvested in better equipment and built the company's first real factory in 1922, which initially focused on producing four products: mosquito coils, tooth powder, food flavorings, and soap. At that time, Fang not only relied on the absence of foreign products but also sought to capture the allure of imports. In 1922, when creating the first Chinese toothpaste, a product that was quickly overtaking tooth powder in popularity, his company consciously imitated the formula and packaging of the most popular foreign brand and quickly became the market leader among the Chinese-made options. The boycott of 1925 removed his primary competition, an American company, from the toothpaste market and allowed his Guanyin (觀音粉) and Flavor's Origin (味生) brands of flavor-enhancement powders to overtake the products of his Japanese competitors. The profits allowed his company to build three additional factories (Ma Bingrong 1996b: 103).

Fang Yexian was representative of a type of movement participant, the domestic manufacturer of mass consumer goods, in three respects. First, the leaders of these companies were active participants in movement organizations and events. Fang, for example, was a co-founder and first general manager of the China National Products Company (中國國貨公司) in Shanghai, which was originally located on Nanjing Road in the building that became the New China Bookstore after 1949. Under his guidance, the store grew into a national chain. Second, in managing these consumer product companies, individuals such as Fang became indirect activists, simultaneously marketing specific national products while raising awareness of product-nationality in general. Fang aggressively promoted his goods as national products, contrasting, for instance, his Three Star mosquito coils with Japanese brands. In marketing his goods, he also helped introduce movement ideology into urban commercial visual spaces by supplying shops selling his products with storefront flags, a traditional means of advertisement, that read: "National Product: Three Star Mosquito Coil" (Ma Bingrong 1996b: 102). Such flags were subtle, everyday reminders of nationality, a form of what Michael Billig (1995) terms "banal nationalism." Last, and most important for the company, the movement placed constraints on Chinese companies to live up to the often impossibly high ideal of creating pure national products (see Chapter 8). Companies such as China Chemical gained from boycotts and the movement, but the same pressures also compelled these companies to find or create domestic substitutes for key imported elements. In the case of China Chemical's Three Star mosquito coil, the most important raw materials came from Japan. However, during the massive boycotts that followed the Japanese invasion of Manchuria in 1931, the company decided it needed to build its own factory (Ma Bingrong 1996b: 105).

The boycott culture produced by the movement also profoundly affected the choice of company and product names. Many products named "national humiliation" (國恥) appeared during boycotts (see the advertisement for National Humiliation cigarettes in Kong Xiangxi 1929). Other names had only slightly more subtle associations with anti-imperialism. China's first manufacturer of electrical products, which was producing tens of thousands of electric fans by the late 1920s, bore the name China Survival Electric Fan Manufacturers (華生電扇制造廠). The founders intentionally selected this name as an abbreviation of the term "for the survival of the Chinese race" (為中華民族之生存) (Lou Dexing 1996a). To cite another example, throughout the 1920s, foreign brands of spun wool continued to dominate the market. Zhao Zizhen 趙子貞, a native of Tianjin, recognized that clothing made from wool, including Western-style suits, had a future in China and suspected that a domestic substitute for these foreign brands would be popular. In 1932, he co-founded the East Asia Wool Textile Company. According to his own account, in choosing a name for his wool products, he consciously attempted to appeal to patriotic Chinese consumers at home and abroad in several ways. First, he ingeniously selected the name Diyang 抵羊, which does not have a specific meaning but translates roughly as "resist sheep" (trademarked in English in 1993 as "Dear Young"). He selected this name because it was a homonym of *diyang* 抵洋, the abbreviated form of the expression *dizhi yanghuo* 抵制洋貨 (boycott foreign products). Second, he extended the patriotic appeal of the name by placing a fragment of a traditional Chinese symbol of resistance to invasion, the Shanhaiguan pass of the Great Wall, along with two rams with locked horns, in the company's logo. The name and logo was a powerful symbol of economic resistance, and Zhao himself credited it for the immediate success of his wool (Zhao Zizhen 1996).

There are countless examples of commodity names that reflected movement ideology. Diyang was not the only wool product with such a name. The national humiliation of the Manchurian Incident was also commodified in product names. For instance, "match king" Liu Hongsheng also owned the Zhanghua Wool Factory (章華毛紡廠), which began producing a brand of serge, a twilled wool fabric, named "November Eighteenth" (the date of the incident) in 1933 (Yang Chengqi 1996). With this and other domestically manufactured wool, some twenty years after the NPPA had argued for continued use of silk clothing on economic grounds because China did not then have a spun wool industry, there were now serious competitors to imported wool. Diyang and November Eighteenth wool immediately became popular fabrics for men's Sun Yatsen–style suits (Mao suits) and women's long-gowns.

However, presenting products as Chinese did not guarantee success. The history of a Chinese light bulb highlights the difficulty a national product could encounter upon entering a market closely associated with and dominated by imports. Light bulbs began to replace oil lamps in China in 1879, when German, Dutch, and American companies began to import them, and imported bulbs dominated the market well into the early twentieth century.

Hu Xiyuan 胡西圓 (1896–1983) expressed an interest in making light bulbs while in high school, and during the 1919 boycott he vowed to make a Chinese light bulb "as a means of expressing patriotism." Nearly two years later, in spring 1921, he made his first light bulb and, after purchasing secondhand Japanese machinery, began to produce Yapuer (亞浦耳) brand bulbs in the summer of that year. At first, the quality of his products was very low, and he lost much money. In the early 1920s, he found it difficult to develop a market for his product. Owners of stores selling imported bulbs claimed that "consumers already have faith in English, German, and other foreign products" and that selling Yapuer's bulbs might ruin the reputation of the store and send customers elsewhere (Hu Xiyuan 1996: 179). Hu slowly began building a customer base through direct marketing, particularly in smaller towns and cities away from Shanghai's more discriminating consumers. Hu gradually developed a market in thirty such smaller cities in the Lower Yangzi region.

The Yapuer light bulb illustrates the central irony of national product manufacturing. Whereas foreign companies often attempted to hide their foreignness, manufacturers such as Hu had to associate their national products with imports to gain a market share. Indeed, his company's name demonstrated the predicament of national product producers who wanted to help save China by manufacturing goods but often found customers wary of domestic goods. According to Hu, it was difficult to overcome the reputation of imports as superior to Chinese products, especially for recent inventions like light bulbs. In the hope of solving this problem, he named his company Yapuer because it was meaningless in Chinese and sounded like a German or a Dutch word. Indeed, many consumers thought Yapuer was the name of a German who they believed owned the company. Hu knew this misunderstanding would at least serve him well initially. And he encouraged this misperception by mentioning German engineers in his employ in his advertisements. Such associations with imports, however, made his products a movement target, especially outside Shanghai. Hu later claimed to have felt uncomfortable about the charade and, after the brand had been successfully launched, elected to add "China" to the name (中國亞浦耳) and the words "national product" on the packaging (Hu Xiyuan 1996: 180–81).

Although Yapuer sought to misrepresent itself as foreign, the company was active in the movement. In recognition of the growing importance of the company, Yapuer was invited to join the NPPA in summer 1923. By this time, the NPPA had evolved into a much larger organization and expanded beyond the silk-industry interests it had represented a decade earlier. Nascent consumer goods industries also had a stake in the success of the movement, and Hu Xiyuan became an enthusiastic participant in the NPPA. In this relationship, each side gained from the involvement of the other. For the NPPA, the success of Hu Xiyuan and Yapuer in competing against imports proved that China could prevail despite the presence of imports. It placed stories in *Shenbao* informing readers that China now had its own light bulb industry and lionized Hu for creating a new Chinese industry. The NPPA's use of the Yapuer story provides a good example of the organization's tactic of publicizing success stories as a part of its long-term goal of promoting movement ideology rather than a single national product. Naturally, such promotions explicitly encouraged Chinese to buy Yapuer bulbs. Hu's company also gained in other ways. The NPPA, for instance, insisted that its members buy one another's products, including Yapuer bulbs. Hu credited the NPPA with playing an important role in the success of the company (Hu Xiyuan 1996: 182).[38]

BOYCOTTS AND
THE MOVEMENT

Boycotts were critical to the development of the movement. They not only provided the passion and muscle to promote and enforce a nationalistic consumer culture but also gave entrepreneurs an incentive to create new industries. During these boycotts, consumers across China first learned to put to use the categories underlying this culture; merchants were forced to identify and sell in terms of product-nationality and either remove or camouflage foreign goods; and national product manufacturers came to dominate domestic markets. Above all, boycotts were important to the movement because they forced people to visualize commodities in terms of product-nationality.

As with queue-cutting during the Revolution of 1911, boycotts created an environment that empowered individuals, groups, and even the state to enforce a single interpretation of material culture through violence and intimidation. Boycotts made it much more difficult to deny the pre-eminence of

---

38. For a more thorough examination of the mutually beneficial relationships between manufacturers and the movement, see Chapter 8.

product-nationality. To be sure, it was still easy for merchants and their customers to avoid the boycott environment by figuratively hiding under the counter, in much the way the economist H. D. Fong initially avoided having his queue forcibly removed. Throughout the boycotts of the late 1920s and the 1930s, in which the Nationalists were heavily involved during and after their successful Northern Expedition (1926–28), the boycotts were never universal.[39] Boycott institutions continued to operate in the ad hoc manner reminiscent of the queue-cutting campaigns, forcing some merchants and consumers into compliance while others escaped. At the same time, however, new and more powerful institutions developed within the movement. The most important of these was a major institutional contribution of the Nationalists to solving the fundamental problem underlying boycotts and indeed the entire movement: What constituted a "national product" and, by implication, what did not?

PART II

STANDARDIZING THE MEANING

OF "NATIONAL PRODUCTS"

The process of nationalizing consumer culture that lay at the heart of anti-imperialist boycotts intensified the need for a system of determining the nationality of products. The creation of such a system required the formulation or adoption of a whole new language of nationalism. The early twentieth century was a critical time for the formulation and spread of modern Chinese nationalism itself. The period witnessed not only the establishment of nationalistic activities and organizations but also the concurrent emergence of vocabularies and narratives that defined the Chinese nation. These new linguistic resources were used to reinterpret China's history, analyze its present situation, and formulate agendas for nation-making.[40] These histori-

---

39. On the Nationalists' changing relationship to boycotts, see Jordan 1976; 1991.

40. Indeed, this is the time when Mandarin became the "national language" (國語); see DeFrancis 1950. On the introduction of physical and social science vocabularies, see, among others, L. H. Liu 1995 and Y.-N. Li 1971. Prasenjit Duara (1995: 5) makes a similar point: "It was these new linguistic resources, both words and narratives, that secured the nation as the subject of History and transformed the perception not only of the past but also of the present meaning of the nation and the world: which people and cultures belonged to the time of History and who and what had to be eliminated."

cally based discursive practices defined the activities and agendas of the movement organizations discussed throughout this study.

Movement organizations, to affirm their interpretation of the Chinese nation, coined or further popularized words and narratives such as "national product," "enemy product," and the notion that China was engaged in a "commercial war" in which it needed to recover "economic control." Such words supported the movement's division of the world of commodities into Chinese and foreign. In short, the movement created and embodied a discourse of nationalistic consumption. Similar to the contemporary academic debates over creating fixed boundaries for socially constructed groupings based on ethnicity, this discourse enabled the movement to produce increasingly sophisticated definitions—and eventually a classification system—to define exactly what constituted a "national product" and, by implication, what was a "foreign product." At the same time, in events ranging from boycotts to exhibitions, movement activities became performances that both depended on and reproduced this discourse and, more specifically, its classifications.

The remainder of this chapter examines the development of a classification system that attempted to stabilize the binary of "national" and "foreign" products and specifies a few of the ways movement activities reproduced and reinforced this bifurcation. Above all, the movement attempted to polarize this opposition and make the two categories of "foreign" and "domestic" mutually exclusive. As part of this effort, the movement sought to limit any overlap by establishing the ideal of the "pure" (單純) "national product" and by denying or masking the interstices between the two categories. As with other binary pairs, this one contained and reinforced a hierarchy. The codification and normalization of "national product" as the sacred manifestation and repository of authenticity was opposed to its diametrical other in "foreign products." This distinction became increasingly enforced through symbolic and physical violence, as the spread of these categories simultaneously provided the basis for self-surveillance and the policing of consumption.

However, Chinese industry could never have sustained the complete separation of these categories. There were simply too many ambiguous areas of overlap, hybrid commodities that resisted an environment in which they had to adopt one label. Japanese factories in China, Chinese-owned factories using imported machinery or technicians, and foreign-financed factories were just a few of the combinations of "Chinese" and "foreign" capital, management, raw materials, and workers spreading throughout the Chinese economy. Some of the more articulate (and realistic) participants in the movement realized these problems and openly acknowledged the need to relax the sharp distinctions.[41] But even these people did not oppose the underlying notion of product-nationality itself.

Associating each side of this duality with other powerful binaries circulating in contemporary Chinese discourse helped sharpen the distinction between Chinese and foreign. The category of national products was linked to nationalism, authenticity, and modernity, as well as to traditional concepts such as propriety (理), righteousness (義), integrity (廉), and shame (恥). In contrast, the category of foreign products was associated with imperialism, treason, inauthenticity, weakness, and immorality. This was never an easy distinction to maintain or even support. Moreover, although this language aided resistance to imperialist economic and *discursive* domination, this was not the whole story. Participants ranging from students to merchants who sold only national products to politicians who stressed the importance of developing national industry all helped build new structures of surveillance.

The Practical Problem of Determining Product "Purity"

Movement participants saw an obvious need for an explicit system for defining "national products." With the spread of brand-name commodities in the early twentieth century, Chinese consumers could not rely simply on visual signs to determine a product's nationality because labels rarely provided straightforward information. Throughout the movement, especially during the frequent anti-imperialist boycotts, producers and merchants regularly attempted to camouflage goods that might have been considered foreign (see Fig. 4.5).[42] Likewise, counterfeit Chinese products were found all over the country (Allman 1924: ii).[43]

---

41. Sun Yatsen himself vacillated on the issue. Despite some misgivings, he saw foreign capital as essential to China's economic development. At the same time, he also expressed fears of imperialist economic domination. See Myers 1989.

42. "Suqian xuelian jinggao shangjie bumai Rihuo" (Suqian Student Association respectfully informs commercial circles not to sell Japanese products), *Ningsheng* 1919.8.16; reprinted in ZDLDG 1992: 231–32.

43. Allman and other foreigners blamed the widespread infringement problem on weak or nonexistent protection of intellectual property. Although China made an effort to codify trademark regulations in 1904, it was not until 1923 that China issued a law on trademarks and other intellectual property. By this time, there were some 25,000 applications on file for

Fig. 4.5 The Myth of the Pure Product
(*Guohuo yuebao* 1, no. 2 [1934.6])

This illustration underscores the practical problem of producing pure national products. Here "Japanese products" (*left*) enter a Chinese "national product factory" (so identified on the smokestack), but what emerges is labeled a "Completely Chinese Product" and "Made in China." The illustration both acknowledges this common practice and serves as another warning to manufacturers to live up to the stated product purity goals of the National Products Standards and the movement.

The open hostility expressed toward goods perceived as foreign also posed a threat to Chinese manufacturers and retailers of these goods as well as to their consumers. Chinese manufacturers themselves often compounded identification problems. Domestic companies occasionally imitated or copied popular imports. As noted, in 1922, when Fang Yexian's China Chemical Industries Company followed market preferences and became the first Chinese manufacturer to switch from making tooth powder to toothpaste, it

---

trademarks, most of which were foreign-owned (Allman 1924: 6). Even after the promulgation of intellectual property laws under the Nationalist government, little changed, and these laws "failed to achieve their stated objectives" (Alford 1995: 53). Alford's study of Republican-era legal reform also uncovers differential treatment of Chinese intellectual property; see esp. "Learning the Law at Gunpoint: The Turn-of-the-Century Introduction of Western Notions of Intellectual Property," in Alford 1995: 30–55.

imitated the formula and packaging of the leading imported brand. This change from powder to paste allowed Fang's company to overtake its domestic competitors (Ma Bingrong 1996b: 102–3).

At the same time, many movement companies grew by using foreign materials or associating their products with foreign goods, even by intentionally misrepresenting their products as imports. To take one example, in the late 1920s, despite decades of growth in the popularity of Western-style clothing, even fashion-conscious urban consumers still considered gauze undergarments luxury items. However, in 1930, a prominent Shanghai importer imported French sheer long-sleeved undershirts, which became an immediate hit in Shanghai. The son of a founder of the Five Cordials Textile Plant (五和制造廠), a Shanghai enterprise active in the movement since its founding in 1924, decided to produce an imitation using imported gauze. The Five Cordials product retailed for half the price of its imported counterpart and became so widely accepted that even the original importers bought garments from the company and then added their own trade name and passed the finished product off as an import (Ren 1996: 78). Within the movement, the next best thing to producing a pure Chinese product was producing one with imported raw materials that displaced imports (see Chapter 8).

Because imports were associated with luxury and quality among urban elites, the labels of popular Chinese items often featured romanized product and company names and occasionally a descriptive statement in a foreign language. However, this association with foreign products cut both ways. Chinese manufacturers frequently complained that the movement erroneously targeted their products. For example, during the 1915 boycott, a Shanghai soap manufacturer ran into problems in Changsha when protestors saw the "foreign characters" (洋字, i.e., alphabetic script) in its trademark and mistook it for a foreign product. In a meeting to discuss the issue, the NPPA suggested that all products certified by it use Chinese characters in their trademarks so that their products would be easily identifiable as Chinese (*SB* 1915.5.16: 10). To some movement enthusiasts, then, even foreign scripts unambiguously signified foreign products.[44] Hybrid products

---

44. Liang 1934. Liang argued that the presence of foreign letters on Chinese products only fueled the "craze for imports" (洋貨的迷) and rejected the idea that Chinese products needed romanized names to succeed in foreign markets, citing the lack of Chinese names on many popular imports.

added a final complication. What, for instance, was the nationality of an item such as imported Japanese cloth made from Chinese cotton?[45]

The history of pencils in China demonstrates the tension between the need for imported components and the desire to appear completely Chinese. Germany began exporting pencils to China in the late nineteenth century, and by World War I, American and Japanese products were also available. The use of pencils spread throughout the country. The major Japanese manufacturer tried to protect itself from attack by using the name "Chinese brand" (中華牌). As with so many products (see Chapter 1), once again, the origin of a "pure" Chinese pencil lay in attempts to develop a domestic equivalent that began with the production of hybrids. In 1932, the China Pencil Company (中國鉛筆公司) was set up in Beiping (Beijing) and the Chinese Literatus Pencil Factory (華文鉛筆廠) in Shanghai. Because both companies used imported leads, neither of these was considered completely Chinese by movement standards. They soon went out of business. In 1934, Wu Gengmei 吳羹梅 (b. 1909) set up the first truly national product pencil company, the China Pencil Factory (中國鉛筆廠). To further promote sales and capitalize on its standing as a national product company, the name was changed to the China Standard National Product Pencil Factory (中國標準國貨鉛筆廠) (Ma Bingrong 1996c: 226).

China Standard intensified its use of movement ideology following the Manchurian Incident, when it adopted the slogan "Chinese people use Chinese pencils" (中國人用中國鉛筆). It also promoted itself as a Chinese company by informing consumers that it was run by Chinese technicians, used Chinese raw materials, and had been established with Chinese capital. Furthermore, the company asked Shanghai education department head Pan Gongzhan 潘公展 (1895–1975) to write its slogan in his own hand and then printed Pan's calligraphy on the pencils and used it in advertisements. Pan's office ordered schools in Shanghai to use these national product pencils and had the national Education Department encourage their use throughout the country's schools (Ma Bingrong 1996c: 229).

The confusion over commodities frequently left Chinese consumers at a loss. A prominent Chinese businessman expressed his consternation over the difficulty of distinguishing Chinese and foreign products. His sentiments reveal the frustration of manufacturers of Chinese products that

---

45. For one argument that such a product was still an "enemy product" (i.e., Japanese), see "Wo jia de riyongpin," 1932.

would have benefited from the sharp differentiation of domestic and imported commodities:

When China restricted international intercourse [i.e., before the Treaty of Nanjing of 1842], it was easy to differentiate between Chinese and foreign products because the material and manufacturing methods of foreign products were different from local products [土貨]. With just a glance, one could see these differences. However, in recent times, the situation is not nearly the same. There are national products that use foreign materials and techniques, while other products disguise foreign products as Chinese; and there are foreigners who imitate Chinese techniques and produce identical items as Chinese ones. Take silk as an example. One hundred years ago, foreigners did not produce silk. With a single look at a silk product, one could determine that it was a national product. But nowadays, not only are French, Italian, Japanese and many others producing raw silk, but there is also so-called man-made silk (人造絲 [i.e., rayon]), which resembles genuine silk. This is really "passing fish eyes off as pearls," and it is difficult to distinguish between them. (Zhu Boyuan 1936)

Movement records are full of such anecdotes and controversies surrounding the definition of "national product." The uncertainty presented a practical problem for boycotts and other movement activities, and movement groups such as the Citizens Association were routinely asked to settle product-nationality issues. Shortly after the establishment of the group in 1923, for instance, they received a letter from ginseng merchants in Xiamen. These merchants were trying to clarify whether Korean ginseng should be boycotted, as the Xiamen Citizens Association (廈門市民大會) demanded. The county chamber of commerce, which received the letter from the Shanghai Ginseng Merchants Association, forwarded the case to the association, which decided to look into the matter. It determined that because the Japanese trading company Mitsui monopolized the Korean ginseng trade, ginseng should be considered a Japanese product. After confirming this with Koreans living in Shanghai, the association sent a telegram to the Xiamen group and other ports informing them of its findings and encouraging them to boycott Korean ginseng (Cao 1925: 51).

The wide array of signs attached to commodities hindered the movement's inculcation of nationalistic categories of consumption, which depended on at least the *possibility* of distinguishing foreign and Chinese. Its activities were, in essence, efforts to make these distinctions and inculcate a nationalistic consumer literacy. For instance, movement commodity spectacles (discussed in Chapters 5 and 6) inculcated a new nationalistic visuality on two levels. First, it taught Chinese consumers to identify individual commodities and sidestep the allure of imports. Spectacles such as national product exhibitions were organized around the notion that the looks of products—slick packaging, eye-catching illustrations, and foreign-language text—were deceiving. Unless consumers learned to recognize national products, movement participants warned, these technologies of desire would mesmerize Chinese consumers into "treasonous" consumption. Nationalistic commodity spectacles aided patriotic consumers by supplying approved nationalized visuals.

Second, movement activities and spectacles reinforced the notion of the nation rather than the locale as one's natural economic community. National exhibitions in particular produced visions of the Chinese nation as an integrated agglomeration of authenticated (or "cleansed") national commodities. The idea of the nation as the primary unit was reinforced by the widespread perception that imports were inundating Chinese markets. Movement activities and spectacles thus functioned to stimulate a common response or preferred reading of heterogeneous urban spectacles and life and helped Chinese avoid oppositional codings (that is, the underreading or incorrect interpretation of commodity texts). The intended consequences of this new literacy were, of course, consumer self-regulation and self-surveillance, the internalization of the nationalist gaze, as constructed by the movement, through the insertion of a discourse of nationalistic consumption between consumer and consumed.

The Formulation of National Products Standards

Movement activities and spectacles designed to teach people to distinguish Chinese and foreign products, then, were only the second half of the solution. A more fundamental problem lay in determining which products should be promoted as "Chinese." The formulation of National Products Standards in 1928 was intended to provide the foundation for creating national channels for solving the thorny issue of what constituted a "national product." The standards attempt not to codify the shapes or sizes of products (which were themselves becoming standardized with the advent of mass production) but to fix the symbolic content or meaning of these goods. As a result, a seamless nationalized product chain was emerging in which the standards first established the basis for authenticating commodities as "national products" (and by extension excluding those that were not); movement spectacles provided the visual training that made these items desirable;

and, finally, a growing variety of markets and stores made them available. In the Republican era, movement advocates did *not* come close to achieving this integration and awareness across the entire country. However, the creation and widespread dissemination of the standards became one more mechanism underlying the nationalization of consumption and, consequently, the construction of nation-conscious consumers.

As the National Products Movement began to unfold during the first decade of the twentieth century, its success in popularizing the notion of a Chinese national product naturally raised the issue of what exactly made a product Chinese. As the number of organizations investigating and publishing findings on national products proliferated, so did the ways of defining such products. In trying to establish a particular good as an authentic national product, companies frequently offered multiple, official-looking "certifications." The issue became even more pressing in 1928, as the new Nationalist government, along with many other organizations, expanded movement activities such as hosting exhibitions, providing tax incentives to Chinese manufacturers, and establishing stores to sell exclusively Chinese products. Such actions depended on explicit definitions of what constituted a national product.

As suggested in Chapter 3, the movement had long attempted to develop a process for authenticating products. A few years after its establishment in 1911, the NPPA began providing national product certifications. Before the rapid increase of commodity spectacles requiring certified national products in the late 1920s, boycotts provided incentives for obtaining certifications. As noted above, the volume of certification activity by movement organizations such as the NPPA corresponded closely to boycotts. In 1914, the first year the NPPA provided certification services, the organization validated only four products in all categories. But during the tumultuous 1915 boycott, the number of certifications jumped to 69. Activity tapered off until 1925, when it soared from 24 certifications the previous year to 105, before falling by half for the next two years. Naturally, the combination of a major boycott and other movement events created record demand, as the 238 certifications issued in 1928 suggests.[46] Although these certifications were initially restricted

---

46. Many other movement groups experienced similar increases. See, e.g., "Guohuo gongchang lianhehui kaimu ji" (Meeting notes of the Association of National Products Factories), *SB* 1928.10.13: 13.

to NPPA members, the organization soon began providing these popular services to anyone.[47]

The National Products Standards of 1928

In September 1928, the newly established Nationalist government built on earlier movement efforts to define "national products" by issuing the Chinese National Products Tentative Standards (中國國貨暫定標準). Movement channels quickly began to disseminate the standards, and the appropriate government publications invariably included a copy of them. Because of these efforts, the line separating pure nationalized commodities from their profane foreign counterparts grew increasingly explicit, with far-reaching implications. At the same time, the growing repertoire of movement activities ranging from physically violent boycotts to more subtle nationalistic commodity spectacles simultaneously reinforced the necessity of having National Product Certifications as well as raised awareness of the categories underlying such certifications.

The immediate inspiration for the establishment of the Chinese National Products Tentative Standards was the government's desire to participate in the certification process. On July 8, 1928, Minister of Industry and Commerce Kong Xiangxi 孔祥熙 (known in English as H. H. Kung) (1881–1967) sent the order to Chinese chambers of commerce and announced the purpose of the certifications:

Since the establishment of this ministry, we have spared no efforts to promote national products. Recently, when one investigates market conditions for various products, one discovers that foreign products are being falsely labeled national products and deceptively sold for unethical profits. Unless we carefully examine and verify genuine articles and fakes, we will be unable to protect capital and stem its outflow. For this reason we have stipulated and issued nine regulations governing the issuing of National Products Certifications [國貨證明書; see Fig. 4.6]. (Kong Xiangxi 1928a)

Although movement organizations such as the NPPA had been issuing national product certifications for over a decade, the ministry's participation

---

47. ZGWH 1932: "Huiwu jilu" section, which provides a yearly record of NPPA activities, contains an endless listing of requests for certifications as well as requests from certified companies to have their products promoted.

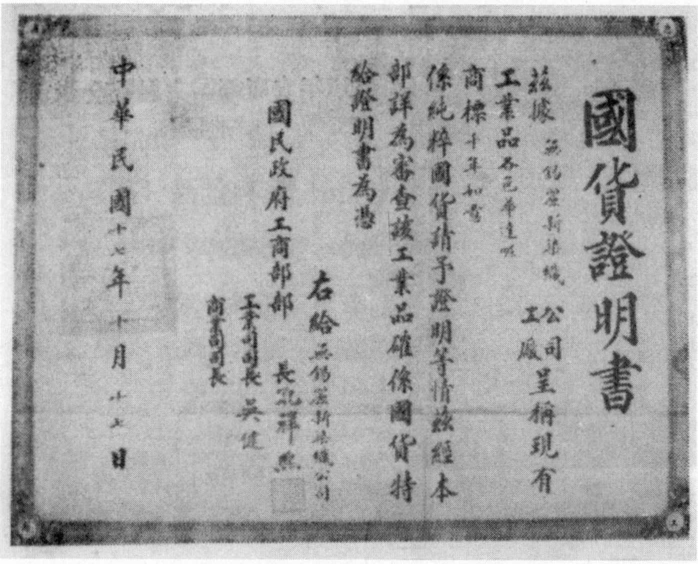

Fig. 4.6 National Product Certification, 1928

Here is an example of the National Product Certifications (國貨證明書) issued by the Nationalist government. Companies used these certifications, which movement organizations also issued, to verify to boycott organizations, local governments, and overseas Chinese that their products were indeed authentic Chinese products and, therefore, deserving of special treatment.

signaled much greater state involvement as well as the attempt to make these certifications universal. In the name of "promoting national products" (提倡 國貨), the state intervened in areas of the economy formerly controlled by local elites. Whereas companies had earlier sought these certifications of their own accord or had been pressured to do so by the movement, companies were now required to do so by the state. Moreover, every company had to apply for such authentication for each of its products. After completing its investigation, the ministry issued a certificate to those products deemed "Chinese" and published the product and company names in its official gazette. Subsequently the ministry and other approved organizations periodically reinspected the company. Companies were required to mention that they had been certified in their advertisements. Finally, the ministry threatened to expose and confiscate any counterfeit national products and penalize their manufacturers (Kong Xiangxi 1928b).[48]

---

48. On enforcement, see "Gongshang bu pai yuan diaocha guohuo," 1928. The ministry's archives at the Institute of Modern History, Academia Sinica, has copies of these certifications.

Because these standards were so widely disseminated and so central to the movement, it is worth discussing them in detail here.[49] First, the standards identified what the movement considered the four basic components of any product: capital, management, raw materials, and labor. The standards required that investment capital come completely from Chinese citizens. When it was absolutely necessary to use foreign capital, then non-Chinese investors were not allowed to participate in management. The standards also stipulated that, with the exception of foreign experts, enterprises be run completely by Chinese citizens. Raw materials were to be Chinese in origin; foreign materials were permitted only in the absence of Chinese sources. Ideally, all the workers were to be Chinese, but the rules granted an exception when foreign "technicians" (技 師) were absolutely necessary; even then, these foreigners were not permitted to have managerial powers.

Based on these criteria, national products were organized into seven official grades, with grade one the purest and grade seven the least pure:

Grade 1: Chinese capital, management, materials, and labor.

Grade 2: Chinese capital, management, and labor, but the use of small amounts of non-Chinese raw materials or a few foreign technicians.

Grade 3: Chinese investment using capital borrowed from abroad, but Chinese management, materials, and workers; or the analogous situation with foreign technicians.

Grade 4: Chinese capital, management, labor, and primarily foreign materials; or the analogous situation with foreign technicians.

Grade 5: Chinese capital borrowed from abroad, Chinese management and labor, primarily foreign materials; or the analogous situation with foreign technicians.

Grade 6: Chinese capital borrowed from abroad, Chinese management and labor, and mainly foreign raw materials; or the analogous situation with foreign technicians.

Grade 7 (added within a few years): Chinese labor, management, and workers, but all foreign materials; or the analogous situation with foreign technicians. (SSGC 1933; see also Zhu Boyuan 1936)

---

49. "Gongshang bu wei Zhongguo guohuo zhanding biaozhun zhi Guomin zhengfu cheng" (Ministry of Industry and Commerce petitions National government with Chinese National Products Tentative Standards), 1928.9; reprinted in Zhongguo di'er lishi dang'an guan 1991: 742–44. Movement publications such as the *Jilian huikan* also often reprinted the standards. See, e.g., "Guohuo zhidao," 1931. On these revisions, see Guoshiguan (Academia Historica), Presidential archives, 267: 1838–51.

Foreign manufacturers operating in China posed a problem. Drafters of the standards wanted to differentiate "completely foreign products" (完全外國貨) from products not qualifying as national products but still manufactured in China with Chinese labor and materials. The standards accomplished this by including two supplemental categories: Honorary National Products (參國貨) and Foreign Products (外國貨). Technically, Honorary National Products were those manufactured with Chinese capital, foreign management, Chinese raw materials, and Chinese labor; or by joint ventures run by foreigners that made use of Chinese materials and laborers; or by foreign-financed companies, managed by foreigners, that made use of Chinese materials and laborers. In contrast, Foreign Products were ones that used foreign capital, management, raw materials, and workers; or just Chinese laborers or materials.

Four things emerge from this hierarchical scheme. First, and most obviously, the standards required higher-grade National Products to be as completely "Chinese" as possible. Second, the standards included a practical bent. Except at the highest grade, products manufactured with the assistance of foreign technicians were not penalized severely. Although their presence did not drop products down a notch, these products were acknowledged as a separate, parallel category that quietly stigmatized the products and acted as a continual reminder that the ideal workplace was one in which Chinese replaced foreign technicians. The honorary category was an even larger compromise, and not surprisingly it was dropped in some movement publications.[50] Third, the introduction of Grade 7 reflected the movement ideal of creating a value-added commodity-producing nation rather than one that supplied raw materials and an abundant consumer market to foreign countries. Finally, in a reflection of the perennial problem of sharply distinguishing domestic and foreign, the standards were vague and left much room for judgment calls and corruption. But the problem of implementing these standards is not the issue here. Rather, the emergence of the standards reveals yet another highly visible means of spreading nationalistic categories of consumption through the actual redefinition of commodities.

---

50. See, e.g., "Gongshang bu yiding zhi guohuo biaozhun yilan," 1930.

THE SPREAD AND USE
OF THE STANDARDS

The quick circulation of the standards was a simple means of raising awareness of the categories Chinese and foreign. Within months, bureaucratic networks had disseminated the official standards. In October 1928, for example, the Ministry of Industry and Commerce ordered chambers of commerce to use the standards as the basis for investigating the nationality of products produced in their areas (SZMA File 1334: 67–73).[51] Similarly, in a November 1928 order, the Hebei provincial government forwarded copies of the standards to local organizations such as the Tianjin General Chamber of Commerce and directed them to adopt the standards.[52] The results of such investigations were widely publicized. In spring 1931, for instance, Tianjin's Social Affairs Bureau (社會局) circulated a list of the companies and trademarks of newly certified national products (Wu Ou 1931; "Shiyebu shencha," 1931).

Although the government's symbolic and financial incentives for issuing the standards seem clear, it is not obvious why manufacturers bothered to comply by submitting their products when the new government was too weak to enforce the law. The Nationalist government was, after all, notoriously desperate to generate revenue, and companies were suspicious of a registration process that would surrender confidential information to political authorities that one historian has labeled "gangsters and extortionists" (Eastman 1974: 230; see also Coble 1980: 56–89). Movement events, such as exhibitions and museums, along with later government policies helped persuade producers to participate on more than legal or patriotic grounds.

Movement organizations and institutions, of course, encouraged compliance and regularly explained the advantages of doing so. For instance, in a large advertisement that chronicled the history of the movement and the place of company registration within it, the newly formed Shanghai Association of Mechanized National Products Manufacturers (上海機制國貨工廠聯合會), which was established in 1927 as an offshoot of the NPPA, volunteered to help companies prepare registration materials for free.[53] Commodity spec-

---

51. The order included a copy of the standards. Similarly, in December 1929, a NPPA telegram prompted the ministry to order Hankou to investigate product nationality (NJ613-68-1).

52. "Hebei sheng zhengfu xunling di 1992 hao," 1928.

53. "Geming hou zhi guohuo yundong," 1928.

tacles, discussed in Part III, were a key means of disseminating the standards. By 1933, the Shanghai Municipal National Products Museum suggested that there was a long list of informal and sporadic non-tariff barriers to foreign commodities that certifications helped companies avoid. For example, the museum claimed that its certification enabled products to circulate throughout China "without incident." The certification would be especially helpful during one of the frequent anti-imperialist boycotts, when radical organizations detained commodities in Chinese ports. The museum also enumerated the variety of goodwill measures granted by the national, provincial, and municipal governments to certified products, such as reduced taxes and lower advertising rates. Finally, the museum's certification made products eligible for Ministry of Industries certification and movement awards.[54]

Although there was a growing acceptance of the standards, many movement participants acknowledged their weaknesses. For example, one businessman criticized them as emphasizing form without spirit. He, like many others, feared that simply restricting the domestic market to national products would inhibit the continual improvement of Chinese goods (an amazingly prescient observation given the post-1949 history of Chinese commodities). This writer suggested that three more properties should be added to the four already acknowledged. In addition to labor, capital, management, and raw materials, true National Products ought to be "refined," "durable," and "inexpensive." Superior products, he claimed, would be worthy of the name National Product and lead to the ultimate protection of the domestic market. Speaking of the Shanghai Chamber of Commerce Commercial Products Display Hall, the writer said: "Only if all exhibited National Products represent the 'national essence' [國粹] of the Chinese Republic can we achieve the goal of promoting national products" (Zhu Boyuan 1936).

The National Products Standards solved on paper the central problem of defining consumption as a means of resistance to imperialism. They provided movement supporters with an explicit mechanism for identifying foreign products, the objects to resist; in effect, they created centrifuges

---

54. On the certification process, see "Kaoding zhangze" (Verification rules and regulations) and "Zhengming guohuo" (Certifying national products), in SSGC 1933. The NPPA encouraged its members to certify products for similar reasons (ZGWH 1932: "Huishi" section, 14).

for removing foreign impurities from a market now marked Chinese. The standards enabled the rationalization of every aspect of the movement by facilitating the creation of more targeted and effective activities. Boycott enforcers now had explicit guidelines for determining the nationality of a product; similarly, merchants had a better idea what was contraband, and consumers had guidelines for their desires. As the next chapters demonstrate, the standards became the core of a growing number and variety of nationalistic commodity spectacles organized around the standards.

The standards became a principal mechanism for shaping consumer behavior around the nascent nationalistic consumer culture. These explicit government-approved standards became an emblem of authenticity that lent an aura of legitimacy to movement activities. Indeed, in a new age of material culture, this mechanism produced its own material embodiment, an official piece of paper certifying the authenticity of products. The Nationalist government, with the support of formal and informal movement organizations, reinforced these certificates with incentives for applying for them. Elaboration of such institutions made escaping the nationalistic net more difficult. As we have seen in this and the previous chapter, boycotts lay at the more violent end of the movement's spectrum of activities aimed at nationalizing consumer culture. But the very intensity and ultimate flagging of boycott support continually affirmed in the minds of movement participants that they needed additional mechanisms to guide, coax, and demand nationalistic consumer behavior.

PART III

The Exhibitionary Complex

CHAPTER FIVE

Nationalistic Commodity Spectacles

In industrially backward countries . . . , people develop the habit of using foreign products. Without realizing it, they come to worship foreign things, even when the same kinds of national products exist in the marketplace. . . . What should we do to promote and get everyone to be aware of national products and destroy the average person's reverence for foreign products? . . . Exhibiting and enthusiastically promoting national products will give everyone a deep awareness of them. Then they will happily buy and use national products.

—Xiang Kangyuan 1936

This exhibition is established to promote national products. If an item is not a national product, then it will not be permitted in the exhibition and the competition. Moreover, in the event that there are counterfeits, as soon as they are discovered, they will be immediately removed from the exhibition grounds and confiscated.

— From "Rules for the Summer and Autumn
Exhibition of National Products" (1928)

During the 1920s and 1930s, what I will call "nationalistic commodity specta-cles," ranging from fashion shows to parables about product-nationality that appeared in popular newspapers and magazines, represented a more subtle way of nationalizing consumer culture than the violent anti-imperialist boy-cotts that have attracted more attention from scholars. This diverse range of spectacles attempted to inculcate a new kind of consumer culture through a nationalistic visuality. In one such parable, a young boy attending a boarding school receives a letter from his mother informing him that she is sending him some handmade long underwear. The news excites the boy who, with the onset of winter, has begun to feel cold. The thoughtful gesture rekindles his feelings for his distant mother. As he anticipates the imminent arrival of the long johns, however, he grows anxious and begins to lose sleep. Has his mother understood the importance of using Chinese materials and of avoid-ing imported fabrics? When the silk underwear arrives, the label on the in-seam reveals the bad news. His mother used Japanese silk.

The nationality of the fabric creates a dilemma for this schoolboy. On the one hand, the boy's teacher had instructed students to abstain from consuming imported products as a way to affirm Chinese nationalism and participate in the anti-imperialist struggle. On the other hand, not wearing the clothes his mother has sewn would be disrespectful to a parent, the worst transgression within traditional Chinese ethics. The boy decides that the nation comes first. Although his legs are cold, "his heart is warm!" The dénouement confirms that this unfilial act was the correct thing to do. To keep from freezing, he takes up running. By the time spring arrives, he has become such an excellent runner that he wins the school race.[1]

Before opting for patriotism, the boy had to visualize his underwear as having a nationality. The frequent anti-imperialist boycotts periodically forced Chinese to view nationality as a characteristic of commodities. However, it was often difficult to convince Chinese to embrace product-nationality as the primary basis for desiring and consuming things. During the early twentieth century in China, an explosion of commodity spectacles supplied many competing interpretations of material culture. The power of advertising, movies, fashion shows, museums, state rituals, and many other spectacles to create associations not only influenced public perceptions of particular products but also, in fact, often overturned or undermined the ways people thought about products in general. Light bulbs, thermoses, women's dresses, traditional men's long-gowns, Western-style suits, and many other items of everyday life came to have multiple, often antithetical, associations. Depending on the observer and context, the same item might signify cosmopolitanism, a Western education, fashion consciousness, cultural treachery, or political conservatism. Against these competing meanings, the fictional schoolboy was advanced as a model for a new and pre-eminent meaning of consumption that placed patriotism above all else, even filial piety.

This and the following chapter (Part III of this book) identify and examine an interlocking complex of nationalistic commodity spectacles that articulated and propagated the ethic of nationalistic consumption through a nationalistic visuality. The commodity spectacles examined here were borrowed from abroad and then transformed into symbols of nationalism; these

---

1. "You zi" (The son away from home), *Jilian huikan* 92 (Apr. 1, 1934): 63–64. This journal was published by one of the most important movement organizations of the late 1920s and 1930s, the Shanghai Association of Mechanized National Products Manufacturers. The journal was distributed throughout China and carried many such stories.

spectacles aimed to "nationalize" Chinese spectators who encountered them and transform them into patriots of a particular sort. By linking a variety of seemingly disparate spectacles, the chapter demonstrates how the movement shaped a nascent consumer culture into a central site in the creation of the nation. The critical issue here is not the reception or interpretation of these spectacles by individual Chinese (that is, how individuals made sense of the intended message). Rather, the main issue is how the movement *set the stage* for any such interpretation through the proliferation of nationalistic commodity spectacles, which thereby engendered (and enforced) the nationalistic consumption practices of the consumer culture itself.

Remaking Commodity Spectacles for the Nation

The National Products Movement appropriated commodity spectacles from Europe and America, often by way of Japan. As with many other modern institutions, Japan helped introduce industrial exhibitions to China, for example. The Japanese government began organizing industrial exhibitions and smaller bazaars (*kankōba* 勧工場) within Japan around the time of the 1868 Meiji restoration (Yoshimi 1992: 107–44; Morley 1974: 160–64). Early Chinese reformers such as Kang Youwei, a leader of the Hundred Days Reforms of 1898, suggested that China follow Japan's lead by holding trade fairs (商學比較場) (Hsiao 1975: 311). Indeed, Chinese consistently referred to the need to emulate the Japanese use of commodity spectacles to promote nationalistic consumption (see, e.g., Lu Guiliang 1915 and "Zhanlankuang Riben"). In a memoir of anti-Japanese boycotts in the Yangzi river city of Yichang, Wen Zhengyi (1996) writes that Japanese merchants held a three-months-long exhibition there of nearly 1,000 products in 1900. Additionally, official Chinese inspection tours of Japan at the turn of the twentieth century visited other types of displays, including educational exhibitions (Borthwick 1983: 135–36). In any case, Chinese saw such displays not only as an element in Japan's rise to industrial power but also as a tool in its imperialistic designs on China. As one author suggested, Japan was subtly using invitation-only exhibitions in China to promote its products (Cheng Heqiu 1934). China sought to appropriate this same institution.

The spread of commodity displays in East Asia was part of the larger development of the institution of massive world exhibitions. Following London's Crystal Palace Exhibition of 1851, the world witnessed an increasing number of international exhibitions, to which China usually sent a display.

between 1855 and 1914, there was an exhibition involving at least twenty countries on average every two years; after that, although their number declined, their size and scope increased (Greenhalgh 1988: 15). At the same time as major cities throughout the world were holding these cosmopolitan events, the National Products Movement in China held dozens—even hundreds—of exhibitions limited strictly to "national products."[2] Scholars generally interpret world exhibitions as "the spectacle that is the quintessential expression of the capitalist era" (de Cauter 1993: 1). In China, however, these spectacles served other ends.

The rise of commodity spectacles in China was not a rush to imitate but a selective process that turned the technologies of imperialism against itself.[3] Chinese national, regional, and local exhibitions naturalized the notion of consumption based on nationalism and anti-imperialism rather than "exchange-value" (market value). Likewise, the movement transformed other imported commodity spectacles to benefit a national(istic) economy: among other acts, it established museums devoted to national products, created markets and stores that sold only national products, promoted an advertising culture that constructed and emphasized product-nationality, and elided pre-existing definitions of commodities, such as the notion of commodities as "local products" (土貨). Collectively, these efforts projected onto commodities such movement aspirations as national unity against foreign imperialism and domestic division, economic strength and self-sufficiency, and, above all, the possibility of following a "modern" lifestyle without surrendering to imperialist economic penetration.[4]

---

2. Ironically, French merchants and manufacturers in China inadvertently promoted the notion of "national commodities" and commodity spectacles by holding their own exhibition in 1923 in Tianjin. According to the U.S. consulate in the city, this exhibition "was organized for the specific purpose of exhibiting French products, or products manufactured in China under French supervision. No other foreign or native merchandise of any sort whatsoever was permitted to be exhibited. Note that like the Chinese classification of "national products" (see Chapter 4), the French also recognized goods made in China by French companies as "French" rather than "Chinese" (see "The French Fair in Tientsin [Tianjin]," Tianjin Vice Consul Woodard to U.S. Secretary of State, Jan. 1, 1924, CRDS File 893.607E: 2 and 20. On earlier U.S. efforts, see Dollar 1912: 70–71).

3. My argument here parallels the trend in anthropology away from simply writing elegies to eroding and lost cultures and toward finding new forms of local appropriation and agency (see D. Miller 1995a).

4. For a contemporary example of the role of one type of commodity spectacle, the department store, in inculcating nationality in consumers, see Creighton 1991.

The establishment and proliferation of these nationalistic spectacles suggest that the movement did not rely on the patriotism of individual Chinese; rather, it began to create an environment in which patriotic practice became inescapable. This larger goal was the fundamental difference between these national product commodity spectacles and their much more frequently studied Western counterparts. In the process of nationalizing consumption, products deemed "foreign," indeed any item deemed to be contaminated with foreign elements and therefore insufficiently Chinese, were deliberately expunged from these spectacles, symbolically exiled from the ideal consumer consciousness (as defined in these nationalistic commodity spectacles).[5]

Thus, the examination of these commodity spectacles reveals one of the central themes of this study: how the movement presented a representation of—and took the initial steps toward creating—an economy that co-opted imperialism and asserted Chinese sovereignty. Commodity spectacles in Europe and America have been viewed primarily as "celebrations of merchandise" that stripped away the individual characteristics of goods and promoted them in universal terms for their exchange-value (de Cauter 1993: 9). In contrast, national product spectacles were celebrations of Chinese *national* merchandise that institutionalized a nationalistic visuality.

---

5. Naturally, the immense social pressure to sinify spectacles applied to the companies themselves, because they more than any other spectacle wanted to publicly portray themselves as patriotic. This effort to purge China of things (or elements of things) deemed foreign existed in other areas of Chinese life. For instance, throughout this period and especially during the 1920s, there was an active anti-Christian movement (反對基督教運動) that depicted mission colleges and universities as "tools used by Western imperialists to consolidate and perpetuate their domination of China" (Lian 1997: 152). Although some participants wanted to rid China of Christianity, many others simply fought for Chinese control of missionary institutions as part of an "educational rights recovery movement" and, to use contemporary terms, the "indigenization" or "sinification" of the Christian church in China (中國本色教會; 中國化的基督教會). On the use and translation of these terms, see J. Chao 1986: 4–7. For brief summaries of the anti-Christian movement, which included the looting of churches and the murdering of missionaries, particularly during the Northern Expedition of the Nationalists in early 1927, see P. Wang 1996: 293–95 and J. Chao 1986: 188–92.

Components of the Exhibitionary Complex

Over the past several decades, scholars of American and European history have demonstrated that Western commodity spectacles developed in what might be termed an "exhibitionary complex" (see Bennett 1995).[6] Similarly, national product exhibitions emerged out of and contributed to many other spectacles, both domestic and international. As in Europe and America, institutions in China such as department stores, museums, zoos, advertising, and movie houses placed things on display as visual entertainment. A history of the national product exhibitions would be incomplete without reference to these complementary components within China's exhibitionary complex. Rather than spectacles in general, the focus here is the nationalistic aspects of four institutions comprising the exhibitionary complex of nationalistic commodity spectacles: exhibitions, museums, stores, and advertising.[7] A brief introduction to each will reveal their nationalistic purposes.[8]

Museums devoted to displaying national products multiplied throughout China during the early twentieth century. According to a 1936 survey conducted by the Chinese Museum Association, there were at least 62 such museums (broadly defined) in China by the mid-1930s, ranging from national museums in Beiping and Nanjing to provincial forums such as the Shanxi Mass Education Institute, which had displays on hygiene and children's toys. Institutions could be found in Shanghai, China's most populous city, as well as in small cities in the interior (for example, the Hechuan County Museum of Science in Sichuan province). The links between the more familiar types of museums and those specifically oriented toward the display of national products were apparent to contemporaries: several national products museums were included in a group of specialized museums (專門博物館) in the survey (Zhongguo bowuguan xiehui 1936: 4–5).

Stores and markets dealing exclusively in national products formed a third institution in this exhibitionary complex. Although an analysis of stores is outside the scope of this chapter, a brief introduction will serve to

---

6. For studies that treat several exhibitionary institutions, see, e.g., Harris 1978. On the relationship between fairs and stores, see Lewis 1983. Bennett 1995 examines museums with reference to other institutions.

7. Of course, many other spectacles performed a similar function. On the numerous national product fashion shows, for instance, see Chapter 7.

8. For articles and primary documents, see Pan Junxiang 1996c. The little that has been written has been confined almost exclusively to the Nanjing exhibition of 1910.

suggest their important role. On one level, these stores simply added to consumer culture in general by increasingly putting goods on display for casual visual entertainment and by providing opportunities for Chinese to observe commodities and one another without an obligation to buy. In other words, to a limited degree, urban China began to experience the revolution in retail marketing occurring in America and Western Europe and forming the basis of new "consumer societies" (cf. Leach 1993 and M. Miller 1981). Indeed, the Chinese entrepreneurs who introduced department stores to Hong Kong and China consciously and openly modeled their stores on Western models (W. Chan 1999: 34).[9]

Yet the movement reinvented this institution as well. From the beginning, the movement tried to provide nationalized channels for moving national products from manufacturers to consumers. Distributors and retailers were a critical yet undependable link. Savvy department stores in Shanghai, frequently targeted during anti-imperialist boycotts for selling imports, carried and promoted national product lines, including ones they themselves developed. However, these stores were famous for carrying, not excluding, imports. On the eve of the Manchurian Incident (September 18, 1931), an estimated 70–80 percent of the stock of the three main department stores (Wing On, Sincere, and Sun Sun) in Shanghai consisted of imported products (Shanghai baihuo gongsi et al 1988: 145).[10]

Movement activists wanted to create markets that sold exclusively "national products." As discussed below, exhibitions and museums early on aided the development of national product stores by establishing adjoining marketplaces. This was only a temporary solution. Once the exhibition disappeared, so did the marketplace. The movement repeatedly attempted to establish not only permanent exhibitions (museums) but also permanent marketplaces (stores). Periodically, zealous individuals and movement organizations even tried to set up stores selling exclusively national products. The establishment of "national product companies" (國貨公司) that sold

---

9. The four most famous department stores in Shanghai were known as the "four great companies" (四大公司). Located on or right off Nanjing Road, the "retailing showcase of Shanghai," these four were: Sincere (or Xianshi 先施), opened in 1917; Wing On (or Yong'an 永安), opened in 1918; Sun Sun (or Xinxin 新新), opened in 1926; and Sun (or Daxin 大新), opened in 1936. For an overview, see Huebner 1988: 222–25.

10. This is the most comprehensive introduction to department stores, including the Shanghai National Products Company. See also Yang Tianliang 1991*b*.

Fig. 5.1　Nationalized Retail Space
(*Shanghai zong shanghui yuebao* 1925.10)

Counterfeit products posed a continual problem for the National Products Movement. The prevalence of counterfeits undermined movement morale because even patriotic consumers were fooled into buying foreign products. The movement responded to this problem by creating its own stores, including Shanghai's Chinese National Products Store, photographed here on its opening day in 1925. Temporary "national product" markets were set up during national product exhibitions and movement organizations (here the NPPA) established stores to create permanently nationalized spaces that displayed and sold exclusively Chinese products. Within such stores, consumers enjoyed the commodity spectacle without fear of inadvertently desiring or buying foreign products.

only Chinese products was a common component of anti-imperialist boycotts. For instance, many such stores opened throughout Jiangsu province during the boycott of 1919.[11] In other instances, protestors created such stores by removing and burning Japanese products from a shop, as students at Qinghua University in Beijing did.[12] Likewise, the NPPA set up a large store for national products during the boycott of 1925 (see Fig. 5.1). The idea

---

11. On the Jiangsu stores, see "Danyang sheli guohuo gongsi" (Danyang establishes national products company), *XWB* 1919.9.15; "Changzhou Wu Jiru deng kaishe guohuo gongsi" (Changzhou's Wu Jiru and others start a national products company), *XWB* 1919.9.20; "Zhenjiang shangren zuzhi guohuo gongsi" (Zhenjiang merchants organize a national products company), *SB* 1919.9.30; and "Liyang xian shangjie chuangshe guohuo gongsi" (Liyang county commercial circles found a national products company), *XWB* 1919.11.9; all republished in ZDLDG 1992: 264–65. On such a store in Nanjing, which "met with considerable success," see Jordon to Curson, F.O. 405/226/72 (1919.7.7).

12. "Tsing Hua Students Declare Boycott," *North China Star* 1919.5.11; in "Zai Shi gaijin hai Nichi sendō no ken."

of establishing a nationwide network that extended into the countryside was constantly discussed and periodically attempted.[13]

These stores met with mixed results, but efforts continued. Movement groups always established special markets to commemorate "national humiliations" and pressured department stores to promote national products.[14] By 1934, stores such as Shanghai's China National Products Company, which billed itself as the "entire nation's most magnificent and most comprehensive national products emporium," had assembled a catalog listing thousands of Chinese goods that it marketed nationally and internationally.[15] Finally, during the mid-1930s, an international network of stores selling national products grew out of such isolated efforts (see Fig. 5.2).[16] As these stores spread throughout the country and among ethnic Chinese communities abroad, they became an important symbolic and practical step in the process of nationalizing consumer culture.[17]

---

13. See, e.g., "Neidi sheli guohuo shangdian zhi guanjian" (1925).

14. One important example was the special market that emerged to commemorate the anniversary of the Manchurian Incident. Beginning on the first anniversary on September 18, 1932, each year movement groups set up such a market. For a brief history that tracks the growing prominence of this event, see "Jiu yiba yu jiuchang guohuo shangchang" (1934). On collaboration among Shanghai department stores in the movement, see the newspaper clippings in the SMA in an uncataloged collection.

15. For one such catalog, see *Zhongguo guohuo gongsi huoming huilu* 1934. Likewise, the number of national products sold at a Tianjin national products store grew from 300 in 1913 to 8,000 by 1926 (Rinbara 1983: 28).

16. For photographs and a brief description of store branches, see SMA Q0-13-226: "Shanghai Zhongguo guohuo gongsi" (The Shanghai China National Products Company); and Zhongguo guohuo lianhe yingye gongsi 1947. This company was an outgrowth of earlier efforts to produce and market Chinese products cooperatively. The two most important predecessors of this organization were the Chinese National Products Manufacturers and Distributors Cooperative (國貨產銷合作協會), and the cooperative's wholesale and retail operation, the Chinese National Products Company Introduction Office (中國國貨公司介紹所). Movement literature published information on these organizations, including their bylaws, throughout the 1930s; see, e.g., *Guohuo banyue kan* 7 (1934.3.15): 26–28. For a brief history of China Chemical founder Fang Yexian's stint as the first general manager, see Ma Bingrong 1996*b*: 107–8.

17. Movement publications and Chinese newspapers regularly carried stories on these stores. See, e.g., "Choushe gedi guohuo gongsi zhi wojian" (1934), which describes the role of such stores, of which there were 24 by mid-1934, in providing reliable retail sources of national products.

Fig. 5.2 The Chinese National Products Company (est. 1937)
(Zhongguo guohuo lianhe yingye gongsi 1947)

By the late 1930s, the institutions of the National Products Movement had developed considerably. The creation of temporary markets devoted to selling only national products had evolved into a fast-growing chain of stores linking patriotic Chinese consumers at home and in Southeast Asia (*see map*); this gradually created a nationalized economy from below by connecting local stores. The company logo (*upper left*) superimposes the Chinese characters "national products" on a silhouette of China, symbolically linking geographical and economic space.

The fourth and most portable of these institutions was advertising, which took commodity spectacles outside controlled spaces to individual consumers, producing what could be called a micro-exhibition. Although a scholarly history of modern advertising has yet to be written for China, its development seems similar to that in other countries.[18] After the introduction of new printing technologies, advertising grew in tandem with the rapid proliferation of newspapers and periodicals early in the Republican era. The first Chinese-language newspaper advertisement appeared around 1872 in *Shenbao*. Although these advertisements initially promoted imported products, Chinese manufacturers soon began to use newspapers and later radio, billboards, automobiles, and calendars to advertise their products.[19]

The movement had a reciprocal relationship with the development of advertising in China. On the one hand, modern advertising provided a means for disseminating the movement agenda.[20] On the other hand, the movement deeply influenced the shape of this advertising culture by helping to define the new language of advertising and generating advertising revenue by intensifying Sino-foreign competition (Zhen 1997: 44).[21] Very early in the movement, participants began using advertising to promote national products and to attack competitors as purveyors of foreign products (see, e.g., Cochran 1980: 61–70). Chinese manufacturers not only incorporated the

---

18. For an overview of the development of advertising in the Republican era, see Zhen 1997: 36–66 and Li Shaobing 1994: 205–21. On the critical role of the British-American Tobacco Company in introducing new forms of advertising, see Cochran 1999*a*. On calendars, see Dal Lago 2000. For the memoir of an American actively involved in developing the modern advertising industry in China, see Crow 1937.

19. On the various types of advertising used by movement participants, see *Guohuo yanjiu yuekan* 1.4 (1932.9): 35–50. For examples of newspaper and magazine advertising as well as billboards, calendars, cigarette collectors' advertising cards, and other forms of printed or posted advertising, see Yi Bin 1995. Cigarette collectors' cards made use of images both of Chinese classical stories and of modern machines such as automobiles, airplanes, and trains to stimulate interest (and sales). For an illustrated overview, see Feng Yiyou 1996.

20. "Guohuo yu guanggao" (1934). For introductions to the semiotics of advertising, which were critical to my understanding of the imputation of social ideas onto commodities, see Williamson 1995 and Jhally 1990. For an analysis of a recent use of advertising to promote national consciousness, see R. J. Foster 1995*b*. The Foster article notes the significance of national content even in the production of advertisements themselves, which under a 1985 criminal law in Melanesia had to be created by local agencies and talent.

21. Likewise, the movement promoted advertising as a way of combating the dominance of imports; see, e.g., "Guohuo guanggao yu boyin" (1934).

Fig. 5.3 Nationalized Visual Spaces
(SB 1929.2.17)

This collective advertisement is one of many that joined numerous "national products" into a single advertisement (see also Fig. I.1, p. 16). The Shanghai Association of Mechanized National Products Manufacturers, which invented this form of advertisement, placed them in major Chinese newspapers during the late 1920s and 1930s. As with national product stores, this form of advertisement created a pure nationalistic commodity spectacle because every item within its boundary was a certified national product. Such advertisements made advertising affordable to smaller Chinese companies and demonstrated that China produced a wide range of products that "everyone welcomed." The advertisement suggested that national products satisfied the consumer desires of individuals ranging from traditional elders (*upper right*), through urbane adults (*lower left*), to pampered children (*lower right*). At the same time, the array of goods demonstrated that one could be both fashionable and patriotic. Product-nationality remained more important than style. Indeed, most of the items displayed here (e.g., toothbrushes, cloth umbrellas, cosmetics, leather shoes, and cotton shirts) had first appeared in Chinese markets only during the previous decades.

term "national product" but also frequently used symbols of nationalism and anti-imperialism, especially the anniversaries of national humiliations, in their advertisements.[22] In addition, movement organizations such as the

---

22. Chinese advertising also incorporated the powerful symbols of the republic, including the national flag and the image of Sun Yatsen, sometimes even in the same advertisement with movement tropes. On the commodification of national symbols, see H. Harrison 2000: 182–84.

Fig. 5.4 Patriotic Smokers
(*SB* 1935.8.8)

Nanyang Brothers Tobacco Company, a major sponsor of National Product Movement organizations and activities, placed this advertisement. Sino-foreign competition over the domestic cigarette market was particularly intense and tobacco advertisements became a common means for disseminating movement ideology. This advertisement makes the familiar
movement argument for the practice of Chinese nationality through the consumption of national products. The banner at the top reads: "Chinese people should smoke Chinese cigarettes." The image on the right reinforces this imperative to consume Chinese by showing a
map of a single Chinese space, undifferentiated by province or any other subnational tie, surrounded by ships laden with imports. The image reinforces the juxtaposition of two primary
categories, Chinese and foreign. The text reads, "With ring upon ring of foreign products surrounding China, how can national products develop? If everyone energetically works together,
perhaps economic privileges won't flow abroad."

Shanghai Association of Mechanized National Products Manufacturers
pooled their resources for advertisements that displayed dozens of authenticated national products to create nationalized visual space as part of the
larger project of creating a nationalistic visuality (for examples, see Fig. 5.3
and Fig. I.1).[23] Another advertisement (Fig. 5.4) illustrates this confluence of
patriotism and products by depicting China surrounded by ships carrying
imports. Finally, by the late 1920s, the Chinese government itself began to
categorize advertisements for national products and for foreign products

---

23. The association explains the purpose of these "collective advertisements" (聯合廣告)
in "Tonggao ge guohuo gongchang" (1937). These ads began running in the newspaper *Shenbao* in 1929.

separately; it even gave special permission for national product promotions to appear on public walls free-of-charge (rates for advertisements for luxury items and entertainment were reduced).[24] More radical participants in the movement, especially during boycotts, nationalized visual spaces by destroying advertisements for foreign products and signs for foreign companies.[25]

COMMODITY SPECTACLES
BEFORE NATIONALISM

The consumer culture forming within the movement was not completely new. Even before the movement began around 1905, three critical elements for the creation of nationalistic commodity spectacles were in place: a basic level of national economic integration, numerous festivals promoting consumption, and brand-name commodities. As a result, Chinese already had ample opportunities to view things as commodities, interact with them as sources of entertainment during festivals, and differentiate among similar products through brand-name associations.

Before importing and remaking these four exhibitionary institutions, Chinese had long had regular exposure to commodities. As far back as the Song dynasty (960–1279) and certainly by the end of the Qing dynasty in 1912, China had a commercialized economy with an extensive and, in many places, intensive circulation of commodities and traders. Likewise, by the eighteenth and nineteenth centuries, Chinese officialdom increasingly turned to market mechanisms to solve state problems (see Dunstan 1996 and Lin Man-houng 1991). China may have even had a "national marketing system" or a "national market" by the mid-Qing.[26] Farmers throughout China participated in periodic markets, buying and selling surplus produce, cash crops, and handicraft goods. According to one estimate, by the early twenti-

---

24. For this and similar measures, see ZGZZW 1929b, pt. VII: 52–53. On the specific regulations for Shanghai, see "Hushi guohuo guanggao mianshui banfa" (1930).

25. See, e.g., "Destruction of British Advertising Signs" (Nanjing, 1925.6.6), CRDS File 893.6385: 2–3; and "Humiliation Day Observed at Changsha" (Changsha, 1925.5.16), CRDS File 893.6273: 2.

26. In the commercial center of Hankou, these commodities "were not luxury goods bearing high per-unit prices, but low-priced, bulk commodities such as rice, other grains, vegetable oil, beans, and raw cotton, as well as only slightly more precious tea, salt, and timber" (Rowe 1984: 60). The level of integration varied by region and commodity. For an introduction to the diversity among ten Chinese "macroregions" during the Qing, see Naquin and Rawski 1987: 138–216.

eth century, there were some 63,000 local markets linked to regional and central trading centers (Skinner 1965: 227).[27]

In addition to local markets, annual festivals connected with both the lunar and solar calendars presented opportunities to examine and consume seasonal and specialty commodities.[28] Several of these festivals were celebrated throughout China.[29] Cities, towns, and villages celebrated regional and local festivals that were often connected with the birthday of a deity. A comprehensive description of annual festivals and rituals in Beijing identifies dozens of events, including national festivals, local temple festivals, festivals for specific industries, festivals involving particular products, and festivals held in specific areas of the city. For instance, at the beginning of each lunar year, a Beijing neighborhood famous for its shops selling paintings, books, stone rubbings, and curios held a fifteen-day fair. Each year, "long lines of carriages of rich and noble people" descended on the area in search of fashionable luxury items (Bodde 1936: 17–18).

Finally, nothing was more important for assigning nationality to commodities than identifying labels or brand names. In late imperial times, brand names ranging from simple words and images to numbers and symbols were used to identify items as basic as rice, tea, and cloth as well as more complex goods such as pharmaceuticals (for example, Shanghai's "Famous Pills of Lei Yushang's Drugstore," which have been around since at least 1700) (Hamilton and Lai 1989: 253, 258–59).[30] Before the twentieth century, brand names were usually confined to local "specialty items" (特產): porcelain from Jingdezhen, the wine of Shaoxing, paper from Fuzhou. Chinese elites not only had access to brand-name goods but also used such goods for status competition.[31]

---

27. Even China's most industrially developed and commercialized province of Jiangsu continued to hold county fairs well into the twentieth century (NII 1935: 49).

28. For a general description and examples of the ritual paraphernalia associated with these events, see Naquin and Rawski 1987: 83–88.

29. These included lunar New Year's Day, Lantern Festival, Tomb-Sweeping Festival, Dragon Boat Festival, Mid-Autumn Festival, and a few others.

30. According to Hamilton and Lai (1989: 258), branded items included: "cotton cloth, items of clothing, porcelain, boots, tea, wine, medicine and herbs, scissors, needles, copper locks, copper mirrors, gold and silver bullion, hair ornaments, jewelry, jade items, writing brushes, writing paper, ink sticks, ink stones, lacquerware, books, and bank drafts." On pre-Opium War forms of advertising in China, see Zhen 1997: 9–35.

31. For the use of material culture in status competitions during the late Ming and early Qing dynasties (1500–1800), see Clunas 1991.

Within the National Products Movement, economic integration pursued for its own sake became the symbolically significant "national economy," festivals, both new and old, became ways to encourage and practice nationalistic consumption, and "China" as a higher geographical identification became the "brand" that subsumed local and provincial items under the category of "national product."[32]

FROM A WORLD OF GOODS
TO A NATION OF PRODUCTS

Despite many similarities, Chinese exhibitions differed fundamentally from both traditional Chinese fairs and world expositions held in places such as London, Paris, New York, San Francisco, and Sydney.[33] Historians usually interpret exhibitions produced by the imperial powers as grand legitimizing performances that symbolized the power of the host-nations and generated national definitions of themselves and others on an international stage.[34] These exhibitions have also been viewed as playing an important part in creating a universal consumer culture. In recent years, scholars have been inspired by Walter Benjamin's pronouncement that late nineteenth-century "world exhibitions are the sites of pilgrimages to the commodity fetish" that "glorify the exchange value of commodities" and "create a framework in which commodities' intrinsic value is eclipsed" and have increasingly explored the links between events such as world's fairs and the emergence of consumer cultures or "consumer societies" (Benjamin 1979: 151–52). For instance, the transformative and symbolic power of such events has been noted by historians such as Rosalind Williams (1982), who sees exhibitions as playing a central role in creating the "dream world of mass consumption" in late nineteenth-century France (see also Rydell 1993: 15–18). Similarly, it is often argued that events such as the Crystal Palace exhibition were "perfectly suited to legitimate the capitalist system, and the class whose interests it served" (Richards 1990: 4).

---

32. As with native-place affiliations, national affiliations did not replace local ones.

33. I follow Findling's (1990: xviii) lead in using the American term "fair," the British term "exhibition," and the French term "exposition" interchangeably.

34. For an example of this line of interpretation, see Greenhalgh 1988. More specifically, Robert Rydell (1984) and others emphasize their role in subordinating colonial possessions and legitimizing expansion into new territories. Japan used the world exhibitions to distinguish itself from China so that the two would be treated differently by the imperialist powers (Schwantes 1974: 161).

In contrast, the history of Chinese national product exhibitions—along with the entire exhibitionary complex of which they were a part—reveals co-optations of the incursions of the imperial powers. Unlike those inspired by Benjamin, I focus on the role of comparable *national* pilgrimages in the creation of a *nationalistic* commodity fetish. The reigning idea (as expressed by Benjamin) suggests that world exhibitions eclipsed the "intrinsic value" of commodities by glorifying exchange-value (Benjamin 1979: 152). The Chinese commodity spectacles examined here redirected this process by attempting to bind this market value to the nation and create a "dream world" of nationalistic consumption.

The tension between the international and the national orientations of industrial exhibitions was there from the beginning. Although exhibitions of manufactured goods began even earlier, the first *national* industrial exhibitions in Europe were held in France under the First Republic (1792–1804).[35] Like the Chinese a century later, the French initially restricted participation to domestic goods. By 1849, on the eve of the first international exhibition in 1851 at the Crystal Palace, the French were seriously considering inviting foreigners to participate in these exhibitions but ultimately decided against it. They feared, as did many other countries holding national industrial exhibitions in the first half of the nineteenth century, that their domestic markets would be overrun with inexpensive foreign (primarily English) products.[36] Despite these fears of foreign penetration, the French and other governments ultimately decided that participating in international fairs such as the Crystal Palace and allowing international participation in their own exhibitions supplied an important opportunity for domestic manufacturers to compare and improve their products (Greenhalgh 1988: 3–26; Walton 1992: 11–12). The French never looked back.

It is not clear exactly when or how Chinese became interested in the idea of putting everyday commodities on display. Clearly the Chinese had plenty of exposure to international exhibitions. Under the auspices of the foreign-managed Imperial Maritime Customs Administration, China sent exhibits

---

35. On the spread of the idea of holding exhibitions in England before the Crystal Palace, see Kusamitsu 1980. In contrast, Mitchell (1988: 5–6) identifies panoramas as the forerunners of world exhibitions.

36. Munich (1818), Stockholm (1823), Dublin (1826), Madrid (1827), New York (1828), Moscow (1829), and Brussels (1830) were just a few of the places that followed the French example of holding national exhibitions. For a more complete list, see Mandell 1967.

to many late nineteenth-century and early twentieth-century exhibitions. The country was represented in major European events and was one of the 34 nations that participated in the first international exhibition in London.[37] Between 1867 and 1905, China was represented in at least 25 international exhibitions (S. F. Wright 1950: 431n16). It also participated in the two huge Parisian exhibitions of 1878 and 1900, as well as in major and specialized events throughout the world.[38] Chinese students and officials living overseas visited the major exhibitions in Europe and America and recorded their impressions in widely read letters, articles, and books.[39]

QUANTIFYING NATIONAL PRODUCT EXHIBITIONS

The practice of holding special exhibitions to promote "national products" spread so rapidly and so widely that it is difficult to establish how many there

---

37. Gibbs-Smith 1981: 56, which includes an illustration, "Great Exhibition from the Celestial Empire." The comments of a contemporary observer echo those of the Qianlong emperor's comments on the British goods sent to him some fifty years earlier (see Chapter 1): "We need envy nothing that they have" because their goods are all very old-fashioned or primitive. It is not clear who was responsible for this Chinese pavilion, but most likely British traders organized it.

38. In addition, China sent exhibits to specialized shows, such as the International Health Exhibition in London in 1884. It also attended exhibitions held in Asia, for example, at Osaka (1903) and Hanoi (1902–3). In the United States, China had pavilions at the Centennial Exposition in Philadelphia in 1876 and the Louisiana Purchase International Exposition in St. Louis in 1904. It also sent large delegations and elaborate displays to the Panama Pacific International Exposition in San Francisco in 1915. For brief introductions to Chinese participation in late nineteenth-century world's fairs in the United States, see Rydell 1984: 29–32, 49–52, 95–97, 202–3, 228–29. See Chinese Maritime Reports, #13, for a description of China's exhibit at the International Health Exhibition in London in 1884; and Chinese Maritime Reports, #14, for the catalog of Chinese products sent to the New Orleans Exhibition of 1884–85.

39. Perhaps the first such account came from Li Gui, a young Customs official who wrote about the Centennial Exhibition (1876) in Philadelphia. He published articles in major Chinese papers such as *Shenbao* and *Wanguo gongbao* and published a book about his travels, *Huanyou diqiu xinlu* (Travel around the globe) (1877). On Li and his impressions of the exhibition, see Ningping Yu 1999: 24–57. Many others published similar accounts. For instance, the late nineteenth-century Qing reformer Ma Jianzhong included a description of his visit to the Paris Exhibition of 1878 in a letter to the famous official Li Hongzhang. He noted that the Chinese display was an embarrassment and that it "could not even match up to the islands of Japan." He recommended that Chinese pay more attention and not entrust their display to foreigners (working in the Customs); see "A Letter to Li Hongzhang on Overseas Study" (1878), trans. in Bailey 1998: 42–44.

were. A list from 1929 that covers the years 1907–29 names 31 of the larger ones. However, during the final years of the Qing dynasty, there were also many smaller exhibitions mandated as part of the New Systems Reforms.[40] In addition, the Qing also helped to establish permanent exhibition halls. For example, in 1906, the Ministry of Agriculture, Industry, and Commerce set up the Jingshi Industrial Promotion Exhibition Hall (京師全工陳列所) in Beijing "to display exclusively each sort of product that China itself makes." Similar institutions soon appeared in cities such as Suzhou and provinces such as Zhili (modern Hebei) (Ma Min 1995: 293–94).[41]

The records of movement organizations such as the NPPA provide evidence of many more exhibitions during the Republican era. Immediately after its establishment in 1911, the NPPA began to organize, promote, and participate in local, regional, and national exhibitions of Chinese commodities and to attend ones organized by ethnic Chinese communities in Southeast Asia (ZGWH 1932, "Kaihui tongji" section: 14).[42] Moreover, the growing power of the movement contributed to the spread of its institutional forms, including exhibitions. As national product exhibitions became a meaningful and politically acceptable form of expressing nationalism and anti-imperialism, many student groups, women's clubs, native-place associations,

---

40. These were the Tianjin Promote Industry Exhibition of 1907, the Wuhan Industrial Exhibition of 1909, the Songjiang Products Exhibition of 1909, and the Beijing Products Exhibition of 1910. For the complete list of 31 exhibitions held between 1907 and 1929, see C. Y. W. Meng, "'Waking Up' Industrial China," p. 124. The Zhili [Hebei] Industrial Exhibition of 1919 is incorrectly listed as occurring in 1909. On the early industrial exhibitions and model factories, see Xu Dingxin and Qian Xiaoming 1991: 100–107 and, in Tianjin and Zhili, see MacKinnon 1980: 163–79. According to MacKinnon, the first exhibition in the region was held in 1904, and tax-free bazaars for Chinese-made goods soon followed.

41. The province of Zhili, for instance, held an exhibition that began on the eleventh anniversary of the start of the Republican revolution (October 10, 1922). See "Chili [Zhili] Industrial Exposition," Tianjin Consul to U.S. Secretary of State, 1922.7.31, CRDS File 893.607C.

42. According to the NPPA's records, the association sent items to exhibitions in Beijing (1915), Shanghai (1921), Fuzhou (1921), Nanjing (1925), and Kaifeng (1928), to name a few. For a complete list of exhibitions in which the NPPA played an active role between 1912 and 1931, see ZGWH 1932, "Huiwu jilu" section: 1–33. Branch organizations in cities such as Suzhou played central roles in organizing local exhibitions. See SZMA File 1324: 6–13. They also encouraged participation in other cities such as Chongqing (SZMA File 1324: 104). The NPPA sent items to major exhibitions in Manila (1914), the United States (1915), Singapore (1922), and Chile and Argentina (1928).

and other social organizations sponsored small exhibitions.[43] As noted above, movement activists also organized traveling national product displays that visited smaller towns and villages (Cao 1928).[44]

Finally, exhibitions proliferated even more after the establishment of the Nationalist government in 1928, which immediately ordered the creation of local, regional, and national exhibitions (SZMA Files 593, 1331, 1345).[45] These years also saw the formation of many new movement organizations that supported these exhibitions. By the 1930s, local, regional, and national exhibitions—along with ones sponsored by overseas Chinese—had become so common that they are, indeed, too numerous to count.[46]

Creating Nationalized Exhibitions

These exhibitions and museums produced carefully controlled nationalized spaces that created and naturalized the notion that the items on display were "Chinese." In the history of these institutions, two trends stand out. First, despite constant civil war and endemic economic instability, the scope, size, and number of participants in exhibitions, museums, and the entire exhibitionary complex grew rapidly. Second, this growth relied heavily on both

---

43. For example, to commemorate the May Thirtieth Incident of 1925, on the second anniversary, Hujiang University in Shanghai held the May Thirtieth National Products Exhibition (五卅國貨展覽會) ("Huda guohuo zhanlanhui zuori kaimu"). Many exhibitions set up during boycotts became permanent museums for Chinese products. The Fuzhou National Products Museum, which had some 200 visitors a day by the mid-1920s, for instance, grew out of student and merchant exhibitions organized during the 1919 boycott ("Permanent Industrial and Commercial Exhibitions, Foochow [Fuzhou], China," Fuzhou Consul Price to U.S. Secretary of State, 1924.4.28, CRDS File 893.607L).

44. Cao Muguan includes a brief (and occasionally inaccurate) history of traveling exhibitions by one of the main organizers in Shanghai. Fifty to eighty local companies participated in these exhibitions, which were held at least once a quarter. In 1929, the Nationalist government made mobile national products exhibitions a basic part of its efforts to promote the collection of national products and the circulation of national product displays (ZGZZW 1929b, pt. VII: 48).

45. As if invoking patron saints, exhibition organizers frequently republished in their own literature government orders and regulations on exhibitions to justify their events and encourage others to follow suit. This and related government orders are republished in, for example, Guohuo zhiyin 1934. For an overview of the place of the movement in Nationalist economic plans, see Guo Feiping 1994: 60.

46. The weekly news summaries published in Shenbao in the early 1930s about the movement mention one or two exhibitions nearly every week and from all corners of the country.

governmental and non-governmental initiatives. The movement did receive state support at the end of the Qing dynasty and under the Republic. At the same time, movement organizations—often led by members of chambers of commerce—kept finding new ways to link "national salvation" to "national products."

THE NANYANG INDUSTRIAL
EXHIBITION OF 1910

China did not exclude foreign products from its first major exhibition, although it was clearly heading in that direction. As noted above, the Qing dynasty supported numerous exhibitions throughout China. The high point of what historian Ma Min has termed the Qing's "exhibition fever" (賽會熱) came at the very end of the dynasty, when China held a world's fair in the Yangzi river city of Nanjing, the Nanyang Industrial Exhibition of 1910 (Ma Min 1995: 294).[47] Foremost in the minds of the organizers was the goal of national economic self-strengthening. The event was the brainchild of Governor-General of Liangjiang Duanfang 端 方 (1861–1911), who hoped to inspire economic competition, which he believed to be at the heart of Western wealth and power. Soliciting foreign participation served several ends. First, as Duanfang acknowledged, the "affair was not really intended to show Chinese products to the world but to spy at foreign ways so as to encourage domestic improvements" (Godley 1978: 515). Second, the event countered foreign and domestic criticism of the crumbling dynasty. As historian Michael Godley has concluded, this was the "last, and most monumental, effort undertaken by the Manchu house to prove to the foreign powers and growing numbers of domestic critics that the traditional leadership was capable of modernizing the country" (Godley 1978: 504).[48]

---

47. The Nanyang quanye hui 南洋勸業會 is also known in English as the "South Seas Exhibition." This was the only fair in all of East Asia deemed sufficiently international to be included in a reference book on world's fairs before the Osaka one of 1970 (Findling 1990: 212–13). As with later national exhibitions, this one represented a culmination of provincial exhibitions held across China (Nanjing vice-consul to U.S. Secretary of State, 1910.2.23, CRDS File 893.607A).

48. Outside Western Europe and the United States, other countries also adopted this strategy. For example, Mexico at the same time also tried to use world's fairs to demonstrate its modern status and national potential (Tenorio-Trillo 1996: 8–11). On this count, the Nanyang Exhibition was somewhat successful. For an example of foreign coverage, see "The Nanyang Exhibition: China's First Great National Show," *FER* 1910.4: 503–7.

The exhibition, which opened in June 1910 and continued until November, was the first national pilgrimage to Chinese commodities. Nearly 200,000 people visited the exhibition. Although only fourteen other nations and 78 private companies participated, the fairgrounds themselves were very impressive, covering 156 acres and encompassing some 36 buildings. The *North-China Daily News* concluded that the effort was a "credible imitation on a smaller scale of the great exhibitions of America and Europe."[49] Although a financial failure, the experiment became a template for later national product exhibitions.[50] It encouraged local and regional competitions and organizing committees and stimulated groups in many locales to create exhibitions with the support of newly established chambers of commerce (Zhongping Chen 1998: 272–74; Wu Kangling 1994: 164–66). Its legacy can be seen in the persistence in subsequent decades of local, non-governmental groups organizing exhibitions in support of higher-level efforts.

EARLY REPUBLICAN EFFORTS

After the Revolution of 1911, collecting and displaying national products represented an effort to do what the new leaders of the Republic could not do militarily: unify China and resist imperialism. These activities also demonstrated to domestic commercial and industrial critics that the government was actively trying to develop the Chinese economy. Thus, despite the unstable polity, ambitious local and national leaders promoted the spread of "exhibition fever" during the early years of the Republic (see "Shangpin chenliesuo zhangcheng"). These efforts expanded following the popular outrage and nationwide boycott protesting Japan's May 1915 attempt to gain more control over China (see Chapter 3). Shortly thereafter, Zhou Ziqi 周 自齊 (1871–1932)—a former Columbia University student and an assistant to Wu Tingfang (the famous diplomat and an early NPPA leader)— persuaded President Yuan Shikai to establish a government bureau to encourage the development of national products. The petition to the president argued that China needed to take action: "Wealth is being lost because no concerted effort is being made to advance domestic commerce and industry."

---

49. Findling 1990: 212–13; "The Nanking Exhibition," *North-China Daily News* 1910.2.22, reproduced in CRDS File 893.607: 1. This file contains many newspaper clippings and a consular report on the Exhibition.

50. NCH 1910.9.30: 801–2; "China's First World's Fair," *American Review of Reviews*, June 1910, pp. 691–93; Godley 1978: 509, 517, 521.

With the president's approval, the Ministry of Commerce, Industry, and Agriculture set up a Commercial and Industrial Commission with three divisions: one for gathering statistical information, another for conducting experiments, and a third for collecting national products and organizing displays ("The Resources of China" [1915]).[51]

Throughout 1915, this commission significantly enlarged the exhibitionary complex by supporting the establishment of permanent spaces for nationalistic commodity spectacles. The first of these was attached to the ministry in Beijing, the Commercial Products Exhibition Hall (商品陳列所). Although Beijing was not China's most industrialized city, it was thought that having a permanent exhibition there would serve to educate China's rulers. The ministry also had ambitious plans to establish branches in the major industrial cities, including Guangzhou, Tianjin, Hankou, Shanghai, and Shenyang (Mukden) ("Home Products Exhibit" [1915]). The Division of Exhibits prepared a complete annual catalog of its holdings for the ministry, facilitated exchanges with other museums, helped establish exhibits in towns and cities throughout China, and hosted an annual national exhibition ("Industrial Exhibition" [1915]).

The success of the inaugural exhibition in autumn 1915 reflected the growing power of the movement. In what became a common practice, the commission used this exhibition to collect products for a permanent hall. Similar to the Nanyang Exhibition of 1910, this event was designed to promote national products. Although imports were displayed, the intent was not to encourage their consumption but to create a reference room for Chinese manufacturers.[52] Within three months, the Division of Exhibits managed to put together an impressive event, the All-China National Products Exhibition (全國國貨展覽會), which ran from October 1 to October 20. Eighteen provinces and two special zones sent approximately 100,000 items (*Nongshang bu* [1918]).[53]

---

51. This article includes a translation of the June 10, 1915, memorial to the president on the commission.

52. Indeed, the name given to the foreign pavilions reflected this purpose. As discussed in the following chapter, at the 1929 exhibition in Hangzhou, an English-language sign on the building read "Foreign Exhibits," whereas the Chinese sign labeled the exhibit a "reference display" (參考陳列所).

53. Such exhibitions led directly to the establishment of new industries. For example, the display of Shandong lace products inspired Beijing entrepreneurs first to sell these products and then to manufacture their own (Dingle and Pratt 1921: Report #116).

Government organizers could not have successfully prepared the exhibition or established the exhibition hall without the assistance of movement organizations. In Shanghai and the surrounding area, groups such as the NPPA and the recently established Society to Encourage the Use of National Products (全用國貨會) helped gather, certify, and submit national products. In summer 1915, to promote the exhibition and the movement as a whole, the NPPA and this society began publishing the *National Products Monthly* (國貨月報), which featured extensive reports on the 1915 exhibition in Beijing.[54] The monthly also published the Ministry of Finance's assurance that products shipped to the exhibition would not have to pay transit taxes ("Fu hui zhi tiaogui"). As with other NPPA activities, this journal spread the movement to Chinese far beyond Shanghai.[55]

SHANGHAI COMMERCIAL PRODUCTS DISPLAY HALL

"National humiliations" such as Japan's presentation of the Twenty-One Demands in 1915 prompted immediate reactions, but movement activists and sympathizers also responded to economic trends. After World War I, the return of Western soldiers, diplomats, merchants, and commodities to China quickly ended what contemporary Chinese observers called the country's Golden Age of self-reliant economic growth.[56] The creation of a permanent display hall in Shanghai reflected this renewed sense of national economic crisis. Although plans began as early as October 1915, the Shanghai General Chamber of Commerce finally established the Shanghai Commercial Products Display Hall (上海商品陳列所) in 1921.[57] In the face of the dumping of products by hostile powers, one critic reminded readers of the

---

54. "Zhonghua guohuo weichi hui zuzhi quanguo guohuo zhanlanhui canguantuan xuanyanshu ji zhangcheng" (1915).

55. Because this journal was distributed to 29 cities and provinces and to overseas Chinese in such places as Singapore, it became an early and important vehicle for disseminating the movement agenda, particularly the idea of organizing nationalized spectacles. For an introduction, see Chen Zhengshu 1987.

56. The development of domestic industry in this period is extensively documented in Du 1991. The amount of autonomy was relative, because the Japanese actively filled the vacuum created by the departure of Western business interests. By one estimate, between 1914 and 1919, the number of Japanese companies increased from 955 to 4,878 (Remer 1933a: 421, 451).

57. The idea for creating such a hall, however, had been proposed as early as 1902 (Xu Dingxin and Qian Xiaoming 1991: 263).

central tenet of the movement and the abstract purpose of the hall: "We believe that military invasion definitely cannot destroy China but we fear that economic invasion can" (Pei Yunqing 1936).[58] In a petition to Chinese officials regarding the plans for the opening of the hall and the launching of an inaugural exhibition, organizers underscored their fear that the reintroduction of foreign consumer goods would destroy China's nascent light industrial sector. Once again, the writers warned, China would be relegated to providing raw materials to foreign powers and importing finished products ("Ben suo lici juban zhanlanhui zhi jingguo" [1936]). To the hall's organizers, it had helped prevent a reversal.

The nationwide search for authentic Chinese goods itself disseminated nationalistic categories of consumption while helping to identify and collect suitable products. Organizers used five techniques to find national products. They sent requests to the Ministry of Agriculture and Commerce and provincial leaders soliciting samples, wrote letters to the general chamber of commerce and local notables in each city asking for assistance, requested schools and individuals to submit model goods, obtained products from famous factories, and dispatched their own investigators. Thanks to these methods, the hall received over 30,000 items from 870 business leaders in over 100 locations. Although the goods came primarily from cities and counties in the surrounding and nearby provinces of Jiangsu and Zhejiang, more distant provinces such as Yunnan and Sichuan also sent items ("Diyi ci zhanlanhui" [1923]).[59]

The Display Hall quickly became a central institution in the burgeoning movement in Shanghai, and a steady flow of pilgrims to the nationalistic commodity fetish made their way to the hall. The activities of the hall began in November 1921. Several hundred officials, industrialists, and foreign dignitaries gathered at the Shanghai General Chamber of Commerce auditorium for the opening ceremony of speeches and a guided tour of the grounds. Over the 30 days of the event, some 61,500 people visited ("Ben suo lici juban

58. SSC 1936, a commemorative volume for the fifteenth anniversary of the founding of the hall, contains many different types of documents: an organizational chart, lists of members, charts of the different types of products displayed and other activities of the hall, essays by prominent government officials and members of the business community, copies of official correspondence, bylaws of the organization, and photographs of prominent leaders of the hall, exhibits, and conferences. The collection is unpaginated.

59. For a complete list of these locations and the number of participants, see "Ben suo lici juban zhanlanhui zhi jingguo" (1936).

zhanlanhui zhi jingguo" [1936]). The number of visitors to the hall varied by time of year. During 1922, each day anywhere from a few dozen to several thousand visited ("Chongxin qiyao hou" [1923]). In 1923, several thousand visited each month ("Yinian nei" [1924]).

The hall provided year-round access to thousands of objects of everyday life deified as talismans for national salvation. These were mundane items. The hall categorized the vast majority of these products as manufactured goods, dyed and woven goods, chemical products, horticultural items, entertainment goods, food and drink products, and pharmaceuticals. In addition, the hall displayed a smaller number of art objects, scientific instruments, hunting and shepherding tools, and aquatic products. Reflecting the growth of the national economy, the total number of objects displayed rose from approximately 5,300 items in 1922 to 8,695 items in 1936 ("Ben suo gezhong chenliepin" [1936]).

The presentation of these items underscored that they were much more than commodities defined strictly by their exchange-value. Throughout the industrializing world, the introduction of plate glass windows and display cases was subtly and decisively altering the relationship between commodities and consumers. Glass shut down the access of two senses, smell and touch, and transferred more power to sight. The introduction of plate glass windows had the same effect in China.[60] Encasing Chinese articles in fancy glass display cases in an elegant and sanitized environment simultaneously provided access and created distance (see Fig. 5.5). As historian William Leach has noted for American department stores, "the result was a mingling of refusal and desire that must have greatly intensified desire" (1993: 63). Within the spectacles nationalized by the movement, however, this desire was valued not only for satisfying individual wants and selling goods but also for aiding "national salvation" (Xiang Kangyuan 1936; Tao Leqin 1936).

The Shanghai Display Hall—along with other halls established in 1915—helped build a rudimentary national foundation for the exhibitionary

---

60. On the introduction of glass displays to storefronts in China in the 1920s, see Zhen 1997: 49. For an example of the dramatic impact of the introduction of plate glass windows in one Chinese town in this period, see Thomas 1931: 147–49. Thomas writes that the whole town turned out at night to see the illuminated display, and many of the other shops in this town quickly followed suit.

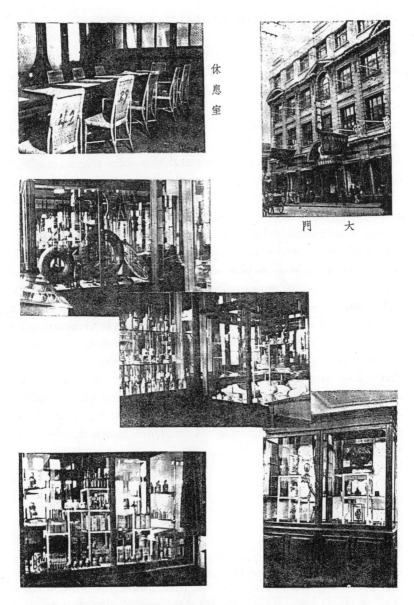

Fig. 5.5 Shanghai Commercial Products Display Hall (est. 1921)
(SSC 1936)

These photographs show the hall's lounge (*upper left*), main entrance (*upper right*), and display cases of national products. By excluding foreign products from a building housing only certified Chinese national products and by putting these mundane commodities (which included automobile tires, bicycle wheels, kitchenware, and canned foods) in glass cases, nationalistic commodity spectacles such as this one helped define nationalistic categories of consumption in China.

complex. The halls provided representative commodities to regional, national, and international exhibitions. Between its founding in 1921 and its fifteenth anniversary in 1936, the Shanghai Display Hall helped collect products for seventeen domestic fairs and organized delegations for fifteen overseas expositions.[61] For instance, in 1929, the hall provided 9,842 articles to the West Lake Exhibition in Hangzhou.[62] It also organized five major exhibitions of its own, such as the inaugural exhibition of 1921 that coincided with the opening of the hall and later displays of the products of important Chinese industries such as silk, chemical, and seasonal goods.[63]

Even before the establishment of a relatively stable central government in 1928, an exhibitionary complex that generated nationalistic commodity spectacles had emerged. Major display halls such as the one in Shanghai played a direct role in organizing similar halls and extending the notion of nationalistic consumption into other cities. In 1923, for the Suzhou Display Hall, for instance, organizations such as the NPPA not only supplied information on how to set up a hall but also helped collect product samples and publicize the event.[64] In short, exhibitions already enjoyed widespread support among Chinese politicians, business leaders, student activists, and others attempting to promote Chinese nationalism through the strengthening of nationalistic categories of consumption. This base provided a strong foundation for an even more comprehensive and organized complex of displays that developed during the following decade.

---

61. For a complete list, see "Ben suo linian juxing zhanlanhui ji daizheng chupin yi lan" (A look at each year that this hall hosted exhibitions and helped solicit products), in SSC 1936.

62. "Lici daizheng chupin shuliang bijiao mian" (A comparative graph of the numbers of products solicited each time), in SSC 1936. The hall also organized delegations to participate in the International Silk Expositions held in New York in 1921 and 1923. The extensive preparations undertaken by the hall are exhaustively documented in Shanghai zong shanghui 1923: pt. II.

63. For full reports on these exhibitions, including photographs, see Shanghai zong shanghui 1924.

64. SZMA File 589: 20–41, 70–72. Moreover, the NPPA continued to play an active role in establishing such national product exhibitions. On its role in an exhibition in Wu county, Jiangsu province, for instance, see SZMA File 1349: 1–9, 12–17, 57–94.

Expansion Under the Nationalist Government

In 1928, two events accelerated and expanded the National Products Movement and its use of nationalistic commodity spectacles: the establishment of a new central government under the Nationalists (Guomindang or GMD) and the massive nationwide boycotts that followed the outbreak of fighting with Japanese troops in Shandong province. This anti-imperialist environment intensified the demand for certified national products and stimulated Chinese leaders to accede to popular demands to impede imports by endorsing the movement.[65]

The restoration of central state power had an immediate impact on the movement. Under the leadership of its activist minister, Kong Xiangxi, the Ministry of Industry and Commerce supported the inculcation of nationalistic consumption by placing Chinese commodities on temporary and permanent display (ZDLDG 1991: 745–58).[66] Indeed, the organization of industrial exhibitions was part of a much larger ministry effort to promote industrial production. Among other efforts, the ministry created rules for rewarding and encouraging Chinese manufacturers, distributed instruments such as weights and rulers to help standardize production, and commissioned special investigations of various industries. At the same time, it also drafted trademark laws, established rules for government takeovers of failing industries, and created quality-control bureaus in commercial ports to prevent exports of poorly manufactured goods (on these efforts, see Tyau 1930: 191–209).

Although Kong's ministry was the most active, other government organs also supported the movement. For example, the Ministry of the Interior circulated detailed proposals specifying how every Chinese social and political

---

65. Many types of evidence confirm this heightened level of movement activity. For instance, commercial and industrial operations, for fear of being labeled foreign, sought membership in these organizations as well as certifications of national product authenticity.

66. The ministry also circulated these suggestions in the 1928 booklet *Guohuo yundong* (The National Products Movement). This ministry was formally established in March 1928, after the successful completion of the Northern Expedition, and was an amalgamation of the Beijing government's Ministry of Agriculture and Commerce and the Ministry of Industry. In 1931, the ministry merged with the Ministry of Agriculture and Mining to form the Ministry of Industries. Kong Xiangxi resigned from the ministry in 1931 but later became minister of finance. Of course, other ministries participated and promoted efforts to collect and promote national products. For an overview, see ZGZZW 1929b, pt. VII.

organization should contribute to the movement.[67] These proposals provide a comprehensive introduction to the ways in which movement terms and goals circulated throughout government and society. In July, the central government issued a set of recommendations for promoting national products that set specific responsibilities for fifteen different social and government groups.[68] For example, Nationalist Party members and student groups were asked to organize teams to travel to towns and villages to lecture on the meaning of buying national products. The recommendations also suggested that party members contact commercial publications and request that national product advertisements receive reduced rates and that publishers use national product newsprint whenever possible. For their part, chambers of commerce were requested, among other things, to "promote morality among business people" by teaching them "not to sell imports, unless they are essential" and not to grant chamber membership to anyone who sold imports. The Ministry of the Interior also instructed public security bureaus to pay special attention to the protection of national product manufacturers and shops and to allow them to hang national product advertisements and movement slogans on public-notice boards for free. All government departments were instructed to include a page urging the consumption of national products in each of their publications.[69]

NATIONAL PRODUCTS MUSEUMS:
NATIONALIZED CONSUMER SPACES

With the cooperation of movement organizations, the new government immediately moved to expand another central element in the exhibitionary complex. In October 1927, the Ministry of Industry and Commerce issued

67. A copy was published as "Fuyu: Neizheng buzhang tichang guohuo zhi juti banfa" (1928). Several pieces of Nationalist government correspondence on this matter during the summer of 1928 are republished in ZDLDG 1991: 737–39.

68. These included the Nationalist Party, chambers of commerce, trade unions, student organizations, women's organizations, Ministry of Interior, Ministry of Finance, Ministry of Industry and Commerce, Ministry of Agriculture and Mining, Ministry of Communications, universities and colleges, and the military, among others. For information on the "state corporatist" social management style introduced by the Nationalist government, see Fewsmith 1985: 159–66.

69. During 1928 and 1929, in accordance with these guidelines, many local and provincial government organs and movement organizations published similar recommendations. The Nationalists published many guides to the movement, including ZGZZW 1929a, b.

the "Rules for National Product Museums" ("Guohuo chenlieguan tiaoli"), which required each province and city to establish a "national products museum." Although the ministry lacked the resources to enforce the rules, the initiative met with widespread acceptance (Lin Zhimao 1928). Shanghai, the leading city in the movement, soon established a museum. So did many other cities. In 1928 alone, twelve cities and provinces, among them Beiping, Zhejiang, Shandong, Shanxi, Fujian, Hebei, and Jiangsu, set up national products museums. Within two years after the establishment of a national government in Nanjing, there were some 21 new or reorganized museums.[70] Even the remote northwestern province of Ningxia and the southwestern city of Guizhou eventually set up such museums (Zhongguo bowuguan xiehui 1936: 121–28, 161–62).

Nanjing, the new capital of China, established one of the most ambitious museums. Following a week of activities designed to encourage citizens to adhere to the principles of nationalistic consumption, the Capital National Products Museum (首都國貨陳列館) held an opening ceremony on a September afternoon in 1929.[71] Addressing over a thousand representatives from the government, the Nationalist Party, and the business world, Kong Xiangxi called the museum "the first step" in developing industry and commerce.[72] Events such as this were in effect a national convention for movement activists, as organizations in other cities sent representatives to the opening ceremonies. For example, the Shanghai Citizens Association for the

---

70. For the complete list, see Dong 1930: 2–3. Sometimes these institutions grew out of earlier ones. For example, at the end of 1928, the Hebei provincial government's Industrial and Commercial Affairs Office (工商廳) responded to the ministry's order by reorganizing the Tianjin Commercial Products Exhibition Hall (天津商品陳列所) and renaming it the Hebei Provincial National Products Museum (河北省國貨陳列館). Shanghai manufacturers also planned to send a team to help with the reorganization. See Hu Guangming et al. 1994: 1511–12. For additional information on this museum, including a list of its award-winning products, see ibid.: 1512–24.

71. "Gongshang bu guohuo chenlieguan zhanqi kaimu" (Opening ceremony postponed for the Ministry of Industry and Commerce's National Products Museum), *Gongshang banyue kan* 1.7 (1929.4): 1; "Gongshang bu guohuo chenlieguan kaimu" (Opening ceremonies of the Ministry of Industry and Commerce's National Products Museum), *Gongshang banyue kan* 1.17 (1929.8): 1; and Guoshiguan (Academia Historica) Presidential archives, 267: 1663–77.

72. "Gongshang bu guohuo chenlieguan kaimu" (Opening ceremonies of the Ministry of Industry and Commerce's National Products Museum), *Shangye zazhi* 4.9 (1929.9): 2. For a collection of essays discussing the significance of the new museum, see Kong Xiangxi 1929.

Promotion of National Products sent a large delegation.[73] In its first year, the highly popular museum displayed over 7,000 objects and welcomed nearly a million visitors.[74] In addition, as with museums in other cities, the Capital Museum also organized special exhibitions. For example, in spring 1930, the hall hosted a month-long All-China Silk and Satin Exhibition. As with most such exhibitions, foreign products were not permitted to participate ("Guohuo chenlieguan jinxun" [1930]). The museum also set up a permanent national products marketplace that quickly attracted over fifty shops that rented space there ("Gongshang bu guohuo chenlieguan jishou zhunxing banfa" [1929]). Gradually, and through these museums and exhibitions, the idea of consecrating national products markets was taking hold.[75]

Changsha, the capital of Hunan province, established an even more impressive institution. After several years of preparations, in 1931, the province began building the Hunan National Products Museum, a massive three-story building at the site of the former imperial examination grounds (a fitting symbol of the new importance of commodity consumption as a path to status).[76] The project was finally finished in January 1934. The largest national products marketplace in the province occupied the first floor, along with a movie house, three restaurants, and a barbershop. The second and third floors exhibited products collected from major cities throughout China as well as the province's specialty products. Organizers hoped to attract consumers year-round by using fans in the summer and heating in the winter

73. For photographs of this delegation, see *Shangye zazhi* 5.3 (1930.3): Inside front cover. "Guohuo gongchang daibiao dahui canjia Gongshang bu Guohuo chenlieguan kaimu jinian Guozhanhui" (National product manufacturers delegation to participate in the Ministry of Industry and Commerce's exhibition to commemorate the opening of the National Products Museum), *SB* 1929.8.14: 13.

74. "Guohuo guan juxing jinian hui" (National Products Museum hosts anniversary meeting), *Gongshang banyue kan* 2.18 (1930.9): 2; and "Xuyan" (Introduction), in Shiye bu, Guohuo chenlieguan 1931: 1–8.

75. One active participant in the movement asserted that selling national products at museums was essential to creating in the museum—and by extension in the products—a dynamic and up-to-date environment; see Tianxu Wosheng (pseud. of Chen Diexian), "Gongxian yu guohuo chenlieguan" (Contributing to the National Products Museums), *Jilian huikan* 105 (1934.10.15): 3–5.

76. Similarly, Nanjing had used the former examination grounds for the Jiangsu Industrial Exhibition of 1921. This exhibition became the basis of the first permanent industrial museum in Nanjing; see "Kiangsu Industrial Exposition," Nanjing Consul to U.S. Secretary of State, 1921.2.9, CRDS File 893.607B: 1.

and added to the festive environment by broadcasting music throughout the building. This building was a conspicuous fortress for the nationalized economy, and it drew the attention of local Japanese, who complained about the official reference to prohibiting "Japanese products" (日貨). Japanese pressure forced museum managers to replace the offending characters with the broader term "foreign products" (洋貨) (Dai 1996: 420–21).

THE ESTABLISHMENT OF
THE SHANGHAI MUNICIPAL
NATIONAL PRODUCTS MUSEUM

A closer look at one museum reveals how these institutions operated.[77] Founded in August 1928, the Shanghai Municipal National Products Museum was one of the earliest within this new network of government-sponsored national products museums. In contrast to the Shanghai Commercial Products Display Hall set up by the Chamber of Commerce in 1921, the Social Affairs Bureau of the local government, working under the direction of the Ministry of Industry and Commerce, ran this museum.[78] In Shanghai, as in other cities, the museum had two express purposes: generally, to promote the consumption of national products and, more specifically, to investigate the nationality of products and display only certified Chinese ones.[79] Thus, the museum represented the visible culmination of a much larger process that separated and then displayed national products. In achieving these purposes, the museum created nationalized spaces and in the process contributed critical elements to the emerging nationalistic exhibitionary complex.[80]

---

77. Museums and other movement institutions frequently published and circulated detailed reports, as well as copies of their rules and official correspondence; this may account for the similarity of rules and events among these institutions.

78. This museum was not entirely new. It was created by the Shanghai municipal government in August of 1928 and based on the Bureau of Agriculture, Industry, and Commerce's Industrial Products Exhibition Room. Christian Henriot singles out Shanghai's Social Affairs Bureau, and its chief, Pan Gongzhan, as especially effective agents within a very active municipal government (1993: 211–28).

79. "Zhengli jingguo ji jihua" (Undertakings and plans), in SSGC 1933: "Guanwu" section, 9–10.

80. The procedures for investigating and certifying "national products," a critical component in the evolution of the exhibitionary complex, are discussed in detail in Chapter 4.

The museum reflected Shanghai's importance to the movement. According to the second director of the museum, Dong Keren 董克仁, Shanghai was the "staging ground for foreign commercial economic invasion of China; therefore promoting national products in Shanghai was especially important" (Dong 1930: 3–4). To promote these products, the museum director and his staff carefully regulated the relationship between the observer and the observed ("Shanghai shi guohuo chenlieguan guicheng" [1930]). As with other sites in the nationalized exhibitionary complex, the museum had strict regulations governing the display of products. The first rule limited access to Chinese citizens and their national products.[81]

To return to the *national* pilgrimage metaphor adapted from Walter Benjamin, the museum operators consciously worked to create a sacred space for national products, the modern equivalent of holy relics. The museum was open every day to all Chinese citizens, but it strictly regulated the personal appearance and deportment of visitors and staff. For instance, visitors were asked not to chew tobacco or spit. Nor did it admit "drunkards, the insane, the improperly dressed, those with livestock or dangerous articles, unaccompanied children under 10" or anyone deemed by the staff to be a nuisance. Inside the museum, patrons were requested to proceed through the building in an orderly manner and not to shout or impede the viewing of others.[82] As Thomas Richards has remarked on the Crystal Palace, putting commodities on display in this way generated reverence for the objects, and elevated "the commodity above the mundane act of exchange" (1990: 39).

Because they were permanent institutions, these national products museums became bases for the regular circulation of information and commodities. As the record of museums such as the one in Shandong confirms, a growing number of these institutions throughout China participated in product exchanges that enabled museum visitors to inspect certified Chinese

---

81. "Shanghai shi guohuo chenlieguan zhengji chupin guize" (1930). The process aimed to be transparent, and the regulations were reprinted in many places; see, e.g., *Gongshang banyue kan* 1.8 (1929.4): 19–20. See also "Shanghai shi guohuo chenlieguan shencha chupin guize" (1930). Similar rules applied to products sold at the museum (see "Shanghai shi guohuo chenlieguan shoupin guize" [1930]). These regulations applied to museums in other cities, too (see "Gongshang bu guohuo chenlieguan jishou zhanxing banfa" [1929]).

82. "Shanghai shi guohuo chenlieguan canguan guize" (The rules for visitors to the Shanghai Municipal National Products Museum), in SSGC 1933, "Guanwu" section, 3–4; and SSGC 1930: 136–37.

commodities manufactured outside their region.[83] Moreover, the circulation of these national products extended outside China. Ethnic Chinese communities in other countries regularly participated in this movement to establish museums or display halls for Chinese products; the ways national products solidified connections between overseas Chinese and China await further study.[84] These institutions, then, became an important venue in which even illiterate Chinese could make the nation a product of their imaginations.

A SPECTACULAR WEEK

National product exhibitions were often at the center of broader movement events. The first of many combined local and Nationalist government efforts was the National Products Movement Week of July 7–13, 1928. The week inculcated the nationalistic categories of consumption through three primary areas of activity: public entertainment, the Summer and Autumn Articles National Products Exhibition, and the Conference on Improving Products. These areas corresponded roughly to the three stated objectives of the week: generating broad public support for the movement, cultivating the domestic market for national products by raising awareness of the range of such goods, and improving the quality and competitiveness of products by encouraging cooperation among producers.[85]

An impressive array of carefully planned spectacles supported the week: a parade, parties, rallies, the scattering of fliers from airplanes, and the posting of slogans throughout the city. Both Shanghai business circles and the new

---

83. For a 1935 exhibition, for example, the museum displayed scores of products from the Shanghai Display Hall as well as from other cities. For a complete list of products displayed from other museums, see "Yinian lai lixing gongzuo" (Routine work of this past year), in Shandong sheng guohuo chenlieguan 1936.

84. Shanghai, Suzhou, and other major cities routinely received requests for information about locally produced goods. For example, in winter 1928, the Jiangsu provincial government forwarded a letter to the Shanghai General Chamber of Commerce from the Chinese Products Museum of Thailand. The letter explained that the museum was trying to help market national products to the many ethnic Chinese living overseas who wanted to express concern for their "ancestral land" (祖國) through consumption ("Xianluo Huahuo chenlieguan zhengji guohuo" [1928]).

85. Many sources list these three goals; see, e.g., "Guohuo yundong dahui taolun gailiang pinzhi huiyi ji" (1928). For a non-Chinese perspective on the week, see "National Products Exhibition, Shanghai, China," Shanghai Consul Huston to U.S. Secretary of State, 1928.7.26, CRDS File 893.607.

government made elaborate preparations for the week, which the Social Affairs Bureau intended to be the first of an annual series.[86] Under the bureau's direction, nearly every division within the Shanghai municipal government participated. A special preparatory committee consisted of some of the most powerful men in Shanghai, including many national product manufacturers. Collectively, these bodies convinced famous individuals and scholars to give speeches and write articles, and they persuaded all the major papers to publish special articles on the week. Movie theaters and radio stations also agreed to promote it. In preparation, the city printed tens of thousands of copies of the official slogans for the week and required that during the week all stores fly the national flag and post the slogans. Organizers even asked that all chamber members fly a "Use National Products" pennant on their (imported) automobiles.[87]

Shanghai's leading figures participated in the spectacle. The opening ceremonies were held on the afternoon of July 7, 1928, at the Shanghai General Chamber of Commerce headquarters. Prominent officials and industrialists attended, including Mayor General Zhang Dingfan 張定璠 (1891–1945), the chief of public security, the head of the local sanitation bureau, and the head of the municipal industrial office. Members of commercial organizations such as the general, county, and local chambers of commerce also attended. The three major movement organizations that had participated in the preparations urged their members to attend. In addition to groups that might be expected to participate enthusiastically in movement events, every conceivable social group was required to send representatives. Altogether more than a thousand people attended ("Shanghai guohuo yundong zhou" [1928]).

Everything about the event reinforced the central messages of the movement. The chamber's auditorium was decorated for the occasion, and posters with movement slogans were hung throughout the hall. The mayor, in the opening speech, outlined his vision of comprehensive social participation in creating a nationalized economy: agricultural laborers would produce national products, merchants would sell only national products, Chinese consumers would "wholeheartedly" use them, and the government would sustain this cycle by continually promoting them. Another speaker reminded everyone that the events of the week were to be more than just an advertise-

---

86. On these and other preparations, see "Guohuo yundong dahui tiaoli" (National Products Movement Rally preparations), SB 1928.6.29: 14.

87. "Guohuo yundong dahui" (National Products Movement rally), SB 1928.7.5: 13.

ment, not something seen and soon forgotten. As the head of the Social Affairs Bureau explained, organizers hoped this week would "change the psychology of the people by causing them to develop a deep appreciation of national products."[88]

The introduction of Nationalist Party and state resources politicized many movement events, including the National Products Movement Week. At the opening ceremony, for instance, a Nationalist representative attempted to claim as much credit for the party as possible. He reminded those assembled that this sort of event would have been impossible just a few years earlier during the warlord period preceding the reunification of China under Nationalist rule. As did other movement supporters, he argued that three major social goals of China depended on the success of the movement. "First, if China desires international economic independence, it must promote national products. Second, if China wants wealth and power, its citizens must stimulate industry. And third, if Chinese desire freedom and equality, then everyone must cherish and use national products." He predicted that under the leadership of the new Nationalist government and the party these long-cherished goals would be realized.[89]

After several hours of speeches, the opening ceremony concluded with the mayor of Shanghai leading everyone in shouting the week's ten official slogans:[90]

1. The National Products Movement is a movement of national salvation!

2. Chinese people should not welcome foreign products!

3. Promoting national products is the responsibility of all citizens!

4. To resist the foreign economic invasion, we must promote national products!

5. To stimulate national products, we must have lasting and genuine preparations!

6. Workers must energetically improve national products and improve production!

7. Merchants must energetically market national products!

8. The masses must energetically buy national products!

9. National product manufacturers and merchants forever!

10. Shanghai Special Municipality National Products Movement forever!

---

88. For a description of the opening ceremonies, excerpts of the speeches, and a photograph, see "Dahui kaimu qingxing" (Rally opening ceremony events), *SB* 1928.7.8: 13.

89. Ibid.

90. Ibid., p. 14.

Mass media extended the reach of the message to those who did not attend. Newspapers printed excerpts from the speeches, and a movie company filmed many of the events.[91] In addition, a Chinese record company recorded and distributed the speeches by Mayor Zhang Dingfan and Social Affairs Bureau Chief Pan Gongzhan.[92] Because the recordings were aimed at ethnic Chinese living abroad, they also included English translations of the speeches so that non-Mandarin speakers could understand them. The mayor told listeners that the promotion of national products required adherence to a simple principle: "If it doesn't exist, quickly make imitations; if it already exists, then quickly make improvements." Pan devoted his speech to explaining the ambitious goal of the week and the movement: to stimulate nationalistic consumption throughout China "from Shanghai to every province, every county, every town, and every village, until throughout the country there isn't a single place that does not strive to promote national products."[93]

Organizers of the week used many techniques to attract attention, often by creating spectacles within spectacles to disseminate the movement message. One of the best-attended events began on the morning of the second day, when movie stars and workers from the China Film Company led an official National Products Week parade. Some thirty industrial and commercial enterprises participated, assembling nearly fifty vehicles. The parade followed extensive routes through the two areas of the city.[94] Because the event was not considered political, the International Settlement authorities permitted the procession to cross the Settlement ("National Products Week" [1928]). Along the routes, participants in the parade passed out fliers advertising the week to some of the over 100,000 people lining the streets. According to the reporter for a local paper, it was the largest parade to date in Shanghai.[95]

---

91. "Guohuo xuanchuan yingpian" (National product dissemination movie), SB 1928.7.9: 14.

92. Excerpts of speeches printed in "Guohuo huapian shouyin jiangci" (National products album records speech), SB 1928.7.8: 14.

93. For copies of all three speeches, see "Guohuo huapian yanshuo ci" (Texts of speeches on the national products records), SB 1928.7.11: 14.

94. The Nanshi and Beishi parade routes were published in advance (see SB 1928.7.7: 14).

95. "Zuori Nanbei shi qiche da youxing" (Grand vehicle parade yesterday in the South and North cities), SB 1928.7.9: 13. This article has the complete list of participating companies and several photographs of the parade. Smaller spectacles included the "amusement parties" (友誼會) hosted by the General Chamber of Commerce throughout the week. The elaborate entertainment programs included plays, musical performances, skits, speeches, and many other forms of entertainment that usually promoted movement ideas. For example, one party

The main event of the week was the Summer and Autumn Articles National Products Exhibition (夏秋用品國貨展覽會), held at the Chamber of Commerce's Display Hall. Although the chamber hosted the event, many government and movement organizations helped organize it, including the NPPA and the Shanghai Association of Mechanized National Products Manufacturers. Altogether, some sixty industrial enterprises exhibited their national products on the two floors of the hall.[96] On the afternoon of the second day of the week, nearly five hundred people attended a separate opening ceremony for the exhibition, which featured hours of the now ritualistic speeches on the importance of promoting national products. Following the opening ceremony, the mayor and other officials led a tour of the display grounds. In addition to these guests of honor, over 25,000 people viewed this representation of a purely Chinese nation.[97]

Because China was unable to confront and expel the imperial powers and their commodities from the domestic market, these exhibitions displayed what might be termed "displaced anti-imperialism," in which the desire for the nationalized market was achieved in miniature. The strict rules governing participation reflected this dream. The first rule of the exhibition grounds made the goal of displaying only pure national products explicit: "This exhibition is established to promote national products. If an item is not a national product, then it won't be permitted into the exhibition and the competition. Moreover, in the event that there are counterfeits [i.e., non-national products], as soon as they are discovered, they will be immediately

---

included a performance by the Boycott Japan Quintet. For a more complete description of the entertainment, see "Di'er ci youyi hui zhuiji" (Recollecting the second amusement party), *SB* 1928.7.13: 13; "Disan ci youyi" (The third amusement party), *SB* 1928.7.13: 13; "Moci youyi hui zhi jianbian" (Highlights of the last amusement party), *SB* 1928.7.14: 14; and "Qianwan Zong shanghui relie youyi hui" (The festive party the night before last at the General Chamber of Commerce), *SB* 1928.7.9: 13.

96. See "Xiaqiu yongpin guohuo zhanlanhui mingri kaimu" (Summer and Autumn Articles National Products Exhibition opening ceremonies tomorrow), *SB* 1928.7.7: 16, for the names of exhibitors. "Xiaqiu yongpin guohuo zhanlanhui jinri kaimu" (Summer and Autumn Articles National Products Exhibition opening ceremonies today), *SB* 1928.7.8: 14, includes a layout of the exhibition and a photo of the entrance.

97. "Ben suo lici juban zhanlanhui zhi jingguo" (The course of each exhibition hosted by this hall), in *SSC* 1936: 20–21; "Xiaqiu yongpin guohuo zhanlanhui zuori kaimu" (Summer and Autumn Articles National Products Exhibition opening ceremonies yesterday), *SB* 1928.7.9: 14. The article has a photograph of the speakers. With the exception of one person, all are wearing the long-gown, the male uniform of the movement.

removed from the exhibition grounds and confiscated."[98] Many similar rules were designed to ensure that the exhibition displayed only Chinese goods. Exhibitors were required to submit a signed statement guaranteeing the purity of their products and to agree not to exhibit or sell anyone else's products. These same strict regulations applied to other aspects of the exhibition. For example, all advertisements by participating businesses had to be approved by the organizers.

During the week, organizers continued to use various promotional techniques to stimulate interest in the exhibition. Attendance at the exhibition grew by the day. On the third day, for example, the organizers gave away thousands of free samples.[99] By the middle of the week, attendance was so large that the organizers decided to extend the hours of operation.[100] To expand the reach of the exhibition, the bureau also arranged for the publication of a *National Products Catalogue* (國貨樣本) of the exhibited goods.[101] Several months after the event, the Commercial Products Display Hall compiled and printed a commemorative volume of the week, which it distributed to government organs and social organizations throughout China.[102]

By this time, in addition to displaying objects, exhibitions such as this one often created spaces to sell authenticated national products. These exhibition marketplaces served two purposes. First, like the exhibitions themselves, they were miniature models of a nationalized market. Second, they made money by giving Chinese consumers an opportunity to buy national products on the spot. To facilitate this transformation of nationalistic sentiment into consumer desire, the Chamber of Commerce's Display Hall arranged for the articles of some seventy companies to be sold. Items included popular consumer goods, especially cosmetics, toiletries, foodstuffs, cooking condiments, pharmaceuticals, straw goods, and children's toys. Sales were

---

98. For this and other rules of the exhibition, see "Xiaqiu zhanlanhui juxing weiyuan hui ji" (Minutes from the committee meeting for the Summer and Autumn Exhibition), *SB* 1928.7.2: 14.

99. "Xiaqiu guohuo zhanlanhui xiaoxi" (News of the Summer and Autumn National Products Exhibition), *SB* 1928.7.11: 15.

100. "Xiaqiu yongpin guohuo zhanlanhui xiaoxi yishu" (A roundup of news of the Summer and Autumn National Products Exhibition), *SB* 1928.7.12: 13.

101. The movement produced many such catalogs. See, e.g., the one published by the Shanghai Association of Mechanized National Products Manufacturers, *Guohuo yangben* 1934.

102. "Xiaqiu guohuo zhanlanhui yuwen" (Additional news of the Summer and Autumn National Products Exhibition), *SB* 1928.9.16: 14.

very brisk.[103] The exhibition earned an estimated $100,000 in just seven days, making this the most profitable national products sale up to this time.[104] The success and utility of the exhibition marketplace convinced many government officials and business leaders of the need to establish permanent marketplaces devoted to selling exclusively national products.

Exhibitions held in other cities provide additional evidence of the spread of a complex of nationalistic spectacles. In the beginning of August, shortly after the end of the Shanghai National Products Movement Week, the Nationalist capital of Nanjing hosted the Capital National Products Traveling Exhibition. In some ways, this event was a continuation of the Shanghai week. It relied heavily on the support of movement organizations from Shanghai. All the members of the powerful Shanghai Association of Mechanized National Products Manufacturers sent products.[105] As with other exhibitions, this one also set up a temporary marketplace to sell the certified national products of more than eighty companies. Despite the hot weather, the event was very popular. On the first day, over 3,000 people visited. To promote the event, organizers posted placards with movement slogans throughout the city and hired sound trucks to roam the streets of Nanjing advertising the event.[106] Most important, products collected for this exhibition formed the basis for the permanent national products museum that opened in the capital the following year. This museum, in turn, became the headquarters for many movement activities in Nanjing during the following decade.[107]

Before Chinese could "consume nationalism," they had to learn to visualize commodities as belonging to one of two categories: national and foreign. They had to learn a nationalistic visuality. In the first third of the twentieth century,

---

103. "Xiaqiu yongpin guohuo zhanlanhui xiaoxi yishu" (A roundup of news of the Summer and Autumn National Products Exhibition), *SB* 1928.7.12: 13.

104. "Xiaqiu guohuo zhanlanhui xiaoxi" (News of the Summer and Autumn National Products Exhibition), *SB* 1928.7.14: 14.

105. "Ji shoudu guohuo liudong zhanlanhui" (Notes on the Capital National Products Traveling Exhibition), *SB* 1928.8.5: 14.

106. "Shoudu guohuo zhanlanhui jinri kaimu" (Capital National Products Museum opening ceremonies today), *SB* 1928.8.9: 17.

107. For instance, the museum organized a week of activities on March 16–22, 1931. For descriptions and photographs, see "Shoudu tichang guohuo yundong xuanchuan zhou" (1931). The museum also hosted numerous special exhibitions (see "Jiangsu techan zhanlanhui" [1931]). For a summary of all the activities during 1930, see "Ben guan zuijin yinian" (1931).

an exhibitionary complex of nationalized product museums, exhibitions, advertisements, stores, and marketplaces emerged to constitute the institutional core of the movement. This burgeoning complex transformed commodity spectacles into events that enacted the movement's goal of nationalizing consumption—that is, conferring nationality on commodities—and thereby setting the foundation for persuading, even compelling, Chinese to consume nationalistically. Through these carefully orchestrated spectacles, the exhibitionary complex helped produce and internalize nationalistic categories of consumption that underlay the imperative to buy national products. As a result, the power of price, quality, and especially fashion—the twentieth century's most enigmatic signifier—to convey the essential or primary meaning of material culture was challenged. Created by and channeled through the movement, anti-imperialist outrage and nationalist pride as well as profits and political propaganda prevented commodities from simply being interpreted as nation-less commodities circulating as pure exchange-values.

Domestic manufacturers and Chinese consumers who were the initial supporters of the movement welcomed the rapid expansion of nationalistic commodity spectacles made possible by the re-establishment of central state power. As Chiang Kai-shek, then chairman of the new government, noted in his opening speech for the huge Chinese National Products Exhibition of 1928, such a large and comprehensive event would have been unthinkable had the Nationalist Party and army not been successful in reunifying the country (GSB 1929, 2: 8a–10a; SB 1928.11.2). The new leaders not only helped bankroll and organize nationalistic spectacles but also became increasingly willing and able to enforce nationalistic consumption through government-supported boycotts as well as through more customary means such as tariffs. Thus, state power added considerably to the social pressure, suggestive spectacles, and onging boycotts underlying the movement's efforts to encourage and force individuals in the Chinese state to consume nationalism.

The appropriation of the movement by the state reveals a larger trend that unfolded in subsequent decades of Chinese history. As Chiang Kai-shek also intimated in his speech, state support came with the premise that the economy served the nation, not vice versa. The Chinese business community—as part of a much broader social movement—had tied its identity closely to the nation-state. But that identity had a cost. As products became "national," they undermined the assumption that profits should remain private. Chinese capitalists steadily lost control and ownership of their enterprises (see Bergère

1986 and Coble 1980). Furthermore, by launching and participating in the movement, they unintentionally helped supply the instruments for their own destruction. Private capital itself was increasingly "nationalized" in the more traditional sense of the word. In the late 1920s and early 1930s, the state turned from taxes and extortion to outright expropriation. The exigencies of the Second Sino-Japanese War and the ongoing civil war with the Communists accelerated the Nationalist regime's takeover.[108] Moreover, more than one political party linked commodities and the nation-state. After the Communists gained control in 1949, they quickly nationalized Chinese capitalists by confiscating private property during the early 1950s and formally abolishing the capitalists as a class later that decade. Ironically, under the Communists, the isolation of imported products in special "friendship stores" (友誼商店) limited the exposure of Chinese consumers.

Chinese consumers, too, had been captured within the narrative of nationalistic consumption. After the Communist revolution in 1949, they were to consume nationalistically not for "national salvation" by way of Chinese manufacturers and at their own discretion but directly through inescapable participation in the national socialist economy. The movement had helped open private and family consumption to wider scrutiny decades before the height of the Cultural Revolution, when nonfictional boys and girls not only refused to wear the figurative Japanese long johns but also turned their mothers over to the people's courts for treason.

---

108. On the Nationalist government's dramatic expansion of economic mobilization and control, see Kirby 1992. According to Kirby's estimates, by 1942 the main arm of the government's economic bureaucracy, the National Resources Commission, controlled 40 percent of the industry in the territories under Nationalist rule.

CHAPTER SIX

Creating a Nationalistic Visuality

in the Exhibition of 1928

The construction of material things as "objects" of a particular character is not perceived as problematic. Things are what they are. There is little idea that material things can be understood in a multitude of different ways, that many meanings can be read from things, and that this meaning can be manipulated as required. Although we are familiar with the way in which advertisements, for example, select and manipulate images of material objects in relation to their associative and relational potentials, it is not understood that the ways in which museums "manipulate" material things also set up relationships and associations, and in fact create identities.

—Roland Barthes, *Image, Music, Text* (1977)

If you want to understand patriotism, it is completely incorporated in these three words: Use National Products [用國貨].

—Minister of Industry and Commerce Kong Xiangxi at the opening ceremonies of the Chinese National Products Exhibition of 1928

The National government wants to promote national products, revive industry and commerce, and recover rights in order that foreign products have no markets in China and that everyone uses national products to destroy imperialism.

— Chiang Kai-shek at the opening ceremonies of the Chinese National Products Exhibition of 1928

As Roland Barthes would have expected and the quotes of Kong and Chiang confirm, the commodity spectacles of the National Product Movement had an agenda. In November 1928, less than four months after the National Products Movement Week, Shanghai hosted a much larger commodity spectacle. Organizers crammed over 7,000 rigorously authenticated national products from 24 provinces into a refurbished three-story building. In the next two months, well over half a million people visited the Chinese National Products Exhibition.[1] This exhibition was the most spectacular commodity fair in China since the Nanyang Industrial Exhibition of 1910 and was a milestone in the movement's efforts to create nationalized spaces and spectacles. In many ways, it was the culmination of the two decades of work described in the previous chapters: the use of a sophisticated system for identifying and certifying "national products" (Chapter 4), the complete regulation of exhibition space, the extensive use of entertainment and attendance programs, and, most significant, the growing manipulation of the exhibitionary complex by the state (Chapter 5).

As with other spectacles organized in conjunction with the central government, the exhibition of 1928 joined the underlying ideology of nationalistic consumption and a newer, more centralized sociopolitical force: the Nationalist state. This chapter brings these two forces—the movement and the Nationalist state—together around the notion of the myth-making embedded in the event. There were two myths (or stories based on fact and fantasy that became, in the notion of Roland Barthes, society's "common sense") at work in the exhibition: the myth of national political/territorial integration and the myth of economic integration.[2] These mutually reinforcing myths created a third myth, directly inscribed on the exhibition's spectators, or ideal subjects, themselves. From the exhibition, organizers hoped, spectators would learn to align themselves as "Chinese" citizens of a Chinese nation-state (replete with a Father of the Nation in Sun Yatsen) and members of a Chinese economy, represented by every "national product." The establishment of the Nationalist state in 1928 intensified the politicization of commodity spectacles.

The organizers intended the exhibition to promote the political myth by commemorating the nominal unification of China under Chiang Kai-shek and his National Revolutionary Army in the Northern Expedition.[3] To be sure, the toppling of the corrupt and discredited Beijing-based national government was a significant symbolic and military accomplishment. The army and its allies destroyed several of the deeply entrenched regional militarists,

---

1. GSB 1929, vol. 6: "Benhui meiri guanlan renshu tongji biao" (A statistical table of daily visitors).

2. Of course, the larger myth underlying both was that of "national unity," that "China" should be a single political unit. For a contemporary's observations on the centrality of this concept in Chinese life, see "Watchwords" in Morgan 1930: 166–71.

3. Led by Chiang Kai-shek, the Northern Expedition of the National Revolutionary Army began in the southeast province of Guangdong in June 1926 and ended with the capture of Beijing in the summer of 1928; see Jordan 1976.

known as "warlords," such as Wu Peifu 吳佩浮 (1874–1959), Sun Chuanfang 孫傳芳 (1885–1935), and Zhang Zuolin 張作霖 (1873–1928). However, new warlords sprang up in their territories, and the Nanjing government's actual control over most of China remained tenuous or nonexistent. The total number of provinces increased during 1928 from 22 to 28.[4] Of these, the Nationalist government directly controlled only a handful in the Lower Yangzi valley and worked constantly to maintain alliances with the warlords controlling other areas.[5] In addition, China was severely constrained by the unequal treaties and would lose the provinces of Manchuria to Japan in 1931–32.

Nationalist leaders used the visual forum of the product exhibition to represent symbolically what they hoped to accomplish in practice: genuine national reunification and integration under the Nationalists and the exercise of complete national sovereignty. Given the fragmented state of China, any claim that an exhibition was national in scope was certainly a fantasy. Indeed, many pavilions and activities at the 1928 exhibition contradicted the central message of national unity by emphasizing provincial and native-place affiliations. In many respects, the exhibition was a weak and anxious claim to national representation and internal coherence.[6] Still, considering the obstacles, it was quite an accomplishment. When placed alongside the commodity spectacles explored in the previous chapter, its size, scope, and number of participants are striking. This exhibition went further than earlier ones in developing the symbolism of the pure Chinese nation. In more practical terms, it also inspired many similar myth-making spectacles that followed both throughout China and in ethnic Chinese communities.[7]

---

4. By 1936, the Nationalist government controlled only ten provinces (Tien 1972: 89–95).

5. In 1928, there were five primary centers of regional power: (1) the Lower Yangzi–based Nationalists; (2) the Guangxi faction, in control of most of Hubei, Hunan, and Guangxi; (3) the "Christian General" Feng Yuxiang 馮御香 (1882–1948), who occupied Shaanxi and Henan as well as parts of Shandong and Hebei; (4) Yan Xishan 閻錫山 (1883–1960), who ruled Shanxi and indirectly the Beijing-Tianjin area; and (5) Zhang Xueliang 張學良 (1898–2001), who dominated the northeast. Moreover, local warlords still dominated large areas, including the southwestern provinces of Guizhou and Yunnan as well as Sichuan (Wilbur 1983:191–94).

6. Indeed, it is possible to view entire spectacles such as this one as temporary and volatile alliances. See Paul Kramer's revisionist article on Philippine participation in the St. Louis World's Fair of 1904, in which he argues that this and other American fairs are best considered "fractured and cobbled together" and "shot through with irresolvable contradictions" rather than "centrally coordinated 'events'" (1999: 77).

7. The speeches—indeed the 1928 exhibition itself and the entire movement—provide an opportunity to plumb one of the more contentious questions in the historiography of the

Making the Mythical

On November 1, 1928, more than 50,000 people attended the opening ceremonies of the two-month-long Ministry of Industry and Commerce's Chinese National Products Exhibition (工商部中華國貨展覽會) (NCH 1928.11.3). The long list of powerful people attending the opening ceremony underscores the importance of the event. Political leaders turned out in force. Among the attendees were the chairman of the newly established Nationalist government (國民政府), Chiang Kai-shek; the new president of the Control Yuan and founder of China's most prominent research institution, Cai Yuanpei 蔡元培 (1868–1940); banker and Minister of Finance Song Ziwen 宋子文 (1894–1971; better known in English as T. V. Soong); and the Nationalist elder statesman Wu Zhihui 吳稚輝 (1864–1953). National and local industrial and commercial leaders, such as Shanghai General Chamber of Commerce leaders Feng Shaoshan 馮少山 (b. 1894) and Yu Xiaqing 虞洽卿 (1867–1945), also participated. Many other leading Chinese figures attended, including the influential widow of Sun Yatsen, Song Qingling 宋慶齡 (1893–1981) ("Zhonghua guohuo zhanlanhui kaimu shengkuang" [1928]).

The sights and sounds of the opening ceremonies were rich in movement symbolism. The event began during the afternoon with a procession leading from the nearby South Railway Station along the newly built National Products Road (國貨路) to the main gate of the exhibition grounds on the former site of the New Puyu Benevolent Association (新普育堂) (Fig. 6.1). As the head of the ministry that had organized the exhibition, Minister of Industry and Commerce Kong Xiangxi led a procession of several thousand people who carried banners, passed out leaflets, and shouted slogans urging their compatriots to use national products. When the parade reached the entrance to the grounds, the organizers held elaborate opening ceremonies, which featured firecrackers, gun salutes, and ten different brass bands.

Nanjing Decade (1927–37): What level—if any—of institutionalized and informal accountability was imposed on the Nationalist regime by such classes and social groupings as landlords, merchants, industrialists, and intellectuals? The issue is beyond the scope of this book, but the evidence supports the views of Richard Bush (1982) and Joseph Fewsmith (1985) that there was significant interpenetration of business and Nationalist interests in the Nanjing Decade.

Fig. 6.1 Chinese National Products Exhibition
(GSB 1929)

Photographed are some of the guests at the opening ceremonies for the Chinese National
Products Exhibition in Shanghai in 1928. At this and other movement events, most industrialists and politicians chose to represent themselves in the long-gown, rather than Western-
style suits, as they often did in other situations. Earlier, movement participants had reinterpreted the long-gown as a symbol of Chinese nationalism, and it became the de facto male
uniform of the movement.

Immediately before the ceremonies, two airplanes flew overhead and
dropped leaflets promoting the idea of nationalistic consumption. Chiang
Kai-shek, who had made a special trip to Shanghai just for the event, cere-
moniously hoisted the Nationalist flag, Minister Kong officially opened the
gate to the grounds, and the students of the Shanghai Jinde Girls School
sang the official "Song of the National Products Exhibition" ("國貨展覽會
歌"), which began: "Arise! Arise! Chinese people quickly rise with enthusiasm! If we fail to pay attention to national products, foreign products will
abound" (GSB 1929, 2: 7b).

Nationalist government symbols also enveloped the event, a sign of the
growing support for the movement among the new rulers. During the exhibition, party and Nationalist flags blanketed the grounds, Revolutionary
Army soldiers lined the entranceway, party members frequently gave

speeches, and Nationalist holidays, such as the birthday of Sun Yatsen, were officially observed.[8] Originally, the exhibition had been scheduled to begin on the most sacred holiday of the Republic, National Day or Double Ten Day (October 10), on the anniversary of the Wuchang Uprising and the start of the Revolution of 1911, which proponents of the movement hoped to link to economic nationalism.[9] However, the Nationalists had already planned to use this day to formally launch their government in the new capital of Nanjing and the inauguration of the Five-Power system of government formulated by Sun Yatsen. Because this presented scheduling conflicts for the national leaders who wanted to participate in the opening ceremonies of the exhibition, it was postponed.

The speeches and essays that accompanied the opening set the tone for the event and reveal the messages China's leaders delivered through this and other movement events. Above all, they expressed the desire to transform the Chinese permanently into patriotic consumers. In a foreword to a special supplement of a nationally distributed newspaper published on the opening day, one writer warned that support for the movement had often waned with the close of earlier exhibitions: "Although Shanghai had just had a very successful National Products Week and Summer and Autumn National Products Exhibition, since then, enthusiasm for national products has dwindled. This exhibition is intended to revive the spirit." He and other planners hoped that the much more comprehensive scope of this exhibition would make it "easier for consumers to select and buy national products."[10]

At the opening ceremonies, Minister Kong reminded everyone that the exhibition had three purposes, all of which linked patriotism and consump-

---

8. November 12, 1928, was the sixty-third anniversary of the birth of Sun Yatsen. On the commemorative activities at the exhibition, see *SB* 1928.11.13: 15.

9. Attempts to connect state holidays to the movement were as old as the Republic. In 1919, for instance, one Jiangsu orphanage celebrated the holiday by parading children through the streets singing the song "Use National Products" ("用國貨") and having them go door-to-door selling items from specially prepared boxes of national products ("Zhenjiang pin'er fufantuan juxing fanmai guohuo kaimu yishi" [Zhenjiang orphan peddler teams hold Sell National Products inauguration ceremony], *Min'guo ribao* 1919.10.13; republished in ZDLDG 1992: 233). On Nationalist attempts to connect the Double Ten holiday to the movement, see ZGZZW 1929a, pt. VII: 47. On the creation of National Day and its importance as a symbol, see H. Harrison 2000: 93–125.

10. Chong Gan, "Yinyan" (Preface). For these and other speeches and photographs of the exhibition organizers and the grounds itself, see "Zhonghua guohuo zhanlanhui tekan" (Chinese National Products Exhibition special publication), *SB* 1928.11.1: 12.

tion. Events such as this one, Kong argued, developed "the patriotic spirit of the Chinese people," which could be measured by import statistics. The Chinese, he suggested, had much to learn from the Japanese, who "wouldn't think of betraying their country by using imports" and who demonstrated their patriotism by choosing domestic products over superior foreign ones. In summary, "If you want to understand patriotism, it is completely incorporated in these three words: Use National Products." Patriotic purchases also aided one's compatriots. Once again, Kong invoked Japan as the model to follow. The Japanese either did without foreign products or quickly learned to manufacture substitutes. The Chinese also needed to improve the quality of domestic products to compete with foreign ones and thereby keep China's wealth within the country. Finally, Minister Kong informed those assembled that patriotic consumption would improve China's international standing by eliminating its foreign trade deficit (GSB 1929, 2: 2b–4a; SB 1928.11.2).

Other speakers underscored the usefulness of exhibitions in teaching Chinese to identify everyday opportunities to practice patriotism. The famous educator Cai Yuanpei emphasized that the exhibition would provide the necessary visual clues to decipher China's increasingly complex consumer culture. Cai argued that the Chinese understood the close connection between economic productivity and national welfare, but they simply did not know "which things were national products." As with the popularization of the National Products Standards, the exhibition, he claimed, would remedy this problem because it took "the best national products and put them on display" in Shanghai, the commercial heart of China (GSB 1929, 2: 7a–b; SB 1928.11.2).

Profiting from a National Polity

At the opening ceremonies of the exhibition, the new chairman of the Nationalist government gave, by far, the longest and most acerbic speech (GSB 1929, 2: 8a–10a; SB 1928.11.2). On one level, Chiang Kai-shek's speech simply echoed the ideas of other speakers by emphasizing the importance of the movement for teaching Chinese the need to learn to see the nationality of products. Chiang's recitation of these movement points demonstrates the extent to which the discourse of the National Products Movement had permeated China. However, he also adapted the message of the movement to suit his particular political concerns.

Chiang began by reminding those assembled not to trust their eyes in the marketplace because the things found there might mesmerize them into acts of unpatriotic consumption: "Ladies and gentlemen, . . . today is the opening day of the Shanghai National Products Exhibition. All of us know that . . . when we come to Shanghai, we see mile after mile of foreign stores and tens of thousands of foreign products—so much so that the scene almost completely fills our eyes." He reminded Chinese to sensitize themselves to the national origins of goods and, therefore, to what the movement advanced as the pre-eminent meaning of these things: "If we consider where these things come from, everyone certainly understands that in the end these are imported by foreigners. How much money do we want to hand over to foreign countries?" As had so many others, Chiang reminded his listeners that individual purchases of imported products added up to a staggering total. But, in contrast with speakers earlier in the movement's history, he frequently referred to the writings of Sun Yatsen to bolster his position:

Every compatriot must have seen in our president's Three People's Principles in the Nationalism section where he says that every year we Chinese give foreigners $1.2 billion. This $1.2 billion is thus money we Chinese reverently present to foreigners, and it's destroying the nation. . . . Yet this still isn't enough—we humiliate ourselves by allowing foreigners to suppress us to the point that we have no food to eat, no clothes to wear, and no houses to live in. It has reached the point that we Chinese can't even travel on our own roads. What sort of logic is this? This comes from the fact that foreigners have seized economic power and have used it to suppress us and destroy China. If every Chinese person continues to use foreign products, and if everyone promotes foreign products, then we Chinese won't need foreigners to use weapons to attack us. In another ten years, one by one all of us will have starved to death. . . . Even the police are foreigners! We Chinese already have almost no powers of independence and freedom and yet we wish to turn ourselves over completely to management by foreigners.

Chiang then raised the catastrophic consequences of unpatriotic consumption and the primary means of redress: "What should we do if we don't want foreigners to come and humiliate us? This is very simple. If one by one each compatriot does not buy foreign products, then foreigners won't humiliate China. Otherwise, the Chinese race [中華民族] will soon be destroyed by foreigners." The opening of the exhibition was a sign both of great hope and of despair:

I don't know about the feelings of my compatriots, but yours truly from birth until now has been around forty-two years, and I have never seen such a glorious day. So today, as we open the National Products Exhibition, it is the most glorious day for all four hundred million Chinese. All of us should understand that today, when we come to the National Products Exhibition, we are not here to see beautiful things nor to participate in the excitement. . . . Today our opening of this event is a glorious thing because, on the one hand, we bring together in one place national products from over twenty provinces. Indeed everyone is thrilled and jubilant. But, on the other hand, we still have deep pains. For one thing, national products are not in every way good. And for another, because our national products are in this state, we still cannot develop the economy to realize [Sun Yatsen's] Principle of the People's Livelihood [民生主義]. . . . So we are excited and thrilled, but at the same time we are filled with grief and sadness. Compatriots, how can we rid ourselves of this grief and sadness? It's very easy. Each compatriot need only return to his or her household and tell those [friends and relatives] who didn't come to the exhibition that the Ministry of Industry and Commerce has opened a National Products Exhibition in Shanghai. The National government wants to promote national products, revive industry and commerce, and recover rights, so that foreign products have no markets in China and that everyone uses national products to destroy imperialism. . . . Compatriots, if we don't want foreigners to come and humiliate us, then the only thing to do is single-mindedly and collectively make national products, sell national products, use national products. Only with this sort of economy will we achieve independence and only then will we achieve the Principle of the People's Livelihood, and only then will we solve the suffering of four hundred million compatriots. This is the purpose of the National Revolution.

Most important, Chiang acknowledged the large amounts of money that the new government had squeezed out of the Shanghai business class. But, he claimed, they were getting their money's worth:

My compatriots probably are aware that in taking Shanghai over a year ago and thereafter gaining control of Beiping and reuniting China, our Nationalist Revolutionary Army used much money from our Shanghai compatriots. For this I apologize to my Shanghai compatriots. . . . Everyone certainly knows that if the Nationalist Revolution had not been successful, today this place of ours would still be the barracks of warlord armies, and we would be unable to open this exhibition. Nobody would be able to visit this festive grand opening.

The new government, he added, had not only contributed nearly half the funding for the event but also supplied something more fundamental: "an orderly, clean, and disciplined" environment. Closing on a note of optimism, he noted that although the exhibition grounds were small, the event was an impressive achievement for a few months of work and a huge initial step for which his party and government deserved much credit.

The Preparations

The extensive preparations for the exhibition reflected the growth of the exhibitionary complex of nationalistic commodity spectacles within the movement, the political support such events enjoyed, and the spread of the spectacles into everyday life outside the actual exhibition grounds. Although the stated goal for much of this work was the rounding up of participants, these efforts also served a more subtle purpose. In the end, the numbers of exhibitors and spectators were impressive, but these numbers represent only a small fraction affected by the exhibition. Each attempt to attract participants also publicized the notion of nationalistic consumption. The details of this preparatory work reveal the avenues for disseminating the notions of nationalistic consumption underlying the National Products Standards in 1928 and the larger movement of which they were a part.

In contrast to earlier, hastily prepared events, the preparations for this one took nearly four months. The first organizational meeting convened in late June 1928, and many distinguished Chinese attended. The four leading members of the organizing group were Shanghai mayor Zhang Dingfan; the head of the Shanghai branch of the Ministry of Industry and Commerce, Zhao Xi'en 趙錫恩 (b. 1882); the leading Shanghai merchant, Yu Xiaqing; and the head of the municipal Social Affairs Bureau, Pan Gongzhan (Xu Youqun 1991: 1329). Several different committees attended to specific areas, and a smaller committee oversaw day-to-day preparations for the event (*SB* 1928.9.3: 14). The organizers began promoting the event during the Summer and Autumn Articles National Products Exhibition during the July National Products Week and established branch committees throughout China to assist in the collection of appropriate articles (GSB 1929, 1: 1a–3b).[11] Organizers repeatedly used the by now well-established networks to disseminate word of the exhibition to officials, chambers of commerce, business people, and organizations throughout China in the months preceding the

---

11. These pages contain copies of the official correspondence. On the initial meetings of the preparatory committee, see "Zhonghua guohuo zhanlanhui choubei ji" (1928).

opening.[12] They encouraged local governments and businesses to send products, or to encourage others to send products; the general message was "This is a matter of commerce and industry rescuing the nation" (SB 1928.8.5: 14).

To further publicize the exhibition, the committee published and circulated a special collection, with essays by leading intellectuals and politicians, including Chiang Kai-shek. The book placed the event in the larger narrative of the movement by publishing trade statistics "to awaken the attention of citizens." It tried to reach a wider audience by incorporating less serious articles, such as the reflections of Tianxu Wosheng, the pseudonym of Chen Diexian, the head of a major Chinese manufacturer of consumer goods, Household Enterprises (SB 1928.9.16: 14). Despite these efforts, it seemed increasingly improbable that organizers could pull everything together in time for the originally planned opening on October 10. Even participants from nearby cities such as Hangzhou stated that they could not deliver their products so quickly (SB 1928.9.20: 14).

At the end of September, the pace of preparations intensified. Event managers set up offices on the grounds, and groups such as the Shanghai Bank and the Post Office established temporary branch outlets there. The number of goods arriving at the exhibition hall from Shanghai and other commercial ports increased rapidly. Telegrams from provincial offices throughout China informed the preparatory committee that goods had been selected and were in transit. The relatively prosperous coastal province of Fujian informed the committee that it was sending money (SB 1928.9.26: 13). In late September, the committee inserted advertisements in local papers to announce that tickets for the exhibition were on sale and asked participating companies in Shanghai to sell them (SB 1928.9.30: 14). The pace of preparations picked up still further in late October. At the end of the month, Shanghai's three major department stores moved into facilities at the exhibition (SB 1928.10.26: 13).

The financing for the exhibition reveals the diverse geographical and institutional support for the event and the movement. Of a total budget of $121,468, about half came from government sources. The Ministry of Indus-

---

12. See, e.g., the pamphlet organizers sent to the Suzhou Chamber of Commerce, which informed chamber members of the event and invited them to advertise in a commemorative volume: "Gongshang bu zhuban guimo zuida zhi Zhonghua guohuo zhanlan jinian tekan" (The Ministry of Industry and Commerce–sponsored and largest Chinese National Products Exhibition commemorative volume), SZMA File 1346.

try and Commerce provided an initial $50,000, and provincial and city governments supplied an additional $11,277. In addition, Chiang Kai-shek raised an additional $12,460 in donations (Chiang himself ceremonially bought the first ticket for $10,000).[13] The exhibition itself generated the other half through several different methods; $11,275, for example, came from rents on exhibition and sales pavilions, advertising within the exhibition grounds, and money raised by the mail order department. In addition, the ticket sales raised over $30,000 for the exhibition. Finally, city and county general chambers of commerce donated $2,420.[14]

Just getting the products to Shanghai was an accomplishment in itself. Even with the three-week delay in the opening of the exhibition, not all products reached Shanghai before the opening, and products continued to arrive throughout the exhibition. Items from the remote southwestern province of Yunnan arrived during the second week of the exhibition, only to be held up by Shanghai customs (SB 1928.11.10). Some items from Hunan province and Tianjin did not arrive until the beginning of the second month. By that time, the East Hall was completely full, and organizers were forced to find space for the overflow on the third floor of the West Hall, which had previously been used only as a sales hall (SB 1928.11.28: 14).

Despite these obstacles, the exhibition succeeded in keeping the myth of a territorially unified China alive. All provinces, most of which were not under Nationalist control, sent products. Even poor and remote regions such as Inner Mongolia, Tibet, Hainan Island, and Xinjiang sent a few dozen items. Altogether, the 24 provinces sent 7,321 items. Jiangsu province, which surrounded and included the Shanghai Special Municipality, sent by far the most products, 1,772, or about 25 percent of the total. But the more distant province of Hebei, which included the former capital, now known as Beiping,

---

13. There was considerable symbolism built into the sale of the first few tickets. The ceremonious purchase of the first exhibition ticket by "royalty" went all the way back to Prince Albert, who had bought the first ticket for the Crystal Palace in 1851. Minister of Finance Song Ziwen bought the second ticket for $2,000. As had been the case in the 1910 exhibition, an overseas Chinese participant bought the third ticket for $10,000. Madame Chiang Kai-shek (Song Meiling 宋美齡; b. 1897) also visited the exhibition on the first evening, along with the wives of other officials ("Zhonghua guohuo zhanlanhui zuori kaimu shengkuang" [1928]).

14. GSB 1929, vol. 5: "Gongshang bu Zhonghua guohuo zhanlanhui Zhonghua minguo shiqi niandu shouru jisuan shu" (Income of the Ministry of Industry and Commerce Chinese National Products Exhibition, 1928). On early fund-raising for the exhibition, see "Zhonghua guohuo zhanlanhui changweihui jiyao" (1928).

sent the second highest number, 1,447, or about 20 percent of the total. Four provinces sent between 500 and 900 items: Guangdong, Fujian, Jiangxi, and Zhejiang, or collectively 35 percent of the total.[15] The geographic distribution of exhibited goods was far from even, but the exhibition accomplished a symbolic unification.

Creating a Nationalized Space

The exhibition grounds constituted a self-sufficient nation in miniature. Creating this nationalized space involved both preparation of the facilities and strict regulation of the exhibition space. The organizing committee poured money into providing impressively clean and renovated facilities, including the new National Products Road leading to the entrance. The exhibition grounds formed a large rectangle (see Figs. 6.2–4). The main building occupied three sides; in its center was a courtyard divided almost completely down the middle by a large building. The grounds were completely enclosed along their southern perimeter by a one-story building, with the main gate at its center. The main gate opened into the courtyard directly opposite the central building. This building at the heart of the grounds housed spacious performance areas on the first floor and two large pavilions on the second. The main building, the National Products Hall, had two wings of three stories each. The exhibitions were housed primarily on the second and third stories of the East Wing in individual rooms. The first floor of the West Wing was devoted to sales. Other areas were devoted to housing for employees, a cafeteria, a fire department, and a nursery.

The division of the exhibition rooms by province, industry, and company reflected the mixed public and private financing of the event (Figs. 6.5 and 6.6). Most of the rooms housed products of a particular industry and often featured special displays for the most prominent companies. For example, in addition to the articles of other companies, the Building Materials Display had a special section for the powerful China Cement Company (中國水泥公司). In some cases, one major company represented an entire industry.

---

15. GSB 1929, vol. 6: "Benhui chupin zhongshu fen sheng fen lei zhao biao" (A brief chart of the total products of this exhibition by province and by type). Not surprisingly, remote provinces had a particularly difficult time getting their products to Shanghai. The 40-odd items from Xinjiang, for instance, arrived over a month after the start of the exhibition (SB 1928.12.9: 14).

Fig. 6.2 Main Gate of the Exhibition
(with the Ceremonial Hall in the background) (GSB 1929)

Nationalist Party and government symbols co-existed with consumer culture within the exhibition. At the apex of the Ceremonial Hall, symbolically presiding over the event, were the new official flag (brilliantly illuminated at night) of the Nationalist government and a portrait of Sun Yatsen, later known as the Father of the Nation (國父). Also visible are three of the dozens of flagstaffs that flew this flag. At the same time, closer to earth, advertisements for certified national products covered all the walls of the grounds.

Fig. 6.3 West Wing of the Exhibition (Sales Wing)
(GSB 1929)

The exhibition grounds formed an enclosed rectangle. The main building occupied three sides. In the center of the grounds was a giant courtyard, divided in half by the Ceremonial Hall (*top, center*).

In other cases, major manufacturers rented their own pavilion. Modern commodities were usually housed together, and the larger provinces had their own displays, especially for arts and crafts.[16] Spread throughout these rooms was an impressive array of thousands of products classified into fourteen categories.[17]

The event provided an opportunity for businesses to demonstrate their patriotic credentials by associating themselves and their goods with national

---

16. For a complete description of the various pavilions, see GSB 1929, vol. 1: "Huichang zhinan" (A guide to the exhibition grounds): 60a–64b.

17. GSB 1929, vol. 6: "Benhui chupin zhe tongji biao" (A statistical table of product categories in this exhibition). The fourteen categories were edible raw materials, raw materials for manufacturing, leather, intermediary industrial goods, food and beverage products, textile goods, building materials, personal items, household goods, artistic objects, educational and printed items, medical supplies, machines and electrical goods, and miscellaneous things.

Fig. 6.4 East Wing of the Exhibition (Display Wing)
(GSB 1929)

Two types of "advertisements" covered the exhibition grounds, political and commercial. In addition to the dozens of flagpoles, commercial advertisements blanketed the facades of all the buildings.

products. Each of the three major Chinese department stores in Shanghai set up a pavilion. Known primarily for selling foreign luxury goods and offering "Western" forms of leisure such as dance halls, coffee shops, and bars, the stores seized the opportunity to remind locals that they manufactured many of the national products they sold. Although Shanghai's most

Fig. 6.5 Textile and Beverage Displays
(GSB 1929)

Fig. 6.6 Nested Identities Within Pavilions
(GSB 1929)

The ideology of nationalistic consumption that underlay movement commodity spectacles trained spectators to visualize and appreciate objects as imbued with nationality. These spectacles acknowledged but subordinated other identities such as the province and native-place to nationality. The exhibition encouraged visitors to see themselves in similar terms. In this way, Chinese spectators and objects figuratively consumed and mutually defined each other. The spectator was both surveyor and surveyed. Dressed in the Chinese long-gown, the man here presented himself before Fujian province's "national products" pavilion.

important publisher (at least until its 1932 destruction by Japanese bombs) did not need to establish its patriotic credentials, the Commercial Press (商務印書館) maintained a strong presence at the exhibition. The press had two different booths, one to display and sell its publications and the other to sell miscellaneous articles. Business at both was brisk (*SB* 1928.11.7: 13).

As at other exhibitions, this event capitalized on the enthusiasm for national products generated by the displayed goods by providing an opportunity to purchase them. And as at other commodity spectacles, the dividing line between display and consumption was frequently traversed. For instance, in late November, in coordination with other events at the exhibition, the sales department set up a special exhibition of ritual goods for the upcoming winter solstice (*SB* 1928.11.30: 13). In addition to specialty goods, popular sales items were silk, cotton, and wool fabrics; books, stationery, and other printed matter; food and drink; personal hygiene products; household goods; artistic goods; cigarettes; and electrical appliances. Over the eight weeks, the sales department sold over $100,000 worth of merchandise.[18]

The regulation of exhibition space began immediately upon entering. Lined up on either side of the entrance were soldiers and police. A huge portrait of Sun Yatsen was placed at the crest of the Ceremonial Hall, just below the recently adopted National flag. Dozens of flagpoles throughout the exhibition grounds flew the flag. In this way, the Nationalists also advertised themselves to spectators and exhibitors. The environment was nationalized throughout—even the towels and washcloths in the men's and women's washrooms on each floor were provided by a major participant in the National Products Movement, Three Friends Enterprises. The process of nationalizing the event and of creating a nationalistic visual feast extended to the smallest commodity spectacles on the exhibition grounds, advertising. The buildings were covered with advertisements, which the company in charge, the Great China Advertising Agency (大中華廣告社), restricted to certified national products.[19]

Even after the opening ceremonies, politicians continued to use the event to promote the new local and national government. The most overt manifestation of these efforts was the display of Shanghai's municipal government (Fig. 6.7). Spectators entered this pavilion celebrating Shanghai's future by walking through the emblem of the party and government, its flag. Inside, a three-dimensional advertisement for the city included descriptions and models of ambitious plans to build schools, playgrounds, and public works such as a model of a bridge that would span the Huangpu River to connect Shanghai with the more rustic Pudong ("National Products Exhibition" [1928]; "Guohuo zhanlanhui zhong zhi shi zhengfu chenlie shi" [1928]).

---

18. GSB 1929, vol. 6: "Benhui shoupin geye yingye zong'e an zhou fenlei tongji biao" (A statistical chart of the weekly sales of each industry at this exhibition's sales department). This volume includes numerous statistical charts that break sales down by day, week, and totals for various products.

19. GSB 1929, vol. 3: "Da Zhonghua guanggao she qishi" (Great China Advertising Agency notice).

Fig. 6.7 Microcosm of Nationalist Modernity
(GSB 1929)

The Shanghai Municipal government used its pavilion (*above*) to display the benefits of its rule by connecting its own vision of modernity to this movement spectacle. The pavilion suggested that the Nationalist government would create the conditions for industrial development by building modern roads, bridges, dams, and so on. The path to this modernity led directly through the Nationalist Party. One entered this pavilion (*top*) by passing through its chief symbol, the twelve-ray star.

This pavilion served the municipal government and the movement simultaneously. It allowed local authorities an opportunity to represent themselves through their ambitious plans as grander than they presently were. At the same time, the pavilion served the movement by linking this spectacular future to the message of the exhibition itself: there would be no modern streets and sanitation, no good life for the citizens of Shanghai without the development of Chinese industry under the leadership of the local and Nationalist government. National products became the key to creating a modern China.

Mass Mediated Spectacle

Even more than earlier movement events, the 1928 exhibition made complete use of the media to promote the event, including both formal and informal writings, recordings, broadcast and print journalism, word-of-mouth and advertisements, airplanes, and parades (GSB 1929, vol. 3). With the encouragement of event organizers, Chinese media transmitted this image of a pure Chinese nationalistic spectacle beyond Shanghai. Publicity began in the months before the opening. Members of the organizing committee sent letters to newspapers and periodicals informing them of the upcoming event and asked these publications to help promote the exhibition by publishing special editions at the time the exhibition opened. Coverage was particularly extensive in Shanghai-based publications. Beginning on November 3, 1928, and continuing until the end of December, Shanghai's most important newspaper, the *Shenbao*, published a 61-part series covering every aspect of the exhibition. Other publications such as the Shanghai General Chamber of Commerce's monthly, *The National Journal of Commerce* (商業月報), devoted an entire issue to the exhibition and, more generally, to the promotion of national products. Distributed across China, these articles ranged from theoretical discussions of the importance of national products to detailed information about the exhibition, its organization, the rules for identifying national products, and application forms to submit products (*Shangye yuebao* 1928.9).

City officials and organizers also created media events to generate publicity. For instance, on November 22, city officials gave twenty reporters a special tour of the exhibition grounds and hosted a reception. Local officials used this opportunity to explain why the municipal government was participating in this event and discussed the link between the development of national products and local governments; they urged the reporters to help develop these links in the minds of all Chinese (*SB* 1928.11.23: 13).

The exhibition organizers also produced an impressive array of special publications to extend the message and deepen the impact of the event. Among the hundred-plus different publications supporting the event were a special commemorative volume, daily press releases, and sundry promotional materials. During the first month of the exhibition, the municipal government's Social Affairs Bureau published 20,000 copies of a book that described investigations of national products and provided basic information intended to improve the circulation of these products, such as where to buy them and how to identify national products company trademarks (*SB* 1928.11.6: 13). The China Press produced a special pamphlet for children entitled *Going to the National Products Exhibition* (到國貨展覽會去). It included a copy of the official song, photographs of the grounds, and a map. Over a thousand copies were sold every day (*SB* 1928.11.9: 13).

The exhibition even had its own newspaper, the *National Products Daily* (國貨日報). The paper informed visitors and participants of news related to the event, and many of the 5,000 copies printed each day were sent to government offices throughout China. Sixty-four issues of the newspaper appeared, in some 320,000 copies. In addition, many provinces and municipalities published their own overviews or introductions to their province and its products. Several places distributed multiple publications. The relatively prosperous province of Zhejiang, for instance, published several guides to its products, reports on important provincial industries such as silk, and introductions to the next major national exhibition at the famous tourist destination of West Lake in the city of Hangzhou.[20] The most impressive publication was a special commemorative volume, a veritable encyclopedia of the movement. This massive volume contained over six hundred pages of national product advertisements, photographs of national political and industrial leaders, tributes from famous figures, essays by leading intellectuals and businessmen, reports on specific industries, histories of famous factories and businesses, and general commercial information.

Finally, the spectator took the message of the spectacle home through symbolically charged mementos. One of the most graphic (Fig. 6.8) was a button that featured charging Nationalist soldiers clutching rifles with

---

20. See GSB 1929, vol. 3: "Kanwu" (Publications).

Fig. 6.8 Mementos from the Exhibition
(SB 1928.11.21)

(*left*) This button was one of the thousands of commemorative items distributed at the exhibition. It brought together the two myths of national unification underlying the exhibition: military/political unification under the Nationalist Revolutionary Army (whose soldiers and flags are pictured) and economic integration (the characters in the upper left corner read: "Memento of the Chinese National Products Exhibition"). A toy company, named on the right, donated this button. (*right*) The Post Office, which set up a temporary branch on the grounds, participated in promotional activities for the exhibition by issuing a special stamp. The stamp prominently displays the words "Chinese National Products Exhibition," yet one more way of transmitting the message of this spectacle to Chinese well beyond Shanghai.

bayonets, with the new National flag fluttering in the background. The button simultaneously symbolized the two mutually reinforcing mythical unifications underlying the exhibition: territorial and economic. On one level, the button commemorated the Northern Expedition and national reunification. The text on the upper left side connected the item with the event by identifying the item as a memento from the exhibition. Significantly, the item was linked to a sponsoring national product manufacturer, in this case, a toy company, named in the upper right corner. As I argue throughout this book, the movement frequently depicted the consumption of national products as an active form of resistance to imperialism, a way for ordinary Chinese to fight for their nation. This memento conveyed the notion that Chinese consumers could express their patriotism not only through military service but also through the discriminating consumption of national products.[21]

People and Products on Display

Attendance at the exhibition was impressive, especially considering the modest size of the exhibition grounds and its timing during the uncomfortably cool winter season.[22] Throughout the opening week, visitors flocked to the exhibition grounds. On the second day, approximately 30,000 people attended. In addition to ordinary citizens, representatives from Chinese organizations and overseas Chinese organizations viewed the exhibition (*SB* 1928.11.3: 13). By one estimate, between 200,000 and 300,000 people visited the exhibition during the first week, and well over 30,000 people attended each day, with the exception of late in the week when bad weather kept all but some one thousand away (*SB* 1928.11.9).[23] Attendance was higher on days with good weather and on weekends. On November 18, which was a warm Sunday, as many as 100,000 people toured the site (*SB* 1928.11.19: 13). After the first week, attendance averaged between 3,000 and 5,000 people during the weekdays and over 10,000 on the weekends. In addition, organizers sold over 21,000 passes that permitted multiple entries. In total, well over a half a million people saw the exhibits, including nearly a thousand "special guests."[24]

---

21. Most mementos were less complex. Chinese companies such as the China Press (中華書局) printed 50,000 copies of the omnipresent photograph of President Sun and his Will as well as a journal for children. Several Chinese cigarette companies provided tens of thousands of packs of cigarettes; see "Canjia zhanlanhui zhi yongyue" (1928).

22. In fact, the overwhelming success of the event caused administrative problems. Much like an amusement park, the exhibition had daily and seasonal entrance passes, along with a separate admission for the elaborate entertainment program. Initially, organizers hoped to stimulate interest in the movement by setting ticket prices very low. However, because of the unexpected popularity of the exhibition, especially its entertainment programs, too many people crowded into the modest grounds. As a result, organizers doubled prices and set additional regulations for attending the entertainment programs (*SB* 1928.11.4: 13).

23. Such estimates were, of course, difficult to make. These estimates were based primarily on ticket sales.

24. For the exact number of paying visitors, see GSB 1929, vol. 6: "Benhui meiri guanlan renshu tongji biao" (A statistical table of daily visitors). For the number of people who visited

Movement commodity spectacles often targeted young consumers, citi-zens-in-the-making, especially schoolchildren. Organizers hoped to reach these Chinese at a young age and link their identities to the consumption of national products. As a result of special efforts to attract them, students from schools throughout Shanghai, other cities, and overseas Chinese com-munities visited the exhibition every day (*SB* 1928.11.11: 13–14). Every type of school sent students. On one particularly busy day, a local primary school sent 700 students, a middle school 100, a university 40, a native-place asso-ciation with its own school 60, a missionary school 50, a girls school 30, and another local university 150. Even a local orphanage sent a few dozen chil-dren (*SB* 1928.11.21: 13). In many cases, entire student bodies of schools visited (*SB* 1928.12.7: 14).

As the speeches by politicians and organizers made clear, these exhibi-tions were intended to be factories for the production of national conscious-ness. In a suggestive photograph (Fig. 6.9) taken during the Beiping Na-tional Products Exhibition of 1933, students lined up at the entrance to the exhibition. Organizers imagined the young spectators as raw material for the production of nationalist consciousness. As they made their way through the exhibition, a narrative of national economic integration, self-reliance, and imperialist resistance through consumption of national products was etched onto their young minds, or so the organizers hoped. It would, after all, re-quire much more to ensure that these young consumers, like their adult counterparts, consumed nationalistically. Yet these spectacles became an-other new dimension of the larger movement of teaching Chinese to distin-guish between Chinese and foreign products.

The market for national products was built on connections, and for many adults attending the event, national exhibitions served a concrete purpose by creating networking opportunities for movement institutions and other or-ganizations across China. To promote such networking, exhibition organiz-ers regularly sent telegrams and letters to government offices and social or-ganizations throughout China informing them of activities at the exhibition and the success of the event (*SB* 1928.11.8: 13). National product institutions

---

with passes for the duration of the exhibition, see GSB 1929, vol. 5: "Gongshang bu Zhonghua guohuo zhanlanhui fashou changqi ruchang quan mingxi biao" (A detailed chart of the Ministry of Industry and Commerce Chinese National Products Exhibition sales of long-term entrance tickets).

Fig. 6.9 Students Visiting an Exhibition
(Bai Chenqun 1933; courtesy of the Tōyō Bunko)

Students were a common sight at national product exhibitions and museums. In this photograph, students of the Northern School (北方學院) lined up at the entrance to the Beiping National Products Exhibition to learn the meaning of nationalism through the identification of Chinese "national products."

in other cities used such information to help organize their own events. In addition, these institutions sent representatives to Shanghai to collect information about certified national products from across China. For example, Nanjing's National Products Museum, which had not yet opened, sent a delegation to look for appropriate samples.

The exhibition was a mandatory destination for a long list of influential foreigners and ethnic Chinese visiting from overseas, similar to the obligatory visit to the model commune and factory of later decades. As with these later models, the exhibition represented a symbol of the nation at its best or the national vision in a microcosm, a place to demonstrate national progress (*SB* 1928.11.6: 13).[25] And there is evidence that the spectacle had the

---

25. This article includes the visit and speech by Tianjin's Nankai University founder and president Zhang Boling 張伯苓 (1876–1951). Over the course of two months, many others spoke, including heads of universities and medical colleges, prominent party leaders, and academicians. See, for instance, the talk by Nationalist Party honcho and mayor of Shanghai Wu Tiecheng 吳鐵城 (1888–1953) (*SB* 1928.11.7: 13). Ironically, Wu's father had owned a shop that sold foreign goods (Wu Tiecheng 1969: 2).

intended effect. Through the image of "industrializing China" produced by the exhibitions, these overseas observers concluded that China was making great strides in its economic development. According to one visitor, Chinese agricultural and textile machines were nearly as good as imported machines and would soon displace imports in the domestic market.[26] One foreign observer was so impressed with the products on display that he found it "difficult in many instances to distinguish between goods of Chinese make and foreign manufactured articles" ("National Products Exhibition" [1928]). Another foreigner was particularly impressed with China's ambitious industrial and modern vision displayed in the models of roads and designs for bridges.[27] An ethnic Chinese observer from the Philippines commented favorably on the Shanghai municipal pavilion, which he saw as emblematic of the emerging spirit of cooperation between rulers and the people within China.[28]

Finally, most people went to consume the spectacle itself, to which they themselves contributed. Movement organizations such as the NPPA successfully lobbied exhibition organizers to mandate that all visitors (with the exception of foreigners) wear clothing (either Western or Chinese styles) made exclusively from Chinese material.[29] In this way, the nationalizing process underlying the event was extended into the lives of spectators, who had to make consumption choices long before they arrived at the exhibition grounds. For these participants, adhering to nationalistic categories of consumption became a prerequisite for participating in these areas of public life rather than an individual decision. Chinese were, to some degree, forced to think in these categories of consumption. By dressing up in national product clothing, exhibition-goers put themselves on display as authentic nationalistic consumers. In other movement events, Chinese had put themselves on a literal fashion catwalk to demonstrate their national consciousness through the consumption of certified national products (as with national products fashion shows). More commonly, however, spectators at these events put themselves on display as part of a crowd of nationalistic consumers. Such actions through appearances (in both senses of the term) should be considered

---

26. "The National Products Exhibition" (1929): 12.

27. "A National Products Exhibition," *American Chamber of Commerce Bulletin*, no. 158 (Nov. 1928): 5.

28. For the text of the speech of this observer, see "Jianian guohuo zhanlanhui" (1929).

29. For a specific example of such lobbying, see "Guohuo hui baju zhi weihui ji" (1929).

a public protest against imperialism, or at least a sign of the growing social requirement to be seen to be in favor of nationalistic consumption.

Communities of Commodities Within the Nation

Commodity spectacles attracted attention and an audience because they were about more than just the articles on display. These spectacles embedded objects of everyday life in larger narratives that promised to fulfill more than immediate material needs. In a sense, these spectacles operated in much the same way as modern advertising, which figuratively enlarges commodities by associating them with famous figures, catchy slogans, and elaborate images. The spectacles of the movement did this at two extremes: on one level, organizers hoped to appeal to a burgeoning sense of national identity and have consumers believe in nationalistic consumption as an emblem of resistance to imperialism and as a sign of good citizenship. But, as with an appealing advertisement, spectacles such as the 1928 exhibition also operated on a more mundane level. They attracted attention by juxtaposing mundane commodities with other, flashier spectacles (analogous to the way advertisements connect beer with sexual and athletic prowess).

The daily entertainment program provided one more way to incorporate diverse elements of Chinese society into the spectacle, both as performers and as spectators (Fig. 6.10). Every night different entertainers performed. On the third night, for instance, in addition to Chinese opera and comedy performances, students from several schools sang and danced for large audiences.[30] These performances often had content designed to promote the movement. On the afternoon of the tenth day of the exhibition, performers sang a song that lamented China's inability to boycott foreign products successfully and stem the influx of foreign products, a situation that the performers described as a "national humiliation." As with other movement messages, the singers asserted, "To be patriotic one must begin by using national products."[31] On December 1, girls from the Jinde Girls School performed a play entitled *The End of the Road for Treasonous Merchants* (奸商末路) (*SB* 1928.12.2: 14). Nor were performances limited to the stage: ten local schools

---

30. The daily papers regularly printed the entertainment programs of the exhibition. See, e.g., *SB* 1928.11.4: 13.

31. For the complete song, see *SB* 1928.11.12: 13.

Fig. 6.10 Ceremonial Hall of the Exhibition
(GSB 1929)

The hall was the literal and figurative center of the exhibition. The first-floor auditorium enticed people to visit the exhibition. The hall's varied programs, spectacles within a larger spectacle, promoted the agenda of the movement through a wide range of traditional (e.g., Chinese opera) and new (e.g., plays) forms of entertainment.

sent teams to participate in a basketball competition held as part of the exhibition (SB 1928.11.6: 13, 11.12: 13). This was one of the many ways the movement incorporated local youth and channeled their commitment to nationalistic activism into approved movement activities.

The creation of special "promotion days" (宣傳日) was one of the many tactics designed to stimulate interest in the exhibition. These days focused attention on participating provinces and cities, which were recognized with their own official promotion day. Each such day featured prominent figures from a given locale (who were often members of Shanghai native-place associations). At a minimum, the speakers discussed the industrial and commercial strengths of their area.

The focus on native-place identities was a clever way to attract attention and subsume regional to national identity. The organization of the exhibition into provincial displays allowed for the expression of powerful native-place affiliations while placing them within a national system of representation. Institutions such as museums have long created "natural" categories through such inherently arbitrary placement strategies (D. Miller 1994: 400). In the 1920s, 70–85 percent of the inhabitants of Shanghai came from outside the area; most maintained close practical and sentimental relations to their native places (Wakeman and Yeh 1992a: 4; Perry 1993: 17). A representative from Hebei province gave the first such speech (SB 1928.11.6: 13). Later, similar days were held for cities such as Shantou and provinces such as Anhui (SB 1928.11.8: 13). In addition to speeches, some areas distributed literature. For example, on Beiping Day, representatives handed out a booklet that introduced the displayed products, another publication that explained specialty items, and a third that provided an overview of economic conditions in the city (SB 1928.11.15: 14). Not surprisingly, in a form of regional conspicuous consumption, the wealthy and influential native-place associations from the southern coastal provinces organized especially elaborate days.[32] Specific industries also organized such days, such as Porcelain Ware Day (November 25) and Culture Industries Day (December 14) (SB 1928.12.5: 16).[33]

---

32. See, e.g., the lengthy programs for Jiangsu, Guangdong, and Fujian days in GSB 1929, vol. 3: "Fenchu xuanchuan" (Disseminating by area).

33. For information on these and other days focused on specific industries, see GSB 1929, vol. 3: "Fenye xuanchuan" (Disseminating by industry).

ENDING AS BEGINNING

On the last official day of the event, December 31, the spectacle wound down the way it began—with elaborate closing ceremonies and speeches underscoring movement themes.[34] The Social Affairs Bureau made a final push to extend the impact of the event by distributing a special catalog of the exhibited products, which it hoped would "act as a reference" (SB 1928.12.28: 12). That evening more than 4,000 people concluded the ceremonies by marching in a lantern parade.[35] The ideas and objects circulated at the exhibition continued to spread by word-of-mouth even after the event, as spectators and exhibitioners from outside Shanghai returned home with firsthand accounts. In late December, for instance, the Social Affairs Bureau of the Tianjin municipal government arranged a banquet to hear the report of the Tianjin delegation to the Shanghai Exhibition. The bureau also used the opportunity to discuss preparations for participating in upcoming exhibitions in Chile, Argentina, and Manila (Hu Guangming et al. 1994: 1503–4).[36]

The spectacle itself did not end; rather, it was broken into parts and sent to form new nationalistic commodity spectacles in other parts of Shanghai, China, and Chinese communities abroad. During the course of the exhibition, other regions began organizing similar events, and immediately after the close, organizers began sending the collected products to exhibitions elsewhere in Shanghai, and in Wuhan, Hangzhou, and Manila, as well as to the new Capital National Products Exhibition Hall in Nanjing (SB 1929.1.10: 14, 1.12: 13).

New spectacles immediately appeared in Shanghai. On New Year's Day 1929, just as the National Exhibition was ending on the southern side of Shanghai, a smaller exhibition opened in the far northern (Zhabei) section of

---

34. For a description of the activities and copies of the speeches at the closing ceremonies, see GSB 1929, vol. 3. Although the exhibition was scheduled to end on December 31, organizers decided to take advantage of the New Year's Eve holiday by expanding the exhibition for an additional three days. The additional days were also well attended. On January 1, 20,000 people visited the exhibition; despite inclement weather, many people visited on the final days ("Bimu hou zhi Zhonghua guohuo zhanlanhui" [1929]; SB 1929.1.1:26). Fittingly, the final day was Shanghai Day (SB 1929.1.1:26).

35. Larger companies and organizations such as the General Chamber of Commerce carried 80 lanterns; the Commercial Press marched with 50. They were part of a much larger celebration organized by the local government (SB 1928.12.31: 13, 1929.1.1: 26).

36. Tianjin had organized its own much more modest one-week exhibition in early October (Hu Guangming et al. 1994: 1504, 1505, and 1507–10).

Shanghai, the Zhabei National Products Circulating Exhibition. Over 5,000 people attended the opening ceremonies for the two-week event, including representatives from all the major movement organizations, such as the omnipresent NPPA leader Wang Jie'an, who represented an umbrella group, the National Products Alliance (國貨大同盟會) ("Zhabei guohuo zhanlanhui san ri ji" [1929]). This exhibition was organized and run largely by members of the Shanghai Citizens Association for the Promotion of National Products, with the help of the Zhabei Chamber of Commerce (these were overlapping organizations).[37] Not surprisingly, considering the duplication in organizations between the Shanghai exhibition and this one, there were many similarities. The Zhabei exhibition also held an extensive and diverse entertainment program every afternoon to attract visitors and on New Year's Day hosted a lantern parade throughout the northern part of the city.[38]

The success of the Shanghai Exhibition encouraged ambitious leaders in other cities such as Wuhan and Hangzhou to plan similar events, and Minister Kong received numerous invitations to host the Shanghai exhibition in other commercial and industrial centers. The powerful chairman of the Wuhan Branch Political Council, Marshal Li Zongren 李宗仁 (1891–1969), arranged with Minister Kong to fold part of the Shanghai Exhibition into one organized for Hunan and Hubei provinces, slated to begin in early February in Wuhan. In a telegram to Minister Kong, Li explained, "We believe that to hold the national exposition here after its closing at Shanghai will be of immeasurable benefit to the development of native industries here." He added: "All expenses will be paid by us" ("Trade Exposition in Hankow" [1928]).[39] In preparation, organizers of Wuhan's Chinese National Products Exhibition (中華國貨展覽會) regularly sent delegates to Shanghai to speak with officials, national product manufacturers, and representatives of the Shanghai General Chamber of Commerce (*SB* 1929.1.5: 14, 1.6: 14). Large-scale exhibitions spread to other cities in the following decade. In 1936, the treaty port city of Xiamen, which had had active movement organizations

---

37. Organizers also actively sought and gained the support of many other organizations and companies in their planning (*SB* 1928.12.18: 14, 12.22: 16, 12.30: 14).

38. *SB* 1928.12.24: 14, 1929.1.1: 28, 1.5: 14, 1.6: 15, 1.8: 14, 1.10: 14. On the closing ceremonies, which were in effect a movement rally, see "Zhabei guohuo liudong zhanlanhui bimu" (1929).

39. Minister Kong also made tentative preparations to hold an exhibition in Beiping on the grounds surrounding the Temple of Heaven ("Trade Exposition in Peking" [1928]; see also *SB* 1928.11.28: 14).

since at least the early 1910s, organized the Xiamen National Products Exhibition, which hosted 350,000 visitors (Hong and Liu 1996: 427).

Overseas Chinese communities also used the Shanghai Exhibition to arrange similar events. Philippine Chinese took advantage of the Shanghai exhibition to stimulate interest in their country's own upcoming exhibition, Manila's Far East Commercial Products Exhibition (遠東商品展覽會). In addition to this Philippine government-sponsored event, the ethnic Chinese community there and China's Ministry of Industry and Commerce organized a National Products Activities Exhibition to tour Chinese communities in Southeast Asia to "encourage overseas Chinese to use national products" ("Guohuo fu Fei zhanlan" [1929]). In Manila, the Philippine Chinese General Chamber of Commerce had already begun building an exhibition space for Chinese products. The chamber sent representatives to Shanghai specifically to collect products and invite Minister Kong to attend the exhibition (held January 26 to February 10, 1929) (SB 1928.12.2: 14; 1929.1.6: 14). In early January, the work of the Philippine delegates paid off, as nearly 200 prominent Shanghainese attended a dinner and pledged to send items to the upcoming event.[40]

Finally, there was an institutional legacy. The success of the Shanghai Exhibition and the growing number of places requesting permission to hold exhibitions inspired Chinese officials to codify their support for participation in domestic and foreign exhibitions. The Ministry of Industry and Commerce circulated these rules in an official letter (no. 18) that promoted the idea of greatly expanding all levels of exhibitions throughout China.[41] For its part, the ministry decided to hold an international exhibition (國際實業展覽會) in the former capital of Beiping in 1930 or 1931 and, as part of the preparations, began organizing the All-China Products Exhibition (全國物品展覽會).[42] In preparation, provinces, cities, and counties were ordered to collect products and hold exhibitions.[43]

---

40. Altogether, 42 crates of products from the Shanghai Exhibition were sent to Manila (SB 1929.1.10: 14).

41. Letter based on proposal by Tianjin representative Lu Mengyan. The rules also had the support of higher levels of government including the National Congress, which passed the general rules for holding exhibitions during its eleventh session. The Suzhou Chamber of Commerce archives contain many invitations to participate in exhibitions across China; see, e.g., SZMA File 1324: 104, which describes a planned event in Chongqing in 1932.

42. See Guomin zhengfu (National government), order 208 (1928.11.17).

43. For the letter announcing the new rules and complete copy, see "Xingzheng yuan guanyu banxing quanguo juban wupin zhanlanhui" and "Guomin zhengfu Gongshang bu

FITTING THE MOLD?

These two chapters on the exhibitionary complex underlying the movement have provided a framework for interpreting the commodity spectacle in pre-communist China. With only slight modification, the largest and most spectacular of these—Hangzhou's West Lake Exhibition of 1929—also fits into this framework.[44] As the previous chapter makes clear, these nationalistic commodity spectacles were innumerable. At the same time, any account of such spectacles, particularly exhibitions, would be incomplete without reference to the largest exhibition of the era, the Hangzhou event, especially because it seemingly challenges the notion of nationalized spectacles.

Between its opening in early June and its close nearly six months later at the end of the year, some twenty million people visited this exhibition, which took advantage of Hangzhou's status as the primary tourist destination in China.[45] This event was unique in many ways.[46] However, it included all the

---

gonghan." The types of exhibitions were listed in three categories: all-China (全國物品展覽會); local products (地方物品展覽會); and specialty items (特種物品展覽會). According to the plans, the national exhibition would be the capstone. It was to be organized in conjunction with provinces and cities, whereas provinces and cities would organize their own local exhibitions lasting two weeks to two months. Specialty exhibitions on things such as soap, tea, and other items would be organized by each industry and last a week to a month. All-China products exhibitions were to be held every year; local ones would be scheduled at the discretion of the provinces and cities. It also suggested that various groups and industries create touring exhibitions of national products. Provinces were required to execute the ministry's order to establish national products museums and then exhibitions. In addition, during government-sponsored campaigns such as the New Life Movement of the mid-1930s, local organizations were ordered to make national products exhibitions part of their agendas (SMP File 5727, 1937.4.15: "New Life Movement Acceleration Association").

44. This was not, of course, the first such movement event in Hangzhou. A year earlier, for instance, Hangzhou had held a more modest, but very successful, event (see "The Exhibition at Hangchow" [1928]). For an overview of the exhibition of 1929, see Luo Jiping 1997.

45. The estimated attendance of over twenty million is problematic. The total number of visitors to all ten pavilions was slightly under eighteen million. Most of these people undoubtedly visited more than one pavilion. At the same time, many people had passes that allowed multiple entries. In any case, this was the best-attended commodity spectacle. For attendance statistics, see "Canguan tuanti ji renshu" (Number of visiting groups and persons) in Zhejiang jianshe ting 1931, vol. 1, chap. 2: 55–57.

46. Many things made this exhibition unique: the size of the grounds and number of buildings, which included private houses, temples, public buildings, and even a zoo scattered throughout the West Lake and Solitary Hill area; the number of exhibited items was in the

key features of a movement-sponsored event, and discussions of it must contend with its relationship to the broader movement. First, the Hangzhou Exhibition clearly was linked to other events, particularly the Shanghai Exhibition.[47] It was also tied to movement organizations outside Hangzhou, which helped find participants.[48] In addition, this event continued the appropriation of the movement by the Nationalists. As with the Shanghai Exhibition, there was full party-state participation in its organization and execution, including speeches by leaders at ceremonies, symbols such as flags, and most conspicuously a Revolutionary Memorial Exhibits Pavilion.[49]

At first, one of the unique aspects of the Hangzhou Exhibition seems to undermine the interpretation of nationalized spectacles advanced here. This exhibition had a designated building for foreign articles. However, its Chinese name, *Cankao chenliesuo* 參考陳列所, which translates as "reference display room," suggests that its purpose was confined to providing foreign models for domestic emulation.[50] This was in line with the movement's goals and addressed the desire of those who saw the need to import certain goods as necessities (for example, foreign technical expertise—see the Introduction). The things displayed in this building, one Chinese observer noted, were intended to "serve as objects of comparison and study with a view toward the improvement of our native industries" ("The Westlake Exposition" [1929]). The regulations for the hall limited the exhibits to machinery and raw materials deemed "essential" to economic development. It did not include commodities competing with Chinese consumer goods.

---

tens of thousands; the large budget ($400,000); the amount of coverage in foreign newspapers; the duration (nearly six months); and finally the limited inclusion of foreign products.

47. Exhibition organizers made frequent visits to the Shanghai exhibition to study its strengths and weaknesses as well as solicit product submissions. Originally scheduled to begin in March, organizers decided to postpone the event for one month, so that it would not overlap completely with the Wuhan Exhibition (*SB* 1928.11.29: 13, 12.9: 14).

48. For instance, in late December, as the Shanghai exhibition concluded, Shanghai movement organizations such as the Association of Shanghai National Products Manufacturers (上海國貨工廠聯合會), one of the few Shanghai movement organizations devoted exclusively to small and medium-sized national product manufacturers, began rounding up its members to participate in the West Lake Exhibition ("Changlian hui canjia Xihu bolanhui").

49. The West Lake Exhibition also generated the most impressive report, a comprehensive six-volume set that includes details on every aspect of the event (Zhejiang jianshe ting 1931).

50. For a photograph of this pavilion, see *Xihu bolanhui canguan bixie* 1929.

Conclusion: A Commodity Nation

Creating national consciousness is always about creating boundaries—linguistic, physical, cultural, mythical, and visual. It is about creating and maintaining differences with foreign countries and creating bonds to overcome or make sense of domestic differences. The movement participated in this process by promoting and naturalizing the idea that all products from the different parts of the geographical entity known as "China" somehow constituted a complete system of commodities superior to any and all other classifications. Locales and provinces still produced commodities. But these goods were now represented as subclassifications of a larger, more important whole. They were made in China and made "China." By collecting, classifying, and juxtaposing these objects, nationalistic commodity spectacles naturalized (however tenuously) the notion that these things had a genuine relationship, that they created a bounded and natural unit. Chinese exhibitions at all levels were less about demonstrating to the rest of the world that China had made the leap to modern industry by producing commodities defined by price than they were about creating and sustaining the myth for domestic audiences that China could and should meet its own industrial needs by consuming goods defined by nationality. They were about giving the universal term "industrial civilization" a national inflection.

Imperialism made it impossible for China to enact its industrial vision on its own terms for the nation as a whole. At the same time, however, imperialism also provided the representational means for articulating nationality through the very same spectacles intended to privilege exchange-value. Within the visual and physical spaces Chinese did control, nationalistic spectacles became a miniature representation of the movement's more ambitious goals for the nation-state. During the first three decades of the twentieth century, nationalistic commodity spectacles—museums, retail stores, advertisements, fashion shows, exhibitions—expanded and proliferated, forming the complex web of institutions described above. These spectacles allowed participants in the movement to implement a strategy for creating a wealthy and powerful nation despite the constraints of imperialism. Participants in the movement did not simply wait to recover sovereignty from the imperialist powers; rather, they began actively to construct it from below in the minds of Chinese consumers through these nationalized visual and physical spaces.

PART IV

Nation, Gender, and the Market

CHAPTER SEVEN

Nationalizing Female Consumers

I consider wearing national products to be the most noble and honorable thing; in contrast, covering oneself in foreign products is to consider one's body as an inferior product and is an unsurpassably shameful thing to do.

—Participant in the Women's National Products Year of 1934

As for making use of national products, of course there is no distinction between men and women, but the vast power to use them is entirely in the hands of women.

—Statement of a Shanghai municipal government official

If women want to enjoy equal rights between the sexes, they must first demonstrate equal strength. Because women are not as effective on the battlefield, they must use all their might to promote national products.

— An official slogan of the Women's National Products Year

Women were critical to the National Products Movement not only as participants but also as representations of an ideal nationalistic consumer. From the start, movement organizations encouraged women to consume nationalistically, and women participated in the earliest movement activities, such as the creation of nationalistic commodity spectacles (see, e.g., Beahan 1981: 231).[1] Indeed, movement organizations formed by businesspeople, students, and government officials and their wives actively courted female participation; indeed they often portrayed women as the linchpin of the movement. Movement advocates contended that if women could learn to consume

---

EPIGRAPHS: (1) "Guohuo yu jinü" (1934); (2) Pan Yangyao 潘仰堯, a male Shanghai city official, quoted in "Funü guohuo nianzhong zhi liangdian xiwang" (1934).

1. In addition to women's movement organizations formed during boycotts (see Chapters 3 and 4), women established groups in other years; e.g., the Women's Circles Society to Encourage the Use of National Products (女界全用國貨會), formed in August 1911 in Jiaxing (in Jiangsu province) (see Lü and Zheng 1990: 173).

nationalistically, China would not only survive the incursions of imperialism but also grow rich and powerful. One article put the relationship this way: "People pay attention to every move a woman makes; so if she is able to promote and earnestly buy national products, she will earn everyone's respect" ("Funü yu zhuangjin" [1934]). Within these representations, women played the potential role of national saviors.

Women were also the chief problem. As China continued to import items deemed unessential by the movement, fashionable female consumers came under attack as agents of imperialist penetration and as catalysts of national destruction. Women became models of how not to consume. Such female consumers were "unpatriotic" because they were obsessed with frivolous surfaces over meaningful substance, as seen in their pursuit of fashions based on imports and because they desired instant gratification over long-term gain, as seen in their decisions to buy goods based on price or quality rather than national origin. Most damning of all, however, they were the antithesis of the "virtuous wife and worthy mother" (賢妻良母) archetype: they mismanaged their household and raised their children without considering the importance of consuming nationalistically. In these representations, their consumption came at the expense of a Chinese nation struggling to rebuff the imperialist powers and their armies of products, which were mesmerizing Chinese females and destroying the markets for Chinese goods. Proponents of the movement asserted that if female consumers remained devoid of national consciousness, they would blindly accelerate the destruction of the nation one coin and one imported item at a time.

These contradictory representations of women as heroic "patriotic consumers" and incorrigibly "unpatriotic consumers" were especially prominent during the Women's National Products Year (婦女國貨年) of 1934.[2] By exploring the events, participants, and discourse surrounding this year, we can not only uncover the complexities of pre-WWII consumption but also see how representations of women within the movement reinforced patriar-

---

2. The movement included other "national products years" directed at specific groups of consumers. The first, named simply the National Products Year (國貨年), was in 1933. The Students National Products Year (學生國貨年) of 1935 followed the Women's Year of 1934. And the next year was the Citizens National Products Year (市民國貨年). For extensive coverage of the activities of these years, see journals such as the *Guohuo yuebao*, weeklies such as *Daxia zhoubao*, and newspapers such as the *Shishi xinwen* and *Shenbao*. In addition, the SMA possesses uncataloged files of local newspaper clippings that cover each year.

chy, under the guise of nationalism, in an emerging consumer culture.[3] By loudly denouncing the inability of women consumers to attain the patriotic ideal, the organizers of the year helped reinforce the assumption that women were barely able to carry out their domestic responsibilities on behalf of the nation. This in turn justified the continued move away from earlier, more radical agendas for women's emancipation. At the same time, movement advocates sought to redefine women's roles in the household by emphasizing their potential contribution to national salvation. Thus, rather than dismantling the family, proponents urged women to embrace their reformulated roles as "virtuous wives and worthy mothers" by producing nationalistic consumers (see Fig. 7.1).[4]

The message of nationalistic consumption underlying the Women's National Products Year was also intended for men. The proliferation of these gendered representations of consumption constructed as unpatriotic also served as a warning to male consumers, who, left to their own devices, might consume in equally unpatriotic ways. These negative representations warned men not to valorize unpatriotic female consumers by viewing them with approval. In these representations, Chinese female consumers came to embody a nationalized set of "eternal Chinese civilizational virtues of self-sacrifice and loyalty" that were specifically linked to consumption (see Duara 1998). They represented the pure or authentic patriotic consumer, much as a handful of their male counterparts (discussed in the following chapter) represented authentic "patriotic producers." The ideal female patriotic consumer was a valorized model for emulation by other women and a sanctioned object of male desire.

---

3. I use the term "patriarchy" in its most comprehensive sense. Maggie Humm supplies a broad but helpful definition: "A system of male authority which oppresses women through its social, political and economic institutions. . . . Patriarchy has power from men's greater access to, and mediation of, the resources and rewards of authority structures inside and outside the home" (1995: 200–202). I see patriarchal relations in the way the editors of the *Engendering China* volume do, "not as static, ahistorical configurations, but . . . as contingent social arrangements that were always being contested and, in turn, required a great deal of cultural and political force to keep in place" (Gilmartin et al. 1994: 5–6). See also Gilmartin 1995: 235*n*17.

4. In a strikingly similar way, halfway around the globe, black housewives in Detroit launched a campaign in 1930 advocating "directed spending" by fellow blacks "to retain higher proportions of material resources in their own communities" (Hine 1993).

Fig. 7.1 Women as National Saviors
(*Guohuo pinglun kan* 1, no. 2 [1926.1])

Representations of women were critical to the National Products Movement, which tried to
define women through nationalistic consumption. Here the close relationship between
movement supporters and national industrial development is metaphorically represented as a
nurturing mother who, the text on the left informs us, "loves her son." This image published
by the NPPA shows a movement "advocate" (written on the blouse) as a mother breast-
feeding "national product enterprises" (on the baby). In these representations, women aided
the nation not only through their own nationalistic consumption but also by rearing children
who did the same.

There are three important reasons for devoting a chapter on gendered
consumption primarily to women. First, the movement aimed to nationalize
the consumption practices of all Chinese, but it approached various social
roles differently. This part of the study shows how diverse groups (men,
women, children, students, merchants, industrialists, and especially prostitutes) related to one another within the movement. Second, as the epigraphs
and the creation of a national products year targeted at women suggest, the
movement paid special attention to female consumers. Proponents of nationalistic consumption understood that two of the roles traditionally played
by women shaped household consumption. First, women were the primary
consumers on behalf of their families. Second, their child-rearing responsibilities meant that they were in the best position to instill nationalistic consumption practices in their children.

These two reasons suggest a third reason for focusing on women. By the
1930s, a new female archetype—the "modern woman" (摩登婦女)—was

emerging as a primary threat to the goals of the movement.[5] This largely urban and internationally oriented phenomenon personified a new form of femininity closely linked to consumption practices antithetical to those of the movement. Destroying the attractiveness of this representation became a key concern of the movement. This chapter demonstrates how the state and businesses—while claiming to represent national interests—intervened in the domestic lives of both men and women by opening what had once been relatively independent purchasing decisions to public scrutiny. Indeed, the movement—especially the Women's National Products Year—sought to justify this by denying distinctions between public and private. Making individual consumption practices an explicitly political act laden with nationalistic overtones was precisely the point of the year and of the movement.

This chapter explores the role of women and representations of women in nationalizing consumer culture. The first section examines representations of female consumers. Exploring what the movement hoped Chinese would see as unpatriotic about female consumption, and why, helps explain how the movement endeavored to correct this behavior. The second section embeds these issues in the Women's Year of 1934, a year in the life of a model female consumer. Three major gift-giving holidays provide an opportunity to see how the movement thought women should manage their households and interact with relatives and friends. Likewise, the celebration of International Women's Day (March 8) provides an opportunity to explore the growth of the view that women's ties to the nation were the highest form of loyalty and allegiance. The movement and the year commandeered these events to produce new norms for national female subjects as mothers, daughters, and consumers who engaged in fashion and, more broadly, consumption, with the interests of the nation in mind. A final section discusses the few women who openly challenged these representations.

The Image of the Consuming Woman

The conflict between female consumers and patriarchal "national interests" has been part of a larger battle over gender relations in modern history. A truism of the study of feminism and other social movements in the twentieth century is that women's movements consistently took, willingly or under du-

---

5. On the representations of "modern women" in 1930s film, see Yingjin Zhang 1996: 185–231.

ress, a backseat to nation-state-building projects (see Jayawardena 1991).[6] In the process, women's rights advocates have continually subordinated or sacrificed their goals to the purported prerequisites of a larger nationalistic discourse.[7] National liberation, in such master narratives, becomes the primary objective on which women's emancipation would (or should) follow. The history of the interaction between nation-state building and the changing roles of women in China is just being written. Starts have been made on relating women's emancipation to revolutionary political movements, labor movements, and even psychological change (Gilmartin 1995; Hershatter 1986; Honig 1986; Collins 1976).[8] I hope to contribute to this literature by linking women's emancipation agendas to the burgeoning urban consumer culture. The emphasis here is on how the nexus of intensely anti-imperialist and nationalistic discourses of consumption subordinated the goals of the women's movement to nationalism.

Women's emancipation and nationalist discourses have long been joined, and the co-optation of women's goals by nationalism was a constant threat. Male contributions to the discourse on women's emancipation (婦女解放運動) from the late Qing on emphasized empowering women, alongside men, so that they might better help serve the nation; they rarely discussed the granting of intrinsic or inalienable rights.[9] This justification for changing women's social roles is clearly seen in two major issues at the turn of the twentieth century: footbinding and education for women (Lü and Zheng 1990: 150–68). The famous reformer Liang Qichao was one of the best-known and earliest proponents of this formulation. He argued that China's backwardness was due to the manifold ways it constricted the potential physical and intellectual contributions of its people. He paid special attention to the physical limitations imposed on women. For example, Liang severely criticized the practice of footbinding because crippling women pre-

---

6. Not only have emancipation agendas been set aside, but, some would also argue, women's bodies have been further colonized by the needs of the nation. See, e.g., the collection of articles in Yuval-Davis and Anthias 1989.

7. Ania Loomba remarks of this trade-off: "The self-fashioning of the nationalistic male thus required his fashioning of his wife into a fresh subservience, even though this new role included her education and freedom from some older orthodoxies" (1998: 221).

8. On the role of Chinese women in introducing and defining nationalism, see Judge 2001.

9. On the application of such terms during the early twentieth-century women's movement in China, see Gilmartin 1995: 6–8. On early twentieth-century anarchism and its attempts to break this link between nationalism and feminism, see Zarrow 1988.

vented them from contributing to the welfare of the country.[10] The other major focus of earlier reformers was women's education. Even when women participated in these initial discussions toward the end of the Qing dynasty, they invariably reproduced the male-dominated discourse on the supreme importance of the nation. For instance, of the reasons given in the early twentieth century for educating women, historian Charlotte Beahan observes, "Women were to be educated because they would be the mothers of the Chinese race and the Chinese citizens of the future. Education was not justified as an inherent right of women, but as an absolute necessity for the good of the nation as a whole" (1975: 385).[11]

Justifying the reform of women's social roles and status as a prerequisite for nation-state building was a double-edged sword, however. The connection legitimized reform in the minds of a much broader audience, particularly among men who could implement such views. The popular appeal allowed reformers to make significant gains in women's emancipation, as the demise of footbinding and the proliferation of women's schools demonstrate (Borthwick 1983: 114–18; Ma Gengcun 1995: 127–41). But the link ultimately proved fatal to reformers. During the iconoclastic New Culture Movement and May Fourth era of the late 1910s and early 1920s, social critics launched a broad criticism of the existing patriarchal system. To save the nation, reformers such as Chen Duxiu 陳獨秀 (1879–1942) called for a host of revolutionary social and political changes, including the abolition of the family as the basic social unit. However, as reform goals broadened, they met resistance from those who questioned the nation's need to empower women in general and their own wives and daughters in particular.

In the late 1920s, tension between the more radical elements of the women's emancipation movement and the proponents of the national welfare came to a head. The reinforcement of gender norms in the 1930s is best seen as part of the ongoing reaction to May Fourth radicalism, which from the start had only limited appeal. Although advocates of women's emancipation were active before and after this time, in the 1920s radicals used "revolu-

---

10. For a summary, see Collins 1976: 239–40. For another example of a similar linking of national survival and women's emancipation, see Rofel 1994: 236. On the struggle for physical emancipation, see Fan and Mangan 1995.

11. For a list of new journals created to disseminate these positions from 1898 to 1919, see Ma Gengcun 1995: 160–63.

tionary action as a means to consciously refashion China's gender order"
(Gilmartin 1994: 201). They failed in their immediate goals, but their activism did successfully publicize women's issues—as demonstrated in the rise
of events such as International Women's Day, the expansion of public discourse on gender roles, and the spread of new social organizations. At the
same time, the history of the decade reveals how quickly and easily politicians trying to build broader male support sacrificed these initial successes.
At the end of the decade men still predominately controlled women, as well
as the production and distribution of representations of women. Both sides
of the Nationalist (GMD)–Communist (CCP) political divide had quickly
backpedaled from earlier and more radical positions on women's emancipation. Both sides found it a political liability to promote issues such as equal
employment opportunities, the freedom to divorce, and expanded legal
rights. In fact, sexual politics became one of the ways the two parties sought
to differentiate themselves, as each side tried to portray the other as endorsing the more extreme social agenda.[12]

THE NEW LIFE MOVEMENT
AND THE MILITARIZATION
OF THE HOUSEHOLD

To historians of Republican China, the year 1934 is primarily known for the
inauguration of the New Life Movement (新生活運動).[13] Officially
launched in February 1934—reportedly after Chiang Kai-shek witnessed a
boy urinate in front of Madame Chiang (Payne 1969: 162)[14]—this Nationalist government–led effort represented Chiang Kai-shek's attempt to inculcate individual self-discipline, group responsibility, and national loyalty by
popularizing a combination of "traditional" Chinese neo-Confucian views
and foreign-inspired ideology. The New Life Movement's foreign models

---

12. See Gilmartin 1994: 212 for an extreme version of the punishing of women for their
clothing and hairstyles. In 1927, in the Changsha Horse Square Incident, women with bobbed
hair were killed on the pretext that they were Communist radicals. For other examples of
controversy surrounding bobbed hair in China, see Lung-kee Sun 1997. Bobbed hair created
controversy in countries around the world during the 1920s and 1930s; on France, see M. L.
Roberts 1994: 63–87 and Zdatny 1997.

13. Historians in the West often conclude that this was the most widespread social
movement in the Republican era. For instance, Samuel Chu calls it "unique" (1980: 38).

14. For a similar account of the origins of the New Life Movement, see Furuya 1981: 434–35.

were the Fascist regimes of Italy and Germany—along with the military ethic Chiang himself had experienced as a cadet in Japan.[15]

On one level, the New Life Movement is useful to the study of the National Products Movement as another example of Republican-era attempts to regulate personal behavior on behalf of the nation and to inculcate the idea that national salvation lay in dictating behavioral norms for individual Chinese. What it demanded was nothing less than the inner transformation of every Chinese for the sake of national salvation (Eastman 1976: 202).[16] Nationalist literature frequently linked China's strength to the cultivation of self-restraint, self-sacrifice, loyalty, and obedience. Chiang himself frequently connected national survival and personal behavior: "If we are to restore the nation and gain revenge for our humiliations, then we need not talk about guns and cannon, but must first talk about washing our faces in cold water" (quoted in Eastman 1976: 202).[17] As historian Arlif Dirlik notes, this was the Nationalist "version of the 'cultural revolution'" (1975: 945).[18]

---

15. On the German inspiration for the New Life Movement, see Kirby 1984: 145–85. On the domestic context, see Chu 1980. For a close reading of its ideology, see Dirlik 1975.

16. There are innumerable accounts from contemporary sources of groups empowered by the New Life Movement to monitor the behavior of others. See, e.g., SMP File 5729, 1935.3.25: "The Youth Service Group," which tells of squads of boys wearing badges canvassing the streets and alleyways around Shanghai "persuading persons found smoking and others who were improperly clad to correct their behavior." Many such groups were established to "advise the people to live a 'rational' life" (File 5729, 1934.6.5: "Inspection of New Life Movement Persuading Corps"). In Shanghai, these "Persuasion Corps," which included members of the police force, were ordered to parade individuals caught violating New Life dictates (File 5729, 1934.5.29: "Violators of Rules of 'New Life' May be Paraded in Streets"). See also File 5729, 1935.3.22: "Activities of the Inspection Group," 1935.2.19: "The First Anniversary of the New Life Movement," and 1935.1.12: "Propagating the New Life" (this SMP file contains extensive coverage on the New Life Movement, including translations of clippings from local newspapers). The official history of the New Life Movement enumerates the various social practices targeted for elimination (*A Brief Historical Sketch of the New Life Movement* [1937]). All the countless movements or campaigns in China during this time sought to change Chinese behavior. Many of these movements overlapped. During the New Life Movement, for instance, the Anti-Tuberculosis Movement tried to persuade Chinese to "refrain from spitting at random on the streets" (SMP File 5729, 1935.3.17: "Anti-Tuberculosis Movement").

17. In some cases, these hygiene campaigns contributed directly to the creation of new Chinese industries. Carl Crow (1944: 134–35) observed that the "Kill Flies!" campaign of the New Life Movement, which rewarded boys for killing flies, initiated a huge demand for a new consumer product, flyswatters.

18. In a chapter devoted to the "successful" and "widespread" New Life Movement, Crow provides colorful examples of the growth of awareness of hygiene and sanitation and its suc-

The National Products Movement used the New Life Movement to spread its agenda. For instance, the thousand-plus branch organizations within the New Life Movement were conduits for the call to promote national products.[19] The movement also re-interpreted the vaunted traditional Chinese virtues at the heart of New Life rhetoric to suit its interests. New Life leaders combined the hallowed Chinese virtues of propriety, justice, integrity, and shame (理, 義, 廉, and 恥) with militarization (軍事化) in an attempt to foster a disciplined, patriotic, and energetic population.[20] Movement participants, however, defined these same traits within the context of nationalistic consumption, citing, for instance, the wearing of foreign-manufactured clothing as an example of a lack of shame and arguing that one should foster these traditional virtues through patriotic consumption. As a female junior high school student put this: "One who uses national products has a sense of shame; and one who does not use national products lacks a sense of shame." This same student also reinterpreted the other virtues in light of the movement by suggesting, for instance, that one could cultivate and demonstrate integrity through a willingness to buy national products "even when they cost more than imports" (Zhang Mingdong 1934) (see Fig. 7.2).[21]

More broadly, the movement helped define the purpose of this universal militarization of Chinese society and attendant attempts to create a common purpose among all Chinese. Scholars have already examined the widespread

---

cess in making polygamy disreputable. Downplaying the coercive aspects of the campaign, Crow called Chiang's government the "Emily Post of China" (1944: 127–29).

19. The widely circulated and posted slogans of the New Life Movement, for instance, included "Promote the National Products Movement" (SMP File 5729, 1935.4.10: "The New Life Movement—General Principles for the Organization of the New Life Public Service Corps," Article 6, no. 16; see also Walter Chen 1937: 210, 219; Dirlik 1975: 950, 955, 973; and Chu 1980: 46). On the number of branch organizations in the New Life Movement, see Walter Chen 1937: 200.

20. The four terms are difficult to translate. Madame Chiang Kai-shek rendered them as "behavior," "right conduct," "integrity," and "self-respect" (Chiang 1934: 7–8). Indeed, Chiang Kai-shek proposed "Militarization Movement" as an alternative name for the New Life Movement (Dirlik 1975: 972; Kirby 1984: 176). Chiang himself said: "In the home, the factory, and the government office, everyone's activities must be the same as in the army. . . . And everyone together must firmly and bravely sacrifice for the group and for the nation" (quoted in Eastman 1976: 202).

21. See also Benson 1999, which demonstrates how Nanjing Road merchants used songs to subvert the New Life message.

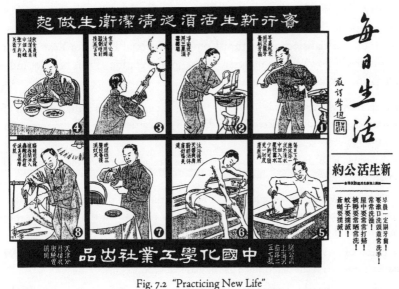

Fig. 7.2 "Practicing New Life"
(*SB* 1934.6.29)

This advertisement for the personal grooming and hygiene products manufactured by China Chemical demonstrates the swift co-optation of the New Life Movement by the National Products Movement. While reproducing slogans from the New Life Pledge such as "definitely brush your teeth every morning" and "frequently sweep your rooms" (*lower right corner*), this advertisement placed by a major supporter of the movement also promotes the consumption of products as the means to achieving "New Life." The advertisement suggests how one might use China Chemical's national products from the first thing in the morning to the last thing at night: "(1) When you get up in the morning, use Three Star toothpaste to brush your teeth; (2) When washing your face and hands, use Three Star antiseptic soap; (3) When a room must be sanitized, use Housefly Killer; (4) When food and drink must be cleaned, add Flavor Life to your vegetables. Adding a bit is tasty and hygienic; (5) Every afternoon, you should bathe. Add Three Star cologne water to a tub of clean water. Just a bit can protect you from skin aliments; (6) After bathing, lightly sprinkling Heavenly Scented talcum powder on your body and skin will leave you relaxed and refreshed; (7) In the evening, light a Three Star mosquito coil to kill mosquitoes; (8) Just before going to bed, sprinkle Bug Enemy medicated powder between the crevices of the bed and the bedding to kill bugs and ensure a peaceful sleep."

militarization of the Nationalist Party and its government.[22] However, the National Products Movement's co-optation of military forms and rhetoric reveals an attempt to extend this militarization even more deeply into

---

22. Representative publications by these "New Military historians" include Waldron 1993 and van de Ven 1996*a*, 1996*b*, 1997.

society.[23] This militarization reached into the family and to the way women were expected to connect their roles as housewives to national salvation. Indeed, the official slogans for the Women's National Products Year of 1934 (translated below) clearly illustrate the re-interpretation of this broader militarization on behalf of the movement:[24]

1. A woman who commands her family to use national products is the equivalent of someone commanding officers and soldiers on the battlefield to kill the enemy for the country.

2. A woman who absolutely refuses to purchase foreign products is the equivalent of a warrior recovering lost territory.

3. If women want to enjoy equal rights between the sexes, they must first demonstrate equal strength. Because women are not as effective on the battlefield, they must use all their might to promote national products.

4. National survival is the duty of everyone. The weapon of women in the fight for national survival is the determined use of national products.

5. Last year [1933], imports topped $1,345,000,000. Because this year is the Women's National Products Year, imports should drop as an expression of women's patriotism.

6. Last year, food and flour imports occupied the top spot, with a total exceeding $275,000,000. Silk fabrics accounted for over $10,000,000, and perfume in Shanghai over $1,000,000. These monies largely came from the hands of women.

7. During the previous year, over 300 Chinese factories closed, leaving 330,000-plus workers without jobs; including their families, this leaves hungry and cold over 2,000,000 people—if women can lead family members to use national products, then they can save the lives of over 2,000,000 persons.

8. Women! Sacrifice a bit of beauty! Thereby save the country and save the people! This is even a greater way to act!

---

23. Indeed, even the body itself was conceptualized as a battlefield (Dikötter 1995: 123–26). On the reflection of this militarization of Chinese society in the fashions of college students, who increasingly chose to wear military uniforms beginning in the late 1920s, see W.-H. Yeh 1990: 222–26. See also "Xin shenghuo zhifu yu guohuo" (1934).

24. *Funü gongming yuebao* 3, no. 12 (1934.12): 27. This list of Women's National Products Year slogans was widely reprinted. See, e.g., "Funü de guohuo biaoyu" and *Guohuo yuebao* (Shanghai edition) 2, no. 2–3 (1935.2–3): 82, which credits the Women's National Products Association (婦女國貨會) with creating these fifteen slogans. These were not the only slogans circulated during the year. For others, see "Funü guohuo nian qiche youxing canjia yongyue," which states such slogans were plastered throughout Shanghai.

9. Considering foreign products as stylish and as beautiful—that is the most shameful attitude.

10. Wasting money buying foreign products is the most immoral act. Hereafter, let's buy national products.

11. Although Chinese products are not as beautiful as imports, we should respectfully use these products because Chinese people make them.

12. We should teach our sons and daughters never to buy foreign products.

13. We should use promoting national products as a means of awakening national consciousness.

14. China has over seventy million struggling farmers; all of them are the result of imperialists exploiting us.

15. If we want to resist the exploitation of imperialists, we must earnestly promote national products.

These slogans neatly summarize the four central tensions, explored in this chapter, between the movement and its representation of female consumers. First, echoing the fascistic Nationalist Party rhetoric, military metaphors abound.[25] In this case, the market was a battlefield dominated by women on one side and nationality-bearing commodities on the other (especially, slogans 1–4, 15). Exemplary men proved their patriotism on the battlefield, and exemplary women on the figurative battlefield of the marketplace.[26] Second, just as a military battlefield was for men, the market was the proving ground for an idealized femininity and motherhood (slogans 3 and 12). As another movement slogan put it, "Women are the mothers of the citizenry; using national products is the mother of national wealth and power" (Zhang Jian and Wu Linwu 1996: 441). Third, the slogans underscore the growing hostility to "unpatriotic" female consumption—and invoke the purportedly indisputable evidence provided by trade statistics to justify this hostility (slogans 5–7, 14). Finally, the movement saw a tremendous need to integrate

---

25. Such military metaphors were parts of many movement slogans. For instance, among the official slogans of the Capital National Products Museum in Nanjing was: "Promoting national products is our greatest weapon for smashing the entire economic invasion of our country" ("Womende kouhao").

26. Indeed, this sentiment grew after the Japanese invasion of Manchuria in 1931, and this line frequently appeared in movement literature: "During the National Crisis, the only responsibility of women is to use national products"; see, e.g., "Guonan zhong funü weiyide zeren."

nationalism into female aesthetics and fashions by arguing that beauty was dependent on nationality (slogans 8–11).[27]

FROM LIVED TO
IDEALIZED DOMESTICITY

The initial stages of the women's emancipation movement in the early twentieth century had some successes. Formerly, "respectable" women had been severely physically limited in mobility by footbinding and customs that discouraged the intermingling of the sexes. By the end of the 1920s, women interacted more commonly outside the home in places such as new-style schools, theaters, native-place associations, and groups for returned students.[28] Moreover, in contrast to earlier periods, women themselves took an active role in the transformation of social roles. By one estimate, over a hundred women's organizations were founded in the first two decades following the Revolution of 1911. This new visibility was striking to foreign residents in China. Japanese and Western visitors to China before 1911 frequently noted the absence of middle- and upper-class women in public places.[29] According

---

27. Sun Mengren (1933: 33) concludes that the beauty of modern women was "artificial beauty" (不自然的美) because it was based on imports. One can find similar attempts to link aesthetics to nationality in other countries. In India, for example, Gandhi made a similar connection in 1925. Biographer Judith Brown summarized his view: "The product of the [traditional Indian spinning] wheel, being Indian rather than foreign, should have a particular beauty in the eyes of anyone who loved the Indian nation" (1989: 203).

28. Participation in native-place associations developed gradually. Here I refer not necessarily to membership, which seems to have been restricted to men until the 1920s, but more generally to events and organizations within association halls. Bryna Goodman notes that by the 1930s women not only could join these associations but also were active participants (1995: 221, 221n9, 282).

29. The Meiji-era leader Tsuda Mamichi, for instance, observed the strict separation of the sexes: "When I passed through the crowded intersections of Shanghai, [Tianjin], and [Beijing], the jams were even more confused than those I had seen even in London and Paris. Yet, I saw not a single Chinese wife on the streets. Nor did I see females sitting in the shops" (Meirokusha 1976: 278). For representative accounts by Westerners, see, e.g., Denby 1906: 163–65, White 1897: 152, and Speer 1870: 91–92, who cited their "inability to walk with ease" as the primary reason for their absence in public. Emile Bard noted: "Except in the open ports, one never sees a native in company with his wife and daughters. We have never met a Chinese woman at a dinner party, with the exception of singers and dancers hired to entertain the company" (1905: 36–37). Recent research, however, suggests that even upper-class women engaged in life outside the home to a greater degree than previously acknowledged; see Ko 1994: 12–14.

to one long-time observer, by the 1930s, women had become much more visible: "Women, especially of the younger generation, now accompany their husbands to restaurants and places of entertainment and sit with them in public theaters. Only five or six years ago [i.e., the mid-1920s] if women attended public meetings at all, they were carefully segregated on one side of the hall" (van Dorn 1932: 242–43).

As women increasingly participated in life outside the home, the New Life Movement and discourses of domesticity became increasingly idealized representations divorced from urban social realities. They were prescriptions for what women ought to do rather than accurate descriptions of what women were increasingly doing. The discrepancy generated the social power to vilify and victimize women not pursuing these normative roles. Attempts to force women back into more narrowly defined social environments centered on the family. But there was a difference. Women were told to return to the household in an attempt not to exclude them from public life but to persuade them to *participate* in public life in a certain way. Moreover, women's organizations joined in emphasizing the national significance of women's domestic roles.

AUTHENTIC AND INAUTHENTIC MODERN WOMEN

Although the movement sought to inculcate its values into every Chinese woman, it had priorities. Movement literature defined its target audience as primarily urban "middle- and upper-class women" (中上階級的婦女) ("Duiyu funümen jiju ni'er zhonggao" [1934]).[30] In other words, the movement focused on what sociologist Pierre Bourdieu terms "tastemakers" or "cultural intermediaries," which in Shanghai were middle- and upper-class women and prostitutes. As with tastemakers in general, these women possessed more than merely money. They also had "differential access to knowledge," cultural capital, and resources that were available in greater supply in major cities, especially in Shanghai, which provided more ways of knowing

---

30. In an interview, Mrs. Pan Gongzhan, a leader of the Women's National Products Year and the wife of a prominent Shanghai politician, also identified these women as the primary targets (Yu Qiacheng 1934). For an overview of the different social classes in Shanghai in this era, see Witke 1980. However, this article does not discuss the role of consumption in forming these classes.

through things such as fashion magazines and more places to learn such as department stores and other public venues (Bourdieu 1984).[31] The National Products Movement considered these women to be the worst offenders—they had the knowledge to know better and the power to make a difference, yet too infrequently did so. Moreover, as tastemakers, their choices were imitated by lower classes in the cities and throughout the country. Converting these women to role models for the construction of new nationalistic Chinese women became a central objective. Indeed, some of these women were the most active in the movement—wives and daughters of politicians, professionals, and merchants.[32]

Although this discourse collectively blamed the social category "woman," the primary transgressor was the "modern woman/gal/girl" (摩登婦女 / 摩登小姐 / 摩登女郎).[33] Like other social categories created in an emerging consumer culture, such women were most easily identified through consumption and leisure habits. In contrast to rural women, who bought primarily Chinese goods, "modern women" consumed almost exclusively imports.[34] Their leisure activities centered around imports and wasteful habits such as frequenting movie houses, dance halls, and hair salons and riding around in automobiles.[35] According to one article, these women were "worse

---

31. For an introduction to the social role of "tastemakers," see Finkelstein 1996: 80–86. On the role of Shanghai in producing fashion knowledge through magazines specifically about women's clothing, see Garrett 1995: 89–90 and Warra 1999.

32. These women were often referred to as "women of the educated class" (知識階級的婦女); see, e.g., SB 1934.5.24.

33. The term modeng 摩登 is difficult to translate. "Flapper" in many ways covers the meaning and was used by contemporaries to describe these women (E. T. Williams 1927: 424). However, as historian Miriam Silverberg (1991: 247–48) argues in an article on the Japanese "modern girl" (moga or modan gaaru), the term is not completely transferable. Although the Chinese "modern girl's" relationship to the flapper is ambiguous, her ties to her Japanese counterparts are more discernable. By the early 1930s, Japan and Tokyo in particular had already become a major source of information and inspiration for urban Chinese fashions. Participants ranged in age from teenagers to middle-aged consumers. On the role of these women and their male counterparts (modan bōi, "modern boys") in disseminating fashion knowledge in Japan, see Shimada 1962.

34. One writer even calculated that "imports constitute 70–80 percent" of the purchases of modern women; by contrast, "national products comprised 70–80 percent" of the items "village women" (鄉村婦女) consumed (Lu Qing 1932).

35. "Modeng funü: juewu ba!" (1934); "Guohuo yu wuchang" (1934), which describes the culture of imports within the halls; and "Modeng nüzi han maoduan nüzi" (1934).

than beggars and drifters." Like these two disparaged social groups, they produced nothing. Worse still, these women adversely influenced society through their example ("Duiyu funümen jiju ni'er zhonggao" [1934] and "Zhenzhengde modeng funü" [1934]). An examination of these representations reveals how patriotic and unpatriotic consumption produced authentic and inauthentic women.

The image of the "modern woman" is central to both movement efforts to nationalize consumption and state attempts to reassert control over women's behavior. This image came to represent everything both the movement and the new patriarchal nation-state claimed to oppose: reckless cosmopolitanism, superficiality, and disregard for social conventions.[36]

These representations also had deeper racial, class, and gender significance. These women showed themselves to be traitors to their race and evinced a "slave's mentality" (奴隸的心理) by blindly pursuing foreign trends; they were traitors to their gender because they apparently rejected state-sponsored interpretations of femininity; and they posed a danger to their social class by disrupting its conventions, undermining its authority, and heightening class tensions through conspicuous consumption. These seemingly apolitical women posed more of a threat than did more vocally political ones, most of whom were still bound by nationalistic narratives ("what is good for us is good for the nation" and, vice versa, "what is good for the nation is good for us"). Moreover, because these women often lacked or were denied an explicit political affiliation, they were much harder to target and control. Ironically, the more the political establishment attacked, the worse the situation seemed to become. Because shunning social conventions was part of the attitude associated with these women, the state undermined its objective by continually identifying these social conventions. Transgression was the point, and it was easier to transgress when rules and expectations were explicit.[37]

---

36. Indeed, in the short story "Cosmetics," a daughter rejects her father's admonitions to use only Chinese products and argues that "only workers did so" ("Huazhuangpin" [Cosmetics], *SB* 1934.1.18).

37. On the ways fashion systems encompass the fashionable, anti-fashionable, and non-fashionable, see Hollander 1980. For an entertaining elaboration of fashionable transgression in a very different context, see Klein 1993.

OBJECTS AND OBJECTIVITY
IN THE POLITICS OF BLAME

The discourse of trade statistics was an animating force not only in the movement (see Chapter 1) but also in these attacks on "the modern woman" and other consumers labeled unpatriotic. Many articles began their critiques of unpatriotic female consumers by invoking the metasignifier, or overarching referent, within this discourse, China's trade deficit.[38] Of the anticipated 1933 trade deficit of $900 million, one article said: "It's as if each Chinese gave more than $2 to foreigners" (SB 1934.1.1).[39] Such statistics were accepted as unmediated scientific proof of the lack of patriotism of Chinese women, particularly the self-described modern ones.[40] These statistics provided concrete evidence of the exact magnitude of the female betrayal. Nearly every article throughout this and other years during the movement makes explicit or implicit reference to China's annual trade deficit, as well as to the specific numbers for the targeted commodity. With this undeniable proof of unpatriotic consumption, movement advocates had a basis for attacking the lifestyles these forms of consumption produced—and, indeed, the movement provided this basis to others as well (for example, the New Life Movement). Moreover, the magnitude of this and other numbers became the primary justification for a gendered national product year—that is, a year devoted to publicizing and correcting the behavior of China's statistically most unpatriotic consumers: women (see Fig. 7.3).[41]

---

38. For instance, Shi Pu 1934 and "Jiagongzhong de fendou" (1934). China had run a trade deficit since the mid-eighteenth century. During the late 1920s and 1930s, this deficit grew quickly; see Table 1.1, p. 44.

39. At a movement fashion show in 1930, for instance, the speaker, Yu Qingtang 俞慶棠 (1897–1949), contextualized the establishment of the Shanghai Women's National Products Promotion Society (上海婦女提倡國貨會) by arguing that China's growing deficits were "passing through the hands of Chinese women" ("Nüjie tichang guohuo shengkuang" [1930]: 36).

40. See, e.g., "Funü guohuo nianzhong zhi chouhuo qingxiao wenti" (1934).

41. Some writers specifically blamed women's obsession with imported fabrics and clothes for the deficit and, therefore, the need to conduct a movement: "The money that every woman every year spends on clothing, I can say, occupies the greatest portion of the money spent that year . . . therefore it is absolutely necessary for the National Products Movement to begin with women's clothing." The author concluded that women "bear the greatest responsibility" for the success of the movement (Ba Ling 1934a: 13). The issue of Jilian huikan in which this article appeared (no. 92, Apr. 1, 1934) was a special issue devoted to the "clothing prob-

Fig. 7.3 Fashionable Traitors
(*Guohuo yuebao* 1, no. 1 [1934.5])

This is a typical representation of a fashionable urban woman circulated during the Women's National Products Year of 1934. The illustration portrays "China" (indicated by the Chinese characters on her blouse) as a well-dressed female in the hand of "foreign economic forces" (on the hand). The caption on the left side explains the reason for China's dire predicament: fashion controls Chinese women.

The movement did not consider all imports or all consumers equally blameworthy. There was an implicit product hierarchy—some desires were more socially acceptable than others. The most treasonable items were those aimed at satisfying female self-indulgence, particularly perfume and cosmetics.[42] These products became common metaphors for national disintegration. In these representations, China was on the verge of "national destruction" (亡國) because women could not control their impulses. The trade deficit was a scorecard for all Chinese and measured in specific terms the success or failure of the movement as a whole. However, in the early 1930s, specific

---

lem" (服裝問題) and contains over a dozen articles that make similar connections. See especially "Fuzhuang yu funü" (Clothing and women): 3–5.

42. "Funü guohuo nian yu huazhuangpin" (1934). For a brief history of the cosmetics industry in Shanghai and its link to the movement, see "Shanghai zhi huazhuangpin gongye" (1933).

Fig. 7.4 Conduits of Imperialism
(*Guohuo yuebao* 1, no. 2 [1934.6])

Here is another example of the many images, stories, articles, and other texts produced during the Women's National Products Year of 1934. These texts vilified middle- and upper-class women for popularizing the consumption of "foreign products" and, consequently, for supporting imperialism. The text (*upper right*) accuses women of acting as the "faithful marketing representatives of foreign products."

numbers were invoked to identify the culprits behind the culprits—or those primarily responsible for the national failure that the number demonstrated. These objects and their consumers, then, became central targets (see Fig. 7.4).[43]

Attacks on "modern women" became a central feature of the Women's Year. The notion of a new or modern woman (新婦女), since its inception at the start of the twentieth century, has always included the idea that there were widespread social "fakes," women who looked "new" but harbored traditional views (Edwards 2000: 120–25). Movement articles participated in this critique by excoriating women who misread modernity. These foolish women blindly equated anything and everything Western with modernity.[44]

---

43. This representation was a common theme in writings throughout the movement. For 1934, see, e.g., "Funümen! Xingba!" (1934) and *SB* 1934.5.24. An article in the latter derisively suggested that the year should be known as the "Women's Foreign Products Year."

44. Eileen Chang observed this equation between things Western and modernity: "The indiscriminate importation of things foreign went to such an extent that society girls and pro-

This mistake threatened the continued existence of the nation, as represented by its national products. As one writer put it, "We must make clear that the kind of modernity and fashion that foreign products express is an inauthentic [不真正] modernity and fashion. This type of expression really demonstrates one's own ignorance and stupidity. With the call to promote national products, this is shameful behavior."[45]

PROSTITUTING THE NATION

Even more than the "modern woman," the category of "prostitute" (妓女) provided the Women's National Products Year and the National Products Movement with the antithesis to its ideal nationalistic female consumer. Expressed in media sympathetic to the movement, the image of the prostitute was an especially potent symbol to associate with unpatriotic consumption, given the growing interpretation of prostitution in the 1920s and 1930s as a hindrance to both women and national development (Hershatter 1992: 146).[46] The movement strengthened the contrast between sacred national products and profane imports in many ways; perhaps the most visible of these was clothing. Within the movement, the two types of clothing produced antithetical social identities. As one writer expressed this relationship, "I consider wearing national products to be the most noble and honorable thing; in contrast, covering oneself in foreign products is to consider one's

---

fessional beauties wore spectacles for ornament, since spectacles were a sign of modernity" (1943: 59).

45. "Guohuo yu modeng funü" (1934). Not everyone wanted the movement to abandon the term "modern." Although some movement critics rejected "modern" clothing altogether, others suggested that "modern" clothing had to be defined strictly in terms of national products. In other words, if an article of clothing was made of imported fabrics, it was *ipso facto* not "modern"; whereas national products clothing always was. For an example of the former argument, see "Wo duiyu fuzhuang shang de sanbu zhiyi" (1934). The first of these three principles was "not modern" (不摩登). For an example of someone trying to redefine modern clothing around national products, see "Modeng fuzhuang de tiaojian" (1934), which includes as its first point: "As for the raw materials of clothing, only if an article of clothing makes use of national products does it count as modern." See also "Shizhuang yu meihua" (Fashion and beautification), SB 1933.5.11, which discusses "authentic fashion" (真正的時裝) in terms of national products.

46. For a review of works that explore representations of prostitutes as allegorical threats to national interests and as "metaphors of modernity," see Gilfoyle 1999. On the early twentieth-century replacement of elite prostitutes, or courtesans, with common prostitutes, see Henriot 1994.

body as an inferior product and is an unsurpassably shameful thing to do" ("Guohuo yu jinü" [1934]).

This author, like most movement advocates, sought to use the visual cues provided by appearance to shame women wearing foreign clothing into compliance and coined a new name to describe women who wore national products. Because prostitutes were famous for wearing fashionable foreign dress, the author suggested labeling all women who wore imports "prostitutes" and urged the circulation of a new slogan: "Women who wear foreign clothing are prostitutes." As the author put it, "I despise them. One knows at a glance that these women are unprincipled and disreputable." In contrast, women who conformed by wearing national products should be deemed "contemporary" or "hip women" (時代的婦女) ("Guohuo yu jinü" [1934]).[47] Unfortunately, the article did not reveal the secret of discerning a fabric's nationality "at a glance."

The term "prostitute" became a twin marker of social decadence and imperialist penetration.[48] Linking the consumption of imports with such potent symbols such as prostitution established the groundwork for treating consumers of imperialist products as non-human, a further check on behavior deemed unpatriotic. The movement needed to cleanse both the prostitute and her representative consumption habits.

AUTHENTIC MODERNITY, AUTHENTIC CHINESE WOMEN

Movement advocates were anxious to reverse the popular appeal of the "modern woman," for fear that an epidemic of emulation would quickly spread across China. As an article published on the first day of the Women's National Products Year warned, "Smaller cities and the countryside imitate the consumption trends of major cities" (SB 1934.1.1).[49] Another

---

47. In fact, even Chinese female mission school students who had contact with foreign men were accused of being unpatriotic and prostitutes. For an example, see Graham 1994: 35–36. Male anxiety that women would prefer the "foreign" to the "Chinese" appears to apply to both products and people.

48. For other uses of the changing categories associated with prostitutes in emerging nationalist discourse, see Hershatter 1994, which focuses on how prostitutes, especially their consumption habits, provided definitions of urbanity.

49. Throughout the movement, the countryside—in sharp contrast to the cities—represented both a place of authentic nationalistic consumption where consumers naturally

article cited the spread among women of the habit of powdering their legs as a specific example of this urban-rural system of disseminating fashion knowledge. The article blamed prostitutes for initiating the habit, "modern women" for adopting it, and rural women for emulating urban women ("Funü guohuo nian huichangwei biaoshi").[50] The movement sought to reverse these trends by denouncing loudly and frequently the "modern woman" and by offering a competing and nationalized alternative, such as the "contemporary" or "hip woman." However, as the final third of this chapter shows, movement sympathizers who set personal examples and organized a year of special events such as fashion shows and makeup education campaigns also waged this battle.

The movement attempted to break the association of the "modern" with international fashion and products by providing portraits of foreign women as role models of nationalistic consumers. These foreign role models invariably came from countries considered the most modern, the United States, Germany, Japan, and France. Fashion, in these examples, was intensely nationalistic rather than superficially cosmopolitan. Newspaper articles told of heroic efforts made by women from these leading countries to consume nationalistically, even while abroad. One role model was a famous Hollywood actress, identified only by the Chinese transliteration of her name, who visited France. While there, the actress used American products exclusively, dined only at American-style restaurants, and expressed absolutely no interest in French products. According to a newspaper article devoted to the story, the outwardly indignant French secretly admired her patriotism. In another parable, a Japanese mother living in Shanghai directed her son to buy a notebook at a distant store run by Japanese. Instead, the child bought

---

chose to buy Chinese goods and also the greatest source of anxiety that foreign product preferences would develop there. For an example of the former, see "Xiangcun tongbao de xialing guohuo yongpin" (1933). For an example of the latter, see "Guohuo tuixiao dao neidi qu" (1933).

50. On the role of high-class prostitutes as tastemakers, see also Gronewold 1985: 17, 59–60. In the 1930s, Carl Crow (1937: 41) commented that Shanghai set fashion trends not only for China but also for overseas Chinese communities. Japanese geisha similarly influenced urban fashions in their country (Dalby 1993: 328–35). A. C. Scott (1960: 59) also notes the coastal/urban to interior/rural path of the spread of fashion trends. In contrast to Scott, I do not equate or measure this spread by the appearance or disappearance of Western and Chinese styles. Definitions of what was Chinese and what was foreign were fluid throughout this period (see Part I).

a Chinese-made notebook at a nearby store run by Chinese. When he returned, his mother promptly inspected the article and discerned its Chinese identity. Thereupon she tore the notebook in two and scolded her son for his unpatriotic act.[51]

Such articles made clear to Chinese readers that theirs was not the only country encouraging strict reliance on national products. Rather, the citizens of every powerful country considered such measures appropriate and natural. As one writer put it, "I'm afraid that the only country that likes to use foreign products is China" (Zhao Yizao 1932: 39). *Authentic* modernity, as practiced in Japan and the West, relied on nationalistic consumption. Therefore, ran the argument, the wealth and power of China turned on the loyalty of its female consumers.

REACHING WOMEN
BEYOND SHANGHAI

Finally, although this chapter focuses on Shanghai, the Women's National Products Year and representations of women had a much broader impact. By 1934, there were many well-established channels for spreading the movement to other parts of China and abroad. Other chapters examine these paths more closely. Here it is simply important to note that many cities and towns reported activities associated with the Women's National Products Year. The specific objectives of the year were disseminated in print and in person. For example, in the spring, committee members such as Mrs. Pan Gongzhan and Ms. Tang Guanyu 唐冠玉 led tours of national product factories in Beiping, Tianjin, Ji'nan, and Qingdao, among other places, and worked to establish connections with fellow advocates of the National Products Movement (SB 1934.5.3).[52] Later during the year, activist Lin Kecong 林克聰 led a delegation to other port cities to promote the year (SB 1934.9.6). Women's monthly magazines such as the *Funü gongming yuebao* 婦女共鳴月報 kept activists in other cities abreast of ac-

---

51. "Zhe shi yimian jingzi" (This is a mirror), SB 1934.5.10. Another article, on the author's visit to Japan, describes how Japanese primary school teachers bully children into wearing only Japanese products and suggests that Chinese teachers do the same ("Xiaoxue jiaoshi zeren jiazhongle" [1934]).

52. Such tours were very common. See also "Funü guohuo hui zu guohuo kaocha tuan" (1934).

tivities in Shanghai and encouraged them to follow suit.[53] Groups in many places did so. In the Jiangsu provincial city of Zhenjiang, for example, December 3–9 was declared Women's Use National Products Promotion Week by the provincial assembly. Local household investigation teams, long a central part of boycotts, were set up to visit housewives and explain the importance of national products.[54] These teams also visited girls schools and encouraged them to set up their own teams to cover more territory. Later, all these teams joined in a mass rally to report the results of their work.[55] Likewise, during this year, Zhejiang province's Women's Association (婦女會) embraced the objectives of the Women's Year by compiling bylaws for the establishment of Women's Use National Products Associations and ordering every county and city to establish a branch ("Gedi funü jiji tichang guohuo" [1934]).[56]

A Year in the Life of a Patriotic Female Consumer

The movement coaxed women to practice the ideals of nationalistic consumption through the Women's National Products Year of 1934. Many of the activities during the year came from a long list of well-established methods for advancing the movement—setting up temporary markets, giving

---

53. New women's organizations were established frequently during the early 1930s to promote the development of the movement. Although there are no specific numbers, the pages of journals devoted to women's issues such as *Funü gongming* provide evidence of growing interest in forming such groups. In August 1930, for instance, it reported on the origins of a branch of the Women's National Products Association (婦女國貨會) in Guangzhou. Wu Zhimei 伍智梅 (1898–1956) of Guangzhou went to Nanjing to investigate the various women's organizations operating there and became especially interested in the Women's National Products Promotion Association (婦女提倡國貨會). The Nanjing organization supplied her with copies of the group's bylaws, minutes, investigative reports, and other information. In addition, executive committee member Chen Shuying 陳淑英 (1893–1990), the wife of Sun Ke (the son of Sun Yatsen who, at the time, was president of the Legislative Yuan), traveled to Guangzhou to help set up the branch and discuss plans for organizing similar groups throughout China ("Funü guohuo hui choushe Guangzhou fenhui" [1930]).

54. "Zuzhi guohuo xuanchuandui de jianyi" (1934). On female students who frequently visited housewives during the boycott in 1919 to help these women identify their Japanese possessions as well as teach them to look for domestic substitutes, see Lü and Zheng 1990: 298–99, 303.

55. *Funü gongming yuebao* 3, no. 12 (1934.12): 56; SB 1934.12.13.

56. Important cities such as Ningbo had already established a branch.

Fig. 7.5 National Product Fashion Shows
(Huang Yiting 1934)

Since its inception, the movement did not reject the idea of fashion, even fashion based on Western styles; rather, it rejected any notion of fashion divorced from nationality. Fashion shows were among the commodity spectacles appropriated from the imperialist countries to promote fashion based on product-nationality. By the late 1920s, such shows had become a regular part of movement events. At a show sponsored by the Chinese National Products Store on Nanjing Road, Shanghai's most famous shopping district, some of the most famous actors of the day modeled national product dresses, including (*on the far left*) Hu Die 胡蝶 (1908–89), (*fourth from the left*) Ai Xia 艾霞 (1912–34), and (*to Ai's right*) Xuan Jinglin 宣景琳 (b. 1907).

public lectures, organizing exhibitions, printing journals, convening rallies, investigating manufacturers and marketers, and visiting activists in other cities and countries.[57] Some of the activities were designed specifically for women, such as fashion shows, cosmetics exhibitions, and children's events (see Fig. 7.5).[58] Others, for example, commemorations of national humiliation days,

---

57. For instance, during the year women in Shanghai organized a temporary market and hired a promotional truck; see "Funü guohuo nian hui chou she lanshi shangchang" (1934) and "Funü guohuo nian hui zhi shixi shangchang kaimu" (1934). Also, "to improve the ability of students to recognize national products," the organizers of the year established the "circulating display of national product samples" (國貨樣本流動展覽會) ("Funü guohuo nian yundong weiyuanhui" [1934]). For a summary and brief description of the main activities of the Women's Year, see Lin Kanghou 1935.

58. I cover only a handful of the year's activities. For a brief overview of planned activities, see "Funü guohuo nian zhi yingyou gongzuo" (1934). The ties between women, fashion, and

were adapted to target women.[59] However, the Women's National Products Year also introduced new events.[60] In contrast to the focus on highly politicized national humiliation days in Chapters 3 and 4, the emphasis in this

---

the movement extend back over several decades. Many references to earlier fashion shows explicitly state the need to teach fashionable women to distinguish between Chinese-made and foreign products, for instance, the show hosted by the NPPA in 1913 (Pan Junxiang 1996c: 534). The most comprehensive report, with many photographs and the texts of speeches given at the event, is "Guohuo shizhuang zhanlanhui" (1930). See also Shanghai guohuo shizhuang zhanlan huiji 1930 and She Ying 1930: 2, who attacks as shameful fashion shows that include foreign articles. The shows were often part of national product exhibitions; see "Hushi guohuo shizhuang zhanlanhui kaimu shengkuang" (1930), for an event hosted by Kong Xiangxi. Often movie stars modeled the clothing at movement fashion shows. On one show during the National Products Year (國貨年) of 1933, see Lin Kanghou 1935 and "Shizhuang zhenyi" (1933). On the NPPA establishment of a "cosmetics lecture team" (化妝演 講團), see ZGWH 1932, "Huishi" section: 3.

59. See, e.g., "Furen xiaojie, ni wangjile ma" (1934), which accuses urban women of consuming Japanese imports and thereby forgetting that country's invasion of China. Movement organizations also organized a yearly week of commemorative activities on the anniversary of the Shanghai Incident of January 28, 1932, when Japanese troops caused massive destruction in that city. See, e.g., "Yi erba guohuo yundong zhou" (1934).

60. I discuss only a handful of the many days redefined by the movement. The movement, for instance, connected its agenda to celebrations of China's National Day, which commemorated the start of the Revolution of 1911 on October 10. On the commemorations of 1935, see "Shuangshijie yu guohuo yundong" (1935) and "Guoqing yu guohuo" (1935). Of course, the participants in the movement were not the only ones redefining the calendar. The veteran China observer Carl Crow noted, for instance, that the New Life Movement of the same year "did not attempt to end old superstitious practices by ridiculing them, but instead offered something new." For instance, it attempted to replace the Tomb-Sweeping Festival and the custom of burning of "ghost money" to one's ancestors with an Arbor Day and a new tradition of planting saplings (Crow 1944: 129). The Chinese Communist Party also actively defined these and other anniversaries. Nevertheless, because the CCP emphasized destroying international capitalism by attacking imperialism in China, their commemorative activities during 1934 and other years incorporated movement themes. SMP archives contain innumerable examples. The CCP, for instance, included the slogan "Intensify the boycott and confiscation of Japanese goods!" in a list circulated on the second anniversary of the Shanghai Incident (SMP 5641, 1934.1.28: Jiangsu Provincial Committee of the CCP, "Slogans Relating to the Second Anniversary of January 28"). On this date, the party also circulated a letter to "young men throughout the country," urging them to commemorate the anniversary: "Confiscate Japanese goods and properties of traitorous merchants for the benefit of unemployed workers and anti-Japanese military fund!" (SMP 5641, 1934.1.11: Central Committee of the Chinese Communist Youth League, "Letter to Young Men throughout the Country Relating to the Second Anniversary of January 28"). Likewise, May Day anniversaries also included reminders to boycott imports; see, e.g., SMP 4801, 1933.4.24: "Outline of Propaganda for the May 1 Anniversary": 4b. On other anniversaries, see SMP 4844.

chapter is on the link between a few of the less overtly politicized days to representations of consumption by women, such as using holidays to celebrate idealized female roles in managing household budgets, raising children, and representing the family.[61]

SETTING THE TONE
ON NEW YEAR'S DAY

On New Year's Day, 1934, the Women's National Products Year began with a parade and a rally. Before beginning the parade, the organizers held an opening ceremony for members of the sponsoring organizations and representatives of national products manufacturers.[62] One of the activists behind the Year, Lin Kecong, made a speech and stated that all of China's problems could be solved if the year were successful.[63] The speech set the tone: Lin did not stipulate what would constitute a successful year, an omission that would continually trouble participants. This was also a feature of the movement as a whole, which often implied that there was no such thing as a good import or a bad national product.

The parade passed through much of Shanghai and attracted large crowds. It began at 1:00 P.M. in the Chinese city (Nanshi). Thanks to the assistance of Du Yuesheng 杜月笙 (1885–1951), best known as the leader of Shanghai's notorious Green Gang, the organizing committee obtained permission to parade along the Bund and through Shanghai's foreign concessions.[64] The key associations of national product manufacturers and marketers, including the Shanghai Citizens Association for the Promotion of National Products and the NPPA, urged their members to participate. More than forty of the most important Chinese retailers and manufacturers of national products

---

61. Similarly, I do not discuss many of the ordinary rallies, tea parties, and other events organized during the year. For instance, the organizers held a rally at the Shanghai General Chamber of Commerce headquarters on January 17; see "Funü guohuo yundong dahui" (1934) and "Funü guohuo xuanchuan dahui" (1934).

62. "Funü guohuo nian jinri juxing qiche youxing" (1934); *SB* 1934.1.5. The lead movement organization involved in the year was the Women's National Products Promotion Association. Many other civic organizations as well as branches of the government participated, including the Shanghai Local Self-governance Association and the Shanghai Municipal Chamber of Commerce (Gu Bingquan 1993: 294–95).

63. *Funü gongming yuebao* 3.1 (1934.1); see also *SB* 1934.1.5.

64. "Funü guohuo nian qiche youxing canjia yongyue" (1933).

provided over fifty floats. Because of extensive coverage in local papers preceding the event, over 100,000 people lined the parade route and loudly cheered the procession.

Events such as this parade served two purposes. Most visibly, these events aimed to promote the consumption of specific items deemed to be national products. But more generally they promoted a nationalistic interpretation of consumption practices. In addition to advertising products, the parade provided an opportunity to link symbols of Chinese nationalism and anti-imperialism to products. For instance, the float of the Nanyang Brothers Tobacco Company was a truck decorated in the shape of the Great Wall. The message was clear: China needed to build up its defenses against a primary threat to the nation, foreign products. And the way to do so was to buy domestic goods such as this company's tobacco products. The floats of two important retailers of national products also linked the idea of defense of the country to products. Both the Shanghai and the Chinese National Products companies sent floats resembling tanks.[65]

THE WOMEN'S NATIONAL PRODUCTS
YEAR FRIENDSHIP RALLY

After two hours, the parade ended near the corner of Beijing and Guizhou roads with an even larger rally at the Huzhou (Zhejiang province) native-place association. In addition to major national product manufacturers and retailers, many of the most prominent women in Shanghai attended the Women's National Products Year Friendship Rally, including the wife of Shanghai mayor Wu Tiecheng. At this rally, Zhou Yanghao 周養浩, the wife of the famous Chinese educator Cai Yuanpei, further refined the day's message by explicitly blaming insufficient participation by women for the failures of the movement: "Although national products have been promoted for many years, the results are small. The biggest reason for this is that women have yet to promote national products wholeheartedly. Women determine the majority of all the products needed by a household. From now on women need to consider buying foreign products a disgrace."[66]

---

65. For photographs of several floats, see *Liangyou* 12.85 (1934.2): 2–3; these photos also appear in SB 1934.1.5. See also Lin Kanghou 1935: 4–5.

66. See the brief coverage in SB 1934.1.5, which includes one photo.

The rally was emblematic of the Women's Year in another sense. Throughout the year, organizers would present their central messages in popular forms of entertainment in the hope of attracting and reaching broader audiences. In addition to vitriolic speeches, the rally delivered its messages in slightly more subtle ways, by, for example, showing a domestically produced movie, presenting a fashion show, and hosting performances of traditional opera, comic dialogues, and a play entitled *Awake* (覺悟), which featured clothing manufactured by one of the main backers of the year. Both traditional and contemporary productions were modified to deliver the messages of the movement and of the year. After four hours, the rally ended (Lin Kanghou 1935: 5–6).[67]

LINKING NATIONAL INTERESTS
TO HOUSEHOLD MANAGEMENT

Throughout the year, movement advocates not only recommended changing one's attitudes toward consumption but also urged implementing or reforming specific consumption practices. One key idea was to monitor not only one's own consumption but also that of one's family, friends, and fellow Chinese. The goal was for Chinese consumers to internalize a particular form of behavior—an ethic of nationalistic consumption—and to reinforce this ethic in others. Women were seen as playing a crucial role in cultivating this attitude in themselves and in others. This section examines one specific practice of monitoring household consumption and the logic behind the attempt to make women see the adoption of patriotic consumption practices as an empowering form of participation in national public life, rather than simply as a new form of intrusive state domination over households.[68] As wives, for instance, women were encouraged to monitor their husbands' consumption. Many articles suggested specific tactics. One offered three ways wives could encourage proper consumption: "(1) If your husband brings home foreign products, refuse to use them; (2) if your husband brings home foreign products, a proper wife should say to him 'This product's not bad.

---

67. The event was heavily publicized beforehand; see, e.g., "Jiji choubei zhong zhi funü guohuo nian" (1933).

68. One article even stated that in their spheres, women were the equivalents of "interior ministers" and "finance ministers"; see "Furen zhi dao" (How to be a wife), SB 1933.6.8; and "Guohuo jiating" (1933).

Unfortunately, the money has gone to finance the foreigners' invasion!'; and (3) when your husband is considering buying something, urge him to buy national products and discuss with him the advantages of these products."[69] Rather than gaining face by giving wives imports as presents, another article suggested that a husband would lose face, especially since foreign products had come to signify "traitor" rather than "superior quality."[70]

A new approach to the housewife's traditional tasks of managing household budgets and account books gave women a way to participate in national salvation. On New Year's Day, the *Shenbao* suggested how those women not busy participating in the parade and rally could support the Women's National Products Year.[71] By reconceptualizing the household budget, one author explained, women could play a major role in national salvation. The author began by establishing the connection between household management and national salvation, a link that elevated the importance of women by stressing the centrality of the household to national salvation. Because women controlled this domain, the argument ran, they were fundamental agents in nation-making.

A nationalistic form of budgeting and planning was at the heart of personal and national salvation. The article urged daily, monthly, and yearly planning. This sort of planning, it claimed, would suppress impulse buying and eliminate "absent-minded and flighty" (糊里糊涂) acts. Such behavior, which was implicitly described as female and anti-modern, was selfish and must be replaced by socially responsible thinking that took into account one's responsibilities to one's family and ultimately one's "compatriots."

The author linked this model to practice through management of the household, a domain in which women were urged to implement rationality

---

69. "Zhufu zenma quandao zhangfu fuyong guohuo?" (1934). Other articles argued that properly run households were the key to the movement. In contrast to "so-called modern households" (所謂摩登的家庭), such households kept abreast of new national products on the market ("Jiating guohuo yundong" [1933]). For additional recommended tactics, see SB 1934.3.1.

70. Tianxu Wosheng, "Gongxian yu funümen" (Offerings to women), *Jilian huikan* 87 (1934.1.15): 2–5. The author, the editor of the journal, reinforced the idea that women should respond to a gift of an import from their husbands with the line: "That's nice. It's just too bad you have handed over our China's money to foreign countries."

71. Portraits of similar model nationalistic consumer families were published around other significant holidays, including the anniversary of the Japanese invasion of Manchuria (e.g., "Jiu yiba yihou de He furen jiating" [1934]).

and suppress impulsive behavior.[72] As others have shown, many new household practices being promoted at this time exhibited this rationality. These ranged from monitoring household temperatures to using new cleaning products to altering cleaning habits to preparing more nutritious meals to drinking milk.[73] As these scholars show, such new practices abstractly linked well-being or rational Chinese subjects to national wealth and power. Rationalizing the household budget—and indeed the Women's Year and the National Products Movement—was explicitly linked to economic rejuvenation and anti-imperialist activism.

The article illustrated this ideal and rational national consumer household through the example of another famous Chinese educator, Huang Yanpei 黃炎培 (1878–1965), and his wife, both active in the movement. Each New Year's Eve, the Huangs set aside time to discuss the previous year's expenditures and the following year's financial plans. With the household account book before them, the couple together identified "irrational" (不合理的) and uneconomical purchases; using this information, they decided where to cut back. Next, they made a budget for the following year, noting the items on which they expected to spend less.

Most important, the author demonstrates how the Huangs nationalized this practice by stressing the absolute importance of national products. It was not enough simply to save money. The article linked household budgeting practices to the movement by urging families to keep close track of expenditures on food, clothing, and daily items. In each category, consumers were told to keep track of daily, monthly, and yearly costs and to note which goods were national products and which were not. They were urged to replace foreign products with domestic substitutes and to abstain from consuming an item if there was no domestic equivalent. This exercise was intended to demonstrate that even small purchases of foreign goods added up. Moreover, these expenditure totals were to provide each movement sympathizer, each "authentically" or nationalistically modern Chinese, with explicit measurements of the depth of one's commitment to the movement, of one's "modern" dedication to the nation, and of one's Chineseness. Previously

---

72. For a similar definition of using national product clothing as part of rationalizing one's wardrobe, see Ba Ling 1934b. This article also cites the trade deficit as the justification for this interpretation of rationality.

73. For instance, on the concept of cleanliness and the creation of the modern homemaker, see Forty 1986: 169. On the Chinese housewife, see Orliski 1998 and Glosser 1995.

families may have used expense books to control spending; now they were urged to do so in the interests of the nation and its national products. Such an exercise pushed the categories of "national" and "foreign" products further into the lives of women in charge of the household budgets.

NATIONALIZING FESTIVALS
OF CONSUMPTION

Annual holidays gave Chinese families opportunities to shape their public image, but imperialism made doing so more complicated. Historian Leora Auslander has noted that one of the chief responsibilities of bourgeois women in nineteenth-century France was "to constitute and represent the family's social identity through goods" (1996: 83). Chinese women targeted by the movement faced an even more complex challenge. The movement compounded the problems of representing oneself and one's family by trying to force women to see consumption as a decision between products that were either treasonously foreign or patriotically domestic. In practice, this created a conflict between the desire to establish and reinforce social position through foreign goods and the demands that one do so via domestic ones of lower status. Put another way, it was competition between national/racial and class-based tastes—the need to strike contradictory poses vis-à-vis foreigners and vis-à-vis Chinese of other social statuses. Imperialism made this tension acute by simultaneously delivering the goods while undermining the ability of consumers to embrace them fully.[74]

The objective of the Women's Year was to impute unpatriotic meanings to foreign products and thereby force women to confront this tension and settle it in favor of the nation. In other words, the movement wanted housewives not just to transform traditional holidays into "festivals of consumption" but to make these festivals opportunities to express nationalism.[75] Three major holidays provided especially important opportunities for women to make

---

74. It is ironic that Chinese middle- and upper-class women, as one learns indirectly through the female characters in stories such as Mao Dun's classic *Midnight*, were consciously choosing class-based representations for themselves via objects, while their staunchly anti-communist husbands were often working feverishly to dismiss class as a legitimate basis for the analysis of Chinese social problems.

75. For the classic treatment of the commodification of holidays such as Christmas and the use of the term "festivals of consumption," see Boorstin 1973: 157–64. There is a growing literature on the general commodification of American holidays (see, e.g., Schmidt 1995).

these choices for themselves and for their families: the Lunar New Year, Dragon Boat Festival, and Mid-Autumn Festival. Preparing for these holidays was one of the central tasks of women at these times of the year. There were an endless number of chores—meals to prepare, cleaning to do, clothing to mend, and visits to pay. Naturally, there were also products to buy and consume. These holidays became especially important yearly opportunities for movement advocates to link the activities traditionally associated with these festivals to new measures of morality and proper feminine behavior.

The movement attempted to nationalize the association between goods and sentiments for each of these festivals. For instance, an article in a leading national paper discussed the different types of New Year's purchases. Failure to purchase only national products revealed multiple moral shortcomings— one dishonored oneself and one's ancestors, was dishonest toward one's children, condescended to relatives, brought shame on one's household, and was rude to one's guests. Once again, a writer invoked the previous year's import statistics for cosmetics to confirm that women as a category were failing this test. The author suggested that women owed China much more on holidays to compensate for their failure to stem the influx of cosmetics.

GIFTS AND THE MONITORING OF OTHERS

To the movement, gift-giving, especially around Chinese holidays, was a good opportunity for differentiating patriotic from self-indulgent consumption.[76] In 1934, the New Life Movement officially introduced frugality to the national discourse, but the movement qualified it. As one article on the Dragon Boat Festival acknowledged, eradicating traditional holidays would be nearly impossible, even though "enlightened people" (明白人) knew that they were wasteful and irrational. Despite this excess, the article continued, these holidays presented good opportunities for promoting nationalistic consumption, and it provided two guidelines: monitor the gifts one gave to others and the gifts one received. Friends did not let friends give enemy products. Moreover,

---

76. During the Women's National Products Year, the *Jilian huikan* 98 (1934.7.1) devoted an entire issue to the question of gift-giving. Most of the articles argued that Chinese nationality was an essential part of a thoughtful and rational gift; see, e.g., Pei Ji 1934. Ba Ling (1934c), for instance, argued that giving national products not only expressed patriotism but also had the practical effect of undermining the popularity of imports while introducing a friend to a Chinese product. In addition to holidays, articles also explained the importance of giving national products as wedding presents; see, e.g., Gan Chunquan 1934.

the movement expected consumers to ensure they were buying national products and not imitations, even if this meant traveling further to a store specializing in such products. When receiving a gift, one was expected to take note of its nationality. To promote such nationalistic practices, the movement suggested that when receiving a national product, one should pointedly give extra thanks for the thoughtfulness. On the other hand, if one received something other than a national product, one should refuse to accept it and explain one's reasons for doing so in writing. As one author pointed out, "The next time that person certainly won't give foreign products!"[77]

The movement attempted to extend such monitoring of the consumption habits of friends and relatives beyond the holidays. Many articles urged women to inspect one another's households even when paying casual visits. If these inspections uncovered foreign products, women were urged to inform their hostess of the need to avoid such products or find domestic substitutes. Moreover, the article asserted that such monitoring practices should be considered patriotic rather than intrusive. The writer claimed to have used these methods with great success ("Funü duiyu guohuonian de zeren" [1933]).[78]

Movement advocates recognized that the changing seasons also presented the opportunity to promote nationalistic consumption. Autumn, for example, was the time to bring out blankets and add extra layers of clothing. As with the American holiday of Thanksgiving, the increased variety and lower food prices that usually accompanied the harvest encouraged more consumption. The movement sought to insert its objectives into these cyclical needs and celebrations and stressed the importance of being extra vigilant during the Mid-Autumn Festival. Articles and advertisements specifically reminded Chinese to fill these needs with national products (see Fig. 7.6).[79]

---

77. "Duanjie han guohuo" (1934). Most of these articles, however, did not address what one ought to do with previously accepted or purchased foreign articles, although one article stated that these should be replaced as soon as possible ("Wo jia de riyongpin" [1932]).

78. Inspections that were more formal were also carried out under the New Life Movement: sanitary inspectors visited houses and posted their findings outside the house (SMP File 5729, 1934.4.9: "New Life Movement"). In addition, New Life followers were encouraged to "listen for the telltale click of the mah-jongg tiles in a Chinese home" (Crow 1944: 134–36). Crow did not record the extent of such visits but observed that New Life Movement exhortations, such as "Brush your teeth" and "Buy native goods," were posted "everywhere."

79. "Funü guohuo nian zai qiuji" (1934); "Qiuling de yiliang yongpin wenti" (1934); and "Guozhi qiuling yongpin de wojian" (1934). Similar articles predated and followed the Women's Year and also appeared each season. See, e.g., "Funü yu dongling yongpin" (1933);

Fig. 7.6 Bashing Foreign Beer
(*SB* 1934.7.12)

The movement did not attack drinking, leisure, or even pleasure. Rather, it opposed any forms of consumption centered on imports. In this illustration, an angry cudgel-wielding bottle of "national product beer" and two drinking glasses chase after three bottles of "foreign beer." The illustration and its title, "The Victory of Nationally Produced Food and Drink" (*upper right*), underscore the movement's persistent sanctioning of violence.

INTERNATIONAL WOMEN'S DAY IN
A NATIONALISTIC WOMEN'S YEAR

The movement transformed the celebration of Women's Day (March 8) to serve its goals (see Tang Shunqing 1937). The way it did so illustrates the subordination of the women's emancipation agenda to a national agenda defined by the movement. The holiday was introduced into China in 1924 (Sun Zhendong 1982: 147–48). Initially, Women's Day addressed many issues central to women's emancipation, such as forced female labor and equality in wages.[80] With the support of the Nationalists and the Commu-

---

"Caiyong xialing yongping ge" (1934); and "Helihuade xialing yongpin" (1935). As noted in Chapters 5 and 6, the movement organized exhibitions to promote the seasonal consumption of national products, a practice that continued throughout the movement. For a report on one such exhibition in the 1930s, see "Xialing yongpin zhanlanhui" (1933).

80. Links between the women's movement and politics had explicitly been made during earlier International Women's Days as well. In 1925, for example, women in Beijing gathered

nists, both the size of the rallies and the radicalism of the agendas increased in the following years. By 1927, for example, more than 100,000 women marched in a government-backed parade in Wuhan.[81] Over time, the celebrations came to feature attacks on such sensitive issues as capitalism and the lack of freedom of choice in marriage and divorce. In Guangdong, women's organizations worked hard to spread awareness of the day both in urban centers such as Guangzhou and in the surrounding areas (Gilmartin 1995: 153–54).[82] The awareness so painstakingly built through such networks by women activists would later be used to disseminate a radically different interpretation of women and of this day.

This new way of commemorating the day was on full display during the afternoon of International Women's Day, March 8, 1934.[83] The Women's National Products Year Movement Committee arranged to use the main ceremonial hall of the Huzhou native-place association to hold a rally that would further conflate the role of women and the movement. Over a thousand people attended the event, including the wives of local and national notables. Cai Yuanpei, then head of Academia Sinica, went with his wife, Zhou Yanghao, who was an official host of the rally (Sun Changwei 1997: 513). Her speech emphasized the disastrous shift in women's fashions from reliance on domestic articles to the increasing use of imports over the last few decades. This trend, she asserted, undermined women's claims for

---

outside the home of Prime Minister Duan Qirui and shouted slogans such as "Down with imperialism" and "Women of the world, unite" (Collins 1976: 557).

81. See Z. Wang 1999: 300–301, which records the impressions of the organizer of the event, Huang Dinghui 黃定慧 (b. 1907).

82. The original idea for a holiday to honor working women came from the German socialist Clara Zetkin in 1907; the first day in the United States was in 1909. During the 1910s, the day became linked to the promotion of international peace. The exact date was not standardized internationally until Zetkin persuaded Lenin to do so in 1922. March 8 marked the anniversary of the beginning of the 1917 revolution in Russia with the food protests by women and children (Kaplan 1998; Navarro 1998). See also Gilmartin 1995: 257n17.

83. Activities actually began the evening before under the sponsorship of another national products organization; the National Products Production and Marketing Cooperative Association (國貨產銷合作協會) sponsored an afternoon tea party for leading female figures in Shanghai. As in the West, department stores in Shanghai also became important spaces for other activities. This group held a party at the Mainland Emporium (大陸商場), a department store that also housed a designated national products store. More than a hundred people showed up; the organizers announced the formation of a Women Wear National Products Society (婦女服用國貨會).

equality in citizenship (SB 1934.3.9). To extend the reach of such messages, the Shanghai Women's National Products Promotion Association also arranged to have speeches by Cai Yuanpei and two other noted Shanghai residents broadcast on radio stations that same afternoon. One after another, the speakers called for women to use consumption to aid the nation (SB 1934.3.8).

One of the many articles in local newspapers devoted to this international holiday made some national comparisons. A decade earlier women from countries such as France, the United States, and the Soviet Union had served as models for Chinese women. Details of their emancipation agendas and tactics provided a road map for Chinese struggling with similar issues. Now, however, women of these same foreign countries illustrated the relative weakness of Chinese women in terms of nationalistic consumption. As the author explained, French, American, and Russian women used their own country's goods—only Chinese women did otherwise. The article asked: "What does that say about women's national attributes?" The author further admonished Chinese women to live up to international women's standards in the realm of nationalistic consumption and show some self-control by boycotting foreign products and using only Chinese ones (SB 1934.3.8). Similarly, other articles warned women not to be tricked by treasonous merchants (e.g., "Funüjie yu guohuo" [1934]).

Movement companies reinforced the idea that nationalistic consumption was the focal point of the day. For example, the Women's Year Committee arranged for three of the most powerful marketers of national products— the Shanghai National Products Company, the Chinese National Products Company, and the Shanghai Chamber of Commerce's National Products Market (國貨市場)—to hold a one-day, 10 percent–off sale to show their solidarity with the aims of the Women's Year.[84] Other movement companies published advertisements linking the day and nationalistic consumption (see, e.g., the advertisement in Jilian huikan 92 [1934.4.1]). A silk association also took out advertisements to explain a new system of identifying fabrics to help consumers ensure the product was a genuine national product (SB 1934.3.8).

---

84. The Chinese National Products Company often provided large-print reminders that this was the Women's National Products Year. See, e.g., the advertisements in SB 1934.3.1. These sales also achieved equality between the sexes—advertisements promised men that they would also receive 10 percent off (SB 1934.3.8).

NATIONALIZING CONSUMPTION
ON CHILDREN'S DAY

The year also sought to nationalize childhood through appeals both to mothers and to children. It redefined women's role as "worthy mothers" by strengthening their bonds to the home and by shaping the form of that bond. Children, the movement taught, were also consumers, although their consumption usually came through the parents, especially their mothers. The movement attempted to nationalize children's consumption habits with stories, comics, and events targeted at them. But the movement directed even more attention to mothers. A mother's job, it was asserted, was to make the primary task of childhood the acquisition of skills for, and loyalty to, the nation: "Last year's trade deficit topped $700,000,000 . . . so we must raise [children] with the good habit of using national products."[85] Model children learned to put the nation first from an early age through consumption habits and attitudes.[86]

Saving the nation through its children was the general theme of the Fourth Annual Children's Day held on April 4, 1934.[87] In the morning, Shanghai mayor Wu Tiecheng presided over opening ceremonies in front of city hall. Speakers included Cai Yuanpei and Nationalist Party elder statesman Li Shizeng 李石曾 (1881–1973) (Sun Changwei 1997: 514). Despite rainy weather, over 10,000 people showed up, including at least two student representatives from every public and private school in the city. In his opening address, Mayor Wu informed the assembled that the event was aimed primarily at parents, who needed to understand the importance of children

---

85. "Gailiang ertong fuzhuang tan" (1934): 39. Another article made this connection between childrearing and national salvation: "If we want to save the nation and strengthen the race, we must begin with childrearing. We must raise children with good habits. They must enjoy using national products" (Pan Yingmang 1933).

86. As with appeals for virtuous women to imitate women of other countries by favoring domestic products, the movement also argued that children around the world were being taught to consume their own national products. One article even reproduced slogans purportedly taken (and translated) from the major powers. The article claimed, for instance, that Russian children learned the slogan "The person who does not use Russian products is not only ignorant but also the unpatriotic slave of a vanquished nation!" ("Tichang guohuo ying cong ertong zuoqi" [1933]: 17).

87. Children's Day was first proposed by two Shanghai children's welfare and educational associations in 1931. After gaining official approval, the first official nationwide Children's Day was held on April 4, 1932 (Sun Zhendong 1982: 207–8).

to the nation. Parents, he said, "should ensure that their children understood that they had obligations to the nation and to the people; children should know that they were the nation's and the people's, and not just their family's [possession]."[88]

The city-run rally emphasized the need to build physically, intellectually, and emotionally strong children to save the nation. In contrast, the Women's Year Committee's "Children's Day Commemoration Rally," which followed the morning event, concentrated more narrowly on the ways that consumption linked mothers and children. Sometime after 2:00 P.M., over 1,000 children and parents attended the rally, which was again hosted at the Huzhou native-place association. To emphasize the participation of children in the movement, the daughters of two committee members gave the opening comments.

Like most movement events, this one was a verbal and visual assault of nationalized spectacles, including displays of educational toys and a model household with a bedroom, kitchen, and living room. These spectacles were intended to display not just a particular lifestyle but a *nationalistic* lifestyle— all the products were aggressively advertised as national products. The rally also featured instruction in household management. All the speakers explicitly connected improving lifestyles through nationalistic consumption and national salvation. Zhou Yanghao reminded children and parents that the first step in "cleansing the national humiliations" (雪國恥) was the use of national products. Her husband, Cai Yuanpei, reinforced this by urging children to keep the use of national products "in their hearts." These speeches were also directed at mothers, who, as heads of households, were instructed to give their children only items that were national products and aim to raise "completely national products children" (完全國貨兒童). After prizes were awarded to the winners of an essay contest on the importance of national products, the meeting wound down with performances of plays and songs and a children's fashion show featuring national products. As was common at such events, national products companies supplied small gifts for the attendees.[89]

---

88. "Wanyu ertong zuo zai shifu relie qingzhu ertong jie" (1934); "Quanshi gejie relie jinian ertong jie" (1934).

89. "Funü tuanti" (1934); "Funü tuanti qingzhu dahui" (1934); and "Quanshi gejie relie jinian ertong jie" (1934). For copies of two different "Women's National Products Songs"

NATIONALIZING FAMILY
RELATIONSHIPS

Shaping the relationship among family members, particularly mothers and children, was an important part of movement activities and an integral part of the Women's Year. In addition, fiction and nonfiction frequently addressed this issue and delineated the social role of family members toward one another. These representations reveal how each role and each relationship was defined by its relationship to the nation through the values of the National Products Movement.

The many elements common to each role within movement literature were most clearly explicated in an article that covered the entire model nationalized family.[90] The article insisted that the mother was the head of the household, but it began by describing the role of the father. The production of national products defined this ideal nationalistic father. Because he had hated imperialism and its material representatives since childhood, naturally he chose to work for a national products manufacturer. And because he devoted his life to producing national products, he spent his spare time working with his compatriots to develop additional products to displace foreign ones from Chinese markets. The model mother contributed to national goals from within the household. However, as such articles quickly pointed out, this was a powerful position in terms of the potential impact both on family members and on the nation. This ideal nationalistic mother was educated and therefore better able to assist her husband. She worked tirelessly to promote national products and avoid all foreign products. Needless to say, she forbade all foreign items entry into her domain. Her final and, in some representations, most important responsibility was to raise children who understood the importance of national products.

This model nationalistic family had two types of children: a relatively independent teenager and younger children. The family's eldest child, a daughter, was the antithesis of the vilified "modern girl." She had graduated from middle school and worked for a national products company, a tea company. The clearest sign of her proper upbringing was her love for na-

---

("Funü guohuo ge") sung during the year, see *Guohuo banyue kan* 3 (1934.1.15): 41–42 or *Guohuo yuebao* 1.1 (1934.2.1).

90. This portrait of a model family of nationalistic consumers/producers comes from "Guohuo de yijiao" (1934).

tional products, which were the only things she wore. In contrast to her misguidedly "modern" counterparts, she did not engage in unpatriotic consumption, such as wearing lipstick from Paris or cosmetics from New York. She also dressed conservatively and did not own high-heel shoes, perfume, or silk stockings. Outside of work, she actively participated in movement activities. The family had two younger children; both frequently demonstrated the correct behavior regarding consumption. Because they had been raised to cherish Chinese goods, they carefully inspected all items. For example, on receiving new clothing, they promptly took the articles to their mother to confirm their nationality, asking "Is this article Chinese?" and stating "I won't wear foreign clothing."

Empowering children to interrogate their parents on behalf of the nation was a common theme of the Women's Year and of the National Products Movement. The idea was not only common in major publications, such as *Shenbao*, but also disseminated much more broadly through movement publications. The theme that fealty to nation takes precedence over filiality to parents was prominent in the story that opens Chapter 5. It was published in an April 1, 1934, work devoted to linking clothing and the movement. In the story, a student living in a boarding school refuses to wear the long underwear made of Japanese silk sent to him by his mother. The student decides that the needs of the nation transcend filial piety.

Stories such as this circulated nationalistic ideas about how children and mothers should interact. Instilling nationalistic consciousness was now a primary objective of good childrearing. The proper mother set an example by ensuring that the family consumed nationalistically. She also ensured that her children's physical world was surrounded with national products—from clothing to toys. If domestically produced objects were unavailable or too expensive, children should be taught to make their own toys.[91] Movement literature recommended taking children to national products stores, where children would naturally develop an appreciation for these products simply by browsing ("Ertong yu guohuo shizhuang" [1933]). The surest sign of a good upbringing was a child who was not only content to consume exclusively Chinese products but played a role in ensuring that the rest of the family did the same. Thus, the mechanisms for ensuring nationalistic con-

---

91. "Cong guohuo shengzhong shuodao ertong wanju" (1933). See also, e.g., the article by Shi Jixiong in SB 1934.1.18. Many such articles assigned responsibility for instilling this ethic of nationalistic consumption to elder sisters and others responsible for childrearing.

sumption worked from older to younger and from younger to older. Children were to act as agents of the nation by inspecting products, and mothers were to encourage this sort of behavior. The highest form of loyalty in the mother-child relationship was now conceived to be that between individuals and the nation. This relationship in turn was to structure other relations, including that of child to parent.[92]

SANTA'S LITTLE HELPERS

As noted above, the movement redefined all types of yearly events, particularly holidays. The extreme nature and comprehensive scope of these reinterpretations was most poignantly on display at the end of the Women's Year. Movement advocates accused Santa Claus of being the "puppet" not simply of the forces of commercialization, as Western critics have argued, but of the international economic powers trying to gain access to Chinese markets.[93] This linking of Christmas gift-giving to the penetration of foreign capital is not surprising. Since at least the anti-Christian campaign of 1922, a growing number of Chinese intellectuals had come to see Christianity as a conduit for imperialism and capitalism. For their part, Chinese Christians attempted to circumvent these associations by creating a "Chinese" church.[94]

One middle-aged female author advanced this interpretation by relating her Christmas Day experiences as an elementary student at a missionary school some twenty years earlier. Each Christmas Day students convened in the gymnasium, and each year someone dressed as Santa distributed gifts to all the children. These gifts were invariably foreign products. The children became deeply attached to these gifts. As they advanced through the school, gifts went from simpler items such as pencils and stationery to the perfumes, soaps, lace, bracelets, and other items desired by older students. According to the author, these children grew to admire and prefer foreign products instead

92. This legacy of children monitoring the behavior of their parents and grandparents on behalf of the nation-state can be seen in virtually every memoir of the Cultural Revolution. See, e.g., N. Cheng 1986: 55, 57, 112, 119, 293; and Gao Yuan 1987: 77–78. The Canadian reporter Jan Wong (1996: 108) also encountered stories of children denouncing their parents, among them the famous Chinese film director Chen Kaige.

93. On the commercialization of Santa in the West, see Nissenbaum 1997: esp. 169–72.

94. The growth of this sentiment and the concurrent attempt to create a "Chinese" church is covered in many places; see, e.g., Jonathan Chao 1986.

Fig. 7.7 Santa Selling Cigarettes
(SB 1934.12.20)

This advertisement uses the images of Santa Claus and cherubs to promote Nanyang Brothers' Golden Dragon cigarettes. This use of Santa highlights the ambivalent place of "the
West" within the movement and within China's nascent consumer culture. Santa was casti-
gated as a puppet of imperialism who promoted imports but, as with other images of "the
West," also recognized as an appealing pitchman for national products.

of Chinese ones; decades later, many still preferred the brands that Santa had
introduced to them as children. Moreover, through their example, such consumers passed these unpatriotic habits to their children and grandchildren.
Once a Chinese consumer developed an addiction to foreign goods, the author maintained, the preference was difficult to change. But there was hope.
In writing this piece, the author hoped to warn Chinese of the darker side of
Santa through the issues and consciousness of patriotic consumption introduced in the Women's National Products Year (see Fig. 7.7).[95]

Contesting Representations of Women as Treasonous Consumers

It is hard to gauge the reactions of women to Women's Year representations
of them as unproductive and treasonous consumers. Explicit rejection of the
logic behind the movement as a whole or the utility of the year itself was extremely difficult. By the 1930s, patriotic consumption was simply too closely
tied to contemporary configurations of the Chinese nation for anyone to
proclaim publicly that consumption of national products had nothing to do

---

95. "Shengdan laoren yu funü guohuonian" (1934); see also "Shengdan laoren de liwu"
(1934).

with nationalism, civic responsibility, and the creation of a wealthy and powerful country.[96] Throughout the history of the National Products Movement, consumers had options. They could ignore it, subvert it, redirect it, and even use it to advance their own interests. But there were limits. As has been suggested throughout the book, consumer opposition to the movement usually took a quieter and simpler form: whenever possible, some consumers simply ignored movement dictates to consume patriotically.[97] The greatest evidence of this can be found in the constant citation in movement literature of the trade statistics that underscored the failure of Chinese to consume patriotically. The movement itself recognized that many consumers were not buying into the movement.

The most common form of overt dissent came from within the movement itself and concerned the issue of assigning responsibility. From the start of the Women's Year, women and schoolgirls challenged the virulent attacks in movement literature on women ("Funü shou ma nian" [1934]). A good example occurred during one of the year's organized events. In May 1934, the Capital [Nanjing] Women's National Products Promotion Association hosted a speech contest to promote the Women's Year among schoolchildren. On the afternoon of May 20, over 800 people attended a speech contest at Jinling University. Five high school and six junior high students delivered ten-minute speeches with titles such as "The Responsibility That Girls Have to Promote National Products" and "The Promotion of National Products and National Revival."[98] Most of the speeches repeated movement and Women's Year rhetoric, including the widely held attitude that women were undermining the movement.[99] But one high school stu-

---

96. Ironically, however, other observers praised fashion-conscious women for their "ready adaptability" demonstrated in their quick adoption of new trends such as hair perms, high-heel shoes, and silk stockings (Ren Dai 1936: 178).

97. Additionally, female mission students did not merely follow male-dominated protest scripts; they occasionally opted for different forms of protest, such as traveling through the surrounding countryside to explain the importance of national products to rural women rather than marching in male-organized demonstrations (Graham 1994: 40–42).

98. For a reprint of a few of the speeches and a photo of the proud winners, see "Jing funü tichang guohuo hui" (1934), which appeared in *Funü gongming yuebao*. Transcripts of other speeches appeared in subsequent issues of this journal.

99. See, e.g., Zhang Mingdong 1934 and Wang Jingming 1934. Wang did, however, point out that intellectuals were often hypocritical when it came to consuming only national products. She suggested that intellectuals (including the assembled students and officials) need to lead by example rather than concentrating on persuading the folks in the countryside: "Look

dent, Wu Jinyun 吳錦芸, went further. She countered this dominant representation of women by asserting that the movement was the responsibility of both women *and* men. As she put it, "Don't blame all of society's problems on women." Her speech undermined movement attempts to subordinate the women's movement. The speaker acknowledged the importance of the movement but forcefully rejected the assertion that promoting nationalistic consumption was or should be the primary objective of the women's movement. The movement, she asserted, insulted women by representing them as capable only of mindless consumption. In fact, the author turned the tables on the movement by suggesting that women's liberation was essential for developing national industries and products. Consequently, she rejected the underlying premise of the Women's Year that women were obligated to participate enthusiastically as a form of atonement. She called it "inhuman" to blame women for "the destruction of the country, the loss of territory, and losses in battle" and went on to point out that foreign things became fashionable because *men* encouraged their use (Wu Jinyun 1934).

On the most basic level, the goal of the Women's Year was to teach female consumers to privilege the nationality of commodities. Once women had learned to interpret objects through the lens of nationality, the movement expected them to consume accordingly and make purchases based on the "Chineseness" of products, rather than on price, quality, style, or any other criterion deemed less important by the movement.[100] This chapter suggests, however, that this demystification, which identified product-nationality as pre-eminent, was simultaneously a remystification. The claims of the Women's Year and the movement to have peeled back the surface meaning of objects to reveal their "true" nationalistic and imperialistic interiors as "national products" and as "foreign goods" created a new world of goods with their own racial, class, and gendered meanings. These meanings came to be

---

at the farmers—they aren't the ones wearing wool, panama straw hats, and leather shoes, riding around in foreign cars, living in foreign-style buildings, and using all those imported products. We are."

100. The great irony here is that this attempt to persuade women to appreciate the non-market values of commodities was occurring exactly as so many more aspects of Chinese life were being commodified. Christian Henriot (1994), for example, explores the impact of accelerating commercialization on prostitution in Shanghai and concludes that the money-for-sex union came to subsume all other relationships between men and female escorts.

an important part of the resources determining the social identities of Chinese consumers, both female and male.

Nationalism and anti-imperialism, however, were never the only meanings attached to consumption. Some women, for example, openly challenged (occasionally, even in print) these representations of unpatriotic female consumers, calling into question the crass commercial motives of movement backers and the hypocrisy of some foreign-dressed participants. Many more women simply ignored movement dictates and continued to wear and consume imported items. Urban elites faced competing demands that often pitted the need to buy "national products" against the desire to look cosmopolitan or foreign-educated. Not surprisingly, the local battle to look as fashionable as one's social peers and the desire to derive power from imports and foreign-inspired styles often won out over movement appeals to dress for the nation.

Nevertheless, no one openly opposed the goals of the Women's Year or the National Products Movement. Nobody argued that consumption was a completely private or family matter, outside the purview of the nation-state. Indeed, even verbal acts of defiance helped nationalize consumption. The women who objected to the representations of women never openly denied the centrality of product-nationality or suggested that buying cheaper imports was better. Rather, critics rejected the notion that women were primarily or exclusively responsible for undermining the Women's Year and the movement. They insisted there was plenty of blame to go around. They continued to circulate the blame for unpatriotic consumption. And, as we have seen throughout these chapters, the accusations alone had social lives of their own and were regularly co-opted for personal, local, and national purposes. In purely statistical terms, the success of the movement in nationalizing female consumption was uncertain in 1934. However, the Women's Year did not include an explicit numerical goal, and import statistics continued to remind Chinese that there were traitorous female consumers in their midst.[101] At the same time, other observers discerned successes within the Women's Year and the movement outside trade statistics and cited the growth in the number of national products, improvements in promoting

---

101. See, e.g., "Modeng funü: juewu ba!" (1934), which uses monthly trade statistics from 1934 to "prove" that unpatriotic female consumers were still out there. For a mixed assessment of the Women's Year, see "Song funü guohuo nian" (1934).

these products, changes in the attitude of citizens toward buying Chinese, and expansion of state efforts to protect and develop domestic industries.[102]

In any case, the twentieth-century history of Chinese consumption reminds us that the re-emergence of a strong, central state would eventually take the *option* of consuming things defined as "national," "foreign," or "nationless" out of the hands of such unreliable Chinese consumers, male and female. In the meantime, the "failure" of women to nationalize their consumption continued to be used to undermine their demands for greater civic responsibility outside the home and, indeed, increased the pressure on them to integrate national interests into their roles as women, wives, and mothers.

---

102. For the most optimistic assessment of the movement, see the speech by movement leader Wang Xiaolai 王曉賴 (1886–1967), reprinted as "Zuijin guohuo de qushi" (Recent trends in national products), *SB* 1934.7.5. Other writers disaggregated the data, used anecdotal evidence, or pointed to specific movement developments to suggest that the movement was succeeding. See, e.g., "Funüjie zhi tuixing guohuo tan" (1934) and "Choushe gedi guohuo gongsi zhi wojian" (1934).

CHAPTER EIGHT

Manufacturing Patriotic Producers

Wu Yunchu is a shining star in the world of national products.

National Products Movement discourse targeted many enemies: imperialist powers who "dumped" products on Chinese markets, women and children who consumed without regard to the national origin of products, and merchants who sold foreign products. Yet the movement also had its heroes, male and female exemplars of a new nationalistic ethic of consumption and production. This chapter examines the creation and dissemination of (largely male) archetypes of patriotic *producers* through a case study of one of the most famous, Wu Yunchu 吳蘊初, the Chinese-educated scientist and entrepreneur whose flavor-enhancing powder made of monosodium glutamate (MSG) successfully replaced an "enemy product," the Japanese Ajinomoto 味の素 (or Weizhisu 味之素, as Chinese consumers knew it), in the Chinese marketplace.

The widely disseminated biographies of patriotic producers such as Wu Yunchu emphasized China's ability to fight imperialism. In contrast to the "treasonous merchants" described in Chapter 4, Wu Yunchu and dozens of other patriotic producers were positive role models for commercial behavior; they showed how Chinese could combine commercial activity and national rejuvenation. These patriotic producers became the industrial world's equivalents to the heroic Chinese resistance fighters battling Japan in Manchuria during the 1930s. The reality behind the myth of resistance—both military and industrial—was always more complicated (see Mitter 2000). An examination of Wu Yunchu's biography and representations of him within the movement will not only reveal the mythogenesis of one patriotic producer but also explore the role of the movement in creating cultural constraints on Chinese companies, which were alternately praised for participat-

---

EPIGRAPH: Guohuo shiye chubanshe 1934: 221.

ing in the movement and expected to live up to its high standards. To be sure, such biographies helped legitimize capitalism in China by highlighting the utility of private enterprise for national salvation. However, as with many other projects (such as the women's emancipation movement discussed in the previous chapter), the interests of the nation were always placed first. Biographies of Chinese capitalists served to sanction not just any form of capitalism or masculinity but only those forms closely tied to the interests of the nation-state. Myth constrained manufacturers.

National Products Movement Biographies

In the late nineteenth and twentieth centuries, import statistics became the primary tool for measuring China's success or failure in regaining sovereignty (on the notion of commercial war in China, see Chapter 1). These statistics, which were constantly recited, became the single most widely used icon for spreading the ideology of "commercial warfare." Invoking these statistics was intended to remind all Chinese that the nation was losing what movement participants considered to be the most insidious and contemporary form of imperialism, commercial warfare. Although the numbers invariably confirmed China's overall weakness, the data on certain products were cause for hope. China had been consistently losing the war for decades. However, its limited successes in industrializing revealed the nation's potential (see Fig. 8.1).

The biographies of national product manufacturers provided a roster of Chinese who were successfully defending the nation by producing national products and displacing imports. Among these capitalists, Wu Yunchu was, as the biography cited in the epigraph to this chapter labeled him, "a shining star in the world of national products" (Guohuo shiye chubanshe 1934: 221). His life story was a model for others to follow, a primer for defending China. In fact, these biographies explicitly called on others to emulate his life (see, e.g., "Tianchu wei chang jing" [1936]).[1] Publications intended for specific National Products Movement events, such as the commemorative volumes for exhibitions, invariably included such biographies.[2]

---

1. This was the forty-ninth "model history" published in this journal, *Jilian huikan*. See also Guohuo shiye chubanshe 1934: 221.

2. E.g., "Tianchu weijing zhizaochang shi" (A history of Heaven's Kitchen) in Kong Xiangxi 1929.

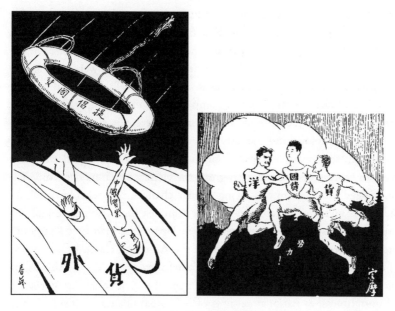

Fig. 8.1 Commercial War
(GSB 1928)

These are two of the illustrations produced during the movement to spread the notion that China was losing the "commercial war." On the left, "Chinese industry" (written on the man's arm) is drowning in an inundation of "foreign products." The solution is, according to the text on the life preserver, the "promotion of national products." The illustration on the right continues this theme. A "national product," represented by the runner in the center, competes against the dirty tactics of "foreign products," represented by the other two runners. The text (below the Chinese runner) commands him—and implicitly the Chinese audience—to "Strive!" The styles of both illustrations owe much more to Western artistic traditions than to Chinese. Within the movement, product-nationality rather than product style was the key to determining what was "Chinese." This, it seems, extended to artwork. Ironically, as "foreign companies" such as British-American Tobacco began adopting Chinese artistic styles to sell products (see, e.g., Cochran 1980: 37), "Chinese companies" were using Western styles to promote the exclusion of imports.

In considering these heroes of Chinese industry, it is tempting to point to what at first appear to be their American counterparts. Americans have certainly had similar industrial heroes—the Carnegies, the Rockefellers, and the other robber barons come to mind (see Catano 2001). Like their Chinese counterparts, these American industrialists accumulated vast fortunes and donated substantial sums to charities. There are, however, fundamental differences in the representations of their Chinese counterparts. Neither Wu Yunchu nor the industrialist Rong Desheng was simply the "Rockefeller of China," even though they were referred to as such in their day (Bergère 1986: 1). These men held a greater place of honor in nationalistic histories of China. Entrepreneurs such as Wu were seen as underdogs who had to create industries in an economically backward country in the face of nearly overwhelming competition from the imperialist powers. The victories of these Chinese industrialists were not simply cast as triumphs of technology and industry over the previous limits of commodity production; they were not just economic progress. More significant, their successes represented national progress, the victory of China over imperialism. Indeed, other countries facing similar changes also remade this "self-made man myth" of nineteenth-century America for nation-state-building purposes. In a study of this reinvention in Japan, historian Earl Kinmonth notes that for the Japanese translator of the American classic of this genre, *Self-Help* (1867) by Samuel Smiles, the "chief attraction . . . was this assertion by Smiles: 'National progress is the sum of individual industry, energy, and uprightness, as national decay is of individual idleness, selfishness, and vice'" (1981: 20).

Thus, Wu's success and the proliferation of his company's commodities were immediately enshrined as a major victory of the movement and of China as a whole. Indeed, the nationalistic import of Wu's story is so strong that even Chinese Communist leaders recognized the contribution of capitalists such as Wu to nation-building in China. After 1949, Wu was classified as a "patriotic businessman" (愛國實業家) and therefore part of China's "democratic capitalist" (民族資本主義) development. On October 1, 1950, the first anniversary of the founding of the People's Republic, Premier Zhou Enlai himself referred to Wu as the "MSG king" (味精大王) (Wang Pilai and Wang Yu 1994: 345).

Nor did the Maoist attack on capitalism completely destroy the image of "patriotic capitalists." Indeed, in the past two decades, it has become progressively easier to find materials to support investigations of such figures. Following the death of Mao Zedong in 1976 and the rise of Deng Xiaoping, China has once again found a use for entrepreneurs as well as for laudatory biographies of earlier Chinese capitalists (see Tim Wright 1993). For instance, Wu's life story was recently recounted in a series published by the People's Liberation Army called, somewhat incongruously, "Chinese Red Capitalists" (中國紅色資本家) and was the basis for a television miniseries (see Wang Daliang 1995).[3] In addition, recent scholarly publications have retold his story in similarly glowing terms (see, e.g., Du 1991: 148–49). The government even went so far as to finance the re-establishment of a class of capitalists. In 1979, the Chinese government spent U.S.$600 million to recompense the former Chinese bourgeoisie for earlier confiscations of their property. Prominent members of this class, including the members of the Rong family, were given government posts and charged with facilitating the growth of private enterprise and foreign investment in China (Bergère 1986: 2). Today the Chinese government praises Wu Yunchu and Fan Xudong, who established China's first soda factory in 1917, as the founders of the modern Chinese chemical industry. But, as this chapter demonstrates, the production of patriotic producers did not begin under the Communists.

A Capitalist with Chinese Characteristics

Three aspects of Wu Yunchu's life story were featured in all the biographies produced during (and since) the movement, especially in the 1920s and 1930s. These aspects are the key to understanding his biography's utility to the movement. First, Wu was educated in modern science. Second, he received his education in China. Finally, and most important, Wu used his modern education to displace a popular Japanese product from the Chinese market. In other words, his education and his business success translated directly into a practical and substantial form of resistance to Japanese economic encroachment. One biography claims that by the mid-1930s, Wu's enterprises were earning over $3 million a year. Wu's companies, in effect, "intercepted [that sum] from the hands of the Japanese" because the money would have been spent on Japanese imports (see Fig. 8.2) (Guohuo shiye chubanshe 1934: 21).[4]

Wu Yunchu's rags-to-riches biography begins outside Shanghai (for a chronology, see Wang Daliang 1995: 268–70). He was born in 1891 in the Jiangsu county of Jiading, now a part of Shanghai Municipality, and was the

---

3. In 1991, Chinese state television ran a series on Wu's businesses, *Tianzihao fengyun lu* (The trials and tribulations of the Heaven Conglomerate), which praised Wu for his significant contributions to his industry and to his country.

4. Other biographies of Wu use a similar or the same line. See, e.g., Chenbao 1933: 53. Even articles that do not use this phrase emphasize that Wu's MSG stemmed the influx of Japanese products on the flavoring powder front; see, e.g., Wang Dongyuan 1928 and "Wu Yunchu xiansheng xiaoshi."

Fig. 8.2 Patriotic Footwear
(*Jilian huikan* 46 [1931.11.16: cover])

Movement literature and advertisements told Chinese producers and consumers that they could participate in the national salvation of China by producing and consuming national products. This advertisement placed by the Great China Rubber Company, taken from the cover of a movement journal, shows a prominent Chinese brand shoe, Double Coin (雙錢牌), bayoneting a Japanese shoe. The silhouette of a Chinese soldier bayoneting to death a Japanese soldier invokes the movement's analogy between commercial and military warfare.

eldest of six children. Wu's movement biographers invariably emphasize that, despite poverty, Wu was able to excel—with the aid of his "model mother" (see, e.g., Chenbao 1933: 52). At an early age, he demonstrated his academic prowess. By the age of ten, Wu was well on his way into the traditional Chinese examination system. In that year, he obtained the preliminary *xiucai* 秀才 degree in the imperial examination system. This was an uncommon distinction for someone so young. Because his father got a job in Shanghai in 1899 as a teacher of Chinese literature at a local university, young Wu had the opportunity to study with better teachers; at the same time, he was exposed to new areas of knowledge.

Despite his early success in the traditional examination system, Wu decided to become a translator and enrolled in Shanghai's Guangfang Foreign Language School against the wishes of his father, who "feared his son would become a tool of foreigners" (Wang Pilai and Wang Yu 1994: 348). His education and career path were typical of many students of new subjects. From 1904 to 1905, he continued his studies of modern subjects as a student in Shanghai; in 1906, he returned to his home county to teach English in a local primary school. The New Systems Reforms around this time greatly expanded opportunities to study Western subjects, and in the following year Wu gained admission to the Qing army's Shanghai Munitions Academy, where he studied chemistry for four years until 1911.

Wu's history as a model producer extended to his personal conduct. Although he won scholarships, biographers emphasize that he was always giving and producing rather than taking and consuming; he did whatever he could to be self-sufficient. At one point, he also taught mathematics at a local primary school to earn money to support his family. For ten years following his graduation in 1911, Wu held a variety of jobs as a teacher and chemical engineer in several of China's nascent industrial centers. Through an arrangement with the Munitions Special School, Wu took a one-year apprenticeship at a Shanghai manufacturer and simultaneously taught at his alma mater. In the chaos following the Second Revolution (a conflict between the GMD and Yuan Shikai) in 1913, however, both the school and the enterprise closed and Wu was unemployed. A teacher of his (who was German) gave him a job as a chemical engineer at China's premier iron works, the Hanyang Iron & Steel Works, which had been established by the famous late Qing reformer Zhang Zhidong several decades earlier but was now controlled by Germans. After a year there, Wu took charge of a brick factory but soon grew dissatisfied with the work and, in 1915, left for a job at a nitric alkali factory in Tianjin. The company, however, never got off the ground, and once again Wu was unemployed. In 1916, Wu returned to Wuhan, where he helped devise a method for manufacturing silicon and manganese tiles. His contributions to this first successful effort to manufacture these items in China established him as one of China's foremost chemical engineers and led to his appointment as the director of a silicon tile plant.

"I AM A LOCAL PRODUCT"

The movement was obsessed with producing, circulating, and consuming products that would be considered completely Chinese. This effort to create pure Chinese objects extended to the figures it lionized. Every biography of Wu Yunchu emphasizes his pure Chinese background and stresses that Wu was educated in China, unlike other industrialists such as Fan Xudong, who studied chemistry in Japan (see Han Yin 1996). As one biography put this, "From the time this gentleman invented MSG, his countrymen were very attentive and respectful toward him. Most common people thought he had studied abroad . . . and thus was able to have this sort of success." But this was not the case. His life story showed readers that it was not necessary to study abroad to contribute to strengthening China. Wu's background was used to signify China's growing strength. In correcting the mistaken impression that he must have studied overseas, Wu himself emphasized his domestic credentials with the oft-quoted line: "I am a local product [土貨]. I have never gone abroad."[5]

Wu also participated in defining himself as an authentic and pure Chinese product. He tried, for instance, to promote his own biography as a lesson in pursuing an alternative path to helping oneself and one's country, in direct contrast to the traditional path through the Chinese bureaucracy, which, Wu suggested, had in recent years slowed China's industrial progress: "Among China's returned students, the number who have studied chemistry abroad certainly is not small. However, after returning to China, because they are anxious to become officials, they forget their enthusiasm for the chemical industry that China desperately needs" (Chenbao 1933: 52).

His newfound reputation and position afforded him many opportunities, and he quickly gained management experience and contacts. At this time, China's oldest and largest munitions manufacturer, the Hanyang Arsenal, hired Wu to supervise its chemistry and physics section. And a short time later, in 1918, Song Weichen 宋偉臣, who owned a match factory, formed a partnership with Wu and founded the Prosperity Nitric Alkali Company (熾昌硝堿公司), which manufactured a key ingredient in matches, a product introduced by Europeans in the second half of the nineteenth century and first manufactured by the Japanese at that century's end.

Through these initial experiences in Chinese industry, Wu concluded that China lacked the basic elements of a domestic chemical industry. Moreover, foreign competition, which soon destroyed Wu's company, was to blame. During World War I, Chinese industries of all sorts experienced what contemporaries themselves saw as a Golden Age of economic development. However, immediately following the war, the imperialist powers began re-entering or expanding their presence in the Chinese markets they

---

5. Nearly every biography of Wu quotes this line; see, e.g., Chenbao 1933: 53, Guohuo shiye chubanshe 1934: 21, and "Wu Yunchu xiansheng xiaoshi" (1934).

had temporarily abandoned.[6] The Golden Age ended and a new, highly competitive environment emerged that bankrupted undercapitalized Chinese companies such as Wu's. Because his new company could not compete, Wu switched his energy to manufacturing glue for matches. But this strategy also failed. In 1920, Wu went to Shanghai and set up the Prosperity New Ox-Glue Works (熾昌新牛皮膠廠) with Shi Gengyin 施耕尹, whom Wu had met when Shi was the manager of the Shanghai Armaments Rifle Factory. Through Shi, Wu met the famous industrialist and match manufacturer Liu Hongsheng, whom Wu convinced to finance the establishment of a glue factory in Shanghai, which Wu planned to manage (Wang Pilai and Wang Yu 1994: 375).

DISPLACING JAPANESE PRODUCTS IN CHINA

The changes wrought by the introduction of mass consumer products extended to a seemingly impregnable bastion of Chinese culture, the kitchen. Flavoring powders enhance the taste of even the most mundane dishes, and the use of such products spread quickly. The condiment and flavor-enhancer monosodium glutamate (also called sodium glutamate or simply MSG) is the crystalline sodium salt of glutamic acid. It is made from water, sodium, and glutamate. Glutamate is an amino acid found in all protein-containing foods, including meat, fish, cheese, milk, and many vegetables. The human body also produces glutamate, which is vital for metabolism and brain function. Monosodium glutamate is the sodium salt of glutamate. Added to foods, MSG performs a flavoring function similar to that of the glutamate that occurs naturally in food.

Frequent anti-imperialist violence and boycotts pressured Chinese consumers to seek domestic substitutes for imports and encouraged Chinese entrepreneurs to try to create such products (Chapters 3 and 4). However, the National Products Movement and Chinese boycotts of foreign products could only do so much to aid these new companies. Each industry faced its own problems in using nationalistic sentiments to market its products as "national products." Foodstuffs, for instance, were quickly consumed, and

---

6. On the three-way competition among Chinese, Japanese, and Swedish companies, see Cochran 2000: 147–76. James Reardon-Anderson (1991: 168) concludes that Wu's initial enterprise was successful.

therefore their purchasers were not subject to long-term social scrutiny. Whereas parading around the streets in the latest London-style clothing would have left one wide open to charges of unpatriotic consumption, mixing Japanese Ajinomoto into one's dinner dishes easily escaped notice. Not surprisingly, even during the most contentious anti-imperialist boycotts, Chinese continued to use products such as Ajinomoto secretly rather than switch to Chinese substitutes, which even by the early 1920s were considered inferior (Yang Dajun 1938, vol. 1, pt. II: 1154–55; Shanghai tebieshi, Shehuiju 1930: 95–99).

Although MSG became popular in the United States only in the 1950s, East Asian cooks have added seaweed to soup stocks and then used extracts of this to enhance the taste of foods for over a thousand years. A German chemist, however, first synthesized MSG in the late nineteenth century. Nevertheless, it was Japanese chemist Ikeda Kikunae 池田菊苗 (1864–1936) in 1907, who extracted MSG from *kombu* (kelp). The Tokyo University Chemistry Department chair, who had studied in Germany, began mass production in 1908 through Suzuki Pharmaceuticals. In 1909, the product went on sale in Japan under the brand name Ajinomoto. By 1917 Ajinomoto was sold throughout the world.[7] Wu was not the first or only person to challenge Ajinomoto. Production in China of similar products began in Shanghai in the early 1920s, and by the end of the decade a dozen or so Chinese companies were manufacturing competing products (see the survey of "gourmet powder" in NII 1935: 589–94). Of these manufacturers, by the late 1920s, Wu was already widely known as the "MSG king" (Gao Shi 1996: 118–21).

According to the nationalistic biographies of Wu Yunchu, his brilliance and patriotism lay in identifying the inexhaustible market potential and nationalistic significance of producing a Chinese version of Ajinomoto. Indeed, decades later, his daughter tied his life history directly to this domination, beginning with the line: "[At the time of my father's birth] Japanese products pervaded the Chinese market" (Wu Zhilian, "Xu" [Foreword], in Wang Daliang 1995: 1–2). In 1920, Wu noted the virtual monopoly enjoyed

---

7. After World War II Suzuki Pharmaceuticals became Ajinomoto Company, Inc., which netted over U.S.$6 billion in sales in 1999 and is still the world's largest producer of L-monosodium glutamate (MSG) and other amino acid products used in pharmaceuticals, foodstuffs, and feed additives (http://www.ajinomoto.co.jp/ajinomoto/company/other/other1.htm, consulted on April 18, 2002). For a chronology of the company, see http://www.ajinomoto.co.jp/ajinomoto/company/eajino/history.htm.

by the Japanese company Suzuki Pharmaceuticals and Ajinomoto in the Chinese market; this was one of the many low-priced Japanese consumer goods that had entered the Chinese market during and immediately after the war. The sudden spread of these products in China was conspicuous, and the advertisements for them that had sprung up throughout Chinese cities expanded the visual dominance of imperialism in the marketplace.

Although Wu Yunchu did not understand how Ajinomoto was produced, he suspected the process was simple, and because the additive was widely used, he knew its production would be enormously profitable. Moreover, the introduction of a Chinese substitute for Ajinomoto would allow Chinese to boycott a product that many found irresistible.[8] After conducting extensive experiments over the course of a year in his house, by the end of 1922, Wu, with his wife's assistance,[9] not only had identified the chemicals in Ajinomoto, but also had mastered a technique for manufacturing MSG (for a detailed description, see Wang Pilai and Wang Yu 1994: 355).

Of course, this was only half the battle. Wu still needed to figure out how to mass-produce and market his creation. Securing capital was particularly difficult in the unstable environment created by incessant fighting among the warlords. Through Wang Dongyuan 王東圓, the marketing representative of a soy sauce manufacturer, Wu met the owner of a dozen-odd soy sauce shops, Zhang Yiyun 張逸云 (b. 1871), and convinced him to run the company and invest $5,000 in helping Wu manufacture MSG.

The first problem the two tackled was selecting a name for their product and enterprise. The name they chose, *weijing* 味精, combines the Chinese term for "flavor" (味 / 味道) and "essence/heart" (精) to form "heart of flavor." The two added the term *tianchu* 天廚, an abbreviation for the term *tianshang paochu* 天上庖廚, "heaven's kitchen," to form the Tianchu Weijing Factory (天廚味精廠)—"The Heart of Flavor from Heaven's Kitchen Factory" or simply "Heaven's Kitchen." To secure the name and product, Wu and Zhang registered the names with the Ministry of Agriculture and

---

8. According to some, in addition to four basic tastes—sweet, sour, bitter, and salty—MSG and Ajinomoto produced another, known in Japanese as *umami* 旨味 and approximated by the English term "savory."

9. In biographies such as Wang Pilai and Wang Yu 1994: 354–55, Wu's wife, Wu Daiyi 吳戴儀, plays an important role—despite a "low level of education," she recognizes the national importance of competing with Japan and opening up the domestic food additive market to a Chinese competitor.

Commerce in Beijing and obtained a patent.[10] In early 1923, operations began on a very modest scale, in a couple of rented rooms, and with only seven or eight workers. Monthly production was initially only about 500 pounds, but output rapidly expanded. Despite the ongoing economic, political, and military chaos in China, production climbed to nearly 20,000 pounds in 1924. By 1929, Heaven's Kitchen produced over 140,000 pounds of MSG.[11]

The managers of Heaven's Kitchen immediately began to take advantage of the National Products Movement by advertising their product as a "completely Chinese product." From the start, Wang Dongyuan handled the marketing of the new product. He immediately began to post advertisements throughout the city and used Zhang Yiyun's soy stores as retail outlets. At one point, Wang decorated a pickled vegetable seller's cart with flags that proclaimed that Heaven's Kitchen's MSG was of superior quality compared to the Japanese Ajinomoto and pushed the cart throughout Chinese neighborhoods, calling out the name of the product and offering taste tests (Wang Pilai and Wang Yu 1994: 363).

The market for the new product developed quickly, but Heaven's Kitchen had to overcome the initial suspicions of consumers about the ingredients and origins of the product. Earlier Chinese flavoring powders were of suspect quality and had failed to win the confidence of Chinese consumers. Heaven's Kitchen overcame this problem by listing the ingredients and the company's address on each label, all the while stressing that its product was cheaper than Ajinomoto (Yang Dajun 1938, vol. 1, pt. II: 1154).

The success of Heaven's Kitchen spawned competition from other Chinese companies. Wu and Zhang responded by reorganizing and expanding their company from an informal company wholly owned and run by them. To raise the necessary capital, they formed a joint-stock company and raised $50,000 (Wu lacked the necessary capital and used his invention of the product as a basis for claiming a share of the company). They also registered their "Hand of Buddha" (佛手) brand name and product at the Shanghai patent office. With the new capital, they rented space in a former cigarette factory through the Taizhou native-place association and purchased more

---

10. "Nongshangbu banfa weijing zhipin hege yi zhangcheng jiangli baozhuang" (1923.5.24) in SSD 1992: 2.

11. For the production figures of Heaven's Kitchen MSG from 1923 to 1937, see "Tianchu chang 1923 nian zhi 1937 nian linian weijing chanliang biao" (1992). Production expanded from around 7,000 pounds in 1923 to over a half-million pounds in 1937.

than ten machines. Although the enterprise was modest by today's standards, in its day it was the largest food additive factory in China.

Wu's Japanese competitor tried to undermine Heaven's Kitchen. Through the Japanese embassy in Beijing, for instance, Suzuki Pharmaceuticals lodged a protest against Heaven's Kitchen's registration of the term "heart of flavor" (*weijing* 味精). Suzuki argued that the name was simply the second and third Chinese characters drawn from the generic description used in Ajinomoto's own advertisements, *diaowei jingfen* (調味精粉 or "flavoring powder") (Wang Dongyuan 1928). They demanded that the Chinese patent office cancel Heaven's Kitchen's copyright. The managers of Heaven's Kitchen feared that changing their product's name would confuse consumers, and they dispatched their marketing expert, Wang Dongyuan, to Beijing to lobby Chinese officials. Other Chinese manufacturers of similar products also petitioned the government on Heaven's Kitchen's behalf (Wang Pilai and Wang Yu 1994: 368; Chen Zhengqing 1992: 388). After a year of lobbying officials with expensive gifts and dinners—and with the aid of nationalistic sentiment in China—Wang won after the Japanese realized the futility of their efforts and gave up.

The Limits of Patriotic Production

What were the obligations of national product producers to the nation? What were the obligations of the managers to the shareholders? And what happened when the needs of the company and those of the country came into conflict? Companies such as Heaven's Kitchen frequently had to navigate between their own interests and the demands of the movement. To be sure, the movement provided critical opportunities for Heaven's Kitchen to develop market share. The May Thirtieth Movement of 1925 was clearly a turning point for the company. The boycott crippled Ajinomoto's sales. As a result, prices for the product dropped. At the same time, Heaven's Kitchen took advantage of the situation by widely advertising itself as a "national product" and reminding compatriots of their need to consume Chinese products. It also expanded its participation in movement events such as exhibitions (Gao Shi 1996: 119; see also Chapters 5 and 6). For instance, the company won a prize at the Third Jiangsu Province National Local Products Exhibition of 1925.[12] Sales skyrocketed as orders poured in from

---

12. "Tianchu weijing huode Jiangsu sheng" (1925).

throughout the country and from patriotic Chinese communities overseas. The company also gained a toehold in the Hong Kong market, which developed quickly.

Heaven's Kitchen took full advantage of the movement, even to the extent of undermining movement objectives. The anti-imperialist boycotts of the spring and summer led to the doubling of production in 1925. Still, production could not keep up with demand. To meet some of the additional demand, Heaven's Kitchen bought Ajinomoto and then repackaged and sold it under its own brand (Wang Pilai and Wang Yu 1994: 367). These tactics helped investors in the company make enormous amounts of money from the enterprise. Following the boycott of 1925, after deducting for production expenses, every six months the stock yielded dividends of $17,500 silver dollars per share.

Not surprisingly, Wu and his colleagues were active in movement organizations such as the NPPA.[13] Indeed, for his frequent contributions to movement causes, Wu was included in a list of prominent Shanghai business and political leaders named honorary chairmen of the organization (ZGWH 1932: "Huishi" section, 21).[14] In the aftermath of the May Thirtieth Movement, Heaven's Kitchen was also a leading contributor to anti-Japanese organizations such as the Shanghai Citizens Association on Sino-Japanese Relations (Cao 1925: 53). Indeed, even after World War II, Wu and his companies continued to oppose imports, especially of Japanese consumer goods.[15]

Ironically, the international success of Heaven's Kitchen's MSG—due in large part to the anti-imperialist boycotts—aided the product's domestic growth by giving the company credibility. Even after the height of the 1925 boycott, company operations continued to expand. In 1926, it began to eye lucrative Western markets and prepared for eventual entry into these

---

13. In 1924, for instance, Wu gave a lecture at the Shanghai Commercial Products Display Hall; see Pan Junxiang, "20 niandai Zhongguo guohuo yundong kaizhan," in idem, 1996: 24.

14. Based on an executive committee decision in 1930–31, the NPPA invited Chinese luminaries to become honorary chairmen of the organization. The honored "led the masses through their example." Among the 82 persons named was the notorious Shanghai Green Gang leader Du Yuesheng, prominent economist Liu Dajun 劉大鈞 (1891–1962; known in English as D. K. Lieu), and many Nationalist leaders.

15. See SMA Q38-1-219, for a handbill produced by Wu Yunchu in 1946 on why China should not open its markets to Japanese products.

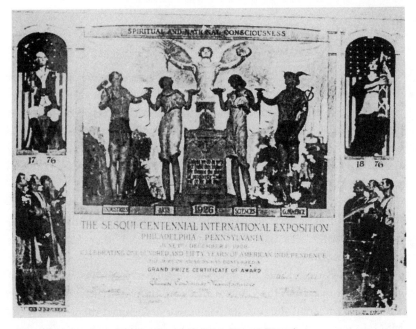

Fig. 8.3 Domestic Status Earned Abroad
(SSD 1992)

The Sesqui Centennial International Exposition Award won by Heaven's Kitchen's MSG in
Philadelphia in 1926.

markets by applying for patents in England, France, and the United States
in the following years. As contemporary biographies of Wu Yunchu proclaim, these were the first international patents awarded to the products of
the nascent Chinese chemical industry.

Further boosts to the company's domestic credibility came in 1926 at
the Sesqui Centennial International Exposition in Philadelphia, when
Heaven's Kitchen won a prize (see Fig. 8.3), and in 1932, when the
company won an award at the San Francisco Exposition. These awards
helped Wu's company navigate difficult waters. On the one hand, the
movement pressured Chinese consumers to select only national products.
At the same time, these consumers wanted to consume the best products,
which were often automatically associated with imports. International
awards gave the company's MSG credibility as a world-class product and
reassured Chinese consumers that they were buying the best, not merely
the most Chinese.

PURIFYING NATIONAL PRODUCTS
OF THEIR FOREIGN COMPONENTS

The movement also placed constraints on Heaven's Kitchen in ways that fundamentally altered its business strategy. Although Wu continually advertised his MSG as "completely Chinese," this was not the case. From the start, he relied heavily on imported raw materials. Initially, for instance, he used inexpensive Chinese gluten, which was the primary ingredient of MSG. As sales soared, the domestic supply was inadequate, and the company began using Canadian wheat, which yielded a high level of gluten. Such compromises ensured the company's continued growth and profitability. Using imported Canadian wheat also gave Wu's MSG a competitive advantage over Ajinomoto, which was made from fish, soybeans, and other more expensive sources of protein.

Heaven's Kitchen's use of imported ingredients helped it force its primary foreign rival from the Chinese market. Throughout most of the 1920s, the need to undercut the price of Ajinomoto determined the price of Wu's MSG. In 1928, each pound sold for about $7, but cost only $3.50 to produce. That changed. In 1928, the new Nationalist government sought to register the company and grant it a five-year monopoly. In the following year, Wu, however, surrendered the domestic patent rights, as the Ministry of Industry and Commerce put it, "so that we may collectively develop national products."[16] Immediately, dozens of Chinese competitors sprang up.[17] Although the new competition exerted downward pressure on the price of MSG, it also forced Ajinomoto from the Chinese market (except for the Japanese controlled provinces in Manchuria).

As a supporter of the National Products Movement and as an astute businessman, Wu had both social and business reasons to sinify his national product by finding or creating domestic substitutes for his imported ingredients.[18] The success of Heaven's Kitchen spawned ancillary chemical

16. "Gongshangbu banfa Wu Yunchu fangqi bufen weijing zhuanliquan baojiang ling" (1929.5.16), in SSD 1992: 15–16.

17. For an exhaustive list of these new Chinese companies, see Wang Pilai and Wang Yu 1994: 370. For translations of these companies' names, their addresses, amount of capitalization, and other information, see NII 1935: 590; for production figures, see ibid., pp. 593–94.

18. Indeed, Wu used his fame and fortune to reinforce movement objectives. A clear articulation of Wu's desire to control foreign involvement in the Chinese market and preserve that market for Chinese is a petition he wrote for the Nationalist government's Industrial and

industries in the Shanghai area. In fact, Wu himself played a direct role in this development. The production of MSG involved seven raw materials: gluten, usually made from wheat flour; hydrochloric acid; caustic soda; alcohol; carbon powder; sodium sulfide; and sodium carbonate. Most of these raw materials were imported. Initially, the company obtained gluten from Shanghai's spinning factories, which manufactured starch to use as sizing. Although Heaven's Kitchen soon exhausted this supply and turned to imported Canadian wheat, it worked to become as self-sufficient as possible by using alternative materials. Ironically, the company initially bought its hydrochloric acid, which reacts with gluten to form MSG, from Japanese suppliers. In 1928, Wu moved to end his company's need for Japanese products by establishing the Tianyuan Electrochemical Factory (天原化工廠) with $200,000 raised from stockholders in Heaven's Kitchen. The factory was immediately successful, and by 1933, Heaven's Kitchen was consuming 2.5 million pounds of the hydrochloric acid produced by this plant (NII 1935: 591).[19]

As Heaven's Kitchen made other efforts to supply its own raw materials, Wu's reputation as a national producer grew. The company's expansion was clearly linked to the growing National Products Movement. The boycotts following the Manchurian Incident of 1931 and the Shanghai Incident of 1932 again fueled demand for products from Wu's companies. Demand was so great among Chinese living in Southeast Asia that Wu's Hong Kong distributor could not fill it. In 1931, he decided to set up a factory in Hong Kong to meet the demand from ethnic Chinese in Southeast Asia as well as to develop new markets in America, Australia, and elsewhere. By the mid-1930s, the Heaven Conglomerate (or Tianzihao 天字號), as Wu's group of enterprises became known because each company name began with the character *tian* 天 ("heaven"), included four companies. The Tianyuan Electrochemical

---

Commercial Conference held at the end of 1930. At the conference, Wu submitted a petition that called for limiting the number and type of factories set up by foreigners in China. According to Wu's petition, in the aftermath of China's recent recovery of tariff autonomy, foreigners had expanded plans to establish factories in China in order to avoid the stiff new tariffs. Wu argued that while China's industry was in its infancy, it should be protected for Chinese. For the text of the petitions, see "Wu Yunchu guanyu dizhi wairen zai Hua shechang ti'an," in SSD 1989: 153–54.

19. For an overview of Tianyuan's output in its first four years, see "Tianyuan dianhua chang sinian lai jingguo qingxing jianming biao (1931–34)," in SSD 1989: 89. In that brief period, production climbed 332 percent, from under 2,000 tons to over 6,000 tons by 1934.

Factory manufactured hydrochloric acid (a fundamental ingredient used to make corn syrup and glucose from cornstarch), caustic soda (used in the manufacture of, among other things, paper, rayon, and photographic film), bleach powder (a standard bleaching agent used to whiten or remove natural colors), and other chloride products. In 1932, Heaven's Kitchen itself was reorganized and opened up two more MSG factories and two additional plants to produce starch and fructose. In response to tremendous domestic pressure to manufacture its own containers, in 1934–35 the Heaven Conglomerate launched the Tiansheng Ceramics Factory (天盛陶器廠).[20] Finally, in 1935–36, the conglomerate formed the Tianli Nitrogen Plant (天利氮氣廠) to use the byproducts of Tianyuan's operations, such as hydrogen and ammonia.

BROADER PATRIOTIC ACTIVITIES

A few other aspects of Wu's life are regularly invoked to solidify his nationalistic credentials. Indeed, his patriotic activities extended beyond the production of chemical products. He engaged in numerous philanthropic activities during these years, such as funding the establishment of the Chinese Industrial Chemistry Research Institute in 1929 and acting as its first head. The institute aimed to address the persistent problem of a lack of knowledge in ancillary fields. In addition, recalling his own past, Wu helped establish a fund for indigent students and contributed several hundred thousand *yuan* to schools throughout China.

Wu contributed directly to China's defense. Following the Shanghai Incident of 1932, Wu briefly attempted to manufacture poisonous gas, but he dropped these efforts and instead helped arrange the production of gas masks (Wang Pilai and Wang Yu 1994: 372; Guohuo shiye chubanshe 1934: 21). Wu also purchased several airplanes in 1933–34 and donated them to the Nationalist army, an act for which he received considerable press at the time (see Fig. 8.4). Finally, after the outbreak of the Second Sino-Japanese War in 1937, Wu moved his Tianyuan and Heaven's Kitchen enterprises,

---

20. Outside Shanghai, movement activists who assumed that a product packaged in Japanese-manufactured materials must itself be a Japanese product frequently challenged the authenticity of Tian commodities as "national products." The SMA files on the Tian Conglomerate contain many references to such disputes. For instance, see SMA Q38-2-148, on the efforts of Tianyuan to get its manufactures certified as national products in Nanchang.

Fig. 8.4 Heaven's Kitchen MSG Bomber

On March 18, 1934, at least 30,000 people attended a ceremony at Hongqiao Airport in Shanghai. Many of the most powerful men in the city assembled for a ceremonial presentation (*upper photo*: Huang Yiting 1934) of a bomber to the Nationalist government by Wu Yunchu (*third from the left in front row*). Those in attendance included (*from right to left in front row*) mayor Wu Tiecheng, Secretary General of the Executive Yuan Zhu Minyi 褚民誼 (1884–1946), Wu Yunchu, Green Gang leader Du Yuesheng, movement leader Wang Xiaolai, and (*in back*) entrepreneur Shi Liangcai 史量才 (1879–1934), Chamber of Commerce head Yu Xiaqing, and newspaperman Zhu Shaoping 朱少屏 (1881–1942). Lest Chinese patriots forget the origin of the airplane, the factory name was painted on the side of the plane (*lower photo*: SSD 1992). And one banner at the airport explicitly linked patriotic consumption and defense: "These airplanes were indirectly purchased by patriotic Chinese who love to use Heaven's Kitchen's Flavoring" (*SB* 1934.3.19).

including its Hong Kong branch, to Sichuan province. He returned to Shanghai after the war.[21] And he stayed in China following the Communist victory and held municipal posts on science committees in the new government. However, the Communists' embrace of "patriotic capitalists" did not last. Wu's companies were, effectively, nationalized in the early 1950s, and capitalists were persecuted. He died on October 15, 1953, at the age of 62.

BIOGRAPHIES AS PACKAGING
FOR PATRIOTIC PRODUCTS

The nationalistic biography of Wu Yunchu was literally attached to the commodities his companies produced. Indeed, product, person, and biography converged on the labels of his Buddha's Hand Flavoring Powder, which by 1928 advertised the product as "devised by Mr. [Wu Yunchu]" (see Fig. 8.5).[22] In earlier times, one way to describe someone as successful was to say that his or her name had spread far and wide. One's "name" or reputation was what became known throughout China. In this emerging consumer culture, the branded commodities of Chinese capitalists carried their names and reputations throughout China. Because Heaven's Kitchen products were so widely known ("there was not a person who did not know of its products"; Chenbao 1933: 53), word of Wu's virtue and his contribution to national survival spread throughout China and into ethnic Chinese communities overseas.

There were many forums for these nationalistic biographies during the movement. Indeed, they often became integral parts of the other movement events discussed in this book, particularly commodity spectacles. On the one hand, they rewarded the primary patrons of such events. On the other hand, these biographies also urged others to follow the lead of China's patriotic producers. With increasing regularity during the movement, national products were put on public display and held up to would-be manufacturers as standards to emulate, to distributors and merchants as the only products

---

21. Wu became a member of several important Nationalist committees that managed China's economy, including the National Economic Council (全國經濟委員會), the National Resources Commission (資源委員會), and the Ministry of Finance's Planning Committee (計劃委員會).

22. For a copy of a label, see "Changhao fazhan xiaoshi" (Brief histories of industrial developments), in Shanghai shangye zazhi 1928.

Fig. 8.5 Packaging Nationalism

The labels on bottles of Heaven's Kitchen's Buddha's Hand brand MSG marketed more than the products themselves. Associating Wu Yunchu's heroic biography as a patriotic producer with the product (which proclaims itself as "devised by Mr. [Wu Yunchu]") offered consumers the possibility of participating in his and, by extension, the nation's struggle against imperialism through nationalistic consumption. The package also reveals a central irony of the movement. Even national product manufacturers understood the allure of the foreign and often used foreign words (here, English) to stimulate desire and sales. Such tactics, however, did not contradict the primary goal of the movement of promoting the consumption of Chinese products.

worth selling, and to consumers as properly nationalistic objects of desire. Through such events, the public also consumed images of nationalistic individuals and their companies as role models.[23] Inclusion in the exhibitions, which required passing a certification process, made this point. It was reinforced by the publications accompanying major movement events, which invariably included biographies and company profiles of prominent producers of national products. For instance, the massive volume commemorating the

---

23. A less formal exhibition grounds was the Tian Conglomerate's factories themselves. The conglomerate frequently hosted groups of students from across the country. For a collection of requests to visit the factories, see the "Jiaotong daxue deng yaoqiu canguan Tianyuan chang zhi Wu Yunchu deng han," in SSD 1989: 65–68.

Ministry of Industry and Commerce's Chinese National Products Exhibition of 1928 included articles contributed by national product producers that expressed support for the goals of the exhibition and, more broadly, the movement. A final section of the volume recounted one more time, in heroic terms, the histories of these patriotic producers and their struggle to secure the national market for authentic Chinese products.[24]

Movement discourse permeated every aspect of Chinese economic life before 1949. The notion of foreign and domestic products—and of patriotic and unpatriotic consumers and producers—defined relationships in an increasingly nationalistic, nationalized Chinese marketplace. Such an environment made heroes out of producers who were deemed to manufacture sufficiently Chinese products and villains out of those facilitating the entry and spread of foreign commodities in the Chinese marketplace. For participants in the movement, defining the world of goods in terms of nations of commodities was not a defense against participating in modern life. Rather, movement advocates saw erecting strong national economic boundaries as an essential step toward emulating Western and Japanese industrial success and toward becoming an equal member of an international community of nation-states.

---

24. See "Gongchang xiaoshi" (Brief factory histories), in GSB 1928.

Conclusion

"Then why did you choose to work for a foreign firm? Don't you know that foreigners have never had any good intentions towards us? They exploited the Chinese people for economic gain or tried to enslave us politically. Only the scum of China work for foreigners. You should know that. You were offered a job teaching English at the Institute of Foreign Languages. But you preferred to work for Shell. Why?"

— Nien Cheng 1986: 88–89

"What has dancing got to do with patriotism?" I was genuinely puzzled.

"You were dancing with a foreigner. And you looked quite happy dancing with a foreigner. That's decidedly unpatriotic."

— Nien Cheng 1986: 264

Was the National Products Movement a success? Did the movement reach its goal of integrating nationalism and consumerism? The answers to these questions depend on the criteria for success. It would certainly be easy to interpret the movement as a dramatic failure. Indeed, this book might have been entitled "the impossibility of nationalizing consumer culture in modern China." Given the tremendous obstacles the movement confronted, the view that it was a failure would have been understandable. China's lack of statecraft tools such as tariff autonomy and, indeed, genuine sovereignty allowed imports to pour into the country. Likewise, the powerful associations between imports and fashion/modernity heightened demand, as did price and the mechanized uniformity and quality of imports. Most important, a weak sense of national identity among the vast majority of Chinese consumers who evaluated their interests also in terms of themselves, their families, lineages, communities, and regions made sacrificing on behalf of the nation difficult, even unthinkable. Not surprisingly, the movement never convinced or forced consumers to avoid imports completely and buy only certified national products. Nor did the movement persuade consumers that they ought to consume something called "national products." In short, the movement did not instill product-nationality as the pre-eminent attribute of a commodity. Appeals for Chinese compatriots to consume Chinese products often went unanswered. Import statistics substantiate this fact. Indeed, the movement's own incessant pleas for treasonous consumers, merchants, officials, and others to heed the call to buy national products confirm that the movement was an ongoing war, to use its own metaphor, rather than a single battle.

On other, subtler cultural, institutional, and discursive grounds, however, the movement was much more successful. The movement insinuated nationalism into countless aspects of China's nascent consumer culture, and this combination of nationalism and consumerism became a basis for what it meant to live in "modern China." This is visible throughout China: from the growing hostility toward and negative perception of imports in the nineteenth century through the establishment of a nationalistic male appearance and visuality in the late Qing to the repeated anti-imperialist boycotts and the development of an exhibitionary complex of nationalistic commodity spectacles in the Republic to the proliferation of gendered representations of unpatriotic consumption and patriotic producers. This nationalized consumer culture influenced Chinese life from top to bottom, from elite discussions of political economy to individual students' decisions of what to wear to school. The movement did have an immediate impact on fashion, business, appearance, and language. Its legacies include the representations of unpatriotic consumption and patriotic production that persist in present-day China. This pervasive cultural influence is the movement's chief success. The general principle, if not the individual practice, of nationalistic consumption is deeply rooted. The breadth, depth, and creativity of the movement described here make it difficult to deny a central role to this movement in the making of the modern Chinese nation.

Again, the legacies of the movement are visible across the twentieth century, particularly after the Communist Revolution in 1949. The effects of decades of Communist historiography, which emphasized the singularly exploitative nature of the imperialist presence in China, are easy to identify. The two epigraphs to this chapter, which come from the interrogations that Shanghai businesswoman Nien Cheng endured during the Cultural Revolution (1966–76), demonstrate the Chinese Communist government's overt hostility to foreign products and practices. This same sort of nationalism and anti-imperialism permeates textbooks, museums, and popular consciousness down to the present. To the Communists, their victory over the

Nationalists in 1949 was always a dual liberation: both from the political oppression of class domination at home and from the economic control of imperialist powers.

The history of the movement captures China's long-standing ambivalence toward foreign involvement in the Chinese economy. True, direct state-sponsored attacks on the evils of foreign involvement in Chinese life have become less frequent since Deng Xiaoping's decision in the late 1970s to "open China to the outside world" (對外開放) and permit the use of private foreign capital to develop the economy. But the deep suspicion of foreign capital is still there. China remains concerned with "self-reliance" (自力更生), even as the definition of the term changes (Pearson 1991: esp. chap. 2). Moreover, this lingering concern regularly manifests itself outside government activity. Runaway best-sellers such as *China Can Also Say No* (中國也可以說不), for instance, passionately plead for renewed anti-American boycotts and urge readers not to fly on Boeing airplanes (Song Qiang et al. 1996; see also Wang Xiaodong et al. 1999). Demonstrations in the mid-1980s railed against Japanese "neo-economic imperialism" and the "second occupation" of China. Likewise, the "war of the chickens"—between Kentucky Fried Chicken and domestic fast-food competitors—called on the "Chinese people to eat Chinese food." These contemporary "national product" campaigns reflect the deep ambivalence over the role of foreigners in the Chinese economy even as China's "new middle class" flocks to these restaurants.[1] Domestic manufacturers continue to use nationalistic appeals to win customer and state approval.[2]

---

1. On the well-known battle between Kentucky Fried Chicken and local businesses in Beijing over the fast-food market, see Yunxiang Yan 2000 and the essays collected in Zhao Feng 1994. In "Changyong guohuo gai bu gai" (Should national products be promoted?), a Chinese author once again browbeats fellow Chinese for their unpatriotic consumption, citing patriotic South Korean consumers as models to emulate. The author states that even while academics debate the merits of fully opening China to foreign products, and even if imports are widely available, "every Chinese person" has the responsibility to favor Chinese products (Zhao Feng 1994: 171).

2. For an example from the late 1990s, see Zhao Yang 2000. Zhao's case study also reveals the ongoing ambivalent relationship between Chinese consumers and imports: "The Wahaha Group's decision to emphasize its drink's indigenous character was followed by the company's determination to depict itself as a staunch defender of the domestic food and beverage industry against what Wahaha's executives called an 'unhealthy tendency' in mass consumption: the public's fascination with Western and Japanese consumer goods" (Zhao Yang 2000: 189).

How Widely Elaborated Was the Movement?

The National Products Movement was a nationwide effort. What, however, did it mean to be "nationwide" in a largely agricultural country of 400 million people? The primary geographical focus here has been on Shanghai for three reasons (see also Chapter 1). First, foreigners and foreign capital were highly concentrated in this city. In fact, a third of all foreign investment and almost half of all direct business investment went to Shanghai (Remer 1933a: 111–12). Second, Shanghai had the most numerous and active movement organizations, many of which became models for other cities.[3] Like the city itself, these organizations were made up of individuals from other places—sojourners who became conduits for spreading the movement agenda across China.[4] Third, Shanghai was both the Hollywood and the Wall Street of its day, the country's capital of both glamour and industry, and was consequently the focus of a great deal of attention within China.[5] By the twentieth century, as historian Hanchao Lu observes, "highly commercialized cities came to be seen as better places than small towns and villages" (1999: 5). Shanghai was at the top of this hierarchy. Not only did the city provide economic opportunities for all classes, but its events, fashions, and habits were also widely publicized and promoted and consequently discussed and emulated throughout China.

Although Shanghai is a principal focus because of its flagship role in the movement, the movement was national in scope. This, however, does not

---

3. See, e.g., "Jingji juejiao de fangfa yu shouduan" (1928), which explains the functioning of two Shanghai organizations and how they promoted national products and anti-Japanese boycotts.

4. During the 1930s, for instance, more than 70 percent of Shanghai's population originated from outside the area (Wakeman and Yeh 1992a: 6).

5. Many of China's most important newspapers and periodicals were based or published in Shanghai. These publications had national readerships. Moreover, publications based in other cities invariably covered Shanghai extensively. "This publicity," Shanghai historian Xiong Yuezhi notes, "promoted a sense in many parts of China that Shanghai and the Shanghainese were the model of the future" (1996: 103). For an extended examination of this role of Shanghai, which was at the center of "modern Chinese imagination," see Yingjin Zhang 1996. Of course, Shanghai had not been the fashion center of China for long. The nearby city of Suzhou, long a wealthy center of silk production, had played this role in earlier centuries (Brook 1998: 221). In addition, elite circles throughout the country had looked to Beijing and the imperial court and courtesans for both official and informal guidance on fashion (Scott 1960: 61).

mean that the movement was uniform across China. Preliminary research on the movement in various cities reveals significant local differences. The northern city of Tianjin, for example, provides a distinct case, particularly given its closer financial and industrial ties to Japan (see Rinbara 1983). Likewise, major commercial centers such as Guangzhou undoubtedly had local economic interests that conflicted with national ones. Although these cities supported the movement to different degrees, all of them participated actively. Chinese and foreign newspaper reports, records from Japanese consulates throughout China, the participation of scores of cities and towns in anti-imperialist boycotts, the proliferation of nationalistic commodity spectacles from Ningxia to Guangdong provinces, and archival records of the communication between movement organizations in various cities confirm that the movement was national in scope.[6]

"China" remains a controversial term. In general, however, the term is valid in this study. First, the participants in this history clearly and expressly saw themselves as operating on behalf of the entire country. As we have seen, their goal was to communicate the aims of their movement to the entire population. Second, even though I refer to processes and events as occurring "across China," I do not mean to suggest that in a country as vast as China, with a population of some 400 million in the mid-twentieth century, or even all of Shanghai's three million residents, every man, woman, and child participated. Many of the major changes of modern Chinese history took place without the knowledge of millions, especially the 300-some million living outside the major cites. Travel accounts alone confirm that customs and diseases long thought dead persisted in out-of-the-way locations. Nonetheless, the National Products Movement involved more than the 40–80 million urban residents. The term "urban" misleadingly downplays the close connections and communications between cities and countryside. Third, I intentionally generalize for "China" as a way of beginning to reaggregate China by considering the centripetal forces pulling China together after several decades of analyses that focused on divisions and differences. Admittedly, there

---

6. To cite three final informal pieces of evidence, the lists of winners of raffles published in the movement magazine *Jilian huikan* reveals that they lived in cities and towns across China; see, e.g., *Jilian huikan* 48 (1931.12.16): 45–48. Second, movement publications carried reports on movement organizations and activities in other cities; see, e.g., "Suiwei niantou zhi guohuo xiaoxi" (1935). Third, organizations and individuals throughout China sent congratulatory messages to the opening ceremony of major movement events; see, e.g., the thirteen pages of such messages reprinted in Kong Xiangxi 1929.

was no single "National Products Movement" for all of China. Politics is always local. And that dictum certainly applied to the politics of consumption. Nevertheless, most of the topics discussed here—such as fashion, boycotts, and commodity spectacles—are difficult to appreciate without first uncovering their connections to national and international issues of nation-making.

A Meta-Movement

The National Products Movement was a matrix that formed, disseminated, and provided the means for practicing modern Chinese nationalism. It was much more than the project or tool of a single segment of Chinese society, more than the handiwork of Nationalist officials or Chinese entrepreneurs. The movement subsumed these and many other diverse social elements—even antagonistic ones—into a shared program of nationalism that transformed commodities into miniature representations of China's aspirations for survival, wealth, and power. As such, the movement is best understood not simply as any of the four parts discussed in this book but as all of them and many others combined.

In each segment of Chinese life, there is evidence for the explicit or, as seen in the widespread use of the movement's vocabulary, implicit support for movement objectives. When identifying the participants, it is easy to find political patrons. From the earliest days of the Republic, government administrations supported aspects of the movement. In fact, as Chapters 5 and 6 demonstrate, the Nationalist commitment to the movement and, specifically, to the expansion of nationalistic commodity spectacles, intensified with that party's ascension in the late 1920s. From financing major national product exhibitions to sponsoring national product years, the Nationalists saw the utility of aligning themselves with the movement.

And yet the movement was clearly not a Nationalist government creation. Its roots stretch back into the late Qing dynasty and extend beyond the rise of the Nationalists. Chinese Communist Party literature was rife with movement vocabulary and arguments. In the CCP's view, denying foreigners access to the Chinese market was a crucial step in undermining imperialism and capitalism and creating the conditions for communism in China. Tens of thousands of handbills confiscated by treaty port authorities and labeled "Communist literature" called for the boycotting of foreign products and the promotion of national products.[7] Consequently, we cannot see the movement as a subordinate part of the history of one side of the Nationalist-Communist struggle for legitimacy and power. Both sides drew on elements of the movement.

The obvious economic patrons were also an integral part of the formation and spread of the movement. In Shanghai, Chinese entrepreneurs, particularly those threatened by foreign competition, actively supported the movement and often assumed key leadership roles. The most powerful movement organizations—the NPPA, the Citizens Association, and the Association for National Products—were bankrolled and run largely by such entrepreneurs. Given the financial resources, national communication networks, and political clout of these people, it is impossible to imagine an influential movement without them.

Yet Chinese industrialists did not monopolize control of the movement. From the formation of the first major group in 1911, the leadership included non-business elites. Moreover, the movement quickly became a vehicle for mass organizations such as student groups, Communist activists, and women's associations. Throughout the movement, many other organizations, often less visible and certainly more ephemeral, participated. Ten-person groups and radical student organizations, for instance, appeared and disappeared within weeks or months. In a fundamental way, these radical organizations shared the objectives of their more conservative and high-profile counterparts; all these groups wanted to apply the categories of Chinese/foreign to all commodities. In this general sense, they were comrades-in-arms. At the same time, however, they did not always use the discourse of nationalistic consumption in the same way. Accounts from boycott years demonstrate that the notion of "pure" national products was not only used against imports and "enemy products" but also against targeted domestically manufactured goods deemed insufficiently Chinese. Moreover, the moral authority to label certain goods and consumers suspect was not solely in the hands of movement organizations headed by Chinese entrepreneurs. During boycotts, for instance, students and even gangsters enforced more radical definitions of national products and interpretations of the movement.

---

7. There are countless examples of such handbills in the Shanghai Municipal Police records; see, e.g., SMP Files 3261, 3360, 3752/21, and 4851.

The movement provided immediate concrete benefits to Chinese manufacturers by developing markets. Moreover, the movement allowed manufacturers to recast private profit-seeking as an action on behalf of the Chinese nation. By downplaying price and quality as the pre-eminent ways of evaluating products and urging their compatriots to privilege product-nationality as the single most important determinant in any market choice, participants in the movement undermined fashion and consumption trends that favored imported goods by questioning the patriotism of those who consumed these things.

The link between national survival and the health of Chinese industries was powerful. Over the course of the movement, China's future seemed increasingly dismal. By the early 1930s, Japan had, in effect, annexed Manchuria and was quickly extending its control over north China. Japanese imperialism in China created a sense of desperation among Chinese anxious to find a means of national salvation. Animosity toward Chinese who aided the Japanese in any way grew. At the same time, both the fear of Japanese military superiority and the desire to consolidate domestic control left Chinese leaders unwilling to confront Japan on the battlefield. Popular and elite expressions of anti-imperialism had to find other outlets.

The movement became a common outlet for the expression of nationalism. It resonated across Chinese life because so many Chinese were seeking a way to express their nationalism in an environment in which doing so was difficult and even deadly. As Japan expanded its control over China, the Chinese intensified their search for "traitors." Traitors were seen as those with contacts with Japanese, and these contacts came to include any consumption of Japanese products. Indeed, as part of a project recording one day in the life of the Chinese nation, an anonymous high school student characterized advertisements for foreign products and services in Japanese-occupied Manchuria as visible reminders of China's lost sovereignty.[8] Everywhere, popular sentiments urged the prohibition of anything Japanese. China's inability to carry out such a prohibition only added to the frustration.[9]

Chinese capitalists could demand that Chinese consumers buy exclusively Chinese products, but this same logic could also be applied to Chinese capi-

---

8. Yuanqie (pseudonym), "May Twenty-First in Tangshan [Hebei province]," in Cochran and Hsieh 1983: 220.

9. See, e.g., Jiangfeng, "Benevolent Elixir," in Cochran and Hsieh 1983: 244.

talists themselves. From national wholesalers to local shopkeepers, Chinese merchants were increasingly held to the standard of handling only Chinese goods. Chinese manufacturers, too, were vulnerable to the same accusations they helped to create. As we saw in the case of Wu Yunchu (Chapter 8), the difficulty (and often impossibility) of adhering to the National Products Standards—producing "pure" Chinese products with exclusively Chinese management, labor, raw materials, and capital—placed manufacturers in a quandary.

Chinese who made and sold commodities came under attack from more than one segment of society. Students, frustrated by their country's continual appeasement of Japan, accused merchants of lacking national consciousness and providing a ready market for Japanese products, which, they argued, created a reason for Japan to be in China in the first place. Hooligans used movement discourse as a pretext for shakedowns, as did local officials. At the highest political level, Nationalists used their support for the movement—from commodity spectacles to anti-imperialist boycotts—to legitimize their polity and its formal and informal taxing of capitalists. Chiang Kai-shek's words at the opening of the National Products Exhibition of 1928 foreshadow the subsequent record of state extractions and takeovers. From top to bottom, the movement provided a flexible matrix for expressing nationalism and anti-imperialism that variously empowered or victimized Chinese. However, even the most cynical manipulations of movement discourse strengthened the movement by reproducing the hegemony of the underlying categories of a nationalistic consumer culture.

Nationalistic Consumerism Viewed from North America

The centrality of nationalism in Chinese consumer culture may be difficult for some non-Chinese to understand. Nationalism is probably a central part of every consumer culture, including that of the United States. However, despite the many "Buy American" campaigns from the Revolutionary War to the present, there remains something *comparatively* a-nationalistic about the *recent* conception of products in the United States. Times change the relationship between nationalism and consumerism. In contrast to the late 1980s, Americans now seem unconcerned by annual trade deficits, which reached record levels for goods in 2002 (U.S.$484 billion). To be sure, Americans continue to define products by nationality. The categories of domestic and foreign remain intact. Many people think of Boeing, for instance, as a U.S. company. Yet there were no popular protests when American Airlines bought European-made Airbuses. Likewise, some retailers such as Wal-Mart cater to Buy American sentiments by loudly proclaiming their "American First" policies and promising to choose domestic vendors when goods are equally priced. But the U.S. government does not require Wal-Mart to do so.[10] Nor does Wal-Mart suggest that its customers ought to buy a more expensive domestic product over a cheaper import.[11] We might well say that individuals predominantly base purchasing decisions on price and quality more often than nationality. Increasingly, other interpretations persistently challenge the supremacy of price and quality, notions of "healthy living," "environment friendly," and "not-made-in-sweatshops." But Americans rarely construct the meaning of commodities as *pre-eminently* about nationality.

Even if one wanted to buy something "American," doing so would be difficult. Advocates of globalization remind consumers that nationality is an increasingly irrelevant category for products. A Detroit-based company may market a car, but that same car may have been designed by German engineers, manufactured with a Japanese engine, and assembled in Mexico with parts imported from around the world. Similarly, how does one classify a Toyota "made" in the United States? What nationality is a Chrysler now that German-based Daimler has acquired the company? Simpler products do not seem to fare any better. Do Americans classify light bulbs as either "domestic" or "foreign"? Do Americans think of soap or any of the other thousands of commodities that they regularly consume in these terms? Or do such distinctions seem much less important than price, quality, and personal taste?

In many countries, the embrace of "nationless products" and a global consumer culture that shuns product-nationality—or actively embraces the

---

10. Under certain circumstances, however, the U.S. government does impose such restrictions. Following the collision of a U.S. surveillance plane and a Chinese fighter jet in April 2001, the Defense Department announced it would recall and "dispose of" its stock of Chinese-made black berets. Tellingly, a spokesperson downplayed product-nationality and emphasized "quality" as a determining factor (see Gary Sheftick, "No Chinese Berets," Army News Service, 2001.5.2).

11. Joseph Kahn, "Snapping up Chinese Goods Despite Qualms on Trade Bill," *New York Times* 2000.5.17: 1 and 12. Kahn interviewed American consumers at a Wal-Mart and discovered that despite the common desire to buy American and avoid Chinese-made products, few were willing to pay more to do so.

"foreign" as fashionable—is a much more recent and tentative development. India, Korea, Brazil, and Malaysia are but a few of the many post-colonial states in which there has been a strong push to assert cultural and economic autonomy through material culture. In the mid-1990s, when the Asian economic crisis began, many of these countries again openly linked consumption of domestic goods to patriotism. One memorable photograph in an international paper pictured Korean students smashing imported Japanese pencils, and another showed Thais lined up to convert their gold and hard currencies into *baht*.[12] In these countries, the domestic/foreign division still matters. Government policies and public appeals to come to the nation's aid by making patriotic purchases reverberate across a deep social-historical foundation.

It may strike contemporary observers as odd to think of China in these terms. China, it seems, hardly needs to worry about its domestic markets being overrun with inexpensive foreign goods. But the multibillion-dollar trade deficit the United States currently runs with China each year is a recent development. Early in the twentieth century, Chinese anxiously noted their own trade debts and sought ways to limit imports.

As Chapter 1 explains, China could not simply ban imports. The British ensured access to Chinese markets in the mid-nineteenth century through agreements following the Opium War. The unequal treaties freed most foreigners from Chinese laws and fixed Chinese tariffs at very low rates. These privileges greatly enhanced the ability of foreigners to sell products and lifestyles in China. The Chinese national political leadership, whenever there was any, lacked the power to ban the consumption of foreign products and to control the embrace of Western lifestyles. The ability to enact such policies came only after the establishment of a powerful centralized state in 1949.

As I have shown, before 1949 resistance took another form: the construction of cultural constraints on consumerism in the National Products Movement. Within the movement, consumption became a way for ordinary Chinese to practice nationalism and anti-imperialism every day. The social forces generated by the movement, eventually including state apparatuses, worked to define and regulate consumerism, channeling consumption into

---

12. *International Herald Tribune* 1997.12.27–28: 1; "Thailand's Gold Campaign Nets 24kg of Metal," *China Post* 1998.1.27: 9. On Koreans' exchanging foreign currencies for *won*, see Andrew Pollack, "Will Korean Frugality Help or Hurt?" *International Herald Tribune* 1997.12.19: 11.

acceptable nationalistic pleasures. But in the environment created by the movement, consuming incorrectly could have caused anything from being teased by classmates to being killed by an irate mob.

Nationalistic Consumerism in Contemporary China

Where did this continual appropriation and expansion of the movement lead? The ultimate proof that Chinese capitalists did not control the movement lies outside the scope of the present inquiry. Yet it seems possible to suggest, as I do throughout the book, that the movement helped legitimize the abolition of private enterprise in China—in other words, that the Communists used the logic of the movement to justify the destruction of capitalism in China. If products were national, why should profits be private? If consumers within the nation as a whole should buy Chinese products, why should the wealth derived from patriotic purchases go to particular citizens of that nation?

Perhaps the CCP was one more interest group legitimizing nationalistic consumerism for its own purposes. In the 1950s, in the name of the new People's Republic, the Communist government pressured Chinese business owners to demonstrate their patriotism by donating their enterprises to the state. In 1956, capitalism was formally abolished. But "fear of the Communists" is inadequate to explain the speed, thoroughness, and popular acceptance of the state's takeover.

The movement never ended. As the opening of this chapter suggests, elements of the National Products Movement agenda—judging national wealth and power through production and assessing patriotism through consumption—continue to this day. Indeed, its themes continue to shape interactions between Chinese, their material culture, and their sense of nation. The relevance of nationalistic consumption did not die with Mao Zedong in 1976, although the irony of China voluntarily ceding tariff autonomy by joining the World Trade Organization (WTO) suggests so. Nevertheless, it is doubtful that a treaty alone can undo the deep connection between China's nationalism and its consumer culture. Rather than eliminating the issue of nationalistic consumption, China's entry into the WTO may reinvigorate it. China may open itself to international trade in the short term, but what will happen if China stops running massive trade surpluses? And how will Chinese react when the WTO demands lower tariffs and the abolition of informal restrictions on foreign management and control?

New interest groups will embrace the notion of nationalistic consumption for their own reasons. As tariffs decline and less expensive imports again threaten Chinese enterprises, the plight of millions of workers at state-owned enterprises undoubtedly will be invoked to attack imports and foreign capital. Indeed, there are already outspoken Chinese critics of the nation's growing international capitalist relations (Fewsmith 2001). Nor is this criticism directed solely at traditional imported commodities. Cultural goods have come under attack as undermining domestic industries. Dai Jinhua 戴錦華, a well-known Beijing University professor and cultural critic, for instance, bemoans the "invasion of Hollywood blockbusters," which "have dealt a destructive blow to the home film industry" (Jin Bo 2002). Likewise, a new generation of students continues to invoke the language of nationalistic consumption, as did those protesting the U.S. bombing of the Chinese embassy in Belgrade in 1999, with poems that include lines such as "Resist America Beginning with Cola, Attack McDonald's, Storm K.F.C." (Rosenthal 1999). Plans for a boycott directed against American companies active in China soon fizzled (Watson 2000). However, the attempt itself renewed the central place of nationalism in China's consumer culture.

Reference Matter

Bibliography

Abend, Hallett Edward. 1943. *My Life in China, 1926–1941*. New York: Harcourt, Brace & Co.

Abend, Hallett Edward, and Anthony J. Billingham. 1936. *Can China Survive?* New York: Washburn.

Adedeji, Adebayo, ed. 1981. *Indigenization of African Economies*. New York: Africana Publishing Co.

Adshead, Samuel Adrian M. 1997. *Material Culture in Europe and China, 1400–1800: The Rise of Consumerism*. New York: St. Martin's Press.

"Aiyong guohuo fengqi zhi puji" (The spread of an atmosphere of cherishing national products). 1932. *Shangye zazhi* 5, no. 10 (Feb. 1932).

Alford, William P. 1995. *To Steal a Book Is an Elegant Offense: Intellectual Property Law in Chinese Civilization*. Stanford: Stanford University Press.

Allen, G. C., and A. G. Donnithorne. 1954. *Western Enterprise in Far Eastern Economic Development: China and Japan*. New York: Macmillan.

Allman, Norwood F. 1924. *Handbook on the Protection of Trade-marks, Patents, Copyrights, and Trade-names in China*. Shanghai: Kelly & Walsh.

Anderson, Benedict R. 1983. *Imagined Communities: Reflections on the Origin and Spread of Nationalism*. London: Verso.

Appadurai, Arjun. 1986a. "Introduction: Commodities and the Politics of Things." In Appadurai 1986b: 3–63.

Appadurai, Arjun, ed. 1986b. *The Social Life of Things: Commodities in Cultural Perspective*. Cambridge, Eng.: Cambridge University Press.

Atwell, William S. 1977. "Notes on Silver, Foreign Trade, and the Late Ming Economy." *Ch'ing-shih wen-t'i* 3, no. 8: 1–33.

Auslander, Leora. 1996. "The Gendering of Consumer Practices in Nineteenth-Century France." In de Grazia and Furlough 1996: 79–112.

Ayers, William. 1971. *Chang Chih-tung and Educational Reform in China*. Cambridge, Mass.: Harvard University Press.

Ba Ling. 1934*a*. "Funü guohuo nianzhong zhi fuzhuang wenti" (The clothing problem in the context of the Women's National Products Year). *Jilian huikan* 92 (Apr. 1): 13.

———. 1934*b*. "Fuzhuang de helihua" (The rationalization of clothing). *Jilian huikan* 92 (Apr. 1): 15–16.

———. 1934*c*. "Zenyang song liwu?" (How to give a present). *Jilian huikan* 98 (July 1): 15–17.

Bai Chenqun, ed. 1933. *Guohuo jian* (National products). Beiping: Beiping gejie tichang guohuo yundong weiyuanhui.

Bailey, Paul J. 1998. *Strengthen the Country and Enrich the People: The Reform Writings of Ma Jianzhong (1848–1900)*. Richmond, Eng.: Curzon.

Balabkins, Nicholas. 1982. *Indigenization and Economic Development: The Nigerian Experience*. Greenwich, Conn.: JAI Press.

Ball, J. Dyer. 1911. *The Chinese at Home*. London: Religious Tract Society.

———. 1925. *Things Chinese; Or, Notes Connected with China*. 5th ed. Shanghai: Kelly & Walsh.

Bao Tianxiao. 1973. *Yi shi zhu xing de bainian bianqian* (One hundred years of change in food, clothing, housing, and travel). Hong Kong: Dahua chubanshe.

Bard, Emile. 1905. *Chinese Life in Town and Country*. Trans. H. Twitchell. New York: G. P. Putnam's Sons.

Barkai, Avraham. 1989. *From Boycott to Annihilation: The Economic Struggle of German Jews, 1933–1943*. Hanover, N.H.: University Press of New England.

Barnard, Malcolm. 1996. *Fashion as Communication*. New York: Routledge.

Barnett, Robert W. 1941. *Economic Shanghai: Hostage to Politics*. New York: Institute of Pacific Relations.

Barthes, Roland. 1972. *Mythologies*. New York: Hill & Wang.

———. 1977. *Image, Music, Text*. New York: Hill & Wang.

Baudrillard, Jean. 1998. *The Consumer Society: Myths and Structures*. London: Sage.

Bauman, Zygmunt. 1988. *Freedom*. Minneapolis: University of Minnesota Press.

Bayly, C.A. 1986. "The Origins of Swadeshi (Home Industry): Cloth and Indian Society, 1700–1930." In Appadurai 1986*b*: 285–321.

Bays, Daniel H. 1978. *China Enters the Twentieth Century: Chang Chih-tung and the Issues of a New Age, 1895–1909*. Ann Arbor: University of Michigan Press.

Beahan, Charlotte L. 1975. "Feminism and Nationalism in the Chinese Women's Press, 1902–1911." *Modern China* 1, no. 4: 379–416.

———. 1981. "In the Public Eye: Women in Early Twentieth-Century China." In *Women in China: Current Directions in Historical Scholarship*, ed. R. W. L. Guisso and S. Johannesen, 215–38. Youngstown, N.Y.: Philo Press.

Bean, Susan S. 1989. "Gandhi and Khadi, the Fabric of Indian Independence." In *Cloth and the Human Experience*, ed. Annette B. Weiner and Jane Schneider, 355–76. Washington, D.C.: Smithsonian Institution Press.

Bell-Fialkoff, Andrew. 1993. "A Brief History of Ethnic Cleansing." *Foreign Affairs* 72, no. 3: 110–30.

Belsky, Richard D. 1992. "Bones of Contention: The Siming Gongsuo Riots of 1874 and 1898." *Papers on Chinese History* 1: 56–73.

"Ben guan zuijin yinian zhong zhi gongzuo gaikuang" (An overview of the work of our museum over the previous year). 1931. In Wang Keyou 1931: 5–11.

Benjamin, Walter. 1979 [1935]. "Paris, Capital of the Nineteenth Century." In idem, *Reflections*, ed. P. Demetz. New York: Harcourt, Brace, Jovanovich.

Bennett, Tony. 1995. *The Birth of the Museum*. New York: Routledge.

Benson, Carlton. 1999. "Consumers Are Also Soldiers: Subversive Songs from Nanjing Road During the New Life Movement." In Cochran 1999*b*: 91–132.

"Ben suo gezhong chenlie pin linian xiao zhang mian" (A chart of the rise and fall of each kind of displayed item in this hall by year). 1936. In SSC 1936.

"Ben suo lici juban zhanlanhui zhi jingguo" (The course of each exhibition hosted by this hall). 1936. In SSC 1936.

Bergère, Marie-Claire. 1986. *The Golden Age of the Chinese Bourgeoisie, 1911–1937*. Cambridge, Eng.: Cambridge University Press.

Billig, Michael. 1995. *Banal Nationalism*. London: Sage.

"Bimu hou zhi Zhonghua guohuo zhanlanhui" (After the close of the Chinese National Products Exhibition). 1929. SB, Jan. 4: 13–14.

Blue, Gregory. 2000. "Opium for China: The British Connection." In Brook and Wakabayashi 2000*b*: 31–54.

Bocock, R. 1993. *Consumption*. London: Routledge.

Bodde, Derk, ed. 1936. *Annual Customs and Festivals in Peking*. Beiping: Henri Vetch.

Booker, Edna Lee. 1940. *News Is My Job: A Correspondent in War-Torn China*. New York: Macmillan.

Boorman, Howard L., and Richard C. Howard, eds. 1967–71. *Biographical Dictionary of Republican China*. 4 vols. New York: Columbia University Press.

Boorstin, Daniel J. 1973. *The Americans: The Democratic Experience*. New York: Random House.

Borthwick, Sally. 1983. *Education and Social Change in China: The Beginnings of the Modern Era*. Stanford: Hoover Institution Press.

Bourdieu, Pierre. 1977. *Outline of a Theory of Practice*. New York: Cambridge University Press.

———. 1984. *Distinction: A Social Critique of the Judgement of Taste*. Cambridge, Mass.: Harvard University Press.

Bourne, Kenneth; Donald Cameron Watt; and Michael Partridge, eds. 1996. *British Documents on Foreign Affairs—Reports and Papers from the Foreign Office Confidential Print*. Frederick, Md.: University Publications of America.

Breen, T. H. 1988. "'Baubles of Britain': The American and Consumer Revolutions of the Eighteenth Century." *Past and Present* 119: 73–104.

A Brief Sketch of the New Life Movement. 1937. Hankou: New Life Movement Headquarters.

Brook, Timothy. 1998. *The Confusions of Pleasure: Commerce and Culture in Ming China*. Berkeley: University of California Press.

Brook, Timothy, and Bob Tadashi Wakabayashi. 2000a. "Introduction: Opium's History in China." In Brook and Wakabayashi 2000b: 1–27.

Brook, Timothy, and Bob Tadashi Wakabayashi, eds. 2000b. *Opium Regimes: China, Britain, and Japan, 1839–1952*. Berkeley: University of California Press.

Brown, Arthur J. *The Chinese Revolution*. New York: Student Volunteer Movement, 1912.

Brown, Judith M. 1989. *Gandhi: Prisoner of Hope*. New Haven: Yale University Press.

Burke, Timothy. 1996. *Lifebuoy Men, Lux Women: Commodification, Consumption, and Cleanliness in Modern Zimbabwe*. Durham, N.C.: Duke University Press.

Bush, Richard C. 1982. *The Politics of Cotton Textiles in Kuomintang China, 1927–37*. New York: Garland Publishing.

Cai Qian. 1936. *Jin ershi nian lai zhi Zhong Ri maoyi ji qi zhuyao shangpin* (Sino-Japanese trade and trade commodities in the past twenty years [1912–1931]). Shanghai: Shangwu yinshu guan.

"Caiyong xialing yongping ge" (The "make use of summer articles" song). 1934. *SB*, June 1.

"Canjia zhanlanhui zhi yongyue" (Enthusiasm for participating in the exhibition). 1928. *SB*, Sept. 1: 13.

Cao Muguan. 1928. "Lijie guohuo zhanlanhui zhi jinguo" (The ins and outs of successive national product exhibitions). In GSB 1928.

Cao Muguan, ed. 1925. *Shanghai dui Ri waijiao shimin dahui erzhou nian huikan* (Second anniversary volume of the Shanghai Citizens Association on Sino-Japanese Relations). Shanghai: privately published.

Carlson, Ellsworth C. 1957. *The Kaiping Mine (1877–1912)*. Cambridge, Mass.: Harvard University Press.

Catano, James V. 2001. *Ragged Dicks: Masculinity, Steel, and the Rhetoric of the Self-Made Man*. Carbondale: Southern Illinois University Press.

Chan, F. Gilbert, ed. 1981. *Nationalism in East Asia: An Annotated Bibliography of Selected Works*. New York: Garland.

Chan, Wellington K. K. 1977. *Merchants, Mandarins, and Modern Enterprise in Late Ch'ing China*. Cambridge, Mass.: Harvard University Press.

———. 1978. "Government, Merchants and Industry to 1911." In *The Cambridge History of China*, vol. 11, *Late Ch'ing, 1800–1911, Part 2*, ed. J. K. Fairbank and K.-C. Liu, 416–62. New York: Cambridge University Press.

———. 1999. "Selling Goods and Promoting a New Commercial Culture: The Four Premier Department Stores on Nanjing Road, 1917–1937." In Cochran 1999b: 19–36.

Chandra, Bipan. 1966. *The Rise and Growth of Economic Nationalism in India: Economic Policies of Indian National Leadership, 1880–1905*. New Delhi: People's Publishing House.

Chang, Chia-ao. 1943. *China's Struggle for Railroad Development*. New York: John Day Co.

Chang, Eileen. 1943. "Chinese Life and Fashions." *XXth Century* 4, no. 1: 54–61.

Chang, Hsin-pao. 1964. *Commissioner Lin and the Opium War*. Cambridge, Mass.: Harvard University Press.

Chang, John K. 1969. *Industrial Development in Pre-Communist China: A Quantitative Analysis*. Chicago: Aldine Publishing Co.

"Changlian hui canjia Xihu bolanhui" (Association of National Products Manufacturers to visit West Lake Exhibition). 1928. *SB*, or Dec. 26: 14.

Chao, Buwei Yang, and Yuen Ren Chao. 1947. *Autobiography of a Chinese Woman, Buwei Yang Chao*. New York: John Day Co.

Chao, Jonathan T'ien-en. 1986. "The Chinese Indigenous Church Movement, 1919–1927: A Protestant Response to the Anti-Christian Movements in Modern China." Ph.D. diss., University of Pennsylvania.

Chen, Joseph T. 1971. *The May Fourth Movement in Shanghai: The Making of a Social Movement in Modern China*. Leiden: Brill.

Ch'en Li-fu. 1994. *The Storm Clouds Clear over China: The Memoir of Ch'en Li-fu, 1900–1993*. Trans. S. H. Chang and R. H. Myers. Stanford: Hoover Institution Press.

Chen, Walter Hanming. 1937. *The New Life Movement*. Nanjing: Council of International Affairs.

Chen Zhen, ed. 1957–61. *Zhongguo jindai gongye shi ziliao* (Materials on the history of modern Chinese industries). 4 vols. Beijing: Sanlian chubanshe.

Chen Zhengqing. 1987. "Shanghai Zhongguo guohuo gongsi zai zhanshi de houfang" (On the China National Products Company of Shanghai behind the frontlines during the Anti-Japanese War). *Dang'an yü lishi*: 64–71.

———. 1992. "Tianchu weijing chang de liushiwu nian" (65 years of the Heaven's Kitchen MSG Factory). In SSD 1992.

Chen Zhengshu. 1987. "Guohuo yuebao" (National products monthly). In *Xinhai geming shiqi qikan jieshao* (An introduction to periodicals of the 1911 Revolution era), ed. Zhongguo shehui kexue yuan, 5: 362–69. Beijing: Renmin chubanshe.

Chen Zhenyi. 1928. *Tichang guohuo lun* (An essay on the promotion of national products). Shanghai: Taipingyang shudian.

Chen, Zhongping. 1998. "Business and Politics: Chinese Chambers of Commerce in the Lower Yangtze Region, 1902–1912," Ph.D. diss., University of Hawai'i.

Chenbao, ed. 1933. *Shanghai zhi gongye* (The industry of Shanghai). Shanghai: Chenbao.

Cheng Heqiu. 1934. "Rihuo qin Hua zhi xin zhanlüe" (The new strategy for Japanese products' invasion of China). *Jilian huikan* 107 (Nov. 15): 11–15.

Cheng, Lin. 1935. *The Chinese Railways: A Historical Survey.* Shanghai: China United Press.

Cheng, Nien. 1986. *Life and Death in Shanghai.* New York: Grove Press.

Cheng, Pei-kai, and Michael Elliot Lestz, with Jonathan D. Spence. 1998. *The Search for Modern China: A Documentary Collection.* New York: Norton.

Cheng Shouzhong and Zhou Jiezhi. 1996. "Guohuo yundong zhong de Shanghai jizhi guohuo gongchang lianhehui" (The Association of Mechanized National Products Manufacturers in the National Products Movement). In Pan Junxiang 1996c: 458–67.

Cheng, Weikun. 1998. "Politics of the Queue: Agitation and Resistance in the Beginning and End of Qing China." In *Hair: Its Power and Meaning in Asian Cultures,* ed. A. Hiltebeitel and B. D. Miller, 123–42. Albany: State University of New York Press.

Ch'i, Hsi-sheng. 1976. *Warlord Politics in China, 1916–1928.* Stanford: Stanford University Press.

Chi, Madeleine. 1970. *China Diplomacy, 1914–1918.* Cambridge, Mass.: Harvard University Press.

Chiang Kai-shek. 1934. *Outline of the New Life Movement.* Trans. Madame Chiang Kai-shek. Nanchang, Jiangxi: Association for the Promotion of the New Life Movement.

"Chongxin qiyao hou zhi canguan renshu tongji biao" (A statistical table of visitors since the re-opening). 1923. In Shanghai zong shanghui, Shanghai shangpin chenliesuo.

"Chōsho, taisaku ikken, chinjō-sho, oyobi kō-shi dantai hōkoku, kyūmin kyūsai, zatsu" (Miscellaneous documents relating to research papers, opinions concerning countermeasures, petitions, the reports of public and private organizations, measures for the relief of the distressed, etc.). Gaimushō. Meiji–Taishō Documents, file 3.3.8.6–2.

"Choushe gedi guohuo gongsi zhi wojian" (My opinion on preparations to establish national product stores everywhere). 1934. *SB*, Feb. 4.

Chow, Kai-wing. 1997. "Imagining Boundaries of Blood: Zhang Binglin and the Invention of the Han 'Race' in Modern China." In *The Construction of Racial Identi-*

ties in China and Japan, ed. Frank Dikötter, 34–52. Honolulu: University of Hawai'i Press.

———. 2001. "Narrating Nation, Race, and National Culture: Imagining the Hanzu Identity in Modern China." In *Constructing Nationhood in Modern East Asia*, ed. Kai-wing Chow, Kevin Michael Doak, and Poshek Fu, 47–83. Ann Arbor: University of Michigan Press.

Chow Tse-tsung. 1960. *The May Fourth Movement: Intellectual Revolution in Modern China*. Cambridge, Mass.: Harvard University Press.

Chu, Samuel C. 1980. "The New Life Movement Before the Sino-Japanese Conflict: A Reflection of Kuomintang Limitations in Thought and Action." In *China at the Crossroads: Nationalists and Communists, 1927–1949*, ed. F. G. Chan, 37–68. Boulder: Westview Press.

Ch'ü, T'ung-tsu. 1961. *Law and Society in Traditional China*. Paris: Mouton.

Clammer, J. R. 1997. *Contemporary Urban Japan: A Sociology of Consumption*. Oxford: Blackwell Publishers.

Clarke, Alison J. 1999. *Tupperware: The Promise of Plastic in 1950s America*. Washington, D.C.: Smithsonian Institution Press.

Clunas, Craig. 1991. *Superfluous Things: Material Culture and Social Status in Early Modern China*. Urbana: University of Illinois.

Coble, Parks M., Jr. 1980. *The Shanghai Capitalists and the Nationalist Government, 1927–1937*. Cambridge, Mass.: Harvard University, Council on East Asian Studies.

———. 1991. *Facing Japan: Chinese Politics and Japanese Imperialism, 1931–1937*. Cambridge, Mass.: Harvard University, Council on East Asian Studies.

Cochran, Sherman. 1980. *Big Business in China: Sino-Foreign Rivalry in the Cigarette Industry, 1890–1930*. Cambridge, Mass.: Harvard University Press.

———. 1999. "Transnational Origins of Advertising in Early Twentieth-Century China." In Cochran 1999b: 37–58.

———. 2000. *Encountering Chinese Networks: Western, Japanese, and Chinese Corporations in China, 1880–1937*. Berkeley: University of California Press.

Cochran, Sherman, ed. 1999b. *Inventing Nanjing Road: Commercial Culture in Shanghai, 1900–1945*. Ithaca, N.Y.: Cornell University, East Asia Program.

Cochran, Sherman, and Hsieh, Andrew C. K., with Janis Cochran. 1983. *One Day in China: May 21, 1936*. New Haven: Yale University Press.

Cohen, Lizabeth. 1990. *Making a New Deal: Industrial Workers in Chicago, 1919–1939*. Cambridge, Eng.: Cambridge University Press.

Cohen, Myron L. 1994. "Being Chinese: The Peripheralization of Tradition and Identity." In *The Living Tree: The Changing Meaning of Being Chinese Today*, ed. Wei-ming Tu, 88–108. Stanford: Stanford University Press.

Cohen, Paul A. 1963. *China and Christianity: The Missionary Movement and the Growth of Chinese Antiforeignism, 1860–1870.* Cambridge, Mass.: Harvard University Press.

——. 1987. *Between Tradition and Modernity: Wang T'ao and Reform in Late Ch'ing China.* Cambridge, Mass.: Harvard University Press.

Cohn, Bernard S. 1989. "Cloth, Clothes, and Colonialism: India in the Nineteenth Century." In *Cloth and the Human Experience,* ed. Annette B. Weiner and Jane Schneider, 303–53. Washington, D.C.: Smithsonian Institution Press.

Collins, Leslie. 1976. "The New Woman: A Pyschohistorical Study of the Chinese Feminist Movement from 1900 to the Present." Ph.D. diss., Yale University.

Confucius. 1994. *Lunyu* (Analects of Confucius). Beijing: Huayu jiaoxue chubanshe.

Conger, Sarah Pike. 1909. *Letters from China, with Particular Reference to the Empress Dowager and the Women of China.* London: Hodder & Stoughton.

"Cong guohuo shengzhong shuodao ertong wanju" (From hearing about national products to speaking of children's toys). 1933. *SB,* May 18.

Constantine, Stephan. 1981. "The Buy British Campaign of 1931." *Journal of Advertising History* 10, no. 1: 44–59.

Corrigan, Peter. 1997. *The Sociology of Consumption.* London: Sage Publications.

Crapol, Edward P. 1973. *America for Americans: Economic Nationalism and Anglophobia in the Late Nineteenth Century.* Westport, Conn.: Greenwood Press.

CRDS (Central Records of the U.S. Department of State relating to the Internal Affairs of China, 1910–1929). "Record Group 59." Microfilm from the U.S. National Archives.

Creighton, Millie R. 1991. "Maintaining Cultural Boundaries in Retailing: How Japanese Department Stores Domesticate 'Things Foreign.'" *Modern Asian Studies* 25, no. 4: 675–709.

Cross, Gary S. 2000. *An All-Consuming Century: Why Commercialism Won in Modern America.* New York: Columbia University Press.

Crossley, Pamela Kyle. 1999. *A Translucent Mirror: History and Identity in Qing Imperial Ideology.* Berkeley: University of California Press.

Crow, Carl. 1937. *Four Hundred Million Customers.* New York: Harper.

——. 1944. *China Takes Her Place.* New York: Harper.

CWR. Appeared under various names: *Millard's Review of the Far East,* 1917–May 28, 1921; *The Weekly Review of the Far East,* June 4, 1921–July 1, 1922; *The Weekly Review,* July 8, 1922–June 16, 1923; *The China Weekly Review,* June 23, 1923–Apr. 7, 1947. Shanghai.

Dagong bao. Daily. Tianjin, 1925–37.

Dai Zheming. 1996. "Hunan sheng guohuo chenlieguan" (Hunan Provincial National Products Museum). Reprinted in Pan Junxiang 1996c: 420–22.

Dalby, Liza. 1993. *Kimono.* New Haven: Yale University Press.

Dal Lago, Francesca. 2000. "Crossed Legs in 1930s Shanghai: How 'Modern' the Modern Woman?" *East Asian History* 19: 103–44.

Davidson, James N. 1998. *Courtesans & Fishcakes: The Consuming Passions of Classical Athens*. New York: St. Martin's Press.

Davis, Deborah, ed. 2000. *The Consumer Revolution in Urban China*. Berkeley: University of California Press.

Davis, Fred. 1992. *Fashion, Culture, and Identity*. Chicago: University of Chicago.

Daxia zhoubao. Weekly. Shanghai, 1935.

Debord, Guy. 1994. *The Society of the Spectacle*. New York: Zone Books.

de Cauter, Lieven. 1993. "The Panoramic Ecstasy: On World Exhibitions and the Disintegration of Experience." *Theory, Culture & Society* 10: 1–23.

Deetz, James. 1996. *In Small Things Forgotten: An Archaeology of Early American Life*. Rev. and exp. ed. New York: Anchor Books.

DeFrancis, John. 1950. *Nationalism and Language Reform in China*. Princeton: Princeton University Press.

de Grazia, Victoria. 1996. "Introduction." In de Grazia and Furlough 1996: 1–10.

de Grazia, Victoria, and Ellen Furlough, eds. 1996. *The Sex of Things: Gender and Consumption in Historical Perspective*. Berkeley: University of California.

Denby, Charles. 1906. *China and Her People*. Boston: L. C. Page & Co.

Dennerline, Jerry. 1981. *The Chia-ting Loyalists: Confucian Leadership and Social Change in Seventeenth-Century China*. New Haven: Yale University Press.

Dernberger, Robert. 1975. "The Role of the Foreigner in China's Economic Development. In *China's Modern Economy in Historical Perspective*, ed. D. H. Perkins, 19–47. Stanford: Stanford University Press.

Des Forges, Alexander. 2000. "Opium/Leisure/Shanghai: Urban Economies of Consumption." In Brook and Wakabayashi 2000b: 167–85.

Dickinson, Frederick R. 1999. *War and National Reinvention: Japan in the Great War, 1914–1919*. Cambridge, Mass.: Harvard University Asia Center.

Dickinson, Gary, and Linda Wrigglesworth. 2000. *Imperial Wardrobe*. Berkeley: Ten Speed Press.

Dikötter, Frank. 1992. *The Discourse of Race in Modern China*. Stanford: Stanford University Press.

———. 1995. *Sex, Culture, and Modernity in China: Medical Science and the Construction of Sexual Identities in the Early Republican Period*. Honolulu: University of Hawai'i Press.

———. 1997. *The Construction of Racial Identities in China and Japan: Historical and Contemporary Perspectives*. Honolulu: University of Hawai'i Press.

———. 1998. *Imperfect Conceptions: Medical Knowledge, Birth Defects, and Eugenics in China*. New York: Columbia University Press.

Ding Lanjun and Yu Zuofeng, eds. 1993. *Wu Tingfang ji* (The collected writings of Wu Tingfang). Beijing: Zhonghua shuju.

Ding Shouhe and Yin Xuyi. 1979. *Cong Wusi qimeng yundong dao Makesi zhuyi de chuanbo* (From the May Fourth Movement to the spread of Marxism). Beijing: Sanlian shudian.

Dingle, Edwin J., and F. L. Pratt, eds. 1921. *Far Eastern Products Manual.* Shanghai: Far Eastern Geographical Establishment.

Dirlik, Arif. 1975. "The Ideological Foundations of the New Life Movement: A Study in Counterrevolution." *Journal of Asian Studies* 34, no. 4: 945–80.

"Diyi ci zhanlanhui zhi jieshu" (A summary of the first exhibition). 1923. In Shanghai zong shanghui, Shanghai shangpin chenliesuo 1923: 5–6.

Diyi Jiaotong daxue fan Ri yundong weiyuanhui, Jingji juejiao bu, ed. 1928. *Guohuo Rihuo duizhao lu* (A comparison of national products and Japanese products). Shanghai.

Dollar, Robert. 1912. *Private Diary of Robert Dollar on His Recent Visits to China.* San Francisco: W. S. Van Gott & Co.

Dong Keren. 1930. "Shanghai shi guohuo chenlie yingyou zhi sheshi" (The facilities that the Shanghai Municipal National Products Museum should have). In *Shanghai shi guohuo chenlie guan niankan*, 1–4. Shanghai: Shanghai shi guohuo chenlie guan.

Dongfang zazhi (Eastern miscellany). Monthly (1904–19); semi-monthly, 1920–47. Shanghai, 1904–48.

Du Xuncheng. 1991. *Minzu zibenzhuyi yu jiu Zhongguo zhengfu* (National capitalism and the old Chinese government). Shanghai: Shanghai shehui kexue yuan chubanshe.

"Duanjie han guohuo" (The Dragon Boat Festival and national products). 1934. *SB*, June 24.

Duara, Prasenjit. 1995. *Rescuing History from the Nation: Questioning Narratives of Modern China.* Chicago: University of Chicago Press.

———. 1998. "The Regime of Authenticity: Timelessness, Gender, and National History in Modern China." *History and Theory* 37, no. 3: 287–308.

"Duiyu funümen jiju ni'er zhonggao" (To women, a few sentences of good advice that may be hard to swallow). 1934. *SB*, May 10.

Dunstan, Helen. 1996. *Conflicting Counsels to Confuse the Age: A Documentary Study of Political Economy in Qing China, 1644–1840.* Ann Arbor: University of Michigan, Center for Chinese Studies.

Eastman, Lloyd E. 1974. *The Abortive Revolution: China Under Nationalist Rule, 1927–1937.* Cambridge, Mass.: Harvard University, Council on East Asian Studies.

————. 1976. "The Kuomintang in the 1930s." In *The Limits of Change: Essays on Conservative Alternatives in Republican China*, ed. C. Furth, 191–210. Cambridge, Mass.: Harvard University Press.

————. 1984. "New Insights into the Nature of the Nationalist Regime." *Chinese Republican Studies Newsletter* 9, no. 2: 8–18.

Eckstein, Alexander. 1977. *China's Economic Revolution*. Cambridge, Eng.: Cambridge University Press.

Economic Yearbook of China. 1934–36. Shanghai: Ministry of Industry.

Edwards, Louise. 2000. "Policing the Modern Woman in Republican China." *Modern China* 26, no. 2: 115–47.

Elias, Norbert. 1994. *The Civilizing Process: The History of Manners and State Formation and Civilization*. Cambridge, Mass.: Blackwell.

"Ertong yu guohuo shizhuang" (Children and national product fashions). 1933. *SB*, May 18.

Esherick, Joseph. 1976. *Reform and Revolution in China: The 1911 Revolution in Hunan and Hubei*. Berkeley: University of California Press.

Ewen, Stuart, and Elizabeth Ewen. 1982. *Channels of Desire*. New York: McGraw-Hill.

"The Exhibition at Hangchow." 1928. *NCH*, May 12: 231.

Fan, Hong, and J. A. Mangan. 1995. "'Enlightenment' Aspirations in an Oriental Setting: Female Emancipation and Exercise in Early Twentieth-Century China." *International Journal of the History of Sport* 12, no. 3: 80–104.

Fang Xiantang. 1996. "1933 nian guohuo nian" (The 1933 National Products Year). In Pan Junxiang 1996c: 429–36.

Fang Xiantang, ed. 1989. *Shanghai jindai minzu juanyan gongye* (Shanghai's modern national cigarette industry). Shanghai: Shanghai shehui kexueyuan chubanshe.

Farjenel, Fernand. 1915. *Through the Chinese Revolution*. Trans. Margaret Vivian. London: Duckworth & Co.

Feng Yiyou, ed. 1996. *Lao xiangyan paizi* (Old cigarette cards). Shanghai: Shanghai huabao chubanshe.

FER. The Far Eastern Review. Monthly. Shanghai, 1904–41.

Feuerwerker, Albert. 1958. *China's Early Industrialization: Shen Hsuan-huai (1844–1916) and Mandarin Enterprise*. Cambridge, Mass.: Harvard University Press.

————. 1968. *History in Communist China*. Cambridge, Mass.: M.I.T. Press.

————. 1969. *The Chinese Economy, ca. 1870–1911*. Ann Arbor: University of Michigan, Center for Chinese Studies.

————. 1976. *The Foreign Establishment in China in the Early Twentieth Century*. Ann Arbor: University of Michigan, Center for Chinese Studies.

————. 1977. *Economic Trends in the Republic of China, 1912–1949*. Ann Arbor: University of Michigan, Center for Chinese Studies.

Feuerwerker, Albert, and S. Cheng. 1970. *Chinese Communist Studies of Modern Chinese History.* Cambridge, Mass.: Harvard University Press.

Fewsmith, Joseph. 1985. *Party, State, and Local Elites in Republican China: Merchant Organizations and Politics in Shanghai, 1890–1930.* Honolulu: University of Hawai'i Press.

————. 2001. "The Political and Social Implications of China's Accession to the WTO." *China Quarterly* 167: 573–91.

Field, Margaret. 1957. "The Chinese Boycott of 1905." *Harvard Papers on China* 2: 63–98.

Findling, John E., ed. 1990. *Historical Dictionary of World's Fairs and Exhibitions, 1851–1988.* New York: Greenwood Press.

Finkelstein, Joanne. 1996. *Fashion: An Introduction.* New York: New York University Press.

Fitzgerald, John. 1996. *Awakening China: Politics, Culture, and Class in the Nationalist Revolution.* Stanford: Stanford University Press.

Fogel, Joshua A. 1996. *The Literature of Travel in the Japanese Rediscovery of China, 1862–1945.* Stanford: Stanford University Press.

Fong, H. D. 1975. *Reminiscences of a Chinese Economist at 70.* Singapore: South Seas Press.

Forty, Adrian. 1986. *Objects of Desire.* New York: Pantheon Books.

Foster, Hal, ed. 1988. *Vision and Visuality.* Seattle: Bay Press.

Foster, John W. 1906. "The Chinese Boycott." *Atlantic Monthly* 97, no. 1: 118–27.

Foster, Robert John. 1995a. "Introduction: The Work of Nation Making." In *Nation Making: Emergent Identities in Postcolonial Melanesia,* ed. R. J. Foster, 1–30. Ann Arbor: University of Michigan Press.

————. 1995b. "Print Advertisements and Nation Making in Metropolitan Papua New Guinea." In *Nation Making: Emergent Identities in Postcolonial Melanesia,* ed. R. J. Foster, 151–81. Ann Arbor: University of Michigan Press.

Fox, Richard Wightman, and T. J. Jackson Lears. 1983. *The Culture of Consumption: Critical Essays in American History, 1880–1980.* New York: Pantheon.

Frank, Dana. 1999. *Buy American: The Untold Story of Economic Nationalism.* Boston: Beacon Press.

Frank, Thomas. 2000. *One Market Under God: Extreme Capitalism, Market Populism, and the End of Economic Democracy.* New York: Doubleday.

Friedman, Milton, and Rose D. Friedman. 1982. *Capitalism and Freedom.* Chicago: University of Chicago Press.

Friedman, Monroe. 1999. *Consumer Boycotts: Effecting Change Through the Marketplace and the Media.* New York: Routledge.

"Fu hui zhi tiaogui" (Regulations for attending the exhibition). 1915. *Guohuo yuebao* 2 (Sept. 9): 12–13.

Fujimoto Hirō and Kyōto daigaku, Jinbun kagaku kenkyūjo. 1983. *Nihon shinbun go-shi hōdō shiryō shūsei* (Collected materials from Japanese newspapers on the May Fourth Movement). Kyoto: Kyōto daigaku, Jinbun kagaku kenkyūjo.

Funü banyue kan. Semi-monthly. Shanghai, 1938.

"Funü de guohuo biaoyu" (Women's national products slogans). 1935. *SB*, Feb. 21.

"Funü duiyu guohuonian de zeren" (Women's responsibilty to National Products Year). 1933. *SB*, Mar. 9.

Funü gongming yuebao. Monthly. Chongqing, 1934–36.

"Funü guohuo hui choushe Guangzhou fenhui" (The Women's National Products Association prepares to establish a Guangzhou branch). 1930. *Funü gongming* 34 (Aug.): 44.

"Funü guohuo hui zu guohuo kaocha tuan" (The Women's National Products Association organizes an inspection group). 1934. *Guohuo banyue kan* 8 (Apr. 1): 24.

"Funü guohuo nian huichangwei biaoshi" (Feelings of a member of the Women's National Products Year Committee). 1934. *SB*, Aug. 13.

"Funü guohuo nian hui chou she lanshi shangchang" (The Woman's National Products Year group plans to establish temporary markets). 1934. *Guohuo banyue kan* 11 (May 15): 30.

"Funü guohuo nian hui zhi shixi shangchang kaimu" (The opening of a market by a Women's National Products Year group in west Shanghai). 1934. *Guohuo banyue kan* 12 (June 1): 24–25.

"Funü guohuo nian jinri juxing qiche youxing" (The Women's National Products Year hosts an automobile parade today). 1934. *SB*, Jan. 1.

"Funü guohuo nian qiche youxing canjia yongyue" (Energetic participation in the Women's National Products Year automobile parade). 1933. *SB*, Dec. 29.

"Funü guohuo nian yu huazhuangpin" (The Women's National Products Year and cosmetics). 1934. *SB*, Feb. 1.

"Funü guohuo nian yundong weiyuanhui" (The Women's National Products Year movement committee). 1934. *Guohuo yuebao* 1, no. 8 (Aug.): 52–53.

"Funü guohuo nian zai qiuji" (The Women's National Products Year in the autumn). 1934. *SB*, Oct. 4.

"Funü guohuo nian zhi yingyou gongzuo" (Work that should be done in the Women's National Products Year). 1934. *SB*, Jan. 11.

"Funü guohuo nianzhong zhi chouhuo qingxiao wenti" (The problem of the dumping of enemy products during the Women's National Products Year). 1934. *SB*, Feb. 8.

"Funü guohuo nianzhong zhi liangdian xiwang" (Two hopes for the Women's National Products Year). 1934. *SB*, Mar. 22.

"Funü guohuo xuanchuan dahui" (Women's national products dissemination rally). 1934. *SB*, Jan. 17.

"Funü guohuo yundong dahui" (Women's National Products Movement rally). 1934. *SB*, Jan. 12.

"Funüjie yu guohuo" (Women's Day and national products). 1934. *SB*, Mar. 8.

"Funüjie zhi tuixing guohuo tan" (A discussion of the marketing of national products by women's circles). 1934. *SB*, July 12.

"Funümen! Xingba!" (Women! Wake up!). 1934. *SB*, May 3.

"Funü shou ma nian" (Women-Get-Cursed Year). 1934. *SB*, Jan. 25.

"Funü tuanti" (The women's group). 1934. *SB*, Apr. 4.

"Funü tuanti qingzhu dahui" (The women's group celebration rally). 1934. *SB*, Apr. 5.

"Funü yu dongling yongpin" (Women and winter articles). 1933. *SB*, Dec. 14.

"Funü yu zhuangjin" (Women and clothing expenses). 1934. *Jilian huikan* 92 (Apr. 1): 6–7.

Funü zazhi. Monthly. Shanghai, 1915–31.

Furen huabao. Monthly. Shanghai, 1933–36.

"Furen xiaojie, ni wangjile ma?" (Ladies, have you forgotten?). 1934. *SB*, Feb. 22.

Furuya, Keiji. 1981. *Chiang Kai-shek: His Life and Times*. Trans. C. Zhang. Abridged English ed. New York: St. John's University.

"Fuyu: Neizheng buzhang tichang guohuo zhi juti banfa" (Appendix: The Minister of the Interior's concrete ways to promote national products). 1928. *Shangye yuebao* 8, no. 9 (Sept.): 3–7.

"Fuzhuang jiuguo" (Saving the nation with clothing). 1933. *Jilian huikan* 71 (5.15): 29–33.

"Gailiang ertong fuzhuang tan" (A discussion on improving children's clothing). 1934. *Jilian huikan* 92 (Apr. 1): 37–39.

Gaimushō. 1937. *Shina ni okeru kō-Nichi dantai to sono katsudō* (Anti-Japanese organizations and their activities in China). Tokyo: Gaimushō.

Galbraith, John Kenneth. 1990. *A Tenured Professor: A Novel*. Boston: Houghton Mifflin.

Gamble, Sidney D. 1921. *Peking: A Social Survey*. New York: George H. Doran Co.

Gan Chunquan. "Hunying han songli" (Weddings and giving presents). 1934. *Jilian huikan* 98 (July 1): 36–37.

Gan Gu, ed. 1987. *Shanghai bainian mingchang laodian* (A hundred years of famous companies and old stores of Shanghai). Shanghai: Shanghai wenhua chubanshe.

Gao Shi. 1996. "Tianzihao xitong chanpin yu waihuo de douzheng" (The struggle between the products of the Heaven Conglomerate and foreign products). In Pan Junxiang 1996c: 118–21.

Gao Yuan. 1987. *Born Red: A Chronicle of the Cultural Revolution*. Stanford: Stanford University Press.

Gardella, Robert. 1994. *Harvesting Mountains: Fujian and the China Tea Trade, 1757–1937*. Berkeley: University of California Press.

Garrett, Shirley S. 1970. *Social Reformers in Urban China: The Chinese Y.M.C.A., 1895–1926*. Cambridge, Mass.: Harvard University Press.

Garrett, Valery M. 1987. *Traditional Chinese Clothing*. Hong Kong: Oxford University Press.

———. 1990. *Mandarin Squares: Mandarins and Their Insignia*. Hong Kong: Oxford University Press.

———. 1994. *Chinese Clothing: An Illustrated Guide*. Hong Kong: Oxford University Press.

———. 1995. "The Cheung Sam—Its Rise and Fall." *Costume* 29: 88–94.

"Gedi funü jiji tichang guohuo" (Women throughout China actively promote national products). 1934. *Funü gongming yuebao* 3, no. 11: 52–53.

Geisert, Bradley Kent. 1979. "Power and Society: The Kuomintang and Local Elites in Kiangsu Province, China, 1924–1937." Ph.D. diss., University of Virginia.

———. 1982. "Toward a Pluralist Model of KMT Rule." *Chinese Republican Studies Newsletter* 7, no. 2: 1–10.

"Geming hou zhi guohuo yundong" (The National Products Movement since the Revolution). 1928. *SB*, Feb. 24.

Gibbs-Smith, C. H. 1981. *The Great Exhibition of 1851*. London: Her Majesty's Stationery Office.

Gilfoyle, Timothy J. 1999. "Prostitutes in History: From Parables of Pornography to Metaphors of Modernity." *American Historical Review* 104, no. 1: 117–41.

Gilmartin, Christina Kelly. 1994. "Gender, Political Culture, and Women's Mobilization in the Chinese Nationalist Revolution, 1924–1927." In Gilmartin et al. 1994: 195–225.

———. 1995. *Engendering the Chinese Revolution: Radical Women, Communist Politics, and Mass Movements in the 1920s*. Berkeley: University of California Press.

Gilmartin, Christina Kelly; Gail Hershatter; Lisa Rofel; and Tyrene White, eds. 1994. *Engendering China: Women, Culture, and the State*. Cambridge, Mass.: Harvard University Press.

Glennie, Paul. 1995. "Consumption Within Historical Studies." In *Acknowledging Consumption: A Review of New Studies*, ed. D. Miller, 164–203. New York: Routledge.

Glickman, Lawrence R. 1997. *A Living Wage: American Workers and the Making of Consumer Society*. Ithaca, N.Y.: Cornell University Press.

Glickman, Lawrence R., ed. 1999. *Consumer Society in American History: A Reader*. Ithaca: Cornell University Press.

Glosser, Susan L. 1995. "The Contest for Family and Nation in Republican China." Ph.D. diss., University of California at Berkeley.

Godley, Michael R. 1978. "China's World's Fair of 1910: Lessons from a Forgotten Event." *Modern Asian Studies* 12, no. 3: 503–22.

————. 1994. "The End of the Queue: Hair as Symbol in Chinese History." *East Asian History* 8: 53–72.

Golay, Frank H., et al., eds. 1969. *Underdevelopment and Economic Nationalism in Southeast Asia.* Ithaca: Cornell University Press.

Goldstein, Joshua. 1999. "Mei Lanfang and the Nationalization of Peking Opera, 1912–1930." *positions: east asian cultures critique* 7, no. 2: 377–420.

Gongmin jiuguo tuan, ed. 1919. *Guochi tongshi* (A general history of national humiliations). N.p.: n.p.

Gongshang ban yüekan. Semi-monthly. Shanghai, 1929–33.

"Gongshang bu guohuo chenlieguan jishou zhanxing banfa" (How to sell on temporary consignment at the Ministry of Industry and Commerce National Products Museum). 1929. *Gongshang banyue kan* 1, no. 15 (July): 13.

"Gongshang bu guohuo chenlieguan nishe yongjiu shangchang" (The Ministry of Industry and Commerce National Products Museum plans to establish a permanent marketplace). *Gongshang banyue kan* 1929. 1, no. 20 (Oct.): 2.

"Gongshang bu pai yuan diaocha guohuo" (The Ministry of Industry and Commerce sends staff to investigate national products). 1928. *Shangye zazhi* 3, no. 11 (Nov.).

"Gongshang bu yiding zhi guohuo biaozhun yilan" (A look at the National Products Standards determined by the Ministry of Industry and Commerce). 1930. In SSGC 1930.

Goodman, Bryna. 1995. *Native Place, City, and Nation: Regional Networks and Identity in Shanghai, 1853–1937.* Berkeley: University of California.

Goto-Shibata, Harumi. 1995. *Japan and Britain in Shanghai, 1925–31.* New York: St. Martin's Press.

Graham, Gael. 1994. "The *Cumberland* Incident of 1928: Gender, Nationalism, and Social Change in American Mission Schools in China." *Journal of Women's History* 6, no. 3: 35–61.

Greenberg, Cheryl. 1999. "'Don't Buy Where You Can't Work.'" In Glickman 1999: 241–73.

Greenberg, Michael. 1951. *British Trade and the Opening of China, 1800–42.* Cambridge, Eng.: Cambridge University Press.

Greenhalgh, Paul. 1988. *Ephemeral Vistas: The Expositions Universells, Great Exhibitions and World's Fairs, 1851–1939.* Manchester: Manchester University Press.

Gronewold, Sue. 1985. *Beautiful Merchandise: Prostitution in China, 1860–1936.* New York: Harrington Par Press.

GSB. 1928. Gongshang bu, Zhonghua guohuo zhanlanhui, ed. *Zhonghua guohuo zhanlanhui jinian tekan* (A special commemorative volume for the Chinese National Products Exhibition). Shanghai: Taidong tushuju.

———. 1929. Gongshang bu, ed. *Gongshang bu Zhonghua guohuo zhanlan hui shilu* (A record of the Ministry of Industry and Commerce's Chinese National Products Exhibition). 6 vols. Nanjing: Gongshang bu, Zhonghua guohuo zhanlan hui.

Gu Bingquan, ed. 1993. *Shanghai fengsu guji kao* (An investigation of Shanghai's traditional customs). Shanghai: Huadong shifan daxue chubanshe.

Gu Weicheng. 1996. "Bisheng zhili yu suliao gongye de Gu Zhaozhen" (Gu Zhaozhen's lifetime devotion to the plastics industry). In Pan Junxiang 1996c: 122–66.

Guangdong jianshe ting, ed. 1930. *Guohuo diaocha baogao* (Reports on national product investigations). Guangzhou: Guangdong jianshe ting.

Guha, Ranajit. 1991. *A Disciplinary Aspect of Indian Nationalism*. Santa Cruz: University of California Santa Cruz, Merrill College.

Guo Feiping. 1994. *Zhongguo minguo jingji shi* (An economic history of the Chinese Republic). Beijing: Renmin chubanshe.

Guo Xianglin et al. 1995. *Zhongguo jindai zhenxing jingji zhi dao de bijiao* (A comparison of China's modern methods of reviving its economy). Shanghai: Shanghai caijing daxue chubanshe.

Guochan daobao. Monthly. Shanghai, 1928–34.

Guochi jiannian xiangqi xinju. 1916. Shanghai: Shangwu yinshu guan.

Guochi ribao. Daily. Beijing, 1925.

Guoguang. Weekly. Shanghai, 1928.

"Guohuo chenlieguan jinxun" (Recent news of the National Products Museum). 1930. *Gongshang banyue kan* 2.5 (Mar.): 5.

"Guohuo de yijiao: women de dianxing" (A perspective on national products: our model). 1934. *SB*, May 24.

"Guohuo fu Fei zhanlan" (National products attend Philippine exhibition). 1929. *SB*, Jan. 12: 13.

"Guohuo guanggao yu boyin" (National product advertising and broadcasting). 1934. *SB*, Dec. 13.

"'Guohuo' he 'guomin'" (National products and national people). 1933. *SB*, Jan. 1.

"Guohuo hui baju zhi weihui ji" (Minutes of the eighth meeting of the executive committee of the National Products Association). 1929. *SB*, June 16: 14.

"Guohuo hui qing nüjie wuyong waihuo" (National Products Association requests that women's circles not use foreign products). 1934. *Guohuo banyue kan* 8 (Apr. 1): 24.

"Guohuo jiating" (National product households). 1933. *SB*, Apr. 20.

"Guohuo lifu yundong zhi tuijin" (The advancement of the national products formal attire movement). 1935. *Guohuo yuebao* 2, no. 1 (Jan.): 36–38.

Guohuo pinglun kan. Monthly. Shanghai, 1925–31.

Guohuo ribao. Daily. Beiping, 1934–35.

Guohuo ribao. Daily. Hankou, 1935.

Guohuo ribao. Daily. Shanghai, 1932.

Guohuo Rihuo duizhao lu (A comparison of national products and Japanese products). 1932. Hangzhou: Zhejiang sheng Hangzhou shi gejie fan Ri jiuguo lianhehui.

Guohuo shiye chubanshe, ed. 1934. *Zhongguo guohuo shiye xianjin shilüe* (Brief histories of model Chinese national product enterprises). Shanghai: Guohuo shiye chubanshe.

"Guohuo shizhuang zhanlanhui" (The national products fashion show). 1930. In SSGC 1930: 155–86.

"Guohuo tuixiao dao neidi qu" (National products marketed in the interior). 1933. *SB,* June 8.

Guohuo yangben. 1934. Shanghai: Jizhi guohuo gongchang lianhehui.

Guohuo yanjiu yuekan. Monthly. Tianjin, 1932–33.

Guohuo yuebao. Monthly. Guangzhou, 1934–37.

Guohuo yuebao. Monthly. Nanjing, 1936.

Guohuo yuebao. Monthly. Shanghai, 1915–16.

Guohuo yuebao. Monthly. Shanghai, 1924–25.

Guohuo yuebao. Monthly. Shanghai, 1934–35.

Guohuo yuekan. Monthly. Changsha, 1933–37.

"Guohuo yu guanggao" (National products and advertising). 1934. *Guohuo yuebao* 1, no. 5/6 (June 15): 21–22.

"Guohuo yu jinü" (National products and prostitutes). 1934. *SB,* June 7.

"Guohuo yu modeng funü" (National products and modern women). 1934. *SB,* Jan. 18.

"Guohuo yundong dahui taolun gailiang pinzhi huiyi ji" (Notes on the National Products Movement Rally's conference to discuss improving quality). 1928. *Shangye yuebao* 8.8 (Aug.).

"Guohuo yu wuchang" (National products and dancehalls). 1934. *SB,* Nov. 1.

"Guohuo zhanlanhui zhong zhi shi zhengfu chenlie shi" (The exhibition room of the municipal government in the National Products Exhibition). 1928. *SB,* Nov. 1.

"Guohuo zhidao" (National product guidance). 1931. *Jilian huikan* 47 (Dec. 1): 36–38.

Guohuo zhiyin (A guide to national products). 1934. Shanghai: n.p.

Guohuo zhoubao. Weekly. Nanjing, 1932.

Guoli lishi bowuguan bianji weiyuanhui, ed. 1988. *Qingdai fushi* (Qing dynasty dress). Taibei: Guoli lishi bowuguan.

"Guomin zhengfu Gongshang bu gonghan" (Official letter of the Central Government Ministry of Industry and Commerce). 1929. *SB,* Jan. 9: 14.

"Guonan zhong funü weiyide zeren" (The only responsibility of women during the National Crisis). 1933. *SB,* June 13.

"Guoqing yu guohuo" (National Day and national products). 1935. *SB,* Oct. 10.

Guowen zhoubao. Weekly. Shanghai and Tientsin, 1924–37.

"Guozhi qiuling yongpin de wojian" (My view on buying autumn articles). 1934. *SB*, Oct. 4.

Gutzlaff, Karl. 1838. *China Opened; or, A Display of the Topography, History, Customs, Manners, Arts, Manufacture, Commerce, Literature, Religion, Jurisprudence, Etc. of the Chinese Empire.* 2 vols. London: Smith, Elder & Co.

Hamashita Takeshi. 1990. *Kindai Chūgoku no kokusaiteki keiki* (The China-centered world order in modern times). Tokyo: Tōkyō daigaku shuppankai.

Hamilton, Gary G., and Chi-kong Lai. 1989. "Consumerism Without Capitalism: Consumption and Brand Names in Late Imperial China." In *The Social Economy of Consumption*, ed. H. J. Rutz and B. S. Orlove, 253–79. Lanham, Md.: University Press of America.

Han Yin. 1996. "Yongli 'Hong sanjiao' guochan chunjian kudou ji" (A record of the struggle to produce Forever Advantageous Red Triangle national product soda ash). In Pan Junxiang 1996c: 111–17.

Hansson, Harry Anders. 1988. "Regional Outcast Groups in Late Imperial China." Ph.D. diss., Harvard University.

Hao, Yen-p'ing. 1970. *The Comprador in Nineteenth Century China: Bridge Between East and West.* Cambridge, Mass.: Harvard University Press.

———. 1986. *The Commercial Revolution in Nineteenth-Century China: The Rise of Sino-Western Mercantile Capitalism.* Berkeley: University of California Press.

Hardy, E. H. 1905. *John Chinaman at Home.* London: T. Fisher Unwin.

Harrell, Paula. 1992. *Sowing the Seeds of Change: Chinese Students, Japanese Teachers, 1895–1905.* Stanford: Stanford University Press.

Harris, Neil. 1978. "Museums, Merchandising and Popular Taste: The Struggle for Influence." In *Material Culture and the Study of American Life*, ed. I. M. G. Quemby, 140–74. New York: W. W. Norton.

Harrison, Henrietta. 2000. *The Making of the Republican Citizen: Political Ceremonies and Symbols in China, 1911–1929.* New York: Oxford University Press.

Harrison, James. 1969(?). *Modern Chinese Nationalism.* New York: Hunter College of the City of New York, Research Institute on Modern Asia.

Hatsuda Tōru. 1993. *Hyakkaten no tanjō* (The birth of the department store). Tokyo: Sanseidō.

Hazama Naoki et al. 1996. *Dāta de miru Chūgoku kindai shi* (Modern Chinese history through data). Tokyo: Yūhaikaku sensho.

He Yiting. 1989. "Wusa yundong zhong de Shanghai zong shanghui" (The Shanghai General Chamber of Commerce in the May 30th Movement). *Lishi yanjiu* 1: 85–100.

He Yu and Hua Li. 1995. *Guochi beiwanglu: Zhongguo jindai shishang de bu pingdeng tiaoyue* (Memoranda on national humiliations: unequal treaties in Chinese modern history). Beijing: Beijing jiaoyu chubanshe.

"Hebei sheng zhengfu xunling di 1992 hao" (Hebei provincial government order no. 1992). 1928. (Nov. 21). Reprinted in Hu Guangming et al. 1994: 1480–81.

"Helihuade xialing yongpin" (Rationalized summer articles). 1935. *SB*, July 15.

Henan sheng difangzhi bianji weiyuanhui, ed. 1983. *Wusi yundong zai Henan* (The May Fourth Movement in Henan). Zhengzhou: Zhongzhou shuhuashe.

Henriot, Christian. 1993. *Shanghai, 1927–1937: Municipal Power, Locality, and Modernization.* Trans. N. Castelino. Berkeley: University of California Press.

————. 1994. "Chinese Courtesans in Late Qing and Early Republican Shanghai (1849–1925)." *East Asian History* 8: 33–52.

Hershatter, Gail. 1986. *The Workers of Tianjin, 1900–1949.* Stanford: Stanford University Press.

————. 1992. "Regulating Sex in Shanghai: The Reform of Prostitution in 1920 and 1951." In Wakeman and Yeh 1992b: 145–85.

————. 1994. "Modernizing Sex, Sexing Modernity: Prostitution in Early Twentieth-Century Shanghai." In Gilmartin et al. 1994: 147–74.

Hevia, James Louis. 1995. *Cherishing Men from Afar: Qing Guest Ritual and the Macartney Embassy of 1793.* Durham, N.C.: Duke University Press.

Hine, Darlene Clark. 1993. "The Housewives League of Detroit: Black Women and Economic Nationalism." In *Visible Women: New Essays on American Activism*, ed. N. A. Hewitt and S. Lebsock, 223–41. Urbana: University of Illinois Press.

Hinsley, Curtis M. 1990. "The World as Marketplace: Commodification of the Exotic at the World's Columbian Exposition, Chicago, 1893." In *Exhibiting Cultures: The Poetics and Politics of Museum Display*, ed. Ivan Karp and Steven D. Lavine, 344–65. Washington, D.C.: Smithsonian Institution Press.

Hirschmeier, Johannes, and Tsunehiko Yui. 1975. *The Development of Japanese Business, 1600–1973.* Cambridge, Mass.: Harvard University Press.

Ho, Virgil Kit-yiu. 1991. "The Limits of Hatred: Popular Attitudes Towards the West in Republican Canton." *East Asian History* 2: 87–104.

Hodgson, James Goodwin. 1933. *Economic Nationalism.* New York: H. W. Wilson Co.

Hollander, Anne. 1980. *Seeing Through Clothes.* New York: Avon.

"Home Products Exhibit at Peking." 1915. *FER*, Oct.: 174.

Hong Buren and Liu Huazhang. 1996. "1936 nian Xiamen guohuo zhanlanhui shimo" (All about the 1936 Xiamen National Products Exhibition). In Pan Junxiang 1996c: 423–28.

Honig, Emily. 1986. *Sisters and Strangers: Women in the Shanghai Cotton Mills, 1919–1949.* Stanford: Stanford University Press.

Hook, Brian, ed. 1998. *Shanghai and the Yangtze Delta: A City Reborn.* New York: Oxford University Press.

Hou, Chi-ming. 1965. *Foreign Investment and Economic Development in China, 1840–1937*. Cambridge, Mass.: Harvard University Press.

Hsiao, Kung-ch'uan. 1967. *Rural China: Imperial Control in the Nineteenth Century*. Seattle: University of Washington Press.

———. 1975. *A Modern China and a New World: K'ang Yu-wei, Reformer and Utopian, 1858–1927*. Seattle: University of Washington Press.

Hsiao Liang-lin. 1974. *China's Foreign Trade Statistics, 1864–1949*. Cambridge, Mass.: Harvard University, East Asia Research Center.

Hsü, Immanuel Chung-yueh. 1983. *The Rise of Modern China*. 3rd ed. Oxford: Oxford University Press.

Hu Guangming et al., eds. 1994. *Tianjin shanghui dang'an huibian (1928–1937)* (A collection of Tianjin Chamber of Commerce archives), vol. 2. Tianjin: Renmin chubanshe.

Hu Jining. 1996. "Guochan xiangliao gongye de xianqu—Shanghai Jianchen xiangliao chang" (The forerunner of the national perfume industry—Shanghai's Jianchen Perfume Factory). In Pan Junxiang 1996c: 136–41.

Hu Wenben and Tian Geshen, eds. 1980. *Wusi yundong zai Shandong ziliao xuanji* (A selection of materials on the May Fourth Movement in Shandong). Ji'nan: Shandong renmin chubanshe.

Hu Xiyuan. 1996. "Guohuo dengpao Yapuer zhi meng" (The dream of the national product light bulb Yapuer). In Pan Junxiang 1996c: 178–87.

Hua Mei. 1989. *Zhongguo fuzhuang shi* (A history of Chinese clothing). Tianjin: Renmin meishu chubanshe.

Huang Hanmin. 1996. "Guohuo yundong zhong de Rongjia qiye" (The Rong family enterprises in the National Products Movement). In Pan Junxiang 1996c: 54–64.

Huang Nongfu and Chen Juanjuan, eds. 1995. *Zhongguo fuzhuang shi* (A history of Chinese clothing). Beijing: Zhongguo lüyou chubanshe.

Huang Shilong, ed. 1994. *Zhongguo fushi* (Chinese dress). Shanghai: Shanghai wenhua chubanshe.

Huang Yiping and Yu Baotang. 1995. *Beiyang zhengfu shiqi jingji* (The economy during the Northern government). Shanghai: Shanghai shehui kexue yuan.

Huang Yiting, ed. 1934. *Guohuo gongshang daguan* (An overview of national product enterprises). N.p., n.p.

"Huda guohuo zhanlanhui zuori kaimu" (Hujiang University National Products Exhibition opened yesterday). 1928. *SB*, May 30: 14.

Huebner, Jon W. 1988. "Architechure and History in Shanghai's Central District." *Journal of Oriental Studies* 26, no. 2: 209–69.

Huenemann, Ralph William. 1984. *The Dragon and the Iron Horse: The Economics of Railroads in China, 1876–1937*. Cambridge, Mass.: Harvard University, Council on East Asian Studies.

Humm, Maggie. 1995. *The Dictionary of Feminist Theory.* 2nd ed. Columbus: Ohio State University Press.

"Hushi guohuo guanggao mianshui banfa" (How to avoid taxes in Shanghai for national product advertisements). 1930. *Gongshang banyuekan* 2.10 (Apr.): 18.

"Hushi guohuo shizhuang zhanlanhui kaimu shengkuang" (Opening ceremonies of the Shanghai Municipal Fashion Exhibition). 1930. *Gongshang banyue kan* 2.20 (Oct.): 16–19.

"Industrial Exhibition in Peking." 1915. *FER* Aug.: 96.

Isaacs, Harold. 1938. *The Tragedy of the Chinese Revolution.* London: Secker & Warburg. Rev. ed., 1951. Stanford: Stanford University Press.

Israel, John. 1966. *Student Nationalism in China, 1927–1937.* Stanford: Hoover Institution Press.

Jang, Sukman. 1998. "The Politics of Haircutting in Korea: A Symbol of Modernity and the 'Righteous Army Movement' (1895–96)." *Review of Korean Studies* 1: 26–52.

Jansen, Marius B. 1975. *Japan and China: From War to Peace, 1894–1972.* Chicago: Rand McNally College Publishing Co.

Jardine, Lisa. 1996. *Worldly Goods: A New History of the Renaissance.* New York: Doubleday.

Jayawardena, Kumari. 1991. *Feminism and Nationalism in the Third World.* New York: St. Martin's Press.

Jhally, Sut. 1990. *The Codes of Advertising: Fetishism and the Political Economy of Meaning in the Consumer Society.* New York: Routledge.

"Jiagongzhong de fendou" (The struggle while being attacked from both flanks). 1934. *Jilian huikan* 90 (Mar. 1): 5–6.

Jiang Weiguo. 1995. "Jindai Zhongguo guohuo tuanti chuxi" (Modern Chinese national products organizations). *Minguo dang'an:* 75–83.

"Jiangsu techan zhanlanhui" (Jiangsu specialty products exhibition). 1931. In Wang Keyou 1931: 25–27.

"Jianian guohuo zhanlanhui mingri anqing ge jie" (Jianian National Products Exhibition hosts dinner for various circles). 1929. *SB*, Jan. 10: 14.

"Jiating guohuo yundong" (The Household National Products Movement). 1933. *SB*, Feb. 16.

"Jiji choubei zhong zhi funü guohuo nian" (Amidst the busy preparations for the Women's National Products Year). 1933. *SB*, Dec. 31.

Jilian. Semi-monthly. Shanghai, 1930–52.

Jin Bo. 2002. "Imported Movies: Entertainment or Hegemony?" 2002. *China Daily,* Apr. 8.

"Jing funü tichang guohuo hui zhuban zhi zhongdeng xuexiao nüsheng jiangyan jingsai hui" (On the secondary schoolgirls' speech contest sponsored by the

Women's National Products Association). 1934. *Funü gongming yuebao* 3, no. 5: 49–50.

"Jingji juejiao de fangfa yu shouduan" (The ways and means for severing economic relations). 1928. In Zhongguo guomindang, Hebei sheng dangwu zhidao wei-yuanhui 1928: 9–18.

Jiuguo zhoubao. Weekly. Shanghai, 1929.

"Jiu yiba yihou de He furen jiating" (Mrs. He's household after 9-18). 1934. *SB*, Sept. 18.

"Jiu yiba yu jiuchang guohuo shangchang" (The 9-18 nine-factory national products market). 1934. *SB*, Sept. 18.

Johnson, David G.; Andrew J. Nathan; and Evelyn Sakakida Rawski, eds. 1985. *Popular Culture in Late Imperial China*. Berkeley: University of California Press.

Johnson, Linda Cooke. 1995. *Shanghai: From Market Town to Treaty Port, 1074–1858*. Stanford: Stanford University Press.

Jones, Andrew. 1999. "The Gramophone in China." In *Tokens of Exchange: The Problem of Translation in Global Circulations*, ed. Lydia H. Liu, 214–36. Durham, N.C.: Duke University Press.

Jones, William C., trans. 1994. *The Great Qing Code*. Oxford: Clarendon Press.

Jordan, Donald A. 1976. *The Northern Expedition: China's National Unification of 1926–1928*. Honolulu: University Press of Hawai'i.

———. 1991. *Chinese Boycotts Versus Japanese Bombs: The Failure of China's "Revolutionary Diplomacy," 1931–32*. Ann Arbor: University of Michigan Press.

———. 2001. *China's Trial by Fire: The Shanghai War of 1932*. Ann Arbor: University of Michigan Press.

Judge, Joan. 1996. *Print and Politics: 'Shibao' and the Culture of Reform in Late Qing China*. Stanford: Stanford University Press.

———. 2001. "Talent, Virtue, and the Nation: Chinese Nationalisms and Female Subjectivities in the Early Twentieth Century." *American Historical Review* 106, no. 3: 765–803.

Kaplan, Temma. 1998. "International Women's Day." In *The Reader's Companion to U.S. Women's History*, ed. W. Mankiller, G. Mink, M. Navarro, B. Smith, and G. Steinem, 281–82. New York: Houghton Mifflin Co.

Karl, Rebecca E. 2002. *Staging the World: Chinese Nationalism at the Turn of the Twentieth Century*. Durham, N.C.: Duke University Press.

Kawakami, Kiyoshi Karl. 1932. *Japan Speaks on the Sino-Japanese Crisis*. New York: Macmillan.

Kellner, Douglas. 1989. *Jean Baudrillard: From Marxism to Postmodernism and Beyond*. Stanford: Stanford University Press.

Kent, Percy Horace. 1912. *The Passing of the Manchus*. London: Edward Arnold.

Kikuchi Takaharu. 1974. *Chūgoku minzoku undō no kihon kōzō: Taigai boikotto no ken-kyū* (The historical background of the Chinese national movement: a study of anti-foreign boycotts). Tokyo: Daian.

King, S. T., and D. K. Lieu. 1929. *China's Cotton Industry: A Statistical Study of Ownership of Capital, Output, and Labor Conditions.* Shanghai(?): Institute of Pacific Relations.

Kinmonth, Earl H. 1981. *The Self-Made Man in Meiji Japanese Thought.* Berkeley: University of California Press.

Kirby, William C. 1984. *Germany and Republican China.* Stanford: Stanford University Press.

————. 1992. "The Chinese War Economy." In *China's Bitter Victory: The War with Japan, 1937–45,* ed. J. C. Hsiung and S. I. Levine, 185–212. Armonk, N.Y.: M. E. Sharpe.

————. 1995. "China Unincorporated: Company Law and Business Enterprise in Twentieth-Century China." *Journal of Asian Studies* 54, no. 1: 43–63.

————. 1997. "The Internationalization of China: Foreign Relations at Home and Abroad in the Republican Era." *China Quarterly* 150: 433–58.

Kirby, William C., and Stephen C. Averill. 1992. "More States of the Field." *Republican China*: 206–55.

Klein, Richard. 1993. *Cigarettes Are Sublime.* Durham, N.C.: Duke University Press.

Ko, Dorothy. 1994. *Teachers of the Inner Chambers: Women and Culture in Seventeenth-Century China.* Stanford: Stanford University Press.

Kong Xiangxi. 1928a. "Guomin zhengfu Gongshang bu ling gongzi di 55 hao" (National Government Ministry of Industry and Commerce order no. 55) (July 8). In Hu Guangming et al. 1994: 1475.

————. 1928b. "Guomin zhengfu Gongshang bu fagei guohuo zhengmingshu guize" (The "National Products Certification Regulations" of the National Government Ministry of Industry and Commerce) (June). In Hu Guangming et al. 1994: 1475–76.

Kong Xiangxi, ed. 1929. *Gongshang bu guohuo chenlieguan kaimu jinian tekan* (Special commemorative volume of the opening of the Ministry of Industry and Commerce's National Products Museum). Nanjing: Gongshang bu.

Koo, V. K. Wellington. 1932. *Memoranda Presented to the Lytton Commission.* New York: Chinese Cultural Society.

Kramer, Paul. 1999. "Making Concessions: Race and Empire Revisited at the Philippine Exposition, St. Louis, 1901–1905." *Radical History Review* 73: 74–114.

Kubo Toru. 1980. "Nankin seifu no kanzei seisaku to sono rekishiteki igi" (Tariff policy of the Nanjing government and its effect on China's industrial development). *Tochiseido shigaku* 86: 38–55.

Kuhn, Philip A. 1975. "Local Self Government Under the Republic: Problems of Control, Autonomy, and Mobilization." In *Conflict and Control in Late Imperial China*, ed. F. Wakeman and C. Grant, 257–98. Berkeley: University of California Press.

———. 1990. *Soulstealers: The Chinese Sorcery Scare of 1768*. Cambridge, Mass.: Harvard University Press.

———. 2002. *Origins of the Modern Chinese State*. Stanford: Stanford University Press.

Kusamitsu, Toshio. 1980. "Great Exhibitions Before 1851." *History Workshop* 9: 70–89.

Kwong, Luke S. K. 1984. *A Mosaic of the Hundred Days: Personalities, Politics, and Ideas of 1898*. Cambridge, Mass.: Harvard University, Council on East Asian Studies.

Lach, Donald F., and Edwin J. van Kley. 1993. *Asia in the Making of Europe*, vol. III, pt. 4. Chicago: University of Chicago Press.

Laermans, Rudi. 1993. "Learning to Consume: Early Department Stores and the Shaping of the Modern Consumer Culture (1860–1914)." *Theory, Culture & Society* 10: 79–102.

La Fargue, Thomas E. 1937. *China and the World War*. Stanford: Stanford University Press.

———. 1942. *China's First Hundred*. Pullman: State College of Washington.

Lai, Chi-kong. 1994. "Li Hung-chang and Modern Enterprise: The China Merchant's Company, 1872–1885." In *Li Hung-chang and China's Early Modernization*, ed. S. C. Chu and K. C. Liu, 216–47. Armonk, N.Y.: M. E. Sharpe.

Latourette, Kenneth Scott. 1929. *A History of Christian Missions in China*. New York: Macmillan.

Lauer, Robert H., and Jeanette C. Lauer. 1981. *Fashion Power: The Meaning of Fashion in American Society*. Englewood Cliffs, N.J.: Prentice Hall.

Leach, William. 1993. *Land of Desire: Merchants, Power, and the Rise of a New American Culture*. New York: Vintage.

Lee, Chae-Jin. 1994. *Zhou Enlai: The Early Years*. Stanford: Stanford University Press.

Lee, En-han. 1977. *China's Quest for Railway Autonomy, 1904–1911: A Study of the Chinese Railway-Rights Recovery Movement*. Singapore: Singapore University Press.

Lee, Leo Ou-fan. 1999. *Shanghai Modern: The Flowering of a New Urban Culture in China, 1930–1945*. Cambridge, Mass.: Harvard University Press.

Lee, Leo Ou-fan, and Andrew J. Nathan. 1985. "The Beginnings of Mass Culture: Journalism and Fiction in the Late Ch'ing and Beyond." In D. Johnson et al. 1985: 360–95.

Lee, Yok-shiu F., and Alvin Y. So, eds. 1999. *Asia's Environmental Movements: Comparative Perspectives*. Armonk, N.Y.: M. E. Sharpe.

Lensen, G. A., ed. 1966. *Korea and Manchuria Between Russia and Japan*. Tallahassee: Diplomatic Press.

Levenson, Joseph Richmond. 1965. *Confucian China and Its Modern Fate: A Trilogy.* Berkeley: University of California Press.

Lewis, Russell. 1983. "Everything Under One Roof: World's Fairs and Department Stores in Paris and Chicago." *Chicago History* 12, no. 3: 28–47.

Li Daofa. 1996. "Quanli sanyu guohuo yundong de Sanyou shiyeshe" (The Three Friends Enterprises wholehearted participation in the National Products Movement). In Pan Junxiang 1996c: 65–70.

Li Jianhong. 1925a. "Beitong de huigu" (A retrospective on sorrow). In Cao Muguan 1925: 27–30.

———. 1925b. "Women zenma qu quxiao zhe guochi" (How we can abolish this national humiliation). In Cao Muguan 1925: 36–38.

Li, Lillian M. 1981. *China's Silk Trade: Traditional Industry in the Modern World, 1842–1937.* Cambridge, Mass.: Harvard University, Council on East Asian Studies.

Li Maosheng. 1992. *Kong Xiangxi zhuan* (A biography of Kong Xiangxi). Beijing: Zhongguo guangbo dianshi chubanshe.

Li Shaobing. 1994. *Minguo shiqi de xishi fengsu wenhua* (Western customs and culture in the Republican period). Beijing: Beijing shifan daxue chubanshe.

Li Wenhai and Liu Qingdong. 1991. *Taiping tianguo shehui fengqing* (Taiping social customs). Taibei: Yunlong chubanshe.

Li, Yu-ning. 1971. *The Introduction of Socialism into China.* New York: Columbia University Press.

Li Yushu. 1966. *Zhong Ri ershiyi tiao jiaoshe* (Sino-Japanese negotiations over the Twenty-One Demands). Taibei: Academia Sinica, Institute of Modern History.

Lian, Xi. 1997. *The Conversion of Missionaries: Liberalism in American Protestant Missions in China, 1907–1932.* University Park: Pennsylvania State University Press.

Liang Xiaohong. 1934. "Guohuo shang de yangzi—shifou biyao?" (Foreign letters on national products—is it necessary?). *SB,* July 12.

Liao Heyong. 1987. *Wan-Qing ziqiang yundong junbei wenti zhi yanjiu* (A history of the issue of armaments in the late Qing Self-Strengthening Movement). Taibei: Wenshizhe chubanshe.

Liao, Kuang-sheng. 1984. *Anti-foreignism and Modernization in China, 1860–1980.* Hong Kong: Chinese University Press.

Lieu, D. K. (Liu Dajun). 1927. "China's Industrial Development." *Chinese Economic Journal,* July: 654–74.

———. 1936. *Growth and Industrialisation of Shanghai.* Shanghai: n.p.

———. 1937. *Zhongguo gongye diaocha baogao* (Research reports on Chinese industries). 3 vols. Nanjing.

Lin Kanghou, ed. 1935. *Zhongguo guohuo nianjian* (China national products yearbook). Shanghai: Guohuo shiye chubanshe.

Lin Man-houng. 1991. "'A Time in Which Grandsons Beat Their Grandfathers': The Rise of Liberal Political-Economic Ideas During the Monetary Crisis of Early Nineteenth-Century China." *American Asian Review* 9, no. 4: 1–28.

Lin Qinfang. 1996. "Shiye bu Guohuo chenlieguan yu guohuo yundong" (The Ministry of Industry's National Products Museum and the National Products Movement). In Pan Junxiang 1996c: 412–19.

Lin Zhimao. 1928. "Lun woguo yi nonggongshangye liguo jiying pushe guohuo chenlieguan" (In using agriculture, industry, and commerce to build the nation, our country should quickly and widely establish national product museums). In GSB 1928.

Liu Dajun, *see* Lieu, D. K.

Liu, Kwang-Ching. 1962. *Anglo-American Steamship Rivalry in China, 1862–1874.* Cambridge, Mass.: Harvard University Press.

Liu, Lydia H. 1995. *Translingual Practice: Literature, National Culture, and Translated Modernity—China, 1900–1937.* Stanford: Stanford University Press.

Liu, Ta-Chung and Kung-Chia Yeh. 1965. *The Economy of the Chinese Mainland: National Income and Economic Development, 1933–1959.* Princeton: Princeton University Press.

Lodwick, Kathleen L. 1995. *Educating the Women of Hainan: The Career of Margaret Moninger in China, 1915–1942.* Lexington: University Press of Kentucky.

————. 1996. *Crusaders Against Opium: Protestant Missionaries in China, 1874–1917.* Lexington: University Press of Kentucky.

Loh, Pichon Pei Yung. 1955. "The Popular Upsurge in China: Nationalism and Westernization, 1919–1927." Ph.D. diss., University of Chicago.

Loomba, Ania. 1998. *Colonialism/Postcolonialism.* New York: Routledge.

Lou Dexing. 1996a. "Huasheng dianshan zai guohuo yundong zhong feisu fazhan" (China Survival Electric Fans' rapid development in the National Products Movement). In Pan Junxiang 1996c: 172–77.

————. 1996b. "Huacheng yan gongsi zai guohuo yundong zhong fazhan" (China Success Cigarette Company's impressive development in the National Products Movement). In Pan Junxiang 1996c: 213–18.

Lu Baiyu. 1931. "Guonan shengzhong wuren yingyou zhi juewu" (The awareness that we should have during the national crisis). *Jilian huikan* 44 (Oct. 16): 12–14.

Lu Guiliang. 1915. "Riben guochan huowu jiangli an" (The Japanese plan for promoting nationally produced products). *Dongfang zhizhi* 12, no. 9 (Sept.): 30–33.

Lu, Hanchao. 1999. *Beyond the Neon Lights: Everyday Shanghai in the Early Twentieth Century.* Berkeley: University of California Press.

Lü Meiyi and Zheng Yongfu. 1990. *Zhongguo funü yundong (1840–1921)* (China's women's movement). Zhengzhou: Henan renmin chubanshe.

Lu Qing. 1932. "Tuixiao guohuo yingzheng shei shixing qi" (With whom should the promotion of national products begin?). *Jilian huikan* 59 (Oct. 1): 33–35.

Lu Shouqian. "Tichang guohuo zhi yuanyin" (The reasons for promoting national products). *Zhongguo shiye jie* 2, no. 6 (1915.6.10).

Luo Jialun, ed. 1968. *Zhonghua minguo shiliao congbian* (A collection of historical materials on the Chinese Republic). Taibei: Zhongguo Guomindang zhongyang weiyuanhui.

Luo Jiping. 1997. "Ji quanguo jingpin kai kongqian shenghui: Xihu bolanhui" (Collecting the nation's best goods, launching an unprecedentedly magnificent fair: the West Lake Exhibition). In *Minguo shiqi Hangzhou* (Hangzhou during the Republican era), ed. Zhou Feng, 503–11. Hangzhou: Zhejiang renmin chubanshe.

Luo Zhiping. 1996. *Qingmo minchu Meiguo zai Hua de qiye touzi (1818–1937)* (American foreign direct investment in China during the late Qing and early Republic). Taibei: Guoshiguan.

Luo Zhufeng, ed. 1990. *Hanyu dacidian* (Chinese dictionary). 12 vols. Shanghai: Hanyu dacidian chubanshe.

Lust, John. 1964. "The *Su-pao* Case." *Bulletin of the School of Oriental and African Studies* 27, no. 2: 408–29.

Lynn, Hyung Gu. Forthcoming. "Distinguishing Dress: Clothing and Identity in Colonial Korea, 1910–1945." In *East Asia and Fashion Theory*, ed. Lise Skov. Honolulu: University of Hawai'i Press.

Lynn, Jermyn Chi-hung. 1928. *Social Life of the Chinese in Peking*. Tianjin: Tiantsin Press.

Ma Bingrong. 1996a. "Yongyu duiwai kaituode Meiya zhichou chang" (Meiya Silk Weaving Factory's courageous expansion abroad). In Pan Junxiang 1996c: 71–76.

———. 1996b. "Fang Yexian yu Zhongguo huaxue gongye she" (Fang Yexian and the China Chemical Industries Company). In Pan Junxiang 1996c: 99–110.

———. 1996c. "Qianbi puxia de guohuo songge" (A national product ode composed in pencil). In Pan Junxiang 1996c: 225–32.

Ma Bohuang, ed. 1992. *Zhongguo jindai jingji sixiang shi* (A history of Chinese modern economic thought), vol 3. Shanghai: Shehui kexue yuan chubanshe.

Ma Gengcun. 1995. *Zhongguo jindai funü shi* (A history of modern Chinese women). Qingdao: Qingdao chubanshe.

Ma Guangren, ed. 1996. *Shanghai xinwen shi (1850–1949)* (A history of the Shanghai press). Shanghai: Fudan daxue chubanshe.

Ma Min. 1995. *Guanshang zhijian: shehui jubianzhong de jindai shenshang* (Between mandarins and merchants: modern gentry-merchants in a rapidly changing society). Tianjin: Renmin chubanshe.

MacKinnon, Stephen R. 1980. *Power and Politics in Late Imperial China: Yuan Shi-kai in Beijing and Tianjin, 1901–1908*. Berkeley: University of California Press.

MacPherson, Kerrie L., ed. 1998. *Asian Department Stores*. Surrey, Eng.: Curzon.

MacPherson, W. J. 1987. *The Economic Development of Japan, 1868–1941*. Cambridge, Eng.: Cambridge University Press.

Mandell, Richard D. 1967. *Paris, 1900: The Great World's Fair*. Toronto: University of Toronto Press.

Mann, Susan. 1987. *Local Merchants and the Chinese Bureaucracy, 1750–1950*. Stanford: Stanford University Press.

Mao Zedong. 1990. *Report from Xunwu*. Trans. Roger R. Thompson. Stanford: Stanford University Press.

Maritime Customs, Statistical Series, Annual Reports on Trade.

Marshall, Byron K. 1967. *Capitalism and Nationalism in Prewar Japan: The Ideology of the Business Elite, 1868–1941*. Stanford: Stanford University Press.

Martin, Luther H., Huck Gutman, and Patrick H. Hutton, eds. 1988. *Technologies of the Self: A Seminar with Michel Foucault*. Amherst: University of Massachusetts Press.

Marx, Karl. 1967. *Capital: A Critique of Political Economy*. 3 vols. New York: International Publishers.

Mathews, R. H.; M. Y. Wang; Yuen Ren Chao; China Inland Mission; and Harvard-Yenching Institute. 1966. *Mathews' Chinese-English Dictionary*. Cambridge, Mass.: Harvard University Press.

Matsumoto Shigeharu. 1933. *The Historical Development of Chinese Boycott, Book 1, 1834–1925*. Tokyo: Institute of Pacific Relations, Japanese Council.

Matsumoto Tadao, comp. 1908–23. *Matsumoto bunko Chūgoku kankei shimbun kirinukishū* (A collection of newspaper clippings on China from the Matsumoto collection). Microfilm. Tokyo: Yūshōdō shoten, 1967.

McCracken, Grant David. 1988. *Culture and Consumption: New Approaches to the Symbolic Character of Consumer Goods and Activities*. Bloomington: Indiana University Press.

McDonald, Angus W. 1978. *The Urban Origins of Rural Revolution: Elites and the Masses in Hunan Province, China, 1911–1927*. Berkeley: University of California Press.

McDowell, Colin. 1992. *Hats: Status, Style and Glamour*. New York: Rizzoli.

McKee, Delber L. 1986. "The Chinese Boycott of 1905–1906 Reconsidered: The Role of Chinese Americans." *Pacific Historical Review* 55, no. 2: 165–91.

McKendrick, Neil; John Brewer; and J. H. Plumb. 1982. *The Birth of a Consumer Society: The Commercialization of Eighteenth-Century England*. Bloomington: Indiana University Press.

Medley, Margaret. 1982. *The Illustrated Regulations for Ceremonial Paraphernalia of the Ch'ing Dynasty*. London: Han-Shan Tang.

Meirokusha. 1976. Meiroku Zasshi: *Journal of the Japanese Enlightenment.* Issues 1–43. Trans. William Reynolds Braisted. Cambridge, Mass.: Harvard University Press.

Meng, C. Y. W. 1929. "'Waking Up' Industrial China." *CWR*, Sept. 21.

Mi Jucheng. 1980. *Diguo zhuyi yu Zhongguo tielu* (Imperialism and Chinese railroads). Shanghai: Shanghai remin chubanshe.

Miller, Daniel. 1994. "Artefacts and the Meaning of Things." In *Companion Encyclopedia of Anthropology,* ed. T. Ingold, 396–419. New York: Routledge.

————. 1995a. "Consumption and Commodities." *Annual Review of Anthropology* 24: 141–61.

————. 1995b. "Consumption as the Vanguard of History." In Miller 1995c: 1–57.

————. 1998. "Why Some Things Matter." In *Material Cultures: Why Some Things Matter,* ed. D. Miller, 3–21. Chicago: University of Chicago Press.

Miller, Daniel, ed. 1995c. *Acknowledging Consumption: A Review of New Studies.* New York: Routledge.

Miller, Michael B. 1981. *The Bon Marché: Bourgeois Culture and the Department Store, 1869–1920.* London: George Allen & Unwin.

Mills, Sara. 1997. *Discourse.* London: Routledge.

Misra, O. P. 1995. *Economic Thought of Gandhi and Nehru: A Comparative Analysis.* New Delhi: M D Publications.

Mitchell, Timothy. 1988. *Colonising Egypt.* Berkeley: University of California Press.

Mitter, Rana. 2000. *The Manchurian Myth: Nationalism, Resistance, and Collaboration in Modern China.* Berkeley: Univeristy of California Press.

"Modeng funü: juewu ba!" (Modern women: wake up!). 1934. *SB,* Aug. 2.

"Modeng fuzhuang de tiaojian" (The prerequisites of modern clothing). 1934. *Jilian huikan* 92 (Apr. 1): 55.

"Modeng nüzi han maoduan nüzi" (Modern gals and bobbed-hair gals). 1934. *SB,* Sept. 1.

Moore, Barrington, Jr. 1966. *Social Origins of Dictatorship and Democracy: Lord and Peasant in the Making of the Modern World.* Boston: Beacon Press.

Morgan, Evan. 1930. *A New Mind, and Other Essays.* Shanghai: Kelly & Walsh.

Morley, James William, ed. 1974. *Japan's Foreign Policy, 1868–1941.* New York: Columbia University Press.

Morse, Hosea Ballou. 1910. *The International Relations of the Chinese Empire.* London: Longmans Green & Co.

Morse, Hosea Ballou; F. L. Hawks Pott; and A. T. Piry. 1908. *The Trade and Administration of the Chinese Empire.* Shanghai: Kelly & Walsh.

Mui Hoh-cheong, and Lorna Mui. 1984. *The Management of Monopoly: A Study of the English East India Company's Conduct of Its Tea Trade, 1784–1833.* Vancouver: University of British Columbia Press.

Murphey, Rhoads. 1970. *The Treaty Ports and China's Modernization: What Went Wrong?* Ann Arbor: University of Michigan, Center for Chinese Studies.

Myers, Ramon H. 1989. "The Principle of People's Welfare: A Multidimensional Concept." In *Sun Yat-sen's Doctrine in the Modern World*, ed. Chu-yuan Cheng, 225–43. Boulder: Westview Press.

Nakai Hideki. 1996. *Chō Ken to Chūgoku kindai kigyō* (Zhang Jian and Chinese modern enterprise). Sapporo: Hokkaidō daigaku tosho kankōkai.

Namikata Shōichi, ed. 1997. *Kindai Ajia no Nihonjin keizai dantai* (Japanese business groups in modern Asia). Tokyo: Dōbunkan.

Naquin, Susan, and Evelyn S. Rawski. 1987. *Chinese Society in the Eighteenth Century.* New Haven: Yale University Press.

"National Products Exhibition." 1928. *NCH*, Nov. 3: 189.

"A National Products Exhibition." 1928. *American Chamber of Commerce Bulletin*, no. 158 (Nov.): 5.

"The National Products Exhibition." 1929. *Chinese Economic Journal* 4, no. 1 (Jan.): 1–20.

"National Products Week." 1928. *NCH*, July 14: 60.

Navarro, Marysa. 1998. "International Feminism." In *The Reader's Companion to U.S. Women's History*, ed. W. Mankiller, G. Mink, M. Navarro, B. Smith, and G. Steinem, 209–10. New York: Houghton Mifflin Company.

NCH. 1895–1937. *North-China Herald and Supreme Court and Consular Gazette.* Shanghai.

"Neidi sheli guohuo shangdian zhi guanjian" (My humble opinion on setting up national product stores in the interior). 1925. *SB*, Oct. 12.

Nelson, Laura C. 2000. *Measured Excess: Status, Gender, and Consumer Nationalism in South Korea.* New York: Columbia University Press.

NII (National Industrial Investigation), ed. 1935. *China Industrial Handbook: Kiangsu.* Shanghai: Ministry of Industry, Bureau of Foreign Trade.

Nissenbaum, Stephen. 1997. *The Battle for Christmas.* New York: Vintage Books.

NJ. Number Two Historical Archives. Nanjing.

Nongshang bu shangpin chenliesuo yi lan (A look at the Ministry of Agriculture and Commerce's Commercial Products Exhibition Hall). 1918. Beijing: Nongshang bu.

"Nüjie tichang guohuo shengkuang—guohuo shizhuang zhanlanhui" (A glorious occasion in the promotion of national products by women's circles—the national products fashion show). 1930. *Funü gongming* 36: 35–36.

Nüsheng. Semi-monthly. Shanghai, 1932–37.

Nüzi yuekan. Monthly. Shanghai, 1933–37.

Ohnuki-Tierney, Emiko. 1993. *Rice as Self: Japanese Identities Through Time.* Princeton: Princeton University Press.

————. 1995. "Structure, Event and Historical Metaphor: Rice and Identities in Japanese History." *Journal of the Royal Anthropological Institute* 1, no. 2: 227–53.

Ono Shinji. 1994. *Jiuguo shirentuan yundong yanjiu* (A study of the national salvation ten-person group movement). Trans. Yin Xuyi and Zhang Yunhou. Beijing: Zhongyang bianyi chubanshe.

Orchard, Dorothy J. 1930. "China's Use of the Boycott as a Political Weapon." *Annals of the American Academy of Political and Social Science* 152: 252–61.

Orliski, Constance Ilene. 1998. "Reimagining the Domestic Sphere: Bourgeois Nationalism and Gender in Shanghai, 1904–1918." Ph.D. diss., University of Southern California.

Orlove, Benjamin S., ed. 1997. *The Allure of the Foreign: Imported Goods in Postcolonial Latin America*. Ann Arbor: University of Michigan Press.

Orlove, Benjamin S., and Arnold J. Bauer. 1997. "Giving Importance to Imports." In Orlove 1997: 1–29.

Ōsaka shōgyō kaigisho. 1928. *Shina ni okeru hai-Nichi undō* (The anti-Japan movement in China). Osaka: Ōsaka shōgyō kaigisho.

Ōsaka shōkō kaigisho, ed. 1931. *Summary of Political and Economic Relations Between Japan and China*. Osaka: Osaka Chamber of Commerce and Industry.

Pan Junxiang. 1989. "Guohuo yundong zhong de Shanghai minzu zichan jieji" (Shanghai's national capitalist class during the National Products Movement). *Dang'an yü lishi* 1: 55–63.

————. 1996a. "Guohuo yundong pingjia de ruogan wenti" (Several issues in assessing the National Products Movement). In Pan Junxiang 1996c: 577–81.

————. 1996b. "Shanghai zong shanghui shangpin chenliesuo" (The Shanghai Commercial Products Display Hall). In Pan Junxiang 1996c: 391–402.

Pan Junxiang, ed. 1996c. *Zhongguo jindai guohuo yundong* (China's modern National Products Movement). Beijing: Zhongguo wenshi chubanshe.

————. 1998. *Jindai Zhongguo guohuo yundong yanjiu* (A study of modern China's National Products Movement). Shanghai: Shanghai shehui kexueyuan chubanshe.

Pan Yingmang. 1933. "Ertong yu guohuo" (Children and national products). *SB*, Apr. 6.

Park, Soon-Won. 1999. *Colonial Industrialization and Labor in Korea: The Onoda Cement Factory*. Cambridge, Mass.: Harvard University Asia Center.

Payne, Robert. 1969. *Chiang Kai-shek*. New York: Weybright & Talley.

Paystrup, Patricia. 1996. "Plastics as a 'Natural Resource': Perspective by Incongruity for an Industry in Crisis." In *The Symbolic Earth: Discourse and Our Creation of the Environment*, ed. J. G. Cantrill and C. L. Oravec, 176–97. Lexington: University Press of Kentucky.

Peake, Cyrus H. 1932. *Nationalism and Education in Modern China*. New York: Columbia University Press.

Pearson, Margaret M. 1991. *Joint Ventures in the People's Republic of China: The Control of Foreign Direct Investment Under Socialism*. Princeton: Princeton University Press.

Pei Ji. 1934. "Helihua de songli" (Rationalized gift-giving). *Jilian huikan* 98 (July 1): 38–39.

Pei Yunqing. 1936. "Jingji qinlüe Zhongguoren ying you de juewu" (Chinese should be aware of the economic invasion). In SSC 1936.

Perkins, Dwight Heald. 1969. *Agricultural Development in China, 1368–1968*. Chicago: Aldine.

Perry, Elizabeth J. 1993. *Shanghai on Strike: The Politics of Chinese Labor*. Stanford: Stanford University Press.

Peterson, Willard J. 1994. "What to Wear? Observation and Participation by Jesuit Missionaries in Late Ming Society." In *Implicit Understandings: Observing, Reporting, and Reflecting on the Encounters Between Europeans and Other Peoples in the Early Modern Era*, ed. S. B. Schwartz, 403–21. Cambridge, Eng.: Cambridge University Press.

Polachek, James M. 1992. *The Inner Opium War*. Cambridge, Mass.: Harvard University, Council on East Asian Studies.

Pomerantz-Zhang, Linda. 1992. *Wu Tingfang (1842–1922): Reform and Modernization in Modern Chinese History*. Hong Kong: Hong Kong University Press.

Pomeranz, Kenneth. 2000. *The Great Divergence: Europe, China, and the Making of the Modern World Economy*. Princeton: Princeton University Press.

Pong, David. 1985. "The Vocabulary of Change and Reformist Ideas of the 1860s and 1870s." In *Idea and Reality: Social and Political Change in Modern China, 1860–1949*, ed. D. Pong and E. S. K. Fung, 2–61. New York: University Press of America.

Pott, F. L. Hawks. 1913. *The Emergency in China*. New York: Missionary Education Movement.

Pusey, James Reeve. 1983. *China and Charles Darwin*. Cambridge, Mass.: Harvard University, Council on East Asian Studies.

Qin Shaode. 1993. *Shanghai jindai baokan shilun* (A history of the Shanghai modern press). Shanghai: Fudan daxue chubanshe.

Qin Xiaoyi. 1981. *Zhonghua minguo wenhua fazhan shi* (The history of cultural development in Republican China), vol. 4. Taibei: Jindai Zhongguo chubanshe.

Qiu Zongzhong. 1936, 1938. "Bianzi jing" (The passing of the queue). 2 pts. *Miaojing*, Oct. 20, 1936: 17–20; Sept. 5, 1938: 11–13.

"Qiuji guohuo yongpin" (Autumn national product articles). 1934. *SB*, Oct. 4.

"Qiuling de yiliang yongpin wenti" (The question of autumn clothing and food articles). 1934. *SB*, Oct. 4.

"Quanshi gejie relie jinian ertong jie" (Circles from the entire city to celebrate Children's Day warmly). 1934. *SB*, Apr. 4.

Quanye chang. Daily. Shanghai, 1918.

Quanye huibao. Daily. 1909–10.

Rankin, Mary Backus. 1971. *Early Chinese Revolutionaries: Radical Intellectuals in Shanghai and Chekiang, 1902–1911.* Cambridge, Mass.: Harvard University Press.

———. 1990. "The Origins of a Chinese Public Sphere." *Etudes chinoises* 9, no. 2: 13–60.

Rawski, Evelyn Sakakida. 1998. *The Last Emperors: A Social History of Qing Imperial Institutions.* Berkeley: University of California Press.

Rawski, Thomas G. 1989. *Economic Growth in Prewar China.* Berkeley: University of California Press.

Reardon-Anderson, James. 1991. *The Study of Change: Chemistry in China, 1840–1949.* New York: Cambridge University Press.

Reinsch, Paul S. 1922. *An American Diplomat in China.* London: George Allen & Unwin.

Remer, Charles F. 1933a. *Foreign Investments in China.* New York: Macmillan.

———. 1933b. *A Study of Chinese Boycotts, with Special Reference to Their Economic Effectiveness.* Baltimore: John Hopkins Press.

Ren Bingdao. 1996. "Jiji canyu guohuo yundong de Wuhe zhizao chang" (Five Cordials Textile Plant's active participation in the National Products Movement). In Pan Junxiang 1996c: 77–81.

Ren Dai. 1936. *The Status of Women in China.* Nanjing: Council of International Affairs.

Renmin chubanshe ditu shi, ed. 1997. *Jindai Zhongguo bainian guochi ditu* (Maps of one hundred years of modern Chinese national humiliations). Beijing: Renmin chubanshe.

"The Resources of China: The Work of the Newly-Created Commercial and Industrial Commission." 1915. *FER*, July: 53–56.

Reynolds, Douglas R. 1993. *China, 1898–1912: The Xinzheng Revolution and Japan.* Cambridge, Mass.: Harvard University, Council on East Asian Studies.

Rhoads, Edward J. M. 1975. *China's Republican Revolution: The Case of Kwangtung, 1895–1913.* Cambridge, Mass.: Harvard University Press.

———. 2000. *Manchus & Han: Ethnic Relations and Political Power in Late Qing and Early Republican China, 1861–1928.* Seattle: University of Washington Press.

Ribeiro, Aileen. 1988. *Fashion and the French Revolution.* New York: Holmes & Meier.

"Riben de tichang guohuo fangfa" (Japanese methods of promoting national products). 1936. *Guohuo xunkan* 2 (July 1): 47.

Richards, Thomas. 1990. *The Commodity Culture of Victorian England: Advertising and Spectacle, 1851–1914.* Stanford: Stanford University Press.

Rigby, Richard W. 1980. *The May 30 Movement.* Canberra: Australian National University Press.

Rimmington, Don. 1998. "History and Culture." In Hook 1998: 1–29.

Rinbara Fumiko. 1983. *Sō Sokkyu to Tenshin no kokka teishō undō* (Song Zejiu and Tianjin's Promote National Products Movement). Kyoto: Dōhōsha.

Roberts, Claire. 1997*a*. "The Way of Dress." In C. Roberts 1994: 12–25.

Roberts, Claire, ed. 1997*b*. *Evolution & Revolution: Chinese Dress, 1700s–1990s*. Sydney: Powerhouse.

Roberts, Mary Louise. 1994. *Civilization Without Sexes: Reconstructing Gender in Postwar France, 1917–1927*. Chicago: University of Chicago Press.

Robinson, Michael Edson. 1988. *Cultural Nationalism in Colonial Korea, 1920–1925*. Seattle: University of Washington Press.

Rofel, Lisa. 1994. "Liberation Nostalgia and a Yearning for Modernity." In Gilmartin et al. 1994: 226–49.

Rosenthal, Elisabeth. 1999. "Chinese Students Are Caught up by Nationalism." *New York Times*, May 12: 1, A13.

Rossabi, Morris. 1997. "The Silk Trade in China and Central Asia." In *When Silk Was Gold: Central Asian and Chinese Textiles*, ed. J. Watt and A. Wardwell, 7–19. New York: Metropolitan Museum of Art.

Rowe, William T. 1984. *Hankow: Commerce and Society in a Chinese City, 1796–1889*. Stanford: Stanford University Press.

Rowling, Nick. 1987. *Commodities: How the World Was Taken to Market*. London: Free Association Books.

Rydell, Robert W. 1984. *All the World's a Fair*. Chicago: University of Chicago Press.

————. 1993. *World of Fairs: The Century-of-Progress Expositions*. Chicago: University of Chicago Press.

Ryū Kaori. 1990. *Danpatsu: Kindai higashi Ajia no bunka shōtotsu* (Haircuts: cultural conflict in modern East Asia). Tokyo: Asahi shinbunsha.

Sanetō Keishū. 1939. *Chūgokujin Nihon ryūgaku shi* (A history of Chinese studying in Japan). Tokyo: Nikka gakkai.

Sarkar, Sumit. 1973. *The Swadeshi Movement in Bengal, 1903–1908*. Cambridge, Eng.: Cambridge University Press.

SB (*Shenbao*). Daily. Shanghai. 1898–1937.

Scanlon, Jennifer, ed. 2000. *The Gender and Consumer Culture Reader*. New York: New York University Press.

Schafer, Edward H. 1963. *The Golden Peaches of Samarkand: A Study of T'ang Exotics*. Berkeley: University of California Press.

Schlesinger, Arthur Meier. 1957 [1918]. *The Colonial Merchants and the American Revolution, 1763–1776*. New York: Frederick Ungar Publishing.

Schmidt, Leigh Eric. 1995. *Consumer Rites: The Buying and Selling of American Holidays*. Princeton: Princeton University Press.

Schneider, Laurence A. 1976. "National Essence and the New Intelligentsia." In *The Limits of Change: Essays on Conservative Alternatives in Republican China*, ed. C. Furth, 57–89. Cambridge, Mass.: Harvard University Press.

Schrecker, John E. 1971. *Imperialism and Chinese Nationalism: Germany in Shantung*. Cambridge, Mass.: Harvard University Press.

Schwantes, Robert S. 1974. "Japan's Cultural Foreign Policies." In *Japan's Foreign Policy, 1868–1941*, ed. J. W. Morley, 153–83. New York: Columbia University Press.

Schwartz, Benjamin Isadore. 1964. *In Search of Wealth and Power: Yen Fu and the West*. Cambridge, Mass.: Harvard University Press.

Scott, A. C. 1960. *Chinese Costume in Transition*. New York: Theatre Arts Books.

"Senden yō sensu" (Fans used for propaganda). 1924–25. Gaimushō. Meiji–Taishō Documents, file 3.3.8.6–3.

Shandong sheng guohuo chenlieguan, ed. 1936. *Shandong sheng guohuo chenlieguan guohuo niankan* (The national products yearbook of the Shandong Provincial National Products Museum). Ji'nan: Shandong sheng guohuo chenlieguan.

Shanghai baihuo gongsi et al., eds. 1988. *Shanghai jindai baihuo shangye shi* (A history of Shanghai's modern department stores). Shanghai: Shanghai shehui kexueyuan chubanshe.

Shanghai fazheng daxue xuesheng hui, ed. 1925. *Xuechi tekan* (Cleanse the humiliation special edition).

"Shanghai guohuo shizhuang zhanlan huiji" (Notes from the Shanghai National Products Fashion Show). 1930. *Shangye zazhi*, 5, no. 7.

"Shanghai guohuo yundong zhou zhi shengkuang" (Grand events of the Shanghai National Products Movement Week). 1928. *Shangye zazhi* 3, no. 9 (Aug.): 4–5.

Shanghai Hualian shangxia dang wei, ed. 1991. *Shanghai Yong'an gongsi zhigong yundong shi* (A history of the Shanghai Yong'an Company's workers movement). Beijing: Zhonggongdang shi chubanshe.

Shanghai jizhi guohuo gongchang lianhehui, ed. 1937. *Shinian lai zhi jilianhui* (A decade of the Association of Mechanized National Products Manufacturers). Shanghai: Shanghai hongxing huiji yinshuasuo.

Shanghai shangye zazhi, ed. 1928. *Shanghai tebieshi guohuo yundong dahui jinian kan* (Commemorative volume for the Shanghai Municipal National Products Movement Rally). Shanghai: Taidong tushuju.

Shanghai shehui kexueyuan, ed. 1981. *Xinhai geming zai Shanghai shiliao xuanji* (A selection of historical materials on the Revolution of 1911). Shanghai: Renmin chubanshe.

Shanghai shehui kexueyuan, Lishi yanjiusuo, ed. 1960. *Wusi yundong zai Shanghai shiliao xuanji* (A selection of materials on the May Fourth Movement in Shanghai). Shanghai: Renmin chubanshe.

————. 1986. *Wusa yundong shiliao* (Materials on the May Fourth Movement), vol. 2. Shanghai: Renmin chubanshe.

"Shanghai shi guohuo chenlieguan guicheng" (Bylaws of the Shanghai Municipal National Products Museum). 1930. In SSGC 1930: 125–27.

"Shanghai shi guohuo chenlieguan shencha chupin guize" (Regulations for investigating products for the Shanghai Municipal National Products Museum). 1930. In SSGC 1930: 130–33.

"Shanghai shi guohuo chenlieguan shoupin guize" (Regulations for products sold at the Shanghai Municipal National Products Museum). 1930. In SSGC 1930: 134–35.

"Shanghai shi guohuo chenlieguan zhengji chupin guize" (Regulations for collecting products for the Shanghai Municipal National Products Museum). 1930. In SSGC 1930: 127–30.

Shanghai shimin bao. 1931.

"Shanghai shimin tichang guohuo hui huizhang" (Bylaws of the Shanghai Citizens Association for the Promotion of National Products). 1934. *Guohuo banyue kan* 5 (Feb. 15).

Shanghai shi zhengfu, Shehuiju, ed. 1933. *Jin shiwu nian lai Shanghai zhi bagong tingye* (Strikes and lockouts in the past fifteen years in Shanghai). Shanghai: Shanghai shi zhengfu.

"Shanghai shi zhengfu tichang guohuo shiyong shixing banfa" (Methods for implementing the promotion of national products of the Shanghai Municipal government). 1930. In SSGC 1930: 165–66.

Shanghai tebieshi guohuo yundong dahui huikan (The Shanghai Municipal National Products Movement Rally). 1929. Shanghai.

Shanghai tebieshi, Shehuiju, ed. 1930. *Shanghai zhi gongye* (The industries of Shanghai). Shanghai: Zhonghua shuju.

"Shanghai zhi huazhuangpin gongye" (Shanghai's cosmetics industry). 1933. *SB*, Apr. 20.

Shanghai zong shanghui, Shanghai shangpin chenliesuo, ed. 1923. *Shanghai zong shanghui Shanghai shangpin chenlie suo dier ci baogao shu* (The second report of the Shanghai Chamber of Commerce Commercial Products Display Hall). Shanghai: Shanghai jiaotong yinshuasuo.

————. 1924. *Shanghai zong shanghui Shanghai shangpin chenliesuo disan ci baogao shu* (The third report of the Shanghai Chamber of Commerce Commercial Products Display Hall). Shanghai: Shanghai jiaotong yinshua gongsi.

Shanghai zong shanghui yuebao. Monthly. Shanghai, 1921–27.

"Shangpin chenliesuo zhangcheng" (Commodity display hall regulations). 1914. *Zhengfu gongbao*, Sept. 25: 859. Reprinted in Zhao Ninglu 1986: 665–66.

Shanhai Nippon shōgyō kaigisho, ed. 1915. *Hainichinetsu to Nikka haiseki no eikyō* (Anti-Japanese mania and the effects of the Japanese boycott), vol. 1. Shanghai: Shanhai Nippon shōgyō kaigisho.

She Ying. 1930. "Nüjie you tichang waihuo zhi kekai." *Funü gongming* 25: 1–2.

Shen Zuwei. 1989. "Jin jinian guonei jindai Zhongguo zichan jieji yanjiu shuping" (A survey of recent studies of the Chinese bourgeoisie in modern China). *Lishi yanjiu* 2: 87–102.

"Shengdan laoren de liwu" (Presents from Santa Claus). 1934. *SB*, Sept. 20.

"Shengdan laoren yu funü guohuonian" (Santa Claus and the Women's National Products Year). 1934. *SB*, Dec. 3.

Sheridan, James E. 1975. *China in Disintegration: The Republican Era in Chinese History, 1912–1949*. New York: Free Press.

Shi Pu. 1934. "Funü guohuo nian zhi zhanwang" (The prospects for the Women's National Products Year). *Guohuo banyue kan* 3 (Jan. 15): 1–5.

Shih Min-hsiung. 1976. *The Silk Industry in Ch'ing China*. Trans. E-tu Zen Sun. Ann Arbor: University of Michigan, Center for Chinese Studies.

Shimada Tomiko. 1962. "Clothing Habits." *Japan Quarterly* 9, no. 3: 352–63.

"Shina ni oite teikoku shōhin dōmei haiseki ikken" (Documents relating to the boycott of Japanese goods in China). Gaimushō. Meiji–Taishō Documents, file 3.3.8.7.

Shiratori Kurakichi. 1929. "The Queue Among the Peoples of North Asia." *Memoirs of the Tōyō Bunko* 4: 1–69.

Shiyebu. 1933. *Riben zai Hua jingji nuli* (The economic efforts of Japan in China). Shanghai: Zhonghua shuju yinshuasuo.

Shiyebu, Guohuo chenlieguan, ed. 1931. *Shiyebu Guohuo chenlieguan er zhounian baogao* (Second anniversary report of the Ministry of Industry's National Products Museum). Nanjing: Shiyebu, Guohuo chenlieguan.

"Shiyebu shencha hege fagei guohuo zhengmingshu zhi guohuo yi lan biao" (A brief list of national products that the Ministry of Industries investigated, found up to standard, and gave national product certifications). 1931. In Hu Guangming et al. 1994: 1483–91.

"Shizhuang zhenyi" (The true meaning of fashion). 1933. *SB*, May 11.

Shoudu guohuo daobao. Semi-monthly. Nanjing, 1935–37.

"Shoudu tichang guohuo yundong xuanchuan zhou" (The Capital [Nanjing] Promotes the National Products Movement Week). 1931. In Wang Keyou 1931: 20–25.

"Shuangshijie yu guohuo yundong" (Double Ten Day and the National Products Movement). 1935. *SB*, Oct. 10.

Silverberg, Miriam. 1991. "The Modern Girl as Militant." In *Recreating Japanese Women, 1600–1945*, ed. G. L. Bernstein, 239–66. Berkeley: University of California Press.

Skinner, G. William. 1965. "Marketing and Social Structure in Rural China, Part II." *Journal of Asian Studies* 24: 195–228.

Skotnes, Andor. 1994. "'Buy Where You Can Work': Boycotting for Jobs in African American Baltimore, 1933–1934." *Journal of Social History* 27: 735–62.

Slater, Don. 1997. *Consumer Culture and Modernity*. Oxford: Polity Press.

SMA (Shanghai Municipal Archives). Shanghai, China.

Smith, Anthony D. 1991. *National Identity*. Reno: University of Nevada Press.

———. 1998. *Nationalism and Modernism: A Critical Survey of Recent Theories of Nations and Nationalism*. New York: Routledge.

Smith, Arthur H. 1894. *Chinese Characteristics*. New York: Fleming H. Revell.

———. 1901. *China in Convulsion*. New York: Fleming H. Revell.

SMP (Shanghai Municipal Police [International Settlement]) Files. Microfilm from the U.S. National Archives.

Snow, Edgar. 1968. *Red Star over China*. rev. rev. and enl. ed. New York: Grove Press.

Sokusha, ed. 1929. *Anti-Foreign Teachings in New Text-books of China*. Tokyo: Sokusha.

Song Feifu, ed. 1994. *Hunan tongshi: xiandai juan* (A general history of Hunan province: the contemporary period). Changsha: Hunan chubanshe.

"Song funü guohuo nian" (Closing out the Women's National Products Year). 1934. *SB*, Dec. 27.

Song Qiang, Zhang Zangzang, and Qiao Bian. 1996. *Zhongguo keyi shuo bu* (China can also say no). Beijing: Zhonghua shehui kexue chubanshe.

Speer, William. 1870. *The Oldest and the Newest Empire: China and the United States*. Hartford: S. S. Scranton and Co.

Spence, Jonathan D. 1992. *Chinese Roundabout: Essays in History and Culture*. New York: W. W. Norton.

———. 1999. *Mao Zedong*. New York: Viking.

SSC (Shanghai shangpin chenliesuo), ed. 1936. *Shanghai shi shanghui shangpin chenliesuo shiwu zhou jinian tekan* (The fifteenth anniversary commemorative volume of the Shanghai Municipal Chamber of Commerce Commercial Products Display Hall). Shanghai: Shanghai shangpin chenliesuo.

SSD (Shanghai shi dang'anguan), ed. 1989. *Wu Yunchu qiye shiliao: Tianyuan huagong chang* (Historical materials on Wu Yunchu's business enterprises: The Tianyuan Electrochemical Factory). Shanghai: Dang'an chuban.

———. 1992. *Wu Yunchu qiye shiliao: Tianchu weijing chang* (Historical materials on Wu Yunchu's business enterprises: The Heaven's Kitchen MSG Factory). Shanghai: Dang'an chuban.

SSGC (Shanghai shi guohuo chenlieguan), ed. 1930. *Shanghai shi guohuo chenlieguan niankan* (Yearbook of the Shanghai Municipal National Products Museum). Shanghai: Shanghai shi guohuo chenlieguan.

————. 1933. *Shanghai shi guohuo zhanlan dahui jinian kan* (Commemorative volume for the Shanghai Municipal National Products Exhibition). Shanghai: Shanghai shi guohuo chenlieguan.

Strasser, Susan. 1989. *Satisfaction Guaranteed: The Making of the American Mass Market.* New York: Pantheon Books.

Struve, Lynn A. 1984. *The Southern Ming, 1644–1662.* New Haven: Yale University Press.

"Suiwei niantou zhi guohuo xiaoxi" (National products news from the end and beginning of the year). 1935. *Guohuo yuebao* 2, no. 1 (Jan.): 49–51.

Sun Changwei. 1997. *Cai Zimin xiansheng yuanpei nianpu* (A chronicle of Mr. Cai Yuanpei). Taibei: Yuanliu chuban gongsi.

Sun Fanjun and He Husheng, eds. 1991. *Minguo shi da cidian* (An encyclopedia of Republican history). Beijing: Zhongguo guangbo dianshi chubanshe.

Sun, Lung-kee. 1997. "The Politics of Hair and the Issue of the Bob in Modern China." *Fashion Theory* 1, no. 4: 353–66.

Sun Mengren. 1933. "Shei shi lixiangzhong de qizi?" (Who is the ideal wife?). *Jilian huikan* 80 (Oct. 1): 33–35.

Sun Yutang, ed. 1957. *Zhongguo jindai gongye shi ziliao, 1840–1895* (Materials on the history of Chinese modern industries). 2 vols. Beijing: Wenhai chubanshe.

Sun Zhendong, ed. 1982. *Zhongguo jinian jieri shouce* (A handbook of Chinese anniversaries and holidays). Taibei: Cuijin caise yinshua gongsi.

Suzhou Wusi, Wusa yundong ziliao xuanji (A selection of historical materials on Suzhou's May Fourth and May Thirtieth Movements). 1984. Suzhou: Suzhou shi dang'an ju.

SZMA (Suzhou Municipal Archives). Collection 2.1: Suzhou zong shanghui quanzong (Suzhou General Chamber of Commerce).

Tagore, Rabindranath. 1931. *The Home and the World.* London: Macmillan.

Takamura Naosuke. 1982. *Kindai Nihon mengyō to Chūgoku* (The modern Japanese cotton industry and China). Tokyo: Tōkyō daigaku.

T'ang, Leang-Li. 1930. *Inner History of the Chinese Revolution.* London: Routledge.

Tang Shunqing. 1937. "Jinnian sanbajie funü duiyu tichang guohuo de zeren" (The responsibility of women for the promotion of national products on this year's Women's Day). *Shoudu guohuo daobao* 38: 9–12.

Tang Weikang and Huang Yixuan, eds. 1991. *Sun Zhongshan zai Shanghai* (Sun Yat-sen in Shanghai). Shanghai: Shanghai renmin meishu chubanshe.

Tao Leqin. 1936. "Shangpin chenliesuo zhi quanwei" (The authority of the Commercial Products Hall). In SSC 1936.

Tarlo, Emma. 1996. *Clothing Matters: Dress and Identity in India.* Chicago: University of Chicago Press.

Teng, Ssu-yü, and John K. Fairbank, eds. 1954. *China's Response to the West: A Documentary Survey, 1839–1923.* Cambridge, Mass.: Harvard University Press.

Tenorio-Trillo, Mauricio. 1996. *Mexico at the World's Fairs: Crafting a Modern Nation.* Berkeley: University of California Press.

Thomas, James A. 1931. *Trailing Trade a Million Miles.* Durham, N.C.: Duke University Press.

Thompson, Roger R. 1995. *China's Local Councils in the Age of Constitutional Reform, 1898–1911.* Cambridge, Mass.: Harvard University, Council on East Asian Studies.

Thomson, John. 1873–74. *Illustrations of China and Its People in Early Photographs.* 4 vols. London: Sampson Low, Marston, Low, and Searle.

Thomson, John Stuart. 1913. *China Revolutionized.* London: T. Werner Laurie.

"Tianchu chang 1923 nian zhi 1937 nian linian weijing chanliang biao" (A table of the Heaven's Kitchen Factory's yearly MSG production from 1923 to 1937). In SSD 1992: 83.

"Tianchu wei chang jing" (The essence of the Heaven's Kitchen MSG Factory). 1936. *Jilian huikan* 153 (Oct. 15): 9–12.

"Tianchu weijing huode Jiangsu sheng disanci difang wupin zhanlanhui diyi dengjiang jiangping" (Heaven's Kitchen's MSG receives top prize at the Third Jiangsu Provincial Local Commodity Exhibition). 1925. In SSD 1992: 43.

Tianjin lishi bowuguan and Nankai daxue, Lishixi, eds. 1980. *Wusi yundong zai Tianjin: lishi ziliao xuanji* (The May Fourth Movement in Tianjin: a selection of historical materials). Tianjin: Renmin chubanshe.

Tichang guohuo hui huikan. Monthly. Changsha, 1932.

"Tichang guohuo juti banfa" (Concrete ways to promote national products). 1934. *Guochan daobao* 160: 10–11.

"Tichang guohuo ying cong ertong zuoqi" (Promoting national products should begin with children). 1933. *Jilian huikan* 84 (Dec. 1): 15–17.

Tichang guohuo zhoukan. Weekly. Changsha, 1929.

Tien, Hung-mao. 1972. *Government and Politics in Kuomintang China, 1927–1937.* Stanford: Stanford University Press.

Tobin, Joseph Jay. 1992a. "Introduction: Domesticating the West." In Tobin 1992b: 1–41.

Tobin, Joseph Jay, ed. 1992b. *Re-Made in Japan: Everyday Life and Consumer Taste in a Changing Society.* New Haven: Yale University Press.

"Tonggao ge guohuo gongchang" (Notice to all national product manufacturers). 1937. In Shanghai jizhi guohuo gongchang lianhehui 1937: 162–63.

Townsend, James. 1996. "Chinese Nationalism." In Unger 1996: 1–30.

"Trade Exposition in Hankow." 1928. *NCH*, Nov. 24: 304.

"Trade Exposition in Peking." 1928. *NCH*, Dec. 29: 523.

Tsou Mingteh. 1996. "Christian Missionary as Confucian Intellectual: Gilbert Reid (1857–1927) and the Reform Movement in the Late Qing." In *Christianity in China: From the Eighteenth Century to the Present*, ed. Daniel Bays, 73–90. Stanford: Stanford University Press.

Tyau, Min-ch'ien T. Z. 1922. *China Awakened*. New York: Macmillan.

Tyau, Min-ch'ien T. Z., ed. 1930. *Two Years of Nationalist China*. Shanghai: Kelly & Walsh.

Unger, Jonathan, ed. 1996. *Chinese Nationalism*. Armonk, N.Y.: M. E. Sharpe.

van de Ven, Hans J. 1996a. "Recent Studies of Modern Chinese History." *Modern Asian Studies* 30, no. 2: 225–69.

———. 1996b. "War in the Making of Modern China." *Modern Asian Studies* 30, no. 4: 737–56.

———. 1997. "The Military in the Republic." *China Quarterly* 150: 352–74.

van Dorn, Harold Archer. 1932. *Twenty Years of the Chinese Republic*. New York: Alfred A. Knopf.

Varg, Paul A. 1968. *The Making of a Myth: The United States and China, 1897–1912*. East Lansing: Michigan State University Press.

Vollmer, John. 1977. *In the Presence of the Dragon Throne: Ch'ing Dynasty Costume (1644–1911) in the Royal Ontario Museum*. Toronto: Royal Ontario Museum.

Wakeman, Frederic E., Jr. 1966. *Strangers at the Gate: Social Disorder in South China, 1839–1861*. Berkeley: University of California Press.

———. 1985. *The Great Enterprise: The Manchu Reconstruction of Imperial Order in Seventeenth-Century China*. 2 vols. Berkeley: University of California Press.

Wakeman, Frederic E., Jr., and Wen-hsin Yeh. 1992a. "Introduction." In Wakeman and Yeh 1992b: 1–14.

Wakeman, Frederic E., Jr., and Wen-hsin Yeh, eds. 1992b. *Shanghai Sojourners*. Berkeley, Calif.: Institute of East Asian Studies.

Waldron, Arthur. 1993. "War and the Rise of Chinese Nationalism." *Journal of Military History* 57: 87–104.

Walker, John A., and Sarah Chaplin. 1997. *Visual Culture*. Manchester: Manchester University Press.

Walshe, W. Gilbert. 1906. *Ways That are Dark: Some Chapters on Chinese Etiquette and Social Procedure*. Shanghai: Kelly & Walsh.

Walton, Whitney. 1992. *France at the Crystal Palace: Bourgeois Taste and Artisan Manufacture in the Nineteenth Century*. Berkeley: University of California Press.

Wang Daliang. 1995. *Weijing dawang Wu Yunchu* (The MSG king: Wu Yunchu). Beijing: Jiefangjun chubanshe.

Wang Dongyuan. 1928. "Tianchu weijing zhizao chang" (The Heaven's Kitchen MSG Factory). In Shanghai shangye zazhi 1928: "Changhao fazhan xiaoshi" (Brief histories of industrial developments) section.

Wang Ermin. 1981. "Duanfa yifu gaiyuan: bianfa lunzhi xiangzheng zhiqu" (Cutting queues, replacing clothing, and changing reigns: the symbolic objectives of constitutional reform discussions). In *Zhongguo jindaide weixin yundong—bianfa yu lixian taojihui* (China's modern reform movement: a conference on political reform and constitutionalism), ed. Zhongguo jindai de weixin yundong, bianfa yu lixian yantaohui, 59–73. Taibei: Academia Sinica, Institute of Modern History.

———. 1995. "Shangzhan guannian yu zhengshang sixiang" (The concept of commercial warfare and the ideology of emphasizing commerce). In idem, *Zhongguo jindai sixiang shilun* (Essays on modern Chinese thought), 233–381. Taibei: Taibei shangwu yinshu guan.

Wang Guanhua. 1995. "Media, Intellectuals, and the Ideology of the 1905 Anti-Exclusion Boycott." *Chinese Historians* 15: 1–48.

———. 2001. *In Search of Justice: The 1905–1906 Chinese Anti-American Boycott.* Cambridge, Mass.: Harvard University Asia Center.

Wang Hanqiang, ed. 1915. *Guohuo diaocha lu* (Records of national product investigations). 3rd ed. Shanghai: Zhonghua guohuo weichi hui.

Wang Jingming. 1934. "Women yinggai xiaofa Yue wang Goujian tichang guohuo" (We should learn from King Goujian of Yue and promote national products). *Funü gongming yuebao* 3, no. 5: 36–39.

Wang Jingyu, ed. 1957. *Zhongguo jindai gongye shi ziliao, 1895–1914* (Materials on China's modern industries). 2 vols. Beijing: Kexue chubanshe.

Wang Keyou, ed. 1931. *Chuangdao jieyue tuixing guohuo wei Zhongguo dongqian zhi jiwu* (Take the lead in economizing and promoting national products in order to aid China in its current crisis). N.p.

Wang, Peter Chen-main. 1996. "Contextualizing Protestant Publishing in China: The Wenshe, 1924–1928." In *Christianity in China: From the Eighteenth Century to the Present*, ed. Daniel Bays, 292–306. Stanford: Stanford University Press.

Wang Pilai and Wang Yu. 1994. "Dongfang weijing dawang Wu Yunchu" (Wu Yunchu, the king of the East's MSG)." In Zhao Yunsheng 1994: 343–451.

Wang Xiang. 1986. "Minchu 'Fuzhi gaige' dui Suzhou si shiye de yingxiang" (The effects of "Dress Reform" on the Suzhou silk industry in the early years of the Republic). *Lishi yanjiu* 4: 36–48.

———. 1992. "Jindai sichou shengchan fazhan yu Jiangnan shehui bianqian" (The development of modern silk production and social change in Jiangnan). *Jindaishi yanjiu* 4: 1–20.

Wang Xiaodong, Fang Ning, and Song Qiang, eds. 1999. *Quanqiuhua yinyingxia de Zhongguo zhilu* (China's road under the shadow of globalization). Beijing: Zhongguo shehui kexue chubanshe.

Wang Xing. 1992. *Bainian fushi chaoliu yu shibian* (One hundred years of dress fashions and changes). Hong Kong: Shangwu yishuguan.

Wang, Y. C. 1966. *Chinese Intellectuals and the West, 1872–1949.* Chapel Hill: University of North Carolina Press.

Wang, Zheng. 1999. *Women in the Chinese Enlightenment: Oral and Textual Histories.* Berkeley: University of California Press.

"Wanyu ertong zuo zai shifu relie qingzhu ertong jie" (Over 10,000 children gathered at City Hall yesterday to warmly celebrate Children's Day). 1934. *SB,* Apr. 5.

Warra, Carrie. 1999. "Invention, Industry, Art: the Commercialization of Culture in Republican Art Magazines." In Cochran 1999b: 61–89.

Wasserstrom, Jeffrey N. 1991. *Student Protests in Twentieth-Century China: The View from Shanghai.* Stanford: Stanford University Press.

Watson, James L. 1985. "Standardizing the Gods: The Promotion of T'ian Hou ('Empress of Heaven') Along the South China Coast, 960–1960." In D. Johnson et al. 1985: 292–324.

———. 2000. "China's Big Mac Attack." *Foreign Affairs,* May/June 2000.

Weale, Putnam. 1926. *Why China Sees Red.* London: Macmillan and Company.

Wen Zhengyi. 1996. "Dizhi Rihuo, tichang guohuo zai Yichang" (Boycotting Japanese products, promoting national products in Yichang). In Pan Junxiang 1996c: 444–51.

"The Westlake Exposition of China Products." 1929. *CWR,* July 27: 378–86.

White, Trumbull. 1897. *Glimpses of the Orient, or, The Manners, Customs, Life and History of the People of China, Japan and Corea.* Philadelphia: P. W. Ziegler & Co.

Wilbur, C. Martin. 1983. *The Nationalist Revolution in China, 1923–1928.* Cambridge, Eng.: Cambridge University Press.

Williams, C. A. S. 1933. *Manual of Chinese Products.* Shanghai: Kelly & Walsh.

Williams, Edward Thomas. 1923. *China Yesterday and To-day.* London: George G. Harrap & Co.

———. 1927. "The Status of Women." *Current History* 26, no. 3: 420–25.

Williams, Rosalind H. 1982. *Dream Worlds: Mass Consumption in Late Nineteenth-Century France.* Berkeley: University of California Press.

Williamson, Judith. 1995. *Decoding Advertisements: Ideology and Meaning in Advertising.* London: Boyars.

Witke, Roxane. 1980. "Women in Shanghai of the 1930s." In *La donna nella Cina imperiale e nella Cina repubblicana,* ed. L. Lanciotti, 95–122. Florence: L. S. Olschki.

"Wo duiyu fuzhuang shang de sanbu zhiyi" (My "three no" principles regarding clothing). 1934. *Jilian huikan* 92 (Apr. 1): 48–49.

"Wo jia de riyongpin" (Daily necessities in my house). 1932. *Jilian huikan* 49 (Jan. 1): 22–23.

Wolman, Paul. 1992. *Most Favored Nation: The Republican Revisionists and U.S. Tariff Policy, 1897–1912.* Chapel Hill: University of North Carolina Press.

"Womende kouhao" (Our slogans). 1931. In Wang Keyou 1931: supplemental section, 13.

Wong, J. Y. 1998. *Deadly Dreams: Opium, Imperialism, and the Arrow War (1856–1860) in China.* Cambridge, Eng.: Cambridge University Press.

Wong, Jan. 1996. *Red China Blues: My Long March from Mao to Now.* New York: Anchor Books.

Wong, Sin-kiong. 1995. "The Genesis of Popular Movements in Modern China." Ph.D. diss., Indiana University.

Wong, Young-tsu. 1989. *Search for Modern Nationalism: Zhang Binglin and Revolutionary China.* New York: Oxford University Press.

Woodhead, Henry G. W. 1935. *Adventures in Far Eastern Journalism: A Record of Thirty-Three Years' Experience.* Tokyo: Hokuseido Press.

Wright, Mary C. 1957. *The Last Stand of Chinese Conservatism: The T'ung-chih Restoration, 1862–1874.* Stanford: Stanford University Press.

Wright, Mary C., ed. 1968. *China in Revolution: The First Phase, 1900–1913.* New Haven: Yale University.

Wright, Stanley F. 1938. *China's Struggle for Tariff Autonomy, 1843–1938.* Shanghai: Kelly & Walsh.

———. 1950. *Hart and the Chinese Customs.* Belfast: Wm. Mullan & Son.

Wright, Tim. 1984. *Coal Mining in China's Economy and Society, 1895–1937.* Cambridge, Eng.: Cambridge University Press.

———. 1993. "'The Spiritual Heritage of Chinese Capitalism': Recent Trends in the Historiography of Chinese Enterprise Management." In *Using the Past to Serve the Present: Historiography and Politics in Contemporary China,* ed. J. Unger, 205–38. Armonk, N.Y.: M. E. Sharpe.

Wu Baiheng. 1996. "Jingying Baihao lianru chang de huiyi" (Reminiscences on managing the Hundred Happiness Condensed Milk Factory). In Pan Junxiang 1996c: 160–71.

Wu, Chang-chuan. 1974. "Cheng Kuan-Ying: A Case Study of Merchant Participation in the Chinese Self-Strengthening Movement (1878–1884)." Ph.D. diss., Columbia University.

Wu Chengming. 1958. *Diguo zhuyi zai jiu Zhongguo de touzi* (Imperialist investment in old China). Beijing: Renmin chubanshe.

Wu Jinyun. 1934. "Duiyu guohuo yundong yingyou de renshi" (The consciousness one should have toward the National Products Movement). *Funü gongming yuebao* 3, no. 6: 29–32.

Wu Kangling, ed. 1994. *Sichuan tongshi* (A general history of Sichuan), vol. 6. Chengdu: Sichuan daxue chubanshe.

Wu Linsi. 1996. "1928 nian Gongshang bu Zhonghua guohuo zhanlan hui jishi" (A record of the 1928 Ministry of Industry and Commerce's Chinese National Products Exhibition). In Pan Junxiang 1996c: 403–11.

Wu Ou. 1931. "Tianjin Shehuiju xunling" (Tianjin Social Affairs Bureau order). May 7. In Hu Guangming et al. 1994: 1482.

Wu Tiecheng. 1969. *Wu Tiecheng huiyilu* (The memoirs of Wu Tiecheng). Taibei: Sanmin shuju.

Wu Tingfang. 1914. *America through the Spectacles of an Oriental Diplomat.* New York: Stokes.

——. 1915. *Zhonghua minguo tuzhi chuyi* (My humble opinion on the Chinese republic). Shanghai: Shangwu yinshu guan.

"Wuhan guo zhanhui daibiao zhaodai gejie yu zhi" (Wuhan National Products Exhibition representatives host various circles). 1929. *SB*, Jan. 5: 14.

"Wu Yunchu xiansheng xiaoshi" (A brief history of Mr. Wu Yunchu). 1934. *Guohuo niankan*: 3–4.

Xia Dongyuan. 1985. *Zheng Guanying zhuan* (Biography of Zheng Guanying). Shanghai: Huadong shifan daxue chubanshe.

Xia Dongyuan, ed. 1995. *Ershi shiji Shanghai dabolan* (Compendium on twentieth-century China). Shanghai: Wenhui chubanshe.

"Xialing yongpin zhanlanhui" (Summer articles exhibition). 1933. *SB*, June 15.

Xiang Kangyuan. 1936. "Tichang guohuo yu guohuo zhanlan" (Promoting national products and national product exhibits). In SSC 1936.

Xiang Zenan. 1996. "Xianshen guohuo shiye de Xiang Songmao" (Xiang Songmao's dedication to national product enterprises). In Pan Junxiang 1996c: 149–59.

"Xiangcun tongbao de xialing guohuo yongpin" (The summer national product articles of village compatriots). 1933. *SB*, June 29.

"Xianluo Huahuo chenlieguan zhengji guohuo" (Thailand Chinese Products Museum collects national products). 1928. *SB*, Nov. 4: 13.

Xiao, Yanming. 1999. "State and Industrial Development in Early Republican China." Ph.D. diss., Harvard University.

"Xiaoxue jiaoshi zeren jiazhongle" (The responsibility of primary school teachers has become great). 1934. *SB*, Apr. 12.

Xie Guoxiang, ed. 1996. *Beiyang junfa shiliao* (Historical materials on the Beiyang warlords). Tianjin: Tianjin guji chubanshe.

Xie Wenhua. 1994. "'Maiban yanjiu' zhi huigu yu zhanwang" (A retrospective and prospects for research on "compradores"). *Lishi xuebao* 22: 391–412.

Xihu bolanhui canguan bixie (Essentials to take to the West Lake Exhibition). 1929. Shanghai: Shangwu yinshu guan.

Xihu bolanhui rikan. Daily. Hangzhou, 1929.

Xin Ping, Hu Zhenghao, and Li Xuechang. 1991. *Minguo shehui dagang* (An overview of Republican society). Fuzhou: Fujian renmin chubanshe.

"Xingzheng yuan guanyu banxing quanguo juban wupin zhanlanhui tongze de cheng" (The Executive Yuan on the petition to promulgate the general rules governing the hosting of article exhibitions across China). 1991. In ZDLDG 1991: 720–22.

"Xin shenghuo zhifu yu guohuo" (New Life uniforms and national products). 1934. *SB,* Apr. 12.

Xiong Yuezhi. 1996. "The Image and Identity of the Shanghainese." In *Unity and Diversity: Local Cultures and Identities in China,* ed. T. T. Liu and D. Faure, 99–106. Hong Kong: Hong Kong University Press.

Xiong Zongren. 1986. *Wusi Yundong zai Guizhou* (The May Fourth Movement in Guizhou). Guiyang: Guizhou remin chubanshe.

Xiongdi guohuo yuekan. Monthly. Beiping, 1934.

Xu Dingxin and Qian Xiaoming. 1991. *Shanghai zong shanghui shi (1902–1929)* (A history of the Shanghai Chamber of Commerce). Shanghai: Shanghai shehui kexueyuan chubanshe.

Xu, Xiaoqun. 2001. *Chinese Professionals and the Republican State: The Rise of Professional Associations in Shanghai, 1912–1937.* Cambridge, Eng.: Cambridge University Press.

Xu Youqun, ed. 1991. *Minguo renwu da cidian* (A biographical dictionary of the Republic). Shijiazhuang: Hebei renmin chubanshe.

Xuechi zhoukan. Weekly. Guangzhou, 1928.

XWB (Xinwen bao). Daily. Shanghai.

Yamane Yukio et al., eds. 1996. *Kindai Nitchū kankeishi kenkyū nyūmon* (An introduction to the study of modern Sino-Japanese relations). Rev. ed. Tokyo: Kenbun shuppan.

Yan Changhong. 1992. *Zhongguo jindai shehui fengsu shi* (A history of Chinese modern social customs). Hangzhou: Zhejiang renmin chubanshe.

Yan Ruli, ed. 1919 [1915]. *Wangguo jian fu guochi lu* (A warning on extinguished nations with a supplement on national humiliations). Shanghai: Taidong tushuju.

Yan, Yunxiang. 2000. "Of Hamburgers and Social Space: Consuming McDonald's in Beijing. In D. Davis 2000: 201–25.

Yan Zhongping, ed. 1955. *Zhongguo jindai jingji shi tongji zhiliao xuanji* (A selection of statistics on China's modern economic history). Beijing: Kexue chubanshe.

Yang Chengqi. 1996. "'Zhanghua maofang chang de 'Jiu yiba' bo biji'" (Zhanghua Wool Factory's November Eighteenth serge). In Pan Junxiang 1996c: 91–93.

Yang Dajun, ed. 1933. *Jindai Zhongguo shiye tongzhi* (Compendium on modern Chinese industry). N.p.

————. 1938. *Xiandai Zhongguo shiye zhi: zhizaoye* (A record of contemporary Chinese industry: manufacturers). Shanghai: Shangwu yinshu guan.

Yang, Lien-sheng. 1970. "Government Control of Urban Merchants in Traditional China." *Tsing Hua Journal of Chinese Studies* 8, no. 1–2: 186–206.

Yang Quan. 1923. *Wushi nian lai zhi Zhongguo jingji* (The Chinese economy during the past 50 years). Shanghai: Shenbao guan.

Yang Shufan. 1982. *Zhongguo wenguan zhidu shi* (A history of the Chinese civil service). 2 vols. Taibei: Liming wenhua shiye.

Yang Tianliang. 1991a. "Guohuo yundong he guohuo tuanti" (National products and national product groups). In *Minguo shehui daguan*, ed. Xin Ping, Hu Zhenghao, and Li Xuechang. Fuzhou: Fujian remin chubanshe.

————. 1991b. "Shanghai sida baihuo gongsi" (Shanghai's four great department stores). In *Minguo shehui daguan*, ed. Xin Ping, Hu Zhenghao, and Li Xuechang. Fuzhou: Fujian remin chubanshe.

Yang Yonggang, ed. 1997. *Zhongguo jindai tielu shi* (China's modern railroads). Shanghai: Shanghai shudian chubanshe.

Ye Kenzhen. 1935. "Aiguo de xiao Maomao" (Patriotic little Maomao). *Guohuo yuebao* 2, no. 1 (Jan.): 82–84.

Yeh, Catherine Vance. 1997. "The Life-Style of Four *Wenren* in Late Qing Shanghai." *Harvard Journal of Asiatic Studies* 57: 419–70.

Yeh, Wen-Hsin. 1990. *The Alienated Academy: Culture and Politics in Republican China, 1919–1937*. Cambridge, Mass.: Harvard University, Council on East Asian Studies.

————. 1996. *Provincial Passages: Culture, Space, and the Origins of Chinese Communism*. Berkeley: University of California Press.

————. 1997. "Shanghai Modernity: Commerce and Culture in a Republican City." *China Quarterly* 150: 375–94.

Yi Bin, ed. 1995. *Lao Shanghai guanggao* (The advertisements of old Shanghai). Shanghai: Shanghai huabao chubanshe.

Yi Ding. 1996. "Guohuo yundong yu Nanyang shichang" (The National Products Movement and the South Pacific market). In Pan Junxiang 1996c: 376–85.

"Yi erba guohuo yundong zhou" (1–28 National Products Movement Week). 1934. *SB*, Jan. 23.

Yinhang zhoubao. Weekly. Shanghai, 1917–50.

"Yinian nei canguan renshu tongji biao" (A statistical table of visitors during the year). 1924. In Shanghai zong shanghui, Shanghai shangpin chenliesuo 1924.

Yip, Ka-che. 1980. *Religion, Nationalism, and Chinese Students: The Anti-Christian Movement of 1922–1927*. Bellingham: Western Washington University, Center for East Asian Studies.

Yoji, Akashi. 1963. "The Boycott and Anti-Japanese National Salvation Movement of the Nanyang Chinese, 1908–1941," Ph.D. diss., Georgetown University.

Yoshimi Shun'ya. 1992. *Hakurankai no seijigaku: manazashi no kindai* (The politics of exhibitions: a look at modernity). Tokyo: Chūkō shinsho.

"You 'jiu yiba' xiangdaole Gandi" (From September 18 to thoughts of Gandhi). 1934. *SB*, Sept. 18.

"You zi" (The son away from home). 1934. *Jilian huikan* 92 (Apr. 1): 63–64.

Young, Ernest P. 1977. *The Presidency of Yuan Shih-k'ai: Liberalism and Dictatorship in Early Republican China*. Ann Arbor: University of Michigan Press.

Young, Louise. 1999. "Marketing the Modern: Department Stores, Consumer Culture, and the New Middle Class in Interwar Japan." *International Labor and Working-Class History* 55: 52–70.

Young, Marilyn Blatt. 1968. *The Rhetoric of Empire: American China Policy, 1895–1901.* Cambridge, Mass.: Harvard University Press.

Yu Heping. 1995. *Shanghui yu Zhongguo zaoqi xiandaihua* (Chambers of commerce and China's early modernization). Taibei: Dongda tushu.

Yu, Ningping. 1999. "Manufacturing Images: Four Chinese Travelers and Their Writings About America." Ph.D. diss., University of Iowa.

Yu Qiacheng, "Pan Gongzhan furen" (Mrs. Pan Gongzhan). 1934. *SB*, Mar. 24.

Yü Ying-shih. 1967. *Trade and Expansion in Han China: A Study of the Structure of Sino-Barbarian Economic Relations*. Berkeley: University of California Press.

Yu Zuoting. 1935. "Guohuo jiuguo" (National products save the nation). *Guohuo yuebao* 2, no. 1: 7.

Yue Qingping. 1994. *Zhongguo minguo xisu shi* (A history of customs in the Chinese Republic). Beijing: Renmin chubanshe.

Yuval-Davis, Nira, and Floya Anthias, eds. 1989. *Women, Nation, State*. New York: St. Martin's Press.

"Zai Shi gaijin hai Nichi sendō no ken" (Documents relating to anti-Japanese agitation by foreigners in China). Gaimushō. Meiji–Taishō Documents, File 3.3.8.6–1.

Zarrow, Peter. 1988. "He Zhen and Anarcho-Feminism in China." *Journal of Asian Studies* 47: 796–813.

Zdatny, Steven. 1997. "The Boyish Look and the Liberated Woman: The Politics and Aesthetics of Women's Hairstyles." *Fashion Theory* 1, no. 4: 367–98.

ZDLDG (Zhongguo di'er lishi dang'an guan), ed. 1991. *Zhonghua minguo shi dang'an ziliao huibian, diwu ji, diyi bian caizheng jingji (ba)* (A collection of archival materials on the Chinese Republic). Nanjing: Jiangsu guji chubanshe.

———. 1992. *Wusi yundong zai Jiangsu* (The May Fourth Movement in Jiangsu). Nanjing: Jiangsu guji chubanshe.

ZGWH (Zhonghua guohuo weichi hui), ed. 1912. *Zhonghua guohuo weichi hui zhang-cheng wendu huilu* (Organizational materials of the National Products Preservation Association). Shanghai: Zhonghua guohuo weichi hui.

————. 1932. *Zhonghua guohuo weichi hui ershi zhounian jinian kan* (A twentieth year commemorative volume of the National Products Preservation Association). Shanghai.

ZGZZW (Zhongguo Guomindang, Zhongyang zhixing weiyuanhui, Xuanchuan bu). 1929a. *Tichang guohuo yundong xuanchuan gangyao* (Essential propaganda for promoting the National Products Movement). N.p.: Zhongguo Guomindang, Zhongyang zhixing weiyuanhui, Xuanchuan bu.

ZGZZW, ed. 1929b. *Qixiang yundong xuanchuan gangyao* (Essential propaganda for the Seven Movements). Nanjing: Zhongguo Guomindang.

"Zhabei guohuo liudong zhanlanhui bimu" (Zhabei National Products Exhibition closes). 1929. *SB*, Jan. 15: 14.

"Zhabei guohuo zhanlanhui san ri ji" (Notes from three days of the Zhabei National Products Exhibition). 1929. *SB*, Jan. 4: 14.

Zhang Jian and Wu Linwu. 1996. "1934 nian funü guohuo nian" (The 1934 Women's National Products Year). In Pan Junxiang 1996c: 437–43.

Zhang Mingdong. 1934. "Cong fuyong guohuo shuodao fuxing minzu" (From using national products to reviving the nation). *Funü gongming yuebao* 3, no. 5: 40–42.

Zhang Xiaobo. 1995. "Merchant Associational Activism in Early Twentieth-Century China: The Tianjin General Chamber of Commerce, 1904–1928." Ph.D. diss., Columbia University.

Zhang Yinghui and Gong Xiangzheng, eds. 1981. *Wusi yundong zai Wuhan shiliao xuanji* (A selection of materials on the May Fourth Movement in Wuhan). Wuhan: Hubei renmin chubanshe.

Zhang, Yingjin. 1996. *The City in Modern Chinese Literature & Film: Configurations of Space, Time, and Gender*. Stanford: Stanford University Press.

Zhang Yufa. 1992. *Jindai Zhongguo gongye fazhan shi (1860–1916)* (A history of the development of modern Chinese industry). Taibei: Guiguan tushu.

Zhang Zhongli, ed. 1990. *Shanghai chengshi yanjiu* (Studies of Shanghai). Shanghai: Renmin chubanshe.

"Zhanlankuang Riben" (Exhibition-mad Japan). 1931. *Jilian huikan* 34 (May 16): 10–11.

Zhao Feng, ed. 1994. *Guohuo, yanghuo ni ai shei* (National products or foreign products: which do you cherish?). Tianjin: Renmin chubanshe.

Zhao Ninglu, ed. 1986. *Zhongguo minguo shangye dang'an ziliao huibian* (A collection of archival materials on China's Republican industries), vol. 2, *Zhongguo shangye jingji yanjiu congshu* (Research series on the Chinese commercial economy). Nanjing: Zhongguo shangye chubanshe.

Zhao Yang. 2000. "State, Children, and the Wahaha Group of Hangzhou." In *Feeding China's Little Emperors: Food, Children, and Social Change*, ed. Jing Jun, 185–98. Stanford: Stanford University Press.

Zhao Yizao. 1932. "Wei shenma yao gou yong guohuo?" (Why should you purchase and use national products?). *Jilian huikan* 58 (Sept. 16): 38–40.

Zhao Yunsheng, ed. 1994. *Zhongguo da zibenjia zhuan 5: Gongshang dawang juan* (Biographies of major Chinese capitalists, no. 5: captains of industry). Changchun: Shidai wenyi chubanshe.

Zhao Zizhen. 1996. "Dongya maoni fangzhi gufen youxian gongsi kanban qianhou" (The East Asia Wool Textile Company around the time of its start). In Pan Junxiang 1996c: 82–90.

Zhejiang jianshe ting. 1931. *Xihu bolanhui zong baogaoshu* (Complete report of the West Lake Exhibition). 6 vols. Hangzhou: Xihu bolanhui.

Zhen Pei'ai. 1997. *Zhongwai guanggao shi: zhan zai dangdai shijiao de quanmian huigu* (A history of Sino-foreign advertising: a retrospective from a contemporary viewpoint). Beijing: Zhongguo wujia chubanshe.

Zheng Guanying. 1998 [ca. 1893]. *Shengshi weiyan* (Warnings to a prosperous age). Zhengzhou: Zhongzhou guji chubanshe.

Zheng Yougui. 1939. *Woguo guanshui zizhu hou jinkou shuilü shuizhun zhi bianqian* (Guidelines for import duties since our country recovered tariff autonomy). Changsha: n.p.

"Zhenjiang pin'er fufantuan juxing fanmai guohuo kaimu yishi" (Zhenjiang orphan peddler teams hold Sell National Products inauguration ceremony). 1919. *Minguo ribao*, Oct. 13. Reprinted in ZDLDG 1992: 233.

"Zhenzhengde modeng funü" (Authentic modern women). 1934. *SB*, Feb. 4.

Zhichi hui, ed. 1915. *Guochi* (National humiliation). 2 vols. N.p.

Zhonggong, Sichuan sheng wei, Dangshi gongzuo weiyuanhui, ed. 1989. *Wusi yundong zai Sichuan* (The May Fourth Movement in Sichuan). Chengdu: Sichuan daxue chubanshe.

Zhonggong, Tianjin shi wei, Dangshi ziliao zhengji weiyuanhui, ed. 1987. *Wusa yundong zai Tianjin* (The May Thirtieth Movement in Tianjin). Beijing: Zhonggong dangshi ziliao chubanshe.

Zhongguo bowuguan xiehui, ed. 1936. *Zhongguo bowuguan yilan* (A survey of Chinese museums). Beiping: Zhongguo bowuguan xiehui chubanshe.

Zhongguo guohuo gongsi huoming huilu (China National Products Company product names catalog). 1934. Shanghai: Zhongguo guohuo gongsi.

Zhongguo guohuo lianhe yingye gongsi, ed. 1947. *Zhongguo guohuo lianhe yingye gongsi shizhou jinian kan* (Tenth anniversary commemorative volume of the China National Products Company). Shanghai: Tongwen yinwuju.

Zhongguo Guomindang, Hebei sheng dangwu zhidao weiyuanhui, ed. 1928. *Dui Ri jingji juejiao* (Severing economic relations with Japan). N.p.: Huamei yinshua.

"Zhongguo huo xianyao Zhongguoren ziji yong qilai" (Chinese should be the first to use Chinese products). 1935. *SB*, Aug. 12.

Zhongguo shehui kexueyuan, Jindai shi yanjiusuo, ed. 1959. *Wusi aiguo yundong ziliao* (Materials on the May Fourth Patriotic Movement). Beijing: Zhongguo shehui kexueyuan chubanshe.

———. 1979. *Ju E Yundong, 1901–1905* (The Resist Russia Movement). Beijing: Zhongguo shehui kexueyuan chubanshe.

Zhonghua guohuo weichi hui. 1912. *Dazongtong gongbu Canyiyuan yijue Zhonghua minguo fuzhi tu* (Illustrations of the Republic of China's clothing regulations issued by the president and passed by the Provisional Council of Provincial Representatives). Shanghai: Zhonghua guohuo weichi hui.

"Zhonghua guohuo weichi hui zuzhi quanguo guohuo zhanlanhui canguantuan xuanyanshu ji zhangcheng" (Announcement and regulations for the All-China National Products Exhibition tour group organized by the National Products Preservation Association). 1915. *Guohuo yuebao* 1 (Aug. 15): 6–11.

"Zhonghua guohou zhanlanhui changweihui jiyao" (Summary of the Chinese National Products Exhibition ordinary committee meeting). 1928. *SB*, Aug. 9: 13.

"Zhonghua guohuo zhanlanhui choubei ji" (Chinese National Products Exhibition preparatory records). 1928. *Shangye zazhi* 3, no. 9 (Sept.): 1–5.

"Zhonghua guohuo zhanlanhui kaimu shengkuang" (Chinese National Products Exhibition grand opening ceremonies). 1928. *Shangye zazhi* 3, no. 12 (Dec.): 1–4.

"Zhonghua guohuo zhanlanhui zuori kaimu shengkuang" (Festive events surrounding the opening ceremonies yesterday of the Chinese National Products Exhibition). 1928. *SB*, Nov. 2: 13–14.

Zhonghua jiuguo shiren tuan lianhehui tekan. Monthly. 1921–22.

Zhou Shouyi. 1923. "Dui Ri jingji juejiao genben ce" (The basic strategy for severing economic relations with Japan). *Dongfang zazhi* 20, no. 13: 33–43.

Zhou Xibao. 1996. *Zhongguo gudai fushi shi* (A history of dress in ancient China). Beijing: Zhongguo xiju chubanshe.

Zhou Xiuluan. 1958. *Diyici shijie dazhan shiqi Zhongguo minzu gongye de fazhan* (The development of Chinese national industries during World War I). Shanghai: Renmin chubanshe.

Zhu Boyuan. 1936. "Guohuo biaozhun" (National products standards). In SSC 1936: 13–15.

Zhu Chengliang, ed. 1997. *Lao zhaopian: Fushi shishang* (Old photographs: clothing and fashion). Nanjing: Jiangsu meishu chubanshe.

Zhu Gongjing, ed. 1932. *Benguo jinianri shi* (A history of Chinese commemoration dates). 4th ed. Shanghai.

Zhu Hanguo, ed. 1993. *Zhongguo jindai guochi quanlu* (A complete record of China's modern national humiliations). Taiyuan: Shanxi renmin chubanshe.

Zhu Peide. 1996. "Wei tichang guohuo zhizhang zuochu gongxian de Zhu Meixian" (Zhu Meixian's contributions to the promotion of national product paper). In Pan Junxiang 1996c: 233–37.

Zhu Ying. 1991a. "Wan Qing shangren minzu zhuyi aiguo sixiang de mengfa ji qi yingxiang" (The nascent sense of nationalism and patriotic thought among merchants in the late Qing period). *Shixue yuekan* 3: 64–72.

————. 1991b. *Xinhai geming shiqi xinshi shangren shetuan yanjiu* (A study of new-style merchant organizations during the Revolution of 1911). Beijing: Renmin daxue chubanshe.

Zhuanji wenxue (Biographical literature). Taibei, 1962 to present.

"Zhufu zenma quandao zhangfu fuyong guohuo?" (How can housewives persuade their husbands to use national products?). 1934. *SB*, May 3.

Zou Yiren. 1980. *Jiu Shanghai renkou bianqian de yanjiu* (A study of population change in old Shanghai). Shanghai: Renmin chubanshe.

Zumoto, Motosada. 1932. *Sino-Japanese Entanglements, 1931–1932*. Tokyo: Herald Press.

"Zuzhi guohuo xuanchuandui de jianyi" (A proposal for organizing national products dissemination teams). 1934. *SB*, Nov. 12.

Index

Advertising, 38*n*; collective advertisements, 16, 214, 215*n*; calendar posters, 22, 213*n*; and foreign scripts and images, 59, 189, 204, 328; and nationalism, 59, 138, 139, 144, 155, 158, 213*n*, 232, 259, 266, 313, 319, 338; and visual dominance of imperialism, 136, 167, 181, 343, 362; on public notice boards, 151, 216, 232; as part of exhibitionary complex, 208, 213–16, 257; as micro-exhibitions, 213, 244, 281; premodern forms, 216–18; and politics, 261, 264–69 *passim*; biography as, 352, 353. *See also* Commodity spectacles; Nationalistic visuality

"Agricultural warfare," 59

Ai Xia, 310

Airbus, 364

Airplanes, 237, 266, 350–51, 364

Ajinomoto (Weizhisu), 333, 342, 343, 348

Alford, William P., 188*n*

All-China National Products Exhibition, 225

All-China Products Exhibition, 278

All-China Silk and Satin Exhibition, 234

Allure of foreign, *see* Foreign products

America, *see* United States

American Airlines, 364

American First policy, 364

Amherst Mission (1816), 34

Analects, 75

Anarchism, 290*n*

Andong (Fengtian), 133

Anhui, 275

Anqing, 98

Anti-Christian Movement, 177*n*, 207*n*, 327

Anti-Russia Volunteer Army, 65

Anti-Tuberculosis Movement, 293*n*

Appearance, *see under* Clothing

Arbor Day, 311*n*

Argentina, 221*n*

Arnold, Julean, 130*n*

"Artificial beauty," 298*n*

Artistic traditions, 335

Asian economic crisis, 365

Association for National Products (Shanghai Citizens Association for the Promotion of National Products), 163–64, 233–34, 277, 312, 361

Association of Shanghai National Products Manufacturers, 280*n*

Association to Encourage the Use of National Products, 142

Auslander, Leora, 317

Australia, 349

Autarky, *see* Nationalizing Consumer Culture

Authenticity: and capitalists, 8, 340;
and national products, 19, 138, 227,
242; and fashion, 21, 272, 305n; difficulty of determining, 186–97, 200;
and nationalistic consumers, 272,
316; and women, 287, 306–8. *See also*
National products
Automobiles, 213, 300, 330n
Awake, 314
Awareness of the Humiliation Association, 141

Banking, 47
Barbers, 70n, 78, 92
Bard, Emily, 298n
Barthes, Roland, 246, 247. *See also* Na-
tional myths
Basketball, 275
Baudrillard, Jean, 7n
Bauman, Zygmund, 14
Beahan, Charlotte, 291
Beijing (Beiping, Peking): as fashion
capital, 80, 107, 358n; and NPPA, 98,
107–9; and movement activities, 141,
148, 154–55, 170, 173n, 210; and
commodity spectacles, 208, 217, 221,
225, 226, 233, 257, 270–71, 275, 277n,
278, 308; contemporary battles over
imports in, 357n
Beijing Convention (1860), 39
Beijing General Chamber of Com-
merce, 108–9
Beiping, *see* Beijing
Beiping Day, 275
Beiping National Products Exhibition
(1933), 270–71
Belgrade, 367
Benjamin, Walter, 218–19, 236
Beret controversy, 364n
Billig, Michael, 181

Birthday parties, 39n
Bleach powder, 350
Boeing, 363
Book Guild, 149
Booker, Edna Lee, 179
Bourdieu, Pierre, 299
Boxer Uprising, 20, 64
Boycott Japan Quintet, 241n
Boycotts: and the enforcement of nationalistic consumption, 1–3, 9, 12–
13, 24, 127, 143n, 151–54, 159–63 *passim*, 179, 200, 231, 244, 361; targeting
specific countries, 54, 64, 127, 131n,
367; and inculcation of product-
nationality, 125–26, 130, 132, 143, 184;
continuity between, 126, 132, 157, 168;
suppression of, 129n, 136, 140n, 178;
problems evaluating, 130, 132; and
students, 143n, 146–51 *passim*, 271;
and Groups of Ten for National
Salvation, 154–55, 164, 169, 361; and
development of national products,
179–84, 342; and commodity spectacles, 210, 216, 222n, 273; lamenting
weakness of, 273, 322; and CCP, 311n;
continued use in the PRC, 367. *See
also* May Fourth Incident; May 30th
Incident; National Products Movement; *and under* Nationalists
Brazil, 365
British-American Tobacco (BAT),
3, 41n, 45n, 56, 128n, 162, 213n,
335
Brocade Guild, 99
Brown, Judith, 298n
Brussels, 219n
Buddhists, 76
Building Materials Display, 258
Bush, Richard, 249n
Button industry, 66–67

Cai Yuanpei, 249, 252, 313, 321–24 *passim*

Calendar poster, 22, 213*n*

Canada, 21

Canadian wheat, 348

Canton System, 33–34

Cao Muguan, 163, 222*n*

Capital National Products Exhibition Hall, 276

Capital National Products Museum, 233, 234, 297*n*

Capital National Products Traveling Exhibition, 243

Capital Women's National Products Promotion Association, 329

Caustic soda, 350

CCP, *see* Chinese Communist Party

Centennial Exposition (1876), 220*n*

Chambers of commerce, 12, 63, 64*n*, 66, 98, 129, 150*n*, 194, 198, 223, 224, 232, 255

Chang, Eileen, 304

Changsha, 92, 98, 155, 165, 166, 176, 216*n*, 234

Changsha Horse Square Incident, 292*n*

Changsha National Products Preservation Association, 163

Chao, Buwei Yang, 137*n*

Chemical industry, 339–41

Chen Chi, 42*n*

Chen Diexian (Tianxu Wosheng), 11, 55*n*, 256, 315*n*

Chen Duxiu, 291

Chen, Joseph, 157

Chen Kaige, 327*n*

Chen Qimei, 97, 106

Chen Shuying, 309*n*

Cheng, Nien, 355, 356

Chengdu, 176*n*

Chess, Chinese, 145

Chiang Kai-shek (Jiang Jieshi), 178, 247, 292, 293, 294*n*; and commodity spectacles, 244, 249–56 *passim*, 363

Chiang, Kai-shek, Madame, *see* Song Meiling

Children, *see* Women

Children's Day (April 4), 323–24

Children's Day Commemoration Rally, 324

Chile, 221*n*

China Can Also Say No, 357

China Cement Company, 258

China Chemical Industries Company, 11, 55*n*, 180, 188, 211*n*, 295

China Film Company, 240

China market myth, 132

China Merchants' Steam Navigation Company, 46–47, 61, 167

China National Products Company, 181, 211

China Pencil Company, 190

China Pencil Factory, 190

China Press, 267, 269*n*

China Survival Electric Fan Manufacturers, 181

Chinese Communist Party (CCP), 121, 155*n*, 168, 172, 177*n*, 245, 292, 311*n*, 320–21, 336–37, 360, 366–67. *See also* Labor activism

Chinese Industrial Chemistry Research Institute, 350

Chinese Literatus Pencil Factory, 190

Chinese Museum Association, 208

Chinese National Products Company, 212

Chinese National Products Company (Shanghai), 313, 322

Chinese National Products Company Introduction Office, 211*n*

Chinese National Products Exhibition (Ministry of Industry and Commerce, 1928), 363; scope, 244, 246, 256–75, 354; layout, 257–61 *passim*; regulation of space, 258, 264, 272; symbolic national unity, 258, 271; Ceremonial Hall, 259, 264, 274. *See also* Commodity spectacles

Chinese National Products Exhibition (Wuhan), 277

Chinese National Products Manufacturers and Distributors Cooperative, 211n

"Chinese people eat Chinese food," 357

"Chinese people should smoke Chinese cigarettes," 215

"Chinese people use Chinese pencils," 190

Chinese products, *see* National products

Chinese Red Capitalists series, 336–37

Chongqing, 221n

Christmas, 317n, 327

Chrysler, 364

Cigarettes, 51, 56, 213n; and nationalizing consumer culture, 56, 129, 132n, 139, 177, 179n, 215, 313, 328

Circulating display of national product samples, 310n

Citizens Association (Shanghai Citizens Association on Sino-Japanese Relations), 146n, 163, 165–66, 167, 173, 191, 346, 361

Citizenship, 4, 15, 273, 291

Citizens National Products Year (1933), 286n

Cloth for erasing humiliation, 117

Clothing (dress): laws and regulations, 50, 70, 80, 87, 109–12, 121, 204; and appearance, 68, 70n, 72, 74, 91–92;

economic importance, 70, 102; and nationalism, 72, 95, 117, 241n, 250, 263, 316; and hygiene, 113, 293n, 295; tuxedoes, 119. *See also* Fashion; NPPA

Coal mining, 47

Cochran, Sherman, 3, 45n

Commemoration, *see* National humiliation

Commercial and Industrial Commission, 225

Commercial bureaus, 63

Commercial Press, 263, 276

Commercial Products Display Hall, 225, 242

Commercial war, 58–62, 67, 153, 158, 186, 356, 334, 335. *See also* Trade statistics

Commodities, *see* Consumer culture

Commodity spectacles: as national representations, 10, 203, 229, 244, 271, 273, 281, 285, 360; and exhibitions, 151, 193, 198, 353; and national consciousness, 192, 205, 207, 246; and stores, 193, 205, 208–12 *passim*, 234, 310, 326; and product-nationality, 194, 198–99, 206; museums, 198, 204, 208, 209, 275; as institutional core of movement, 203, 208, 216, 244; as integrated exhibitionary complex, 204–5, 208–16; international, 205–6, 220; and coercion and violence, 207, 244; and department stores, 209, 228, 256, 261, 300, 321n; origins, 216–20, 317–18; and nationalistic commodity fetish, 219, 224, 236; quantifying exhibitions, 220–22; and pressure to purify products, 352. *See also* Advertising; Chiang Kai-shek; Consumer culture; Fashion; National humiliation; National Products

Movement; NPPA; Overseas Chinese; Students; Tianjin; United States

Common sense, 247. *See also* National myths

Communist historiography, 149

Communist Party, *see* Chinese Communist Party

Company, defined, 43*n*

"Compatriots," 89

"Completely national products children," 324

Comprador capitalist, 8

Conference on Improving Products, 237

Consumer culture: and nationalism, 1, 3, 4–5, 12, 16, 57–58, 70, 74, 191, 268, 281; defined, 2*n*, 13; and commodities as conduits, 7*n*, 29–36, 330; historiography of, 13–14, 18–19; and free choice, 14–15; appropriation of, 67; and status competition, 70, 217, 317, 234, 330; origins, 71*n*, 209; and agency in, 199, 207, 269. *See also* Commodity spectacles; National Products Movement; Nationalizing consumer culture; Women

Consumer products, 49, 180, 204, 214, 264; pattern of development, 52–56

Consumption, *see* Consumer culture

Control Yuan, 249

Cosmetic education campaigns, 307

Cosmetics, 214, 243, 301*n*, 303, 318, 326; exhibitions, 310

Cosmetics lecture team, 311*n*

Cotton mills, 171

Counterfeits, *see* Disguising product-nationality

Countryside, 232, 300*n*, 306*n*, 307, 329*n*

County fairs, 217*n*

Crow, Carl, 293*n*, 307*n*, 311*n*, 319*n*

Crystal Palace Exhibition (1851), 205, 218, 219, 236, 257*n*

Cultural Revolution (1966–76), 20, 245, 327*n*, 356

Culture Industries Day, 275

Dai Jinhua, 367

Daimler, 364

Dalian (Dairen), *see* Liaodong Peninsula

Dancing, 300, 355

Daoguang emperor, 35

Daoists, 76

Dare-to-Die Corps, 92

Dasheng Cotton Mill, 11

Daxia zhoubao, 286*n*

Deng Xiaoping, 50, 336, 357

Department stores, *see under* Commodity spectacles

Ding Richang, 59–60

Dion, Celine, 21*n*

Dirlik, Arlif, 293

Discourse of trade statistics, *see* Trade statistics

Disguising product-nationality: foreign as Chinese, 144*n*, 152*n*, 162, 187, 203, 210, 346; Chinese as foreign, 183, 191, 192, 197; and packaging, 350*n*, 352, 353. *See also* Advertising; Boycotts; Product-nationality

Dong Keren, 236

Dorgan, 76

Double Coin shoes, 338

Dragon Boat Festival, 217*n*, 318

Dress, *see* Clothing

Du Yuesheng, 312, 346*n*, 351

Duan Qirui, 84, 321*n*

Duanfang, 223

Duara, Prasenjit, 5n, 185n
Dublin, 219n

East Asia Wool Textile Company, 11,
    182
Education Department, 190
End of the Road for Treasonous Merchants,
    273
Enemy Fish Inspection Committee,
    178
Enemy products, *see* Foreign products
Environment-friendly products, 364
Ethic of nationalistic consumption, *see*
    under Nationalizing consumer cul-
    ture
Eugenics, 8–9
Europe, 207, 209, 220, 223n, 224, 340
Examination system, 40, 49, 50n, 234,
    338
Exchange value, *see* Product-nationality
Exhibitionary complex, *see under* Com-
    modity spectacles
Exhibition fever, 223, 224
Exhibitions, *see under* Chinese National
    Products Exhibition; Commodity
    spectacles
Expeditions, 151
Expropriation, 245
Extraterritoriality, 35

Factories: defined, 51n; tours, 353
Family, *see* Women
Famous Pills of Lei Yushang's Drug-
    store, 217
Fan Xudong, 11, 337, 339–40
Fang Yexian, 11, 55n, 180–81, 188,
    211n
Fans: as propaganda, 174
Far East Commercial Products Exhibi-
    tion (Manila), 278

Fashion (style): and western styles, 20,
    53, 73, 93, 119; and authenticity, 21,
    272, 305n; less important than
    product-nationality, 22, 204, 214,
    244, 298; and coercion and violence,
    91, 151, 167, 169, 302n, 331; Sun Yat-
    sen jacket/suit, 93, 116, 182; shows,
    119, 203, 204, 281, 307, 310, 311n, 314,
    324; long-gown as movement uni-
    form, 121, 204; redefined by CCP,
    121; and treasonous consumption,
    286, 321–22; in control of women,
    300, 303, 307, 331, 355, 362. *See also*
    Clothing; Nationalistic visuality;
    NPPA
Feng Shaoshan, 249
Feng Yuxiang, 248n
Fengtian, 166
Festivals: annual, 216–17; of consump-
    tion, 317–18. *See also* Commodity
    spectacles
Fewsmith, Joseph, 129, 249n
Filial piety, 204
Films, 38n
First Sino-Japanese War (1894–95), 33,
    47, 48
Five Continents Dispensary Company,
    12
Five Cordials Textile Plant, 189
Flags, Nationalist, 250, 259, 264
Flapper, 300n. *See also* Women
Flavoring powder, *see* MSG
Flour, 55, 296
Flyswatters, 293n
Fong, H. D., 58, 91, 185
Footbinding, 94, 290–91, 298
Foreigners in China, 33, 45–46, 253–54
Foreign investment, 43n
Foreign products (*yanghuo*): allure and
    fear of, 1–2, 29, 30n, 32, 180, 183, 192,

203, 204, 227, 300, 342, 344, 365; and nation-making, 3–4, 103; signifying, 7n, 139, 235; defining, 20–21, 48–49, 186, 190, 197; as symbols, 33, 38, 47, 155, 333; techniques for removing, 129, 173, 210, 213, 246; and treason, 177, 178–79, 286; and shame, 285, 286, 294, 318; and improving national products, 280; and national destruction, 227, 253. *See also* Japan; National products; National Products Movement; "Treasonous merchants"

Four Great Companies, 209n

400 Million Customers, 45

Four peoples, 161

France, 15, 189, 206n, 219, 307, 317, 322, 347

Freedom cloth, 11

Friendship Stores, 245

Fujian province, 233, 258, 263, 275n

Funü gongming yuebao, 308

Fuzhou, 37, 98, 141n, 166, 217, 221n

Fuzhou Incident (1919), 157

Fuzhou National Products Museum, 222n

Fuzhou Naval Dockyard, 61n

Gandhi, Mohandas, 17–18, 116, 298n

Gas masks, 350

Geisha, 307n

Germany, 15, 52, 134, 147, 182–83, 190, 293, 307, 321n, 339, 342

Ginseng, 191

Glass, 227

Globalization, 364

Glutamate, 341

Godley, Michael, 223

God of the Queue, 89–90

Going to the National Products Exhibition, 267

Golden Age, 58, 226, 340–41

Goodman, Bryna, 298n

Government-merchant joint management, 62

Government-supervised, merchant-run, 61

Grain mills, 55

Great Britain, 15, 160, 168, 170, 176, 219, 347

Great China Advertising Agency, 264

Great China Rubber Company, 338

Great Kanto earthquake, 167

Green Gang, 312, 346n, 351

Groups of Ten for National Salvation, *see under* Boycotts

Guangdong province, 65, 66, 81, 247n, 258, 275n, 321, 359

Guangzhou (Canton), 32, 37, 62, 82–83, 130, 132, 139, 176, 225, 309n, 321, 359

Guilds, *see* Native-place associations

Guizhou, 233

Guohuo, see National products

Guohuo yuebao, 286n

Guohuo yundong, see National Products Movement

Guomindang (GMD), *see* Nationalists

Hainan Island, 257

Hair, 77–78, 79, 83, 135n, 292n, 300. *See also* Queue

Hand of Buddha, 344

Hangzhou, 132, 225n, 230, 256, 267, 276–80 passim

Hankou, 56, 98, 166, 198, 225

Hanoi, 220n

Hanyang Iron & Steel Works, 339

Hanyeping Iron Works, 134

Harbin, 56, 166n

Hats, straw, 53–54, 96, 151, 152, 330*n*
He Jiafu, 96*n*
Heaven Conglomerate (Tianzihao), 349–50
Heaven's Kitchen Factory, 343–44; pressure to sinify products, 348; raw materials, 349. *See also* Wu Yunchu
Hebei province (Zhili), 53, 198, 221, 233, 257, 275, 362*n*
Hebei Provincial National Products Museum, 233*n*
Hechuan County Museum of Science, 208
Hengyu Company, 55
Henriot, Christian, 235*n*, 330*n*
Holidays, 251, 289, 317
Hollywood invasion, 367
Hong Kong, 89, 131, 160, 176, 209, 346, 349, 352
Honolulu, 131
Hou, Chi-ming, 57*n*
Household Enterprises, 55*n*, 256
Household responsibility system, 154*n*
Hu Die, 310
Hu Xiyuan, 183–84
Huang Yanpei, 316
Huanyou diqiu xinlu (Travel around the globe), 220*n*
Hubei Cotton Cloth Mill, 62
Hubei province, 62, 65, 90, 156, 277
Hujiang University, 222*n*
Humiliation, *see* National humiliation
Humm, Maggie, 287*n*
Hunan National Products Museum, 234
Hunan province, 60*n*, 65, 172*n*, 277
Hundred Days Reforms (1898), 84*n*, 205
Hundred Happiness Condensed Milk, 180

Huzhou native-place association, 313, 321, 324
Hydrochloric acid, 349

Ikeda Kikunae, 342
Imitations, *see* Disguising product-nationality
Imports, *see* Foreign products
Import statistics, *see* Trade statistics
Import-substitution, *see* Nationalizing consumer culture
"Incident," 131. *See also individual incidents by name*
India, 137*n*, 298*n*, 365
Indigenization, *see* Nationalizing consumer culture
Industrial and Commercial Conference, 348*n*
Industrial and Commercial Study Society of China for the Preservation of International Peace, 146*n*, 150
Industrial College of Shanghai, 154
Inferior products, *see* Foreign products
Inner Mongolia, 257
Inspections: popularity in 1930s, 319*n*
Inspection tours abroad, 205
Intellectual property, 187*n*
International Health Exhibition (1884), 220*n*
International Settlement, 178*n*, 240
International Silk Expositions (1921, 1923), 230*n*
International Women's Day (March 8), 289, 292, 320–22
Investigations, *see under* National products
Ireland, 15
Iron and Blood Society, 13
Italy, 293

Japan: rice as metaphor for, 9n; as model, 15, 41n, 86, 106, 252, 300n, 307, 308n; as economic competitor, 31, 83, 117, 226n, 341–45; Chinese in, 33n, 65, 89, 133; aggression in China, 135–37, 166, 248, 263, 297n, 311n, 315n, 326, 333, 357, 362; and boycotts, 137, 141, 142, 159, 160, 167, 168–77, 231, 235; and product-nationality, 186, 191, 203; use of nationalistic spectacles, 205, 218n, 220n. *See also* Boycotts; Foreign products; National humiliation

Japanese Ministry of Foreign Affairs, 174

Japanese products, *see* Foreign products; Japan

Jiading county, 337

Jiang Jieshi, *see* Chiang Kai-shek

Jiangnan Arsenal and Shipyard, 61n

Jiangsu Industrial Exhibition (1921), 234n

Jiangsu province, 50–51, 217n, 337; activities in movement, 135n, 143n, 210, 227, 230n, 233, 237n, 251, 257, 275n, 309

Jiaozhou Bay (Qingdao), 147

Jiaxing, 98, 285n

Jilian huikan, 8n, 196n, 204, 302n, 318, 334n, 359n

Ji'nan, 98, 155, 159, 308

Jinde Girls School, 273

Jingdezhen, 217

Jingshi Industrial Promotion Exhibition Hall, 221

Jinling University, 329

June 1 Incident (1923), 176

Kaifeng, 221n

Kaiping Coal Mines, 61

Kang Youwei, 63, 205

Kentucky Fried Chicken (KFC), 357, 367

Kikuchi Takaharu, 126n

Kill Flies! Campaign, 293n

King George III, 30

Kinmonth, Earl, 336

Kirby, William C., 245n

Kong Xiangxi (H. H. Kung), 194–95, 231, 233, 246, 249, 250, 251–52, 277, 311n

Korea, 15, 139, 145, 160, 167–68, 191, 357n, 365

Kramer, Paul, 248n

Kuhn, Philip, 76n

Kuomintang (KMT), *see* Nationalists

Labor activism, 169, 171–72, 296, 367

Lace, 52, 225n

Lantern Festival, 217n

Leach, William, 228

League of China, 142

Lecture teams, 170

Legal reform: of copyright and patent laws, 63, 347

Leg powder, 307

Lenin, V. I., 321n

Li Fan, 59

Li Gui, 220n

Li Hongzhang, 42, 61, 220n

Li Jianhong, 173–75

Li Shizeng, 323

Li Zhuoyun, 98

Li Zongren, 277

Liang Qichao, 8n, 43, 137n, 290

Liaodong Peninsula, 160–67 *passim*, 174. *See also* Twenty-One Demands

Light bulbs, 182–84, 204

"Lin Family Shop, The," 1–3, 161

Lin Kecong, 308, 312

Lin Zexu, 35

Liu Dajun (D. K. Lieu), 62n, 346n

Liu Hongsheng, 11, 341

Liyang county, 210n

Local products, *see under* National products

Local self-government movement, 67n

London, 205, 218, 220n, 298n

Loomba, Ania, 290n

Louisiana Purchase International Exposition (1904), 128n, 220n

Lower Yangzi, 81, 160, 183, 248. *See also* individual cities

Lü Baoyuan, 107–8

Lu Hanchao, 358

Lu Mengyan, 278n

Lunar New Year, 318

Lüshun (Port Arthur), *see* Liaodong Peninsula

Luxuries and necessities, 51

Lytton Commission, 177n

Ma Jianzhong, 42, 220n

Ma Min, 223

Macartney Mission (1793), 34

Madrid, 219n

Mainland Emporium, 321n

Malaysia, 365. *See also* Overseas Chinese

Manchuria, 160, 248, 297n, 315n, 333, 348, 362

Manchurian Incident (1931), 117n, 179, 190, 211n, 349

Manila, 131, 221n, 276, 278. *See also* Overseas Chinese

Mao Dun, 1–2, 51, 317n

Mao suit, *see under* Fashion

Mao Zedong, 54n, 60, 336, 366

Maritime Customs Administration, 42, 156, 219

Marketplace, 208, 242, 309; local, 216–17; as proving ground for women, 297

Marx, Karl, 21, 22

Marxism, 23

Matches, 133, 341

Material culture: definition, 2n; instability of, 68, 118; interpretations of, 88. *See also* Consumer culture

Matsumoto Shigeharu, 140

May Day, 310

May Fourth Movement, 146–47, 291

May Ninth Humiliation Day (5-9), 134, 137–38, 148, 153, 158, 165–67, 173, 174

May Seventh Humiliation Day (5-7), 134, 137n, 147–48, 172n, 173n

May 30th Incident (1925), 158, 168–73 *passim*, 345, 346

May Thirtieth National Products Exhibition, 222n

McDonald's, 365

Mei Zuolü, 71, 72, 94, 120

Melanesia, 213n

Merchants, *see* "Treasonous merchants"

Mexico, 223n

Mid-Autumn Festival, 217n, 318, 319

Midnight (Ziye), 51, 317n

Militarization of society, 285, 292–98, 313, 338

Ming dynasty, 76, 217

Ministry of Commerce, Industry, and Agriculture, 221, 225, 227, 231n, 232n, 343–44

Ministry of Communications, 232n

Ministry of Education, 117

Ministry of Finance, 232n, 352n

Ministry of Industry and Commerce, 108, 194–95, 198, 199, 231–35 *passim*, 249, 254, 278, 348

Ministry of the Interior, 231–32

Missionaries: and spread of consumerism, 37, 39, 79; and schools, 306n, 327

Mitchell, Timothy, 219n

Mitsui, 191

Model commune/factory, 271

Mongolia, 64

Moninger, Margaret, 39n, 152n

Moscow, 219n

Mosquito coil, 295

Movement, the, *see* National Products Movement

Movie houses, 204, 208, 238, 300

MSG (monosodium glutamate), 333, 341

MSG King, 336. *See also* Wu Yunchu

Mukden Incident, *see* Manchurian Incident

Munich, 219n

Museums, *see under* Commodity spectacles

Myth, *see* National myths

Nagasaki, 131

Nanchang, 350n

Nanjing, 98, 166n, 208, 210n, 221n, 223, 233, 234n, 243, 251, 271, 276, 297n, 309n, 329

Nanjing Decade (1927–37), 249n

Nanjing Exhibition (1910), 208n

Nanjing National Products Museum, 271

Nanjing Road, 169, 178n, 181, 294n, 310

Nankai University, 271n

Nanyang Brothers Tobacco Company, 3, 11, 132n, 139, 215, 313, 328

Nanyang Industrial Exhibition (1910), 223–26, 247. *See also* Commodity spectacles

National Assembly, 87, 111, 160

National blood, 8

National content regulations, 21

National Day (Double Ten Day), 251

National drama, 8n

National Economic Council, 352n

National economic integration, 216, 218, 228, 270. *See also* National myths

National essence, 199

National father, 8

National flag, 8

National humiliation (*guochi*): and cleansing of, 19, 135, 175, 192, 324; and trope of national extinction, 71n, 137, 175, 303; construction of, 134, 147, 148–49, 159, 165–66, 172; and advertising as means of constructing, 137–40; and humiliation days, 134n, 146, 170, 173n, 176, 216n, 310–11; and commodity spectacle, 211, 214, 226, 273, *See also* Advertising; Boycotts; Twenty-One Demands; *and individual days by name*

National Humiliation Commemoration Rally, 166

National Humiliation Society, 132n

Nationalism: linked to consumer culture, 1–5 *passim*, 12, 16, 57–58, 70, 74, 191, 268, 281; and national products, 3, 4, 16, 17, 212, 218, 266; and the term "nation-making," 4n, 17, 74, 315; and fashion, 22, 204, 214, 244, 298; measured with trade statistics, 43, 45, 46, 103, 145, 252, 296, 297, 302, 316n, 323, 328, 334, 356; and tariff autonomy, 41n, 169, 349n, 355; and advertising, 59, 138, 139, 144, 155, 158, 213n, 232, 259, 266, 313, 319, 338; and clothing, 72, 95, 117, 241n, 250, 263, 316. *See also* Consumer Culture; Nationalistic visuality; National

Products Movement; Product-nationality; Women

Nationalistic commodity spectacles, *see* Commodity spectacles

Nationalistic visuality, 10, 118, 326; and Western material culture, 37–40 *passim*; and personal appearance, 68–69, 120–21, 306; and boycotts, 125, 191–92; and commodity spectacles, 203–10 *passim*, 214, 215, 216, 226*n*, 243, 252, 263, 264, 281; and glass, 228*n*, 229. *See also* Advertising; Commodity spectacles; National Products Movement

Nationalists, 207, 339, 348, 352*n*; and nationalizing consumer culture, 42*n*, 115–17, 172, 194, 198, 360; and boycotts, 170, 176, 177–79, 185; and commodity spectacles, 222, 231–38 *passim*, 244–45, 246, 259, 264, 323; and women, 292, 320. *See also under individual ministries and politicians by name*

Nationalized nouns, 8

Nationalizing consumer culture: nationalism tied to consumerism, 1–5 *passim*, 16, 70; defined, 15*n*, 19; and cigarettes, 56, 158, 169, 179; and sovereignty, 64, 67, 354, 355; ethic of nationalistic consumption, 74, 101–5, 135, 146, 204, 326*n*, 333; inability to make all-embracing, 211, 365; and categories of consumption, 207, 218, 229, 247, 272, 287, 288, 361; commodity nation, 281; and tensions with class, 317; foreign nations as models of nationalistic consumption, 41*n*, 86, 106, 252, 307–8, 322; and self-surveillance, 186–87, 192. *See also* National Products Movement; Nationalists; Women

National Journal of Commerce, The, 266

National language (Mandarin), 185*n*

National medicine, 8

National myths, 45–46, 249–52, 333; of economic integration, 247, 268; of political integration, 247–48, 257, 268

National opera, 8

National product companies, 209

National product peddler squads, 154

National products (*guohuo*): considered inferior to imports, 2, 192, 342, 344, 347; defining, 2, 7, 22, 118, 186, 196–200, 214, 320, 363; and nationalism, 3, 4, 16, 17, 212, 218, 266; authenticating, 9, 192, 194–97, 252, 255; emphasis on purity, 19, 180, 188, 207*n*, 214, 241, 361; foreign origins of, 52–56, 189–90, 196; collecting and investigating, 100, 144, 226, 227, 235, 242*n*, 266, 271, 276; and tax incentives, 156, 193; and local products, 191, 206, 340; and subnational ties, 215; specialty items, 217; as souvenirs, 267–68, 269*n*; and nationalized distribution, 192–93, 209, 212; and aesthetics, 285, 296–98, 305–6; and gift-giving, 289, 318–19. *See also* Foreign products; National Products Movement; Women

National Products Activities Exhibition (Southeast Asia), 278

National Products Alliance, 277

National Products Catalogue, 242

National Products Daily, 267

National Products Exhibition, *see* Chinese National Products Exhibition

National Products Hall, 258

National Products Monthly, 144, 226

National Products Movement (*Guohuo yundong*): defined, 4–9 *passim*; and Chinese studies, 5, 359–60; as a meta-movement, 5–6, 9–15, 360; origins, 5–6, 52, 57, 64–66, 360; and eugenics, 8–9; coercion and violence in, 12–13, 67, 68, 69, 117, 179, 184, 244, 320; similar movements in other countries, 15, 17–18, 21, 363–64; dissemination techniques, 38, 97–101, 165, 198–99, 240n, 266, 308, 312n, 321n, 314; and foreign companies in China, 48, 197; and capitalism, 62, 218, 245, 334, 361, 366; failures and successes, 120, 312, 329, 330, 332n, 355–56, 361; boycotts as "camouflage" for, 137–40, 145; and pressure to eliminate foreign elements, 207n, 339, 348–50; and the countryside, 222, 232, 300n, 306n, 307, 329n; as displaced anti-imperialism, 241; national and international scope, 246, 266, 268, 306–9 *passim*, 350n, 358–60; and social norms, 291–92, 354, 356; and "traditional values," 294; and surveillance of family and friends, 309, 314, 319, 363; legacies in the PRC, 356–61 *passim*, 366–67. *See also* Advertising; Boycotts; Consumer culture; Foreign products; Militarization of society; Nationalizing consumer culture; National products; Overseas Chinese; Shanghai; Women

National Products Movement Week, 237–43, 246

National Products Preservation Association, *see* NPPA

National Products Production and Marketing Cooperative Association, 321n

National Products Road, 249, 258

National Products Salvation Rally, 101

National product standards, *see under* National products

National Products Week, 251, 255

National Products Year (1933), 286n, 311n

National Resources Commission, 244, 352n

"National salvation," 94, 223, 228, 287

National Salvation Fund, 141

Nationless products, 364

Nation-making, *see under* Nationalism

Native goods movement, *see* National Products Movement

Native products, *see* National products

Native-place associations, 12, 66, 71, 129, 221, 248, 263, 275, 281. *See also individual associations by name*

Needles, 30

Neo-economic imperialism, 357

Nested identities, 263

Netherlands, 182–83

New China Bookstore, 181

New Culture Movement, 291

New Life Movement: and nationalization of consumption, 177n, 279n; co-opted by National Products Movement, 292–98, 318; and attack on lifestyles, 299, 302, 311n, 319n

New military historians, 295n

New Orleans Exhibition (1884–85), 220n

New Puyu Benevolent Association, 249

New Systems Reforms (*Xinzheng*), 63, 84, 221, 339

New Year's, 217n, 312, 315

New York, 218, 219n, 230n, 326

Nie Qigui, 62

Nigeria, 15

Ningbo, 37, 53, 128n, 309n

Ningxia province, 233, 359

North-China Daily News, 224

Northern Expedition (1926–28), 185, 207n, 231n, 247, 268

Not-made-in-sweatshops, 364

NPPA (National Products Preservation Association): efforts to define clothing styles, 71–74, 94–97, 109–11, 120n, 272, 277; national and international links, 98–99, 150, 163–64, 183, 198, 221n; and boycotts, 133, 135, 137, 163–69 *passim*; participants, 143, 346, 361; and women, 143n, 288, 311n, 312; and national products, 189, 193–94; and commodity spectacles, 210, 221, 226, 230, 241, 272

Ohnuki-Tierney, Emiko, 9n

"Open China to the outside world," 357

Opium: addiction as symbols, 31; trade, 34; war, 42, 365

Orphans, 251, 270

Osaka, 220n, 223n

Overseas Chinese: as market for national products, 55, 195, 211, 212, 346, 349; and queue cutting, 85, 86, 90n; and boycotts, 127n, 131, 141; and commodity spectacles, 226n, 230, 237, 240, 248, 267, 272, 278, 352

Pan Gongzhan, 190, 235n, 240, 255

Pan Gongzhan, Mrs., 308

Pan Junxiang, 126n

Pan Yangyao, 285n

Panama Pacific International Exposition (1915), 220n

Paper, 217

Parables of nationalistic consumption, 203, 307, 326

Parades, 237, 240, 249, 266, 312, 313, 321. *See also* Commodity spectacles

Paris, 218, 298n, 326

Patriarchy, 287n, 291

Patriotic associations, 65n

Patriotic blue cloth, 11

Patriotic cloth, 117

Patriotic producers, *see* Wu Yunchu

Patriotic products, *see* National products

Patriotic umbrella, 54

Pawnshops, 96n

Pencils, 190, 327

People's Liberation Army, 336

People's Livelihood Foreign-Style Umbrella Factory, 54

People's Republic of China (PRC), 336, 352, 356, 366–67

Perfume: as symbol of unpatriotic consumption, 296, 303, 327

Pharmaceuticals, 49, 217, 228, 243

Philadelphia, 220n, 347

Philippine Chinese General Chamber of Commerce, 278

Pilgrimages to the nationalistic commodity fetish, 227

Pipe smoking, 51

Pledges, 155

Poland, 137n

Porcelain, 217

Porcelain Ware Day, 275

Port Arthur, *see* Liaodong Peninsula

Posters, 237, 238

Post Office, 268

Pre-eminence of product-nationality, *see under* Product-nationality

Price and quality, *see* Product-nationality

Principle of People's Livelihood, 254

Product-nationality, 2; and nation-making, 3, 4n; and exchange value, 7n, 206, 218–19, 228, 244; difficulty of establishing pre-eminence of, 19, 23, 206, 215, 244, 330–31, 347, 355, 362; pre-eminence of, 74, 184–85, 206, 214, 310, 364; problem of distinguishing, 187–92, 197, 350n. *See also* Disguising product-nationality; National Products Movement; "Treasonous merchants"

Promote National Products Rally, 100

Prosperity New Ox-Glue Works, 341

Prosperity Nitric Alkali Company, 340

Prostitutes, 299, 305–6, 330n. *See also* Women

Provisional Government (Nanjing), 69

Public notice boards, 151, 216, 232

Pudong, 264

Purity of products, *see under* National products

Qianjiang native-place association, 95, 100n

Qianlong emperor, 30, 80

Qingdao, 56, 147, 308

Qing dynasty, 216, 220n, 221, 223, 290–91, 356

Qinghua University, 210

Queue: competition to define significance of cutting, 68–71, 85, 88–93 *passim*; and clothing, 73, 75, 86; and status, 75–79 *passim*; and coercion and violence, 76n, 87–88, 89, 184; and reforms, 84, 90–91, 94. *See also* Hair

Queue Army, 84

Racial hygiene, 8

Radio, 213, 238, 322

Raffles, 359n

Railways, 47–48, 147, 152n

Rawski, Thomas, 45n, 57n

Reardon-Anderson, James, 341n

Records of National Products Investigations, 144

Reference display room, 225n, 280

Reid, Gilbert, 37n

Reinsch, Paul S., 156

Remer, Charles, 126n, 130, 132, 168

Resist Russia Movement, 64

Retailing, *see* Commodity spectacles

Revolution of 1911, 72, 184, 224, 251, 298

Reynolds, Douglas, 84n

Rice, 217

Richards, Thomas, 2n, 236

Rigby, Richard, 175

Rights Recovery Movement, 65, 133

Rong Desheng, 11, 336

Rong family, 337

Rong Zongjing, 11

Rules for the National Products Museum, 233

Rumor, 129

Russia, 160, 174, 321n, 322, 323

Rydell, Robert, 218n

San Francisco Exposition, 218, 220n, 347

Santa Claus, 327–28

School, 293, 298, 309

Scott, A. C., 307n

Second Sino-Japanese War (1937–45), 245, 350

"Self-reliance," 357

Self-strengthening movement, 61
Semi-colonial, 17
Sequi Centennial International Exposition (1926), 347
"Severance of economic relations," 160. *See also* Boycotts
Shamian (Shameen) Incident (1925), 175–76
Shandong, 53, 134, 159, 225n, 231, 233, 236
Shandong Promote National Products Research Association, 154n
Shandong Question, 147
Shang Yang, 59
Shanghai: as center of consumer culture, 11, 37–38, 51, 119, 252, 299–300; leadership in the movement, 20, 71, 87, 358–60; as manufacturing center, 52, 54–56, 61–62, 66–67, 190, 348–50; and boycotts, 130, 139–40, 141, 152, 155, 169–72, 181, 183, 346, 350; and commodity spectacles, 208–211n passim, 217, 221n, 222n, 225, 226, 237–43, 256, 276, 310, 321; and imports, 253, 296; and Wu Yunchu, 337–41, 344, 351
Shanghai Association of Mechanized National Products Manufacturers, 198, 204n, 214, 215, 241, 243. *See also* Jilian huikan
Shanghai Chamber of Commerce, 235, 249, 351; Commercial Products Display Hall, 199; National Products Market, 322
Shanghai Citizens Association for the Promotion of National Products, *see* Association for National Products
Shanghai Citizens Association on Sino-Japanese Relations, *see* Citizens Association

Shanghai Commercial Products Display Hall, 226–30, 235, 346
Shanghai Day, 276n
Shanghai Display Hall, *see* Shanghai Commercial Products Display Hall
Shanghai Federation of Students, 154
Shanghai General Chamber of Commerce, 163, 226, 227, 238, 240n, 241, 242, 266, 276n, 277, 312n
Shanghai Incident (1932), 311n, 349, 350
Shanghai Jinde Girls School, 250
Shanghai Municipal National Products Museum, 199, 235–37
Shanghai Municipal Police (SMP), 361n
Shanghai National Products Company, 209n, 313, 322
Shanghai Tariff Conference (1918), 171
Shanghai Women's National Products Promotion Association, 322
Shanghai Women's National Products Promotion Society, 302n
Shantou, 275
Shanxi Mass Education Institute, 208
Shanxi province, 208, 233
Shaoxing, 217
Shell, 355
Shenbao, 106, 109n, 184, 213, 215n, 220n, 222n, 266, 286n, 315, 326
Sheng Xuanhuai, 62, 66
Shenyang (Mukden), 133, 225. *See also* Manchurian Incident
Shi Gengyin, 341
Shi Jixiong, 326n
Shi Liangcai, 351
Shipping, 46–47, 142, 152
Shishi xinwen, 286n
Shoes, 214, 338
Shuanglun Toothbrush Company, 55
Sichuan province, 65, 208, 227, 352

Silk, 31, 109, 264; and status, 70, 80–81, 82, 326, 329; and foreign competition, 83, 105, 191, 203, 322

Silk and Satin Guild, 108

Silver bullion, 81

Sincere Department Store (Xianshi), 59, 152, 209

Singapore, 221*n*, 226*n*

Sinificiation, *see* Nationalizing consumer culture

Sino-foreign treaties, 35

Skullcap, 53

Slogans, 232, 237, 239, 249, 296*n*

Smiles, Samuel, 336

Smith, Adam, 42

Snow, Edgar, 60*n*

"So-called modern households," 315*n*

Social Affairs Bureau (Shanghai), 171, 235, 238–39, 255, 267, 276

Socialist economy, 245

Society to Encourage the Use of National Products, 226

Song dynasty, 216

Song Feiqing, 11

Song Meiling (Madame Chiang Kaishek), 257, 292, 294*n*

Song Qingling, 249

Song Weichen, 340

Song Zejiu, 11, 117

Song Ziwen (T. V. Soong), 249, 257*n*

Songs, 151, 267, 273, 324*n*; "Song of the National Products Exhibition," 250

Sound trucks, 243

Southeast Asia: Chinese communities in, *see* Overseas Chinese

South Seas Exhibition, *see* Nanyang Industrial Exhibition

Sovereignty, *see under* Nationalizing consumer culture

Soviet Union, 322

Soy sauce shops, 343–44

Space, nationalized, 210, 222, 235, 242, 258–66. *See also* Advertising; Commodity spectacles; Nationalizing consumer culture

Spain, 15

Spectacles, *see* Commodity spectacles

Speech contest, 329–30

Stamps, 268

State rituals, 204

St. Louis World's Fair, 220, 248*n*

Stock, disclosure of ownership, 61*n*

Stockholm, 219*n*

Stories, *see* Parables

Students, 33*n*, 296*n*; role in movement, 117, 146–51 *passim*, 361; as enforcers, 143*n*, 151, 155; and commodity spectacles, 220, 221–22, 267, 271

Students National Products Year (1935), 286*n*

Style, *see* Fashion

Summer and Autumn Articles National Products Exhibition, 203, 237, 241, 251, 255

Sun Chuanfang, 248

Sun Ke (Sun Fo), 73

Sun Mengren, 298*n*

Sun Yatsen (Sun Yixian), 8, 41*n*, 73, 89, 97, 102, 106–7, 109, 187*n*, 214*n*, 247, 251, 253, 259, 264

Sun Yatsen jacket/suit, *see under* Fashion

Sun Department Store (Daxin), 209*n*

Sun Sun Department Store (Xinxin), 209

Suzhou, 99, 221*n*, 237*n*, 256*n*, 278*n*, 358*n*

Suzhou Display Hall, 230

Suzuki Pharmaceuticals, 342–43, 345

Swadeshi movement (India), 15

Sydney, 218

Tagore, Rabindranath, 18n
Tai, Lake, 81
Taiping Rebellion, 75, 79n, 82, 92
Taizhou native-place association, 344
Talcum powder, 295
Tang dynasty, 32
Tangshan, 362n
Tariff autonomy, 35, 40–43; and na-
    tionalism, 41n, 169, 349n, 355. See also
    Trade statistics
Tariffs, see under Trade statistics
Tastemakers, 299–300
Taste tests, 344
Tatsu Maru II, 131
Tax incentives, 156, 193
Tea, 31n, 217
Telegrams, 256
Textbooks, 150n
Thailand, 169, 237n, 365. See also Over-
    seas Chinese
Theaters, 298
Third Jiangsu Province National Local
    Products Exhibition (1925), 345
Three Friends Enterprises, 11, 53n, 264
Three People's Principles, 253
Tiananmen Square, 147
Tian Conglomerate, 353n
Tianjin, 56, 298n, 339, 359; movement
    organizations in, 98, 198; boycotts,
    129, 153n, 154–55, 166, 175n, 177n, 182;
    and commodity spectacles, 206n,
    225, 257, 271n, 276n, 278n, 308
Tianjin Commercial Products Exhibi-
    tion Hall, 233n
Tianli Nitrogen Factory, 350
Tiansheng Ceramics Factory, 350
Tianxu Wosheng, see Chen Diexian
Tianyuan Electrochemical Factory,
    349–50
Tianzihao, see Heaven Conglomerate

Tibet, 257
Toiletries, 54–55, 59, 243
Tokyo, 165, 167, 300n
Tokyo University, 342
Tomb-Sweeping Festival, 217n, 311n
Tonghai, 98
Toothbrushes, 54–55, 214
Toothpaste, 188–89, 295. See also Toi-
    letries
Townsend, James, 4
Toyota, 364
Toys, 208, 243, 268, 326
Trade fairs, see Commodity specta-
    cles
Trademarks, 187n, 198, 231, 267
Trade statistics, discourse of, 366; and
    tariffs, 5, 6, 199, 244, 365, 366–67;
    and symbols of lost sovereignty,
    40–42; and measure of nationalism,
    43, 45, 103, 145, 252, 316n, 323, 328,
    334, 356; and proof of treason, 46,
    296, 297, 302. See also Commercial
    war; Tariff autonomy
Trade unions, 232n
Transit tolls (lijin), 41
"Treasonous merchants": as key prob-
    lem for the movement, 143–44, 149,
    161–63, 177, 178, 239, 322, 333, 356;
    and morality, 232. See also Boycotts;
    Disguising product-nationality
Treaty of Nanjing, 35, 41
Treaty of Shimonoseki (1895), 48
Treaty ports: growth, 36; as showcases,
    37–38
Tsuda Mamichi, 298
Tupperware, 49n
Tuxedoes, 119
Twenty-One Demands, 96, 105, 133–42,
    145, 147, 160, 164, 165, 167, 172, 174,
    224, 226

Umami (savory), 343*n*
Umbrellas, 54, 214
Underwear, 52, 203–4
Unequal treaties, 5
Uniforms, 84, 113, 115. *See also* Clothing
United States, 127–31, 342, 347, 349; as basis of comparison, 13–14, 218, 307, 322, 335, 363–66; and commodity spectacles, 182, 207, 209, 220*n*, 223*n*, 224, 228, 347
Urbanization, 38

Versailles Peace Conference, 146, 147, 150
Virtuous wife and worthy mother archetype, 286, 287, 323
Visuality, *see* Nationalistic visuality

Wahaha Group, 357*n*
Wal-Mart, 364
Wang Dongyuan, 343, 344, 345
Wang Jie'an, 103–4, 167, 277
Wang Jingming, 329*n*
Wang Kangnian, 43*n*
Wang Tao, 58*n*
Wang Wendian, 142
Wang Xiaolai, 332*n*
Wang Zhengting, 42*n*, 108, 142
Wanguo gongbao, 220*n*
Warnings to a Prosperous Age, 60, 103
War of the chickens, 357
Wealth of Nations, 42
Wen Zhengyi, 205
Wenzhou, 177*n*
Western Europe, *see* Europe
Westernization movement, 61
West Lake Exhibition (1929), 230, 267, 279–80
Williams, Rosalind, 218
Wilson, Woodrow, 147

Wine, 217
Wing On Department Store (Yong'an), 152, 170, 209
Women: active in movement, 6, 96, 143*n*, 221, 232*n*, 285, 300*n*, 308, 309, 361; defined by consumption, 7, 288, 291–92, 297–303 *passim*, 306–8; and fashion, 21, 55, 80–81, 111, 303, 307, 331, 355, 362; vilification of, 286, 299, 301, 303; and Women's National Products Year of 1934, 286*n*, 289, 296–97, 309–28; and public life, 287, 290*n*, 298–99; and childrearing, 288, 323–27 *passim*; as modern, 288–89, 299–301, 306–7, 325; as models of nationalistic consumption, 289, 315*n*, 325–27; and International Women's Day (March 8), 289, 292, 320–22; and monitoring of family and friends, 309, 314, 319, 363; and household management, 287, 296, 309, 314–17, 325–27; directly contesting vilification, 328–32. *See also* Fashion; Nationalizing consumer culture
Women's Association, 309
Women's Circles Society to Encourage the Use of National Products, 285*n*
Women's emancipation, 287, 320, 334; and nationalism, 290, 291
Women's National Products Association, 296*n*
Women's National Products Promotion Association, 309*n*, 312*n*
Women's National Products Year Friendship Rally, 313
Women's National Products Year Movement Committee, 321, 322, 324
Women's Use National Products Association, 309

Women's Use National Products Promotion Week, 309

Women's Year Committee, 321, 322, 324

Women Wear National Products Society, 321n

Wong, Jan, 327n

Woodhead, Henry, 163n

Wool, 102, 105, 107, 182

World Trade Organization (WTO), 366–67

Wu Baiheng, 180

Wu Daiyi, 343

Wu Gengmei, 190

Wu Jinyun, 330

Wu Peifu, 248

Wu Tiecheng, 271n, 313, 323, 351

Wu Tingfang, 63n, 224; and clothing, 72, 85–87, 112–15; and the NPPA, 97, 112, 128n, 142, 144n

Wu Yunchu: as archetypical patriotic producer, 11, 333–37, 350–52; and commodity production as anti-imperialism, 334, 341–45; aided by movement, 345–47; as pure national-product, 337–41, 352–54; pressure to produce pure products, 348–50

Wu Zhihui, 249

Wu Zhilian, 342

Wu Zhimei, 309n

Wuchang Uprising, 251

Wuhan, 276, 277, 321, 339

Wuhan Exhibition, 280n

Xiamen, 37, 166, 277–78

Xiamen Citizens Associations, 191

Xiamen National Products Exhibition, 277–78

Xiang Kangyuan, 203

Xiang Songmao, 11–12

Xiao Yanming, 57n

Xinjiang province, 64, 257, 258n

Xiong Yuezhi, 358n

Xuan Jinglin, 310

Xue Fucheng, 42

Xunwu county, 54n

Yan Fu, 42

Yan Xishan, 248n

Yanghuo, see Foreign products

Yao Diyuan, 96n

Yapuer, 183–84

Yichang, 205

Yokohama, 167

Yu Qingting, 302n

Yu Xiaqing, 249, 255

Yuan dynasty, 76n

Yuan Shikai, 224, 339; and regulating appearance, 84, 90, 107, 109, 112–13; and boycotts, 129n, 140n, 174; and Twenty-One Demands, 134, 136, 160

Yung Wing (Rong Hong), 33n

Yunnan province, 227, 257

Zaize, 84

Zaizhen, 87

Zeng Guofan, 33n, 59, 61

Zetkin, Clara, 321n

Zhabei Chamber of Commerce, 277

Zhabei National Products Circulating Exhibition, 276–77

Zhang Boling, 271n

Zhang Dingfan, 238, 240, 241, 255

Zhang Jian, 11, 62

Zhang Xueliang, 248n

Zhang Xun, 84

Zhang Yiyun, 343, 344

Zhang Zhidong, 48n, 62, 63, 339

Zhang Ziyin, 96*n*, 104
Zhang Zuolin, 248
Zhanghua Wool Factory, 182
Zhao Tieqiao, 55
Zhao Xi'en, 255
Zhao Zizhen, 182
Zhejiang province, 227, 233, 258, 267, 313
Zheng Guanying, 60, 103
Zhengzhou, 162

Zhenjiang, 98, 154, 210*n*, 309
Zhifou (Chefoo), 52, 92
Zhou Enlai, 137*n*, 153*n*, 336
Zhou Xuexi, 62
Zhou Yanghao, 313, 321, 324
Zhou Ziqi, 224
Zhu Minyi, 351
Zhu Shaoping, 351
Zoos, 208
Zuo Zongtang, 61

Harvard East Asian Monographs
(* out-of-print)

*1.   Liang Fang-chung, *The Single-Whip Method of Taxation in China*

*2.   Harold C. Hinton, *The Grain Tribute System of China, 1845–1911*

3.   Ellsworth C. Carlson, *The Kaiping Mines, 1877–1912*

*4.   Chao Kuo-chün, *Agrarian Policies of Mainland China: A Documentary Study, 1949–1956*

*5.   Edgar Snow, *Random Notes on Red China, 1936–1945*

*6.   Edwin George Beal, Jr., *The Origin of Likin, 1835–1864*

7.   Chao Kuo-chün, *Economic Planning and Organization in Mainland China: A Documentary Study, 1949–1957*

*8.   John K. Fairbank, *Ching Documents: An Introductory Syllabus*

*9.   Helen Yin and Yi-chang Yin, *Economic Statistics of Mainland China, 1949–1957*

*10.   Wolfgang Franke, *The Reform and Abolition of the Traditional Chinese Examination System*

11.   Albert Feuerwerker and S. Cheng, *Chinese Communist Studies of Modern Chinese History*

12.   C. John Stanley, *Late Ching Finance: Hu Kuang-yung as an Innovator*

13.   S. M. Meng, *The Tsungli Yamen: Its Organization and Functions*

*14.   Ssu-yü Teng, *Historiography of the Taiping Rebellion*

15.   Chun-Jo Liu, *Controversies in Modern Chinese Intellectual History: An Analytic Bibliography of Periodical Articles, Mainly of the May Fourth and Post–May Fourth Era*

*16.   Edward J. M. Rhoads, *The Chinese Red Army, 1927–1963: An Annotated Bibliography*

17.   Andrew J. Nathan, *A History of the China International Famine Relief Commission*

*18.   Frank H. H. King (ed.) and Prescott Clarke, *A Research Guide to China-Coast Newspapers, 1822–1911*

19.   Ellis Joffe, *Party and Army: Professionalism and Political Control in the Chinese Officer Corps, 1949–1964*

*20.   Toshio G. Tsukahira, *Feudal Control in Tokugawa Japan: The Sankin Kōtai System*

21.   Kwang-Ching Liu, ed., *American Missionaries in China: Papers from Harvard Seminars*

22.   George Moseley, *A Sino-Soviet Cultural Frontier: The Ili Kazakh Autonomous Chou*

23.   Carl F. Nathan, *Plague Prevention and Politics in Manchuria, 1910–1931*

Harvard East Asian Monographs

*24. Adrian Arthur Bennett, *John Fryer: The Introduction of Western Science and Technology into Nineteenth-Century China*

25. Donald J. Friedman, *The Road from Isolation: The Campaign of the American Committee for Non-Participation in Japanese Aggression, 1938–1941*

*26. Edward LeFevour, *Western Enterprise in Late Ching China: A Selective Survey of Jardine, Matheson and Company's Operations, 1842–1895*

27. Charles Neuhauser, *Third World Politics: China and the Afro-Asian People's Solidarity Organization, 1957–1967*

28. Kungtu C. Sun, assisted by Ralph W. Huenemann, *The Economic Development of Manchuria in the First Half of the Twentieth Century*

*29. Shahid Javed Burki, *A Study of Chinese Communes, 1965*

30. John Carter Vincent, *The Extraterritorial System in China: Final Phase*

31. Madeleine Chi, *China Diplomacy, 1914–1918*

*32. Clifton Jackson Phillips, *Protestant America and the Pagan World: The First Half Century of the American Board of Commissioners for Foreign Missions, 1810–1860*

33. James Pusey, *Wu Han: Attacking the Present through the Past*

34. Ying-wan Cheng, *Postal Communication in China and Its Modernization, 1860–1896*

35. Tuvia Blumenthal, *Saving in Postwar Japan*

36. Peter Frost, *The Bakumatsu Currency Crisis*

37. Stephen C. Lockwood, *Augustine Heard and Company, 1858–1862*

38. Robert R. Campbell, *James Duncan Campbell: A Memoir by His Son*

39. Jerome Alan Cohen, ed., *The Dynamics of China's Foreign Relations*

40. V. V. Vishnyakova-Akimova, *Two Years in Revolutionary China, 1925–1927*, tr. Steven L. Levine

*41. Meron Medzini, *French Policy in Japan during the Closing Years of the Tokugawa Regime*

42. Ezra Vogel, Margie Sargent, Vivienne B. Shue, Thomas Jay Mathews, and Deborah S. Davis, *The Cultural Revolution in the Provinces*

*43. Sidney A. Forsythe, *An American Missionary Community in China, 1895–1905*

*44. Benjamin I. Schwartz, ed., *Reflections on the May Fourth Movement.: A Symposium*

*45. Ching Young Choe, *The Rule of the Taewŏngun, 1864–1873: Restoration in Yi Korea*

46. W. P. J. Hall, *A Bibliographical Guide to Japanese Research on the Chinese Economy, 1958–1970*

47. Jack J. Gerson, *Horatio Nelson Lay and Sino-British Relations, 1854–1864*

48. Paul Richard Bohr, *Famine and the Missionary: Timothy Richard as Relief Administrator and Advocate of National Reform*

49. Endymion Wilkinson, *The History of Imperial China: A Research Guide*

50. Britten Dean, *China and Great Britain: The Diplomacy of Commercial Relations, 1860–1864*

51. Ellsworth C. Carlson, *The Foochow Missionaries, 1847–1880*

52. Yeh-chien Wang, *An Estimate of the Land-Tax Collection in China, 1753 and 1908*

53. Richard M. Pfeffer, *Understanding Business Contracts in China, 1949–1963*

54. Han-sheng Chuan and Richard Kraus, *Mid-Ching Rice Markets and Trade: An Essay in Price History*

Harvard East Asian Monographs

55. Ranbir Vohra, *Lao She and the Chinese Revolution*

56. Liang-lin Hsiao, *China's Foreign Trade Statistics, 1864–1949*

*57. Lee-hsia Hsu Ting, *Government Control of the Press in Modern China, 1900–1949*

58. Edward W. Wagner, *The Literati Purges: Political Conflict in Early Yi Korea*

*59. Joungwon A. Kim, *Divided Korea: The Politics of Development, 1945–1972*

*60. Noriko Kamachi, John K. Fairbank, and Chūzō Ichiko, *Japanese Studies of Modern China Since 1953: A Bibliographical Guide to Historical and Social-Science Research on the Nineteenth and Twentieth Centuries, Supplementary Volume for 1953–1969*

61. Donald A. Gibbs and Yun-chen Li, *A Bibliography of Studies and Translations of Modern Chinese Literature, 1918–1942*

62. Robert H. Silin, *Leadership and Values: The Organization of Large-Scale Taiwanese Enterprises*

63. David Pong, *A Critical Guide to the Kwangtung Provincial Archives Deposited at the Public Record Office of London*

*64. Fred W. Drake, *China Charts the World: Hsu Chi-yü and His Geography of 1848*

*65. William A. Brown and Urgrunge Onon, translators and annotators, *History of the Mongolian People's Republic*

66. Edward L. Farmer, *Early Ming Government: The Evolution of Dual Capitals*

*67. Ralph C. Croizier, *Koxinga and Chinese Nationalism: History, Myth, and the Hero*

*68. William J. Tyler, tr., *The Psychological World of Natsume Sōseki*, by Doi Takeo

69. Eric Widmer, *The Russian Ecclesiastical Mission in Peking during the Eighteenth Century*

*70. Charlton M. Lewis, *Prologue to the Chinese Revolution: The Transformation of Ideas and Institutions in Hunan Province, 1891–1907*

71. Preston Torbert, *The Ching Imperial Household Department: A Study of Its Organization and Principal Functions, 1662–1796*

72. Paul A. Cohen and John E. Schrecker, eds., *Reform in Nineteenth-Century China*

73. Jon Sigurdson, *Rural Industrialism in China*

74. Kang Chao, *The Development of Cotton Textile Production in China*

75. Valentin Rabe, *The Home Base of American China Missions, 1880–1920*

*76. Sarasin Viraphol, *Tribute and Profit: Sino-Siamese Trade, 1652–1853*

77. Ch'i-ch'ing Hsiao, *The Military Establishment of the Yuan Dynasty*

78. Meishi Tsai, *Contemporary Chinese Novels and Short Stories, 1949–1974: An Annotated Bibliography*

*79. Wellington K. K. Chan, *Merchants, Mandarins and Modern Enterprise in Late Ching China*

80. Endymion Wilkinson, *Landlord and Labor in Late Imperial China: Case Studies from Shandong by Jing Su and Luo Lun*

*81. Barry Keenan, *The Dewey Experiment in China: Educational Reform and Political Power in the Early Republic*

*82. George A. Hayden, *Crime and Punishment in Medieval Chinese Drama: Three Judge Pao Plays*

*83. Sang-Chul Suh, *Growth and Structural Changes in the Korean Economy, 1910–1940*

Harvard East Asian Monographs

84. J. W. Dower, *Empire and Aftermath: Yoshida Shigeru and the Japanese Experience, 1878–1954*

85. Martin Collcutt, *Five Mountains: The Rinzai Zen Monastic Institution in Medieval Japan*

86. Kwang Suk Kim and Michael Roemer, *Growth and Structural Transformation*

87. Anne O. Krueger, *The Developmental Role of the Foreign Sector and Aid*

*88. Edwin S. Mills and Byung-Nak Song, *Urbanization and Urban Problems*

89. Sung Hwan Ban, Pal Yong Moon, and Dwight H. Perkins, *Rural Development*

*90. Noel F. McGinn, Donald R. Snodgrass, Yung Bong Kim, Shin-Bok Kim, and Quee-Young Kim, *Education and Development in Korea*

91. Leroy P. Jones and Il SaKong, *Government, Business, and Entrepreneurship in Economic Development: The Korean Case*

92. Edward S. Mason, Dwight H. Perkins, Kwang Suk Kim, David C. Cole, Mahn Je Kim et al., *The Economic and Social Modernization of the Republic of Korea*

93. Robert Repetto, Tai Hwan Kwon, Son-Ung Kim, Dae Young Kim, John E. Sloboda, and Peter J. Donaldson, *Economic Development, Population Policy, and Demographic Transition in the Republic of Korea*

94. Parks M. Coble, Jr., *The Shanghai Capitalists and the Nationalist Government, 1927–1937*

95. Noriko Kamachi, *Reform in China: Huang Tsun-hsien and the Japanese Model*

96. Richard Wich, *Sino-Soviet Crisis Politics: A Study of Political Change and Communication*

97. Lillian M. Li, *China's Silk Trade: Traditional Industry in the Modern World, 1842–1937*

98. R. David Arkush, *Fei Xiaotong and Sociology in Revolutionary China*

*99. Kenneth Alan Grossberg, *Japan's Renaissance: The Politics of the Muromachi Bakufu*

100. James Reeve Pusey, *China and Charles Darwin*

101. Hoyt Cleveland Tillman, *Utilitarian Confucianism: Chen Liang's Challenge to Chu Hsi*

102. Thomas A. Stanley, *Ōsugi Sakae, Anarchist in Taishō Japan: The Creativity of the Ego*

103. Jonathan K. Ocko, *Bureaucratic Reform in Provincial China: Ting Jih-ch'ang in Restoration Kiangsu, 1867–1870*

104. James Reed, *The Missionary Mind and American East Asia Policy, 1911–1915*

105. Neil L. Waters, *Japan's Local Pragmatists: The Transition from Bakumatsu to Meiji in the Kawasaki Region*

106. David C. Cole and Yung Chul Park, *Financial Development in Korea, 1945–1978*

107. Roy Bahl, Chuk Kyo Kim, and Chong Kee Park, *Public Finances during the Korean Modernization Process*

108. William D. Wray, *Mitsubishi and the N.Y.K, 1870–1914: Business Strategy in the Japanese Shipping Industry*

109. Ralph William Huenemann, *The Dragon and the Iron Horse: The Economics of Railroads in China, 1876–1937*

110. Benjamin A. Elman, *From Philosophy to Philology: Intellectual and Social Aspects of Change in Late Imperial China*

111. Jane Kate Leonard, *Wei Yüan and China's Rediscovery of the Maritime World*

112. Luke S. K. Kwong, *A Mosaic of the Hundred Days:. Personalities, Politics, and Ideas of 1898*

Harvard East Asian Monographs

113. John E. Wills, Jr., *Embassies and Illusions: Dutch and Portuguese Envoys to K'ang-hsi, 1666–1687*

114. Joshua A. Fogel, *Politics and Sinology: The Case of Naitō Konan (1866–1934)*

*115. Jeffrey C. Kinkley, ed., *After Mao: Chinese Literature and Society, 1978– 1981*

116. C. Andrew Gerstle, *Circles of Fantasy: Convention in the Plays of Chikamatsu*

117. Andrew Gordon, *The Evolution of Labor Relations in Japan: Heavy Industry, 1853–1955*

*118. Daniel K. Gardner, *Chu Hsi and the "Ta Hsueh": Neo-Confucian Reflection on the Confucian Canon*

119. Christine Guth Kanda, *Shinzō: Hachiman Imagery and Its Development*

*120. Robert Borgen, *Sugawara no Michizane and the Early Heian Court*

121. Chang-tai Hung, *Going to the People: Chinese Intellectual and Folk Literature, 1918–1937*

* 122. Michael A. Cusumano, *The Japanese Automobile Industry: Technology and Management at Nissan and Toyota*

123. Richard von Glahn, *The Country of Streams and Grottoes: Expansion, Settlement, and the Civilizing of the Sichuan Frontier in Song Times*

124. Steven D. Carter, *The Road to Komatsubara: A Classical Reading of the Renga Hyakuin*

125. Katherine F. Bruner, John K. Fairbank, and Richard T. Smith, *Entering China's Service: Robert Hart's Journals, 1854–1863*

126. Bob Tadashi Wakabayashi, *Anti-Foreignism and Western Learning in Early-Modern Japan: The "New Theses" of 1825*

127. Atsuko Hirai, *Individualism and Socialism: The Life and Thought of Kawai Eijirō (1891–1944)*

128. Ellen Widmer, *The Margins of Utopia: "Shui-hu hou-chuan" and the Literature of Ming Loyalism*

129. R. Kent Guy, *The Emperor's Four Treasuries: Scholars and the State in the Late Chien-lung Era*

130. Peter C. Perdue, *Exhausting the Earth: State and Peasant in Hunan, 1500–1850*

131. Susan Chan Egan, *A Latterday Confucian: Reminiscences of William Hung (1893–1980)*

132. James T. C. Liu, *China Turning Inward: Intellectual-Political Changes in the Early Twelfth Century*

133. Paul A. Cohen, *Between Tradition and Modernity: Wang T'ao and Reform in Late Ching China*

134. Kate Wildman Nakai, *Shogunal Politics: Arai Hakuseki and the Premises of Tokugawa Rule*

135. Parks M. Coble, *Facing Japan: Chinese Politics and Japanese Imperialism, 1931–1937*

136. Jon L. Saari, *Legacies of Childhood: Growing Up Chinese in a Time of Crisis, 1890–1920*

137. Susan Downing Videen, *Tales of Heichū*

138. Heinz Morioka and Miyoko Sasaki, *Rakugo: The Popular Narrative Art of Japan*

139. Joshua A. Fogel, *Nakae Ushikichi in China: The Mourning of Spirit*

140. Alexander Barton Woodside, *Vietnam and the Chinese Model.: A Comparative Study of Vietnamese and Chinese Government in the First Half of the Nineteenth Century*

141. George Elision, *Deus Destroyed: The Image of Christianity in Early Modern Japan*

142. William D. Wray, ed., *Managing Industrial Enterprise: Cases from Japan's Prewar Experience*

143. T'ung-tsu Ch'ü, *Local Government in China under the Ching*

144. Marie Anchordoguy, *Computers, Inc.: Japan's Challenge to IBM*

145. Barbara Molony, *Technology and Investment: The Prewar Japanese Chemical Industry*

146. Mary Elizabeth Berry, *Hideyoshi*

147. Laura E. Hein, *Fueling Growth: The Energy Revolution and Economic Policy in Postwar Japan*

148. Wen-hsin Yeh, *The Alienated Academy: Culture and Politics in Republican China, 1919–1937*

149. Dru C. Gladney, *Muslim Chinese: Ethnic Nationalism in the People's Republic*

150. Merle Goldman and Paul A. Cohen, eds., *Ideas Across Cultures: Essays on Chinese Thought in Honor of Benjamin L Schwartz*

151. James Polachek, *The Inner Opium War*

152. Gail Lee Bernstein, *Japanese Marxist: A Portrait of Kawakami Hajime, 1879–1946*

153. Lloyd E. Eastman, *The Abortive Revolution: China under Nationalist Rule, 1927–1937*

154. Mark Mason, *American Multinationals and Japan: The Political Economy of Japanese Capital Controls, 1899–1980*

155. Richard J. Smith, John K. Fairbank, and Katherine F. Bruner, *Robert Hart and China's Early Modernization: His Journals, 1863–1866*

156. George J. Tanabe, Jr., *Myōe the Dreamkeeper: Fantasy and Knowledge in Kamakura Buddhism*

157. William Wayne Farris, *Heavenly Warriors: The Evolution of Japan's Military, 500–1300*

158. Yu-ming Shaw, *An American Missionary in China: John Leighton Stuart and Chinese-American Relations*

159. James B. Palais, *Politics and Policy in Traditional Korea*

160. Douglas Reynolds, *China, 1898–1912: The Xinzheng Revolution and Japan*

161. Roger R. Thompson, *China's Local Councils in the Age of Constitutional Reform, 1898-1911*

162. William Johnston, *The Modern Epidemic: History of Tuberculosis in Japan*

163. Constantine Nomikos Vaporis, *Breaking Barriers: Travel and the State in Early Modern Japan*

164. Irmela Hijiya-Kirschnereit, *Rituals of Self-Revelation: Shishōsetsu as Literary Genre and Socio-Cultural Phenomenon*

165. James C. Baxter, *The Meiji Unification through the Lens of Ishikawa Prefecture*

166. Thomas R. H. Havens, *Architects of Affluence: The Tsutsumi Family and the Seibu-Saison Enterprises in Twentieth-Century Japan*

167. Anthony Hood Chambers, *The Secret Window: Ideal Worlds in Tanizaki's Fiction*

168. Steven J. Ericson, *The Sound of the Whistle: Railroads and the State in Meiji Japan*

169. Andrew Edmund Goble, *Kenmu: Go-Daigo's Revolution*

170. Denise Potrzeba Lett, *In Pursuit of Status: The Making of South Korea's "New" Urban Middle Class*

171. Mimi Hall Yiengpruksawan, *Hiraizumi: Buddhist Art and Regional Politics in Twelfth-Century Japan*

172. Charles Shirō Inouye, *The Similitude of Blossoms: A Critical Biography of Izumi Kyōka (1873–1939), Japanese Novelist and Playwright*

173. Aviad E. Raz, *Riding the Black Ship: Japan and Tokyo Disneyland*

174. Deborah J. Milly, *Poverty, Equality, and Growth: The Politics of Economic Need in Postwar Japan*

175. See Heng Teow, *Japan's Cultural Policy Toward China, 1918–1931: A Comparative Perspective*

176. Michael A. Fuller, *An Introduction to Literary Chinese*

177. Frederick R. Dickinson, *War and National Reinvention: Japan in the Great War, 1914–1919*

178. John Solt, *Shredding the Tapestry of Meaning: The Poetry and Poetics of Kitasono Katue (1902–1978)*

179. Edward Pratt, *Japan's Protoindustrial Elite: The Economic Foundations of the Gōnō*

180. Atsuko Sakaki, *Recontextualizing Texts: Narrative Performance in Modern Japanese Fiction*

181. Soon-Won Park, *Colonial Industrialization and Labor in Korea: The Onoda Cement Factory*

182. JaHyun Kim Haboush and Martina Deuchler, *Culture and the State in Late Chosŏn Korea*

183. John W. Chaffee, *Branches of Heaven: A History of the Imperial Clan of Sung China*

184. Gi-Wook Shin and Michael Robinson, eds., *Colonial Modernity in Korea*

185. Nam-lin Hur, *Prayer and Play in Late Tokugawa Japan: Asakusa Sensōji and Edo Society*

186. Kristin Stapleton, *Civilizing Chengdu: Chinese Urban Reform, 1895–1937*

187. Hyung Il Pai, *Constructing "Korean" Origins: A Critical Review of Archaeology, Historiography, and Racial Myth in Korean State-Formation Theories*

188. Brian D. Ruppert, *Jewel in the Ashes: Buddha Relics and Power in Early Medieval Japan*

189. Susan Daruvala, *Zhou Zuoren and an Alternative Chinese Response to Modernity*

190. James Z. Lee, *The Political Economy of a Frontier: Southwest China, 1250–1850*

191. Kerry Smith, *A Time of Crisis: Japan, the Great Depression, and Rural Revitalization*

192. Michael Lewis, *Becoming Apart: National Power and Local Politics in Toyama, 1868–1945*

193. William C. Kirby, Man-houng Lin, James Chin Shih, and David A. Pietz, eds., *State and Economy in Republican China: A Handbook for Scholars*

194. Timothy S. George, *Minamata: Pollution and the Struggle for Democracy in Postwar Japan*

195. Billy K. L. So, *Prosperity, Region, and Institutions in Maritime China: The South Fukien Pattern, 946–1368*

196. Yoshihisa Tak Matsusaka, *The Making of Japanese Manchuria, 1904–1932*

197. Maram Epstein, *Competing Discourses: Orthodoxy, Authenticity, and Engendered Meanings in Late Imperial Chinese Fiction*

198. Curtis J. Milhaupt, J. Mark Ramseyer, and Michael K. Young, eds. and comps., *Japanese Law in Context: Readings in Society, the Economy, and Politics*

199. Haruo Iguchi, *Unfinished Business: Ayukawa Yoshisuke and U.S.-Japan Relations, 1937–1953*

200. Scott Pearce, Audrey Spiro, and Patricia Ebrey, *Culture and Power in the Reconstitution of the Chinese Realm, 200–600*

Harvard East Asian Monographs

201. Terry Kawashima, *Writing Margins: The Textual Construction of Gender in Heian and Kamakura Japan*

202. Martin W. Huang, *Desire and Fictional Narrative in Late Imperial China*

203. Robert S. Ross and Jiang Changbin, eds., *Re-examining the Cold War: U.S.-China Diplomacy, 1954–1973*

204. Guanhua Wang, *In Search of Justice: The 1905–1906 Chinese Anti-American Boycott*

205. David Schaberg, *A Patterned Past: Form and Thought in Early Chinese Historiography*

206. Christine Yano, *Tears of Longing: Nostalgia and the Nation in Japanese Popular Song*

207. Milena Doleželová-Velingerová and Oldřich Král, with Graham Sanders, eds., *The Appropriation of Cultural Capital: China's May Fourth Project*

208. Robert N. Huey, *The Making of 'Shinkokinshū'*

209. Lee Butler, *Emperor and Aristocracy in Japan, 1467–1680: Resilience and Renewal*

210. Suzanne Ogden, *Inklings of Democracy in China*

211. Kenneth J. Ruoff, *The People's Emperor: Democracy and the Japanese Monarchy, 1945–1995*

212. Haun Saussy, *Great Walls of Discourse and Other Adventures in Cultural China*

213. Aviad E. Raz, *Emotions at Work: Normative Control, Organizations, and Culture in Japan and America*

214. Rebecca E. Karl and Peter Zarrow, eds., *Rethinking the 1898 Reform Period: Political and Cultural Change in Late Qing China*

215. Kevin O'Rourke, *The Book of Korean Shijo*

216. Ezra F. Vogel, Yuan Ming, and Tanaka Akihiko, *The Golden Age of the U.S.-China-Japan Triangle, 1972–1989*

217. Thomas A Wilson, ed., *On Sacred Grounds: Culture, Society, Politics, and the Formation of the Cult of Confucius*

218. Donald S. Sutton, *Steps to Perfection: Exorcistic Performers and Chinese Religion in Twentieth-Century Taiwan*

219. Daqing Yang, *Technology of Empire: Telecommunications and Japanese Imperialism, 1930–1945*

220. Qianshen Bai, *Fu Shan's World: The Transformation of Chinese Calligraphy in the Seventeenth Century*

221. Paul Jakov Smith and Richard von Glahn, eds., *The Song-Yuan-Ming Transition in Chinese History*

222. Rania Hungtington, *Alien Kind: Foxes and Late Imperial Chinese Narrative*

223. Jordan Sand, *House and Home in Modern Japan: Architecture, Domestic Space, and Bourgeois Culture, 1880–1930*

224. Karl Gerth, *China Made: Consumer Culture and the Creation of the Nation*